The
NEW DEALERS'
WAR

Also by Thomas Fleming

Nonfiction
*Duel: Alexander Hamilton, Aaron Burr and
the Future of America*
Liberty! The American Revolution
1776: Year of Illusions
The Man Who Dared the Lightning
The Man from Monticello
West Point: The Men and Times of the U.S. Military Academy
One Small Candle
Beat the Last Drum
Now We Are Enemies

Fiction
When This Cruel War Is Over
Remember the Morning
Over There
Loyalties: A Novel of World War II
Time and Tide
The Officers' Wives
Promises to Keep
Liberty Tavern

The

NEW DEALERS'
WAR

Franklin D. Roosevelt

and

The War Within World War II

THOMAS FLEMING

BASIC
BOOKS

A Member of the Perseus Books Group

Published by Basic Books,
A Member of the Perseus Books Group

Book Design by Elizabeth Lahey
Text set in 11.5/16pt Sabon

A CIP catalog record for this book is available from the Library of Congress
ISBN: 0–465–024645

01 02 03 04 / 10 9 8 7 6 5 4 3 2 1

In any future great national trial, compared with the men of this, we shall have as weak and as strong, as silly and as wise, as bad and as good. Let us therefore study the incidents of this, as philosophy to learn wisdom from, and none of them as wrongs to be revenged.

–ABRAHAM LINCOLN

The effect of power and publicity on all men is the exaggeration of the self and a sort of tumor that ends by killing the victim's sympathies.

–HENRY ADAMS

There is nothing new in the world but the history you do not know.

–HARRY S. TRUMAN

CONTENTS

ACKNOWLEDGMENTS

No book of this dimension can be written without the help of many people. I would like to express my appreciation to several scholars who assisted me in my research. First is Steven Bernstein, a talented archivist who used the internet and library resources to help me track down numerous leads. Next is F. Kennon Moody, who solved a number of research problems at the Franklin D. Roosevelt Library in Hyde Park and also played a major role in helping me locate pictures that illuminate the text. My son, Richard Fleming, a trained librarian and archivist, as well as the holder of a graduate degree in Russian studies, used the resources of several New York City libraries, notably his alma mater, Columbia University, to provide me with invaluable aid. In Washington, D.C., Mrs. Anne McGovern helped me explore the Fulton Oursler Papers at the Georgetown University Library. I would also like to thank the staff of the Columbia Oral History Collection, who were invariably helpful in my explorations of such treasure troves as Henry Wallace's multivolume recollections. For their skill in helping me with their own fine history collection, as well as their readiness to retrieve out-of-print books for me via interlibrary loan, I am grateful to the staff of the New York Society Library. The librarian of the Century Association, W. Gregory Gallagher, was also helpful in computer searches for such books and swift in obtaining them when located. Also supportive were Kenneth French, head of the New Jersey Room in the Jersey City Public Library, and his colleague, Charles Markey, who shared with me many books and magazines from his personal library. A similar sense of gratitude marks my friendship with Lewis Daniels, head of the Westbrook, Conn., Library, where I spent several summers working on the book. I must also thank my agent, Ted Chichak, for his editorial advice and his enthusiasm for the book, over many years. My wife, Alice, was also invaluable as an inhouse editor and critic. Finally, my editor Don Fehr's encouragement and insights kept me on track and focused over the long haul.

INTRODUCTION

Every time I walked through the vestibule of my family home in Jersey City in the 1940s, I saw Franklin D. Roosevelt's face on the wall, where many devout Irish-Catholic families hung a portrait of the Sacred Heart of Jesus. FDR was the hero of my youth, the almost mythical figure on whom the political fortunes of my father, leader of the gritty working-class Sixth Ward, a vital cog in the city's powerful political machine, depended. The name Roosevelt had a magical aura, inducing total admiration of him and equally total loyalty to the Democratic Party.

But memories, hero-worship, the loyalties of youth, are the stuff of novels, not history. This book owes its existence to my painfully acquired belief that the historian's chief task is to separate history from memory. In our understanding of the cataclysm that historians call World War II, we are in the final stage of celebrating the riches of memory. We are saluting the generation that won the titanic global conflict. There is nothing wrong with this impulse. These men and women deserve the literary and cinematic cheers we are giving them.

But memory is not history. It is too clotted with sentiment, with the kind of retrospective distortion that we all inflict on the past. History gives us, not the past seen through the eyes of the present, but the past in the eyes, the voices, the hearts and minds of the men and women who lived through a particular time, as they experienced it.

For some people, this kind of history is a disturbing experience. When I wrote *1776: Year of Illusions*, which described the unreal assumptions that confused the founding fathers and their British adversaries in that seminal year, as well as the illusory "golden glow" in which Americans viewed the Revolution thereafter, I was accused of *lèse majesté*, sacrilege, unpatriotism. One man rushed up to a platform as I finished speaking about the book and roared that I was one of those people who said a glass was half empty rather than half full.

I could have replied (but I didn't) that if the rest of the glass was full of hot air or some other ingredient that altered the contents, it was not a bad idea to know this. That is a somewhat crude way of explaining why history is more important than memory. I also believe history is valuable because it makes us more sympathetic (or at least, less apocalyptically judgmental) toward the politicians of our own time. They too grope into the future that becomes their history with the same or similar confusions and weaknesses.

This is the spirit in which I have written *The New Dealers' War*. The title has a special significance for me. I first saw it in 1952, when I was working for Fulton Oursler, a many-sided writer who also had an extraordinary career as an editor of national magazines and friend of presidents. I recall the encounter as one of those primary moments that impelled me to become an historian. In a flash the phrase challenged me to think of Franklin D. Roosevelt, the Democratic Party, and World War II not as sacred entities but as historical experiences, to be studied, explored, and eventually understood, like the American Revolution or the Civil War. The words remained alive in my mind throughout the next four decades. I hope this book will give them life and meaning in the minds of my readers.

1

THE BIG LEAK

Blazoned in huge black letters across the front page of the December 4, 1941, issue of the *Chicago Tribune* was the headline: F.D.R.'S WAR PLANS! The *Washington Times-Herald*, the largest paper in the nation's capital, carried a similarly fevered banner. In both papers Chesly Manly, the *Tribune's* Washington correspondent, revealed what President Franklin D. Roosevelt had repeatedly denied: that he was planning to lead the United States into war against Germany. The source of the reporter's information was no less than a verbatim copy of Rainbow Five, the top-secret war plan drawn up at FDR's order by the joint board of the United States Army and Navy.[1]

Manly's story even contained a copy of the president's letter ordering the preparation of the plan. The reporter informed the *Tribune* and *Times-Herald* readers that Rainbow Five called for the creation of a 10-million-man army, including an expeditionary force of 5 million men that would invade Europe in 1943 to defeat Adolf Hitler's war machine. To all appearances the story was an enormous embarrassment to President Roosevelt. When he ran for a third term in 1940, the president had vowed that he would never send American soldiers to fight beyond America's shores.

Neither Roosevelt admirers nor Roosevelt haters, who by this time were numerous, were likely to forget his sonorous words, delivered at the Boston Garden on October 29, 1940, at the climax of his campaign for an unprecedented third presidential term: "While I am talking to you mothers and fathers, I give you one more assurance. I have said this before but I shall say it again and again and again: Your boys are not going to be sent into any foreign wars." In Buffalo three days later he made an even more emphatic declaration: "Your president says this country is not going to war."[2]

The Rainbow Five leak also made a fool or a liar out of Senator Alben W. Barkley of Kentucky, the Senate Democratic majority leader. On August 9, 1941, the president and England's prime minister Winston Churchill had met in Placentia Bay, Newfoundland, to affirm Roosevelt's determination to give England all aid short of war. They had issued a declaration of human rights, the Atlantic Charter, as a rallying cry for the struggle against dictatorship. Manly had written a story based on another leak, reporting plans for an American expeditionary force. Barkley had risen in the Senate and denounced Manly for writing a "deliberate and intentional falsehood." Manly and the *Tribune* now demanded a public apology from Barkley. Colonel Robert R. McCormick, the fiercely antiwar owner of the *Tribune*, reminded readers that in 1919, the paper had leaked the verbatim text of the Versailles Treaty, revealing Woodrow Wilson's abandonment of a peace of reconciliation to Europe's revenge-hungry politicians.[3]

In Congress, antiwar voices, most but not all Republicans, rose in protest. For more than two hours, unnerved House Democratic leaders delayed consideration of the administration's $8.24 billion arms bill, a key element in the expansion of the army and navy to fight the war designed by Rainbow Five. Heretofore this controversial legislation had been disguised as a purely defensive measure. Republican congressman George Holden Tinkham of Massachusetts declared that the nation had been "betrayed" and received unanimous consent for his motion to put Manly's story into the *Congressional Record*.[4] "The biggest issue before the nation today is the *Tribune* story," said Republican congressman William P. Lambertson of Kansas. "If it isn't true, why doesn't the president deny it?"[5]

In the Senate, Democrat Burton K. Wheeler of Montana, a leading critic of Roosevelt's policy of supporting the foes of Germany, Italy, and Japan, declared that the story proved everything he had been saying. On a radio program in early 1941, the sharp-tongued Wheeler had accused the president of having a "New Deal . . . foreign policy" that would "plow under every fourth American boy." Americans of the time immediately got the sarcastic reference to a controversial 1930s federal program that paid farmers to plow under crops to create artificial shortages and bolster prices.

Roosevelt had denounced Wheeler's metaphor as "the rottenest thing that has been said in public life in my generation." The senator was unbothered by this presidential outburst. He had won reelection in 1940 by 114,000 votes. FDR had carried Montana by only 54,000 votes.[6] Moreover, the western Democrat was not the only person to resort to such rhetoric. Antiwar folk artists Pete Seeger, Woody Guthrie, and other members of the group known as the Almanac Singers (forerunners of the Weavers) had recently issued a record featuring the song "Plow Under."[7] During the 1940 presidential campaign, beetle-browed John L. Lewis, head of the United Mine Workers Union, arguably the most powerful labor leader in the country, had urged his followers to vote against Roosevelt, lest he "make cannon fodder of your sons."[8]

II

Although Hitler had crushed France and the rest of Europe except for Great Britain and was now rampaging through Russia, most Americans felt no strong desire to stop him. Disillusion with the American experience in World War I permeated the nation. The soaring idealism with which Democrat Woodrow Wilson had led the country into that sanguinary conflict "to make the world safe for democracy" had ended in the vengeful Treaty of Versailles. Thanks in large part to that document, Europe's statesmen had created a world in which democracy soon became ridiculed and dictatorships of the left and right ran rampant. Worse, America's democratic allies, England and France, had welshed on repaying billions of dollars loaned to them to defeat Germany.

All this had been scorched into American hearts and minds in hearings conducted in the mid-1930s by progressive Republican Senator Gerald P. Nye of North Dakota, who purported to prove that profit-hungry munitions makers and bankers, not Wilsonian idealism, had propelled America into World War I. As a result of these hearings, which the Roosevelt administration had made no attempt to contradict, Congress passed a series of neutrality acts that forbade Americans to loan money or send armaments to any belligerent. These laws had won huge majorities in both the Senate and the House of Representatives and Roosevelt had signed them without a word of disapproval.

If it was difficult for the president to whip up any enthusiasm for fighting Germany, arousing alarm about the threat from Japan seemed next to impossible, except in California, where Japanese (and Chinese) phobia had been endemic for a hundred years. Tokyo was clearly on the march to dominate Asia. Since

1937 Japan's war with China had given her control of virtually the entire Chinese coast, enabling Tokyo to cut off all supplies for China's armies except along a tortuous path through the mountains of south China, known as the Burma Road.

In 1940, Japan's rulers had allied their nation with Fascist Italy and Nazi Germany in the Tripartite Pact. This venture created what some newspapers called "a Rome-Berlin-Tokyo Axis," though no one had a clear idea of how the alliance worked. The pact had emboldened Japan to occupy the northern half of French Indochina (Vietnam) in a bloodless coup that the defeated French accepted as a fait accompli. In 1941 Tokyo seized the southern half of the colony. But Indochina and the rest of Asia were 7,000 miles away in a world that remained murkily mysterious and remote to most Americans.

A majority of those polled favored aid to embattled China and Great Britain, but other polls revealed that 80 percent were opposed to declaring war on Germany or Japan as long as they committed no hostile acts toward America. Many viewed with great uneasiness Roosevelt's escalating belligerence with Germany. U.S. Navy ships were convoying war supplies destined for England as far east as Iceland. This policy had already produced three clashes between U-boats and American destroyers.[9]

III

If the *Tribune* story caused consternation in Congress, its impact in the War Department could be described as catastrophic. General Albert C. Wedemeyer has provided the most vivid recollection. "If I live to be a hundred," he told this writer in the spring of 1986, "December fourth, nineteen forty one, will still seem like yesterday." (He was an erect six feet five and mentally alert at eighty-nine.) Although only a major in the War Plans Division, Wedemeyer, a 1918 graduate of West Point, had already been tabbed by his superiors as a man with a bright future. In 1936 they had sent him to Berlin, where he spent two years studying at the German War College. When Roosevelt ordered the preparation of Rainbow Five, the forty-four-year-old major was given the task of writing it.[10]

General Wedemeyer recalled the atmosphere he encountered when he walked into the War Department's offices at 7:30 A.M. on December 4. "Officers were standing in clumps, talking in low tones. Silence fell, and they dispersed the moment they saw me. My secretary, her eyes red from weeping, handed me a copy of the *Times-Herald* with Manly's story on the front page. I could not have been more appalled and astounded if a bomb had been dropped on Washington."[11]

For the next several days Wedemeyer almost wished a bomb had been dropped on him. He was the chief suspect in the leak of Rainbow Five, which within the closed doors of the War Department was called the Victory Program. He had strong ties to America First, the largest antiwar group in the nation, with 800,000 vociferous members, including Charles Lindbergh and retired General Robert E. Wood, chairman of Sears, Roebuck. Both Wedemeyer and his father-in-law, Lieutenant General Stanley D. Embick, were known to be opponents of Roosevelt's foreign policy, which they thought was leading the United States into a premature and dangerous war.

This was a full year before anyone realized Adolf Hitler might try to exterminate Europe's Jews. Embick and Wedemeyer viewed the world through the realistic eyes of the soldier. They had no use for Hitler's Third Reich and its anti-Semitic policies. But many other European countries, notably Soviet Russia, practiced anti-Semitism, either covertly or openly. The *New York Times* Moscow correspondent had pointed out that Josef Stalin had shot more Jews in his late-1930s purges of supposedly disloyal Communists than Adolf Hitler had thus far killed in Germany.[12]

Embick and Wedemeyer did not believe the United States should fight unless it was attacked or seriously threatened. They scoffed at Roosevelt's claim that Germany planned to invade South America, acidly pointing out that if the Nazi leader were to land an army in Brazil, his reputed prime target, the Germans would be farther away from the United States than they were in Europe. Both men also knew that America was not prepared to take on the German and Japanese war machines.

At the same time, Wedemeyer and Embick (who was descended from German-Americans who had emigrated to America before the Revolution) were men of honor, true to their oaths of allegiance as officers of the United States Army. (Admiral William Leahy, Roosevelt's military chief of staff, praised Embick's "superlative integrity.") Although they disagreed with the president's policy, there was no hesitation to obey his orders. "I never worked so hard on anything in my life as I did on that Victory Program," Wedemeyer recalled. "I recognized its immense importance, whether or not we got into the war. We were spending billions on arms without any clear idea of what we might need or where and when they might be used. I went to every expert in the Army and the Navy to find out the ships, the planes, the artillery, the tanks we would require to defeat our already well-armed enemies."[13]

One conclusion Major Wedemeyer drew from this research was particularly alarming. There was a gap of eighteen months between the present U.S. military posture and full readiness to wage a successful war. To discover this secret splashed across the front pages of two major newspapers for the Germans and Japanese to read was dismaying enough. But it was the "political dynamite" in the revelation that Wedemeyer dreaded even more.[14]

His civilian boss, Secretary of War Henry Stimson, told reporters that the man who had leaked Rainbow Five was "wanting in loyalty and patriotism," and so were the people who had published it. Wedemeyer was summoned to the office of John

McCloy, assistant secretary of war. He was not invited to sit down. He therefore stood at attention. "Wedemeyer," McCloy snarled, "there's blood on the fingers of the man who leaked this information."[15]

IV

Frank C. Waldrop, at that time the foreign editor of the *Washington Times-Herald*, has contributed another recollection of that emotional morning in the War Department. He visited the scene in pursuit of a story that had nothing to do with Rainbow Five and encountered a friend on the War Plans staff, Major Laurence Kuter. "Frank," a white-lipped Kuter said, "there are people here who would have put their bodies between you and that document."[16]

J. Edgar Hoover, the director of the FBI, was summoned to the office of Secretary of the Navy Frank Knox and urged to launch an investigation. Hoover called in the chief of naval operations, Admiral Harold R. Stark, and Rear Admiral Richmond Kelly Turner, who had been in charge of preparing the navy's portion of the Victory Program, and began interrogating them. Hoover asked if there was any dissatisfaction with the plan among naval officers. Turner, exhibiting his talent for political infighting, caustically informed Hoover that all the navy's officers considered Rainbow Five an "army" plan, "impractical of consummation" and "ill-advised." This was Turner's way of saying the navy wanted to fight Japan first, not Germany.[17]

Later in this tumultuous morning two FBI agents appeared in Wedemeyer's office and examined the contents of his safe. Their eyes widened when they discovered a copy of the Victory Program with everything that had appeared in the newspapers underlined. The sweating Wedemeyer explained that he had just done the underlining to get a clear idea of how much had been revealed. The two agents began an interrogation of Wedemeyer and other army and navy officers that continued for months.

Several army staff officers said they strongly suspected Wedemeyer of being the leaker. An anonymous letter, obviously written by an insider and addressed to the secretary of war, accused the harassed major and General Embick. The writer claimed Embick hated the British and "condemns Britain" for Germany's decision to declare war. There was an unfortunate germ of truth in this accusation. Embick, an 1899 West Point graduate, had served in England as a staff officer during World War I. He grew to loathe the arrogance with which the British demanded that Americans feed doughboys into their decimated regiments and abandon plans to form an independent army in France.

Wedemeyer's prospects grew even bleaker when the FBI discovered he had recently deposited several thousand dollars in the Riggs National Bank in Washington. He explained it was an inheritance from a relative. He admitted that he knew General Robert E. Wood, Charles Lindbergh, and other leaders of America First and agreed with some of their views. He often attended America First meetings, although never in uniform.

FBI agents hurried to Nebraska, the general's home state, to investigate his German origins. They were befuddled to discover his German-born grandfather had fought for the Confederacy. His Irish-American mother called him long distance to ask him what in the world he had done. She thought he was in danger of being shot at sunrise. General Wedemeyer smiled when he told this part of the story in 1986 but in 1941 he found nothing about his ordeal amusing.[18]

V

Meanwhile the White House was reacting to the big leak in several ways. Although FDR "approved" Secretary of War Stimson's statement, the president refused to discuss the matter at a press conference on December 5. Stimson had also refused to take any questions from reporters. Roosevelt allowed reporters to question his press secretary, Steve Early, who claimed he was not in a position to confirm or deny the authenticity of the story. Early added that it was customary for both the army and the navy to concoct war plans for all possible emergencies. Sensing that this was an absurd way to discuss Rainbow Five, which included the president's letter ordering its preparation, Early stumbled on to assert that it was also customary to ask the president's permission to publish one of his letters.

The press secretary undercut himself again by admitting that this was an official, not a personal, letter, hence a public document. Then he lamely pointed out that the president's letter made no specific mention of an expeditionary force. But Early did not attempt to deny the president had seen Rainbow Five and given it his tacit approval.

On only one topic did Early seem forthright. He said that the newspapers were "operating as a free press" and had a perfect right to print the material, "assuming the story to be genuine." It was the government's responsibility to keep the report secret. Almost in the same breath he added that other papers were free to print the story too, depending on whether they thought such a decision was "patriotic or treason." Obviously Early was practicing what Washington pundits later called damage control.

After his histrionics with Major Wedemeyer, John McCloy coolly informed Clarence Cannon, the head of the House Appropriations Committee, and John Taber, the ranking House Republican, that there were no plans for an American expeditionary force. They brought his assurance back to their colleagues; Cannon declared that the whole story, which he implied was fictitious, was designed to wreck the appropriations bill. The next day the House voted the more than $8 billion to enlarge the army to 2 million men and expand the navy and the army and navy air forces at a similar rate.[19]

In his diary Secretary of the Interior Harold Ickes recorded his outrage at the leak of Rainbow Five. Few men in Roosevelt's administration, except perhaps Ickes's colleague, Secretary of the Treasury Henry Morgenthau Jr., were more ardently prowar. At a cabinet meeting on December 6, Ickes urged the president to punish the *Chicago Tribune* and the *Washington Times-Herald*. Attorney General Francis Biddle said he thought they could be prosecuted for violating the Espionage Act. FDR asked Secretary of War Stimson if Colonel McCormick, the owner of the *Tribune*, was a member of the army reserve and if so, could he be court-martialed? Stimson said no to both questions, which seem to have been more playful than serious. Ickes recorded his bafflement that Roosevelt, although apparently angry, showed no real interest in taking action against the *Tribune*.[20]

White House speechwriter and Roosevelt intimate Robert Sherwood later described Rainbow Five as "one of the most remarkable documents in American history, for it set down the basic strategy of the global war before the United States was involved in it." The plan had distilled "two years of wartime deliberations" by American army and navy staffs and "upwards of a year of exchanges of information and opinion by British and American staffs working together in secret." In the light of such an opinion, Roosevelt's seeming indifference to the source of the leak becomes even more puzzling.[21]

Elsewhere, the reaction to the big leak was quite different. The U.S. government's Foreign Information Service was staffed by interventionists. Far from exhibiting any embarrassment, they decided to send the story abroad by shortwave radio as proof of America's determination to defeat the Axis powers. The British, struggling to cope with savage German air and submarine offensives, headlined it in their newspapers as a beacon of hope.[22]

Interest in Rainbow Five was at least as intense elsewhere in the world. On December 5 the German embassy in Washington, D.C., had cabled the entire transcript of the newspaper story to Berlin. There it was reviewed and analyzed as "the Roosevelt War Plan." Tokyo also paid considerable attention to the plan. One big daily paper headlined the story with: UNITED STATES LACK OF PREPAREDNESS EXPOSED BY AMERICAN PAPER. Another paper called it: UNITED STATES GIGANTIC DREAM PLAN FOR WAR. A third bannered: SECRET UNITED STATES PLANS AGAINST JAPAN AND GERMANY ARE EXPOSED.[23]

VI

On the same December 4, 1941, in the United States' largest overseas possession, the Philippine Islands, Lieutenant Kemp Tolley was summoned to the Manila waterfront office of Commander Harry Slocum, the operations officer of the U.S. Asiatic Fleet. Tolley had just arrived in the Philippine capital aboard the USS *Oahu*, a Yangtze River patrol steamer that had barely survived a typhoon in the Taiwan Straits. Slocum gave Tolley the strangest order he had ever heard. He was to take command of a two-masted schooner, the *Lanikai*, commission her as a U.S. man-of-war, arm her with a cannon and a machine gun, man her with a mostly Filipino crew, and have her ready to sail under sealed orders in forty-eight hours.[24]

"The rules do not apply here," Slocum continued. "The Navy Yard has been directed to give you highest priority—without paperwork of any kind. Of this you can rest absolutely assured. The President himself has directed it."

At the Cavite Navy Yard, Commander R. T. Whitney greeted Tolley with nervous alacrity. "Sign this receipt for one schooner and tell me what you want," he said. Soon ordnance, supply, and communications technicians were swarming over the decrepit interisland vessel, which the navy had chartered for one dollar a year. They bolted a three-pound Spanish-American War cannon to the afterdeck house roof and added two World War I Lewis machine guns and a radio receiver. There was no transmitter available, so they left onboard the homemade rig the owners used to communicate with nearby islands. It would be useless once the ship was more than a few hundred miles at sea. The five-man Filipino civilian crew was sworn into the U.S. Navy and a half-dozen more sailors were added from the Insular Force, a naval unit of 1,000 Filipinos that were legally forbidden to leave Philippine waters. With a chief boatswain's mate and a chief gunner's mate from the Asiatic Fleet, the *Lanikai* was officially a warship.[25]

On December 6, Manila time—on the eastern side of the international date line it was December 7—the USS *Lanikai* sailed fifteen miles to the mouth of Manila harbor and anchored at dusk. The ship would have to wait until dawn to traverse the minefield at the harbor's mouth. Lieutenant Tolley had not opened his sealed orders; he was technically not yet at sea. But Commander Slocum had already told him where he was going: the waters off Cam Ranh Bay, the big Japanese naval base on the coast of Indochina. Tolley sat on deck watching hundreds of lights begin glowing on the nearby fortress island of Corregidor. What his improvised man-of-war was supposed to accomplish off Indochina was a mystery that only Franklin D. Roosevelt could solve.

At 3:00 A.M. on December 8, Manila time, the *Lanikai*'s radioman awoke Lieutenant Tolley. By flashlight he read an astonishing message: ORANGE WAR PLAN IN EFFECT. RETURN TO CAVITE. As an Annapolis graduate, he instantly knew Japan and the United States were at war. Plan Orange, the strategy for fighting the Japanese in the Pacific, was a familiar term to every officer in the U.S. Navy. (It had been combined with Plan Black—a war with Germany—and various other plans to create Rainbow Five.)

Back in Cavite later on December 8, Tolley shared the stunning surprise of his fellow sailors when they learned that the war had begun with a devastatingly successful Japanese attack on the Pacific Fleet's Hawaiian headquarters, Pearl Harbor.[26]

VII

Pearl Harbor made the question of Rainbow Five's relationship to American politics seemingly moot. But this appearance was deceptive. All-out war with Japan, which the attack triggered, was not part of Major Albert Wedemeyer's Victory Plan scenario. Rainbow Five had envisaged devoting almost all of America's military strength to defeating Hitler. Japan was to be handled by defensive strategies short of war. This posture reflected the perceived danger of an imminent German victory over Russia and Great Britain and a shortage of ships, planes, weaponry, and men to fight a two-ocean war.

In this context, Pearl Harbor seemed a political as well as a military misfortune. With newspapers and newsreels full of images of American ships burning and capsized in the Hawaiian anchorage, how could anyone, even a president as charismatic as Franklin D. Roosevelt, persuade the nation to fight Germany when Japan had dealt this staggering blow to America's pride and military prowess? Had FDR and the men around him blundered?[27]

The gap between what the public knew through their newspaper and radio reporters and the reality of American relations with Japan was vast. After the war historians began piecing together the backstage drama of the failed negotiations that led to the Japanese attack on Pearl Harbor. Even today, some pieces are missing from the puzzle; the leak of Rainbow Five is one of them.

When Japan signed the Tripartite Pact with Germany and Italy in 1940, the problem of how to restrain her ambitions in Asia acquired new dimensions. Tokyo was obviously hoping for a chance to acquire British and French colonies in the Far East, as well as a stranglehold on China. Although bringing the United States into the war against Germany remained Roosevelt's top priority, Japan began receiving serious attention. Roosevelt encouraged Secretary of State Cordell Hull to haul the hulking Japanese ambassador, one-eyed Admiral Kichisaburo Nomura, into his office for almost nonstop lectures on proper international behavior. The retired admiral, a professed friend of America, had the best of intentions, but he was at an enormous disadvantage. American cryptographers had broken Japan's top secret "Purple" code and knew more of what was going on in Tokyo than he did.

Roosevelt had no confidence in Hull or anyone else in the State Department except reserved, ultra-dignified Under Secretary of State Sumner Welles. Like the president, Welles was a product of Groton and Harvard, as well as an old family friend. He had been a page boy at Roosevelt's wedding. In 1915, Roosevelt, assistant secretary of the navy in Woodrow Wilson's cabinet, had helped Welles win his appointment to the diplomatic Service. From the beginning of FDR's administration, the president and his New Deal colleagues took a dim view of the other career diplomats in the department. Sometimes they viewed them as effete snobs, too subservient to the British diplomatic Office. At other times they accused them of being pro-Nazi. The president's aides and cabinet officers leaked a stream of nasty stories against the career men to columnist Drew Pearson, who specialized in character assassination.[28]

The president also made cruel backstage fun of Secretary of State Hull, a gray-haired, dignified but not terribly bright former senator from Tennessee. FDR even mocked his lisp when Hull descanted on "fwee twade," (free trade) the one issue that galvanized him. Roosevelt had put the Tennessean in the job as a gesture to the southern wing of the Democratic Party but he seldom had any interest in Hull's advice. Like many presidents, FDR preferred being his own secretary of state.

The Purple intercepts, code-named "Magic," revealed to the Americans a Japan torn between an expansionist army, a cautious navy (personified by Nomura), and moderate politicians who lived in constant fear of assassination by military extremists. Hull's pompous sermons to Nomura, which were accompanied by demands that Japan abandon all thoughts of an overseas empire, took the moral high ground that Americans loved to occupy. Diplomatically speaking, the secretary's lectures were idiotic. Japan had the third largest navy and the fourth largest army in the world. It was absurd to expect Tokyo to capitulate to the United States' demands when the Americans lacked the muscle to enforce them.

VIII

Other men, watching this diplomatic drama from the sidelines, had more forceful ideas. Secretary of the Treasury Henry Morgenthau Jr. had been arguing for a year that the United States should use economic sanctions to rein in Japan. Tokyo depended on America for a steady supply of scrap metal, copper, and other ingredients vital to her war machine. Even more crucial was oil; Japan imported 90 percent of her needs and the United States supplied half of that amount. Virtually echoing his cabinet colleague, Secretary of the Interior Ickes wrote to Roosevelt in the spring of 1941: "To embargo oil to Japan would be as popular a move in all parts of the country as you could make. There might develop . . . a situation as would make it not only possible but easy to get into the war in an effective way." Whereupon Ickes, who was wearing a second hat as Petroleum Coordinator, unilaterally suspended all shipments of oil to Japan.

When Roosevelt discovered this decision, he hastily counter-manded it and called the pugnacious—and amazingly presumptive—secretary of the interior into the Oval Office for a lecture. He told Ickes any such action was premature. A brawl in the Pacific would mean fewer ships in the far more crucial theater, the Atlantic. But six months later, Ickes was still convinced that starting a war with Japan was the solution to Roosevelt's intervention problem. On October 18, 1941, he wrote in his diary: "For a long time I have believed that our best entrance into the war would be by way of Japan . . . And, *of course,* if we go to war against Japan, it will inevitably lead us to war against Germany."[29]

Instead of an outright embargo, which would have stirred the hard-liners in Japan to fury, Roosevelt chose deception of the murkiest sort. Some historians are inclined to attribute his policy to lack of a policy. Anyone who follows what happened next with any degree of attention is more likely to conclude it was an attempt to combine opposites: the stalling for time that is implied in Rainbow Five, and the interventionist advice the president got from Ickes, Morgenthau, and others.

The idea of using Japan as a back door to war with Germany was already in circulation. Shortly after FDR was reelected in 1940, Chief of Naval Operations Harold Stark wrote a memorandum that became the basis for War Plan Dog. It was, in the words of one historian, the "true parent" of Rainbow Five. Stark envisioned the U.S. fighting a limited defensive war with Japan while Britain and America combined forces to defeat Germany. Plan Dog won the enthusiastic approval of Army Chief of Staff General George C. Marshall, and Stark was told that Roosevelt was "probably delighted" with his thinking. The probable delight became certainty when the president authorized secret conferences with British military men to plan combined operations based on the concept.[30]

In retaliation for Japan's mid-1941 seizure of southern French Indochina, Roosevelt froze all Tokyo's assets in the United States, something he had already done with Germany and Italy. The Japanese now had to obtain a license for any product deemed useful to their war machine and another license to unfreeze the dollars to pay for it. This meant they had to go to both the State Department and the Treasury Department, leaving ample room for maximum bureaucratic foot-dragging.

Meanwhile the Americans were reinforcing the Philippines with all the men and planes they could find, notably B-17 Flying Fortresses, which had the range to hit Formosa, Okinawa, and other parts of Japan's island empire. A new model of the bomber, just going into production, would be able to hit Japan's home islands. The army air forces had been eagerly selling the idea that air power alone could keep Japan at bay because their mostly wooden cities were extremely vulnerable to incendiary bombs. This rush to defend the Philippines was a wild card in the American scenario. Plan Orange had called for the abandonment of the islands as indefensible in a war with Japan.

The man in charge of the Japanese unfreezing process at the State Department was an elegant mustachioed lawyer named Dean Acheson. He was a liberal but not a passionate supporter of FDR; Acheson had resigned as secretary of the Treasury in 1933 in protest against Roosevelt's spendthrift domestic policies. But he was a fervent Anglophile and a wholehearted interventionist. His immediate superior was Under Secretary of State Sumner Welles, Roosevelt's spokesman at the State Department.

The silent embargo began in August 1941, just before Roosevelt sailed to Placentia Bay, Newfoundland, to meet Winston Churchill for a conference that Roosevelt hoped would tilt the United States toward an alliance with England. Roosevelt took Welles with him and left Secretary of State Hull home, a snub that would have caused most men to resign. But Hull was not the

resigning type, except in another sense of the word: he was resigned to Roosevelt ignoring him. Worn out from preaching to
Admiral Nomura, Hull took a long summer vacation and thus
had no idea what his subordinates in the State Department were
doing.

When Roosevelt returned from the conference with Churchill
at which they issued the Atlantic Charter, Sumner Welles informed him of the de facto backstairs embargo and not a demur-
ring word was heard in the Oval Office. On the contrary, on
September 5, 1941, the president persuaded Secretary of State
Hull to accept the situation, arguing that to alter the policy now
would be a sign of weakness. Hull, already convinced from reading the Purple intercepts that the Japanese were bent on war, accepted the secret cutoff.[31]

As the Japanese slowly realized that they were not going to get
any oil, Tokyo's hard-liners argued that this was proof that the
Americans were trying to humiliate them. They began planning
to use their military power to get oil—and much more. It is hard
to believe that Roosevelt, if he was reading the Purple intercepts,
did not see war as an inevitable outcome of this covert policy.

The oil cutoff was public knowledge. *Time* magazine reported
Nomura saying: "All over Tokyo, no taxicab." When he said
that, *Time* noted, "the sparkle goes out of his one good eye. It
means Japan is desperately hard up for oil and gasoline, which
means Japan must say uncle to Uncle Sam or else fight for oil."
Fiercely interventionist and ardently pro-China, thanks to
founder Henry Luce's family ties to that country, *Time* declared
the U.S. had no "morally valid answer" to Chiang Kai-shek's
statement that one drop of oil for Tokyo meant gallons of blood
to China. "The case for Mr. Roosevelt is very simple," *Time*
maintained. "He is committed to destroying aggressors. Japan is
an aggressor. He is committed to destroying Japan unless Japan
changes her ways."[32]

To paraphrase the French general who said the charge of the light brigade was magnificent but it was not war, this kind of thinking was not diplomacy. For one thing, the United States had been supplying oil to this aggressor since Japan went to war with China in 1937. Why should the White House suddenly get this attack of moral principles in mid-1941?

In November, the Japanese sent another negotiator to Washington, Saburo Kurusu, who was married to an American and spoke excellent English. He was an old friend of Admiral Nomura and a spokesman for the dwindling peace party in Japan. Kurusu brought with him orders to reach a settlement before November 25. By the time he arrived in Washington and joined Nomura for their first meeting with Hull, only six days remained to cut some sort of deal. Hull and Roosevelt, still reading the Purple intercepts, knew how little room was left for maneuver.

The final Japanese offer did not amount to anything approaching generosity. They suggested a ninety-day cooling-off period in which both countries would promise not to move troops or warships in the Far East in any direction. The United States would permit Japan to buy oil from America and help her obtain additional oil from the Dutch East Indies. In the meantime, Japan would remove her troops from southern Indochina, reducing the threat to Singapore and Malaya. Other clauses discussed the "restoration of peace" with China without specifying how this goal would be achieved, except for one important point: The Americans would cease aiding China, on the theory that this would force her to negotiate. As soon as the war was concluded to everyone's satisfaction, Japan promised to evacuate Indochina.

This proposal was savagely attacked by the interventionists in the State Department and by the British Foreign Office, which had an intense interest in getting the United States into the war. But another group of State Department officers tried to convince Hull that it was time to stop enunciating lofty principles and use the Japanese offer as the basis for a modus vivendi. This 1941 equivalent of détente not only made sense because it would offer something to the harassed Japanese politicians who wanted to avoid war, it also dovetailed with the increasingly urgent requests from America's military leaders to buy more time. On November 21, the army's War Plans Division told Secretary of State Hull it was a matter of "grave importance . . . that we reach a *modus vivendi* with Japan."[33]

Hull permitted the peacemakers to put together a proposal that had real potential. It offered Japan practical proof of American friendship in the form of a $2 billion loan—if she agreed to end the war in China on reasonable terms. It promised a renewal of the shipments of oil and other minerals and metals she needed for her factories. Hull circulated the document around the State Department and the War Department and everyone on the interventionist side found fault with it. The end product was a feeble ghost of the original proposal, which might well have produced at least a temporary truce.

Throughout this diplomatic debacle, FDR remained a passive spectator, except for suggesting a few ideas such as a six-month cooling-off period, which vanished like most other ideas with a potential for peace in the attack of the interventionist critics. The British and the Chinese were even more hostile, with the Chinese resorting to a leak of the modus along with a condemnation. The president said nothing and let Hull and the State Department take the heat for supposed appeasement of Japan.[34]

In Russia, the Germans were within eighteen miles of Moscow. On November 26, Roosevelt told Secretary of the Treasury Morgenthau the Soviets were beaten, the capital lost. In Egypt, the British were locked in a ferocious struggle with Germany's Afrika Korps led by charismatic General Erwin Rommel. The prize: Britain's lifeline to the Far East, the Suez Canal. Never did American intervention seem more urgent. But General Marshall and other American military leaders continued to implore the president and Hull to accept some form of temporary truce with Japan. The buildup in the Philippines was far from complete.

Caught between these two imperatives, Roosevelt made a fateful decision. Instead of negotiating to get a better offer from the Japanese—or taking charge of the situation and proposing one himself—he let Hull present Nomura and Kurusu with a ten-point virtual ultimatum that included a demand for a total withdrawal from China and Japan's repudiation of the Tripartite Pact. The two diplomats were stunned and dismayed and asked why there was no response to their offer. Hull mumbled some rigmarole about American public opinion and all hopes of temporary peace between Japan and the United States vanished. The next day, Hull told Secretary of War Stimson, "I have washed my hands" of the Japanese and dealing with the situation was now up to the army and the navy.[35]

Some historians have blamed this final lurch toward war on a kind of mental collapse on Hull's part, a psychological burnout. But the situation could have been rescued by the kind of leadership Roosevelt had displayed repeatedly in the past. Instead, FDR uncharacteristically let Hull take charge of the situation. The secretary of state went to the White House on the morning of November 26 and read his ultimatum to the president, who "promptly agreed" with it.

Roosevelt permitted Hull to deliver this document to the dismayed Japanese without any further consultation with the secretaries of the army or navy or the service's military leaders. Even historians who attempt to defend the president describe his conduct on this day of decision as "extraordinary." Crucial to any judgment of FDR's performance is what we now know: thanks to the Purple intercepts, the president was aware that the Japanese, in the words of Foreign Minister Shigenori Togo, one of the peace seekers, saw "the fate of the nation" hanging on the outcome of their final offer, which showed "the limit of our friendship" in this "last possible bargain."[36]

IX

Further Purple decodings revealed that Foreign Minister Togo had persuaded the Japanese military to extend the war deadline from November 26 to November 29. But with Hull's near ultimatum on the table, there was nothing to negotiate and Roosevelt made no attempt to do so. Was he satisfied that the elaborate attempt at a final settlement would deflect any and all criticism? In the Oval Office, Roosevelt met with Admiral Stark, General Marshall, Secretary of War Stimson, and Secretary of the Navy Knox. The chief topic they discussed was how to make sure, in Stimson's words, Japan "fired the first shot."[37]

On November 27, war warnings were sent to American commands throughout the Pacific, with a special emphasis on the Philippines. The army message, which went to General Douglas MacArthur, the commander in the Philippines, contained a sentence missing from the navy warning: "If hostilities cannot, repeat, cannot be avoided, the United States desires that Japan commit the first overt act." The Philippines was obviously considered the place where the shooting war was most likely to start.

On December 1, the president summoned the British ambassador, Lord Halifax, and told him how serious the situation looked. There were reports of Japanese troopships in the South China Sea, suggesting a possible attack on Thailand. He urged the British to take preventive steps to thwart this possibility, and assured Halifax of American backing. As for a Japanese attack on British or Dutch Far East possessions, "we should obviously all be together." Those last words make it clear that Roosevelt now saw Japan as, in Harold Ickes's words, a way to get into the global war in an "effective" way.[38]

The focus on a Japanese thrust south also makes it clear that Roosevelt was as blind as everyone else to the possibility that the American fleet at Pearl Harbor might be the target of an attack. As the president saw the unfolding drama in the last week of November and the first week of December 1941, he was faced with a formidable test of his leadership skills in and out of Congress. He told Lord Halifax he would need a few days "to get things into political shape." He was thinking ahead to the moment when he would call his congressional lieutenants to the Oval Office and order them to begin lining up votes for a declaration of war against Japan.[39]

X

On the same day that Roosevelt assured Halifax of American support, he revealed how unsure he was of delivering on this promise by cabling the order to Manila to outfit the *Lanikai* and two other small ships and send them into the sea lanes supposedly to detect Japanese transports and warships heading south toward Malaya and the East Indies. In Cavite, as the war exploded around him, Lieutenant Kemp Tolley began asking questions that had some potentially disturbing answers. Why had Roosevelt sent a seven-knot ship with no radio worth mentioning on a reconnaissance into hostile waters? Such a voyage might have made sense in the eighteenth or nineteenth century. In 1941, the U.S. Navy and Army had airplanes that could scout the China Sea in one-twentieth of the time and at virtually no risk. Was the *Lanikai* supposed to provide the first shot FDR thought he needed to persuade Congress to declare war? Had the president stipulated that the *Lanikai* be staffed with a mostly Filipino crew because he wanted her destruction to bring the Philippines into the war on the American side? Most disturbing of all, had the commander in chief sent Lieutenant Tolley and his crew on a suicide mission?[40]

2

THE BIG LEAKER

Between a war with Japan and the next step—a declaration of war against Germany, the imperative heart of Rainbow Five—there was a large and mostly inscrutable void. In the scenario Roosevelt had envisioned on the eve of Pearl Harbor, the orders to the *Lanikai* make it clear that the president realized he had a problem. It would be difficult to persuade the antiwar leaders in Congress and the nation that America, with its heritage of opposition to colonialism, enshrined in the American Revolution and restated often in other eras, should go to war to defend British and Dutch colonies in the East Indies and the Malay Peninsula and Singapore.

It was all too easy to envisage a raging quarrel over declaring war against Japan that even if successful would consume almost all Roosevelt's political capital. To pile on a proposal for war against Germany might trigger an unthinkable possibility: a congressional rejection that would make Adolf Hitler invulnerable. There was only one solution to this dilemma. Germany—more specifically, Adolf Hitler—had to declare war on the United States.

How could the Nazi dictator be provoked into such a decision when it was obvious that keeping the United States out of the war was one of his top priorities? He had issued orders to his U-boats and air force to avoid attacks on Americans, and had studiously ignored or downplayed the numerous provocations that Roosevelt had flung his way. Moreover, the Tripartite Pact did not obligate Germany to join Japan in a war Tokyo initiated.[1]

Pondering this awesome problem, Franklin D. Roosevelt decided to capitalize on the one huge advantage he had over his opponents, both at home and abroad. He knew, thanks to the Purple intercepts, that war with Japan was going to start in a few days, a week at most. Why not leak Rainbow Five to one of the antiwar leaders, who would undoubtedly leak it to one of the antiwar newspapers, and inspire all these angry people to fulminate against it in their most choleric fashion? When Japanese aggression exploded in their faces, they would be left speechless with embarrassment—and politically neutered. But that would be a minor triumph, compared to the real purpose of the leak: to provoke Adolf Hitler into a declaration of war.

II

There is no absolute proof for this scenario, but it fits the devious side of Franklin D. Roosevelt's complex personality. He often liked to boast about the way he outwitted his opponents. Six months after Pearl Harbor, he told Secretary of the Treasury Morgenthau: "You know I am a juggler, and I never let my right hand know what my left hand does . . . and furthermore I am perfectly willing to mislead and tell untruths if it will help win the war."[2] The search for the leaker of Rainbow Five offers more than a few clues that point to FDR as the master of the gambit.

One fact is certain: Albert Wedemeyer was not the leaker. He survived the investigation unscathed and went on to high command in World War II, retiring from the army in 1951 as a four-star general. He attributed a good part of his salvation to his innocence. But he admitted that General George C. Marshall's trust in him, which never wavered, also had a lot to do with his subsequent successful career.

In the ensuing years a good deal of information has surfaced about the way Rainbow Five reached the public. We know that the man who passed the war plan to Chesly Manly was Senator Burton K. Wheeler. In his memoirs Wheeler said he got the plan from an army air forces captain. Senator Wheeler's son, Edward Wheeler, a Washington attorney, recalled that the captain told his father, "I'm only a messenger." The same captain had come to Wheeler earlier in the year to feed him secret information about the appalling weakness of the American air forces. Senator Wheeler never had any doubt, his son told this writer, that the man who sent the messenger was General Henry H. ("Hap") Arnold, the chief of the army air forces.[3]

In 1963 Frank C. Waldrop, who rose from foreign editor to managing editor of the *Washington Times-Herald*, published an article recalling his memories of the big leak. He told of having lunch after the war with the FBI man who had directed the investigation. The agent told him the bureau had solved the case within ten days. The guilty party was "a general of high renown and invaluable importance to the war." His motive was to reveal the plan's "deficiencies in regard to air power."[4]

In an interview with this writer, Waldrop added some significant details to this story. The FBI man was Louis B. Nichols, an assistant director of the bureau. Waldrop asked him, "Damn it, Lou, why didn't you come after us?" Waldrop and everyone else at the *Times-Herald* and the *Chicago Tribune* had hoped that the government would prosecute. They had a lot of information about the way the Roosevelt White House was tapping their telephones and planting informants in their newsrooms that they wanted to get on the record. Nichols replied, "When we got to Arnold, we quit."[5]

There are grave reasons for doubting Arnold was the leaker. All available evidence shows the general supported Rainbow Five, which did not, contrary to the imputation, scant a buildup of American air power. Even more significant is General Arnold's continuing friendship with General Marshall. If the FBI had found Arnold guilty, Marshall would certainly have been told. The virtue Marshall valued above all others was loyalty. It is inconceivable that Marshall would have ever trusted or worked with Arnold again, if he had leaked Rainbow Five without Marshall's knowledge and covert approval.[6]

The 1,200 pages of the FBI investigation, made available to this writer under the Freedom of Information Act, are an ironic counterpoint to what Nichols told Waldrop. A memorandum summarizing the probe, sent to Attorney General Francis Biddle with a covering letter from J. Edgar Hoover on June 17, 1942, concluded: "Owing to the number of copies [there were thirty-five copies of Rainbow Five distributed to the army, navy, and army air forces] and the several hundred Army and Navy officers and civilian employees in both the War and Navy Departments having legitimate access thereto, it has not been possible to determine the source."[7]

III

A wild card explanation of the mystery emerged in 1976. In William Stevenson's book, *A Man Called Intrepid*, about the British spy William Stephenson (no relation), the author asserted that the leak was conceived and orchestrated by Intrepid as part of his plan to bring America into the war on Britain's side. "The Political-Warfare Division of the BSC [British Security Coordination, the secret propaganda group that Intrepid led] concocted the Victory Program out of material already known to have reached the enemy in dribs and drabs and added some misleading information," Stevenson wrote. On November 26, James Roosevelt, the president's son, supposedly told Intrepid that negotiations with Japan had collapsed and war was inevitable. But Roosevelt and his advisors realized that a war with Japan did not guarantee the war they wanted, with Germany. The army air forces captain was sent to Wheeler with the supposedly fake document to create a newspaper story that would provoke Hitler into a declaration of war.[8]

Reviewers and some historians swallowed this story in 1976 because elsewhere in the book Stevenson offered documentary proof that the BSC had supplied Roosevelt with a forged letter and a map that the president used in the fall of 1941 to prove the Germans planned to conquer South America. But a closer look at the claim to orchestrating the big leak creates severe doubts. The only verifiable fact in Intrepid's version is the date, November 29, 1941. That was the day the Japanese had named as the deadline for a negotiated truce. As Wedemeyer attests, Rainbow Five was hardly a collection of dribs and drabs from public sources, it was a verbatim copy of what he had written. The reaction of Secretary of War Henry Stimson and others in the War Department makes it clear that they did not regard the war plan as material already known to the enemy. Far from being a fake, Rainbow Five was the unnerving real thing.[9]

Nevertheless, Stephenson's boast suggests in a murky way the identity of the man who engineered the leak. "I have no hard evidence," General Wedemeyer said in 1986, "but I have always been convinced, on some sort of intuitional level, that President Roosevelt authorized it. I can't conceive of anyone else, including General Arnold, having the nerve to release that document."

Frank Waldrop told this writer, "I'd like to believe it, because that confrontation with Larry Kuter in the Munitions Building bothered me for a long time." But Waldrop found it hard to believe that FDR would have "thrown gasoline on a fire." That was the way he and other antiwar advocates regarded the political impact of the big leak.

In spite of these cautionary words, no other explanation fills all the holes in the puzzle as completely as FDR's complicity. Although Intrepid's specific claim to have concocted the leak is full of holes, his presence in the United States and his purpose—to bring America into the war with Germany—are admitted facts. That he was in the country with Roosevelt's knowledge and approval is also an admitted fact. Would a president who had already used faked maps and concealed from Congress the truth about the naval war in the North Atlantic hesitate at one more deception?

This explanation enables us to understand why General Marshall, who was undoubtedly told of the deception after the story broke, never blamed General Arnold. It explains FBI Assistant Director Louis Nichols's cryptic admission that the bureau "quit" when it "got as far" as General Arnold. Nichols would seem to have been implying that the FBI knew the real leaker was someone above Arnold in the chain of command. The explanation also makes sense of Marshall's continuing confidence in Wedemeyer, on whom such dark suspicions had been cast. It explains Roosevelt's reluctance to prosecute the *Washington Times-Herald* and the *Chicago Tribune* for publishing what could justifiably be called vital state secrets. Finally, there is strong evidence from Germany that Rainbow Five played a part in Hitler's declaration of war on the United States.

IV

While his military advisors were digesting Rainbow Five, the German dictator wrestled with this immense political decision.

The Japanese attack on Pearl Harbor surprised him as much as it staggered Franklin D. Roosevelt. The Tripartite Pact had never been supplemented by specific agreements about coordinating Germany, Italy, and Japan's war aims. The German foreign minister, Joachim von Ribbentrop, had promised Hiroshi Oshima, the Japanese ambassador to the Third Reich, that Germany would support Japan if it became embroiled with the United States. Other Germans had quoted Hitler as offering similar assurances and the Führer had promised Japanese foreign minister, Yosuke Matsuoka, Germany's assistance when he visited Berlin in April 1941.

But no guarantees existed on paper and Matsuoka had been ousted from his job when Hitler attacked the Soviet Union without bothering to inform Japan in advance. The two allies soon acquired additional doubts about each other's reliability. The Nazis groused about Japan's failure to attack Russia, which would have forced Stalin to fight a two-front war. Germany had repeatedly urged the Japanese to attack Singapore and the rest of Great Britain's Far East Empire, to no effect. The Japanese coolly informed Berlin that they preferred to wait until 1946 to go after Singapore. That was the year the Philippines would be granted its independence and the American army and navy would withdraw from the islands. (Here, it might be added, was additional evidence of Japan's reluctance to challenge the United States.) The Japanese had smugly lectured the Germans about the original goal of the Tripartite Pact: to keep the Americans from declaring war on Germany. In the summer of 1941, before the undeclared oil embargo began, Tokyo insisted that negotiating with the Americans was the best way "to bring about [their] domestic disintegration rather than to excite and unify them."[10]

In Berlin, after Pearl Harbor, Ambassador Oshima urged Ribbentrop to make good on his promise to join the war against the United States. The German foreign minister replied with cool generalities and urged Hitler to let the Japanese and the Americans fight it out, while Germany mopped up the Russians and the British.[11] There were good reasons, aside from Germany's disappointment with their inscrutable ally, to pursue this course. Hitler viewed the Japanese as an inferior race—far below Germany's supermen—and he never had any compunction about breaking his promises, as his attack on his ally, Josef Stalin, made clear. Moreover, the Germans had assumed that Japan's war with America would begin with an American attack to prevent the Japanese from seizing Singapore, Malaya, and the Dutch East Indies. If Germany joined that version of the war, it would look like the decision of an honorable ally. Japan's ferocious assault on Pearl Harbor now made a German declaration of war on America look like the tail, not the head, of the Axis kite.[12]

Even after Roosevelt had issued orders to American warships to "shoot on sight" at German submarines on October 8, 1941, Hitler had ordered Grand Admiral Erich Raeder, the German navy's commander in chief, to avoid incidents that Roosevelt might use to bring America into the struggle.[13] After the war Colonel General Alfred Jodl, Hitler's chief planner, said that the Nazi leader had wanted Japan to attack Great Britain and the USSR in the Far East but not the United States. He thought there was a very good chance that Roosevelt would not be able to persuade the Americans to go to war to defend Britain's Asian colonies. Hitler had wanted "a strong new ally without a strong new enemy."

On December 8, 1941, President Roosevelt seemed to confirm the wisdom of Hitler's policy in his speech to Congress, calling for a declaration of war against Japan. Condemning the attack on Pearl Harbor as a "date which will live in infamy," FDR did not so much as mention Germany. Hitler's policy of keeping incidents between America and the Reich to a minimum seemed to have succeeded.

On December 6, just before Japan launched its attack, Admiral Raeder became a major player in the Führer's global decision. He submitted to Hitler a report prepared by his staff that pointed with particular urgency to the most important revelation contained in Rainbow Five: the fact that the United States would not be ready to launch a military offensive against Germany until July 1943.

Raeder argued that this necessitated an immediate reevaluation of Germany's current strategy. He recommended an all-out offensive on land and sea against Britain and its empire to knock them out of the war before this crucial date. He envisaged further incidents between American naval vessels and German submarines in the North Atlantic and admitted that this could lead to war with the United States. But he argued that Rainbow Five made it clear that America was already a "nonbelligerent" ally of Great Britain and the Soviet Union and that a declaration of war was no longer something Germany should seek to avoid by restraining her U-boats. Moreover, Raeder concluded that Roosevelt had made a serious miscalculation "in counting upon Japanese weakness and fear of the United States" to keep Nippon at bay. The president was now confronted with a Japanese war two or three years before the completion of a two-ocean navy.

Hitler concurred with Raeder on launching the U-boat offensive. On December 9, he let the German navy suspend its prohibition against attacking American ships. But this was not a declaration of war. On the contrary, it could be justified by the assumption that American voters, having failed to respond to previous unauthorized attacks, would still ignore them.[14]

On December 9 Hitler returned to Berlin from the Russian front and plunged into two days of conferences with Raeder, Field Marshal Wilhelm Keitel, the chief of staff of the Oberkommando der Wehrmacht (usually referred to as the

OKW, the army's general staff), and Reich Marshal Hermann Goering, the commander of the German air force. The three advisors stressed Rainbow Five's determination to defeat Germany. They pointed out that the war plan discussed the probability of a Russian collapse and even a British surrender, whereupon the United States would undertake to carry on the war against Germany alone. By and large they leaned toward Admiral Raeder's view that an air and U-boat offensive against both British and American ships might be risky, but America was unquestionably already an enemy.

V

On December 9, 1941, Franklin D. Roosevelt made a radio address to the nation that is seldom mentioned in the history books. It accused Hitler of urging Japan to attack the United States. "We know that Germany and Japan are conducting their military and naval operations with a joint plan," Roosevelt declared. "Germany and Italy consider themselves at war with the United States without even bothering about a formal declaration." This was anything but the case, and Roosevelt knew it. He was trying to bait Hitler into declaring war, or, failing that, persuade the American people to support an American declaration of war on the two European fascist powers.

FDR added to this accusation of German complicity a string of uncomplimentary remarks about Hitler and Nazism. "Powerful and resourceful gangsters have banded together to make war upon the whole human race," he declared. "Their challenge has now been flung at the United States of America." He saw a pattern of aggression by Japan, Italy, and Germany, beginning as far back as 1931. "Modern warfare, as conducted in the Nazi manner is a dirty business," the president said. "Your government knows Germany has been telling Japan that if Japan would attack the United States Japan would share the spoils when peace came. She was promised by Germany that if she came in she would receive the control of the whole of the Pacific area and that means not only the Far East but all the islands of the Pacific and also a stranglehold on the west coast of North and Central and South America. We know also that Germany and Japan are conducting their naval operations in accordance with a joint plan."[15]

There was very little truth in any of this rhetoric. Germany and Japan did not have a joint naval plan before Pearl Harbor and never concocted one for the rest of the war. Japan never had any ambition or plan to attack the west coast of North, Central, or South America. Her goal was to create a new order in the Far East, with Japan running things instead of the British. Germany did not "promise" Japan anything in the Far East. The Third Reich's power in the region was negligible.[16]

On December 10, when Hitler resumed his conference with Raeder, Keitel, and Goering, the Führer's mind was made up. He said that Roosevelt's speech confirmed everything in the *Tribune* story. He considered the speech a de facto declaration of war, and he accepted Raeder's contention that the unwanted war with Japan made it impossible for the Americans to follow the grand strategy of defeating Germany first that had been laid down in Rainbow Five.[17]

On December 11 Hitler went before the Reichstag and announced that Germany and Italy had been provoked "by circumstances brought about by President Roosevelt" to declare war on the United States. His final decision, Hitler said, had been forced on him by American newspapers, which a week before had revealed "a plan prepared by President Roosevelt . . . according to which his intention was to attack Germany in 1943 with all the resources of the United States. Thus our patience has come to a breaking point." The yes-men in the Reichstag cheered wildly.

Foreign Minister von Ribbentrop grandly approved his leader's decision. "A great power does not allow itself to be declared war upon," he intoned. "It declares war on others."[18]

With a little extra prodding from the White House, the big leak had handed Roosevelt the gift that he desperately needed to proceed with the program outlined in Rainbow Five. Contrary to Raeder's expectations, neither America's military leaders nor the president altered the Europe-first cornerstone of the Victory Program. "That's because it was sound strategy," General Wedemeyer averred in 1986. He went on to plan Operation Bolero, which eventually became Overlord, better known as D day.[19]

VI

For a few more weeks the big leak developed yet a third life in Germany. Berlin greeted Rainbow Five's revelations as "the most profound intelligence value conceivable, enabling [the German High Command] to adapt [its] arrangements to the American program." The offensive against Moscow and Leningrad was faltering in the freezing Russian winter. The generals seized on the Roosevelt war plan to reinforce a suggestion they had already made to Hitler: to pull back to carefully selected defensive positions that would give them time to regroup and reinforce their decimated divisions.[20]

In a postwar memoir, General Walter Warlimont, the deputy chief of the general staff, revealed how little information the generals had on the United States, which made Rainbow Five all the more important to them. Warlimont told of receiving a phone call from Jodl in Berlin on December 11, 1941:

"You have heard that the Führer has just declared war on America?" Jodl asked.

"Yes and we couldn't be more surprised," Warlimont replied.

"The staff must now examine where the United States is most likely to employ the bulk of her forces initially, the Far East or

Europe. We cannot take further decisions until that has been clarified."

"Agreed," Warlimont said. "But so far we have never even considered a war against the United States and so have no data on which to base this examination."

"See what you can do," Jodl said. "When we get back tomorrow we will talk about this in more detail."[21]The OKW staff soon submitted to Hitler a study of the "Anglo-Saxon war plans which became known through publication in the Washington *Times-Herald*." The analysts concluded that to frustrate the Allies' objectives, Germany should choose a "favorable defensive position" and terminate the Russian campaign. Next Hitler should integrate the Iberian Peninsula, Sweden, and France within the "European Fortress" and begin building an "Atlantic wall" of impregnable defenses along the European coast. The "objective of greatest value" should be the "clearing of all British and allied forces out of the Mediterranean and the Axis occupation of the whole of the northern coast of Africa and the Suez Canal."

Admiral Raeder and Reich Marshal Goering joined in this recommendation in the most emphatic fashion. They told Hitler that in 1942 Germany and Italy would have "their last opportunity to seize and hold control of the whole Mediterranean area and of the Near and Middle East." It was an opportunity that "will probably never come again." To everyone's delight Hitler agreed to these proposals.

A few days later, the Nazi leader returned to the Russian front, where he was astonished and enraged to find his armies reeling back under assaults from Soviet armies whose existence his intelligence officers had failed to detect. The Führer flew into a rage and summoned Col. Gen. Franz Halder, the chief of staff of the German army, and Field Marshal Walther von Brauchitsch, the commander in chief. Berating them hysterically, Hitler declared that a "general withdrawal is out of the question." Whereupon he fired Brauchitsch and took over command of the army. A dismayed General Halder filled his diary with lamentations about Hitler's "fanatical rage against the idea of withdrawing to a winter line."[22]

If Hitler had stuck with his original decision and acted to frustrate the objectives of Rainbow Five, he could have freed a hundred divisions from the eastern front for a Mediterranean offensive. Against this force the Allies, including the Americans, could not have mustered more than twenty divisions. Germany's best general, Erwin Rommel, was already in Egypt, demonstrating with a mere nine divisions (three German, six Italian) what he could accomplish against the British and Australians.

There is little doubt that Hitler could have turned the Mediterranean into a German lake and nullified the Allied plan to seize North Africa and attack Europe from the south. The catastrophic German defeat at Stalingrad would never have occurred, and the Allied attempt to invade Europe at any point, particularly across the English Channel, would have been much more costly. This grim possibility explains why men trained to think strategically, like Albert Wedemeyer, were horrified by the leak of Rainbow Five. The Allies were rescued from the worst consequences of Roosevelt's gamble by the emotional instability of another amateur strategist, Adolf Hitler.

VII

On the home front, Pearl Harbor was a political bonanza for Roosevelt and the interventionists. The American public, who saw only the externals in the newspapers—the wily Japanese negotiating until the last moment, while their fleet headed for Hawaii; the surprise attack, easily converted into a "sneak" attack—confirmed all the nasty things Roosevelt and members of his administration had been saying about the Axis powers for years. It ignited a vast rage in the American people, which obliterated all and every hesitation about going to war.

Secretary of Labor Frances Perkins left an account of Pearl Harbor's impact on Roosevelt. She visited him on Sunday night and recalled that on the previous Friday, December 5, 1941, the president had been "tense, worried, trying to be as optimistic as usual, but it was evident that he was carrying an awful burden of decision. The Navy on Friday had thought it likely it [the Japanese attack] would be [on] Singapore. . . . What should the United States do in that case? . . . One was conscious that night of 7 December, 1941, that in spite of the terrible blow . . . he had, nevertheless, a much calmer air. His terrible moral problem had been solved by the event."[23]

FDR's calm was undoubtedly reinforced when he heard about the humiliation of the leading antiwar group, America First. On December 7, they had scheduled a huge rally in Pittsburgh's Soldiers and Sailors Memorial Hall. The principal speaker was Senator Gerald P. Nye of North Dakota, the man who had created the Neutrality Acts. The meeting began at 3:00 P.M. with a rousing speech by Irene Castle McLaughlin, the attractive former wife and partner of dancer Vernon Castle, who had been killed in World War I. Mrs. McLaughlin was a favorite among women antiwar activists. She spoke with her usual passion about the folly of war and the fear that she would lose her son in the conflict Roosevelt was trying to enter.

The next speaker was a local Pennsylvania politician, Hale Sipe, who denounced American aid to Communist dictator Josef Stalin as a betrayal of the national trust. In the middle of Sipe's speech, a man rose to tell the audience that the Japanese had attacked Pearl Harbor. People thought he was a heckler and the ushers escorted him to the door.

At 5:00 P.M. Senator Nye strode to the microphone. By this time almost everyone in America who was near a telephone or a radio had learned about the Japanese attack. But the news had not penetrated Soldiers and Sailors Memorial Hall. Nye unleashed a ferocious diatribe against Roosevelt for fighting Britain's war. He called the British cowards because they feared and avoided heavy casualties whenever possible. About a half-hour into his speech, a local reporter handed him a piece of paper, confirming the Japanese attack on Pearl Harbor.

The flustered Nye kept on talking until he reached the part of his speech where he condemned Roosevelt's attempt to start a war with Japan. Abruptly, he interrupted himself to read the message from the reporter, calling it "the worst news I have had in twenty years." The message read: "The Japanese Imperial Government at 4 P.M. announced a state of war between it and the United States and Great Britain." Like a man drowning in his own incoherence, Senator Nye stumbled back into his speech. When reporters swarmed around him to ask for comments, he snarled: "It sounds terribly fishy to me."

Other members of America First reacted with more dignity and common sense. They called on their members to support the nation in its war on Japan. But there was an undercurrent of bitterness beneath the surface of this patriotism. On Martha's Vineyard, Charles Lindbergh had been working on a speech he planned to give in Boston the following week. He called General Robert E. Wood and they agreed the meeting should be cancelled. "Well," Wood said, "he got us in through the back door."[24]

In the privacy of his White House study, FDR must have taken special delight in thinking of how much egg he had layered over the face of Colonel Robert McCormick, publisher of the *Chicago Tribune*. The colonel had devoted immense amounts of energy and newsprint to painting Roosevelt as a warmonger and a fraud. Tricking him into publishing Rainbow Five three days before Pearl Harbor was exquisite revenge for the Colonel's 1919 leak of the Versailles Treaty, which had wounded Woodrow Wilson's political credibility and his presidency.

Thanks to a bizarre combination of presidential trickery and Japanese aggressiveness, Roosevelt and his followers had won a stupendous political victory over their domestic enemies. But the war had only begun. How the president would wield the immense power now in his hands was far from clear. The temporarily silenced opponents inside and outside the American government were by no means ready to give him a free pass.

VIII

Secretary of Labor Frances Perkins may have seen a calmer, more confident FDR—the face he displayed to the nation and the world for the rest of the war—but other visitors to the White House on December 7 brought away a very different impression. Secretary of the Navy Frank Knox went to the Oval Office on the afternoon of that fateful day. He later told one of his aides that the president "was seated at his desk and was as white as a sheet. He was visibly shaken. You know, I think he expected to get hit; but he did not expect to get hurt."[25]

Frank Knox's recollection was in response to a question from his aide, Admiral Ben Moreell, who had asked Knox whether he had ever seen Roosevelt reveal any inner doubt. Morrell said he thought Roosevelt's complete confidence in himself was one of his most remarkable characteristics. He had never seen FDR "indicate any doubt about the correctness of his position on any issue."[26]

Absence of doubt was a widespread characteristic in the Roosevelt administration. Another trait was a tendency to clothe their policies and decisions in moral garb. Frances Perkins's remark that the Japanese had solved Roosevelt's moral problem is a particularly revealing example. The dilemma of how to get the United States into the war was, morally speaking, not a simple one. No matter how intensely FDR and his supporters believed the United States should become a belligerent, there were serious issues of statecraft and responsibility to the men in the American armed forces involved in the process.

The charge that Roosevelt wanted the Japanese to attack the Pacific fleet in Pearl Harbor remains unproven. But the responsibility for stationing the ships there is another matter. FDR ignored the warnings of the commander in chief of the U.S. Fleet, Admiral James O. Richardson, who wanted to keep the ships in San Diego. Roosevelt argued that the warships' presence at Pearl Harbor would be a "restraining influence" on Japan.

Admiral Richardson found it difficult, if not impossible, to see the logic of the president's argument. At Pearl Harbor, the fleet was 5,587 miles away from the Philippines—the territory the ships were supposed to protect—and even farther from the Dutch East Indies, Singapore, and Malaya, other likely targets of Japanese attack. Moreover, the fleet, already diminished by the withdrawal of many ships to the Atlantic, was not ready for war. It lacked the oilers, supply ships, and training to operate at sea for a long period of time. There were serious shortages of trained enlisted personnel.

The argument between Roosevelt and Richardson reached an ugly climax in the Oval Office on October 8, 1940, when the admiral said: "Mr. President, I feel I must tell you that the senior officers of the navy do not have the trust and confidence in the civilian leadership of this country that is essential for the successful prosecution of a war in the Pacific."

Roosevelt was deeply offended. "Joe," he said, "you just don't understand that this is an election year and there are certain things that can't be done, no matter what, until the election is over."[27]

That was the beginning of the end of Richardson's tenure as commander in chief of the U.S. Fleet. FDR fired him soon after he was reelected for his third term. As Richardson departed from Washington, he spent two hours with Secretary of the Navy Frank Knox, warning him that the fleet was vulnerable at Pearl

Harbor and Roosevelt's idea of a naval offensive to stop the Japanese in the Far East was a fantasy. "J.O." as he was called, was a very popular admiral and his opinion—and his fate—were widely discussed throughout the fleet.[28]

The president replaced Richardson with Admiral Husband Kimmel, who went to his grave declaring he never received adequate warning that the Japanese might attack Pearl Harbor. These cries of distress have concealed Kimmel's true role in the debacle. Although additional transfers to the Atlantic had cost him one-fourth of his ships, the admiral agreed with Roosevelt's idea that the fleet should steam from Pearl Harbor the moment Tokyo committed a hostile act against an American ship or island in the Far East and wipe the Japanese fleet off the strategic map in a twentieth-century version of the battle of Trafalgar.

Kimmel's 113-page battle plan, approved by Roosevelt's complaisant chief of naval operations, Harold Stark, lay in navy files for five decades, until it was revealed in a startling article in the pages of *MHQ*, the *Quarterly Journal of Military History*. So mesmerized were Kimmel and his staff with their offensive plan, they lost sight of the possibility that the Japanese might have offensive plans of their own. The fleet was scheduled to go to sea on Monday morning, December 8, in search of the all-out battle. Admiral Kimmel, yielding to sentiment, decided to let the men have a final Sunday at home with their families and friends, never suspecting they would entertain such unwelcome visitors.[29]

IX

Ironically, the man who invented the idea of attacking Pearl Harbor by air was an American, Admiral Harry Ervin Yarnell. In 1932, on fleet maneuvers off Hawaii, he commanded America's first two aircraft carriers and four escorting destroyers. Operating independently of the navy's array of battleships and cruisers,

Yarnell took this task force north of Hawaii on Sunday, February 7, a day he chose because he knew the defenders would not expect an attack. Launching 152 planes at dawn, Yarnell theoretically "sank" every ship in Pearl Harbor's anchorage and "destroyed" all the defending planes on the ground. (No live ammunition was used, of course.) A report on this astounding demonstration of naval air power was promptly forwarded to Tokyo by the Japanese consulate in Honolulu.[30]

Thereafter, the Americans were jumpy about the possibility of an air attack on the fleet at Pearl Harbor. In June of 1940, when navy intelligence officers lost radio contact with the Japanese fleet, Admiral Richardson immediately ordered the American fleet to sea. The navy, army and army air forces in Hawaii stayed on full alert for six weeks. The chief of army war plans reported to General Marshall later in the same year that an attack on Hawaii by Japan "could not be ruled out because a large part of the fleet was based there."[31]

If an attack on Pearl Harbor was a surprise only in the tactical sense, what lay behind FDR's decision to base the fleet there, in spite of the strenuous warnings by Admiral Richardson against it? A good part of the answer lies in the race-based contempt for the Japanese that too many Americans shared with their British allies. The Anglo-Saxons were convinced that the Japanese could neither shoot, sail, or fly with the skill of Westerners. Myths about Japanese endemic bad eyesight and poor numerical skills abounded. In a 1939 article, military commentator Fletcher Pratt dismissed Japanese warships as top-heavy and poorly built. Pratt also declared that the Japanese "can neither make good airplanes nor fly them well." He claimed that Japanese stupidity made them good infantry because obedience was more important than intelligence in ground battles. But alone in a plane a Japanese pilot was hopeless, and the planes were no good in the first place. Within six months of Pratt's pronouncements, the Japanese fielded the world's most advanced fighter plane, the Zero, against the Chinese. Its existence went unnoticed by the smug American and British military.[32]

A year later, Secretary of the Interior Harold Ickes confided to his diary: "It seems to be pretty well understood . . . that the Japanese are naturally poor air men. They cannot cope with the fliers of other nations." On December 4, 1941, the day of the big leak, Secretary of the Navy Frank Knox told a group of businessmen who had come to Washington to run the defense effort that America would be at war with Japan in a matter of days. But not to worry, Knox assured them. The war would not last much more than six months.[33]

At Pearl Harbor, the Americans were totally amazed, not only by the accuracy of the Japanese bombers, but by the aerial torpedoes that inflicted fearful damage on the anchored battleships. Torpedoes of 1941 required water far deeper than Pearl Harbor's anchorage to be effective. No one dreamed the Japanese were ingenious enough to modify a torpedo to perform in such relatively shallow water. Three days later, when Japanese fighter planes and bombers annihilated most of the American air force on the ground in the Philippines, an agitated General Douglas MacArthur swore they must have acquired Germans or some other white mercenaries to fly their planes. This arrogant mindset explains why FDR expected to "get hit but not hurt" wherever the Japanese attacked—including Pearl Harbor.[34]

X

By maneuvering Japan into a war she did not want, or at least was trying to delay, Roosevelt ignored the warnings, not only of the departed Admiral Richardson, but of his current military chiefs, about the army's and navy's unpreparedness. The president thereby exposed thousands of American servicemen in the Pacific to a conflict they could not win. Within a few weeks, the surface contingent of the U.S. Asiatic Fleet, consisting of three cruisers and a handful of destroyers, would be annihilated by the overwhelmingly superior Japanese fleet in the Java Sea.[35] The Philippines would be invaded and conquered and the 20,000 army and navy men stationed there killed or captured. Their fate—and their attitude—was summed up by General William E. Brougher, commander of the 11th Division in the losing fight against the Japanese invaders: "Who had the right to say that 20,000 Americans should be sentenced without their consent and for no fault of their own to an enterprise that would involve them in endless suffering, cruel handicaps, death or a hopeless future?"[36]

General Brougher was not the only man who recorded the anger these men felt about their abandonment by their commander in chief and their fellow Americans. Lieutenant Ward Bronson of the USS *Chicago* kept a diary, although such unofficial record-keeping was forbidden. It was his way of staying in touch with his wife, Rosemary, whom he had left in Hawaii. He mailed her portions of the diary whenever *Chicago* made port.

In the months after Pearl Harbor, Bronson became more and more bitter about the odds the Americans faced in the South Pacific and the blunders that had started the war so ruinously. "I think of the thousands of men who died at Pearl Harbor and begin to feel very bitter about the fact that Admiral Richardson's two hour talk to Secretary Knox was completely disregarded. . . . I think of the boys in civilian life who were drafted and sent to the Philippines to fight against the overwhelming odds that were to be thrown against them." A few months later, Bronson died when a Japanese torpedo smashed into *Chicago's* engine room.[37]

After the war, Admiral Richardson, the man Roosevelt had relieved because he did not want to keep the fleet at Pearl Harbor, said: "I believe the President's responsibility for our initial defeats in the Pacific was direct, real and personal."[38]

XI

Lieutenant Kemp Tolley, commander of the *Lanikai,* devoted several of his postwar years to proving he had been sent on a suicide mission. Admiral Thomas Hart, the commander of the Asiatic Fleet, refused to discuss it at first. But after Tolley retired as an admiral, Hart was more forthcoming. At lunch with another admiral, Hart said: "I once had the unpleasant requirement to send this young man [Tolley] on a one-way mission."

"Do you think we were set up to bait an incident?" Tolley asked.

"Yes, I think you were bait!" Admiral Hart said. "And I could prove it."

Hart was even more pointed in a postwar letter to Samuel Eliot Morison, official historian of the navy in World War II, who attempted to downplay the *Lanikai* mission. Hart told him either to rewrite it "to accord with facts" or omit it. "It is not a piece of history of which to be proud."[39]

Hart told Admiral Richardson that when he returned to Washington with the sickening knowledge that virtually every ship in the Asiatic Fleet was at the bottom of the Pacific, he was invited to the White House. FDR told him that the army had misinformed him about their ability to defend the Philippines. If he had known the truth, he would have "stalled off the Japs" for another year. The statement contradicted the written evidence that his military chiefs had told the president the precise opposite. Inadvertently, FDR admitted that delaying war with Japan was an option he chose to ignore.[40]

No one has summed up Roosevelt's course better than the State Department's George F. Kennan, a man who would soon emerge as the most trenchant foreign policy thinker of the century. Looking back on the president's performance, he wrote: "Opinions will differ, of course . . . but surely it cannot be denied that had FDR been determined to avoid war with the Japanese, he would have conducted American policy quite differently, particularly in the final period. . . . He would not have tried to starve the Japanese navy for oil. And he would have settled down to some hard and realistic dealings with the Japanese, instead of letting them be deluged and frustrated by the cloudy and unintelligible moralisms of Cordell Hull."[41]

XII

Merlo Pusey, editorial writer for the *Washington Post* and later a distinguished biographer, was a confirmed interventionist. "Inevitably, we had to get into it [the war]," he later said. "I just wish we had done it honestly and openly in our constitutional way of doing things instead of . . . by the back door. I think Roosevelt had a moral responsibility for leadership. If he had been less of a politician and more of a statesman, he would have taken a stand instead of trying to do it covertly."[42]

Using Japan as the back door to war was the only way FDR and his inner circle decided they could achieve their goal. The leak of Rainbow Five and the aborted cruise of the *Lanikai* exemplify their dilemma as they perceived it. Measuring his arguments against the contentions of his domestic opponents, the president decided he lacked the political strength to make a direct appeal to his fellow Americans to join the war against Germany. He had to trick the people into it.

Why had Franklin Roosevelt found himself forced to resort to this immensely risky, morally dubious pattern of deceit? Why was he unable to tell the American people the truth about one of the most important political decisions in the history of the country, for that matter one of the turning points in the history of the world?

3

From Triumph
to Trauma

The answer to that question is the stuff of tragedy, with that central tragic idea, *hubris*, at the center of it.

In 1933, Franklin D. Roosevelt became president of a nation mired in the most horrendous economic depression in American history. It was a global phenomenon, ultimately traceable to the massive wounds that the nations of Europe, with some help from the United States, had inflicted on each other during World War I. England, heretofore the world's richest nation, had seen all the wealth she had accumulated in a century of economic supremacy annihilated in those four nightmare years.

An unparalleled bankruptcy gripped the industrial nations that had created Europe's hegemony. In 1929, after a few years of fevered prosperity that the rest of the world did not share, the American stock market had crashed, wiping out billions of invested dollars. By 1933, the net worth of shares on the exchange had plummeted from $87 billion to $19 billion. Corporations collapsed and banks were closed without prior notice, leaving middle-class and working-class savers penniless. The song "Brother Can You Spare a Dime" was on the way to becoming a national anthem.[1]

Roosevelt's performance as a leader in this crisis was magnificent. At the Democratic convention that nominated him in 1932, he rallied the nation with a call for a "new deal for the American people" that would give the "forgotten man" a more equitable share of America's abundance. In his inaugural address, the president told a shaken populace that the only thing they had to fear was fear itself. Within two weeks of his inauguration, FDR went on the radio to give the first of his mesmerizing "fireside chats" that won support for his policies. Deciding that traditional government mechanisms were inadequate, he launched an alphabet soup of new federal agencies to intervene in the crisis.

FERA, the Federal Emergency Relief Administration, distributed $500 million to the nation's 13 million unemployed. HOLC, the Home Owners Loan Corporation, made $3 billion available to people about to lose their homes through foreclosure. AAA, the Agricultural Adjustment Administration, attempted to raise farm prices by setting quotas on how much growers should produce. The Works Progress Administration, soon known as the WPA, hired millions of unemployed to build hospitals, roads, parks, and monuments. The Public Works Administration (PWA) launched gigantic construction projects such as Colorado's Boulder Dam. The creation of the Securities and Exchange Commission proclaimed Washington D.C. would henceforth punish chicanery on Wall Street. The Civilian Conservation Corps gave work to 250,000 youths in the national parks and forests. The Tennessee Valley Authority (TVA) undertook the challenge of bringing electricity, flood control and economic development to an entire region.

Most ambitious of all was the NRA, the National Recovery Administration, which set out to control wages and prices in American industry. The New Deal's goal, people began to see, was not merely to stanch the wounds of the Depression but to prevent further downturns by increasing the buying power of the people at the bottom and limiting the profits of the people at the top.

In a world where Russia had embraced a form of state control called communism and Germany had opted for another variety of this same nostrum, national socialism, while Italy embraced fascism, yet another variation on authoritarian rule, the New Deal's attempt to insert the government into American business on a broad and apparently permanent scale alarmed not a few people. Their uneasiness was not soothed by the head of the NRA, General Hugh S. Johnson, who was fond of comparing his agency to Italy's "corporate state." People were even less reassured by the way the NRA sprouted like a bad seed producing jumbo-sized weeds. Soon there were 750 wage and price codes for everything from dog food to shoulder pads, plus a jungle of administrative regulations.[2]

For a while, however, the naysayers were ignored. The nation was captivated by the sheer energy of Roosevelt and his New Dealers. They were an unstable mix of Democratic professionals such as Postmaster General James Farley, who had been one of presidential candidate Al Smith's backers in 1928; independents such as crotchety Secretary of the Interior Harold Ickes, who had been heavily involved in Theodore Roosevelt's maverick run for the White House in 1912 on the Progressive Party ticket; and former Republicans such as shaggy-haired Secretary of Agriculture Henry Wallace, whose father had held the same job under Presidents Harding and Coolidge.

II

Beyond the cabinet swarmed a host of eager aides and administrators, many of them young, who enlisted in the New Deal's crusade to change the nation's direction and priorities. At the head of this group was Harry Hopkins, a dark-haired effervescent former social worker from Iowa who had registered as a socialist in 1916 because he was opposed to America getting into World War I. While running a New York State program for the unemployed, Hopkins had impressed then Governor Roosevelt with his administrative ability and his passion to help the troubled and needy. Put in charge of FERA, the Federal Emergency Relief Administration, Hopkins set up a desk in a hallway and gave away $5 million to seven states on his first day on the job.[3]

Hopkins went on to head the WPA, which built 651,087 miles of highways, worked on 124,087 bridges, constructed 125,110 public buildings, 8,192 parks, and 853 airports. Before it expired in 1943, the WPA had employed 8,500,000 people on 1,410,000 projects and spent $11 billion. Obviously Hopkins was a man who got things done. But he did not conform to the conventional image of either a do-gooder or a political operator. He despised most politicians and seldom concealed it. He could be ruthless and inconsistent. He enjoyed expensive living and liked to play the horses. In an unguarded moment at a New York racetrack, he supposedly said: "We shall tax and tax, spend and spend, elect and elect," a remark he frequently denied making. Nevertheless, the words—and his philosophy of largesse to the underclass— earned him the long-running enmity of Roosevelt's opponents.[4]

Less visible than Hopkins were thinkers like Adolf A. Berle, Jr., brilliant Columbia University law professor and coauthor of a landmark book, *The Modern Corporation and Private Property*, a savage attack on big business arrogance. Berle was a member of the original "brain trust," the largely unappointed insiders who gave Roosevelt the ideas that animated the early New Deal. In his later years, Berle summed up the essence of FDR's appeal to him and other intellectuals. "Leave the politics to me," Roosevelt told him. "That's a dirty business. Your business is to find . . . what should be done. I'll have to decide how much of it can be done or whether it can be done at all."

This marriage of idealism and pragmatism was the heart of the New Deal's approach to government.[5]

Balancing the liberals was bulky millionaire Houston newspaper-owner Jesse Jones, conservative head of the Reconstruction Finance Corporation. The RFC was created by FDR's predecessor, Herbert Hoover, but the New Dealers decided it fit perfectly into their scheme of things, thanks to its ability to loan millions to banks and corporations with the stroke of a pen. Jones was there to let businessmen know they had a friend in Washington—if they took the money and kept their mouths shut.

In those heady early days, Roosevelt attracted media support from all points of the ideological compass. Even conservative tycoons such as William Randolph Hearst, owner of a chain of influential newspapers and magazines, and Colonel Robert McCormick, combative publisher of the *Chicago Tribune*, supported the New Deal. One of his most enthusiastic backers was Fulton Oursler, editor of *Liberty*, the second largest weekly magazine in the United States. Oursler, a Baltimore Republican, had played a crucial role in winning FDR the Democratic nomination. Roosevelt's enemies in the Democratic Party had circulated the rumor that he had never really recovered from his 1921 bout with poliomyelitis and would be unable to handle the stresses of the presidency. Some of the rumormongers added the canard that his brain had been affected by the disease.

Oursler arranged for the owner of *Liberty*, Bernarr Macfadden, a fanatic apostle of physical fitness, to visit Roosevelt and declare that he was in excellent shape. Oursler followed this publicity coup with an article written by a reporter who spent four weeks with Governor Roosevelt in the executive mansion in Albany, watching him handle that demanding job with no apparent difficulty. Oursler buttressed the resultant article in *Liberty*, "Is Roosevelt Physically Fit To Be President?" by insisting that FDR submit to an examination by three reputable doctors, all of whom found him in good health. The reporter was thus able to dismiss the fact that Roosevelt was confined to a wheelchair except for public appearances, when he stood with the aid of leg braces attached to a steel belt around his waist. The article made the front pages of almost every newspaper in the country.[6]

III

After FDR's election, Fulton Oursler became a regular on the White House invitation list. He hired Eleanor Roosevelt to edit a magazine, *Babies, Just Babies,* with her daughter Anna as her paid secretary (and de facto editor). But Oursler soon experienced what many others encountered in their dealings with the president, his deviousness. An IRS agent showed up in Oursler's office and went around telling employees that Oursler had not paid any income tax in 1932. Oursler had a ferocious argument with the man, produced photostats of past checks, but made no impression. It dawned on him that the man was not there by accident.

A consultation with Bernarr Macfadden revealed that he had recently refused to give Mrs. Roosevelt a raise for her editorship of *Babies, Just Babies.* Oursler took a train to Washington D.C. and talked his way into the Oval Office. "Fulton I am damned glad to see you!" the president said in his cheeriest tone. Oursler asked if there was something wrong between Macfadden Publications and the Roosevelts. FDR claimed he did not know what Oursler was talking about.

Realizing he was getting nowhere, Oursler decided to take advantage of proximity and ask the president if *Liberty*'s chief Washington reporter could be tipped off five or six weeks in advance of a big story. "The trouble is," Roosevelt replied, "we seldom know six weeks in advance what we are going to do."

While Oursler struggled to digest this revelation of the New Deal's seat-of-the-pants style of governing, the president called in his chief advisor, Louis Howe, a gnome of a man who had devoted the previous decade to making Roosevelt president. Howe dourly concurred with FDR's remark about their impromptu agenda, and Oursler followed him out the door to have a pleasant lunch with Mrs. Roosevelt and Frances Perkins, the new secretary of labor, at which nothing was said about *Babies, Just Babies* or Mrs. Roosevelt's salary.

Afterward, a White House usher summoned Oursler to Louis Howe's office. Pounding a chair on the floor for emphasis, Howe declared in sulphurous terms that Mrs. Roosevelt had been "miserably treated" by Macfadden Publications. Oursler no longer needed an explanation for the appearance of the IRS man in his office. He departed, never expecting to be invited to the White House again.

"In that I was wrong," Oursler later admitted. He was "still a novice in politics." Oursler would gradually learn from his own experience and the experience of others whose stories traveled among political insiders that Franklin D. Roosevelt had a bad habit of using his power to treat people in the most cavalier fashion, relying on his enormous charm to make amends later. Dozens of people commented on this aspect of Roosevelt's personality. Secretary of Agriculture Henry A. Wallace said he had "a great capacity for communicating warmth." Later, a disillusioned Wallace concluded he "turned this on automatically."[7]

IV

In spite of this warmth, Oursler and many others began to cool on Roosevelt as the New Deal shifted from government aid to government control of the American economy. Former enthusiast Ernest K. Lindley of the *New York Herald Tribune* wrote a book, *Half Way with Roosevelt*, spelling out his disillusion.[8] Others left because they had been treated badly. Raymond Moley of Columbia University, another member of the brain trust, quit in disgust after being sent to England on a diplomatic mission that Roosevelt scuttled without bothering to tell him.

Others began having doubts about the governmental style and attitudes of New Dealers in general. Future Harvard sociologist David Riesman lived in one of the several large houses the younger operatives rented, creating an ongoing party atmosphere, shot through with political excitement. In his house, Riesman said, "they were all dedicated New Deal activists." But Riesman began to wonder if these Washington newcomers had "too much contempt for ordinary Americans. They thought it hopeless to try to persuade the country, or even to persuade Congress. Clever and ingenious, they were therefore tempted to use undemocratic means."[9]

Not a little of the growing chorus of critics concentrated on the NRA and its apparently endless attempt to control the economy. The organization was a blunder of major proportions but Roosevelt refused to admit it. Inevitably it was challenged in the courts. The case of choice was a federal prosecution that had sent the four Schechter brothers, New York City kosher chicken merchants, to jail. It was a prime example of the regulatory mania to which the NRA was predisposed. The Schechters had failed to comply with an NRA rule that if a customer refused to buy a full coop of chickens, he could not select the most likely looking fowls to fill a half-coop. He had to close his eyes and haul out his squawking choices at random.

On May 27, 1935, the Supreme Court, which usually divided five to four along a conservative-liberal fault line, voided the Schechters' prison sentences and found the NRA unconstitutional by a vote of 9-0. Still Roosevelt's self-confidence in his own judgment remained unassailable. "Where was Brandeis, where was Cardozo, where was Stone?" he cried, unable to believe that the Court's liberals, Justices Louis Brandeis, Benjamin Cardozo, and Harlan Fiske Stone, had voted with the conservatives.[10]

The NRA was by no means the only New Deal legislation the conservative majority on the Court struck down in that confrontational year 1935. The justices also deep-sixed the Agricultural Administration Act, calling it an attempt to give the federal government "uncontrolled police power in every state in the union." The justices wreaked similar havoc on a bill that attempted to rescue the NRA codes for the bituminous coal industry, calling the regulations "obnoxious" and "intolerable." Inflamed by Roosevelt's determination to assert government power, the Court's conservatives even banned a minimum wage law passed by the Democrats of New York State. [11]

Roosevelt and his Democratic majority in Congress pressed on, passing a graduated income tax frankly aimed at redistributing the nation's wealth, and the Social Security Act, which gave Americans a financial safety net for their old age. The Wagner Act gave labor unions far more power than they had possessed under the NRA. Another law assaulted public utility holding companies, a sacred cow that had produced some of the more outrageous stock frauds of the previous decade. More and more, the New Deal veered toward outright hostility to big business. Roosevelt told Raymond Moley that most businessmen were "stupid." Assistant Secretary of Agriculture Rexford Tugwell called on the government to take over "large blocks of paralyzed industries."[12]

Roosevelt ran for reelection in 1936 in this frame of mind, rallying his New Dealers for what he portrayed as an Armageddon-like conflict between property rights and human rights. He heaped scorn on the opposition, which now consisted not only of Republicans but moderate Democrats such as Al Smith, who had formed a "Liberty League" to protest FDR's supposed assault on the Constitution. He brushed aside cautionary comments from abroad, such as Winston Churchill's observation that there were dangers in "the disposition to hunt down rich men as if they were noxious beasts."[13]

Far from attempting to soothe his critics with talk of compromise and moderation, the president declared a readiness to take on the nation's "forces of selfishness and lust for power." He damned "economic royalists" who were trying to enslave the nation. Not only would he defeat these would-be tyrants, he would "master" them. "I welcome their hatred," he proclaimed.[14]

The results of the 1936 election seemed to promise mastery of the sort not seen since the days of Augustus Caesar. Roosevelt won a second term in one of the greatest landslides in American history, 27,751,612 to 16,681,913. He carried with him enough senators and congressmen to reduce the Republican Party to the vanishing point. The Democrats had majorities of 334 to 89 in the House and 75 to 17 in the Senate.[15]

V

Roosevelt began his second term as the most powerful political figure on the globe. A postelection headline in the *New York Times* declared: ROOSEVELT TOWERS IN THE IMAGINATION OF EUROPE. In Berlin, Adolf Hitler was still struggling to consolidate his grip on Germany. In Moscow, Josef Stalin would soon massacre the elite of the Communist Party in a series of savage purges to maintain his grasp on Russia. In Rome, the hollowness of Benito Mussolini's military pretensions was all too visible. England and France were led by timid politicians with precarious parliamentary majorities. Japan was embroiled in murderous political feuds between military and civilian cliques. Roosevelt alone was a colossus, capable, it seemed, of molding America and the world to his wishes.[16]

Then came the hubris. Two weeks after FDR took his second oath of office and declared he had defeated the Depression but paradoxically still saw a third of the nation "ill housed, ill clothed, ill nourished," he announced to his startled cabinet and the White House press corps his intention to reform the federal judiciary with a law that would permit him to appoint fifty new judges, including seven additional justices of the Supreme Court. On the same day, the bill was sent to Congress with blithe confidence in its immediate approval.

Drawn in total secrecy by a handful of New Deal insiders, the bill was quintessential Roosevelt-the-trickster, full of bogus statistics about Supreme Court justices and other federal judges being overworked and needing a WPA-like infusion of helping hands. The move collided head-on with realities that the landslide-mesmerized president ignored or forgot in his dizzying vision of himself as the voice of the people.

The Democratic majority that Roosevelt had created with his call for a New Deal and his energetic attack on the Depression was a strange hybrid, with drastically different views of political reality. The yellow dog Democrats of the South (so-called because they would vote for anyone or anything, even a yellow dog, if he, she, or it ran on the Democratic ticket) were conservatives with no desire to change the established order, particularly its shibboleths about segregation, black inferiority, and the undesirability of labor unions. In the North new industrial labor unions were often led by radicals if not by outright Communists who viewed the southerners with barely disguised loathing. Somewhere on the right of the middle were millions of northern ethnic voters, still mostly led by Irish-Americans in big city political machines, who suspected ideologues and disliked reformers almost as much as the southerners did.

The court-packing bill, as it soon was called, also collided with an almost mystic reverence for the Supreme Court that was deeply embedded in the psyche of the American people. Various presidents, going all the way back to Thomas Jefferson in 1805, had received bloody noses and black eyes when they tangled with this mind-set. Jefferson had pushed the idea that judges could be removed by a majority vote of Congress and their decisions overruled the same way. Roosevelt's solution seemed to many people more disreputable, because of the trickiness and evasion that surrounded it. The mail to Congress was soon running ten to one against the president's bill.[17]

That was only the beginning of FDR's woes. Senator Burton K. Wheeler of Montana, the same man who would assail Roosevelt as a warmonger, announced his unalterable opposition to the bill. Wheeler was a bona fide liberal who had a long record of defending the rights of the people against the power of property, in particular the politicians who spoke for Montana's giant copper companies. He quickly drew other western liberals into his camp. Southern Democrats, already unnerved by Roosevelt's liberal campaign rhetoric, defected virtually in a body.

In a move that revealed for the first time a glimmer of intelligence in the Republicans' opposition to Roosevelt, the GOP decided to say nothing. They even banned a radio address by former president Herbert Hoover attacking the president's lust for power. The GOP sat on the sidelines while the Democratic Party tore itself into chaotic shreds over the court-packing bill. In

spite of Roosevelt's landslide and the seemingly unassailable support of two-thirds of the American electorate, a majority of the
Democrats in Congress declared their distrust of Roosevelt's
charisma, his unpredictability, his arrogance. They declined to
give him the new power he was demanding.

Crucial to this collapse of Roosevelt's mandate was the Gallup
poll, which had won a sudden endorsement by the media thanks
to its fairly accurate prediction of the 1936 landslide. With maddening regularity, Gallup reported the American people divided,
45 percent for, 45 percent against Roosevelt's plan, with 10 percent undecided. Not even two all-out speeches by Roosevelt managed to change these numbers. The coup de grâce came from a
totally unexpected quarter. Justice Louis Brandeis, the first Jew
appointed to the Supreme Court, and far and away the most respected legal (and liberal) voice on the bench, announced that he
opposed the measure. This revelation, coupled with a canny letter
from Chief Justice Charles Evans Hughes, refuting the claim that
the court was unable to handle the flood of business from the
New Deal's legislation, sent the Roosevelt plan's poll numbers
into a slide from which they never recovered.[18]

Even when the Supreme Court, in a signal that suggested they
were more than willing to compromise, began to approve some
New Deal legislation, Roosevelt persisted in demanding his original bill with its seven extra justices, or nothing. By now the struggle had become personal, a no-holds-barred battle in which the
president was determined to prevail. Not even the desertion of
key members of his coalition, such as Vice President John Nance
Garner, who went home to Texas in the middle of the fight, de-
terred him. Nor did the Senate Judiciary Committee report that
damned the bill as a "needless, futile, and utterly dangerous
abandonment of constitutional principle" give him pause. Then
came the coup de grâce to the coup de grâce. New York's governor, Herbert Lehman, a certified liberal and FDR's handpicked

successor in that powerful office, released a letter to Senator Robert Wagner, urging him to oppose the bill. The Senate soon buried the plan, 70-20. "That this was a terrific defeat for the president cannot be denied," a glum Harold Ickes told his diary.[19]

VI

The failure to pack the court was not the end of Roosevelt's second term travails. On the contrary, it was the beginning of their multiplication. As a result of his obsession with the court bill, he neglected other proposals the New Deal was pushing in Congress, and had to swallow more legislative defeats.

In the 1938 midterm elections, Roosevelt revealed his most unlovely characteristic, his vindictive streak. He set out to defeat a baker's dozen of mostly southern and western Democrats who had led the fight against the court bill. He journeyed to their home states and spoke against them or made hostile statements that resounded in the newspapers, to no avail. All but one of his Democratic enemies were resoundingly reelected. Worse, the media fastened the word "purge" on his vendetta, implicitly likening FDR to Stalin and Hitler. Worst of all, in the 1938 midterm elections the Republicans went from 88 seats in the House to a respectable 170 and gained 8 seats in the Senate. An unspoken coalition between the GOP and southern conservatives began to form before the New Dealers' appalled eyes.[20]

Compounding these political agonies was a return of the Depression in 1937. In October of that year, the stock market went into a nosedive that reminded many people of the collapse in 1929. An agitated Secretary of the Treasury Henry Morgenthau Jr. wrote in his diary that "seven million shares changed hands while prices skidded amid hysteria resembling a mob in a theater fire." By November 1937, unemployment had soared to 11 million, with another 3 million working only part time. Once more the New Dealers resorted to massive government spending to stanch the economic wounds. They also confronted a rising chorus of critics who began telling the nation the New Deal was a fraud and a failure. One of the most outspoken was FDR's erstwhile admirer, Fulton Oursler. In *Liberty* editorials, he began referring to the New Deal years as an era of "Squandermania." Twenty-two billion dollars had been wasted by "starry-eyed idealists, crackpots and political heebie-jeebie boys" who had tried to spend America into prosperity.[21]

Typical was the record of the Resettlement Administration, which had boasted it would relocate a million families from urban slums to small farms. In fact it had resettled a pathetic 11,000—and the most visible of these communities, Arthurdale, West Virginia, remained an economic basket case, supported by charitable handouts procured by First Lady Eleanor Roosevelt.[22]

Even more humiliating were statistics that showed the United States was lagging far behind foreign countries in recovering from the Depression. American national income in 1937 was 85.8 percent of the 1929 high-water mark while England's was 124.3 percent. League of Nations reports found that Japan's employment figure was 75 percent above 1929's numbers. Chile, Sweden, and Australia had growth rates in the 20 percent range. The United States' figure was a dismal –7 percent. Worst of all, America's chief political rival, Adolf Hitler's Germany, was far more successful in cutting unemployment and raising national income.[23]

It is no exaggeration to say the disasters of his second term traumatized Roosevelt. At one point he told Harold Ickes he was convinced that the economic royalists had deliberately triggered the Depression of 1937. At a cabinet meeting, Roosevelt maintained that the new economic collapse was the result "of a concerted effort by big business and concentrated wealth to drive the market down just to create a situation unfavorable to me."[24]

Even more outlandish was Roosevelt's assertion to Secretary of the Treasury Henry Morgenthau Jr. that they were only inches away from a fascist-style takeover of the government by the "interests." More and more, FDR began to see himself as the voice of an embattled liberalism that was imperiled by a conservative counterattack. "He is punch drunk from the punishment that he has suffered lately," Harold Ickes noted in his diary.[25]

VII

In a 1938 cabinet meeting, Jim Farley urged Roosevelt and the administration to take a more positive approach to business. Too many executives thought the New Deal had "no sympathy or confidence in business, big or little," he said. Roosevelt brushed the suggestion aside. "Business, particularly the banking industry, has ganged up on me," he insisted.[26]

"Monopoly power" became the New Dealers' rallying cry in 1938–39. Roosevelt created a new entity, the Temporary National Economic Committee, and put Leon Henderson, one of the most aggressive ideologues in his entourage, in charge of investigating what the agency's flacks portrayed as a rampant corporate conspiracy to defraud consumers by creating industry-wide monopolies. Forgetting all about the NRA's call for cooperation to soften the sharp edges of capitalism, FDR appointed Yale law professor Thurman Arnold, author of a ferocious attack on big business, *The Folklore of Capitalism*, to head the Justice Department's heretofore dormant antitrust division and increased its staff from a few dozen to nearly 300 lawyers.

With Roosevelt's approval, Harold Ickes took to the airwaves to blame the recession on a conspiracy hatched by the sixty richest families in the nation. He condemned the "industrial oligarchy" that controlled the country. There was an irreconcilable conflict between "the power of money and the power of the democratic instinct," Ickes cried. America was lurching toward a "big business fascist America—an enslaved America."

Ickes stole this idea from a book by Ferdinand Lundberg, *America's 60 Families*, which revealed to a supposedly startled world that many if not most of the country's great fortunes had been acquired in less than admirable ways. The book was little more than a rehash of revelations from the earlier decades of the century, when a squadron of journalists dug up dirt on the Rockefellers and others, prompting Theodore Roosevelt to call them "muckrakers." Honest Harold, as Ickes like to style himself, did not mention that Lundberg despised the New Dealers as much as his capitalist targets, dismissing them as exponents of "one camp of great wealth pitted against another." Lundberg even listed two full pages of names of plutocrats, ranging from Du Ponts to Mellons to Goulds, who had contributed to Roosevelt's 1932 campaign. This was New Deal elitism in full flower; Ickes clearly assumed the vast majority of his audience was too dumb to read the book.[27]

Even more headstrong was the rhetoric of Robert Jackson, who moved from antitrust division chief to solicitor general in 1938. A much publicized Roosevelt favorite—in the mid-1930s, he had prosecuted former secretary of the Treasury Andrew Mellon for income tax evasion—Jackson accused big business of conspiring to "liquidate the New Deal." He too dredged up the image of sixty families running the United States as if it were their private plantation. He accused the capitalists of going on "a general strike" against the government and darkly intimated that the government might go on a very different kind of strike against them.[28]

On January 10, 1940, at the Democratic Party's annual dinner celebrating their founder, Andrew Jackson, FDR continued this offensive, using American history to support the contention that the ruinous 1937 recession had been engineered by Wall Street. He compared the current situation to President Jackson's 1832 war with financier Nicholas Biddle over rechartering the Bank of the United States. "Biddle and the Bank sought to create an economic depression in order to ruin the president," FDR declared. But Jackson won an overwhelming reelection victory and the bank was consigned to history's junkyard.

The *New York Times* felt constrained to point out that the "big panic" FDR was talking about came in 1837, five years after Jackson's reelection. The paper of record might have added that many historians blamed the 1837 depression on Jackson for junking the bank, a decision that destabilized the nation's finances.[29]

Thus did the New Dealers, exacerbated by their failure to revive the American economy, drift into declaring war on capitalism.

VIII

Badly battered on the domestic front, Roosevelt had, not surprisingly, little or no success in persuading Americans to take bold steps internationally in his second term. Here the trauma of the Supreme Court–packing debacle was compounded by the memory of his Democratic predecessor, Woodrow Wilson, who had destroyed his presidency and wrecked the Democratic Party with a foreign policy of vaulting idealism that Americans ultimately declined to support. In 1937, as Germany and Italy intervened in the Spanish Civil War and Japan invaded China, Roosevelt gave a speech in Chicago calling for "positive endeavors" to "quarantine" the aggressors. When the British asked for a definition of positive endeavors, they were brushed off with an abrupt reminder that American voters would not tolerate any collaboration with England at the moment. In a press conference, Roosevelt backed even farther away from his own pronouncement, admitting he had no program and thought the real answer might be "a stronger neutrality," whatever that meant. From there FDR drifted to sending a congratulatory telegram, "Good man," to British prime minister Neville Chamberlain the following year as he prepared to fly to Munich to appease Adolf Hitler.[30]

In the vacuum Roosevelt created by his dodging and ducking, isolationists on both the left and right rushed to excoriate the president. The Communists and their fellow travelers in the intelligentsia were at this point violently hostile to overseas adventures, lest they lead to a confrontation with the Soviet Union. Peace groups left over from World War I rediscovered their voices. The leading universities, notably Yale and Harvard, hotbeds of pacifism, joined the chorus. Even the AFL declared that "American labor does not wish to be involved in European or Asiatic wars."

A disconsolate FDR complained to one of his favorite speechwriters, ex–Tammany Hall politician Sam Rosenman, the man who had invented the term "new deal," that it was "a terrible thing to look over your shoulder when you are trying to lead—and to find no one there." It was a graphic admission of the depth of the trauma the failed court-packing plan had inflicted on Roosevelt's presidency.[31]

IX

The preference for trickery and deception persisted as Roosevelt dodged and weaved his way to a decision to seek a third term in 1940. Here a new and more ominous factor intruded: his health. Confined to his wheelchair, his bodily strength already diminished by his 1921 bout with polio, he had begun to show alarming signs that the stress of the presidency was taking a toll. He had repeated bouts of respiratory infection, especially when he was wrestling with a difficult decision.[32] In February of 1940, while having dinner at the White House, he had passed out and his two guests were so alarmed, they summoned the White House doctor, Admiral Ross McIntire, who later told them the president had suffered a "slight heart attack." Those who witnessed the episode thought it was a good deal more than slight, and doubted McIntire's diagnosis. When Eleanor Roosevelt heard about it, she said it reinforced her already strong opinion that her husband should not seek a third term.[33]

On the other side of the argument was a host of New Dealers who foresaw calamitous defeat in 1940 without Roosevelt on the ticket. But the ultimate arbiter was Roosevelt himself, who surveyed the Democratic and Republican parties and decided there was no one on the horizon who could lead a unified America into war with the Axis powers, and rescue liberalism from domestic defeat. These two ideas soon became closely interwoven in his mind.

A climactic moment in this evolution came at Hyde Park on July 7, 1940, when Jim Farley, still the postmaster general and chairman of the Democratic Party, visited the president. Farley was seriously considering a run for the White House and had been assured by Roosevelt that he would be among the first to know if FDR decided not to seek a third term. Instead, Roosevelt had stalled on making the decision until it was impossible for Farley—or anyone else—to launch a serious candidacy.

Roosevelt pointed to the headlines from Europe, where two weeks earlier Hitler had dictated peace terms to the French, the British had evacuated their beaten army from Dunkirk, and Italy had entered the war as Germany's ally. He told Farley the world situation made it imperative for him to seek a third term, and wanted to know what he thought of Secretary of Agriculture Henry Wallace as his running mate. Controlling his anger, Farley coldly informed FDR that Wallace was a terrible choice. Too many people considered him a "wild-eyed fellow," an ideologue and an extremist.

Roosevelt shook his head. He had already recited a long list of possible alternatives and ruled them all out for reasons of age or lack of liberalism. "The man running with me must be in good health because there is no telling how long I can hold out," he said. "You know Jim, a man with paralysis can have a breakup at any time." Whereupon he pulled up his shirt and showed the astounded Farley a large lump under his left shoulder. FDR said it was flesh and muscle that had wandered there because of his sedentary wheelchair life.

Roosevelt expatiated on how much he did not want to run, but felt it was his moral duty. If he thought these avowals would change Farley's mind, he was disappointed. The postmaster general, who had been largely responsible for winning Roosevelt the Democratic nomination over Al Smith in 1932, bluntly informed him that he was totally opposed to a third term, on principle. He added the salient point that if, after eight years of Roosevelt's leadership, the Democratic Party could not produce another viable candidate for the presidency, it deserved to lose.

Roosevelt grimly disagreed. "Jim," he said, "if nominated and elected I could not in these times refuse to take the inaugural oath, even if I knew I would be dead within thirty days."[34] Few have paid much attention to the way FDR linked liberalism to his decision to seek a third term. His readiness to accept death in the Oval Office to make a certified New Dealer his successor is evidence that he expected liberalism to be the centerpiece, the justification, of the war he was determined to fight. Instead, with that irony that history seems to enjoy inflicting on even the greatest personages, the war would destroy the New Deal forever. FDR's run for a third term with Henry Wallace as his vice president was the first step on the road to this largely forgotten destination.

X

In order to win the nomination for a third term, Roosevelt had to seek the support of two of the most hardboiled Democratic politicians in the country, Ed Kelly of Chicago and Frank Hague of Jersey City. Each led political machines that dominated their respective states by stuffing ballot boxes, enfranchising the grave-yards, and paying for straight ticket votes on a per capita basis, tactics that made reform-minded liberal Democrats wince and righteous Republicans sputter.

In the 1920s, Chicago became known as the murder capital of America as Al Capone shot his way to power in the Mafia. In fact, New York had a higher murder rate but Chicago was the city where, in the words of one muckraking journalist, "the Mafia achieved its highest degree of immunity." The Hoover administration put Capone in jail. After FDR's election, federal prosecution of Chicago's mafiosi dropped to zero. Not a little of the reason was FDR's rapport with Kelly, who backed Roosevelt with a wholehearted enthusiasm not shared by other Democrats in Illinois. ("Roosevelt Is My Religion," was the title of a speech Kelly gave repeatedly.) In return, FDR made sure huge amounts of federal money went to Chicago for public projects, ignoring Harold Ickes's plaint that at least 20 percent of the cash would end up in the pockets of Kelly and his cohorts.[35]

In 1937, Frank Hague had compounded his sins in liberal eyes by using police nightsticks to crush an attempt by the CIO (Congress of Industrial Organizations) to organize Jersey City's factories. When Norman Thomas, the leader of the Socialist Party, tried to make a speech in Journal Square, Jersey City's business center, he was pelted with eggs, called a Communist (an epithet Hague applied freely to the CIO) and deported to Manhattan on the first available ferryboat. Liberal lawyer Morris Ernst, who took rooms in a local hotel to supervise the CIO campaign, exploded when he discovered that Hague was opening every letter sent to him at Jersey City's Central Post Office. Postmaster General Farley too was outraged and urged Roosevelt to at least prosecute the Hague underling who opened the letters. FDR shook his head. "We need Hague's support if we want New Jersey," he said.[36]

Working with the bosses at the Chicago convention was WPA director Harry Hopkins, who set up a command post in Chicago's Blackstone Hotel with a direct line to the White House. For a while it looked as if Roosevelt would not be nominated. Shunting Farley aside was an insult that many delegates resented. Fabled for his ability to remember names and personal details of a man's life, the party chairman was very popular among his fellow professionals.

A jittery Harold Ickes sent a telegram to the White House: "The convention is bleeding to death. Your reputation and prestige may bleed to death with it." Secretary of Labor Frances Perkins pleaded with the president to fly to Chicago and take charge of the fratricidal delegates. Instead, Roosevelt arranged for Senator Alben Barkley of Kentucky, the keynote speaker, to read a letter from him in which he claimed he did not want to run and the convention was free to vote for any candidate.

As the sullen delegates tried to digest this startling statement, a stupendous voice echoed through the convention hall. "We want Roosevelt! We want Roosevelt! Everybody wants Roosevelt!" The voice belonged to Chicago's superintendent of sewers, who was in command of the loudspeaker system in the convention hall's basement. Someone handed Senator Barkley a large portrait of the president, which he held aloft. The galleries, which had been packed with city employees and followers of Chicago's boss Ed Kelly, erupted with wild cheers and applause. Other members of the Chicago machine, joined by delegates from many states, swarmed in the aisles under the leadership of Frank Hague, while the sewer superintendent's voice boomed over the loudspeaker: "New York wants Roosevelt! Chicago wants Roosevelt! The world needs Roosevelt!" For more than an hour,

Hague, Kelly, and Harry Hopkins presided over this demonstration. By the time it ended, there was no longer any doubt that Roosevelt had the nomination.[37]

Two nights later, when the delegates learned that the president wanted Henry Wallace as his running mate, something very close to a revolt erupted. There were at least a dozen aspirants to the vice presidency, many with substantial support. Texas millionaire Jesse Jones, now the secretary of commerce as well as head of the Reconstruction Finance Corporation, was in the lead, with the backing of Jim Farley. Already resentful at being manipulated into nominating FDR, the delegates booed and hissed every time Wallace's name was mentioned.

But the word from the White House via Harry Hopkins was: Roosevelt and Wallace or Nobody and Nobody. Frank Hague testified to Hopkins's power by telling a reporter: "I'm just an amateur here. Talk to Hopkins." In fact, as FDR listened to the unruly proceedings on the radio, he wrote out a statement, declining the nomination. Once more it was evident that keeping liberalism alive was at least as important to FDR as remaining in power to fight the Axis.[38]

Wallace was rescued from defeat only by an ultimate reinforcement. At FDR's request, Eleanor Roosevelt flew to Chicago and pleaded with the delegates to give her husband the man he wanted to help him bear "the immense burden" they were placing on his shoulders. Eventually, the secretary of agriculture got 627 votes out of the 1,100 delegates present. That meant nearly half these official spokesman for the Democratic Party went home in an extremely negative frame of mind. Resentment against Wallace was so intense, Harry Hopkins forbade him to give an acceptance speech, lest it be drowned out by hisses and boos.

Even more alarming to some people was a slip of the tongue Roosevelt made in his speech, accepting the nomination for a third term. He thanked the delegates for nominating Wallace for "the high office of President of the United States." This prompted some congressmen and other White House watchers to opine that Roosevelt planned to turn the presidency over to Wallace soon after they were elected. FDR was forced to announce that "God willing" he would serve a full term.[39]

XI

Watching this political circus with extremely jaundiced eyes was Harry S. Truman, the Democratic senator from Missouri. Truman was facing political extinction because FDR, the man who had gotten into bed with Boss Kelly and Boss Hague to win his nomination a third term, had turned on the Kansas City political machine led by Boss Tom Pendergast that had elected Truman in 1934. Prodded by Missouri Governor Lloyd Stark, who had been elected with Boss Tom's backing, FDR appointed a federal task force that put Pendergast in jail for income tax evasion. Soon Stark announced he was going to run for Senator Truman's seat and was frequently in the White House, having his picture taken with the beaming president. Apparently forgotten was Truman's down-the-line support of the New Deal in his six years in the Senate.[40]

Harry Truman grimly vowed to run for reelection with or without Roosevelt's backing. On February 3, 1940, he launched his campaign by defiantly announcing he favored Missouri's senior senator, Bennett Clark, for president and opposed a third term for Roosevelt, although Truman promised to support the president if he won the Democratic nomination. The Bennett Clark puff was pure politics, designed to win support in eastern Missouri, where Senator Clark was strong. But Truman meant what he said about a third term. His study of history had convinced him that in a republic, no man should be indispensable.

His brain inflamed by FDR's backing, Stark veered into hubris worthy of the president's post-1936 landslide seizure. The governor announced that he was running not only for senator but for vice president. Senator Bennett Clark issued a savage statement, wondering if "Lloyd" was also running for Akhund of Swat. Truman persuaded Senate heavyweights such as Foreign Relations Committee Chairman Tom Connally of Texas and Majority Leader Alben Barkley of Kentucky to come to Missouri to speak for him. But Truman never got an endorsement from Roosevelt. When the senator asked Harold Ickes to intercede for him, that quintessential New Dealer curtly informed Truman that he, Ickes, was for Stark.[41]

Showing he was no slouch at political strategy, Truman allowed a friend to persuade Kansas City federal attorney Maurice Milligan, the man whose investigation had put Pendergast in jail, to enter the race, supposedly to stop the obnoxious Stark. The liberal *St. Louis Post-Dispatch* declared that a Truman victory would be "a sad defeat for the people of Missouri." Nevertheless, in a three-way contest, Truman came down the middle and won the Democratic primary—tantamount to election in Missouri in those days—by a slim 8,000 votes.

Back in the Senate, Truman was hailed by Senator Burton K. Wheeler and other anti-Roosevelt Democrats for winning without FDR's endorsement. In a September 1940 letter to his wife, Bess, the man from Independence sounded rather anti-Roosevelt himself. "I'm not going to see the president any more until February 1, and then he's going to want to see me. I rather think from here out I'll make him like it."[42]

XII

As the presidential contest began in 1940, Vice President John Nance Garner, passed over for a third term, went home to

Uvalde, Texas, and let all and sundry know he planned to sit on his hands in the forthcoming election. He urged his many friends in and out of Congress to do likewise. The southern and western senators and congressmen whom FDR had tried unsuccessfully to purge were planning to imitate Garner.

A disgusted Jim Farley, symbol if not spokesman for the better side of the Irish-American political tradition, resigned as postmaster general and chairman of the party. His farewell to Roosevelt was not a pleasant scene. When FDR tried to turn on the charm, Farley gave it to him with the bark on. "Boss," he said, "you've lied to me and I've lost all faith in you."

Roosevelt made no attempt to deny this accusation. He simply shrugged and turned away, as if to say: You don't understand how politics works, Jim. Farley went back to New York and devoted not a little of his leisure time to saying nasty things about Roosevelt.[43]

Almost as anti-Roosevelt was another prominent Irish-American Democrat, Joseph Kennedy. A banker-entrepreneur who had turned to politics, Kennedy had been an able first chairman of the Securities and Exchange Commission, which purged Wall Street of unsavory characters and instituted tough reforms aimed at restoring people's confidence in the stock market. Roosevelt rewarded him with the ambassadorship to London, a role that Kennedy's Irish side savored.

But the American side of Kennedy's hyphen soon soured on FDR's determination to back England at the risk of war with Germany. Kennedy thought this policy was a colossal mistake. He saw nothing in Europe that was worth the lives of young Americans, and he was convinced the British could not win. A stream of messages warning Roosevelt against backing a loser went unheeded. Soon Kennedy was talking to Republicans such as Clare Booth Luce, wife of *Time*'s editor in chief, angrily denouncing FDR's desire to "push us into the war." Henry Luce artfully urged Kennedy to return to the United States and speak out against Roosevelt, "regardless of . . . antiquated rules." Kennedy's oldest son, Joseph Jr., had been a member of the Massachusetts delegation to the Democratic convention, all of whom had backed Jim Farley on the first ballot.[44]

XIII

FDR was rescued from possible defeat as the leader of a badly split party by an internal upheaval in the Republican Party. The eastern wing, deeply influenced by British propaganda, as they had been in World War I, staged a virtual coup d'état at their national convention. Instead of choosing a Midwest conservative such as Senator Robert Taft of Ohio, who would have challenged Roosevelt's domestic and foreign policies, the easterners contrived to nominate a Wall Street lawyer from Indiana named Wendell Willkie. A Democrat until 1938, Willkie said he had no quarrel with the New Deal's reforms and claimed to be as eager to stop Hitler as Roosevelt was, but could do it better. The blunders and disasters of Roosevelt's second term, from the court-packing fiasco to the return of the Depression, were not on Willkie's agenda. (That did not stop Harold Ickes from mocking the candidate's aw shucks style by dubbing him "a simple barefoot Wall Street lawyer.") Foreign policy became the main issue, and even there Willkie surrendered most of the argument.

FDR declined to campaign, claiming he was devoting all his time to building up the nation's defenses. Just before the Republican convention met, he had finessed the GOP by inviting into his cabinet two interventionist members of their party, Henry L. Stimson, who had been Herbert Hoover's secretary of state, and Frank Knox, who had been the GOP nominee for vice president in 1936. They provided cover for the most daring move Roosevelt had yet made toward joining the war: the September 3,

1940, decision to send fifty overage World War I destroyers to Great Britain in return for the right to establish naval bases on seven British territories and islands from Newfoundland to British Guiana. FDR compared the deal to Jefferson's purchase of Louisiana, a rather improbable match of realities and intentions. Even bolder was his decision to proceed with the nation's first peacetime draft, which began on October 29, on the very eve of the election.

By approving these moves, Willkie seemingly conceded the race. FDR felt no compunction about ignoring the GOP candidate's repeated demands for a debate. That left most of the heavy lifting to Henry Wallace, and he revealed an unsettling tendency to say extreme things. "The Republican candidate is not an appeaser and not a friend of Hitler," Wallace declared at one point. "I'll say too that every Republican is not an appeaser. But you can be sure that every Nazi, every Hitlerite, and every appeaser is a Republican."[45]

Such rhetoric cried out for retaliation, and the Republicans soon acquired a weapon, a series of letters that Wallace had written in the 1930s to a Russian mystic named Nicholas Roerich, suspected at one point of being a Japanese agent. The guru pushed a vision of a new world order that would emerge when the people of light triumphed over the forces of darkness. Wallace's letters more than qualified him for Jim Farley's epithet, "wild man." He signed them "G" for Galahad, the name Roerich had assigned him in his pseudochurch. Wallace assured the guru that he awaited "the breaking of the New Day" when the people of "Northern Shambhalla"—a Buddhist term roughly equivalent to the kingdom of heaven—would create an era of peace and plenty. In other letters FDR was called "the Wandering One" and Secretary of State Cordell Hull "the Sour One." Not a little inside government information was passed to Roerich amid the mumbo jumbo. The Republicans had their hands on over 100 of these so called "guru" letters.[46]

Asked about the letters, Wallace lied. He said they were forgeries. Behind the scenes, the White House was using an even less admirable tactic. The Republicans were told that if they published the letters, the newspapers would soon learn about Candidate Willkie's New York mistress, the writer and editor Irita Van Doren. New Deal spokesmen such as Ickes and Hopkins would say nothing, of course. "The people down the line," Roosevelt told one of his aides, "Congress speakers, and state speakers" would "get it out." The guru letters remained unpublished.[47]

XIV

By midcampaign, Wallace's rhetoric made it clear that the New Dealers saw the election as a plebiscite on whether America should enter the war against Hitler. But this stance suddenly became untenable when Willkie moved closer to the majority of the Republican Party and the large minority of disillusioned anti-Roosevelt Democrats and began calling the president a warmonger. Polls showed a huge leap in Willkie's numbers and Roosevelt was soon forced to drop his above-the-battle stance and enter the campaign. Ultimately he was pressured by his worried inner circle into making his historic promise to the mothers and fathers of America: "Your boys are not going to be sent into any foreign wars."

A few days later, FDR more than matched Henry Wallace in the fine art of smearing the Republicans as enemies of democracy. Speaking in Brooklyn, he conjured up the image of a conspiracy between the extreme right and the extreme left. In 1939, Josef Stalin had signed a nonaggression pact with Hitler, and the American Communists and their friends had become as furiously opposed to Roosevelt's support of Great Britain as the staunchest Midwest Republican. FDR noted how Nazis and Communists were collaborating to stifle democracy in Europe. "Something evil is happening in this country," he told his audience, citing a full-page ad in *The Daily Worker,* supposedly paid for by the Republican Party. It was an insult his opponents were unlikely to forgive or forget.[48]

XV

Less well known but almost as important as FDR's "foreign wars" speech was a radio talk by Ambassador Joseph P. Kennedy. Roosevelt took a calculated gamble when he permitted Kennedy to return from London in the closing weeks of the campaign. He knew how alienated and angry the Bostonian had become. When Kennedy called the White House for an appointment, Congressman Lyndon Johnson was in the Oval Office with the president. Pouring on the charm, Roosevelt said: "Ah, Joe, it is so good to hear your voice." For Johnson's benefit, FDR simultaneously drew his finger across his throat, suggesting he was about to commit—or risk—political murder.[49]

At dinner that night, Roosevelt smiled and nodded while Kennedy ranted about the way his advice had been ignored. FDR blamed much of Kennedy's vexation on the New Dealers' favorite whipping boy, the State Department. To prove how highly he regarded Kennedy, FDR confided that Joe was his choice for president in 1944. Then Roosevelt asked the crucial question. Would Kennedy endorse him for reelection on a national radio hookup? Polls showed many Irish-Catholics, influenced by Jim Farley's withdrawal from the administration, were planning to stay home on election day.

In Kennedy's pocket was a letter from General Robert E. Wood, head of the America First Committee, begging Kennedy to tell Americans the truth about Roosevelt's "secret commitments" to Great Britain. The ambassador knew all about these backstairs understandings—and loathed them. But in Kennedy's Irish-American soul, loyalty to the Democratic Party and to his family was more important than telling the truth. He agreed to make the speech if Roosevelt promised to support Joseph Kennedy Jr. for governor of Massachusetts in 1942. The ambassador saw this as a first step toward making his son president. FDR cheerfully guaranteed a ringing endorsement.

Not only did Joe Kennedy back Roosevelt in his nationwide radio speech—"the man of experience is our man of the hour"—he denounced the Republican claim that "the president of the United States is trying to involve this country in a world war. Such a charge is *false*." The Democratic National Committee was so enthralled that they took ads in newspapers across the country pointing out that Ambassador Kennedy had "smashed to smithereens" Wendell Willkie's "brutal charge" that the president planned to send American soldiers overseas. After enduring months of Nazi bombs in London, Joe Kennedy had flown home "to tell Americans the truth."[50]

XVI

The voter turnout on November 5, 1940, was over 49 million, the largest in American history up to that time. Roosevelt won, but it was far from the landslide of 1936. The final count was 27,244,160 for Roosevelt to 22,305,198 for Willkie. Another 6 million voters had been added to Roosevelt's opposition. Still, a 5 million vote edge was a comfortable margin of victory. Yet the president reiterated to Joseph Lash, a young friend of Eleanor Roosevelt's who was at Hyde Park on election night, an opinion he had previously stated to Secretary of the Treasury Morgenthau. "We seem to have avoided a *putsch*, Joe," FDR said.[51]

Apparently FDR saw himself and his New Dealers not merely as America's rulers for another four years, but as her saviors from a domestic fascist takeover. The putsch rhetoric suggests FDR believed the enemy was not only beyond the oceans. They were in the midst of the nation, and they had an alarming grip on the souls of the American people. That would explain why it was necessary—and morally permissible—to lie and evade and deceive to lead the people into the war against Germany.

XVII

Forced to rescue his faltering campaign for a third term by telling an outright lie to the voters about his war plans, Roosevelt found himself trapped into a pattern of evasions and further deceptions for most of 1941. The extreme rhetoric FDR, Wallace, and other New Dealers used during the campaign also did nothing to soothe the animosity of their opponents.

One of the most effective attacks on the administration came in the June 1941 issue of the magazine *Coronet*. Writer John Pritchard said the nation was now in the second stage of the New Deal. The first phase had been a visionary attempt to reshape the American economy into a planned state. The second stage was an entirely new approach, "The New Deal of War." Unable to solve the problems of the American economy peacefully, Roosevelt was taking the nation to war in order to achieve full production—and state control of everything.[52]

The article expounded an idea that had begun to circulate throughout the undefined anti-Roosevelt coalition not long after he was reelected in 1940. There was just enough truth in the notion to inflame a great many people. The New Deal had failed to achieve full employment. The recession of 1937/38 had been a catastrophic blow to its pretensions. Employment had only begun to pick up when the nation began to rearm in 1939 and changes in the neutrality law permitted belligerents to buy planes and other weapons of war on a cash-and-carry basis. In 1940, there were still 10,650,000 people unemployed. Joblessness did not drop below 10 percent until 1941.[53]

Not a little of this combination of suspicion and hostility exploded early in 1941, when Roosevelt proposed in a bill histrionically titled H.R. 1776 that the United States should become the "Arsenal of Democracy" and "lend-lease" $7 billion worth of weaponry to a dollar-short Great Britain. The original proposal gave FDR all but unlimited power to transfer weapons and anything else he considered necessary to making war to any foreign power he deemed an ally. Thomas E. Dewey, running for governor of New York, said the bill would "abolish the Congress for all practical purposes" and incidentally eliminate free government in the United States. Liberal Senator Hiram Johnson of California called it "monstrous."[54] Republican Senator Arthur Vandenberg of Michigan wrote in his diary: "Should the United States become wrecked as a nation, you can put your finger on this precise moment as the time when the crime was committed."[55] Even the CIO opposed H.R. 1776 because it gave the president power to ban strikes and otherwise ignore labor legislation in the new and converted factories that would produce the weaponry.[56]

Although Roosevelt repeatedly insisted lend-lease would aid "the democracies," it was clear that 99 percent of the war materiel would go to Great Britain, and large portions of the American electorate had been taught to look upon the English with suspicion and even loathing. Massachusetts seethed with what a dismayed Roosevelt called "wild Irishmen" led by isolationist Democratic Senator David I. Walsh. Ethnic antagonism was not the only problem. Millions of other Americans were convinced that the British were taking the United States to the cleaners. Outgoing vice president John Nance Garner opined at a cabinet meeting that England could easily pay her bills. Millions of Midwest farmers shared this xenophobic opinion.

The invective in Congress and in anti-Roosevelt newspapers was unbelievably ferocious. The *Chicago Tribune* called lend-lease "the Dictator Bill." The *New York Daily News* ran a cartoon showing a stupid-looking Uncle Sam embracing a death's head figure labeled World War II, with the caption: "Uncle Sap's new girlfriend." When Wendell Willkie told diminutive Roy Howard, head of Scripps-Howard newspapers, that he supported the bill, an enraged Howard vowed to ruin him. The burly Willkie almost punched the publisher out.

The influential Kansas newspaperman, William Allen White, head of the Committee to Defend America by Aiding the Allies, turned against H.R. 1776 and Roosevelt because White was sure it would lead to war. Many others felt the same way. Mothers knelt on the Capitol steps, crying: "Kill Bill 1776, Not Our Sons." At Princeton, "Veterans of Future Wars" urged the president to appoint an unknown soldier, "so we'll know who he is before he gets killed." Charles A. Beard, arguably the most distinguished living American historian, called H.R. 1776 "a bill for waging undeclared war." Robert Hutchins, president of the University of Chicago, feared "the American people are about to commit suicide."[57]

After two months of rancorous debate, Congress passed the lend-lease bill, with significant amendments. Its powers were granted for only two years. Convoying the war materiel to Britain with the help of American warships was forbidden. The British would have to get the guns and planes and ammunition to their embattled island in their own merchant ships, protected by their own fleet. Roosevelt had acceded to this idea in a press conference, saying he never dreamed of using U.S. naval escorts. That could lead to shooting, and "shooting comes awfully close to war, doesn't it? That is the last thing we have in mind."[58]

Eleven days earlier, in England, Harry Hopkins, Roosevelt's special envoy to Winston Churchill, told the British prime minister: "The president is determined that we shall win the war to-gether. Make no mistake about it. He has sent me here to tell you that at all costs and by all means he will carry you through, no matter what happens to him—there is nothing he will not do so far as he has human power."[59]

A delighted Churchill christened Hopkins "Lord Root of the Matter" for his ability to get to the essence of a situation.

XVIII

The passage of lend-lease, which made the United States an active nonbelligerent in England's war against Germany, only made the opponents to Roosevelt's policies more determined. At the heart of the quarrel was Roosevelt's personality. Norman Thomas, head of the Socialist Party, privately saw a connection "between Roosevelt's growing messianic complex and his conception of the emergency." Charles Lindbergh echoed this opinion, marveling at the way Roosevelt could convince himself that his and the nation's interests were identical.

Underlying this emotion was a rancorous suspicion and hostility to the New Deal. Former insider Raymond Moley predicted that the call for a united front against Hitler was a disguised summons for a "counter-revolution as the exact opposite of Nazism." Moley said the New Dealers and their leader hoped to turn the United States into a version of the British Labour Party's socialist state. From there, they would attempt to establish "throughout the world a still more radical New Deal." Even more drastic was the fixed belief of a group of Republican congressmen, who told ex-president Herbert Hoover that "the administration was concerned with war not as war but as a method of destroying the present form of government in the United States." Here was further evidence of the potency of the

Republican Wendell Willkie campaigns for president in 1940 in Elwood, Indiana. Hostile New Dealers dubbed Willkie a "simple barefoot Wall Street lawyer." But his poll numbers leaped when he called President Franklin Roosevelt a warmonger. FDR was forced to deny he had any plans to send American soldiers to fight in "foreign wars." (Acme)

Roosevelt's uneasy partnership with Winston Churchill is visible in this first meeting at Placentia Bay, Newfoundland, in August 1941. At one point Churchill exclaimed, "I believe you are trying to do away with the British empire!" (He was right.) FDR hoped the meeting would persuade Americans to enter the war as Britain's ally. But polls showed 74 percent still opposed such a move.

On December 4, 1941, the leak of Rainbow Five, Roosevelt's plan to send a 5 million man army to Europe, caused an uproar in Washington, D.C. Three days later, the Japanese attack on Pearl Harbor made it yesterday's news. But Adolf Hitler later said the leak was a prime reason he declared war on the United States on December 11.

Albert Wedemeyer was an army major in 1941 when he wrote the secret war plan known as Rainbow Five. When the plan was leaked to the Chicago Tribune and the Washington Times-Herald, Wedemeyer said he could not have been more appalled and astounded "if a bomb had been dropped on Washington, D.C." He later was promoted to general and named American commander of the U.S. Sixth Army in China.

Democratic Senator Burton K. Wheeler of Montana claimed FDR's foreign policy was going to "plow under every fourth American boy." An infuriated president said the wisecrack was "the rottenest thing that has been said in public life in my generation." Wheeler helped leak Rainbow Five to the Chicago Tribune.

Secretary of the Interior Harold Ickes urged FDR to embargo oil to Japan. Ickes thought such a move "would make it not only possible but easy to get into the war in an effective way." With the help of interventionists in the State Department, FDR soon took his advice.

On December 8, 1941, President Roosevelt denounced the Japanese attack on Pearl Harbor as a "date that would live in infamy" and asked Congress to declare war on Japan. Secretary of the Navy Frank Knox later said FDR expected to "get hit but not hurt" when the Japanese attacked. American intercepts of Japanese diplomatic codes had made it clear that Tokyo was going to war.

Japanese bombers wrecked two destroyers in this Pearl Harbor dry dock. In the background is the battleship USS Pennsylvania, *ablaze from enemy bombs. When the commander in chief of the U.S. fleet, Admiral James O. Richardson, warned Roosevelt that the ships were vulnerable at Pearl Harbor, FDR fired him.*

At Pearl Harbor, the Japanese destroyed 180 American planes and damaged 128 others. In the Philippines, General Douglas MacArthur's 277-plane air force was swiftly reduced to similar junk. MacArthur was convinced Germans flew the Japanese planes. He and other American leaders believed the Japanese were inept pilots.

In a fireside chat on February 23, 1942, FDR assured the American people that "your government has unmistakable confidence in your ability to hear the worst, without flinching or losing heart." He then minimized American losses at Pearl Harbor. FDR saw himself as a "juggler" who was "perfectly willing to mislead and tell untruths if it will help win the war." (Photograph by T. McAvoy)

Over the objections of the attorney general and FBI Director J. Edgar Hoover, Roosevelt interned 120,000 Japanese-Americans early in 1942. The American Civil Liberties Union later called the decision "the greatest deprivation of civil liberties in this country since slavery." Here First Lady Eleanor Roosevelt visits a relocation center in an attempt to palliate this injustice.

Fleet Admiral William Leahy was the blunt voice of the military in FDR's Oval Office. He told the president, "We should ... use everybody — good, bad and indifferent — who promised to be of assistance in reducing the length of our casualty list." This view clashed with the desire of many New Dealers to politicize the war. (Corbis)

After a 1942 radio address, FDR chats with Henry Wallace, the man he had handpicked as his vice president in 1940. Wallace had recently seized the leadership of the nation's liberals with his speech "The Century of the Common Man." But FDR dumped him in 1944 and let the Democratic Party bosses nominate Missouri Senator Harry S. Truman. (American Heritage Library/Carousel)

idea that there was a New Deal of War at the secret heart of the president's policy.[60]

A lot of this anti-Roosevelt, anti–New Deal hostility spilled over onto Harry Hopkins. Antagonism to the former head of the WPA was so intense inside the Democratic Party that Roosevelt was forced to remove him as secretary of commerce in 1940 and replace him with Jesse Jones to placate southern conservatives. But in typical Rooseveltian style, the president outflanked the critics by making Hopkins a special assistant to the president and dispatching him first to England to confer with Churchill and then to Moscow to consult with Stalin when Hitler invaded Russia. Because Hopkins's health was precarious (he suffered from a rare form of stomach cancer) FDR gave him a bedroom in the White House as his headquarters. This only redoubled suspicion of the American "Rasputin."

If Hopkins's critics could have read a memorandum he wrote in the White House, they would have fulminated against him even more ferociously. In April 1941, he outlined an apocalyptic vision that seemed to confirm their worst fears. It was entitled: "The New Deal of Mr. Roosevelt is the Designate and Invincible Adversary of the New Order of Hitler."

As Hopkins saw it, the new order of Hitler "can never be conclusively defeated by the old order of democracy, which is the status quo." There was only one way to beat Hitler: "By the new order of democracy, which is the New Deal universally extended and applied." Unless "world democracy" backed Roosevelt's New Deal, they would fail. The peoples of the world were not fighting to preserve the old order "but to build a new one." Only under the leadership of Franklin D. Roosevelt "was a more humane and democratic world order plausible."[61]

A New Deal for the world. Americans would soon discover that Hopkins was not the only follower of Franklin D. Roosevelt who embraced this large idea. Almost as daunting was Hopkins's view of how to achieve this new world order. Democracy "must wage total war against totalitarian war. It must exceed the Nazi in fury, ruthlessness and efficiency."

There were few ideas that Hopkins did not share with FDR. One can reasonably conclude that this proposal was discussed in some detail in the evenings when the president was alone in his White House study with "Lord Root of the Matter."[62]

XIX

During the first six months of 1941, while British and American military staffs met secretly in Washington D.C. to plan a future war, Roosevelt struggled to create the incident in the North Atlantic that he hoped would draw America into the conflict. "I am not willing to fire the first shot," he told Harold Ickes. "I am waiting to get pushed into the situation," he told another cabinet diary keeper, Henry Morgenthau Jr. But the Germans declined to cooperate, even when American destroyers, ordered by FDR on ever more extensive Atlantic patrols, dumped depth charges on their U-boats.

On May 3, a fuming Morgenthau confided to his diary: "The President is loath to get into this war, and he would rather follow public opinion than lead it." As the stalemate continued, interventionists such as Harold Ickes conferred with other prowar cabinet members on issuing a public statement accusing FDR of failed leadership. This would not have been the first time the self-styled Old Curmudgeon quarreled with the president, frequently supplementing his brickbats with a letter of resignation.[63]

In Europe and the Middle East, the Germans looked irresistible in the spring of 1941. They blasted Yugoslavia into submission, flung the British out of Greece, and conquered Crete in a spectacular airborne assault. In North Africa the British abandoned

Libya and retreated into Egypt before General Erwin Rommel's Afrika Korps. "Wolf packs" of German submarines were sinking British ships by the dozen in the North Atlantic. On May 3, 1941, a desperate Churchill begged Roosevelt to declare war. Instead, FDR delivered a fireside chat declaring "an unlimited national emergency" that gave the White House the equivalent of war powers.

Roosevelt's opposition saw, again, a policy that ignored Congress and reached for ever increasing personal power. They pointed to the creation of a Petroleum Coordinator in the person of Secretary of the Interior Harold Ickes as part of the New Deal's long-running ambition to control American industry. "The out and out New Dealers are in the saddle," wrote one critic, "and they are using their power with the same zest they have exercised in the past." Echoing the *Coronet* magazine article, Senator Robert A. Taft of Ohio prophesied: "Entrance into the European War will be the next great New Deal experiment."[64]

XX

The next day, in a press conference, Roosevelt undercut the declaration of an emergency by denying it had any practical implications, such as ordering U.S. Navy ships to convoy British merchantmen, or calling for repeal of the Neutrality Acts, so American ships could carry war cargoes to England. In their diaries, Harold Ickes and Secretary of War Stimson bemoaned Roosevelt's timidity. Stimson fumed that the press conference "undid the effect of his speech."

Not even when Hitler invaded Russia, transforming the war, did FDR, studying the polls as usual, find reason to change his cautious stance. He announced that America would follow Britain's lead and support the Soviet regime. But he was acutely aware that this decision introduced a new cadre of domestic enemies into the quarrel: the leaders of the Catholic Church, who were inveterate foes of Communism. FDR ordered his ambassador to the Vatican, Myron Taylor, to get a statement from Pope Pius XII endorsing his Russian policy. Taylor obtained a wary papal agreement that it was permissible to support the people of Russia, as distinct from their atheistic regime.[65]

In August 1941, when Roosevelt met with Churchill at Placentia Bay in Newfoundland for the Atlantic Charter conference, the British prime minister again pleaded for a declaration of war. Once more, Roosevelt said no. He told Churchill if he "put the issue of peace and war to Congress, they would debate it for months." Graphic proof came from Congress while the two men conferred. On August 13, 1941, the House of Representatives came within a single vote of refusing to extend the 1940 Selective Service Act, which kept a million men in the army's ranks for an additional six months, rather than letting them go home in October. This hesitation was in keeping with Senator Gerald Nye's frequent criticism of "undue military preparedness" as a symptom of Roosevelt's determination to get America into a war.[66] Only an all-out effort by the White House staff and Democratic House leaders prevented a ruinous political defeat.

Nonetheless, at Placentia Bay Roosevelt told Churchill he was determined that the United States would "come in." The president said he "planned to wage war but not declare it," and would become more and more "provocative." He presumed that this would lead to a German attack on an American naval vessel, giving him the incident he needed to demand a declaration of war.[67]

As theater, the Churchill-Roosevelt meeting at Placentia Bay was magnificent. Newspapers and newsreels showed the two leaders side by side on the deck of the British battleship HMS *Prince of Wales*. They issued the eight-point Atlantic Charter proclaiming a postwar world founded on the four freedoms that

Roosevelt had enunciated in his state of the Union address to Congress in January 1941. But as a step toward Roosevelt's goal of getting the United States into the war, Placentia Bay was a failure.

In polls taken before the conference, 74 percent of the people said they would vote to stay out of a war against Germany. In a poll the week after the deluge of publicity about the meeting, the questioners found exactly the same response: 74 percent—three-fourths of the nation—had no desire for war with Adolf Hitler. A month later polls revealed 68 percent of the people preferred to stay out, even if that meant a German victory over England and Russia.[68]

XXI

Roosevelt's plan to create an incident in the Atlantic had failure built into it. Incidents abounded in the fall of 1941. On September 11 Roosevelt reported that the destroyer USS *Greer* had been attacked by a German submarine and henceforth U.S. ships had orders to "shoot on sight" at any German vessel in the proclaimed neutral zone, west of Iceland. The president did not mention that *Greer* had stalked the submarine for three hours, in cooperation with a British patrol plane, before the U-boat fired a torpedo at the destroyer.

A few weeks later, the USS *Kearny* took a torpedo in the engine room, killing eleven men. Next the USS *Reuben James* broke in half when a torpedo exploded in a midship magazine. One hundred and fifteen American sailors died in the freezing North Atlantic. Roosevelt fulminated on the radio and in press conferences. "The shooting has started. And history has recorded who fired the first shot!" he cried. But there was no upsurge of war sentiment for a very simple reason. By insisting he had no desire to enter the war, Roosevelt fatally undercut public indignation. His concept of "all aid short of war" let Americans tell themselves that the loss of some ships and men was inevitable—and even a price worth paying—to stay out of the war.[69]

Playwright Robert Sherwood, who had been persuaded by Harry Hopkins to become a Roosevelt speechwriter, saw the paradoxical failure of Roosevelt's policy all too clearly. "The bereaved families [of the drowned sailors] mourned but among the general public there seemed to be more interest in the Army-Notre Dame football game. There was a sort of tacit understanding among Americans that nobody was to get excited if ships were sunk by Uboats."[70]

The antiwar groups in and out of Congress also played a powerful role in this indifference. They were able to damn the president as a hypocrite for his provocative acts and convince a large percentage of the American people that the dead sailors were Roosevelt's fault, not Hitler's. The German leader, finding the Russians a far larger handful than he had estimated, was even more determined to avoid a war with America. He continued to order his submariners to avoid shooting at American ships whenever possible. The German submarine captains who attacked American ships thought they were British—not surprising, considering their often hostile behavior and the transfer of fifty American destroyers to the Royal Navy.

Not even underhanded deception got the president anywhere. Shortly before the *Greer* narrowly escaped a torpedo, FDR exhibited a letter forged by British intelligence, purporting to prove that a pro-German Bolivian military officer was plotting a coup to set up a Hitler-style dictatorship. After the *Reuben James* was sunk, Roosevelt produced the map that failed to impress General Stanley Embick and Major Albert Wedemeyer. Also forged by British intelligence, it purported to be a Nazi plan to conquer Brazil and the rest of South America. Neither revelation created the hoped-for outrage.[71]

So the situation remained a perilous stalemate throughout the autumn of 1941. The polls continued to show as many as 80 percent of Americans opposed to entering the war. Robert Sherwood, who saw much of Roosevelt during these frustrating months, grew dismayed at the president's helplessness. "He had no more tricks left," Sherwood later recalled. "The hat from which he had pulled so many rabbits was empty."[72]

This was the desperate president who decided Japan was his one hope of getting the United States into the war. It was a tactic that succeeded beyond FDR's most extravagant hopes. Pearl Harbor created furious anger, humiliated the antiwar forces, and made Franklin D. Roosevelt the leader of a seemingly united, grimly determined nation. By the time he celebrated his sixtieth birthday on January 30, 1942, FDR's poll ratings were the highest in his presidency—84 percent.

In Chicago, police arrested a young man named Edwin A. Loss, Jr. for booing a newsreel shot of Roosevelt. The judge fined the penitent Loss $200 for disorderly conduct, the equivalent of $2,000 today. But this kind of unanimity could not and did not last long. Charles Lindbergh confided to his diary that he supported the president of the United States but he had no confidence in Franklin D. Roosevelt. Four days after Pearl Harbor, twenty Republican senators conferred and issued a statement pledging all-out support for the war effort. Behind this boilerplate lay a raging two-hour argument that came very close to ending in a public indictment of the president as a trickster and provocateur. On February 12, 1942, GOP publicity director Clarence Buddington Kelland issued a warning against one-man or one-party rule. He declared that the Republican Party did not intend to let America turn into a copy of the dictatorships that the nation was now committed to destroy.[73]

It was the opening shot of the war within the war.

4

THE GREAT DICHOTOMY

As the war began, Vice President Henry Wallace was the most frustrated man in Washington, D.C. After anointing him as his liberal heir in 1940, FDR had done little to give the vice president a role. Day after day, Wallace dozed on the dais of the Senate while the members orated. After a few months he began handing over the chairman's gavel to any solon willing to play president pro tem. Wallace devoted himself to studying the defense program with the help of specialists in the various agencies and departments.

The gangling Iowan was grateful to Roosevelt for making him vice president but he had no illusions about his party's leader. In 1940, Jim Farley, irked at the cat and mouse game the president was playing with him about running for a third term, told Wallace that Roosevelt was a sadist. "Farley was incorrect," Wallace told his diary. "Although there is a certain amount of that element [sadism] in his nature. The predominant element, however, is the desire to be the dominating figure, to demonstrate on all occasions his superiority. He changes his standards of superiority many times during the day. But having set for himself a particular standard for the moment, he then glories in being the dominating figure along that particular line."[1]

Roosevelt's opinion of Wallace was also somewhat less than one hundred percent positive. The Iowan had hoped to become president in 1940, but after a talk with Roosevelt speechwriter and confidant Sam Rosenman, Wallace had gracefully agreed a third FDR term was necessary and was one of the first to endorse the idea. Roosevelt had dismissed Wallace's backing as of no consequence. He was not "politically minded," FDR said. Earlier, a full year before he told Jim Farley he wanted Wallace for his vice president, Roosevelt had dismissed him because he did not have "it"—the indefinable something that made a good politician. The president apparently changed his mind because of Wallace's vehement prowar stance.[2]

Occasionally, the president seemed to remember Wallace's role in his liberal vision of the future. FDR ordered him to be briefed on the top secret S-1 project, the program to build an atomic bomb, which Roosevelt had authorized in early 1941. In July of 1941, FDR appointed Wallace chairman of the Economic Defense Board, an agency with a resounding name and no authority. Next came the chairmanship of SPAB, which stood for Supplies and Priorities Allocation Board. This entity was supposed to recognize and solve shortages of crucial materials. Roosevelt layered it on top of the Office of Production Management (OPM) in a vain attempt to resolve the ongoing brawl between this supposedly all powerful agency and the War and Navy Departments. SPAB too turned out to be a hollow agency with no real power. It was, from Wallace's point of view, an illustration of Roosevelt's slapdash methods. "The president," Wallace said some years later, "was a very bad administrator"—a conclusion the vice president learned the hard way.[3]

At OPM and SPAB, Wallace dealt with business executives whom the media had dubbed "dollar-a-year men" because they had been sent to Washington by their companies with the understanding that Uncle Sam would pay this tiny gratuity to legalize them as government servants while they remained on their corporate payrolls. Wallace profoundly distrusted these people. He considered them secret agents of monopoly power, interested mainly in profits.

There was no doubt that some of the dollar-a-year men did not forget their companies when they came to Washington. Burly white-haired William Knudsen, the General Motors executive who was head of OPM, spent most of 1941 resisting attempts to reduce the production of automobiles. He thought only about 15 percent of Detroit's assembly lines should be devoted to the defense program. But other dollar-a-year men were committed to helping the government and made an effort to include the vice president in their circle. One of these positive thinkers was the former Sears Roebuck executive, ruddy-faced genial Donald Nelson.

On December 4, 1941, the same day the *Chicago Tribune* and the *Washington Times-Herald* printed the text of Rainbow Five, Nelson hosted a dinner for twenty-four in the Carlton Hotel's North Lounge. Wallace was the undesignated but unquestionably recognized guest of honor. During the cocktail hour, Rainbow Five and what it revealed about the president's interventionist intentions was almost certainly discussed and perhaps debated. After coffee, Donald Nelson sounded the note that was the purpose of the dinner. He wanted his fellow businessmen to get to know Henry Wallace better. "I have [found] our vice president to be a great man and a regular fellow who has contributed much to our defense effort," Nelson said in his usual jovial style.

Bill Knudsen, Nelson declared, "was also a great man and a regular fellow, who had made immense contributions to the defense effort." A note of desperate pleading crept into Nelson's voice. He insisted that the government (a word which every business executive at the table translated into New Dealers) could get along with private industry. He urged everyone to forget their "doubts and mistrusts" and work together to create a defense force "second to none."

Whereupon Nelson introduced Vice President Wallace. During the cocktail hour, he had stood among these corporate chieftains, saying little, nursing a glass of fruit juice. He did not drink or smoke, and had no reason to look forward to the dinner. It was certain to be roast beef or steak, which he, a vegetarian, disdained. As Wallace rose to speak, a newspaperman portrayed him facing the "dominant majority" with an uncertain smile, which some of them might have taken for condescension. As usual, his hair strayed over his furrowed brow.

It was a moment Franklin Roosevelt would have enjoyed and exploited. He would have said grandiloquent things about Americanism and the nation's peril. He would have made extravagant promises about cooperation while mentally translating the crucial word into co-option. But Wallace was a politician who did not believe in politics. He was too aware that he had nothing in common with these men and they disliked the liberalism he personified. Instead of trying to charm his select audience, he told a mildly amusing story that drew a ripple of polite laughter, and sat down. The gulf between him and the dollar-a-year men remained all too visible—and probably, to Donald Nelson's distress, yawned even wider.[4]

II

Henry Wallace personified the profound dichotomy in American life between the soaring idealism of the Declaration of Independence and other documents of America's origins and the often brutal realism with which the heirs of that struggle for liberty subdued a continent and used its immense resources to create the most powerful nation on earth. The clash between these two views of life runs like a tangled often tragic thread throughout American history. It was visible in the compromise that legalized African slavery in the United States Constitution. It killed 600,000 young Americans in the collision that history now calls the Civil War. It roiled the nation with the threat of class war as American entrepreneurs transformed themselves into tycoons with monopoly power and the Republicans, the party that had produced Abraham Lincoln and his call for a new birth of freedom, became their chief defenders. It exasperated reformers who could not understand or respect voters who pledged their fealty to the often corrupt political machines that dominated America's cities.

Henry Wallace combined, he liked to think, the "practical" (read: realistic) side of this great dichotomy, as well as the idealistic side. As a scientist he had perfected a new hardier kind of corn that had multiplied the productivity of America's farms. He and his father before him had spent their lives urging farmers to use the latest science and the best machines to increase their profits. But his roots in the soil of the American heartland gave idealism a larger claim to his emotions. He was a descendant of Thomas Jefferson's dream of a nation of small businessmen and yeoman farmers, a dream that Alexander Hamilton's vision of a continent-wide industrial powerhouse had long since superseded. But Henry Wallace—and many of his fellow New Dealers—remained convinced that Jefferson's idealism was still relevant to the American colossus.

A profoundly intelligent, extremely gifted man, the vice president had blended the simple Christianity of his boyhood with these Jeffersonian ideals. The result was a mystical vision of a world in the process of spiritual transformation from scarcity to abundance, thanks to the miracles of modern science. Wallace's

1934 book, *New Frontiers*, urged Americans to abandon old ideas about religion, science, and human relations. He vehemently backed FDR's attempt to reconstruct the Supreme Court, writing a book on the subject, *Whose Constitution?*, that Roosevelt liked "enormously." It was so liberal, Jim Farley forbade its publication until after the 1936 election and FDR reluctantly went along.[5]

Wallace was probably the most successful secretary of agriculture in the history of the department. He created an "ever normal granary" in which the government worked with farmers to keep prices reasonably high and provide the nation with protection against food shortages. His rural electrification program transformed the American countryside. He had waged an effective war on rural poverty and this had led him to become a proponent of a similar campaign against urban poverty, particularly among American blacks. But as a politician he was a study in ineptitude.[6]

As vice president, one of Wallace's first moves was the abolition of his predecessor John Nance Garner's private capitol saloon—the "bureau of education" where senators relaxed while learning which way the political wind was blowing—or Garner wanted it to blow. Wallace let Majority Leader Alben Barkley deal with the behind-the-scenes politics of the world's greatest deliberative body. Instead Wallace launched a physical fitness program. His goal, he declared, was "to take an inch off the waist of every senator whose girth is above 40 and whose age is below 60."

The vice president as physical training instructor! It swiftly became one of the jokes of Washington D.C. Wallace searched in vain for sparring partners to box in the Senate gymnasium. He found no volunteers for paddleball. He was finally forced to admit that his prospective trainees "were hopeless from the standpoint of using the gymnasium except for taking hot baths and getting a rubdown." Undeterred, Wallace abandoned the Senate gym and played paddleball with young congressmen in the House gym. He stubbornly insisted it was "my equivalent of Garner's bar"—an almost pathetic glimpse of his political unrealism.[7]

Pearl Harbor galvanized the White House into doing something about Wallace's repeated pleas for a job with some real responsibility. On December 17, 1941, FDR made the vice president chairman of the Board of Economic Warfare. This time he had a mandate and, so it seemed at first, significant powers. The BEW was supposed to deal directly with foreign governments to procure scarce commodities such as rubber. It was also assigned a watchdog role to prevent strategic materials from reaching the Axis powers. Unfortunately, FDR did not bother to tell two very powerful conservatives in his entourage, Secretary of State Cordell Hull and Secretary of Commerce Jesse Jones, that Wallace might ignore them in exercising these responsibilities. It virtually guaranteed a confrontation that would make headlines across the country.

III

William Knudsen, head of the Office of Production Management, was immensely proud of his close relationship with the president. He had succumbed totally to the Roosevelt charm. Proudly, he told friends in his odd Swedish-American brogue: "He calls me Bill!"[8] After Pearl Harbor, strange things began happening to this friendship. In the second week in January 1942, Eleanor Roosevelt made a speech to a meeting of 4H Club directors. She told them how she had gone to see Mr. Knudsen and urged him to create retraining programs so people would not lose jobs when the auto industry shifted to defense production. The First Lady did not mention that Knudsen had opposed this shift. Mrs. Roosevelt reported to the 4H directors that the OPM director had "looked at me like a great big benevolent bear as if to say, now Mrs. Roosevelt, don't let's get excited." A month later, when she went to see him again, urging these training programs, she got another brush-off, a bland assurance that something was being worked out.

"I wonder if Mr. Knudsen knows what hunger is, if any member of his family has ever gone hungry," Mrs. Roosevelt asked her audience. She followed this roundhouse right with an upper-cut. "The slowness of our officials in seeing ahead . . . is responsible for the whole [defense] mess."[9]

This was a less than accurate explanation of the widespread public perception that the defense program was a mess. FDR's haphazard administrative methods had not a little to do with it. At OPM Donald Nelson was Knudsen's deputy. On SPAB, Knudsen was Nelson's deputy—a recipe for total confusion. But astute White House watchers knew what Mrs. Roosevelt's harsh words meant: Bill Knudsen's days as head of OPM were dwindling down.

The big Swede remained oblivious for another week. Then, toward the end of January, an associate came into Knudsen's office and slid a bulletin from one of the wire services across his huge glass-topped desk. It announced that OPM had been abolished by presidential order and Donald Nelson was now head of a new organization, the War Production Board, which would have total authority over all aspects of the war effort.

Minutes later, an embarrassed Nelson hurried into Knudsen's office. He had come from the White House, where he and Vice President Wallace had been conferring with the president. Nelson lamely tried to explain why Roosevelt had not had the courtesy to call his friend Bill into the Oval Office and let him down gently.

A lot of men would have gone back to Detroit and denounced Franklin D. Roosevelt and his wife. But Bill Knudsen was made of different stuff. "The president—he is my boss," he said. "He is the commander in chief. I do whatever he wants me to do." The next day, Nelson went back to the White House and persuaded

FDR to make Knudsen a lieutenant general and send him over to the War Department, where he operated as a troubleshooter with a large title, Director of Production, for the rest of the war.[10]

IV

Behind this hugger-mugger of character assassination and abrupt decapitation was a man *Time* magazine curtly described as "gray little Harry Truman." *Time* did not like Senator Truman because he seemed on the verge of making the war, which *Time*'s interventionist owner, Henry Luce, had enthusiastically endorsed, look bad. Soon after Truman's election to a second term in 1940, the senator had gotten into his car and driven around the country, personally investigating the defense program. He found such staggering amounts of waste and corruption in the $13 billion spending spree, he obtained a half-hour in the Oval Office to tell the president about it. Roosevelt gave him a full blast of the charm. He called him Harry and congratulated him on his reelection. But Truman departed without so much as a hint that FDR wanted any further examination of the bungled defense program.

By now, Truman had no illusions about the president. Early in 1941, the senator rose in the Cave of Winds, as some people called the U.S. Senate, and made a speech, proposing a special committee to look into the defense mess. The idea would have died there, but for an angry voice in the House of Representatives. Roosevelt-hating congressman Eugene Cox of Georgia wanted a joint committee to do a similar job. Deciding Truman was a safer choice, the New Dealers backed his proposal—sort of. Senator James F. (Jimmy) Byrnes of South Carolina, who headed the Audit and Control Committee, offered Truman a pathetic $10,000 to conduct the investigation. Truman had asked for $25,000. (To get a realistic idea of the dollar values, these figures should be multiplied by at least ten.) Settling for $15,000, Truman coolly resisted attempts by Majority Leader Alben Barkley and Vice President Henry Wallace to pack the committee with Roosevelt yes-men. The Missourian's choices were all independents like him and—also like Senator Truman—extremely hard workers.

In the business of building army camps, at a cost of $1 billion, the Truman Committee found $100,000,000 had been wasted. This was only a warm-up. As they slogged around the country during 1941, the committee and its investigators uncovered appalling examples of bad planning or no planning at all, of racketeering by labor unions and profiteering by corporations. The army air forces, for instance, did not seem to have a clue about which planes it wanted. It left that up to the manufacturers. Worst of all was the chaotic division of authority between and within the various government agencies. At OPM Roosevelt had given CIO labor leader Sidney Hillman as much power as William Knudsen. Hillman, an emerging Roosevelt favorite, played labor politics with a heavy hand. At one point he refused to approve a low bidder on a defense contract because the company had signed a closed-shop contract with a union that Hillman had secretly agreed to freeze out of government business. "I cannot condemn Mr. Hillman's position too strongly," Truman said in a stinging Senate speech. "If Mr. Hillman cannot or will not" protect the interests of the United States, "I am in favor of replacing him with someone who will."[11]

Within days of the Japanese attack on Pearl Harbor, the Roosevelt administration made another effort to silence Truman. On December 13, 1941, Under Secretary of War Robert Patterson wrote to the president, declaring it was "in the public interest" to suspend the committee. But Truman knew something about political infighting too. On December 10, he had written FDR a letter, assuring him the committee was "100 percent behind the administration" and had no intention of criticizing the military conduct of the war. More important, he sent the president a pre-view of the committee's forthcoming annual report, with its excruciating details of gross mismanagement and corruption. The imminent publication of that document was the reason for Bill Knudsen's sudden beheading. Whether Eleanor Roosevelt's attack was part of the White House game plan is more difficult to determine; the president and his wife did not always work in harmonious tandem. But it seems safe to presume that Mrs. Roosevelt knew that Knudsen's days were numbered, which made him a target of opportunity.[12]

V

In the White House, the president often acted more like a man savoring the Japanese trap he had set for his political enemies than an apostle of national unity. Soon after Pearl Harbor, FDR consulted with financier Bernard Baruch, legendary advisor to presidents since World War I, about how to deal with looming manpower and food shortages on the home front. Baruch recommended putting Herbert Hoover in charge of solving those problems. Baruch added that he had already contacted the former president, and he had evinced an eagerness to serve the country again.

Before the United States entered World War I, Hoover had organized a vast relief program for starving Belgium and other European countries. After America joined the fighting, Hoover had become Woodrow Wilson's "food czar" and done a magnificent job. Few could match the ex-president's expertise as a government administrator. In 1920 the *New York Times* had ranked him among the ten greatest living Americans. Woodrow Wilson reportedly said he hoped the Great Engineer, as he was often called, would run for president on the Democratic ticket. Franklin Roosevelt, Wilson's assistant secretary of the navy, offered himself as vice president on this ticket, which was swiftly abandoned when Hoover revealed he was a Republican.

In Roosevelt's campaign for the presidency in 1932, he acquired a very different view of his erstwhile hero. He gleefully encouraged the Democratic Party's publicity machine, led by a mordant genius named Charles Michelson, to demonize the Great Engineer. The Depression and its immense suffering was wholly Hoover's fault, went this party line. A stream of vituperation portrayed the former savior of starving millions as the cold, cruel, uncaring servant of the ruling class.

One might think that a triumphant Roosevelt, badly in need of an administrator who could talk blunt sense to the dollar-a-year men, would have decided it was time to abandon this fiction and use Hoover's expertise in the war effort. Throughout the domestic battles of the 1930s and in the 1940s furor over intervention, Hoover had remained a hard-hitting critic of FDR and the New Deal. But Roosevelt could have brushed aside these past antagonisms in the name of the wartime unity he supposedly sought. Instead, FDR told Baruch: "Well I'm not Jesus Christ. I'm not going to raise Herbie from the dead."[13]

James Farley was another man who waited in vain for a summons from the White House to join the war effort. Several times, General George Marshall, who admired Farley's executive skills, recommended him for high-level jobs. Each time Roosevelt "just sort of looked at him" and said nothing. Farley, who heard the story from Marshall personally after the war, was convinced that FDR never forgave him for opposing his run for a third term. He was especially angry, Farley thought, because the Democratic Party chairman had gotten a hundred-plus votes at the 1940 Democratic convention, depriving Roosevelt of the privilege of saying he was nominated unanimously.[14]

Even more revealing was the visit of Joseph Medill Patterson, publisher of the *New York Daily News*, to the Oval Office. He was a cousin of Colonel Robert McCormick, publisher of the *Chicago Tribune* and brother of Eleanor Medill ("Cissy") Patterson, publisher of the *Washington Times-Herald*, the two papers that had splashed the big leak across their front pages. With a circulation of 2 million the *Daily News* was the biggest paper in the nation. Patterson had supported Roosevelt during the 1930s and backed him for a third term; he had persuaded his sister to join him. The *Times-Herald* was the only newspaper in Washington D.C. to support FDR's historic break with presidential tradition. But both Pattersons had turned against the president for his postelection attempts to intervene in the war. Joe Patterson had fought in World War I and the prospect of another slaughter appalled him. At one point he became so enraged at Roosevelt, he burst into tears. "He lied to me," he sobbed.[15]

Now, contrite and eager to serve, Patterson came to Washington and was ushered into the Oval Office. Roosevelt was signing documents. He let Patterson stand there for five minutes. Finally, he shook hands and said: "Well Joe, what can I do for you?"

"I am here, Mr. President, to see what aid I can be in the war effort," Patterson said.

Although he was sixty-two, Patterson was still a physically impressive man. He hoped to get an army commission. He had been a captain in World War I.

"There is one thing you can do, Joe," Roosevelt said. "Go back and read your editorials for the past six months. Read every one of them and think what you've done."

For another fifteen minutes, FDR excoriated Patterson as a traitor for opposing his attempts to get America into the war. Finally, FDR dismissed him with a curt: "You can pass the same word to Cissy. Tell her to behave herself."

A wild-eyed Joe Patterson rushed to the offices of the *Washington Times-Herald* and told his sister the story. In a rage they jointly vowed to do their utmost to make Franklin D. Roosevelt's life miserable for the rest of his days on earth.[16]

VI

Soon after Bill Knudsen's decapitation, Mrs. Roosevelt learned that political assassination could work both ways. The First Lady had lobbied vigorously to make her friend, Fiorello La Guardia, the pint-sized effervescent mayor of New York, head of the Office of Civilian Defense. Although he was a Republican, La Guardia was a longtime Roosevelt ally, united by a shared antagonism to New York's Democratic political machine, Tammany Hall.

The First Lady immediately began bombarding La Guardia with ideas on how to run the agency. Still the mayor of the nation's largest city, La Guardia was doing the job with his left hand and suggested Mrs. Roosevelt become his assistant director. It was one of the worst mistakes of both their lives.

Eleanor Roosevelt was, to put it mildly, not a clear thinker. She found fault with the OCD because it concentrated on things like producing gas masks and training air-raid wardens and volunteer firemen. Mrs. Roosevelt thought its goals should be broader. She wanted civilian volunteers to be trained to work in nursery schools, housing projects, and other "meaningful" jobs. She talked incessantly about the importance of building morale. What these ideas had to do with civilian defense was opaque, to say the least.

Mrs. Roosevelt invariably gravitated toward the idealistic side of the great American dichotomy. On some issues, such as race relations, she was a courageous pioneer. On others she personified the old saw that the road to hell is paved with good intentions.

La Guardia, a sensible man, began disagreeing with some of the First Lady's fuzzy OCD projects. She immediately sought the president's backing, a tendency already evidenced in the way she tried to get a raise out of Fulton Oursler. Roosevelt, trying to cope with a losing war and a muddled home-front war effort, found their arguments more than a little trying. At first he recommended various mediators. But Mrs. Roosevelt was relentless, and soon the president resorted to his favorite ploy: he layered another executive on top of the mess in the hope he could straighten things out. His choice was James Landis, a pioneer New Dealer, currently dean of the Harvard Law School. La Guardia got the message and resigned with a farewell blast at Mrs. Roosevelt.

Not surprisingly, Landis made sure not to disagree with the First Lady. Given a free hand, Mrs. Roosevelt soon had on her payroll two old friends, the actor Melvyn Douglas and a dancer named Mayris Chaney who in 1937 had charmed the First Lady by inventing a dance called the Eleanor Glide. Douglas was being paid $8,000 a year, Chaney $4,600. (Again, multiplied by ten, these numbers become rather nice salaries.) What these two contributed to civilian defense was not easy to explain.

Someone in the OCD, perhaps an old La Guardia loyalist, leaked information about Douglas and Chaney to members of Congress. A Republican soon rose to note that General Douglas MacArthur's salary was the same as Melvyn Douglas's. The general was risking his life in the Philippines while no one seemed to know exactly what Melvyn Douglas was doing. The *Washington Times-Herald* gleefully pounced on the story. Other newspapers soon followed suit. One columnist wondered if the OCD had become "a personal parking lot for the pets and proteges of Mrs. Roosevelt."

An attempt to claim Chaney was teaching physical fitness fell flat. The *Times-Herald* and the Hearst newspapers took a dim view of Douglas's connection to numerous left-wing groups. A media feeding frenzy was soon rampaging on the radio and in print. Congress issued a specific ban against having physical fitness taught by dancers, putting Ms. Chaney out of work. Douglas wisely resigned and headed back to California. A humiliated Eleanor Roosevelt also resigned.[17]

The brouhaha seemed, on the surface, an explosion of sheer irrationality on both sides. But it served notice to the nation that Pearl Harbor had not endowed the Roosevelts with immunity to criticism. Its very ferocity revealed just how much antagonism to the president lurked beneath the fragile facade of national unity.

VII

The president's home-front vindictiveness seemed especially misplaced in the light of what was happening on the nation's battle fronts. In the opening months of 1942, the Americans were being humiliated on both oceans. While the Japanese army and navy rampaged through the Far East, German submarines wreaked almost as much havoc along the American east coast. Code named *Pauchenschlag* (Drumbeat), the offensive began in mid-January 1942 with the arrival of five U-boats in the U.S. Navy's home waters. In three weeks they sank a staggering thirty-five ships. Soon a dozen other U-boats joined the "turkey shoot," as the Germans gleefully called it. Ships went down by the dozen and more than half of them were tankers full of precious oil. By June the slaughter had reached a staggering 397 ships. An alarmed General George C. Marshall warned the navy that the losses "threaten our entire war effort."[18]

The Roosevelt administration's first reaction to this catastrophe was a communications stonewall. The sinkings were seldom reported in the newspapers (radio newsmen did somewhat better) and no hint of the cumulative effect and its danger to the war effort ever reached the American public.

For months the U.S. Navy ignored British advice to organize coastal convoys. The administration also refrained from ordering a blackout along the East Coast, because they did not want to admit what was happening. That meant merchant ships were silhouetted against the bright lights of New York, Atlantic City, Charleston, and Miami, turning them into targets in an oceanic shooting gallery. One U-boat cruising off New York sank eight ships in twelve hours. FDR, the self-styled naval strategist, who loved to talk about "my" navy, found it difficult if not impossible to confess how totally unprepared his navy was for the German onslaught.

For over a year, the president had been trying to taunt or trap the Germans into committing a hostile act that would start the war. Yet he and his navy did virtually nothing to prepare for what the Germans would do, if war finally started. To oppose Operation Drumbeat along the 1,500 miles of the East Coast's shoreline, the U.S. Navy had exactly twenty small ships. Not one was well armed enough to survive an encounter with a U-boat in a ship-to-ship surface fight. Among this so-called fleet were two gunboats built in 1905, three 200-foot "Eagle boats" built in 1919, four wooden-hulled submarine chasers of similar vintage, and four converted yachts. Within a few weeks the admiral in command of this matchbox enterprise would report that only three of these ships could withstand the heaving seas of the Atlantic in winter. Of planes with radar and the cruising range to make an impact on the elusive enemy, the Americans had none.[19]

Along with the communications blackout, the administration regularly resorted to good old-fashioned lying. Secretary of the Navy Knox declared the navy was concealing the number of German submarines it was sinking for "security" reasons, when in fact it had sunk none. The *New York Times* was gulled into declaring: NAVY HIDES ITS BLOWS. But it was impossible to conceal what was happening. Off Miami, Florida, and other resorts, such as Virginia Beach, ships were sunk in full view of horrified bathers. Bodies of drowned sailors were regularly encountered in the surf. *Pauchenschlag* contributed not a little to the growing impression that Mr. Roosevelt and his New Dealers were not fighting their war very well.[20]

VIII

Beset by bad news from so many directions, the administration drifted toward a decision that belied its liberal commitments on a truly fundamental level. Pearl Harbor and the rumors of a planned Japanese invasion of the West Coast stirred deep alarm in many minds. This panic coalesced with long-running racist hostility to the 120,000 Japanese Americans living in California, Oregon, and Washington. The only answer, argued prophets of imminent doom, was an immediate evacuation of the Japanese to internment camps in the interior of the country.

Inside the Roosevelt administration, the problem triggered a furious quarrel between the Department of Justice, Congress, and the army. Attorney General Francis Biddle, a balding scholarly descendant of a distinguished Philadelphia family, denounced the idea. He was supported by FBI Director J. Edgar Hoover, who insisted the Japanese were loyal Americans. His G-men had found no evidence of a readiness to betray their adopted country.

West Coast congressmen bombarded the White House and the Justice Department with demands for action. California Attorney General Earl Warren, future chief justice of the U.S. Supreme Court, joined the immediate evacuation chorus as spokesman for the assembled sheriffs of the Golden State. The racism behind this thinking was summed up by John Rankin of Mississippi in the House of Representatives. He claimed Japanese were untrustworthy unto the third generation. "Once a Jap, always a Jap," he declared. "You can't any more regenerate a Jap than you can reverse the laws of nature."[21]

PM, a newspaper founded by wealthy Chicagoan Marshall Field to give New York a liberal voice, was one of the most vociferous callers for internment. Showing an egregious disinterest in the facts, the editors declared, even before Pearl Harbor, that the FBI was ready to "crack down" on Japanese living in Hawaii. After the bombs fell, the paper's cartoonist, Theodore Giesel, future beloved children's book writer Dr. Seuss, drew a picture of a long column of slanty-eyed Japanese lining up to collect TNT at a house labeled "Honorable Fifth Column." Another cartoon showed an evil-looking Japanese carrying a spyglass. It was entitled: "Waiting for the Signal from Home."[22]

Early in February, Secretary of War Stimson went to the White House to discuss the problem. Pressured by the army's generals, the secretary was tilting toward evacuation, even though he feared the idea would "make a tremendous hole in our constitutional system." To his relief, he found FDR had already made up his mind that the Japanese had to go. "He was very vigorous about it," Stimson noted in his diary. When Stimson told Biddle of the president's decision, the attorney general crumpled and agreed to issue the evacuation order. One of Biddle's assistant attorney generals, veteran New Dealer James Rowe, who attended the climactic conference, was "so mad that I could not speak." A few days later, FDR signed executive order 9066, setting in motion what the American Civil Liberties Union later called "the greatest deprivation of civil liberties in this country since slavery."[23]

Quintessential New Dealer Harold Ickes thought the evacuation was "stupid and cruel." But like most of the men who struggled for power and influence around the president, he swallowed his moral qualms—or vented them in his diary. FDR soon demonstrated he was ready to go farther in his Japanese phobia than any of his advisors. On February 26, he told Secretary of the Navy Frank Knox that he wanted Hawaii's 140,000 Japanese evacuated too. The president said he had no worries about "the constitutional question" because Hawaii was under martial law. But the army and the navy objected because so many of the Hawaiian Japanese were skilled workers needed for the local war effort.[24]

The Japanese stayed in Hawaii. It was the first but by no means the last time FDR was forced to give the men who were running the war the final say on a political decision.

IX

The New Dealers and their leader soon produced another demonstration that civil liberties were not on the front burner of their wartime agenda. In the rancorous debate over American entry into the war, a lunatic fringe of anti-Semites and heirs of American white Protestant supremacy played a vociferous part, far out of proportion to the numbers of their followers. Pearl Harbor did not change their minds or shut their mouths or their printing presses. They continued to heap abuse on the president and the war.

Attorney General Francis Biddle had strong liberal principles. He had been shocked by the Chicago judge who fined the young man who booed Roosevelt, noting ruefully that this suppression of free speech had taken place on Bill of Rights Day. He ordered all federal attorneys not to bring any more such cases without specific written authority from him. His stance was based on memories of World War I, when patriotically inflamed judges had imprisoned anyone and everyone who criticized any aspect of the government's performance.

The president did not agree with the nation's chief law-enforcement officer. Biddle started receiving notes from FDR, attached to scurrilous attacks on the president's leadership, asking: "What are you doing to stop this?" When Biddle tried to explain that he felt the government would have to prove the nasty stuff was interfering with recruitment or could be connected to Nazi propaganda, FDR looked very unhappy. "He was not much interested in the theory of sedition or in the constitutional right to criticize the government during wartime. He wanted this anti-war talk stopped," Biddle glumly noted.[25]

In the early months of 1942, when FDR turned to the attorney general at weekly cabinet meetings, there was not a trace of the fabled Roosevelt charm in his manner. "He looked at me, his face pulled tightly together," Biddle recalled. "'When are you going to indict the seditionists?' he would ask." Biddle soon caved under this assault. A federal grand jury began pondering evidence of treason, under the guidance of an aggressive publicity-loving Justice Department attorney, William Power Maloney.

For awhile, Maloney made headlines by leaking that he planned to indict two Roosevelt-bashing congressmen, Clare Hoffman of Michigan and Hamilton Fish of New York. Fish was a promising target. Before Pearl Harbor, the head of his Washington staff had been caught distributing isolationist propaganda furnished by German agents. But Maloney—or more likely, Biddle—had second thoughts about taking on Congress. On July 21, 1942, twenty-eight people, described by Biddle as "native fascists," were indicted, and FDR stopped giving his attorney general that tight-faced look. Some liberal papers such as the *New York Post* cheered. But many people wondered what the government thought it was doing.[26]

Even Biddle admitted the defendants were "a curious assortment." They included Elizabeth Dilling, who had given up a concert career as a harpist to publish something called *The Red*

Network, which accused everyone from the Quakers to the Federal Council of Churches of being under Moscow's control. Ellis Jones was head of the National Copperheads and author of the poem, "Beware the Wily Jew." William Dudley Pelley led the Silver Shirts Legion of America, modeled on Hitler's Brownshirts, and abused Jews, Roosevelt, and Democrats in *Pelley's Weekly.* Gerald Winrod attacked Jews, Blacks, labor unions, and Catholics. The Jesuits (he called them the pope's secret service) were one of his favorite targets.

How to prove these people were interfering with the war effort kept Attorney General Biddle awake nights. He grew even more distressed when he saw the text of William Power Maloney's indictment. The reasoning was so flabby and loose, any judge who had ever read the Constitution and the Bill of Rights would gavel the government out of court. In the Senate, Maloney came under attack by Senator Burton K. Wheeler, who accused him of using these lunatics to smear responsible dissenters such as himself. Still, the attorney general could console himself that he had done something. At cabinet meetings, FDR was smiling at him again.[27]

X

Another far more formidable opponent of the war was silenced extra-legally with the attorney general's energetic cooperation. Detroit-based Father Charles Coughlin, known as "The Radio Priest," had been a strident opponent of the New Deal since he lost his enthusiasm for FDR in 1936. He had a largely Catholic audience of millions who listened to his fervent attacks on bankers, the British and—with mounting intensity as war approached—on Jews.

Biddle had no trouble persuading Postmaster General Frank Walker, a Catholic, to suspend postal privileges for Coughlin's magazine, *Social Justice*. But Biddle grew jittery when Coughlin demanded to appear before William Power Maloney's grand jury. The *Chicago Tribune* and the *New York Daily News* attacked banning *Social Justice* from the mails, fearing it was the first step toward silencing other magazines and eventually newspapers.

At Roosevelt's urging, Biddle sent Assistant Attorney General James Rowe to Secretary of the Treasury Morgenthau to see if they could get the Radio Priest on a tax fraud conviction, a device FDR had used to silence other opponents. As a Jew, Morgenthau was reluctant to tangle with Coughlin. Given the priest's proclivity for anti-Semitism, it was easy to foresee how he would retaliate. Instead, Biddle had lunch with prominent Catholic Leo Crowley, chairman of the Federal Deposit Insurance Corporation. In no time Crowley was on a plane to Detroit, where he conferred with Archbishop Edward Mooney, Coughlin's immediate superior.

Three days later, Crowley was back in Washington, "rubbing his hands with satisfaction," said the grateful Biddle. Archbishop Mooney had ordered Coughlin to shut down *Social Justice* and end his radio broadcasts. "That was the end of Father Coughlin," Biddle later wrote. "FDR was delighted with the outcome."[28]

As the war gathered momentum, idealism repeatedly lost to ruthless realism. Only a dwindling handful of New Dealers groped for high moral ground. Franklin D. Roosevelt was not one of them.

5

WHOSE WAR IS IT
ANYWAY?

The navy's refusal to tell anything even close to the truth about
the German submarine rampage off the East Coast underscored
another large problem the Roosevelt administration faced: how
to deal with the information side of the war. During the days of
the defense buildup the task had been scattered through a half-
dozen agencies such as the Office of Government Reports and
the Foreign Information Service. Roosevelt declared himself opposed to organizing a single propaganda agency such as
Woodrow Wilson founded during World War I. Headed by
newsman George Creel, the Committee on Public Information
preached hatred of "the Hun" and organized a small army of
"Four Minute Men" who hurled patriotic fustian at audiences in
theaters and motion picture houses across the nation. It also
produced films, sponsored books, magazines, and posters, and

otherwise marshaled the nation's creative powers to sell the war
to the American people.

World War I had needed selling. Ten days before Wilson asked
Congress for a declaration of war against Germany, the U.S.
Army had dispatched two intelligence officers to the west. They
had traveled from Kansas City to San Francisco without finding
ten people in favor of fighting. As in World War II, intervention
appealed largely to East Coast anglophiles in both political parties. Harry S. Truman, among many others, later attested it was
Woodrow Wilson's soaring call for a war to make the world safe
for democracy that transformed attitudes in the nation's heartland.

At first, the national outrage generated by Pearl Harbor made
such an all-encompassing propaganda effort seem superfluous.
But the inevitable decline of intense emotion, coupled with the
tidal wave of bad news from the battlefronts, soon changed many
people's minds. Another unsettling problem was the president's
continuing determination to focus on defeating Hitler first. This
did not go down well with many people. One study found that
almost half of American servicemen agreed with the statement: "I
would really like to kill a Japanese soldier." Less than one in ten
said he wanted to kill a German soldier. A poll revealed a startling 30 percent of the American people said they would welcome
peace overtures from Germany if Hitler were overthrown by the
Reich's generals and they renounced the Nazi leader's war conquests.[1]

When Frank Knox, the secretary of the navy, hewed to the administration line in a speech, declaring Germany was our "great
enemy" and Italy and Japan were secondary targets, the Dutch
government in exile in London exploded, revealing their eagerness to get back their oil-producing colony in the East Indies. The
Chinese government was even more negative. Dr. Sun Fo, son of
Sun Yat-sen, founder of the Chinese republic, revered as the

George Washington of China, said his country was so discouraged, they might sign a separate peace with Japan and drop out of the war. Knox hastily ate his words. He claimed he only meant to say Hitler was the evil genius who had hatched the global conspiracy they were confronting. We would not turn our backs on either front.[2]

II

The job of selling the war without George Creel's overkill seemed made to order for an energetic moderate like Fulton Oursler. In his heyday during the 1920s and 1930s, he had supervised a dozen magazines in the Macfadden group, written an occasional novel and a mystery series, had a hit play, "The Spider," on Broadway, and personally edited the weekly, *Liberty*. Moreover, as World War II began, Oursler found himself out of a job. An internal power struggle ousted both him and founder Bernarr Macfadden from the ailing company, which had been badly hurt by the recession of 1937.

Upton Sinclair, the aging California radical, who had contributed to *Liberty* and was an admirer of Oursler's talents, wrote from Pasadena urging him to go to work for the government. "What a magnificent propaganda job you could do in getting the ears of the oppressed peoples of all the world and telling them about Democracy!" he declared. Sinclair added that he presumed Oursler needed no help from him. But he knew "several of the New Dealers" very well. In particular, his old friend, playwright Robert Sherwood, was running the Foreign Information Service out of 270 Madison Avenue in New York City.

On February 11, 1942, Sinclair wrote Sherwood a fulsome letter urging him to hire Oursler. He described him as "one of the most brilliant and capable men I know." He added that he was "too good a man to be used in any sort of subordinate position.

He could do big things and would be interested in doing them. He is one of those day-and-night workers." Moreover, he was "heart and soul for our cause."[3]

Almost a month passed without a word from Sherwood. On March 3, Oursler told Sinclair of the long silence. "I wonder if my criticisms of the New Deal [in *Liberty*] would stand in the way of serving my country. I would not like to think so," he wrote.

Along with describing the New Deal spending sprees of the 1930s as "Squandermania," Oursler had also taken issue with FDR's frequent references to "economic royalists" and attacks by New Dealers such as Harold Ickes on the nation's businessmen. Oursler considered this tactic a flirtation with class warfare, which would ruin America. When the president announced the Four Freedoms as the postwar goal for which the United States was contending, Oursler wondered why FDR had omitted freedom of enterprise.

Sinclair wrote to Sherwood on March 9, 1942, asking if he had received his "important letter about Fulton Oursler." He could only conclude it had gone astray. "I am sure you would not neglect it." This was probably what Sherwood had done. His fellow workers in the Foreign Information Service remembered him as "slow, unpunctual and moody." He hated paperwork. His private secretary often sent in stacks of letters in the morning and got them back that night, untouched.[4]

Prodded by Sinclair, Sherwood telephoned Oursler and offered to see him. But his tone was so unenthusiastic, it was clear to Oursler that he was going to get a brush-off. That conclusion is amply confirmed by a memorandum Sherwood had written the president about personnel policy in the Foreign Information Service. "It is all right to have rabid anti-New Dealers or even Roosevelt haters in the military or OPM, but I don't think it is appropriate to have them participating in an effort which must be expressive of the President's own philosophy." Few pithier statements of the New Dealers' wartime goals exist. Sherwood was saying it was all right to let the conservatives do the fighting and produce weapons of war, but the New Dealers intended to control the ideas.[5]

Writing to Upton Sinclair, Oursler bitterly concluded it was "a New Deal war" and there was no room for him in Washington D.C. Sinclair's reply was another indication of what liberals were thinking about the war. He disagreed with Oursler's claim that it was a "New Dealers' War"—a more exact statement of what Oursler meant. Instead, Sinclair applauded a "New Deal War"— meaning a war for a New Deal for the entire world. "Either the war is a New Deal War or it is not worth winning," Sinclair declared. "Because if we simply get the old deal back, we will have to get ready for the next war."[6]

Oursler, still determined to make a contribution to the war effort, turned to J. Edgar Hoover, who had made numerous appearances in the pages of *Liberty*. Hoover said he needed someone to set up a covert operation to help fight Nazism in South America. Soon Oursler was running something called the American Editors' Syndicate, which sent FBI men to South America disguised as journalists. He took no money for this rather complicated task. To keep food on his table, Oursler became a radio newsman, broadcasting nightly for most of the war years on WOR and other stations.[7]

III

Politically, Upton Sinclair was on the sidelines. He had run for governor of California in 1934 on a program that called for turning all the idle farmlands and factories in the state over to the unemployed. FDR had invited him to Hyde Park and encouraged him at first but withdrew his support when public reaction to his radical proposals showed he was a sure loser. Like the NRA, Sinclair had served as a kind of lightning rod, warning how far to the left the New Deal could go.

In Washington, D.C., in 1942 there was a very active politician who was having thoughts about turning the war into a crusade for a global New Deal: Vice President Henry Wallace. He had long had a penchant for sweeping liberal ideas. His experience as head of the Board of Economic Warfare soon exacerbated this tendency. Thanks to FDR's fondness for dividing power, Wallace found it necessary to go head-to-head with Secretary of Commerce Jesse Jones and Secretary of State Cordell Hull. Both were old pros in the peculiar capital game known as turf wars.

Of the two, the beefy, six-foot-two Jones was by far the more formidable. He used his status as a millionaire, a newspaper owner, and a good old bourbon-drinking boy (from Tennessee, originally) to impress and otherwise befriend dozens of congressmen and senators. His control of the Reconstruction Finance Corporation gave him awesome power to do favors for the politicians' constituents in the form of million-dollar loans. As the defense program expanded and became the war effort, Jones acquired even more power, presiding over his own private alphabet soup of lending agencies, such as the Defense Plant Corporation. Jones had a conservative's approach to government: the money belonged to the people and should be spent as sparingly as possible—a consensus shared by most southern congressmen and senators and most Republicans.

Complicating matters was the man Wallace made the chief operating officer of the BEW, a former aide from the Department of Agriculture, Milo Perkins. Like his boss, Perkins had a mystical streak. He had been a bishop in the Liberal Catholic Church, which was actually a branch of the theosophical movement, the same treasury of spiritual mumbo jumbo that had inspired Wallace to write his politically explosive "Dear Guru" letters. Perkins and Jesse Jones were both from Houston and early in the New Deal Jones had taken a ferocious dislike to him.

Wallace, Perkins, and their staff at the BEW saw themselves as committed to winning the war as quickly as possible, and also to improving the quality of life in the countries from which they were buying raw materials. In their South American contracts, for instance, they specified that the sellers had to guarantee that their workers had adequate food and shelter and let the BEW have a say in determining their wages. The agency also paid outrageous prices for tin, rubber, and other raw materials on the theory that some of the money would trickle down to the workers. They defended this largesse by arguing the Axis powers might buy the stuff first.

Jones maintained that the idea of the Germans or Japanese getting tin or rubber across oceans controlled by the British and Americans was absurd. He saw the BEW's expensive deals as a scheme by "socialist-minded uplifters" to spend American money abroad New Deal–style with no visible return on the investment. He also got Secretary of State Cordell Hull to agree that the BEW had no business telling foreign countries how much their workers should be paid or how much food and shelter they should get.

Hull soon persuaded Roosevelt that the State Department should oversee all BEW contract negotiations. Jones meanwhile saw to it that bureaucratic foot-dragging slowed the money the Wallace-Perkins team requested whenever possible. Jones also used his large influence in other government agencies to delay BEW attempts to get the cash elsewhere.

Milo Perkins filled Wallace's ears with tales of the obnoxious ways Jones and his right-hand man, Texas cotton tycoon Will Clayton, were dealing with him and the rest of the BEW staff. An infuriated Wallace asked FDR to do something. After mulling it over for a month, in April 1942 the president issued an executive order giving BEW the power to make all decisions on major purchases—but the cash would still have to come from Jones. It was a typical Roosevelt solution, and a brooding

Wallace later said it played a major part in "my growing distrust of FDR." Jesse Jones soon made it clear that having a
White House order issued behind his back, with no prior consultation with him, confirmed his growing distrust of Henry
Agard Wallace.[8]

IV

Wallace's irritation with Jones's parsimonious capitalist style undoubtedly played a part in his decision to become a visionary
spokesman for worldwide liberalism. When Mrs. Borden Harriman asked him to address a meeting of the Free World Association on May 8, 1942, the vice president saw an opportunity to go
far beyond Roosevelt's vague goal of the Four Freedoms.

In a speech that combined religious fervor and soaring secular
ideology, Wallace claimed the war was the climactic moment in a
150-year-old people's revolution that had begun on April 19,
1775, with the gunfire at Lexington and Concord. He recounted
the history of other revolutions in France, Germany, and Russia
and insisted World War II was in the same tradition. Out of the
war would come a New Deal for the world, a new abundance
that would guarantee to every child at least a pint of milk a day.
With this abundance would come a new equality, an end to ruling
classes, dictators, and economic royalists.

"Some have spoken of the American Century," Wallace thundered. "I say the century on which we are now entering, the century that will come out of this war, can and must be the century
of the common man. The people's revolution is on the march and
the devil and all his angels cannot prevail against it. They cannot
prevail, for on the side of the people is the Lord."[9]

The speech created a sensation. Columnist Raymond Clapper
compared it to the Gettysburg Address. A friend told Wallace he
was on his way to becoming a second Lincoln. Wallace's delighted

circle of aides and advisors urged him to cultivate a Lincolnesque look and demeanor. It went well with his Midwest background, his unruly hair, and his craggy all-American looks. Wallace seemed like the man who could speak for the aspirations of the old America of small farms and businesses as well as the workers in the giant corporations.

Wallace not only seized the rhetorical leadership of the nation's liberals with this speech. He enraged conservatives and moderates who had long since soured on the New Deal. They said trying to guarantee a daily pint of milk "to every Hottentot" and financing better wages for workers around the world were beyond America's capacity. Even some New Dealers disliked the speech. Former brain truster Adolf Berle, whose duties as assistant secretary of state involved U.S. relationships with South America, rebuked Wallace to his face for "your talk about revolution."[10]

More important, in Wallace's contemptuous reference to an American century, he threw down the gauntlet to another vision of the future, articulated by Henry Luce and his journalists at *Time* and *Life* magazines, with the backing of the 1940 Republican presidential candidate, Wendell Willkie, and Under Secretary of State Sumner Welles. Beginning with an essay in *Life* in February 1941, Luce saw American capitalism rescuing the postwar world from disorder and poverty, and he made it plain that this reinvigorated production machine would have no truck with government planning à la the New Deal or Soviet Communism. Luce even opined that the New Deal had dangerously weakened America. But the American ideals of law, truth, charity, and freedom had remained intact and would lift mankind to a higher plane as Americans, replacing their British cousins, shouldered the white man's burden and became the dominant nation on the planet.[11]

Undeterred by the conservative counterattack, on June 8, Wallace made another speech that projected an even more apocalyptic vision of the future. He called America the "chosen of the Lord." In her the traditions of Judaism and Christianity, ancient Rome's rule of law and England's commitment to freedom were about to come to fruition. He cited America's multiethnic background and saw a similar polyglot heritage in South America, enabling both continents to share in the mission to create a new world order. Reporting on the speech to his superiors in London from his post in the British embassy in Washington, philosopher Isaiah Berlin called it "the most unbridled expression to date of the New Deal as the New Islam, divinely inspired to save the world."[12]

Which of these two versions of the future prevailed meant a great deal to thinkers and writers and politicians, while the men in uniform fought a losing war in the Pacific and German armored columns rumbled toward the Russian oil fields in the Caucasus. No less a personage than Edward R. Murrow, the CBS correspondent who had electrified America with his broadcasts during the 1940 German air blitz against London, told a friend he believed the fate of the world depended on whether Henry Wallace or Henry Luce controlled American foreign policy.[13]

V

Behind this idealistic sound and fury lay an ironic well-concealed reality, a veritable paradigm of the interplay of the great dichotomy in American life.

Franklin D. Roosevelt, the designated leader of the New Deal and putative defender of the "little man," had put the big-business executives he had condemned as economic royalists and crypto-fascists in charge of winning the war. Over two-thirds of the $100 billion in military contracts let in 1942 went to a mere one hundred companies. The thirty-three largest corporations got half the production orders. General Motors got 10 percent of the total outlay all by itself. Secretary of War Henry L. Stimson and his top assistant, Under Secretary of War Robert P. Patterson, a fellow Republican who had resigned from the Court of Appeals to lend his formidable personality to the war effort, virtually ignored attempts by Donald Nelson at the War Production Board and New Dealer Leon Henderson at the Office of Price Administration to play a part in the procurement process.

"When you are going to war in a capitalist country," Stimson said, "you have to let business make money out of the process or business won't work." Stimson and Patterson offered the big corporations risk-free cost-plus contracts, huge loans for plant expansion, and a promise that the new production facilities could be bought at bargain prices when the war ended. Patterson was ably seconded on the navy side of the procurement program by Under Secretary James Forrestal, former president of Wall Street's Dillon, Read and Co. Their policies were warmly supported by their mostly conservative opposite numbers on the army and navy side of the procurement process. Lieutenant General Brehon B. Somervell, head of the Army Service Forces, summed up the military's attitude when he growled that he regarded Roosevelt's alphabet soup of war agencies as a scheme by "Henry Wallace and the leftists to take over the country."[14]

A major component of the president's appeasement of his erstwhile foes was the virtual suppression of the feisty head of the antitrust division, Thurman Arnold. In spite of a noteworthy string of antitrust convictions, Arnold had gotten himself in trouble with the New Dealers by prosecuting labor unions as well as corporations for pursuing anticompetitive practices designed to fill the pockets of their members. Labor unions were sacrosanct to the New Dealers; their members' votes were crucial to victory on election day. The New Dealers shuddered when Arnold, in his usual slashing style, denounced unions for "eliminating cheap methods of distribution . . . preventing organizations of new firms, eliminating small competitors and owner-operators" and other abuses. It was, Arnold concluded, "part of the age old struggle for economic power by men who love power."[15]

As a result, Arnold had few if any supporters in the White House when he attempted to launch antitrust lawsuits against major defense contractors. Arnold tried to outflank his critics by claiming the antitrust division was "one of the nation's vital defense agencies" but this soon proved to be his private fantasy.

Among Arnold's targets were Du Pont, General Electric, and Standard Oil. Army secretaries Stimson and Patterson and the navy's procurement secretary Forrestal rushed to the White House and demanded an immediate end to the prosecutions. Stimson called Arnold "a self-seeking fanatic" who was frightening businessmen and endangering, among other things, munitions production. After conferring with Sam Rosenman, Roosevelt agreed and ordered the preparation of a letter that a humiliated Arnold was forced to sign, agreeing to defer antitrust activity until it "no longer interfere[d] with war production."[16]

A bitter Arnold condemned the dollar-a-year men that the major corporations had loaned to the defense effort for fostering the Roosevelt administration's sudden love affair with big business. He gloomily predicted "a few giants" would end up controlling postwar markets. Roosevelt ignored him. He also ignored Harold Ickes, who moaned in his diary against allowing "private people [a.k.a. capitalists] to make a guaranteed profit for themselves."[17]

FDR—and the New Dealers—were discovering that liberalism and war were not a very good match. The war was an entity with its own rules, its own imperatives. Realism—often brutal realism—almost always prevailed over idealism. Eventually the New Dealers would make the dismaying discovery that Franklin D. Roosevelt was no longer on their side in the war within the war.

VI

Congressional and media snipers, having discovered they could bring down a major target such as Eleanor Roosevelt, soon turned on another likely prospect, Archibald MacLeish, head of the Office of Facts and Figures (OFF). Roosevelt had created this agency in the fall of 1941 to report on the defense program and put MacLeish, a well-known poet and outspoken interventionist, in charge. As the name implied, OFF was not supposed to indulge in propaganda. Yet MacLeish privately confessed that he yearned to follow the example of Lincoln, "who reduced the violence and confusion of his time to the essential moral issue."[18]

This was a serious misreading of the history of the Civil War. Lincoln had in fact done the exact opposite. He had refused to reduce the Civil War to a struggle over slavery. He had declared that if he could save the Union without freeing a single slave, he would do it. The New Dealers had a recurrent tendency to misread American history for their own purposes.

Unable to formulate the essential moral issue, MacLeish fell back on proclaiming that OFF's credo would be "the strategy of truth." The agency would avoid "ballyhoo" and simply give the American people the facts, letting them decide. This formula soon proved as feckless as the search for the single moral issue.

The press hated OFF from the start, instinctively distrusting government handouts, no matter how high-minded. They dubbed the agency "the Office of Fun and Frolic," implying a lot of government jobs were being distributed to literary lightweights. Ideology was another problem. Among his chief lieutenants, MacLeish selected the author Malcolm Cowley, who had a long history of involvement with Communist causes. Cowley came under ferocious attack from conservatives in Congress, which was gleefully reported in the Hearst and McCormick-Patterson papers, and was soon forced to resign.

Worse, MacLeish gradually realized he was another victim of the Roosevelt style of running the government. OFF was supposed to coordinate information from dozens of other agencies, but MacLeish had no authority to stop them from issuing press releases and publications on their own, which sometimes contradicted what OFF was saying. One OFF observer put it pithily: the agency tried to call the signals "but the players ran where they pleased with the ball."[19]

This was particularly true in OFF's relationship with the army and the navy. They had their own information policies and they clashed head-on with MacLeish's. "Under no circumstances [will] the government withhold information simply because it is bad or depressing," MacLeish intoned. When Pearl Harbor exploded in his face, the poet rushed around Washington, D.C., trying to find out something to tell the press. He was soon reduced to asking J. Edgar Hoover what he knew (nothing) because the military refused to talk to him. In the ensuing days, MacLeish frantically tried to persuade the army and the navy to tell the public the truth about the disaster—and got nowhere.[20]

Early in 1941, almost a year before Pearl Harbor, the admirals and generals had revealed their thinking on information. The Joint Army and Navy Public Relations Committee proposed to spend $50 million to set up "complete censorship of publications, radio and motion pictures within the U.S.A." Roosevelt recoiled from this policy, calling it "a wild scheme." But when the war began, he did little to loosen the military's grip on information. During the first twenty-one months of the war, not a single photo of a dead American soldier, sailor, or marine was displayed in any publication on the theory that it might panic the public into calling for a premature peace.[21]

Roosevelt himself revealed his indifference to MacLeish's "strategy of truth." In a fireside chat on February 23, 1942, he solemnly assured the American people that "your government has unmistakable confidence in your ability to hear the worst, without flinching or losing heart." He then proceeded to minimize American losses at Pearl Harbor. Instead of admitting the Japanese had sunk six battleships and damaged two others, plus three cruisers and two destroyers, FDR claimed "only three ships" had been permanently put out of commission. This evasion was based on the navy's determination to raise most of the sunken battlewagons for repairs that would take years. The president added a total whopper about aircraft losses. "To date," he declared, "including Pearl Harbor—we have destroyed considerably more Japanese planes than they have destroyed of ours." At Pearl Harbor, the Japanese obliterated 180 planes and damaged 128 others. Only 43 planes remained operational. Japanese losses were 29 planes. In the Philippines, within two weeks, General MacArthur's 277 plane air force had been reduced to a handful of fighters and a few bombers. By the time FDR spoke, these planes too were goners.[22]

Soon the anti-Roosevelt press was smelling MacLeish's blood. The Hearst newspapers published a searing blast calling the government's information "treacle for children." Hearst reporters declared that 3,000 full-time bureaucrats were involved in putting out as little news as possible, especially if the facts and figures were unpleasant. Thirty thousand other government drones were devoting a large chunk of their forty-hour weeks to assisting them. THE FAT CATS IN WASHINGTON FIDDLE WITH FIGURES WHILE THE PEOPLE PAY WORK AND DIE, roared the Hearst flagship paper, the *New York Journal American*.[23]

MacLeish blasted back at his critics. In a March 1942 speech he accused them of trying to undermine people's confidence in the government and America's alliance with Russia, tactics he characterized as close to treason. He also denounced the *Washington Times-Herald* and *Chicago Tribune* for publishing Rainbow Five. MacLeish soon became the Patterson-McCormick team's favorite whipping boy. In the *Times-Herald*, Cissy Patterson dubbed the poet "the Bald Bard of Balderdash." She said MacLeish was presiding over an "array of literary floozies engaged in turning out hate at salaries equivalent to those of major generals."[24]

When the FBI began investigating two other MacLeish appointees for Communist connections, the poet fired off a letter to Attorney General Francis Biddle, testily demanding that he do something about J. Edgar Hoover. Instead, Biddle passed the letter on to Hoover, instantly converting the FBI director into MacLeish's enemy. He opened a file on the politician-poet, which eventually grew to 600 pages.[25]

Then came a truly disastrous blunder. OFF produced a booklet full of glowing praise for the defense program that appeared only a few days before Harry S Truman dropped his committee's bombshell on Washington, D.C., reporting that several hundred million dollars had already been wasted. Derision and outrage mingled in the storm of criticism that descended on the harried MacLeish. The *St. Louis Post-Dispatch* suggested the Office of Facts and Figures should change its name to the "Office of Alibis and Excuses."[26]

MacLeish fled to a White House insider, Budget Director Harold Smith, and told him the government's information problem needed a new superagency run by someone with the power to make major decisions. "I am NOT the man for that job," the chastened poet confessed. He added a succinct summary of the government's current information setup: it was a "Tower of Babel."[27]

VII

The Foreign Information Service was less vulnerable to congressional criticism. The politicians did not read its commentaries in their daily papers. Under the leadership of playwright Robert Sherwood, the FIS was, comparatively speaking, a safe haven for New Dealers. Like his colleague MacLeish, Sherwood proclaimed that "truth is the only effective basis for American foreign information." He assembled an impressive staff, including such literary big names as poet Stephen Vincent Benet and novelist Thornton Wilder.

At first FIS concentrated on beaming the story of America's enormous productive capacity around the world, on the assumption it would intimidate Axis followers. Also emphasized were the promises of the Atlantic Charter and the Four Freedoms. The ultimate goal was to use words to fight Fascism everywhere. An all-out Roosevelt worshipper, Sherwood thought their message should sound as if "it were a continuous speech from the president."[28]

Things went awry when Sherwood and his aides collided with a human buzzsaw named William J. Donovan. Known as "Wild Bill" for his exploits with the Fighting 69th in World War I, Donovan had talked his way into the Oval Office in the summer of 1941 and persuaded FDR to make him head of the Office of Coordinator of Information. Its focus was supposed to be secret intelligence but Roosevelt put the FIS under this umbrella, making Donovan theoretically Sherwood's boss.

The playwright was appalled to discover that Wild Bill was a Republican with decidedly conservative views. He objected to FIS attacks on the pro-Fascist governments of Spain and Argentina. He also thought the strategy of truth was idiocy. The goal of the FIS should be an all-out propaganda war on the Axis, with plenty of ingenious lying to make it effective. A harried FDR was soon being bombarded with vituperative memos from both sides of this mounting quarrel, which eventually got into the newspapers.[29]

Although the president still resisted the idea, he gradually realized it was time to put all the government's information problems under one roof. His budget director, Harold Smith, prodded by Archibald MacLeish, pushed the idea. So did one of the nation's most popular radio commentators, Elmer Davis. He recommended Edward R. Murrow for the job. But when Roosevelt made the choice, he decided on the man "with the funny voice, Elmer—Elmer something."[30]

In June of 1942, when Davis took over the new Office of War Information (OWI), most newsmen applauded. In public, he was neither a wild-eyed liberal nor a Roosevelt worshipper. (Privately, however, he told Henry Wallace his goal was to sell the Century of the Common Man to America and the world.)[31] At fifty-one, Davis emanated vigor that belied his prematurely white hair. His Midwest accent had survived a two-year sojourn as a Rhodes Scholar at Oxford University and seemed to his radio listeners proof of his common sense Americanism. Before taking to the air waves he had enjoyed a distinguished career as a reporter and editorial writer at the *New York Times*.

The chorus of praise from Davis's fellow journalists helped the Roosevelt administration conceal some brutal behind-the-scenes bureaucratic infighting in the creation of OWI. Wild Bill Donovan had resisted letting the Foreign Information Service out of his grasp. He lost the immediate battle and accepted leadership of a new Office of Strategic Services (OSS), whose murky mandate by no means prohibited him from indulging in psychological warfare by fair means and foul. Nelson Rockefeller, Coordinator of Inter-American Affairs, got Under Secretary of State Sumner Welles to back him in banning OWI from having anything to do with South America.

These ambiguities and eviscerations were only harbingers of Elmer Davis's future problems. Two months after he took charge of OWI, he received a letter from World War I's propaganda chief, George Creel. While he wrote to wish Davis well, Creel pulled no punches in his assessment of the future. He told Davis "your control over Army, Navy and State is not real in any sense of the word." These powerful entities were supposed to confer with OWI and agree on a policy. Creel warned Davis "coordination by conference never worked and never will work." When the military and the diplomats challenged Creel in World War I, Woodrow Wilson had "hammered them down." Creel doubted that Roosevelt would follow this example.

Many months later, an agonized Davis would write at the bottom of Creel's letter: *He was about right on all points.*[32]

VIII

Around the time Elmer Davis was appointed, another newsman was trying desperately to get some time with FDR. His name was Louis Lochner and he too had enjoyed a distinguished career, covering American politics in World War I and the 1920s and then going to Europe where for more than a decade he was the Associated Press's man in Berlin.

In November 1941, Lochner was invited to the house of a Reichstag deputy to meet fifteen members of the Nazi opposition, ranging from politicians to churchmen to a spokesman for certain army generals and key members of the German secret service. They told him that they hoped to overthrow Hitler, renounce his conquests and his war on the Jews, and restore Germany as a peaceful member of the family of nations.

Lochner was deeply impressed and promised to see Roosevelt, whom he knew well, and ask him for his tacit support. The conspirators even solicited FDR's opinion on the kind of government he favored for a post-Hitler Germany. Some of them wanted a constitutional monarchy, others a republic. They gave Lochner a secret radio code, hoping to establish direct communication with the White House.

Unfortunately, before Lochner could leave Germany, Hitler declared war on the United States on December 11, 1941, and the newsman was interned. He did not get back to the United States until June of 1942. He immediately wrote to Roosevelt and requested a meeting. He got nothing but silence. Five subsequent letters and calls were also rebuffed. Lochner was finally told through the AP's Washington office that the president had no interest in his information about a German resistance movement against Hitler. In fact, FDR found his persistence "most embarrassing" and Lochner was told to drop the subject.[33]

Later in 1942, Lochner published a book, *What About Germany?*, in which he vividly described and denounced Nazi barbarism and called for a maximum effort to defeat the German war machine. Patriotically averse to criticizing the president, Lochner made no mention of his rebuff by Roosevelt—but he included a chapter entitled: "Is There Another Germany?" His answer was an emphatic yes. There were millions of Germans who prayed "for deliverance from the Nazi yoke as fervently as any member of the United Nations can pray for the end of Hitler and his system." This Germany is "ashamed and humiliated at the disgrace into which Nazism has dragged the German name."

Alas, these "bewildered German masses" were bereft of leadership and living in a police state. Lochner told of one German friend who came to him for advice. The Gestapo had ordered him to report on everyone in his apartment house. He did not know what to do. If his information sent someone to prison, he would "never be able to sleep again." But if he refused or sent false information, he feared arrest. At least two other people were also performing the same task.

In spite of this police terror, Lochner reported the existence of a "clandestine leadership" working in deep cover that was attempting to guide the Front der anständiger Leute (Front of Decent People). Unfortunately, Lochner could not name any of these courageous men and women without signing their death warrants.[34]

6

Some Neglected Chickens Come Home to Roost

The New Dealers were uneasily aware that the war's timing, from a political point of view, was not propitious. Midterm elections were scheduled for November, 1942, and the stream of military disasters that cascaded into America from the Atlantic and the Pacific did not make for happy voters. Sam Rayburn, the Speaker of the House, told Roosevelt that Americans were very upset because the U.S. had failed to thrash Japan in six weeks—a graphic example of how deeply ingrained was the country's conviction that the Japanese were an inferior people.[1] In June of 1942, *Time* acidly observed that in the first six months after Pearl Harbor, the United States had "not taken a single inch of enemy territory, not yet beaten the enemy in a major battle on land, nor yet opened an offensive campaign."

The Luce men scanted, in this appraisal, two substantial naval victories in the Pacific, Coral Sea, and Midway. There was some justice to the gibe, nonetheless. It would take several years of hindsight to realize how important these victories were. To the Americans at the time they were desperate defensive struggles, in which the U.S. Navy barely repelled Japanese attempts to cut off Australia (Coral Sea) and take a giant step toward Hawaii (Midway).[2]

Even more unsettling were shortages of gasoline and rubber, as Donald Nelson's War Production Board issued draconian decrees sequestering most of the nation's resources for war purposes. Simultaneously, farmers and businessmen large and small were feeling the harsh hand of New Dealer Leon Henderson, head of the Office of Price Administration (OPA), which fought inflation by clamping a lid on retail prices. Not a few Americans found OPA's bureaucrats arrogant and heavy-handed and Henderson himself abrasive. Many farmers grumbled that the New Dealers were coddling their favorite group of voters, the labor unions, by declining to put a ceiling on wages. Millions of Americans were also parting with their sons as Selective Service harvested men for Rainbow Five's 10-million-man army.[3]

Four days after Pearl Harbor, the Democratic National Committee announced the "complete adjournment of domestic politics." On the same day, December 11, 1941, FDR issued an even more resounding declaration: "In time of war there can be no partisan domestic politics." This noble ideal was seconded by liberal journals such as the *New Republic* and by do-gooders such as the League of Woman Voters. But cracks soon appeared in this nonpartisan facade.

Wendell Willkie proposed that both parties back only candidates who had supported intervention before Pearl Harbor. His dislike of isolationists was deep and sincere. FDR said the same thing more obliquely when he urged the election of candidates "who have a record of backing up the government in an emergency." Since he had declared a national emergency months before Pearl Harbor, this too implied America Firsters and their ilk were persona non grata. He bolstered this impression with cutting references to isolationists in press conferences and speeches as "little men of little faith who play petty politics in a world crisis." Emmanuel Celler, a liberal House Democrat from New York, was far less subtle. A week after Pearl Harbor, he taunted ex-isolationists to their faces, declaring they should "apologize to President Roosevelt."[4]

James Farley repudiated Willkie's call for an anti-isolationist coalition, and declared "politics should be adjourned so far as the war effort is concerned but only that far." Not surprisingly, Republicans agreed with him. Many keyed their remarks to National Chairman Clarence Buddington Kelland's warning that America was in danger of one-man rule. Senator Robert Taft of Ohio took a more moderate but still combative stance, declaring. "Criticism in time of war is essential to the maintenance of any kind of democratic government." Senator Harry Truman cautioned his Democratic colleagues, calling post–Pearl Harbor recriminations "unwise and unjust."[5]

II

In May of 1942, Charles Michelson, the publicity director of the Democratic Party, attempted a preemptive strike on the opposition by issuing a history lesson even more dubious than Roosevelt's attempt to find parallels to his battle with economic royalists in Andrew Jackson's war with the Bank of the United States. In a column entitled: "Dispelling the Fog," Michelson asked his readers if they realized that they were worrying about rubber and food shortages and their drafted sons because they had listened to the enemies of Woodrow Wilson in 1918.

Yes, Michelson averred, in that crucial year, voters had deserted the Democrats and elected a Republican majority in the House and Senate. These evil men had rejected Woodrow Wilson's treaty of peace, which included U.S. participation in the League of Nations. Thus the American voters were gulled into giving the government to the Republican isolationists, who "laid the foundation of the present war."

Those careless or emotional voters of 1918 had supposedly destroyed the hope for an international accord "to make such wars as the present one impossible." Worse, the blunder brought us "the Harding administration and its scandals . . . the amiable do-nothing policies of the Coolidge regime . . . [and] the great depression of President Hoover's term [which] promoted . . . the rise of Hitler and Hitlerism [and] . . . the jingoism of Japan." If the United States had not been embroiled with the Germans in the Atlantic, the "Japonification" of the Far East would never have taken place. We would have had enough warships in the Pacific to prevent it. Michelson hoped the voters would "keep this picture in mind" when they went to the polls next November.[6]

The distortions in this statement once more revealed the New Dealers' ignorance of—or indifference to—the facts of history. In 1918, Woodrow Wilson had dug his own political grave by abruptly shifting his political stance. After announcing a suspension of politics for the duration of the war, he suddenly called for the election of a Democratic Congress. The voters had responded by electing a Republican Congress, which promptly claimed Wilson had been repudiated by the American people.

Wilson compounded this blunder by refusing to take any leading Republicans with him to the Paris Peace Conference, thus practically inviting Congress to reject the peace treaty and the League of Nations to which it was attached. At that dolorous gathering in Paris, Wilson had done as much as anybody to torpedo an acceptable treaty. After assuring the American people when he declared war that they were not hostile to the German people but only to their militaristic government, he changed his mind at Versailles and agreed the Germans were guilty en masse. He voted with the vengeful British and French to insert a war-guilt clause in the peace treaty and fasten crippling reparations on the defeated Reich.

Publicity Director Michelson later claimed he wrote his history lesson to infuriate his opponents and thus gain attention for his argument. If publicity was what he wanted, he got it by the train-load. The *Chicago Tribune* editorialized that "Charlie the Smear" Michelson had betrayed the political desperation of the Roosevelt administration. They were trying to use "the blood and sweat of war" for their personal advantage. The *Washington Times-Herald* said Michelson was calling for a Congress "made up exclusively of 1. Congressmen who were interventionists and administration rubber stamps before Pearl Harbor and 2. new Congressman whose chief campaign promise [will be] to yes-yes every war move the Roosevelt administration makes." The *Chicago Daily News* said Michelson's column should be retitled: "Disseminating the Fog." The *New York Sun* thought it was an ominous "blueprint" for coming political campaigns in which loyalty to FDR would be the only criterion. BLAME GOP FOR ALL—TO BE 42 CAMPAIGN, the *New York Daily News* declared in a page 2 headline.[7]

III

The president and his top advisors chose this moment for a display of management ineptitude that soon became known as "the rubber mess." Operation Drumbeat, the hugely successful German submarine campaign along the East Coast, created a serious shortage of gasoline and oil on the Atlantic seaboard. Almost all the supplies of these crucial ingredients of American civilization had been delivered by ship—until the Germans started sinking them by the dozen. OPA's Leon Henderson responded by announcing a rationing program for the seventeen states on or near the coast. Dismayed drivers were told they would have to manage on as little as two and a half gallons a week.

An explosion of criticism from all directions descended on the OPA director. But he grimly decreed that rationing was here to stay, giving ground only on the minimum, which he raised to three gallons a week. He also made no friends by calling critics of his decree "ignorant or intentionally traitorous." Meanwhile, this emergency measure was overtaken by another crisis: the rubber shortage. Another government agency, the War Production Board, had decided the only way to solve this dilemma was nationwide gasoline rationing. They persuaded Roosevelt to float a trial balloon in its favor at a press conference on May 19, 1942, only four days after OPA's East Coast rationing began.

This time the explosion was truly national. Congressmen and senators orated that the rubber shortage was the administration's fault, which was, to some extent, the truth. Confident that the U.S. and British navies could handle the Japanese, the White House had been slow to start a synthetic rubber program until the triumphant soldiers of Nippon had conquered Malaya, cutting off 90 percent of the country's supply of natural rubber. Worse, the president let the East Coast rationing, based on a real gasoline shortage, get mixed up with the national plan, which was based on the rubber shortage. Congress caucused and declared no such plan would be tolerated until they were "convinced" of its necessity.

FDR responded to this onslaught in his next press conference with an offhand dismissal of the "overexcitement" in all quarters about a rubber shortage. He was sure that the problem would be solved by various programs in the works that would produce more than enough synthetic rubber for the armed forces and the civilians. Reporters swarmed to the War Production Board offices to find out what these programs were, forcing a floundering Donald Nelson to contradict the president. No matter how successful the programs were, new civilian tires were going to be nonexistent for the next several years, a red-faced Nelson said.

Henderson, Nelson, and other top bureaucrats involved in this mounting disaster rushed to the White House to get the gasoline rationing program back on track. Only FDR's charisma could persuade Congress and the nation to cooperate. Instead, the commander in chief grandly informed them that "personally" he was not worried about the rubber shortage. As Henderson and Nelson tried to assemble their wits at this turnaround, Harold Ickes, present as the petroleum czar, chimed in with a declaration that the shortage could easily be solved by collecting a million tons of scrap rubber from junkyard owners and other patriotic Americans.

The director of the WPB's rubber program, Arthur Newhall, was a former rubber manufacturer. He goggled at Ickes's figure and told him it was "fantastically high." He was the only rubber expert in the room but that did not matter to FDR, who was thinking politically, not realistically. Roosevelt knew that Ickes required careful handling. If Honest Harold did not get his way, Drew Pearson and other columnists would soon be hearing about ineptitude in the Oval Office. A beaming president announced the rubber problem was solved and told Ickes to launch a nationwide scrap rubber collection drive immediately.

The drive was a fiasco. At the end of five frantic weeks, in which the president made a statement and Ickes ran around like an out-of-control windup toy, the nation had collected only 335,000 tons of scrap rubber. Ickes was reduced to trying to confiscate the rubber mats on the floors of the Interior Department buildings. The Public Buildings Administration blocked him, saying it would lead to an epidemic of broken hips when people started falling on the slippery marble floors. In a last gasp, Ickes was caught stealing a rubber mat from the White House. Compounding the petroleum czar's folly was his apparent ignorance of the fact that rubber mats were made from recycled rubber and were useless in the production of tires.

While the president and one of his cabinet members were thus making fools of themselves in public, the last American bastion in the Philippines, the fortified island of Corregidor, surrendered to the Japanese. General Rommel's Afrika Korps was battering the desperate British back to within sixty miles of the Suez Canal. Compounding the confusion, FDR reversed himself at another press conference and announced the government might have to requisition every tire in the country. But he sugarcoated this bad news with the remark that for the present he saw no harm in anyone using his car for business, if he still had four good tires. The nation's newspaper readers could only conclude that the president and his friends did not know what they were talking about when it came to rubber and gasoline, which led to grave doubts about their competence in other areas of the war effort.[8]

IV

In August, as the fall elections loomed, the *New York Times* noted that the Democrats were charging 85 percent of the Republican candidates with obstructing the nation's foreign policy—a code word for being isolationists. Democratic Party Chairman Edward Flynn declared that the election of a congress hostile to the president would be the equivalent of "a major military defeat." Simultaneously, Roosevelt was saying with a straight face in his Oval Office press conferences that when he saw any evidence of partisanship in his administration, "I step on it with both feet."[9]

The *New Republic*, after calling loudly for an end to partisan politics, showered its readers with pro-Democratic appraisals of various candidates. In May they published a pamphlet, "A Congress To Win the War," produced by the Union for Democratic Action, one of the nation's leading liberal groups. They examined the voting records of the candidates and reported that only 9 of 236 Democratic congressmen and 3 of 23 Democratic senators had been "wrong" (not liberal enough) more than half the time. On the other hand, 152 of 159 Republican congressmen were in this pit of infamy, along with 7 of 8 senators. Ultimately the *New Republic* endorsed 157 Democrats and 8 Republicans.[10]

The Democrats were barely concealing the "I told you so" self-satisfaction they had acquired from Pearl Harbor. They campaigned at first with a complacent assumption that they only had to point out how right they had been about the evil Axis enemies and the electorate would instantly agree with them. Only a few, closer to the voters and more practical about the way elections work, saw difficulties.

In a letter to the president, Mayor Ed Kelly of Chicago, the man who had stage-managed Roosevelt's third-term nomination, reported that Illinois Democrats planned an all-out attack on isolationists. Then, virtually confessing that this formula was far from a guaranteed winner, Kelly added that the vendetta would have to be handled very carefully, "because we recognize most people before Pearl Harbor were against war."[11]

V

The White House's ballooning self-satisfaction was also punctured by unnerving primary election squabbles in several key states. In Illinois, conservative Republican Senator C. Wayland Brooks looked vulnerable—and numerous liberals began jockeying for the Democratic nomination—until they discovered that Boss Kelly himself was thinking of becoming the candidate. Too

late they discovered this was a ploy to discourage other contenders and enable the boss to select the candidate he wanted,
Congressman Ray McKeough, an anti-interventionist who had
voted against the extension of the draft in 1941.

The defiant liberal Democrats put up their own candidate, economics professor Paul Douglas, and begged the White House to
intervene on his behalf. But Roosevelt owed Boss Kelly too much
to say a word. In the primary, Douglas ran well downstate but
was predictably swamped in Chicago, leaving the Democrats
with a candidate that a hefty proportion of the party detested.[12]

Texas offered a similar dilemma. Up for a new Senate term was
W. Lee (Pappy) O'Daniel, a Roosevelt-hater and ally of discarded
vice president John Nance Garner. Daniel had beaten a Roosevelt
favorite, Congressman Lyndon Johnson, in a 1941 special election to fill an unexpired term. The liberals got behind federal
judge (and former governor) James Allred, who agreed to run if
the president asked him, and promised to reappoint him to the
bench if he lost. An indication of Roosevelt's popularity in the
Lone Star State was a solemn compact to keep FDR's support a
secret. It was generally agreed that Johnson had lost because the
president backed him too enthusiastically.

In a three-way race, O'Daniel finished first, Allred second. As
they headed for a runoff, liberals implored FDR to say something
on Allred's behalf. Demonstrating how badly he had been burned
by his failed interventions in congressional elections in 1938,
FDR coolly appraised the situation and decided Allred could not
win. He remained silent while the liberal bit the primary dust.[13]

VI

New York's gubernatorial election was another matter. Here
FDR was personally and politically involved on several levels.
When a president cannot field a winning ticket in his home

state, he looks weak to the rest of the country. Herbert Lehman, the popular five term governor, had announced he was retiring. The Republican candidate was almost certain to be New York City's racket-busting district attorney, Thomas E. Dewey. A big win for this young aggressive politician would make him a presidential prospect in 1944. A strong Democratic candidate was imperative.

Jim Farley was still the New York State Democratic Party chairman, and he had his own ideas about a candidate. John J. Bennett Jr. had been a hardworking scandal-free attorney general since Roosevelt's governorship. Twice he had stepped aside to let Lehman run for reelection. Farley had promised Bennett his backing and had spent months rounding up support for him. A founder of the American Legion, Bennett was popular with veterans and the Democratic rank and file. But he was a devout Catholic and had been a supporter of anti-Communist General Francisco Franco during the Spanish Civil War—a hot-button issue in New York—and had been conspicuously silent about intervening in World War II.

A jittery Roosevelt invited Farley to the White House for a talk. It was the first time the two men had met in fourteen months. Farley, one of the few to whom FDR had confessed his intimations of mortality, eyed Roosevelt from this perspective. He saw evidence of strain. "His eyes had heavy circles under them and his face was chalky. He was more nervous than I had ever seen him. He was continuously reaching for things on his desk and toying with them. He coughed frequently," the ex-chairman later recalled. [14]

They discussed possible candidates, but dismissed them for various reasons. Farley explained why he was backing Bennett. FDR reminisced jovially about how he had chosen Bennett for attorney general over the opposition of the head of Tammany Hall, and urged Farley to get the story into the *New York Times*. The former national chairman emerged to announce that FDR and he had agreed on Bennett.

Harold Moskowitz, a leader of New York's liberals, promptly dubbed Bennett a "fifth columnist" inside the Democratic Party. Assistant Secretary of State Adolf Berle, a charter member of the New Deal, publicly agreed with him. The far left American Labor Party, backer of Congressman Vito Marcantonio, a more or less avowed Communist, announced their opposition to Bennett. An agitated Roosevelt claimed he never told Farley that he backed Bennett; all he said was he would vote for him in preference to Dewey.

Suddenly the Brooklyn Democratic leader, John Kelly, a staunch Bennett man, was summoned to the White House. He and the president discussed various candidates, barely mentioning Bennett. A few days later, National Chairman Ed Flynn read Kelly a tough statement from the president, declaring that FDR had told Kelly if Bennett were nominated, Roosevelt would not campaign for him, or make the slightest effort to persuade the American Labor Party to endorse him. The stunned Kelly claimed FDR had said no such thing.[15]

Next, outgoing governor Herbert Lehman trekked to the White House for lunch with the president. They too discussed candidates, and Lehman emerged to announce that his lieutenant governor, Charles Poletti, was his choice for the Democratic nomination. Lehman claimed FDR had assured him that he had not expressed a preference for any candidate. If this was not pulling the rug out from under Bennett, it was the next worst thing.[16]

Suddenly the liberal and well-regarded U.S. senator from New York, James Mead, became the focus of White House attention. A stream of leaks reported that Roosevelt thought he was the best candidate. Mead repeatedly declared he did not want the nomination but finally said he would run if the president insisted.

Roosevelt ally Fiorello La Guardia backed him. In a few days Mead was a bona fide candidate with the president's unqualified endorsement. "If I were a delegate to the [state] convention, I would cast my vote for Jim Mead," Roosevelt said.[17]

White House pressure soon gave Mead the backing of Tammany Hall and the O'Connell political machine in Albany. Ed Flynn put his Bronx machine behind him. Governor Lehman warned that if Bennett were nominated, he would not endorse or campaign for him. New York's senior senator Robert Wagner, father of the New Deal's popular labor legislation, announced he wanted Mead. Bennett backers said the whole thing was a plot by "a little band of New Dealers" to oust Jim Farley and seize control of the New York Democratic Party.[18]

The Democratic state convention, which took place in the grand ballroom of Brooklyn's St. George Hotel in late August, was "decidedly not a pro-Roosevelt convention," wrote James A. Hagerty of the *New York Times*. Farley and Bennett, playing by the rules, made no attempt to steamroller the opposition. They allowed Lehman to make a vigorous nominating speech on Senator Mead's behalf. The New York *Daily News* reported the convention "greeted in stony silence the Roosevelt thesis that only those should be favored in the forthcoming campaign who had supported his foreign policy before Pearl Harbor."

In a companion story, the *News* told how "Roosevelt desperationists" demanded a grueling two-hour roll call vote, the first in the history of the state's Democratic Party. The result was a solid 623–393 victory for Bennett. A delighted Joe Patterson, the *News* publisher, unleashed his waspish columnist John O'Donnell on the president who had humiliated Patterson in the Oval Office six months earlier. O'Donnell chortled that Roosevelt had suffered "the greatest defeat of his political career at the hands of brother New York Democrats. . . . The myth that the champ could not be beaten was shattered." The usually pro-Roosevelt *Washington*

Post agreed, calling Mead's repudiation "a political slap in the face" and a "humiliating defeat" for FDR.[19]

Arthur Krock of the *New York Times* attacked the president for playing politics-as-usual while Americans were fighting and dying on two oceans. Another columnist opined that Roosevelt's defeat had "diminished his stature and detracted from our national unity." An angry Roosevelt fired back that the "amount of time taken by me from war work in relation to the New York political situation was exactly zero."[20]

Meanwhile, the American Labor Party convened and nominated a liberal, Dean Alfange, as their candidate. He was soon calling himself the only New Dealer in the race. Earl Browder, the head of the Communist Party, told delegates to their convention that Bennett was "the favorite candidate of the advocates of a negotiated peace with Hitler." Mayor Fiorello La Guardia announced he would not back Bennett under any circumstances.[21]

Beneath this reckless rhetoric was a struggle between the Irish-Americans, who had dominated urban politics for almost a hundred years, and the rising anger of Jews, Italians, and other ethnic groups who wanted a voice in the national discourse—and a piece of the action. Ideology meant far more to many of these groups than it did to the Irish-Americans, who saw loyalty to the organization and the party as the prime consideration in most elections.

Elsewhere in the Empire State, a group called Vote For Freedom tried to stampede the Republicans into nominating Wendell L. Willkie for governor on the shaky charge that Thomas E. Dewey was a covert isolationist. David Dubinsky, President of the International Garment Workers and one of the founders of the American Labor Party, wasted his breath (though he undoubtedly startled his followers) by announcing: "If Wendell L. Willkie should get the nomination, I would not only vote for him but would urge his election, even on the G.O.P. ticket." In a frosty statement, the Republican state executive committee condemned "blitzkrieg tactics," a cutting reference to the way Willkie had won the Republican nomination in 1940. Veteran political columnist Mark Sullivan, after surveying the primary debacles, urged Roosevelt to "shelve the isolationist issue" in the upcoming November elections.[22]

VII

Early in the summer, Eleanor Roosevelt remarked to FDR that she was worried about the parlous condition of the Democratic Party. The president grinned and said he had a plan that would reduce the Republicans to an even worse state of desuetude. He was going to make Wendell Willkie part of his administration, instantly subtracting the 6 million extra votes Willkie had turned out for the GOP in 1940.

Even before Pearl Harbor, FDR had converted Willkie into a covert supporter. To bolster his de facto alliance with England, Roosevelt sent the ex-candidate to London with a letter of introduction to Winston Churchill. Willkie came back praising England's courage and determination—exactly what FDR wanted the American people to hear. Thereafter, Willkie made many after-dark visits to the White House through the rear entrance, during which Roosevelt persuaded him to back controversial programs such as lend-lease. Two days after this daring proposal went up to Capitol Hill, Willkie sent telegrams to every member of Congress, telling them "the problem is not how to keep America out of the war but how to keep the war out of America." The line had the very distinctive ring of Roosevelt's ace speechwriter, playwright Robert Sherwood.[23]

Republican professionals were outraged by Willkie's convergence with Roosevelt. "Willkie's statement and his subsequent trip to England," wrote one man, "resulted in a breach between himself and the Republican members of Congress, which in my opinion, is irreparable. . . . Out of the 190 members of the House and Senate, Willkie couldn't dig up ten friends if his life depended on it." Congressman Dewey Short of Missouri seemed to confirm this assessment. When he called Willkie a "belligerent, bombastic, bellicose, bombinating blowhard who couldn't be elected dogcatcher," his fellow Republicans applauded for a full minute.[24]

Nevertheless, polls showed that Willkie remained a very popular figure. Americans liked his forthright honesty and energetic idealism. Late in 1941, Roosevelt sent one of his aides to discuss with Willkie the possibility of joining his administration. He was still thinking about it when the Japanese attacked Pearl Harbor. On December 15, Roosevelt invited Willkie to the White House for lunch and a talk. But the tousled-haired Hoosier backed away from accepting a post in wartime Washington. He may have been influenced by a Gallup poll that showed most Americans expected him to be FDR's successor.[25]

Nevertheless, Willkie found himself unable to resist FDR's charm. He permitted the president to lure him back to Washington a month later, supposedly to discuss becoming head of the War Production Board, the boss of the war effort. Roosevelt apparently toyed with this idea, until Harry Hopkins talked him out of it, probably for the same reason—those sky-high poll ratings—that Willkie had danced away from a lesser job in December. When Roosevelt appointed Donald Nelson head of the WPB without bothering to give Willkie a heads-up, the ex-presidential contender looked foolish—and rejected in the bargain.[26]

Yet in July 1942 Willkie journeyed to Hyde Park for another meeting with Roosevelt. A month later, with the mid-term elections looming, and his standing in the polls still high enough to make his endorsement of individual candidates worth a great deal, Willkie departed on a trip around the world as FDR's personal ambassador. It was a journey Willkie wanted to make—he saw himself as a man summoned by God to scour isolationism from the soul of the American people—but its timing proved his political instincts were virtually nonexistent. The trip would make him world famous—and an electoral dead duck.

VIII

As election day approached, foreboding grew like an unwanted weed among the Democrats. From across the nation came a chorus of complaints about the leadership vacuum in Washington D.C. Much of the overt criticism was aimed at Party Chairman Ed Flynn—one columnist called him "at least three or four cuts below the Farley standard."[27] But the real vacuum was in the White House. Roosevelt was too overwhelmed by the internal politics and the external planning of the war to give the domestic situation much thought—beyond his disastrous dalliance with the New York governor's race.

FDR had devoted most of his mental and physical energy during the spring and summer of 1942 to an acrimonious battle with the British over whether to open a second front in France that year. British resistance was so stiff, and American preparations so inadequate, Roosevelt yielded to Churchill's insistence and agreed to an invasion of North Africa as a substitute that would give the voters a feeling the United States was finally taking the offensive against the enemy. FDR specifically requested Chief of Staff George Marshall to make sure it took place on or about October 30, a week before election day.

"We are face to face with a political Libyia(sic)," Congressman Lyndon Johnson warned the White House, in a reference to recent defeats suffered by the British in the Middle East. There was little or no response as the Democratic Party unraveled in other key states.

In New Jersey, Governor Charles Edison, son of the inventor, had won the governorship with the backing of Mayor Frank Hague's Hudson County political machine. The Mayor had accepted Edison at Roosevelt's urging, swallowing his doubts. Edison had instantly turned reformer and began attacking "bossism." Once more Roosevelt showed how well he remembered who had masterminded his third-term nomination. Over Edison's squawks, FDR appointed a Hague man to a key federal judgeship. When Jersey City Congresswoman Mary T. Norton called Edison "the most arrant hypocrite that ever walked," she got a one-line letter from Roosevelt: "You are a grand girl!" But the brawl dimmed Democratic hopes in New Jersey, where a dedicated New Dealer, Senator William H. Smathers, was up for re-election.[28]

In California, a proven Republican vote-getter, Attorney General Earl Warren, was running against a liberal Democratic governor, Culbert Olson, who was unpopular with the conservative wing of his own party. Thanks to the state's peculiar cross-filing law, Warren got 41 percent of the Democratic votes in the primary, an ominous sign. In New York, polls revealed Dewey so far ahead of Bennett, advisors told him he could stay in bed for the rest of the campaign if he felt like it. Roosevelt issued two lukewarm statements on Bennett's behalf, and, in a swipe at the American Labor Party, said he did not believe in "protest voting." But when a reporter asked him if he planned to cooperate closely with Farley in the campaign's closing days, FDR replied: "I haven't thought about politics for weeks."[29]

IX

Across the country, Democrats were alarmed by the low turnout in primary elections. With money in their pockets for the first time in a decade and war news dominating the headlines, people did not think politics was very important. Low turnout almost always spelled trouble for the Democrats, because the better educated Republicans habitually voted. Despite his supposed indifference to partisan politics, Roosevelt responded to pleas from Democratic politicians in key states and issued numerous statements and press releases, urging people to vote. He called it "one of the essential privileges and duties of the democratic way of life for which we are now fighting." He issued orders to government agencies and requests to corporations to allow their employees time off to vote.

Another symptom of FDR's anxiety was his abrupt announcement in October that henceforth, all salaries would be limited by executive order to $25,000 after-tax dollars (about $200,000 in twenty-first-century money). The goal, the president declared, was "an equality of sacrifice." Given the already stratospheric wartime tax rate, it was a purely political gesture, which would apply to only one in 50,000 Americans. The president was responding to calls from the Congress of Industrial Organizations (CIO) and the United Automobile Workers to make sure labor's agreement to relinquish overtime pay for weekend and holiday work did not create "war millionaires" on the business side.[30]

FDR thought he was making one of his shrewder moves. Polls showed people approved of his executive order by a 2-1 margin. But conservative newspapers and radio stations nonetheless attacked the idea savagely as a menacing step in Roosevelt's plan to convert the war into a new and more aggressive New Deal. They accused him of preaching class hatred and trying to sovietize America, when he was only trying to get Democrats elected. Not even his closest advisor on monetary matters, Secretary of the Treasury Henry Morgenthau Jr. agreed with him. A few months earlier, Morgenthau had written in his diary that he thought it was "stupid . . . in order to satisfy labor . . . to go after rich people."[31]

X

In mid-September, FDR embarked on a two-week "inspection tour" of defense plants that took him across the country. He demanded and got total press silence for the duration of this trip. There was an inescapable political dimension to the journey, as the president was greeted by tens of thousands of defense workers and made speeches hailing their contribution to the war effort. So insistent was FDR about press silence, 30,000 copies of the *Aero Mechanic*, a weekly union publication, were destroyed because they carried a story on the president's visit to the Boeing plant in Seattle.[32]

The theoretical excuse for the silence—the enemy might attack the commander in chief in his armored train or in a car driving to and from the train to defense plants—was obviously a way for FDR to conceal the fact that he was campaigning in spite of his vow to eschew politics for the duration. Returning to Washington in the first week in October, he held a press conference at which he thanked the newsmen for helping him conceal his trip, and then lashed out at "elements" of the radio and newspaper press that were "hurting the war effort" by their hostile attitude toward the administration.[33] One cannot help suspecting FDR was shaken by polls showing the Democrats slipping behind everywhere. Elmo Roper predicted the Republicans would gain up to 53 seats in the House of Representatives.

The attack on the press was a grievous miscalculation, another indication that FDR the war president was finding it more and more difficult to be the shrewd domestic leader. The *New York Herald Tribune* responded with a ferocious editorial, denouncing the enforced press silence about the president's trip. It accused Roosevelt of doing "more to undermine the confidence of his fellow citizens than the gravest danger of any enemy act." On the same day in the *New York Times*, columnist Arthur Krock declared that most newsmen did not think the silence

SOME NEGLECTED CHICKENS 155

was necessary and it aroused the specter of "wholly dictated official publicity."[34]

Meanwhile, Roosevelt's ace in the hole, his invasion of North Africa a week before election, became a mocking joker. The army and navy decided that landing on beaches pounded by the Atlantic Ocean's heavy surf would be a very slow and risky business. If they met resistance, the invasion could become a slaughter. To play it safe, the generals and admirals wanted a moonless night. There was one on October 8, but they could not meet such an early deadline. Too much equipment and too many troops had to be shipped from England, where they had been sent to prepare for a cross-channel invasion of France. The next moonless night would be November 8, five days after the election.

XI

A week before the election, an article appeared in *American Magazine* that did not make good bedtime reading in the White House. It was titled: "We Can Lose the War in Washington." The author was Senator Harry S. Truman, chairman of the Special Committee to Investigate the War Program. The piece was a scathing attack on the maze of conflicting and often contradictory wartime agencies constructed by FDR in standard New Deal fashion.

As an example, Senator Truman told his readers that the committee's investigation of the rubber shortage forced them to visit seven separate agencies, the War Production Board, the Reconstruction Finance Corporation, the Office of Petroleum Coordinator, the Office of Defense Transportation, the Price Administrator, the Board of Economic Warfare, and the Department of Agriculture. All had a finger in the mess. Again and again, Truman said the blame lay not with the fumbling quarreling bureaucrats. The problem was "lack of courageous unified leadership and centralized direction at the top." All Americans wanted or needed to win the war is "that we be intelligently and resolutely led."[35]

Later, the senator claimed never to have read the article. He said it had been ghostwritten by an *American Magazine* writer and sent to him in Washington on the day it was going to press. The magazine's spokesperson, a young woman who pleaded that there was not a second to waste, persuaded him to initial his approval without bothering to check a word. When he (or an aide) finally read it, the senator sent Truman Committee lawyers scurrying to New York to block publication. But it was too late.

The story is plausible on one level. Senator Truman had a bad habit of working himself to the point of exhaustion and the *American Magazine*'s messenger may have caught him at one of these downturns. But he never claimed the entire article was a fabrication. He had obviously told the magazine writer quite a few of the dismaying facts about the bungling and gross corruption the Truman Committee was turning up in their hard-eyed look at the war effort. The senator was inclined to talk freely. Since his 1940 struggle for reelection, Truman no longer thought Franklin D. Roosevelt was a political genius worthy of his worshipful support.

XII

FDR's stealth campaign tour, his frantic maneuvers in New York, his desperate pleas to vote, his dispatch of Wendell Willkie overseas, his salary cap on the rich, failed as totally as his military timetable in Africa. Although Congressman Lyndon Johnson could not spell Libya, he had it right when he saw a debacle looming. On election day, New Dealers toppled by the dozen in a surging Republican tide. Nationally, the GOP gained 44 seats in the House of Representatives, narrowing the Democrats control to a squeaky 8 votes. In the Senate, the Republicans gained 9 seats. Without the Solid South, the Senate would have been a replay of the House disaster. The Republicans won 20 out of 25 Senate races outside that traditional Democratic stronghold. Needless to say, the House would have gone Republican without the South. No less than 103 of the Democrats 222 remaining seats were southern.

Gone was Senator Smathers in New Jersey, along with a half-dozen Democratic stalwarts from the Midwest. (Smathers bitterly informed Vice President Wallace that if he had run as an anti-New Dealer, he would have won.) In Nebraska, eighty-one-year-old progressive icon Senator George Norris, who had backed Roosevelt since 1932, went down before the assaults of conservative Kenneth Wherry. In Illinois, Roosevelt critic Senator C. Wayland Brooks swept to victory over Boss Kelly's handpicked candidate. Liberal congressmen got the electoral equivalent of the guillotine everywhere. In New York, Thomas E. Dewey became the first Republican governor since 1920 and in California Earl Warren became a national name with an overwhelming triumph over hapless liberal Governor Culbert Olson.[36]

Among the bitterest pills the man in the White House had to swallow was the reelection of Congressman Clare Hoffman of Michigan, who once called FDR a "crazy conceited megalomaniac." Before Pearl Harbor Hoffman maintained that Roosevelt had seized the same dictatorial powers as Hitler but Hitler was more efficient. Also returned for another two years was Harlan J. Bushfield of South Dakota, who once proposed a National Debt Week to spur citizens to reflect on New Deal spending.

At least as painful was the return of Hamilton Fish, the right-wing Republican congressman who represented the district that included Hyde Park. Roosevelt had devoted almost as much time to undermining Fish as he had spent trying to sidetrack Jim Farley's gubernatorial candidate. Fish was so far to the right,

Thomas E. Dewey refused to endorse him. Nevertheless Fish cruised to an easy victory, stunning the Democrats by even carrying the Irish-American wards in the Hudson River town of Poughkeepsie. A week after the election, a disconsolate Roosevelt told one correspondent Fish's triumph was a "disgrace."[37]

Raymond Moley, *Newsweek* columnist and disillusioned former brain truster, exulted in the way the Republicans had regained control of the Midwest. He saw a reaffirmation of an American preference for blunt, tough, honest politicians. "There is nothing visionary about these people," Moley wrote, "whereas it had been a bad November for extremists and prophets. The American people have reminded the 'morale builders' in Washington [a dig at Eleanor Roosevelt] that they don't want to be told what to think or how to feel." *Fortune* magazine reported many of the newly elected politicians "think they have a mandate to repeal all New Deal reforms." New congressperson Clare Booth Luce of Connecticut, wife of *Time's* owner, thought the election proved the American people wanted to fight the war with their eyes open, not with "blinders." They also wanted to fight it "without bungling."[38]

Time compared the Republican sweep to the Depression-triggered Democratic avalanche of 1930. They also noted with unconcealed glee that if you subtracted the conservative Southerners, the New Deal Democrats were a minority party. Others pointed out that the Republicans had shown majority strength in 26 states, with 319 electoral votes, leaving the Democrats with 22 states and 212 electoral votes. Joe Patterson's *New York Daily News* gloated that the election meant "there is going to be no fourth term for the Commander-in-Chief."[39]

New Dealers were crushed and dismayed by the election. When Roosevelt urged Secretary of the Interior Harold Ickes to convene a liberal brain trust to begin thinking about a comeback in 1944, Ickes morosely replied that he did not think it would accomplish anything. Vice President Henry Wallace tried to put a brave face on the disaster, claiming the election was a Democratic victory because the party had retained control of Congress. This fatuity only further eroded Wallace's bona fides as a realistic politician. Everyone in Washington knew that a coalition between the conservative southern Democrats and the Republicans would effectively destroy Roosevelt's control of Congress. Moreover, Wallace had fallen on his face in his native Iowa, where he had campaigned for Senator Clyde L. Herring. He too went down in the across-the-board massacre of Democrats in the Midwest.

New Dealer Oscar Ewing could think of only one solution: a better job of "selling" the war, an idea that would soon cause Elmer Davis and the Office of War Information no end of grief.[40]

XIII

What had happened? Many historians have attempted to explain away the 1942 elections, pointing to the low turnout, the millions of young men in the service, the numerous other Americans who had recently moved because of war work and had not had time to register to vote. The turnout was low and many Americans were displaced or in the ranks. But that does not explain why so many Americans repudiated the New Dealers' attempt to claim everyone had a patriotic duty to vote Democratic. Even more counterproductive was the attempt to smear Roosevelt's critics as isolationists, as if the word were synonymous with pro-Hitler. Millions of decent honorable men and women had felt no need to go to war to "stop Hitler" and politicians such as Burton K. Wheeler and Robert Taft were equally honorable in their grave doubts about Roosevelt's interventionist policies.

The isolationist impulse was not necessarily rooted in a contemptuous indifference to the fate of other peoples, such as Germany's persecuted Jews. In the nineteenth century, Americans demonstrated enormous sympathy for oppressed peoples struggling for freedom—the Irish, the Germans, the Italians, the Hungarians—but only a few pugnacious volunteers fought beside them. There was no support for dispatching an army. No one summed up the attitude better than John Quincy Adams in a Fourth of July address in 1821. America, he declared, "well knows that by once enlisting under other banners than her own, were they even the banners of foreign independence, she would involve herself beyond the powers of extrication, in all the wars of interest and intrigue, of individual avarice, envy and ambition which assume the colors and usurp the standard of freedom. The fundamental maxims of her policy would insensibly change from liberty to force."[41]

American antipathy to—or at least wariness of—involvement with Europe was rooted for many people in the sense of exceptionalism that Abraham Lincoln had identified when he called Americans "an almost chosen people." Both Washington and Jefferson had warned Americans against "entangling alliances" with Europe. At least as influential was a repugnance against war as humanity's greatest folly, an attitude that America's experience in World War I had powerfully reinforced.

What the New Dealers needed was a strong dose of realism. They got it from a big California oilman named Ed Pauley. He was not a New Dealer. By instinct and temperament Pauley sided with the professionals who ran the big city machines and chaired the state party organizations. While New Dealers such as Ickes sulked, Pauley polled the Democrats' congressional candidates, both the winners and the losers. From their responses he culled three chief causes for the 1942 debacle: frustration and fury at Roosevelt's Germany-first strategy, which translated into failure to punish the Japanese more aggressively for Pearl Harbor; the resentment of the farmers because of the way New Dealers were "coddling" the labor unions; and dislike of bureaucrats, which often focused on the acerbic head of the Office of Price Administration, Leon Henderson. Roosevelt the realistic politician agreed with Pauley that the Henderson problem was "correctable." Henderson soon departed from Washington, never to return.

Less immediately correctable was the enfeebled Democratic Party organization. Chairman Ed Flynn resigned, confessing his responsibility for the electoral calamity. The new chairman, Postmaster General Frank Walker, took the job with unconcealed reluctance. No wonder—the Democrats were broke. Before the end of the year, most of the personnel in Democratic national headquarters were laid off, including Publicity Director Charles Michelson, the man who had assaulted isolationists with his bogus history lesson in May. One Democrat nervously noted: "It's only 102 weeks until the 1944 election."[42]

XIV

Roosevelt's cup of 1942 woe was filled to overflowing by a final end-of-the-year embarrassment. Harry Hopkins's unpopularity among the Democratic Party's regulars remained intense. Nevertheless, Roosevelt had made him head of lend-lease, responsible for shipping billions of dollars worth of weapons and war supplies to England and Russia. His intimacy with Roosevelt remained unimpaired. He continued to live at the White House and Eleanor Roosevelt tried to be a mother to his young daughter, Diana. When the widowed Hopkins fell in love with svelte Louise Macy, a former *Harper's Bazaar* fashion editor without an iota of interest in politics, FDR insisted she move into the White House too.

No member of the inner circle was closer to Roosevelt than Harry Hopkins. When the ex-social worker spoke, almost everyone assumed it was the president's voice. In December 1942, *American Magazine* published an article by Hopkins, "You Will Be Mobilized." It was a draconian sermon from a man who apparently believed too many people were growing complacent about the war. Its central message portrayed an American Sparta laboring under the grim-visaged bureaucrats of the OPA and other war agencies.

> Through forced savings and taxes, our spending will be limited and priorities far more widespread than at present will determine the kinds of food, clothing, housing and businesses which we will have, and will affect every detail of our daily lives. We should not be permitted to ride on a train, make a long distance telephone call, or send a telegram without evidence that these are necessary.[43]

A few days later, Cissy Patterson, publisher of the *Washington Times-Herald*, proved she was keeping the vow she had sworn with her brother Joe to make Roosevelt's life miserable. The paper's society columnist, Oleg Cassini, reported a dinner dance for sixty people that millionaire advisor to presidents Bernard Baruch had given at the Carlton Hotel for Harry Hopkins and his new bride. The guest list was a who's who of the top echelon of wartime Washington: War Production Board boss Donald Nelson, White House Press Secretary Steve Early, OWI foreign information director Robert Sherwood and ex-Senator James F. Byrnes, who had recently become FDR's home front "czar."

The *Times-Herald* printed the menu that was served to this assemblage of New Deal glitterati. It did not have much resemblance to the spartan lifestyle the author of "You Will Be Mobilized" was preparing to inflict on the rest of the nation.

Bowl of Caviar with trimmings
Pâté de Fois Gras
Cheese Croquettes
Celery, Radishes, Olives, Pecans
Banked Oysters Bonne Femme
Tortue Clair (en terrine)
Crème au Champignons Frais
Profiteroles
Mousse of Chicken
Galantine of Capon
Cold Tongue
Beef à la Mode
Corned Beef in Jelly
Turkey Chicken Virginia Ham
Calves Head Vinaigrette
Truite en Gelée
Homard en Aspic
Terrapin (Baltimore style)
Chicken à la King
Steamed Rice
Sliced tomatoes Crisp lettuce
Mayonnaise French Dressing
Russian Dressing
Mixed Green Salad
Assorted Cheese and Crackers
Socle of Raspberry ice
Petit Fours
Demi Tasse

At every place was an expensive gift from the host. Vintage champagne flowed without stint, along with a plethora of other French wines. The *Times-Herald* estimated the four-hour feeding frenzy cost about a million dollars. For Americans who had voted Republican—or stayed home in silent dissatisfaction with the New Dealers' war—the story more than justified their decision, and bolstered widespread conservative opinion about the New Deal's hypocrisy.[44]

XV

Watching from the vantage point of the British embassy, talking with journalists and politicians from all parts of America, philosopher Isaiah Berlin reached a significant conclusion as 1942 drew to a close: "The war as a necessary evil has been soberly accepted and squarely faced. But it is not a crusade such as we saw in 1917 and [the] average citizen is rarely swept on a wave of patriotic emotion."[45]

OWI research into the attitudes of army draftees confirmed this dour assessment. Fewer than a tenth of the men surveyed in August 1942 had a "consistent, favorable, intellectual orientation toward the war." Later surveys revealed that the Four Freedoms, the slogan Roosevelt had hoped would become the war's battle cry, was a bust. Over a third of a 3,000-man army sample had never heard of them and only 13 percent could name three or four of them. The OWI concluded there was very little trace of "inspired work performance" in the American army.[46]

This grim stoicism, which at times approached cynical indifference, was why Republicans such as Henry Luce and New Dealers such as Archibald MacLeish and Henry Wallace thought the war was desperately in need of "the provision of a moral issue." No one was more likely to be aware of this problem than that inveterate scrutinizer of the nation's political mood, President Franklin D. Roosevelt.

7

IN SEARCH OF
UNCONDITIONAL PURITY

Within a week of the Democratic Party's debacle at the polls, the New Dealers had a war to sell. On Sunday, November 8, at seven o'clock, reporters were summoned to the White House to be told that an American army under the command of an unknown general named Dwight D. Eisenhower was landing in North Africa as part of a giant pincer movement designed to clear the south shore of the Mediterranean of Axis troops. The British had started the process in October with a victory at El Alamein in Egypt that sent General Erwin Rommel and his vaunted Afrika Korps reeling west in chaotic retreat.

The North African assault, code-named Torch, suddenly acquired unexpected political complications. Relations between the French and the British were only a step above the enemy level since Churchill, after the fall of France, ordered the Royal Navy to seize the French fleet at Oran to prevent it from falling into German hands. When the French admiral refused to surrender his ships, the British opened fire on the anchored vessels, a decision Churchill admitted was "the most unnatural and painful in which I have ever been concerned." The reaction to this slaughter in French North Africa and in Vichy, the new capital of defeated France, was profoundly negative.[1]

The United States had maintained an embassy in Vichy, ignoring complaints that the regime, led by aged World War I hero General Henri Petain, was drifting into outright collaboration with the Nazis. Roosevelt had sent an old friend, Admiral William D. Leahy, to serve as ambassador. As his right-hand man Roosevelt chose Robert Murphy, a suave handsome diplomat whose career he had sponsored for many years. There was some payoff on the intelligence side but Roosevelt's idea that the Leahy-Murphy team might also stiffen French spines against Hitler was a dolorous failure. Vichy even enforced Hitler's Nuremberg Laws, depriving Jews of most of their rights as citizens. The regime condemned Free French leader General Charles de Gaulle to death in absentia for his radio broadcasts from London calling for resistance and showed no enthusiasm for cooperating with Americans in ways that might trigger a harsh German reaction.

Attempts to sell Torch as an American operation got nowhere, even though the initial landings were assigned to U.S. troops and their British counterparts were kept in discreet reserve. To bolster this deception, a message from Roosevelt was broadcast and dropped in leaflets: "We come among you to repulse the cruel invaders who would remove forever your rights of self government." With Roosevelt's approval, Murphy had smuggled General Henri Giraud into Algiers on the theory that this supposedly popular World War I hero, who had recently escaped from a German prison, could persuade his countrymen to greet the Americans as comrades.

This carefully planned diplomacy was a disastrous flop. The first wave of American soldiers to hit North Africa's beaches found themselves fighting for their lives against attacking French tanks and infantry. Giraud's call for an immediate cease-fire was ignored. Admiral Jean François Darlan, one of Marshal Petain's chief lieutenants, was visiting his polio-stricken son in Algiers and countermanded the general's appeal. At one beachhead only desperate heroics by Colonel Harry H. Semmes, who had led the first American tank attack in World War I, prevented a French armored assault from driving part of General George H. Patton's Western Task Force into the sea.[2]

Murphy and Eisenhower decided to cut a deal with Darlan. In return for making him high commissioner of North Africa and guaranteeing that the French would continue to control their colonies, the short dapper admiral double-crossed his Vichy cohorts and ordered French troops to stop shooting on November 11—a day that recalled America's role as France's savior in World War I.

Almost instantly, New Dealers and their supporters in the press raised a huge uproar in the United States. Columnists such as Drew Pearson and Walter Winchell called it "a deal with the devil." Walter Lippmann, doyen of American political commentators, deplored the arrangement. In a broadcast from London, Edward R. Morrow said the British were appalled, a claim that may have bolstered his status as a liberal but not his skill as a reporter. The British man in the street may have been perturbed but His Majesty's secret service had been negotiating with Darlan for weeks before the invasion. *Time*, always ready to make trouble for Roosevelt, piously asked how we could do business with one of Hitler's stooges.[3]

II

Secretary of the Treasury Henry Morgenthau Jr. was so undone by the Darlan deal, he told Secretary of War Stimson that he had lost all interest in the war. Stimson invited him and Archibald MacLeish, now a senior official with the OWI, to tea to discuss the matter. The visit became a classic great dichotomy confrontation between the New Dealers' approach to the war and those who rated realism above moral purity. Stimson lectured his guests on the military advantages of the Darlan deal. He stressed the fact that it was a temporary arrangement, not a new departure in foreign policy. Morgenthau tried to make Stimson read Murrow's broadcast. The secretary of war said he could not care less what some (expletives deleted) reporter in London thought. Darlan's cease-fire had saved thousands of American lives and rescued the invasion from potential disaster.

Morgenthau denounced Darlan as a man who had sold thousands of people into "slavery." There were some things more important than "temporary military victories," he ranted. "There is a considerable group of rich people in this country who would make peace with Hitler tomorrow. . . . The only people who want to fight are the working men and women, and if they once get the idea that we are going to favor these Fascists . . . they're going to say what's the use of fighting just to put that kind of people back into power?" The secretary predicted sit-down strikes and production slowdowns would soon be sweeping the country.

Although MacLeish said nothing, Morgenthau could tell that he agreed with him—a hardly surprising reaction. Dealing with Darlan was a long way from MacLeish's dream of reducing the war to the essential moral issue.[4]

III

A few days later, Morgenthau lectured FDR in the Oval Office for twenty minutes, claiming the Darlan deal had fatally impugned the nation's honor. Roosevelt, already acutely disturbed by the press attacks, told him it might have taken ten weeks to subdue the French, giving the Germans time to pour in reinforcements. FDR quoted an old proverb about being permitted to ride on the back of a devil when you are crossing a turbulent river. Still dissatisfied, Morgenthau pressed the president to announce the Nuremberg Laws were suspended in French North Africa and urged him to give everyone the right to vote.[5]

In a tense press conference not long after this meeting with his secretary of the treasury, Roosevelt used the word "temporary" five times, describing the arrangement with Darlan. But the liberal assault on the deal continued. James Warburg, deputy director of OWI's overseas branch, said it would destroy the belief of people everywhere in the good faith of the United States. The head of the OWI office in London chimed in with a similar opinion, declaring "the moral authority of the president is being impaired." Even Eleanor Roosevelt joined the negative chorus in her daily newspaper column. Admiral William Leahy, back from Vichy and now FDR's military chief of staff and liaison to the Joint Chiefs of Staff, noted that at a White House dinner, "Mrs. Roosevelt did most of the talking" and "appeared to be opposed to Darlan's efforts on our behalf."

The crusty Leahy made sure the president stayed on the military's side of the argument. When Roosevelt murmured uneasy comments about Darlan, Leahy told FDR, "We should indefinitely continue to try to use everybody—good, bad and indifferent, who promised to be of assistance in reducing the length of our casualty list."[6]

IV

In a speech on November 17, Wendell Willkie, already running for renomination in 1944, assailed Roosevelt and Eisenhower for doing business with fascists. Willkie had recently returned from his trip around the world and fancied himself an expert on foreign policy. He grudgingly permitted the government to see the speech in advance and Secretary of War Stimson ordered him to remove all direct references to the Darlan deal. The State Department refused to allow the speech to be sent abroad without an "interpretation," claiming it did not refer to the situation in North Africa, infuriating Willkie. He was also less than pleased by a swipe from his party's right wing: Senator Arthur Vandenberg of Michigan, the GOP's chief foreign policy spokesman, declared his complete approval of the Darlan arrangement.[7]

FDR's confidante and speechwriter, Sam Rosenman, later recalled that Roosevelt devoted hours to refuting the liberal assault on his Darlan policy. "He strongly resented this criticism," Rosenman wrote, "indeed I do not remember his ever being more deeply affected by a political attack, especially since it came chiefly from those who usually supported him." At times, FDR "bitterly read aloud" what a liberal columnist or editorialist had said about him, and "expressed his resentment."

Roosevelt was also expressing acute political anxiety. The election had revealed that his traditional allies in the Democratic Party, the Irish and other ethnic groups, were staying home in droves. With the South hostile, the liberals were the only bloc of support he had left. If he lost them he would be isolated.[8]

V

On December 24, 1942, a twenty-year-old Frenchman named Bonnier de la Chapelle assassinated Admiral Darlan in Algiers. A supreme cynic, the admiral had sensed his North African reign would be brief. Shortly before his death, he had written that he expected the Allies would squeeze him dry and then dispose of him. In his diary, Harold Ickes marveled that Darlan's departure was another example of FDR's luck.

There is considerable evidence that the process was a bit more complicated. The British secret service bought the pistol that the witless killer used and the Free French convinced Monsieur Chapelle that Darlan's departure would hasten the return of the heir of Louis XVI, the Comte de France, to the French throne. Shortly before his execution, Chapelle happily informed the priest who heard his last confession that he was glad to die for such a noble cause. Later, FDR made a gesture that suggests he was aware of the way the embarrassing admiral was eliminated. He invited Darlan's polio-afflicted son to the therapeutic hospital he had helped to found at Warm Springs, Georgia, for treatment.[9]

VI

The humiliating election results made Roosevelt doubly sensitive to criticism. Even attacks from acknowledged enemies stirred him to fury. Vice President Wallace recorded in his diary a post-election conversation with FDR in which Roosevelt bitterly denounced an editorial in the *New York Daily News*, asserting that the Japanese occupation of the Aleutian islands of Kiska and Attu raised the ominous possibility of an invasion of the American mainland. Roosevelt fulminated that Joe Patterson had it all wrong; the Japanese presence on these islands was giving the United States a better opportunity to kill their soldiers and sink their ships. This argument was so dubious, Wallace could not resist obliquely disagreeing with the president. He asked FDR whether he would prefer American or Japanese troops on Attu and its rocky Aleutian sister.[10]

The vice president, embroiled in his ongoing private war with Secretary of Commerce Jesse Jones over the prerogatives of the Board of Economic Warfare, wisely declined to criticize the arrangement with Admiral Darlan. Instead, he used the 1942 election debacle to enlarge his role as the voice of the New Deal in the Democratic Party. On November 26, after a Thanksgiving service in the White House, Wallace got Roosevelt alone and told him he wanted to approach him in the spirit of biblical Queen Esther approaching King Ahasuerus, but he was going to speak on behalf of liberals rather than Jews.

Wallace warned FDR that since the election businessmen in the Commerce Department (an oblique dig at Jesse Jones) and their "kindred souls" in the State Department were getting the idea that big corporations were going to run the country. Roosevelt replied that he was "gravely concerned" about the way the army's generals were forming alliances with these same businessmen through their ability to determine where and how weapons and other war material would be produced. Warming to his theme, Wallace told the president there was "an attack against the liberals going on . . . actively in the government."[11]

VII

The defeat at the polls, which put Roosevelt on the defensive in Congress, and the uproar over Darlan, which had New Dealers questioning FDR's credentials as a liberal, were in the forefront of Franklin D. Roosevelt's consciousness on January 9, 1943, when he began a top secret train trip to Florida. There he and his entourage boarded planes for a long flight to North Africa. Waiting for them was Winston Churchill and a much larger entourage of British diplomats and generals.

For ten days the two leaders met and argued amiably and compromised even more amiably in the sunny resort of Anfa, a collection of luxurious villas around a three-story hotel some three miles south of Casablanca. Nearby their numerous staffs argued much less amiably and in some cases declined to compromise. Finally, on January 24, 1943, reporters gathered in the courtyard of Roosevelt's villa to hear the two leaders sum up the historic conclave.

FDR sat with his lifeless legs jauntily crossed, wearing a light gray suit and a dark tie. Churchill was replete with homburg, cigar, and a dark blue suit and vest that seemed more suitable for the House of Commons than a backdrop of waving palm trees and tropical sunshine. Beaming, FDR declared that the two allies had reached "complete agreement" on the future conduct of the war.[12]

The precise opposite was closer to the truth. General George C. Marshall, the U.S. Army Chief of Staff, was so infuriated by the British refusal to agree to a cross-channel invasion in 1943, he was threatening to shift his support to an all-out American effort in the Pacific. The navy's chief, Admiral Ernest King, an advocate of this idea since the war began, was even more hostile to London. Almost all the lower echelon Americans were fuming over the way Churchill had cajoled the president into agreeing to another year of campaigning in the Mediterranean.[13]

He and the prime minister, FDR continued, had also hammered out a policy that would guarantee both victory and a peaceful world for generations to come. "Some of you Britishers know the old story—we had a general called U. S. Grant," Roosevelt said. "His name was Ulysses Simpson Grant but in my, and the Prime Minister's early days, he was called 'Unconditional Surrender Grant.' The elimination of German, Japanese and Italian war power means the unconditional surrender of Germany, Italy and Japan."[14]

As the reporters scribbled, FDR added: "It does not mean the destruction of the population of Germany, Italy or Japan, but it does mean the destruction of the philosophies in those countries which are based on conquest and the subjugation of other people." In subsequent remarks, Roosevelt made it clear that the latter comment was little more than an afterthought. The main message was unconditional surrender. He even suggested calling Casablanca the "unconditional surrender meeting."[15]

Winston Churchill manfully chimed in with a hearty endorsement of their "unconquerable will" to pursue victory until they obtained "the unconditional surrender of the criminal forces who have plunged the world into storm and ruin." It may well have been his finest hour as a political performer. Inwardly, the prime minister was dumbfounded by FDR's announcement—and dismayed by its probable impact on the conduct and outcome of the war.[16]

VIII

Among the prime minister's British colleagues, dismay and alarm were, if possible, even deeper. The chief of the British secret intelligence service (SIS), General Sir Stewart Graham Menzies, considered unconditional surrender disastrous not only to certain secret operations already in progress but because it would make the Germans fight "with the despairing ferocity of cornered rats."[17] Air Marshal Sir John Slessor called it "unfortunate" and maintained to the end of his life that were it not for the policy, air power alone could have ended the war.[18] Lord Maurice Hankey, one of Churchill's senior advisors (he had held important government posts for over three decades) was so perturbed he went back to England and researched fifteen British wars back to 1600. In only one, the Boer War, had the idea of unconditional surrender even been considered, and it had been hastily dropped when the Boers announced they would fight until doomsday. In fact, Lord Hankey could find only one noteworthy example of unconditional surrender in recorded history: the ultimatum that the Romans gave the Carthaginians in the Third Punic War. The Carthaginians rejected it and the Romans felt this justified razing Carthage to the ground—something they had intended to do in the first place.[19]

The feeling of dismay was shared by not a few Americans in the ranks of VIPs standing behind the two leaders. General Dwight

D. Eisenhower thought unconditional surrender would do nothing but cost American lives. Later, he said: "If you were given two choices, one to mount a scaffold, the other to charge twenty bayonets, you might as well charge twenty bayonets."[20] General Albert Wedemeyer, the man who had survived the big leak uproar of December 4, 1941, was even more appalled. He decried unconditional surrender from the moment he heard it. It would, he said, "weld all the Germans together." Having spent two recent years in Berlin attending the German War College, he had heard a lot about the deep divisions between the Nazis and the Wehrmacht's generals.[21]

Even more vehement was Major General Ira C. Eaker, commander of the U.S. Eighth Air Force. He had flown from England to fight off an attempt by the RAF to force the Americans to join them in bombing Germany by night.

> Everybody I knew at the time when they heard this [unconditional surrender] said: 'How stupid can you be?' All the soldiers and the airmen who were fighting this war wanted the Germans to quit tomorrow. A child knew once you said this to the Germans, they were going to fight to the last man. There wasn't a man who was actually fighting in the war whom I ever met who didn't think this was about as stupid an operation as you could find.[22]

Although Chief of Staff General George Marshall never expressed his opinion of unconditional surrender with such vehemence—it would have been out of character, for one thing—he would soon make it clear that he too considered the policy a major blunder. Deliberately excluded from the conference by the president was another opponent, Secretary of State Cordell Hull. Determined as usual to invent his own foreign policy, the president had taken no high-level State Department officials with him to Casablanca.

When the news of unconditional surrender reached Berlin, Admiral Wilhelm Canaris, the silver-haired chief of the Abwehr, the German intelligence service, turned to one his deputies, General Erwin Lahousen, and said, with a sigh:

> You know, my dear Lahousen, the students of history will not need to trouble their heads after this war, as they did after the last, to determine who was guilty of starting it. The case is however different when we consider guilt for prolonging the war. I believe that the other side have now disarmed us of the last weapon with which we could have ended it. Unconditional surrender, no, our generals will not swallow that. Now I cannot see any solution.[23]

Elsewhere in the German capital, Dr. Joseph Goebbels, Hitler's propaganda chief, was in a state of euphoria. He called Roosevelt's announcement "world historical tomfoolery of the first order." To one of his colleagues, he admitted: "I should never have been able to think up so rousing a slogan. If our Western enemies tell us, we won't deal with you, our only aim is to destroy you . . . how can any German, whether he likes it or not, do anything but fight on with all his strength?"[24]

IX

Historians and biographers of Roosevelt have been amazingly reluctant to deal with this epochal statement, which FDR made in the teeth of opposition from his secretary of state, his top military advisors, and his British allies. Let us look first at the reality of a German resistance movement against Hitler, the

subject Roosevelt told newsman Louis Lochner he had no interest in discussing.

Since the war began, Stewart Menzies, head of British Secret Intelligence, and Admiral Wilhelm Canaris, head of the Abwehr,
had been in shadowy touch with each other through emissaries
who shuttled from Berlin and London to the borders of the Nazi
empire. In 1940 the Abwehr leaked Hitler's planned assault on
Holland, Belgium, and France. (The Allies had ignored it.) While
the admiral went briskly about the business of intelligence, running spy networks throughout Europe, evidence accumulated
suggesting the astonishing possibility that Canaris was a secret
enemy of the Nazi regime.

In the spring of 1942, Karl-Friedrich Goerdeler, the gaunt former mayor of Leipzig, had traveled to Stockholm on a passport
supplied by Canaris to have a long talk with the banker Jakob
Wallenberg, scion of a Rothschild-like family whose business often took him to London, where he had contacts with both Menzies and Churchill. Goerdeler had been dismissed as mayor of
Leipzig because he refused to remove a monument to the great
German-Jewish composer, Felix Mendelssohn. In the late 1930s,
the ex-mayor had made several trips to London as an emissary
from Canaris and members of the German general staff to urge
the British to take a firmer stand against Hitler. Goerdeler maintained that neither the German people nor the generals wanted a
war and a serious warning from London would have forced
Hitler into humiliating retreat—or triggered his removal in a
coup d'état.[25]

Now Goerdeler told Wallenberg he and many of these same
generals were part of a formidable conspiracy. They were appalled by Nazism's crimes against the Jews, Poles, and Russians
in the East. They were determined to remove and if necessary kill
Hitler. They wanted to know what terms the Americans and
British would offer them if they accomplished this overthrow.

Wallenberg's response was cautious. He thought the Western allies were unlikely to promise much in advance to any German. If Goerdeler and his friends rid Germany of the Nazis, however, the chances of a decent reception from Churchill were reasonably good. The banker offered himself as a wholehearted intermediary to the prime minister.[26]

The existence of this conspiracy was the reason for Menzies's interference in a plot to kidnap Canaris, only a few weeks before Casablanca. When the Allied invasion fleet began landing men on North African beaches on November 8, 1942, the Abwehr director had rushed to Algeciras on the Spanish coast to galvanize the horde of agents working out of the German consulate in Tangier. The British intelligence leader in nearby Gibraltar decided to grab the admiral and fly him to London—until a message arrived from Menzies: "Leave our man alone."[27]

Not long after, Menzies received a message from Canaris through an Abwehr agent in Spain, asking if they could meet secretly somewhere on the Iberian peninsula. Visions of an ultimate intelligence triumph danced through Menzies's head: he and Canaris could negotiate a peace that would save millions of lives. But when the SIS chief asked his superiors in the British Foreign office for permission, it was stonily refused. The ostensible reason was fear of offending the Russians. That reason, if Canaris had heard it, would have given him a bitter laugh. The Russians had been trying to negotiate a separate peace with Hitler through agents in Stockholm for over a year.[28]

X

There are grave reasons for doubting the British Foreign Office explanation. Throughout World War II, these diplomats were the chief source of virulent German hatred in the British government. Much of the virus can be traced to one man, Lord Robert Vansittart, who had been the permanent under secretary of the Foreign Office from 1930 to 1938, when Foreign Secretary Anthony Eden moved him to the post of chief diplomatic advisor. Like his friend Winston Churchill, Vansittart had begun warning England against German aggression from the day Hitler seized power. Vansittart combined his prophecies with a prejudice against Germans on a par with the Ku Klux Klan's antipathy for blacks, Jews, and Catholics. After he retired from the Foreign Office and accepted a peerage, Vansittart relentlessly called for Germany's total destruction.

Here is Vansittart in full cry, speaking to the British National Trade Union Club. "Let us remember the origin of the word 'assassin' . . . the Arabic word 'hashisheen.' The word meant those who killed after they had taken hashish. The German nation [has] become in the main a nation of killers because they [have] become spiritual dope fiends. The fatal drug [of militarism] has been administered to them for 150 years." In 1940 Vansittart wrote a fellow diplomat: "Eighty percent of the German race are the political and moral scum of the earth." Needless to say, Vansittart was a passionate supporter of unconditional surrender. In his spirit, the Foreign Office issued a blanket order to its representatives to henceforth ignore peace proposals from any and all Germans.[29]

From the point of view of Canaris and the other members of the Front of Decent People, the timing of the unconditional surrender declaration at Casablanca could not have been worse. It was announced on the day that the Russians split in half the German army trapped in the Stalingrad pocket, making its destruction inevitable. For two years the conspirators had been waiting for a defeat of this magnitude, which would force the German generals to admit the war was lost—and agree to support a coup d'état. At the very moment when this precarious hope seemed to be coming true, Roosevelt had delivered it a lethal blow.[30]

On January 22, 1943, Ulrich von Hassell, a senior official in the German foreign office, whose diary is one of the few surviving records of the German resistance, wrote:

> According to people who ... have pipe lines to the Army both on the battle front and at home, there is now a real possibility for peace. The evil of the situation is revealed in the fact that at this same time there come reports from the 'enemy's side' which give rise to ever-increasing doubts as to whether they are now holding out for the complete destruction of Germany.[31]

XI

FDR later claimed that unconditional surrender had just "popped into my mind" at the press conference—an explanation accepted by a dismaying number of historians. In fact, when the president said this, he had in his lap notes he had dictated to prepare for the press conference, which contain virtually identical sentences about the policy.[32]

Unconditional surrender was anything but accidental and its meaning and intent were profoundly serious. It represented FDR's attempt to assuage his liberal critics in America and give the war a moral purpose, a rallying cry it had thus far lacked.

The term first appeared in the American government in the spring of 1942, when the State Department set up a committee to discuss postwar aims. Its chairman was J. P. Morgan banker Norman H. Davis, former under secretary of state in Woodrow Wilson's State Department and a frequent collaborator with FDR on foreign policy matters. In the weeks after FDR's election in 1932, Davis was considered a strong candidate for secretary of state. In 1942 he was president of the influential Foreign Policy Association.[33]

Many people urged FDR to bring Herbert Hoover into his wartime administration. But the Democrats had demonized the Republican former president as the personification of the cold, uncaring capitalist. "I'm not going to bring Herbie back from the dead," FDR said. In this picture, a discouraged Hoover rides with Roosevelt to FDR's 1932 inauguration.

Conservative Republican Congressman Hamilton Fish represented Hyde Park, FDR's home turf. In 1942, FDR devoted many hours to trying to defeat Fish. To the president's chagrin, an anti–New Deal surge reelected Fish, and the GOP came within eight seats of capturing the House of Representatives.

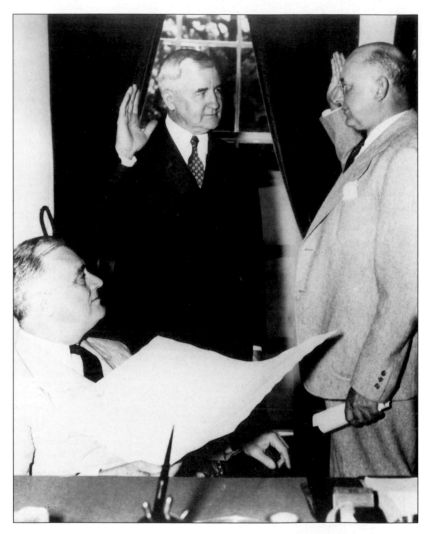

Roosevelt watches as Jesse Jones of Texas is sworn in as secretary of commerce in 1940. Already head of the Reconstruction Finance Corporation, Jones now became one of the most powerful men in Washington, D.C.—and a ferocious enemy of Vice President Henry A. Wallace. The man on the right is Supreme Court Justice Stanley Reed.

After conferring for ten days with Prime Minister Winston Churchill at Anfa, a resort near Casablanca, President Roosevelt declared that they would insist on the "unconditional surrender" of Germany, Italy and Japan. Churchill later said he was "dumbfounded" by the announcement.

At Casablanca and elsewhere, Harry Hopkins was never far from Roosevelt's side. Hopkins believed democracy should wage "total war against totalitarian war. It must exceed the Nazi in fury, ruthlessness and efficiency." He was also a strong advocate of a New Deal for the world. Sitting with FDR is French General Henri Giraud.

American B–17s head for another attack on Germany. At first the Americans rejected British area-bombing, insisting that their superior bombsights would enable them to destroy specific targets. But horrendous losses to German anti-aircraft guns and fighter planes soon forced them to change their policy. (Corbis)

Radio commentator Elmer Davis became head of the Office of War Information in mid–1942. He told Henry Wallace his goal was to sell the Century of the Common Man to America and the world. Instead, Davis was reduced to a figurehead by a hostile Congress, and the OWI became a propaganda arm of the War and Navy Departments.

Playwright and Roosevelt speech writer Robert Sherwood became head of the Foreign Information Service in 1941. He barred all Roosevelt critics from the agency. The New Dealers were determined to retain control of the war's ideas. Congress ousted Sherwood in 1943.

Republican Henry Stimson (right) became FDR's secretary of war in 1940. He had been secretary of state under Herbert Hoover. With the backing of military leaders such as Army Chief of Staff George C. Marshall, Stimson funneled most American war production to major corporations. He dismissed New Dealer objections, calling one critic "a self-seeking fanatic."

Secretary of State Cordell Hull (left) and Under Secretary of State Sumner Welles seldom spoke to each other. FDR frequently ignored Hull and consulted Welles. When rumors of Welles's homosexuality swept Washington, Hull forced Roosevelt to dismiss him. The winner of this nasty feud was Josef Stalin.

Not *until the fall of* 1943 *did the Roosevelt administration let the American people see pictures of battle dead. These soldiers on a beach in Buna, New Guinea, appeared on the cover of* Life *magazine. They were cut down by a hidden Japanese machine gunner. (Photograph by George Strock)*

The Big Three, FDR, Churchill and Stalin, sit for photographers at their summit meeting in Teheran in late November 1943. Stalin looks pleased, Churchill glum. At this conference FDR demoted the British prime minister to a minor partner in the grand alliance. A few weeks later, Stalin told a Yugoslav Communist that the Slavs would soon rule Europe and Asia.

Ferociously anti-German, Davis had gone to the president and told him the committee was inclined to recommend unconditional surrender. FDR said he was in complete agreement with them. Roosevelt had determined to pursue the policy very early in the war. It was foreshadowed in his annual message to Congress on January 6, 1942, a month after Pearl Harbor, when he declared: "There has never been—there can never be—successful compromise between good and evil. Only total victory can reward the champions of tolerance, and decency, and faith."[34]

Another reason for unconditional surrender was Roosevelt's desire to reassure Josef Stalin and dissuade him from making a separate peace with Hitler. Stalin was enormously disappointed when Winston Churchill went to Moscow in August and told him there would be no second front in 1942. The Russian dictator sent stinging cables to Roosevelt and denounced Churchill to his face. The Russians grew even more exercised when they discovered that the massive amount of shipping required to launch Operation Torch meant their lend-lease deliveries would be cut 40 percent for the foreseeable future.

XII

There was also an historic dimension to the unconditional surrender policy. To understand it requires a look backward at Franklin Roosevelt's experience in World War I, when he watched brutal clashes over peacemaking with Germany destroy the presidency and the health of Woodrow Wilson, the man who had named him assistant secretary of the navy, and given him his first chance to win national attention. This ordeal predisposed Roosevelt to absorb the hatred of Germany that was preached throughout America during World War I.

George Creel's government-financed Committee on Public Information was only one of a chorus of voices who called for a war of annihilation against the kaiser and his people. Methodist Bishop William Alfred Quayle declared that Americans fought not merely Junkers, Prussianism, and the kaiser, but the German people, who were perpetrating "the chief barbarity of history." Newell Dwight Hillis, successor to Henry Ward Beecher in Brooklyn's fashionable Plymouth Church, a position that made him a virtual spokesman for Protestant America, told audiences that generals, statesmen, diplomats, and editors were "talking about the duty of simply exterminating the German people." Hillis warmly approved a proposal to sterilize Germany's entire 5-million-man army.[35]

This kind of thinking was not confined to clergymen and propagandists. It infected some of the best minds of the era. No less a personage than Supreme Court Justice Oliver Wendell Holmes wrote to a friend: "Whatever I may think privately, I would do what I could to cherish in my countrymen an unphilosophic hatred of Germany and German ways."[36]

As for the unconditional surrender slogan itself, FDR never revealed its real source because it came from a Republican president whose influence he did his utmost to conceal: Theodore Roosevelt. At the close of World War I, T.R. had differed violently with President Wilson when he offered the reeling Germans an armistice and peace on the basis of his idealistic Fourteen Points. The Republican Roosevelt had insisted that nothing less than the unconditional surrender of the German army would guarantee the peace, an idea that the commander of the American Expeditionary Force (AEF), General John J. Pershing, also endorsed.

Pershing was supporting T.R., the man who had rescued his military career by vaulting him over several hundred senior officers to general's rank in 1906. When Pershing cabled his view to the U.S. War Department and to the French and British governments, everyone reacted with fury and contempt. "Someone put him up to it," snarled David Lloyd George, the British prime minister, which was more or less the truth. Georges Clemenceau, the French premier, dismissed it as "theatrical." The commanders of the French and British armies rejected the idea out of hand.[37]

As for Theodore Roosevelt's embrace of unconditional surrender, it is important to remember that he was planning to run for president in 1920—it was generally agreed that he would get the Republican nomination by acclamation—and he was determined to disagree with Woodrow Wilson on anything and everything. (T.R. died unexpectedly in 1919.) Recent historians have minimized the influence of the issue in the 1918 midterm elections, which gave the Republicans control of Congress, arguing that domestic and local discontents were more important in the Democratic defeat.

T.R. did not think so at the time. On election day, he wrote Rudyard Kipling: "We did an unparalleled thing and took away the Congress from him [Wilson] on the issue that we stood for forcing the Germans to make an unconditional surrender. I took a certain sardonic amusement in the fact that . . . four years ago, to put it mildly, my attitude was not popular, I was now the one man whom they [the Republicans] insisted on following." T.R.'s words were an inadvertent commentary on the progress of German-hatred in America's psyche during World War I.[38]

Adolf Hitler's repudiation of the Treaty of Versailles and his reckless aggressions convinced FDR that Cousin Theodore and General Pershing were correct. Roosevelt was determined to apply this supposed lesson of history to the war he was running. Playwright Robert Sherwood, a close student of FDR, concluded that unconditional surrender was "very deeply deliberated . . . a true statement of Roosevelt's policy." It was also a manifestation of Harry Hopkins's insistence that democracy "must wage total war against totalitarian war" and exceed the Nazis in "ruthlessness."[39]

XIII

Apparently, Roosevelt discussed unconditional surrender with Churchill some five days before he announced it at Casablanca. Churchill—or someone on his staff—sent a cable to the British cabinet, asking if they approved the policy. The cabinet answered in the affirmative, and urged that Italy be included in the decree, a proposal with which Churchill strongly disagreed. There seems to have been even more serious reservations on Churchill's part about making unconditional surrender a public slogan to which the Allies would be tied for the rest of the war. It was Roosevelt's announcement that left Churchill "dumbfounded," as one of Casablanca's British participants later told Cordell Hull. It is not insignificant that the final communiqué on the conference, to which both men gave their approval, did not mention the phrase.[40]

As a student of the past on a level that Roosevelt never approached, Churchill knew the danger of applying so-called lessons of history to statecraft. Such lessons were too often irrelevant to the realities of a new time and a very different situation. Seldom has this been more true than in the case of Nazi Germany and the German opposition to Hitler. Roosevelt's commitment to unconditional surrender led him to disregard the existence of those decent men and women who risked their lives and reputations to redeem their country from one of the most evil regimes in history.

The declaration had a decidedly negative effect on many Germans who were crucial to the Canaris-Goerdeler circle's hopes for a coup d'état. The chief planner of this operation was Brigadier General Hans Oster, Canaris's right-hand man in the Abwehr. Oster had boldly approached men such as Field Marshal Erwin von Witzleben, commander of the Berlin garrison, who loathed Hitler and declared himself ready to do everything in his power to overthrow him. After Casablanca, Witzleben said: "Now, no honorable man can lead the German people into such a situation."[41]

General Hans Guderian, the inventor of panzer warfare, declined to participate for the same reason, when he was approached by Goerdeler. Colonel General Alfred Jodl, chief of the operations staff of the German army, said at the Nuremberg War Crimes trials that unconditional surrender had been a crucial element in his refusal to join the plot.[42]

Some German officers did not take the slogan seriously at first. They were inclined to think—or hope—it was propaganda, aimed at stiffening resolve on the Allied home and fighting fronts. After all, in their own country, Joseph Goebbels had organized a huge rally at the Sportspalast in Berlin, at which he called on 100,000 Nazi Party members to join him in a perfervid response to unconditional surrender and the defeat at Stalingrad. "*Total war!*" screamed the propaganda chief. The audience responded with frantic approval of the cry. A film of the rally was shown in every movie theater in the Reich.[43]

XIV

Little more than six weeks after Casablanca, the German army's branch of the resistance showed just how serious they were. One of the leaders was General Henning von Tresckow, the forty-one-year-old chief of staff of Army Group Center on the Russian Front. He urged the Army Group's commander, Field Marshal Guenther von Kluge, the man who had almost reached Moscow in 1941, to join the conspiracy. Kluge, a brilliant general but a political naif, at first demurred, but finally agreed to a talk with Goerdeler, who visited him disguised as an itinerant preacher. Kluge said he would lend his prestige—and his army—to the plot, if someone killed Hitler. The general was troubled by the oath of loyalty he and the rest of the army's officers had sworn to the Führer.

After Stalingrad, Tresckow approached Kluge again, forced him to admit the war was lost, and implored him to act. Kluge agreed to invite Hitler to visit him at his headquarters in Smolensk, where they hoped he could be seized or murdered. When the Führer accepted—but took the precaution of bringing with him a heavily armed group of bodyguards—Abwehr General Hans Oster flew to Smolensk with the ingredients for a bomb, which Tresckow and another conspirator, Major Fabian von Schlabrendorff, constructed. Wrapping it in a package that looked like two bottles of Cointreau, Tresckow asked one of the members of Hitler's entourage to take the "gift" to a friend in Berlin. The bomb, which depended on a bottle of corrosive acid to release the detonating pin, was set to explode a half-hour after Hitler took off at the close of his conference with Kluge.

The conspirators sent a coded signal to Berlin, where a half-dozen key plotters, led by General Ludwig Beck, the army's former chief of staff, were ready to act. But the heater in the plane's baggage compartment malfunctioned and the temperature fell to near zero, freezing the acid in the detonator. Schlabrendorff managed to retrieve the package before it was opened. But everyone in the conspiracy was shaken by this strange trick of fate.

Grimly, Tresckow summoned another young officer, Baron Rudolph Christoph von Gersdorff, and asked him to volunteer to use a bomb to blow up Hitler and himself at an exhibition of captured Russian weaponry a few weeks later. Gersdorff ignited the bomb, which had a ten-minute fuse, and offered to guide Hitler through the exhibition. He was the intelligence officer of Kluge's army and a logical choice. Instead of spending an hour on the tour as planned, Hitler inexplicably hurried through the rooms in less than five minutes and departed, leaving the stunned Gersdorff with a bomb on the brink of detonation. He rushed to a men's washroom and defused it.

Equally frustrating was an attempt by another army officer, Captain Axel von dem Bussche. Appalled by witnessing an SS massacre of the Jews on the eastern front, he volunteered to wear a bomb under a new uniform scheduled to be shown to Hitler. He would set the fuse, leap on Hitler, and destroy himself and the Führer. But Hitler, again displaying an uncanny sixth sense for danger, postponed the uniform presentation again and again. Finally, the new uniforms were destroyed by a British air raid and Bussche had to return to the front, where he soon lost his leg in combat.

The momentum on the army's side of the plot faltered badly after these setbacks. Soldiers are notoriously superstitious and Hitler's luck seemed to intimate some supernatural protection. Also, the realization that Roosevelt was serious about unconditional surrender soon spread through the army's ranks, making many officers feel Germany's only choice now was a fight to the finish.[44]

XV

Unconditional surrender not only ignored the existence of the German resistance movement; the policy scanted the substantial minority of Americans, many of them of German descent, in the United States, who were eager to support an attempt to rid Germany of Nazism. Shortly before FDR flew to Casablanca, ads appeared in several prominent Eastern newspapers, signed by "Loyal Americans of German Birth," calling on Germans to revolt against the Nazis and urging Germans in the United States to join their committee. The statement was drafted by columnist Dorothy Thompson, wife of Nobel Prize–winning novelist Sinclair Lewis.

Around the same time, columnist Anne O'Hare McCormick wrote a moving plea in the *New York Times*, urging that the "decent anti-Nazi majority" of the German people be not forgotten. She had been encouraged to write the column by Under Secretary of State Sumner Welles. That this Roosevelt ally took such a stance, no doubt knowing Roosevelt's intentions at Casablanca, is another indication of how totally FDR ignored all his top military and diplomatic advisors when he launched the policy of unconditional surrender.[45]

Millions of men and women on both sides of the battle lines would pay a heavy price in the next two and a half years for FDR's attempt to recapture the moral leadership of the New Dealers' war. Not only would unconditional surrender prolong the war, the slogan would pollute the thinking and even the tactics of the leaders of America's armed forces. Unconditional surrender was not the moral rallying cry that Archibald MacLeish, Henry Wallace, and Henry Luce, among many others, sensed the war needed. It was not a soaring vision of reform or rebirth, like Woodrow Wilson's call to make the world safe for democracy. It did not communicate the fervor to transform, only a hate-tinged determination to destroy. Unfortunately, it jibed all too well with most Americans' grimly stoic view of the war as a necessary evil.

8

War War Leads
to Jaw Jaw

Franklin D. Roosevelt returned from Casablanca a tired and sick man. He wrote Churchill a complaining letter, saying he had caught some strange African bug that put him in bed for four days. Sulfa drugs left him feeling like a dishrag for another week, unable to work past 2 P.M. It was the first glimpse of a problem that would gradually grow ominous, the failing health of the leader of the global war.[1]

The situation in North Africa, both military and political, remained a fretful worry. Slowed by their problems with the French and by rainy weather that turned roads and airfields into gumbo, the Allies lost the overland race to seize Tunisia. Hitler poured in some 200,000 troops and planes and inflicted embarrassing defeats on the green Americans in the first few battles. A campaign that was supposed to take weeks began stretching into months, ending any hope of changing British minds about a second front in France in 1943.

Liberals continued to criticize the administration for leaving Frenchmen with strong ties to Vichy in charge of the North African civilian population. Associate Justice Felix Frankfurter of the Supreme Court, a Roosevelt ally who liked to work in deep background, got into the ongoing imbroglio after talking to OWI man Jay Allen, who told him that most U.S. Army officers were not only "ignorant" about politics but were more comfortable with "the *Vichysoisse* [sic] crowd . . . of Nazified Frenchmen."[2]

This was undoubtedly true of some officers. General George Patton became much too friendly with General Auguste Nogues, the governor general of Morocco, who entertained him with lavish dinners and hunting parties. Patton looked the other way while Nogues threw in jail people who had tried to help the Americans when they landed. Patton also took it upon himself to alter the wording of a message from the president to the sultan of Morocco, because the general thought it might give the sultan delusions about early independence.[3]

The liberal attack soon shifted from Roosevelt to the State Department, with the surreptitious encouragement of the president. But the liberals discovered there were people in FDR's war cabinet with the power to hit back. OWI man Edgar Ansel Mowrer was one of the most vociferous State Department critics. As the first American newsman to be expelled from Germany by the Nazis, he felt he had a license to hunt fascist sympathizers everywhere.[4]

When Mowrer asked to go to North Africa to cover the Casablanca summit, Secretary of War Henry Stimson said he did not think it was "wise" for a man with "such decided, not to say passionate views" to be allowed anywhere in a war zone. An outraged Elmer Davis demanded a meeting with FDR to override Stimson. A phone call from Stimson persuaded the president to cancel the appointment. A fuming Mowrer resigned from the OWI.[5]

Not long after Roosevelt returned from Casablanca, Mowrer denounced State's bureaucrats in a speech to the French American Club in New York. Mowrer called them "salonnards" who naturally gravitated to the side of the rich and powerful and looked with suspicion on labor agitators, intellectuals—and New Dealers.

II

Left-leaning columnist I. F. Stone joined the assault, declaring that a New Dealer could not exist in the State Department because the profascist old-line professionals were in control. Columnist Drew Pearson, never hesitant about shooting from the lip, made the "reactionaries" at State a favorite target, using material leaked to him by Harry Hopkins and others. But the journalistic jabs did little to change the situation, because the president did not have the will or the inclination to go head-to-head with Secretary of State Cordell Hull, who disliked New Dealers and grimly backed his conservative professionals and their French appointees.[6]

A diplomatic topper of sorts was provided by the American ambassador to Spain, Carleton Hayes. A highly respected professor of history at Columbia University, Hayes had been told by State to keep General Franco from drifting into Hitler's embrace. To demonstrate his bona fides, Hayes released a report that was largely for Spanish consumption. He announced that the United States was making sure Spain had as much gasoline on hand as the residents of the American East Coast. Additions to this generosity included 25,000 tons of ammonia, 10,000 tons of cotton, and at least as many tons of industrial chemicals and foodstuffs. Hayes said this bounty was being financed by a complicated series of loans because Spain was not on the list for lend-lease. It was all intended to help General Franco build a "peace economy."

In fact, the announcement was designed to keep General Franco from unleashing the large army he maintained in Spanish Morocco on the Allied flank as they battled the Germans, who were pouring into Tunisia. Franco was playing a delicate balancing act between the fiercely anticommunist Falange Party, who wanted to join the Axis powers in gratitude for helping them win the Spanish Civil War, and the millions of Spaniards who shuddered at more bloodshed.

New Dealers and their media allies were predictably apoplectic at Hayes. The *New York Post*, one of FDR's staunchest backers, wondered if there comes a time when "too much is too much." The majority who elected Roosevelt three times "did not put him in there to appease Franco." The *Post* warned that if this policy continued, the Democrats' majority would begin to "wonder" until "the thing in its heart that creates enthusiasm and election victories begins to shrivel."[7]

III

Worsening the *New York Post*'s mood were the latest developments in the sedition indictment of the twenty-eight American fascists whom FDR had pressured Attorney General Francis Biddle into prosecuting. Biddle became more and more dissatisfied with the behavior of the government's attorney, William Power Maloney. He was continuing to leak political attacks on ex-isolationists and Roosevelt critics by linking them to his bizarre defendants. Biddle feared that Maloney's behavior in the courtroom would be so prejudicial, it would be a replay of the farcical sedition trials of World War I.

Early in 1943, Biddle removed Maloney and replaced him with O. John Rogge, a Harvard Law School graduate with a more buttoned-down style. Rogge decided Maloney's porous indictment had to be discarded and began working on a whole new argument. The liberal press, in particular the *Post*, did not approve the change of prosecutors. They raged at Biddle for removing Maloney, accusing him of caving in to Senator Burton K. Wheeler. The *Washington Post* weighed in with an editorial, "Appeasement Is Folly," which made it sound as if Biddle had been cutting deals with Hitler. Further roiling the attorney general's nerves was a note from the president asking: "Why Maloney's removal?"

Early in March 1943, the Supreme Court gave the president an inadvertent answer. It threw out a much publicized conviction Maloney had won against George Sylvester Viereck, a German-American with a history of propagandizing on Germany's behalf, starting in World War I. Viereck had been indicted for failing to register as an agent of the German government. The high court commented that Maloney's behavior was so outrageously prejudicial, the trial judge should have silenced him without an objection from the defense.[8]

IV

These diplomatic and legal headaches and FDR's worries about Josef Stalin's reaction to the news that there would be no second front in 1943 were more than equaled, in the president's perspective, by his relations with the new Seventy-eighth Congress. After the disastrous 1942 election, one of FDR's first moves was to hire a full-time pollster, Hadley Cantril of Princeton University, at the then princely sum of $5,000 a month. (Again multiply by ten for the equivalent in today's dollars.)[9]

Cantril's central discovery from his polls was the need for the president "always to give the impression of cooperation with Congress." While their sons were fighting and dying overseas, Americans did not want to hear that their representatives in Washington and the New Dealers in the executive departments were at each other's throats. Somewhat ominously, Cantril's report added that it was "more necessary for the president to cooperate with Congress than for Congress to cooperate with the president." For a man like FDR, who liked to dominate any relationship, these recommendations must have been hard to swallow.[10]

As a sort of consolation prize, Cantril also urged the president to take credit for any and all good news from the battlefronts, something FDR had no trouble doing. In his January 1943 state of the union address, the president virtually avoided all mention of domestic politics, and talked glowingly of how well things were going in the war zones. Soon Cantril was reporting that 76 percent of the people had more confidence in FDR as a war leader than they had felt a year ago. An Elmo Roper poll showed that 56 percent of the people gave Roosevelt a "good" job performance rating while only 26 percent gave a similar gold star to Congress.

But Cantril's advice was, in the long run, a defensive strategy. It was an attempt to repair the damage done by the New Dealers' arrogance in 1942, when they thought the whole country was going to roll over and vote Democratic because the war had finally begun and they were running it. One of Harry Hopkins's aides, Oscar Cox, put his finger on the looming problem. When did conciliating Congress cross the line into appeasement?[11]

Roosevelt and his New Dealers soon discovered the realism of this question, if not the answer to it. For the first time in a decade, the Republicans and their southern conservative allies felt they held the initiative against the "Champ." They had floored Roosevelt with a roundhouse right in November and now hoped to wipe up the ring with him. Harrison E. Spangler, the new chairman of the Republican Party, summed up the prevailing attitude toward the New Deal. "I have been after that animal since 1932 and I hope that in 1944 I can be there for the kill." Republican Congressman Charles L. Gifford of Massachusetts agreed wholeheartedly. He said it was vital for them to "win the war from the New Deal."[12]

Senator Arthur Vandenberg of Michigan sounded the note that Congress intended to strike as often as possible when he went before the joint committee on the reduction of nonessential federal expenditures. He told of a Kansas farmer who had received a form from the Office of Price Administration to fill out to get a pair of rubber boots. At the bottom of the form was a warning that if he told any lies he was in danger of ten years imprisonment and a $10,000 fine. Interestingly, Senator Vandenberg quoted with enthusiasm a remark by his fellow senator, Democrat Harry S. Truman of Missouri: "Washington has become a city where a large portion of the population makes its living, not by taking in one another's washing, but by unreeling one another's red tape."[13]

Another sign of trouble ahead was a special election in the Sixth Missouri District to replace Republican Philip A. Bennett, who had died suddenly. His son Marion ran for the seat and won with a far larger majority than his father had ever achieved. The son carried every county in his district, including many that were traditionally Democratic. One observer opined that "this large Republican swing indicates that [the] anti-Administration wave is still rising and weakens Democratic claims that the last election might have gone better for them but for lack of good war news."[14]

V

In the face of this rampant Capitol Hill hostility, FDR began his campaign of conciliation with a blunder. He nominated his old friend Ed Flynn, just retired as the National Chairman of the Democratic Party, as ambassador to Australia. This was business-as-usual politics at a time when it was out of sync with the mood of the country and Congress. The opposition on the Foreign Relations Committee shredded Flynn's reputation, dredging up charges that he had once used his prerogatives as boss of the Bronx to have the city of New York pave his driveway with expensive Belgian bricks left over from the 1939 World's Fair. Republican Senator Styles Bridges of New Hampshire called the attempt to transform Boss Flynn into Ambassador Flynn "nauseating" and, losing all sense of proportion, claimed it was the "most despicable appointment" ever made by a president. (In real life, Flynn was a very intelligent, well-read man, the opposite of the stereotypical boss.) The Democratic majority on the committee reported favorably on the nomination but Flynn asked the president to withdraw it, knowing he would only face more abuse and possible defeat in a floor vote.[15]

Meanwhile Flynn's predecessor, Jim Farley, was touring the southern and border states, schmoozing with old friends. Insiders said he was trying to build an anti-Roosevelt coalition within the Democratic Party. Farley serenely downplayed the rumor but did not deny he was blaming Roosevelt for the Democrats' catastrophic defeat in New York. A nervous Henry Wallace told FDR that Farley would control one-third of the delegates at the next Democratic convention. The president agreed with this ominous estimate. Farley went on politicking and the White House began to feel more and more like a besieged fortress, with few friends in sight.[16]

VI

Democratic Congressman Martin Dies of Texas, head of the House Un-American Activities Committee, now weighed in with a charge that he had found forty assorted leftists, communists, and crackpots among the employees of Vice President Henry Wallace's Board of Economic Warfare, including one man who advocated "universal nudism" at home and in the workplace. Dies had made a similar charge in March of 1942 and Wallace had angrily refuted him, declaring he was as dangerous to the war effort as Joseph Goebbels. In a press conference, FDR backed the vice president with a witticism. He said Congress, in the person of Dies, had something worse than a nudist on its hands—an exhibitionist.

Dies was an old thorn in Roosevelt's side. Since 1938, he had won attention and congressional funding with frequent attacks on the New Deal's leftward tilt. Although FDR refused to take him seriously and liberal journals deplored his often crude assaults, the Texan had a following in the conservative press. In the late 1930s his committee had shut down funding for the Federal Theater Project and the Federal Writers Project by finding too many Communists in their ranks.

An expert at sensing the mood of Congress, Dies now urged his fellow legislators to guard their prerogatives and their constituents from the socialistic clutches of Roosevelt's ever multiplying bureaucrats, who now numbered a supposedly staggering 172,736. The new Congress dismayed the White House by taking Dies seriously. Soon hearings were authorized and employees from the FCC and other agencies were being grilled on their political and personal connections before they took their government jobs. The inquisitors took special interest in three former university professors. In spite of their assertions of loyalty and faith in the free enterprise system, the House attached a rider to an important funding bill, ordering the three men to be terminated, unless they were reappointed by the president and confirmed by the Senate.[17]

This latter proviso was part of a wider congressional strategy. In the Senate, a dedicated anti-Roosevelt man, Kenneth McKellar of Tennessee, was pushing a bill that would require senatorial approval for every member of the federal bureaucracy who earned more than $4,500 a year. This would correct, with a vengeance, what Congress perceived as an unconstitutional shift in the balance of power between them and the president, begun early in the New Deal and now grown rampant with the government's huge war-spurred growth.[18]

Roosevelt furiously resisted this congressional assault on his presidential powers. He refused to fire the professors and ordered his followers in the Senate to detach the rider from the funding bill. Eventually, the quarrel ended in the U.S. Supreme Court, which ruled three years later that firing the professors without due process amounted to a bill of attainder, a government abuse of power specifically forbidden in the Constitution.

VII

Unfortunately, the president could do little about assaults on New Deal agencies that had, in Congress's opinion, outlived their usefulness. The lawmaker's first target was the WPA, which had no role to play in an economy where employers were scouring the country in search of workers. Roosevelt acknowledged the point and shut down the agency early in 1943.

FDR did little more to defend one of his wife's favorite agencies, the National Youth Administration (NYA), on which Mrs. Roosevelt had lavished endless attentions in the 1930s, often ignoring her husband's opinion that "youth" did not need a special government agency. The director, southern-born Aubrey Williams, was considered a radical by most Democrats below the Mason-Dixon line because the NYA devoted much of its funds to training young blacks for jobs.

In 1941, Williams made training for defense industries the agency's chief focus. Top executives, presumably Republicans, praised its contribution to the war effort. But the NYA was savagely attacked by two powerful groups, the National Education Association (NEA) and the American Vocational Association (AVA), both of whom accused the agency of a plot to take control of secondary school education away from state and local governments. This was an old-fashioned turf war that had little to do with ideology but it jibed neatly with the antiadministration offensive in Congress.

Eleanor Roosevelt pleaded with FDR to defend Williams but the president had no stomach for taking on the NEA and the AVA. He issued only a few vaguely favorable statements, and made no attempt to rally Congress on the NYA's behalf. A desperate Williams offered his would-be executioners a bare-bones budget and talked grandiloquently about the agency's future importance in helping young people move from the military to civilian jobs after the war. He might as well have whistled in the wind. Congress voted the NYA into oblivion in June of 1943.[19]

VIII

Next in the conservatives' crosshairs was the National Resources Planning Board (NRPB), an agency that had New Deal plastered all over it in capital letters. It was run by aging Frederick Delano, Roosevelt's uncle, and was the headquarters of liberal thinking about government. Its budget was not large, little more than a million dollars a year, most of it doled out to university professors to study the nation's problems. Congress saw it as a nest of collectivists and responded eagerly to calls from the *Wall Street Journal* and other conservative powers for its extermination. In February 1943, the House cut off all funds for the NRPB.

There was more at stake here than the balance of power between the president and Congress and both sides knew it. Roosevelt wrote a letter to "Dear Uncle Fred" telling him he was going to fight to save the NRPB. The president declared there was a vital need for planning for the postwar future and launched a major publicity offensive. Early in March 1943, FDR sent Congress two hefty reports that the NRPB had compiled on postwar planning. The first, *After the War—Full Employment* contained a nine-point economic "bill of rights" that called for the creation of a national transportation agency, the consolidation of the nation's railroads, and a government role in developing air transportation. On top of these ideas the bureaucrats piled calls for vast public works projects on rivers and in harbors, a massive investment in public housing, and tough enforcement of antitrust legislation. The companion report, *After the War—Toward Security* went even further toward revealing the New Dealers' fondness for a government-controlled economy. It called for a permanent public works program, a big expansion in social security benefits, and federally funded medical care for the poor.

The *Wall Street Journal* called the package a "totalitarian plan" and denounced it as an enemy of liberty and prosperity. Senator Taft, the voice of conservative Republicanism, joined with Democrat Millard Tydings of Maryland to deplore the NRPB proposals. A GOP congressman from Oklahoma said they added up to national socialism and Hitler would love it. The *New York Times* obliquely agreed with him, wondering editorially why the United States should be "resigning ourselves to our own brand of totalitarianism after beating back the Nazi brand."

Roosevelt urged various senators to support the $1,000,000 appropriation the NRPB was requesting. The Senate did not entirely ignore him but they came close. The solons shaved the funding to a pathetic $200,000. When the bill went to a conference committee of the two branches, House spokesmen were unrelenting in their demand for the NRPB's extermination. The Senate, having already demonstrated minimal enthusiasm for its survival, consented. To FDR's acute embarrassment, Uncle Fred lost his unsalaried government job—and the nation faced the postwar future relying on the free enterprise system, if your inclinations were rightward—or naked capitalism, if you leaned in the other direction.[20]

In the latter department, FDR's salary cap on the rich also fell victim to the conservative resurgence. Ignoring the polls in its favor, in March of 1943, a majority of House Democrats joined Republicans to repeal the president's executive order by a huge veto-proof margin. The Senate joined the burgeoning anti–New Deal crusade by a vote of 74-3. Equality of sacrifice was as dead as Uncle Fred's NRPB and its visions of a command economy.[21]

IX

In the first six months of 1943, Congress rampaged through several other New Deal agencies, either abolishing them or gutting them to a state of meaninglessness. The Farm Security Administration, dedicated to helping small farmers, shriveled to a near-cipher under meat-ax budget cuts and so did the Rural Electrification Administration—long a bête noire of private power companies. Worst of all was the public battering Congress inflicted on the domestic branch of the OWI.

The trouble started early in 1943, when the agency began publishing *Victory*, a magazine aimed at foreign audiences. One article was entitled: "Roosevelt of America, President, Champion of Liberty, United States leader in the War to Win Lasting and Worldwide Peace." The writer described the president as a benevolent, warmhearted man whose generous political philosophy was sharply contrasted to the "toryism of the conservative reactionary." Numerous senators and congressmen exploded, calling *Victory* Roosevelt campaign literature and expensive in the bargain. OWI chief Elmer Davis earnestly defended portraying the president as a hero for overseas readers. But he was forced to admit the Roosevelt article might have profited from some editing. That did not inhibit Congress from firing volleys at other OWI publications. One pamphlet praised the administration program for fighting inflation before Congress voted on it. Another publication, *Negroes and the War*, made it sound as if the Democratic Party had ended slavery, rather than the Republicans.

The OWI's plight was worsened by a sensational resignation of several of its top writers in April 1943. They exited with a blast at the agency's supposed shift in policy from providing sober information on the war to selling the American cause as if the global struggle was an advertising campaign. The result was turning OWI into the "Office of War Bally-Hoo." Worse, this approach to the struggle was leaving people adrift and confused, the departing protestors charged. There was some truth to their claim. Polls showed as many as 35 percent of the people could not answer the question: "What are we fighting for?"

Elmer Davis revealed his political ineptitude by choosing this moment to attack the press for the way they were reporting the war. Obviously aiming at the Hearst-Patterson-McCormick anti-Roosevelt alliance, he accused the nation's newspapers of being more interested in rivalries between Washington administrators than battles between Japanese and American fleets. The touchy lords of the press replied in kind, making it clear that they had never liked the OWI in the first place and now disliked its putative leader even more. Davis found himself swinging in the wind, a perfect target for congressional sharpshooters.

Representative John Taber called OWI "a haven of refuge for derelicts" (dredging up the old saw that most reporters were drunks) and an Alabama Democrat said it was a "stench in the nostrils of the American people." A few northern Democrats tried to defend the agency but the House Republican–southern Democratic coalition voted to abolish the domestic branch of the OWI completely. The Senate was slightly kinder, persuading the conference committee to restore half the original appropriation of $5,500,000. It was, Davis glumly observed, enough money to avoid "the odium of having put us out of business" while not providing enough "to let us accomplish much."

Along with this starvation budget, which forced the OWI to close its regional offices and abandon production of all publications and motion pictures, Davis had to agree to become strictly a coordinator of information put out by other agencies, over which he had no effective control. He also had to promise not to let a page of the Roosevelt-praising propaganda they sent overseas appear in the United States. "I do indeed feel pretty much like Job at the moment and sit here scraping myself with potsherds," Davis confessed to one friend. He did not comment on the most ominous part of his ordeal: the president had not said a supporting word on OWI's behalf.[22]

X

In Berlin, Admiral Wilhelm Canaris struggled to revive the German resistance by launching a series of initiatives aimed at finding out if unconditional surrender could be modified or abandoned to accommodate the needs and hopes of the Front of Decent People. Discouraged by the Vansittartism of the British Foreign Office, he put his chief effort into contacting Americans. His first move was worthy of a master of intrigue. He persuaded Captain Paul Leverkuehn, an internationally known lawyer serving in the German army mission to Turkey, to try to reach William Donovan, the head of the Office of Strategic Services. Leverkuehn had met Donovan in Washington before the war.

Working through Commander George H. Earle, the American naval attache in Istanbul who was Roosevelt's Special Emissary for Balkan Affairs, Leverkuehn arranged a meeting with Canaris. The Abwehr chief implored Earle to ask Roosevelt to alter the

unconditional surrender formula to revive plans for a coup d'é-
tat. Scion of a distinguished Pennsylvania family, Earle had
thrown his money and influence behind FDR before he was nominated in 1932. Two years later, Earle became the first Democratic governor of Pennsylvania in four decades. Three years later,
after he lost a race for the Senate, Roosevelt had appointed him
minister to Bulgaria, where he became extremely well informed
on the politics of Eastern Europe.[23]

Earle quickly became a Canaris ally. The Pennsylvanian saw
that overthrowing Hitler would save Eastern Europe from Communist domination. He told Leverkuehn he would get in touch
with FDR immediately—and would enlist Donovan's support.
Roosevelt's response was icy: he told Earle and Donovan to dis-
continue all contacts with Canaris and his representatives.[24]

Undeterred, in June 1943 Canaris advanced one of his best
men to Istanbul: Count Helmuth James von Moltke. The great
grandnephew of the general who had beaten France in 1871 and
made Germany a world power, Moltke was a lawyer and a committed idealist who worked in the Abwehr's foreign countries department, where he had firsthand knowledge of the atrocities the
Nazis were committing against the Jews and other captive peoples. Six foot seven, with an intellect that matched his stature, he
was an impressive man. He met with two OSS men to offer another Canaris proposal: a member of the German general staff
was ready to fly to London and make arrangements to open the
western front for an allied landing—if the Casablanca formula
would be retracted or at least altered.

This offer persuaded William Donovan himself to come to Istanbul. Moltke had returned to Germany but Leverkuehn prepared a typed statement of the proposal on German embassy
stationery and signed it. Donovan was so impressed he decided to
tackle Roosevelt again. The president curtly informed him that he
had no desire to negotiate with "these East German Junkers."[25]

Simultaneously, Canaris was developing a seemingly more fruitful contact in Berne, Switzerland, where Allen Dulles had become the OSS station chief. Here the messenger was another tall German, six-foot-four-inch Hans Bernd Gisevius, an Abwehr agent disguised as German vice consul in Zurich. To bolster his case, Canaris leaked reams of secret information about the German war effort to Dulles, who forwarded it to Washington with strong recommendations to cooperate with the resistance movement, whom he code-named "Breakers." Many of Dulles's more breathtaking dispatches—such as an eyewitness report that whole streets in Germany were being plastered at night with signs reading Down With Hitler and Stop The War!—were rushed to the Oval Office. From the White House came only silence.[26]

We now know one reason for that silence, which extends like a shroud across all the German resisters' attempts to establish a fruitful contact with the West, but was particularly damaging to the Dulles-Gisevius relationship. Through their astonishing success at breaking German codes, the British and American Sigint (Signal Intelligence) people already knew most of what Canaris told them to establish his bona fides. The Allies could afford to disdain him as a source of information, an attitude that fit neatly into the German hatred that emanated from the White House and Whitehall. It never seemed to occur to the Allied leaders that Ultra, as the Sigint breakthrough was called, was also a way of establishing the seriousness and basic veracity of the Front of Decent People.

Another large negative influence was the jealousy of other intelligence agencies, especially the British secret service officer on duty in Berne. The State Department also hurled strident tut-tuts around Washington about the danger of compromising the policy of unconditional surrender, which they had now erected into a rule of law to govern all contacts with Germany. In April 1943, William Donovan ruefully informed Dulles that "all news from Berne is being discounted 100% by the War Department."[27]

Nothing came of a new initiative in Stockholm, launched by another civilian member of the conspiracy, the German foreign office diplomat Adam von Trott zu Solz. In many ways he was the most tragic figure of the resistance. As brilliant as he was handsome, he was a descendant, on his mother's side, of the American founding father, John Jay. Trott had visited London and Washington, D.C., before the war, trying to persuade the British and Americans to take a stronger stand against Hitler. Now he sought out the American ambassador to Sweden and pleaded for an alteration in the unconditional formula. The ambassador sent full reports of his visits to Washington and received the same answer as Dulles: silence.[28]

For Canaris, the disappointment was crushing, and it soon became doubly depressing when his enemies in the Nazi hierarchy, who had long suspected the Abwehr of treason, began to strike at some of his most trusted subordinates. First, General Hans Oster and one of his assistants were caught laundering money to aid escaping Jews. Next Moltke attended a garden party at which, the Gestapo soon learned, a number of indiscreet things were said about the regime. After one more futile trip to Ankara in the last weeks of 1943 to try to contact the American ambassador to Cairo, who was an old friend, Moltke too was arrested and Canaris's grip on the Abwehr was threatened by investigators from several branches of the Nazi apparatus. The Gestapo gave the suspected conspiracy a nickname, *die Schwarze Kapelle* (the Black Orchestra), which distinguished it from *die Rote Kapelle* (the Red Orchestra), a Communist conspiracy in the air ministry that the Nazis had smashed earlier in the year.[29]

XI

Meanwhile, the war rumbled into the next phase. Sicily was invaded and conquered in the summer of 1943 and an invasion of

Italy was clearly in the cards Roosevelt and Churchill were holding in their ever more potent hands. Using OWI-manned radio stations in Algiers and elsewhere the British and Americans launched a propaganda offensive aimed at destroying Italian confidence in Mussolini's government. On July 17, the two leaders issued a joint statement that revealed Churchill's disenchantment with unconditional surrender. The British prime minister persuaded Roosevelt to say with him that Italy's only hope lay in "honorable capitulation to the overwhelming power of the military forces of the United Nations." For anyone conversant with the language of war and diplomacy, this was a oblique way of saying Italy would not have to surrender unconditionally.

The psychological assault was combined with devastating Allied air attacks on Italian cities. On July 25, 1943, the Fascist Grand Council deposed Mussolini and appointed retired Field Marshall Pietro Badoglio prime minister. The decree was approved by King Victor Emmanuel. The next day, Churchill cabled Roosevelt that he would "deal with any non-Fascist government that can deliver the goods." The following day, Badoglio dissolved the Grand Council—in effect saying Italy was through with Fascism—and proclaimed martial law throughout the nation. Before the House of Commons on July 27, Churchill said, "It would be a grave mistake . . . to break down the whole structure and expression of the Italian state"—another signal of his readiness to negotiate with Badoglio. Everyone, including Adolf Hitler, expected an imminent acceptance of the call for an honorable capitulation.[30]

That same day, July 27, General Eisenhower broadcast to the Italian people a personal statement prepared for him by his political advisor, Robert Murphy, the man who cut the deal with Darlan, and Harold Macmillan, the British resident minister in Algiers. Eisenhower offered the Italians a chance to surrender "immediately." If the Italians stopped supporting the Germans and returned all Allied prisoners in their hands, "the ancient liberties and traditions of your country will be restored." There was no mention of unconditional surrender.[31]

On July 28, FDR went on the radio and unilaterally declared that "our terms to Italy are still the same as our terms to Germany and Japan—'Unconditional Surrender.' We will have no truck with Fascism in any shape or manner. We will permit no vestige of Fascism to remain." This was ideological warfare with a vengeance. The seventy-two-year-old Badoglio had been Mussolini's field commander in the war with Ethiopia and the architect of the Fascist victory in the Spanish civil war. King Victor Emmanuel had given Mussolini his implicit blessing for over two decades. If they were not Fascists, they certainly qualified as vestiges of the system.[32]

The prospect of a relatively bloodless surrender of Italy went into a swoon. A dismayed Dwight Eisenhower could only follow orders. When Marshal Badoglio flew one of his generals to confer with Ike's chief of staff, General Walter Bedell Smith, in Lisbon, Smith revealed that the surrender would have to be unconditional. An outraged Badoglio hesitated and protested. He had never been much of a Fascist. In one news photo, he stood in a row of generals behind Mussolini while Il Duce and the others gave the Fascist salute. Badoglio's arm remained by his side. When Italy joined the war as Germany's ally, the marshal had resigned in protest.

Not until September 3, the day the Allies invaded Italy at Reggio and Salerno, did Badoglio sign a secret armistice agreement with the Allies, with no reference to unconditional surrender. By that time, the Germans had poured troops onto the peninsula. At Salerno, the Americans found the Wehrmacht and their Tiger tanks and .88 millimeter cannon waiting for them in the hills. Only massive bombardments from the escorting fleet and the in-

sertion of the elite Eighty-second Airborne Division into the col-
lapsing beachhead prevented a debacle.[33]

XII

On September 20, the Allies handed Marshal Badoglio a document entitled "The Unconditional Surrender of Italy." He
protested violently that the title was a humiliation for him and
the Italian people. Nine days later he met with Eisenhower and
urged him to delete the phrase. Eisenhower virtually apologized,
but said his civilian superiors insisted on keeping it. Badoglio
signed, but over the next months continued to make public his
unhappiness with the document. He wrote to both Churchill and
Roosevelt, claiming he had been led to believe the words would
not be in the final surrender. Otherwise he would never have
signed the September 3 armistice. Not a few Italians agreed with
the field marshal and became as disenchanted with the Allies as
they were with the Nazis. One historian summed up the mess in
a few pungent lines: "The policy of unconditional surrender, applied to Italy, had been based on the premise that it would enable the Allies to preserve their moral integrity without
sacrificing military expediency. Its actual result was the loss of
both."[34]

Instead of reaching Rome in a week or two as optimists had
predicted, the British and Americans found themselves up to their
axles in winter mud, confronted by thousands of Germans man-
ning the mountainous Gustav Line one hundred miles south of
the Eternal City. The German commander was one of the Reich's
shrewdest generals, Field Marshal Albert Kesselring. He turned
the already unenthused Italians into neutrals by disarming their
soldiers and letting them go home.[35] So began a war of attrition
that would kill or wound 201,180 American and British soldiers

and leave Italy devastated. It was the first taste of the bitter fruit of unconditional surrender.[36]

XIII

In Washington, D.C., the New Dealers in OWI's foreign branch, already alienated from American policy by the Darlan affair in North Africa, blundered into the contretemps about the application of unconditional surrender to Italy. The U.S. Army and the OWI had already become antagonists in North Africa. The agency's field representatives refused to follow orders either from the generals or their own OWI superiors to downplay the Vichy problem. They were surreptitiously encouraged by the headstrong OWI regional chief, Percy Winner. A short, brisk, pepperpot of a man, Winner had covered European politics for CBS and NBC and found it hard to conceal his strong liberal opinions. General Walter Bedell Smith, Eisenhower's chief of staff, was soon growling: "Europe and Africa together are too small to hold Percy Winner and the U.S. Army."[37]

When Badoglio replaced Mussolini, the OWI's top people saw another Darlan situation emerging and they did not like it. The BBC, reflecting British policy, bombarded Italy with congratulatory messages, hailing the political shift as the end of Fascism. The OWI decided to treat the event "coldly and without any jubilation." They saw no difference in Mussolini, Badoglio, or the king. They did not bother to clear this policy with the U.S. State Department or the U.S. Army. Robert Sherwood defended this lapse with a patently offhand evasion. "It was a nice summer evening and it was Sunday. We couldn't get anybody on the phone."

The OWI soon went even further into making its own foreign policy. One of their commentators, John Durfee, broadcast a column written by Samuel Grafton of the *New York Post*, quoting him with obvious approval. "Fascism is still in power in Italy. . . .

The moronic little king who has stood behind Mussolini for 21 years has moved forward one pace. This is a political minuet and not the revolution we have been waiting for."[38]

Watching in the wings was a powerful spokesman for American public opinion, the *New York Times*. The newspaper had recently begun monitoring the OWI's broadcasts. On July 27, 1943, the *Times* unleashed a front-page blast at OWI's policy for overhauling Italy. The *Times*'s Washington columnist, Arthur Krock, damned the Durfee broadcast for making it difficult if not impossible to use Badoglio and King Victor Emmanuel to build "a bridge to a democratic government."

In a press conference that afternoon, Roosevelt showed no enthusiasm for defending the OWI. He said the broadcast "should never have been done" and declared "Bob Sherwood is raising hell about it now." The president was trying to protect his friend and favorite speechwriter, if not the agency. The next day, July 28, Roosevelt's radio broadcast insisting on unconditional surrender indirectly gave the back of his hand to the *Times* and Arthur Krock, a columnist he hated, and semi-endorsed the OWI's stand. But FDR's switch only succeeded in adding fuel to the controversy. The *Times* had made another discovery, almost as serious from a professional newsman's point of view. The OWI commentator, John Durfee, was a fictitious name. In reality he was James Warburg, deputy director of the OWI foreign branch.

This revelation gave an ugly underhanded cast to the broadcast and Arthur Krock took full advantage of it in the following days. Reminding readers of the Darlan uproar, Krock accused "a group of administration employees" of carrying out "a foreign policy of its own" shaped by the "Communists and fellow travellers in this country." They did not care whether they disrupted top secret diplomatic negotiations or killed thousands of American soldiers, Krock stormed. The only thing that mattered to them was their left-wing ideology.

William Randolph Hearst's *New York Journal American* gleefully joined in denouncing these "half-baked international politicians" and their "Communist lunatic fringe." Drew Pearson, abandoning his liberal inclinations to get in on the story, sneered that the White House should rename the OWI "the Office of Warburg Information." The *New York World Telegram* snapped: "the whole thing smells of dishonesty" and urged the State Department to take charge of the overseas OWI immediately.[39]

XIV

Within two days, FDR demonstrated his ability to dodge a bullet. Abandoning the OWI, the president told another press conference that the Americans would deal with any non-Fascist Italian—"a king, a present prime minister, or a mayor of a town or village." The stunned liberals in the OWI could only swallow hard and complain among themselves about the latest "resort to expedience." They told each other that this second venture into political realism would make Europeans regard the United Nations "not as liberators but as agents of reactionary suppression." Some of them groused that FDR was letting them become scapegoats for a muddled policy that was mostly his fault.[40]

Publicly, however, the OWI ate humble pie by the pound. Robert Sherwood promised Congress the overseas branch would never make such a stupid mistake again. Elmer Davis, having seen the domestic OWI eviscerated by Congress, decided to assert his theoretical authority over the foreign branch, which now had 90 percent of the agency's budget. This led to a spectacular public brawl with Robert Sherwood, which got into the newspapers, and eventually brought the two men to the Oval Office, where an exasperated Roosevelt told them to reach some sort of face-saving agreement.

The result was the departure of the New Dealers. Sherwood went to London on a vague assignment and Warburg and several other top deputies resigned. They were replaced by less ideological newsmen, who meekly accepted the U.S. Army's decree that henceforth the overseas OWI would devote itself to psychological warfare against the enemy, under military direction.[41]

In the war within the war, the New Dealers were suffering catastrophic defeats. They had been routed from the agency in which they had pictured themselves controlling the ideas of the global conflict. Congress had abolished or gutted many other agencies that they had created in their 1930s glory days. Simultaneously, in the first disastrous seven months of 1943, the man who had become the New Deal's chief spokesman, Vice President Henry Wallace, was stripped of his power and publicly humiliated by Franklin D. Roosevelt.

9

FALL OF A PROPHET

Throughout the winter and spring of 1943, Henry Wallace and his chief lieutenant on the Board of Economic Warfare, Milo Perkins, waged an increasingly bitter war with Jesse Jones, secretary of commerce and head of the Reconstruction Finance Corporation. They quarreled repeatedly over the pace of Jones's response to requests for money for BEW purchases and programs, and occasionally over the nature of the programs themselves. When the State Department dragged its feet on issuing passports to BEW administrators assigned overseas, Perkins and Wallace saw a conspiracy between Jones and his fellow conservative Cordell Hull.

Wallace sought FDR's backing in this growing feud. In a conversation at the end of 1942, the vice president had warned the president that the nation's liberals saw the conflict as a symbolic clash between the New Deal and its conservative foes. It was becoming a test of the president's commitment to liberalism. Wallace went away thinking the president wholeheartedly supported him—an error that many people made after a talk with FDR.[1]

Wallace did not seem to appreciate what a formidable opponent he was taking on. FDR's friendship with Jones went back to World War I days, when Jones first entered government service. During the 1920s he had remained a good friend of both Roosevelt and the Democratic Party. In 1928, he personally anted up $200,000 to fund the Democratic National Convention in Houston, and contributed $25,000 to New York Governor Al Smith's cash-short presidential campaign. Behind the scenes, Jones often used his conservative clout to help labor unions get a better deal from their corporate antagonists. "All the bankers depended on him," said Isidore Lubin, head of the Bureau of Labor Statistics. In a labor dispute Jones would call a banker who had influence with the corporation and urge him to prod the executives into settling with the union.[2]

Jones had also done FDR some significant personal favors, at one point loaning money to G. Hall Roosevelt, Eleanor's alcoholic, frequently bankrupt brother, and another time rescuing the president's son Elliott from severe financial embarrassment in Texas when his radio station went bust to the tune of $200,000. Throughout the 1930s, Jones had been a frequent White House guest at poker parties and Potomac cruises. Although the president was occasionally irritated by Jones's determination to do things his way at the RFC—FDR sometimes referred to him as "Jesus H. Jones"—there was a long history of loyalty and friendship on which the Houston millionaire could draw. Add to this White House rapport Jones's clout with Congress, as head of the Reconstruction Finance Corporation and the web of other agencies the RFC funded, and you had a larger than life-sized figure with whom few Washington insiders wanted to tangle.[3]

II

Compounding Wallace's potential peril was Milo Perkins's tendency to extreme opinions. The executive director of the BEW was convinced, he told Wallace, that the big corporations were moving toward "monopolizing the nation in the most extraordinary way that the world has ever seen." Thanks to their common fascination with mystic spirituality and their joint fondness for soaring idealism, Perkins's influence on Wallace was large. One observer said it was often hard to tell which of them was initiating the policies they backed.

Surprisingly, Perkins was also a very tough, able administrator—the best in the New Deal, according to one knowledgeable man's opinion. During his tour in the Agriculture Department, he had created the federal food stamp program and the federal school lunch program and pushed them into national agendas. But he had ended his usefulness in that department when he wrote a fiery letter to the mild-mannered secretary of agriculture, Claude Wickard, calling him an incompetent useless tool of the conservative farmers' lobby, the Farm Bureau.[4]

Wallace had rescued Perkins with a transfer to the Board of Economic Warfare, whose potential for doing good stirred new excitement in his zealot's soul. Like Wallace, he saw the BEW as an opportunity to begin expanding the New Deal to the rest of the world, along with providing vitally needed raw materials for the war effort. At the BEW, Perkins continued to wield a sharp tongue. After several clashes with the State Department over the BEW's determination to play social engineer in foreign countries, he began calling Secretary of State Cordell Hull "an old fuddy-duddy"—not a good idea in a city where Hull was popular with many people and political gossip was a staple of everyday conversation. Perkins also managed to insult Sumner Welles in a 1941 exchange that left the under secretary of state in a permanent rage at him.

At the many meetings between the BEW and the Reconstruction Finance Corporation, Perkins was equally brisk with Jesse Jones, frequently reminding his fellow Texan that the BEW had an executive order from the president giving them the power to make any and all purchase decisions, and brusquely demanding an end to RFC foot-dragging on delivering the cash. The moment Wallace procured FDR's executive order giving BEW the power to close foreign deals, Perkins issued "Directive No. 1" to all agencies and departments involved in foreign economic affairs, declaring that BEW would tolerate no contract unless it was negotiated by them. BEW agents, he announced, would soon be dispatched overseas to take charge of everything in sight. Jesse Jones protested that his people were in the midst of negotiating at least a hundred deals that would come to an abrupt halt if Directive No. 1 was implemented.[5]

III

The BEW and the Jones empire clashed head-on about the rubber shortage. After the public relations debacle of the Roosevelt-Ickes plan to solve the problem by collecting used rubber, Jones favored pouring billions into synthetic rubber plants. Wallace and Perkins objected because they saw a plot by Jones and his friends in the big oil companies to build an industry at government expense and then sell it to the oilmen at bargain rates after the war.

The BEW leaders also wanted to use rubber procurement to advance their New Deal for the world. Over the objections of Jones's men, the BEW launched a program in Haiti to extract rubber from the cryptostegia plant, a dubious source, according to many scientists. Soon a 100,000-acre plantation was in existence, financed by 5 million American dollars. There was talk of converting the plantation into a cooperative run by the workers after the war, raising the island's living standards. But no one had bothered to figure out how to extract the rubber from the plant's leaves mechanically, slowing the business to the tempo of the preindustrial age. Cryptostegia also turned out to be vulnerable to numerous diseases that killed it before it got to the point of producing rubber.[6]

An even bigger effort, involving many more millions, went into the Amazon River Valley project. The statistics were staggering. Wallace was told it would take 40,000 workers, who would bring with them as many as 200,000 family members, to produce 20,000 tons of rubber a year. These people would have to survive appalling conditions in the jungle, not to mention their already bad health because of endemic malnutrition and poor sanitation. Wallace and Perkins undertook to tackle all these problems simultaneously, shipping tons of food and medicine and sanitary equipment to Brazil. RFC complaints of vast expenditures were echoed by the U.S. Army, who wanted to know why they were being told to feed, clothe, and sanitize Brazilians while fighting a global war. Despite these immense efforts, a U.S. government report concluded: "The failure of the rubber program in Brazil is not a matter of dispute."[7]

IV

At the end of 1942, Jesse Jones testified at a Senate hearing requesting extra funds—no less than $5 billion—for the Reconstruction Finance Corporation. He told the senators that not a little of this cash was needed because Milo Perkins was spending money in squandiferous amounts, and no one could or would restrain him because he had an executive order from the president making him the final authority on his murky overseas dealings.

Buoyed by the anti–New Deal outcome of the 1942 elections, the solons were suddenly awake and agog. Senator Charles Tobey of New Hampshire asked Jones to explain why the BEW was spending millions to buy natural rubber abroad when the United States had the scientific know-how and the economic muscle to build synthetic rubber plants and make the nation immune to any future need to ransack the jungles of the Amazon in search of rubber trees. Jones replied that he had always favored synthetic rubber (not entirely true) but Vice President Wallace and his spendthrift right-hand man, Perkins, had overruled him because they wanted to ship American dollars abroad in pursuit of their vision of the century of the common man.[8]

The goal of Jones's testimony became clearer and clearer: he wanted the executive order empowering the BEW to make overseas deals rescinded. The vice president demanded the right to defend the BEW and the Democratic majority leader, Senator Alben Barkley of Kentucky, easily obtained a hearing for him. Wallace strove to dispel the idea that Milo Perkins was in complete charge of the BEW, reducing his boss to the status of a bystander. He argued vehemently that a repeal of the executive order would pose a serious danger to the war effort, because the RFC had demonstrated it was incapable of making the swift and admittedly expensive decisions that characterized the BEW's performance. Perkins followed his leader with a scathing attack on the RFC's failure to perform at a level that the national emergency demanded.

Wallace and Perkins also replied to Jones's congressional foray with a preemptive strike at the bureaucratic level. The president had sent letters to all heads of departments and agencies, urging them to eliminate superfluous projects and programs and study their relationships with other government operations to reduce duplication of effort. FDR was reacting to congressional critics who had made electoral hay lampooning his haphazard style of governance.

Prodded by Perkins, Wallace seized on this presidential letter and issued Directive No. 5, which transferred most of Jones's various loan agencies to BEW control, leaving him only the RFC to function as a mere money supplier, on demand. The move left Jones and his lieutenants predictably outraged and recalcitrant to the point of open defiance.[9]

V

With war more or less declared between the BEW and Jones's financial empire, Wallace departed on a trip to South America. The BEW had spent over $600,000,000 in that part of the world during the previous year—evidence that Jesse Jones's foot-dragging was not quite as ruinous as Milo Perkins claimed. Latin-American public officials and businessmen rolled out red carpets or their equivalents wherever the vice president appeared. In Costa Rica, free trains brought workers and peasants from all parts of the country to the capital, San Jose. In Quito, capital of Ecuador, workers were ordered to join the welcoming parade or else.

Wallace added to the warmth of his reception by visiting public markets and mingling with ordinary people to find out how they were living. He spoke fluent Spanish and his folksy style won him admiration from right and left. He was showered with flowers in Bolivia and wildly applauded by a huge crowd in Lima, Peru. Drew Pearson claimed that no one had received such adulation anywhere in the world since Charles Lindbergh flew the Atlantic in 1927.[10]

Wallace returned to the United States more than ever convinced that he had been singled out by the spiritual forces that presided over history to create a New Deal for the world. He was determined, as he told the Costa Rican congress, "to make freedom from want a reality on earth." He saw his and Milo Perkins's leadership of the BEW as the vanguard of a movement to share America's wealth and productivity with the poor and oppressed everywhere. Imagine his fury when he came home from this triumphant tour to discover Jesse Jones and his friends in Congress were again on the attack, determined to destroy the Board of Economic Warfare.[11]

By this time, the BEW had become a formidable enterprise, employing over 3,000 people in Washington, in a field office in New York City, and in overseas operations in Central and South America and Africa. Wallace's and Perkins's anxiety to protect this power base had been evident from the start. When Martin Dies attacked the BEW for harboring left-wingers and a philosopher of nudism in 1942, Wallace had indignantly denounced the assault for the benefit of the newspapers and enlisted FDR's support. Behind the scenes Perkins axed the nudist, one Maurice Parmalee, in very short order and fired another ideologically unsound man virtually at the request of a congressman on the House Un-American Activities committee.[12]

The renewed attack began on June 4, 1943, when one of Jesse Jones's Senate allies, Kenneth McKellar of Tennessee, presided at a hearing on BEW's funding request for the next fiscal year. Milo Perkins was in the witness chair. McKellar asked him how he justified spending such huge sums of money overseas without asking Congress for so much as a by-your-leave. There should be some sort of congressional control over the BEW, McKellar thundered.

For the rest of the month, other conservative senators and congressmen used the BEW for verbal target practice. Jesse Jones was called to testify and artfully denigrated Perkins and his wasteful projects. His right-hand man, fellow Texan Will Clayton, who disliked Perkins with the same vehemence, told Congress that everything the BEW was doing could be done better by the RFC, for less money.

An anxious Wallace warned FDR that Congress, egged on by Jones, was threatening to torpedo the BEW. But the vice president refused to compromise with Jones. When the RFC chairman intimated he would sign a truce if Wallace withdrew Directive

No. 5, returning the subsidiary loan agencies to Jones's control, Wallace stonily replied: "Complete responsibility for all foreign development and procurement work . . . rests with the BEW and as far as we are concerned, it is going to stay there."

In the midst of this escalating brawl, Milo Perkins suffered an awful tragedy. His eighteen-year-old son, George Perkins, in training as a marine pilot, was killed in a crash. A few years earlier, Perkins's other son had died in a railroad mishap. The distraught BEW director began referring to a letter he had received from his marine son, urging his father to "stay in and slug" on the home front, whatever happened to him in combat. Perkins told a fellow New Dealer: "Jesse didn't wait one week after my boy died until he went up on the Hill and told [those] goddamn lies!" For Perkins the quarrel had acquired Armageddon overtones.[13]

VI

In the BEW files sat a twenty-eight-page memorandum that Perkins had assembled to demolish Jones and his entourage once and for all. Knowing the president had issued a strong statement against public quarrels between his appointees, Wallace had hesitated to release it. But the drumfire of criticism of the BEW in Congress and in the press slowly changed the vice president's mind. Milo Perkins, even more convinced of a conservative plot, urged him to strike back.

On June 29, 1943, against his better judgment, Wallace released this missive to the press. It listed all sorts of derelictions by the RFC and other Jones agencies, making it sound as if they were sabotaging the war effort. One of the nastiest charges was the claim that RFC foot-dragging had crippled the stockpiling of quinine, when General Douglas MacArthur was frantically demanding more of the malaria-fighting drug for his troops in the South Pacific.

Jesse Jones blasted back with predictable fury. He said Wallace's assault was "filled with malice and mis-statements." He intended to answer the charges in detail and, more important, to call for a congressional investigation to determine who was lying. An appalled Roosevelt, deeply involved in plans for the imminent invasion of Sicily, asked former senator Jimmy Byrnes of South Carolina to resolve the dispute. FDR had appointed Byrnes head of the Office of War Mobilization, making him, in newspaper parlance, assistant president for the home front.[14]

VII

Byrnes wrote Wallace a terse letter, stating that it was his duty "to resolve and determine controversies between agencies and departments" and requesting that he and Jesse Jones see him in his East Wing White House office that same day. Wallace arrived at Byrnes's office in a truculent frame of mind. Perhaps he suspected Byrnes would side with his fellow southerner. Before Byrnes could get to the BEW-RFC quarrel, Wallace informed him that BEW lawyers maintained that the executive order setting up the OWM did not give Byrnes any authority over foreign affairs.[15]

This was hardly the voice of sweet reasonableness. Wallace was telling Byrnes he wanted to deal with the president on this matter. He continued in the same unpleasant vein, saying he would not "insist" that Byrnes take back his letter. "But I wanted him to know that I would have been glad to come over in response to a phone call. I also wanted him to know that if he felt he had jurisdiction in this field, he should have gotten into the problem long before this."[16]

As with so many other matters political, Wallace simply did not get it. He seemed to have no awareness that Byrnes, with his office in the White House, might be acting on the president's orders. He apparently thought the OWM boss had entered the quarrel on his own authority.

Wallace's behavior did not improve when Jesse Jones arrived. He told Jones he had read in the *New York Daily News* that Jones was going to punch him out. "Is that true, Jesse? Are you going to hit me?" he asked. At sixty-seven, the paunchy Jones was unlikely to assault the fifty-five-year-old Wallace, a physical fitness fanatic. Jones did not shy away from verbal abuse, however. He accused Wallace of calling him a traitor in his press release, something he would not tolerate.

Jimmy Byrnes asked Wallace if he was willing to make a public statement that Jones was not a traitor. Wallace denied calling the financier a traitor but stonily declined to say so in public. "I am sure there is no statement which I can make that would be satisfactory to Jesse," he said. That may have been true, but, again, Wallace did not seem to realize that he as well as Jones was in serious political peril.[17]

The three men wrangled over Wallace's contention that everything Senator McKellar said against the BEW had been supplied to him by Jones. As an ex-senator, Byrnes had listened to McKellar's rantings on various topics for years; he told Wallace he was being silly to take the Tennessean seriously. Wallace said he wanted a constructive solution to the problem of funding the BEW but he also wanted a promise from Jones that he and his operatives would not reopen their offensive against the agency from Capitol Hill. Jones claimed his people had done nothing to ignite these attacks. Wallace virtually scoffed in his face.

With mounting bitterness, Jones told Wallace he knew Milo Perkins was the real author of the twenty-eight-page missive. It was proof that Milo was out to destroy him. The attack, Jones roared, "was not Christian." Maybe he did not go to church as often as Wallace but he knew that Milo's smear was "not a Christian act." Turning to Jimmy Byrnes, Jones asked why he should be singled out in this way. He had worked hard for the president on Capitol Hill. Byrnes emphatically agreed that Jones had been very helpful on several recent congressional votes.

Again Wallace did not get the message. He insisted on an agreement that would let him go to Congress and get funding for the BEW's procurement programs by direct appropriation, making him and Milo Perkins totally independent of Jones and the RFC. Byrnes reluctantly agreed to let him try it.

Jones departed in a fury. Wallace told Byrnes he would accept any statement of how they had resolved the conflict that the assistant president wanted to issue. Byrnes wrote it out in longhand and Wallace took it back to Milo Perkins, who found several things wrong with it. Making these changes required more telephone negotiations, which could not have charmed the overworked Byrnes. The assistant president suddenly suggested a change of his own: where Wallace had wanted "Mr. Jones agreed," Byrnes wanted, "Mr. Jones did not object" to the decision to seek direct funding from Congress.

The reason for this change became all too apparent later in the day. As Wallace ruefully noted in his diary, "While Mr. Jones did not object between 5 and 6 on June 30, he did object most strenuously by 10:30 that night." At that hour, Jones released a statement denouncing the plan to make the BEW independent and calling Wallace's accusation that he had hindered the war effort "a dastardly charge." Jones reiterated his demand for a congressional investigation, which he was confident would sink Wallace's demand for direct BEW funding. Newspapers and radio reporters rushed to publicize this public brawl between two of the most powerful men in Washington, D.C. Over the July 4 holiday, the Jones camp prepared a thirty-page refutation of the Wallace twenty-eight-page assault, turning the quarrel into a media conflagration all over again.[18]

VIII

On July 5, Milo Perkins issued a biting one-page reply to Jones's assault, for which Wallace congratulated him. But he added in his diary that Milo had released it without his prior approval. Wallace also noted somewhat anxiously that Elmer Davis of the OWI had "called him [Perkins] on the carpet" about it and Perkins had defied the already badly bruised information chief. At least Wallace seemed aware that another major player was turning against them. Consumed by grief and righteousness, Perkins remained oblivious, and Wallace seemed unable to control him.

Jimmy Byrnes made his attitude extremely clear in a letter to Wallace and Jones on July 6, 1943. He warned them that their dispute was liable to "hurt the war effort and lessen the confidence of the people in their government." He wanted no further statements made by either side, unless they were connected to a congressional investigation. A Republican congressman had already asked the House Rules Committee to hold hearings on the feud.

At the BEW, Milo Perkins revealed he was rapidly losing touch with reality. He urged Wallace to call the White House to head off the congressional investigation. It would be too political—meaning Jesse Jones would have all the advantages. Instead, he suggested Wallace persuade FDR to appoint some prestigious neutral party, such as former Chief Justice Charles Evans Hughes, a Republican, to conduct an impartial public hearing. Wallace called Roosevelt, who was escaping the Washington summer heat at Hyde Park. The president said he thought Hughes was a wonderful suggestion and told Wallace to talk it over with Jimmy Byrnes.

The vice president told the assistant president about Milo Perkins's suggestion and added they were not trying to head off the congressional investigation. The BEW had nothing to hide. Byrnes replied that he now opposed this idea. Any investigation that would give anti-Roosevelt congressman such as Hamilton

Fish, Martin Dies, Eugene Cox of Georgia and the like a chance to sling barbs and arrows would be "horrible." Byrnes called Sam Rayburn, the Speaker of the House, who agreed to quash any and all inquiries. But Wallace, still not getting it, told Byrnes he would like an impartial hearing by "any fair committee."[19]

IX

The feud subsided for a week. At a cabinet meeting on July 9, the vice president noted that "the President said absolutely nothing about the unpleasantness between Jesse and myself."

But Wallace could not let lie the murderous sleeping dog he and Jones had created. A *Chicago Sun-Times* reporter sent him a letter, passing on a particularly nasty rumor about Jesse Jones. It seems that Jones boasted in private that he had a prewar letter from FDR telling him to hold back on building up a stockpile of rubber because Winston Churchill had assured him there was no chance of the British losing Malaya. "This was being cited in Texas circles as evidence 1. of Jesse's great devotion to the president—he had taken a cruel public beating in order to shield his boss and 2. as proof that if FDR knew what was good for him, he wouldn't tangle with Jesse on the stockpile issue," Wallace told his diary.[20]

With incredible naïveté, on July 12, Wallace sent this letter to the president, along with a renewed request for a congressional investigation into the BEW-RFC feud. "We have heard similar stories [about Jones] from many quarters," he wrote. "The sum and substance of them is that Mr. Jones has been very careful to get your initials on all questionable programs so that he can escape personal responsibility if any serious investigations of RFC activities is ever undertaken by Congress."

On July 13, Milo Perkins summoned the entire Washington staff of the BEW to a meeting in the auditorium of the Labor Department building. The ostensible reason was to express his gratitude for a fund the men and women had raised to buy an ambulance in memory of Perkins's dead son, George. The combination of a Washington heat wave (the temperature had hovered near 100 for weeks), his lost son, and Perkins's ongoing hatred of Jesse Jones proved to be an explosive combination. His talk went from effusive gratitude to a savage attack on Jones. He told his applauding listeners that Wallace's June 29 assault was "what any red blooded American" would have done when he turned over a rock and saw "slimy things crawling" beneath it. None of these devoted BEWers realized they were applauding the extinction of their agency and their jobs [21].

Two days later, the *Washington Times-Herald* published an article, "Milo the Messiah of Mystic Washington." The reporter claimed the entire story had been sent to her by a mysterious messenger who told her that Milo Perkins had once more attacked Jesse Jones. The reporter claimed she felt sorry for Jones, because he was a mere worldly man to whom "the mysteries of the ancient East" were foreign. Whereas Henry Wallace had as a wielder of the assassin's dagger none other than Milo Perkins, "high priest of his own mystic cult."

The reporter filled in her readers with a fairly accurate account of Perkins's rise to a bishopric in the Liberal Catholic Church. She told how each Sunday the true believers had climbed a ladder to Perkins's Houston attic. The ladder was then retracted, making them feel they had ascended into heaven. The reporter had also gotten her hands on a letter that Perkins had written to Wallace in the early 1930s, asking for a government job so he could help save the world.

Under the article was a large cartoon, showing Jesse Jones staring up into an attic where Henry Wallace in a witch's hat was stirring a cauldron of mystic brew. Around him lay exotic books with titles such as *Exorcism*. In the haze from the cauldron, Milo

Perkins hovered like a deranged angel, beaming half-baked thoughts into Wallace's willing head.[22]

That same day, Franklin D. Roosevelt issued an executive order abolishing the Board of Economic Warfare. In his diary, Wallace attributed the decision to White House insiders, in particular Harry Hopkins, Sam Rosenman, and Jimmy Byrnes, all, he theorized, extremely jealous of him. (Hopkins did, in fact, dislike Wallace intensely.) But any objective student of the account can readily conclude FDR needed no persuasion. A man who said he wanted a congressional investigation and then suggested that Jesse Jones might spring documents ruinous to Roosevelt's presidency was clearly no longer to be trusted with power or responsibility.[23]

X

To soften the blow, the president stripped the RFC and Jesse Jones's other loan agencies of all responsibility for overseas raw materials procurement and regrouped them under a new agency, the Office of Foreign Economic Warfare. FDR put Leo T. Crowley, the man who had helped him silence radio priest Charles Coughlin, in charge of the operation. Crowley worked for Jones and most of the American press saw the appointment as a victory for the RFC chairman, who was quick to agree with them. Jones issued a statement congratulating the president for his "determination to have harmony and cooperation between government officials in the war effort."[24]

Leo Crowley visited the vice president five days later and surprised him by expressing considerable sympathy for his fate. Crowley said Roosevelt had given Wallace "an utterly raw deal." The Wisconsin businessman was unhappy because FDR had told him that Milo Perkins had to go. But in a press conference a few days later, Roosevelt piously informed reporters that it was up to

Crowley to decide Milo's fate. Perkins solved the problem by re-signing before Crowley wielded the ax. In a contrite letter to Wallace, the former bishop obliquely confessed his responsibility for their mutual disaster: "90 percent of the scum inside me has boiled to the surface," he wrote.[25]

Wallace claimed he was not in the least bitter at Roosevelt for his dismissal. He could not say the same for Perkins or another top BEW executive, former New York businessman Morris Rosenthal. They were exceedingly bitter. Milo felt the president had "dealt a blow to the memory of his son," Wallace noted in his diary.

The vice president went ahead with other activities, such as a major speech scheduled for later in the summer in Detroit. He sent a copy to Roosevelt, who read it carefully and made several minor changes in his own handwriting. Wallace confided to his diary that this was FDR's "usual technique of being very nice to a person he has just gotten through hitting." But he added with stubborn faith that it also suggested FDR was "really fond of me except when stimulated by the palace guard to move in other directions."

However, the vice president could not resist adding to his diary the glum conclusion of BEW's Morris Rosenthal. "He feels he [FDR] has betrayed the cause of liberalism."[26]

Watching from the sidelines at the British embassy, philosopher Isaiah Berlin reported that Harry Hopkins had sadly remarked to a member of the embassy staff, "The New Deal has once again been sacrificed to the war effort."[27]

10

WHAT'D YOU GET, BLACK BOY?

The New Dealers' dream of converting the war into a moral crusade at home and abroad soon received other brutal shocks. One of the most jarring occurred in Detroit in the same overheated week in June of 1943 when Henry Wallace, Milo Perkins, and Jesse Jones were lurching toward the climax of their confrontation. Between 1940 and 1943, Detroit's booming war plants had attracted a half-million newcomers, many from the chronically depressed hills and valleys of Appalachia. Some 60,000 African-Americans flooded up from the South, attracted by the higher pay and the possibility of achieving a better life than the segregated Land of Cotton offered them.[1]

These two groups made for an explosive mix in a city where race relations had never been good. In the 1920s, attempts by blacks to move into white neighborhoods had met with riotous resistance. As Detroit's wartime population soared, housing became a critical issue between the races. In the black ghetto, entire families were living in one room, with no indoor toilet facilities. Black infant mortality and tuberculosis death rates were five times Detroit's white rate. A ferocious fight erupted over the status of two hundred (out of a proposed thousand) houses built for blacks by the United States Housing Authority in a part of the city close to Hamtramck, a heavily Polish-American suburb.

After numerous local protests, a Polish-American congressman attacked the "Sojourner Truth Homes" (named for a nineteenth-century black woman activist) on the floor of Congress, declaring that Communists were in control of selecting the tenants. This agitation brought two federal housing officials to Detroit, along with members of the House Committee on Public Buildings. Shortly after Pearl Harbor, the Federal Housing Agency and the new Coordinator of Defense Housing announced the Sojourner Truth Homes would be for whites only.

Black Detroit seethed. A federal housing official told presidential assistant Marvin McIntyre that the agency "now" followed local recommendations, even if they clashed head-on with racial equality. McIntyre blandly agreed, telling black protestors that it was important to avoid "an open fight" lest it interfere with the war effort.

The blacks declined to put the war effort first. Their strenuous protests finally persuaded the Detroit Housing Commission to change its mind. The local bureaucrats were also prodded by a liberal southerner in the Federal Housing Agency. In February 1942, twenty black families tried to move into the Sojourner Truth Homes. They were blocked by a mob of whites who pelted them with curses and stones. The police managed to restore order but declined to take responsibility for the blacks' safety. For the next two months, protests and counterprotests roiled the city.

Not until April were the blacks able to occupy the houses, backed by a regiment of Michigan militia.[2]

For the next year, Detroit was a racial tinderbox waiting for a match. Name-calling and fistfights regularly erupted in the high schools and on streets that bordered black districts. Local defense plants were disrupted by strikes when blacks were promoted to desirable jobs. "I'd rather see Hitler and Hirohito win than work next to a nigger," roared one agitator over a loudspeaker during one of these walkouts.[3]

On Sunday, June 20, 1943, the city was sweltering along with Washington, D.C., and most of the eastern half of the nation in a 100 degree heat wave. Thousands of families, a high percentage of them black, sought relief on leafy Belle Isle, an island in the Detroit River. During the day, fights erupted between groups of blacks and whites, worsening the already ugly mood on both sides.

As the crowd jammed the bridge on the way back to the steaming city at the end of the day, a lot of jostling was inevitable. A jostle judged too hard to be accidental led to a punch and as women and children screamed, a roaring cursing mob of white and black young men began slugging it out. The brawl swirled from the bridge into Paradise Valley, the city's downtown black section, and soon became a major riot. Shop windows were smashed and looted, cars were overturned, guns and ammunition stolen from pawnshops. Snipers began firing at random human targets.

The outnumbered police, their ranks thinned by the draft, tried to contain the trouble in Paradise Valley. They used tear gas and clubs to keep blacks inside and whites outside the roped-off streets. But other inflamed whites roamed downtown and caught blacks driving home from their jobs in war plants. Many were beaten and their cars burned. Other rioters burned black homes.

Around 2:00 A.M. a rumor that a black woman and her baby had been thrown off the Belle Isle bridge by white rioters inflamed Paradise Valley. The upheaval regained its fury as blacks roamed the streets beating up any white unlucky enough to wander within their reach. A white milkman and a doctor making a house call were killed.

By 10:00 A.M. a huge white mob was in action, attacking and often killing any black they caught. By the time 6,000 federal troops arrived to bolster the overwhelmed Detroit police force, 26 blacks and 9 whites had been killed and almost 700 people had been injured. Hospital emergency rooms were jammed with battered bleeding casualties.[4]

II

Like sparks from a bonfire, the story of the riot floated across America, igniting similar upheavals in other cities. In Beaumont, Texas, 3,000 workers abandoned their tools at the Pennsylvania Shipyard and stormed into the city to surround the jail, where a black man was supposedly being held on a charge of raping a white woman. Told that there was no such man, the rioters rumbled through the city's two black districts, beating up anyone they caught on the streets, smashing windows in cars and houses. At the county courthouse, they encountered Sheriff Bill Richardson, hefting a tommy gun. "Give us the nigger raper!" they screamed. Sheriff Richardson, a rangy six-footer, again told them there was no such man and urged them to resume building ships to beat the Germans and the Japanese. The rioters drifted back to the shipyard, leaving one black and one white man dead and fifty injured.[5]

On August 1, 1943, the nation's most famous black ghetto, New York's Harlem, erupted, when a rumor swept the streets that a black soldier had been shot by a white policeman. In this upheaval, no whites were attacked by the black mobs, but a tremendous amount of looting and burning took place. Mayor

Fiorello La Guardia drove through the littered streets, urging people to return to their homes. He ordered his policemen to use their weapons only in self-defense and deputized 1,500 African-American leaders, who patrolled the streets trying to restore order. In spite of the mayor's attempt to restrain unnecessary violence, six blacks died and three hundred needed hospital treatment. Most of Harlem's residents, reported the *Amsterdam News*, secretly condoned the outburst as perhaps the only way to tell white Americans that "Negroes must be made to feel they are a part of this country."[6]

III

Those words revealed the hollowness of the New Deal's commitment to racial equality. Fearful of offending the southern Democrats on an issue that cut to the bone of their daily lives, Roosevelt had relied on lip service, charm, and evasion to maintain a racial status quo. Although Negroes had enlisted in the U.S. Army at a rate well above the white population, they found themselves consigned to segregated construction battalions. Secretary of War Henry Stimson added insult to this injury by decreeing that the officers in these units would be white. "Leadership is not embedded in the Negro race yet," Stimson said. Virginia-born General George C. Marshall, the army's chief of staff, was inclined to agree.[7]

Early in 1941, A. Philip Randolph, the leader of the Brotherhood of Sleeping Car Porters, the biggest black union in the country, had threatened Roosevelt with a march on Washington if he did not take practical steps to give blacks some hope of escaping the shadow world of segregation, with its penumbra of implied inferiority. After some very tense negotiations, Roosevelt created the Fair Employment Practices Commission (FEPC) to enforce a presidential decree barring discrimination in defense industries and the U.S. government's workforce. But segregation remained the policy of the armed forces, and not a few blacks had grave doubts about how much power the FEPC really had to redress civilian grievances.

In and out of Congress, the conservatives of the South immediately claimed the riots of 1943 proved the folly of the New Deal's halfhearted push for racial equality. One southern paper singled out Eleanor Roosevelt for primary responsibility, declaring, "It is blood upon your hands, Mrs. Roosevelt." Others attacked the Fair Employment Practices Commission. One southern congressmen accused the FEPC of "crazy politics." By this he meant trying to mix races on the job. Martin Dies announced he planned to investigate the Detroit riots and root out the undoubted Communist role in the carnage.[8]

Walter White, head of the National Association for the Advancement of Colored People, begged President Roosevelt to say something on behalf of black Americans. Jonathan Daniels, an aide assigned to racial issues, urged a "statement of idealism." From the White House came nothing but silence, as FDR's pollsters tried to assess the impact of the riots on the white majority. After the terrific beating the New Deal had taken in the first six months of 1943 from the southern Democrats and Republicans on Capitol Hill, FDR was in no mood for moral heroics. He was tilting toward the realist pole of the great dichotomy. Talking with Senator Bennett Clark of Missouri, a pre–Pearl Harbor isolationist, Roosevelt reportedly said: "I have had my experience with the professors, the enthusiastic young men, the idealists. They mean well but they are not practical. I am through with them."[9]

Instead of responding to Walter White, Roosevelt wrote a tepid reply to Philip Murray, the president of the CIO, who had urged him to undertake a massive educational assault on race prejudice, using the army, the navy, the OWI, and other government agencies. "I join you," FDR wrote, "in condemning mob violence, whatever form it takes and whoever its victims." This umbrella denunciation enabled the president to express his disapproval of riots in Los Angeles that had preceded the Detroit explosion. There the targets of white hostility had been Mexican-Americans, particularly young men who favored the heavily draped coats and pegged pants of the "zoot suit" style. The president did nothing to implement the government crusade that Murray implored him to launch.

In the magazine the *Crisis*, a young black poet named Pauli Murray published a reply to the president. It did not win her any friends in the White House, but it summed up what a lot of blacks were feeling.

> *What'd you get, black boy*
> *When they knocked you down in the gutter*
> *And they kicked your teeth out,*
> *And they broke your skull with clubs*
> *And they bashed your stomach in?*
> *What'd you get when the police shot you in the back,*
> *And they chained you to the beds*
> *While they wiped the blood off?*
> *What'd you get when you cried out to the Top Man?*
> *When you called the man next to God, as you thought*
> *And you asked him to speak out to save you?*
> *What'd the Top Man say, black boy?*
> *Mr. Roosevelt regrets . . .* [10]

IV

National unity seemed to be evaporating everywhere in that quarrelsome spring and summer of 1943. Another major discord erupted from a sector of the nation that the New Deal had assiduously cultivated for a decade: labor. In May, John L. Lewis, head of the United Mine Workers Union, pulled 530,000 miners out of the pits. The bulky Lewis was a figure of biblical dimensions, fond of thunderous quotations from the Old Testament. The founding father of the UMW, he had also created the Congress of Industrial Organizations to unionize the unskilled in the big corporations. Lewis became the CIO's first president. In 1936, he had put a half-million dollars of the UMW's treasury behind Roosevelt's run for a second term.

By 1943, the union leader hated Franklin D. Roosevelt as passionately as he had once adored him. In the late 1930s Roosevelt had declined to back the CIO in clashes with several major companies. Lewis decided FDR was a double-talking ingrate whose condemnation of economic royalists was political hot air. By 1940 Lewis was opposing a third term and FDR's interventionist foreign policy. Repudiated by other union leaders in the CIO, Lewis had resigned the presidency but retained control of the UMW, where his support bordered on fanaticism.

Lewis was demanding an additional two dollars a day for his miners—a pay raise likely to jump-start inflation—the bugaboo that had haunted the Roosevelt administration since the war began. In World War I, the inflation rate had been 100 percent and labor leaders like Lewis, whose organizing days went back to 1907, never forgot the way the soaring prices had devoured most of the extra dollars the war put in workers' pockets, while big corporations kept most of the stupendous profits they had made. So far, this war's inflation was barely a third of the first war's skyrocket, but it was enough to make workers restless.

Labor leaders nervously informed Roosevelt that Lewis's indifference to the administration's attempt to keep a ceiling on wages was very popular with the rank and file. Equally popular was Lewis's disregard of a December 23, 1941, no-strike pledge that FDR had extracted from the unions in return for a no-lockout promise from the corporations. That outburst of post–Pearl Harbor patriotism had long since cooled as inflation pressures mounted, in spite of the Office of Price Administration's war on gougers. "Discontent and unrest" were rising ominously in the factories, the labor leaders warned. They pointed to the Michigan chapter of the CIO, which had repudiated the no-strike pledge. In the spring of 1943, rubber workers in Akron, Ohio, machinists in San Francisco's shipyards, and assembly-line workers in Chrysler's huge Detroit tank plant had walked out. But none of these strikes caught the public's attention as much as the mine workers' walkout. A coal shortage threatened to bring steel production to a stop, cripple the railroads, and trigger massive layoffs.[11]

At the War Labor Board, the bureaucrats in charge of keeping workers and capitalists from each other's throats viewed Lewis's defiance in Götterdämmerung hues. If the miners' leader could defy no-strike pledges and wage guidelines, any union with similar muscle was going to hit the picket lines. It was not hard to imagine how the fighting men overseas would react to the news that the home front was being swamped by greed. The WLB wanted the president to defy Lewis and send in the army to force the miners to dig coal at gunpoint.

When Lewis first walked out in May 1943, FDR had asked Harold Ickes to negotiate with him. The attempt soon degenerated into name-calling. Lewis claimed Ickes had agreed to a deal and Ickes denied it. But Ickes opposed the WLB's draconian approach; he blamed the mine owners for most of the miners' grievances. The secretary of the interior warned the president "there are not enough jails in the country to hold these men."

Roosevelt privately called Lewis a psychopath, and told another visitor that he would gladly resign as president if Lewis would promise to commit suicide. The Justice Department was ordered to explore an indictment for tax evasion, but an investigation came up dry. The president was equally wary of appealing over Lewis's head to the miners' patriotism, sensing that their first loyalty was to their leader and the union.[12]

V

While the White House dithered, Congress acted. Lewis's tactics had ignited a wave of national fury against him—and the labor movement. Letters from servicemen showed a strong desire to sharpen their marksmanship on Lewis. Among civilians, a poll showed 87 percent had a low opinion of him. More than a dozen state legislatures had already passed laws restricting strikes and curbing the power of labor in other ways, such as banning political contributions by unions. The New Dealers saw their greatest political advantage, their role as advocates of the poor and the underpaid, evaporating in front of their dismayed eyes.

The White House watched helplessly as Senator Tom Connally of Texas pushed a bill through the upper house, giving the president power to take over any strikebound war plant or industry. The House of Representatives was nurturing a much tougher bill proposed by Congressman Howard Smith of Virginia. This version barred unions from giving money to politicians, required a secret ballot when voting on a strike, mandated a thirty-day cooling-off period for a strike, and threatened anyone who encouraged strikes in war plants with jail time. These ideas soon blended with the Senate measure to become the Smith-Connally bill, which was passed by huge majorities in both houses of Congress.[13]

Smith-Connally landed on Roosevelt's desk with a portentous thud. If FDR refused to sign it, he was going to outrage the huge majority of the citizens who saw it as John L. Lewis's comeuppance. If the president vetoed it, he looked as if he was afraid of the UMW boss—and playing labor's game, when most of the country was thoroughly tired of the New Deal's flirtation with economic democracy. Jimmy Byrnes told the president to sign it; southern Democratic congressmen had voted for it en masse. Secretary of War Stimson and Secretary of the Navy Knox, FDR's two Republican cabinet members, also urged a signature. Secretary of the Interior Harold Ickes, Secretary of Labor Frances Perkins, and several other charter New Dealers urged Roosevelt to veto it.[14]

For over a week, Roosevelt brooded and conferred with advisors. During this tense interim, he ordered Harold Ickes to take over the mines and tell the miners they were now working for Uncle Sam. They dribbled back reluctantly; about 50 percent stayed home. Finally, after nine and a half days of indecision, on June 25, 1943, Roosevelt vetoed the Smith-Connally bill, objecting primarily to the ban on labor's political contributions and the secret ballot for strikes, which he claimed would foment more, not fewer, walkouts. The decision reached Congress at 3:15 P.M. Eleven minutes later, the Senate overrode the veto, while servicemen packing the galleries cheered. An hour later the House followed the Senate's lead, 244–108. Liberals such as Claude Pepper of Florida, Carl Hatch of New Mexico and Lyndon Johnson of Texas voted with the majority, political survival overwhelming their usual loyalty to the president.

It was the first time a Roosevelt veto of a major bill had been overridden since 1936. Senator Robert Wagner of New York was so upset, he said he felt as if he were sitting in a "Reconstruction Congress." He was referring to the vengeance-hungry post–Civil War congress that had demonized President Andrew Johnson and destroyed Lincoln's dream of restoring national unity by reconciling the South with mild laws.[15]

The Champ had taken another haymaker. Was he down for the count? Eric Johnson, president of the U.S. Chamber of Commerce, obviously hoped so. He took the opportunity to deliver a slashing attack on the "knock-kneed dilly dallying" of the administration on the home front.[16]

VI

Undaunted by the conservative majority in Congress and his public repudiation by Roosevelt, Vice President Henry Wallace still saw himself as the torchbearer of the New Deal in the fractured Democratic Party and the nation. Wallace was scheduled to speak in Detroit on July 25. In the aftermath of the race riot and Congress's override of FDR's veto of the Smith-Connally bill, the vice president's appearance acquired national significance.

A sarcastic reporter asked Wallace if he agreed with a news magazine that had recently labeled him "the last New Dealer." Wallace coolly replied he did not think the conservatives were going to take over the Democratic Party. However, in a glimpse of what was blowing in the wind, Wallace dodged the label New Dealer, saying he preferred the phrase "the progressive element."[17]

The CIO was strong in Detroit and they turned out a crowd of 20,000 to hear Wallace, making no secret of their determination to label him their favorite politician. Wallace delivered a speech that had the crowd roaring approval again and again. His theme was Nazism, at home and abroad. He denounced the racism behind the recent riot, calling it a perversion of the democratic freedoms for which Americans were dying overseas. Mincing no words, he said those who "fan the fires of racial clashes" at home were "taking the first step toward Nazism." He had equally harsh words for those who attacked labor, calling them "midget Hitlers."[18]

Turning his attention to the postwar world, Wallace said the politicians had to be "more concerned with welfare politics and less with power politics, more attentive to equalizing the use of raw materials of nations than condoning the policies of grab and barter that freeze international markets." To create a "warproof world," Americans would have to devote themselves to eradicating deprivation at home and abroad. Then, throwing down the gauntlet to his critics, he said the isolationists, reactionaries, and imperialistic nationalists (read Henry Luce) in both parties were a form of "American Fascism."

Critical reaction was swift and savage. Harrison E. Spangler, chairman of the Republican Party, roared that Wallace had smeared the "twenty five million voters in America who are opposed to the New Deal." Alfred Landon of Kansas, the Republican presidential candidate in 1936, replied nationwide on NBC radio on July 31. Landon had already labeled Wallace a "mystic" Adolf Hitler in a February speech. He now seized on the American fascism remark to accuse the vice president of declaring a political civil war.

Landon asked his listeners a rhetorical question: "Who, then, are the real Fascists in American Life today?" He offered a plethora of evidence that it was the New Dealers, who never stopped maneuvering behind the scenes to reduce Americans to obedient helots in their elitist command economy. The Kansan said he feared American soldiers would return from foreign battlefields to discover New Deal fascism established on their home soil.[19]

The *New York Times*, among many others, was appalled by this exchange of ideological insults. They saw it rending national unity at a time when it was never more desperately needed. In an editorial, the *Times* rebuked Wallace for his "reckless accusations." Even some of Wallace's liberal backers had second thoughts, urging him to return to "decency and dignity." But other liberals hailed the address as a master stroke that had returned Wallace from the political graveyard and made him a leader of global proportions. Senator Joseph Guffey of Pennsylvania said he could hardly wait to renominate Wallace as vice president in 1944.[20]

VII

Wallace paid no attention to the *New York Times* or other critics. In September, he spoke in Chicago to the United Nations

Committee to Win the Peace. He launched another ferocious assault on isolationists, apparently oblivious to the way this tactic had backfired for the Democrats in 1942. But he spent most of his time damning economic royalists, the New Deal's target of opportunity when their recovery program fell apart in the late 1930s. According to Wallace, these elitists constituted a shadow government that parceled out the resources and markets of the world "so as to control production, prices, distribution and the very lifeblood of world industry." They had the final say on who was given permission "to produce, to buy and to sell."[21]

Still shadowboxing with Jesse Jones, Wallace claimed the nation's rubber shortage was caused by a secret agreement that Standard Oil of New Jersey had signed with I. G. Farben, the German petrochemical giant, in the 1930s, giving Farben the right to control the production of synthetic rubber and Standard Oil the exclusive right to make synthetic gasoline. Wallace implied that this agreement amounted to treason, because a decade later, the Americans got into a war with Japan and lost their access to natural rubber. It was also an oblique way of saying that Jones and his RFC circle were part of this greedy elite who controlled the world's economy. The choice before the American people, Wallace thundered, was "America First" or "Democracy First." America First led to "economic feudalism," an intolerable future for America and the rest of the postwar world.

This not very subtle attempt to resurrect and then smear America's biggest antiwar group continued Wallace's attack on the isolationists, a strategy that must have sent chills through Boss Ed Kelly's Chicago Democratic machine. (Wallace noted in his diary that Kelly was "strategically" out of town when he spoke.) For them and a growing number of other Democrats, Wallace was a liability, no matter how much praise he received in the *Nation* and the *New Republic*.

Wallace and his circle attempted to trump this reaction by embracing Franklin D. Roosevelt with almost blinding fervor. In Detroit, Wallace declared his total loyalty to the president, insisting he was "the symbol the world over of the dearest aspirations of the common man." He also said American fascists hated FDR because he had "stopped Washington from being a way station on the way to Wall Street." When he submitted his Chicago speech for FDR's approval, Wallace wrote: "If I know your heart, Mr. President, this speech, even though awkwardly stated, expresses in its broad principles either that which you have already said or that in which you have long had faith."[22]

FDR did not disagree with this appraisal. In fact, he went out of his way to ingratiate himself with Wallace after he fired him from the BEW and annihilated the agency. On July 28, he wrote him a letter telling him the Detroit speech was "splendid." He added that the "incident"—the imbroglio with Jones—"has not lessened my personal affection for you." In a postscript FDR commented on the uproar over the speech: "You drew blood from the Cave Dwellers!"[23]

Simultaneously, Wallace was listening to liberal friends such as William B. Herridge, the former Canadian minister to the U.S., who lived in Washington. Herridge told Wallace that Roosevelt was finished. "He thinks the President was a gallant figure in the early days of the New Deal but that he has never known what the economic thing was all about," Wallace confided to his diary. "At the present time he [the President] really represents the forces of reaction. Herridge wants me more and more to break loose from the President altogether."[24]

Other liberals sought out Wallace for advice and consolation. Elmer Davis of the OWI came moaning low that Secretary of State Cordell Hull now had complete control over the OWI's international branch and had ordered him not to publish anything with ideology in it. Hull thought the Democrats were going to lose in 1944 and he was trying to make the transition to Republican control as easy as possible. "It was important not to raise the hopes of foreign nations," he said. Davis had tried to get Roosevelt's help but was told that Hull was in charge and the president could do nothing. Wallace told the OWI chief he still thought FDR was "sound at heart" and he would "demonstrate at the right time in terms of action just where he stood."[25]

VIII

While Wallace was pursuing confrontational politics, on another part of the playing field Senator Harry S. Truman was doing the precise opposite. The Truman Committee continued to investigate the war effort, repeatedly turning up evidence that idealism was not always the driving force in the struggle against Nazism and Fascism. Wallace's diary has random entries about the unethical practices and monopolistic tendencies of American corporations such as Standard Oil of New Jersey. Truman could have supplied him with material for a thunderous denunciation every week. Like the vice president, Truman was troubled by the way the dollar-a-year men from the big corporations were making sure that their companies got most of the war contracts. But he chose to correct matters behind the scenes whenever possible and let the malefactors repent in private. His committee reports were submitted to Congress with a minimum of accusatory rhetoric.[26]

In a discussion of a steel shortage, the Truman Committee announced that German submarines had sunk 12 million tons of Allied shipping in 1942, leaving a 3 million ton deficit for the nation's straining shipyards to make up. The U.S. Navy, having stonewalled on the truth about the U-boat offensive along the East Coast, which accounted for a heavy percentage of these staggering losses, issued a furious denial. Secretary of the Navy Frank Knox sneered that the report was based on "common gossip."

Other politicians—Wallace in particular, who loved to issue attacks and rebuttals—would have plunged into a major brawl with Knox and the admirals. Instead, Truman asked one of the Republican members of the committee to warn Knox he was going to be called before the committee to settle the argument. Knox hastily issued a statement saying the figures were correct.[27]

Early in 1943, an investigation revealed almost incredible carelessness and corruption in the manufacture of aircraft engines by the Wright Aeronautical Corporation, a subsidiary of Curtiss-Wright, the second largest defense contractor after General Motors, with over $9 billion in government orders. Again, instead of going public, Truman held secret hearings. To his dismay, the army sent a squadron of generals and colonels who told lie after lie, claiming they never saw or even heard of a defective engine from Curtiss-Wright.

After compiling 1,286 pages of sworn testimony, Truman published a scathing report on the company's defective inspection procedures and malfunctioning engines. The Department of Justice went to court, using these facts to accuse Curtiss-Wright of massive malfeasance. The company spent freely from its $9 billion kitty to launch a ferocious attack on the Truman Committee. For a while even the *New York Times* was convinced that Truman was wrong.

Instead of battling it out in public, Truman sent the committee's chief counsel to the *Times* to tell them the truth. Under Secretary of War Robert Patterson, who had declared that the army air forces had never received a single defective engine from Curtiss-Wright, was invited to Senator Truman's office for a chat. The under secretary, who had tried to disband the committee after Pearl Harbor, soon admitted he was wrong about Curtiss-Wright. The press assaults on the Truman Committee ended a few days later.[28]

Truman had his own run-in with Jesse Jones when the committee began investigating the shortage of aluminum. Truman's investigators found that Jones's RFC had loaned ALCOA (the Aluminum Company of America) a huge sum to expand their production while permitting them to retain a virtual monopoly of the market. When Truman summoned Jones before the committee, Jesse played every trick in his repertoire of Capitol Hill influence to make Senator Truman back down. None of them worked and Jones was soon in the witness chair, humbly admitting that the Alcoa contract was a mistake and would be renegotiated. The exchange was courteous on both sides. Not a voice was raised, not a nasty name was called.[29]

In deep background, a third party helped reassure Jones that he had no fear of being pilloried in the newspapers for admitting a mistake. One of Truman's closest friends, Missouri banker John Snyder, was head of the Defense Plant Corporation, a key component of Jones's lending empire. A conservative Democrat, Snyder shared Jones's dislike for Henry Wallace's attack style of politics, and was equally skeptical about a New Deal for the world.

The senator from the Show-Me state was also unintimidated by the New Dealers who ran the alphabet soup agencies. When the chairman of the War Manpower Commission (WMC), Paul McNutt, demanded the right to draft workers and shift them from New York to California or Texas at his decree, Truman rose in the Senate to call the proposal unnecessary. To prove their point, the WMC's bureaucrats cited the North American Aviation plant in Dallas, Texas, which was supposedly short 13,000 workers. Truman sent investigators to the plant and found no such shortage existed. In fact, the plant had more workers than they could use and a lot of them were loafing while the executives scrambled for new orders. Mr. McNutt's worker draft bill went nowhere in the Senate.[30]

Truman's performance won him attention, even though he did not seek headlines. In March of 1943, *Time*, eating its snide words of dismissal a year earlier, put him on its cover and called him a "billion dollar watchdog." The *St. Louis Post Dispatch*, also eating its previous condemnations, declared Truman "one of the most useful and at the same time one of the most forthright and fearless" politicians in the country. An old Washington hand told *Time*: "There's only one thing that worries me more than the present state of the war effort. That's to think what it would be like by now without Truman." New Dealers liked the way Truman stood up to the generals and admirals. Moderates and conservatives liked the way he declined to kowtow to the New Dealers.[31]

In his quiet way Truman remained unafraid to place the blame for the messy war effort where it really lay. At one point, Republican Senator Arthur Vandenberg of Michigan had the following exchange with the Democrat from Missouri on the floor of the Senate.

> MR. VANDENBERG: *In other words, the Senator is now saying that the chief bottleneck which the defense program confronts is the lack of adequate organization and coordination in the administration of defense?*
>
> MR. TRUMAN: *That is exactly what the hearings before our committee will prove.*
>
> MR. VANDENBERG: *Who is responsible for that situation?*
>
> MR. TRUMAN: *There is only one place where the responsibility can be put.*
>
> MR. VANDENBERG: *Where is that—the White House?*
>
> MR. TRUMAN: *Yes sir.*
>
> MR. VANDENBERG: *I thank the Senator. (Laughter.)*[32]

Ever since Truman had published the article, "We Can Lose the War in Washington," in *American Magazine* on the eve of the 1942 election debacle, he had sensed a distinct chill emanating from the White House. It did not particularly bother him, but he finally decided to ask a member of his committee, Senator Harley Kilgore of West Virginia, to explain to the president that he never intended the article to sound so harsh. The ghostwriter had slanted it far beyond his original intentions. FDR reportedly accepted this apology with good grace. Perhaps it was the president's way of admitting that Senator Truman was a pretty formidable politician in his own right.[33]

IX

Elsewhere in the national arena, another seemingly formidable politician was putting on a display of verbal pyrotechnics during the first half of 1943. Wendell Willkie was making even more speeches than Henry Wallace, and his vision of America's place in the world was equally drenched in perfervid idealism. Willkie was running for the Republican presidential nomination in 1944 in the strangest way any defeated candidate had ever sought another chance: as the secret alter ego of the man who had defeated him.

Willkie's trip around the world in the late summer and fall of 1942 had been a media triumph. In Egypt he had so charmed frosty British general Bernard Montgomery, he was allowed to announce the news of the turning-point victory of El Alamein. In Beirut, he told General Charles de Gaulle that the Free French would win favor in America if he publicly renounced France's overseas empire. De Gaulle was so furious he refused to say good-bye to Willkie the next day. Journalists loved this attack on colonialism.

In Moscow Willkie dined with Joseph Stalin and urged him to stop criticizing the pace of American lend-lease aid, causing knees to knock among the Russian dictator's astonished aides. Willkie made amends with a passionate call for an immediate second front, rattling policy-makers in London and Washington.

In China, he conducted a virtually public affair with beautiful Wellesley-educated Madame Chiang Kai-shek, wife of the country's leader, General Chiang Kai-shek. Willkie's terrified OWI escorts feared they would be shot at any moment by the regime's secret police. Willkie ended his dalliance with a dramatic demand for an end of colonialism and the immediate abandonment of American and British extraterritorial rights in China. After a steamy farewell embrace at the airport, Madame Chiang told confidants that her quondam lover was "a perpetual adolescent."[34]

Since FDR had designated Willkie his personal ambassador, many people presumed he was speaking for the president. But when reporters asked Roosevelt to comment on Willkie's call for a second front, FDR, who was planning to invade North Africa instead of France in a few weeks, said "typewriter strategists" did not have a realistic grasp of military operations. Willkie was deeply offended and retorted that he was speaking only for himself and would continue to say "what I damn please."[35]

Willkie knew he was saying what Roosevelt and many New Dealers thought about colonialism and the need to break up the British empire, but could only whisper among themselves while Britain was a wartime partner. Roosevelt may have taken secret pleasure in letting the Chinese use Willkie's remarks to pressure the U.S. State Department and Great Britain's Foreign Office into completing negotiations already under way to renounce their extraterritorial rights in China.

Back in America, Willkie reported on his trip to a radio audience estimated at 36 million people. He was a sensation. He descanted upon the "reservoir of good will" toward America he had found everywhere and called again for the breakup of the colonial empires. He urged the United States to find "a new world idea," and play a "constructive role" in making it work. Clare Boothe Luce, who had tried to talk her way onto Willkie's plane (only to be told by Mrs. Willkie she did not want her husband to go "around the world" with her) called him "a global Abraham Lincoln." The philosopher of the Republican Party, William Allen White, editor of the Emporia, Kansas, *Gazette*, praised him for demanding "freedom for all mankind."[36]

In the privacy of the Oval Office an angry FDR told Henry Wallace that he had warned Willkie not to say anything that would antagonize America's allies. As far as the president was concerned, the Hoosier "had his chance and has muffed it"—a remark that Wallace, competing for the same audience, heard with no little pleasure.[37]

In early 1943, Willkie topped his radio performance with *One World*, which became one of the best-selling books of all time. His mistress, Irita Van Doren, was the ghost writer. Basically a narrative of his trip, it sold a million copies in the first seven weeks, an unheard of performance for nonfiction in the 1940s. Willkie's message was in the title: America had to guarantee freedom and democracy to the entire world. Only a few people noticed that the content was a bit watery. While he slammed British colonialism with a vigor that brought joy to the hearts of the Irish, the Arabs, the Indians, and the Chinese, he had nothing but kind words for Josef Stalin's Communist dictatorship, which was depriving 240 million people of their freedom.[38]

The momentum of Willkie's popular appeal looked irresistible to almost everyone—except the professional politicians of the Republican Party. While he was playing one-world games in Beirut and Moscow and Chungking, they were getting elected in Terre Haute and Topeka and Omaha—without him. Thomas E. Dewey summed up the prevailing opinion in a letter to his mother, during Willkie's trip. "I hear he is going to Russia . . . where he belongs and I hope he stays there until Christmas." When the *Indianapolis Star* reported on February 28, 1943, that Willkie would seek the presidential nomination in 1944, the *Fort*

Wayne News-Sentinel canvassed 1,693 Republican precinct workers in Indiana and found that only 11.9 percent backed Willkie.[39]

X

Nevertheless, Willkie was a force to be reckoned with, not only by the GOP, but by the Democrats. He rampaged across the country, sometimes criticizing the White House for permitting too much "get mine" in the procurement of lucrative government contracts and just as often assailing the conservatives of the Republican Party, such as FDR's bête noire, Congressman Hamilton Fish. His friends urged Willkie to cut this out and try to build bridges to party regulars. But Willkie's political instincts were on a par with Henry Wallace's: nonexistent. Meeting with a group of freshman Republican congressmen, Willkie roared: "I know you people don't like me. But I am going to get nominated whether you like it or not. Better get right with me. I am going to be your next president."[40]

In the White House, FDR made fun of his embattled alter ego, mimicking his Hoosier-accented declamations about the "resev-wharr of goodwill" for America around the world. When someone worried about how to solve the manpower shortage, FDR drawled: "We'll just draw on our reserv-wharr of woman power"—a dig at Willkie's womanizing. The president also joked about Willkie's fondness for alcohol. FDR told Henry Wallace that Willkie was several sheets to the wind on a recent visit. The president had asked White House reporters if Willkie had been drinking excessively in the forty-five minutes he waited outside the Oval Office. Wallace recorded in his diary that the newsmen said "he only had four or five drinks"—apparently not excessive for Willkie.[41]

XI

During these same crowded months, William Allen White traveled from Emporia, Kansas, to attend a presidential press conference. He stood in the first row and studied Roosevelt carefully to see what changes ten years in the White House had wrought. In many ways White saw the same man he had known and admired in a cautious liberal Republican way since 1932. "He seemed to be gay, sure of himself, indeed festive at times. . . . He has grown notably heavier. . . . His growth has not been in the paunch. It has been above the navel. His shoulders have widened. His neck and jowls have filled out. His head has taken a new form." White concluded he was still "a vital person."

That night, White attended a dinner at Washington's new Statler Hotel at which Roosevelt spoke. The Kansan found a different man. "In the five hours he had grown tired. As his speech went on, his voice seemed to lose its fire. . . . In the final sentences his voice drooped and I could not hear the last three words. . . . I could see that the steam in the old boiler . . . had taken its toll of rust."[42]

Maybe this was why Wendell Willkie, who spent a good deal of time in the Oval Office during his clandestine visits to the White House, was sure he was going to be the next president.

II

LET MY CRY
COME UNTO THEE

While New Dealers and idealists such as Wendell Willkie fretted over the failure to define the war as a moral crusade, an issue of enormous ethical proportions began to emerge from the dark recesses of the Nazi empire. Toward the end of 1942, Eduard Schulte, a German industrialist from Breslau, told a Swiss friend that the Nazis were planning to deport all the Jews in Europe to Poland, where extermination centers were being constructed. Schulte's story confirmed information reaching Gerhart Riegner, the representative of the World Jewish Congress in Geneva. He prepared a cable that he asked the American consulate in Geneva to send to Washington and London, and then to transmit to Rabbi Stephen Wise, head of the American Jewish Congress. The diplomats did so, adding a cautionary statement casting doubt on Riegner's information. In Washington, the skepticism was harsher. The State Department called it "a wild rumor inspired by Jewish fears." The headquarters of American diplomacy decided to stick the cable in a file and forget about sending it to Rabbi Wise.[1]

A copy of the cable reached Wise via London a month later. It was buttressed by information from the Polish government in exile. No less than the prime minister of these stateless politicians, who were in close touch with their homeland, declared the Nazis intended "to slit the throats of all Jews, no matter what the outcome of the war." But Rabbi Wise was counseled by Under Secretary of State Sumner Welles, Roosevelt's chief spokesman at the State Department, to say nothing until the Riegner report could be confirmed. The president himself was cautious at his next press conference, only saying he had heard worrisome stories about Nazi policies that might lead to the extermination of "certain populations." He urged anyone who had more information to send it to him.

Unknown to Roosevelt or anyone else in America, the British were sitting on files that proved what the Nazis were doing in gruesome detail. British cryptanalysts had broken the radio code of the German Order Police, who followed the German armies into conquered territories with the express purpose of massacring Jews. The British had hundreds of pages of information on the leaders of the program, the shift from bullets to gas as the extermination weapon of choice—and the Nazis' evident desire to keep the monstrous crime secret from everyone, including the German people. The British rationalized their silence by telling themselves they did not want the Germans to know they had broken the Order Police code.[2]

Even without this information, the State Department soon gathered evidence from other sources, such as OSS station chief Alan Dulles in Switzerland, that convinced Sumner Welles the Riegner cable was true. He summoned Rabbi Wise to Washington and grimly informed him of this semiofficial but still off-the-record conclusion. Wise immediately went public with a statement that appeared in many newspapers on November 25, 1942. But few editors gave it more than a dozen lines in their back pages.

Neither the American nor the British governments backed Wise with a statement of support. Pressured by his Jewish secretary of the treasury, Henry Morgenthau Jr., Roosevelt met for a half-hour with Wise and other Jewish leaders. In typical fashion, when he was faced with a topic that he wished to evade or avoid, FDR spent most of the time talking about other things and finally confessed he had no idea how to stop the slaughter. All he could offer was another statement condemning the Nazis in general terms and warning them of postwar retribution.[3]

Unlike many upper class WASPs, FDR was not an anti-Semite. He had brought more Jews into the top ranks of his administration than any previous president. Before the war began, the U.S. had admitted more Jewish refugees from Germany and Austria than all the other Western countries combined. Thanks largely to American efforts, 72 percent of all the Jews in Germany had escaped to friendly countries. But turning the war into a crusade to save the Jews was a far different matter. It collided with cruel realities that confounded the seemingly simple morality of the situation.[4]

FDR was uneasily aware of the fragility of the American people's commitment to the war. At times he may have been even more uneasily aware that this state of mind was partly, even largely, his fault. He had seduced America into the war with clever tricks, one-step-forward one-step-back double-talk, and the last resort provocation of Japan. Deceit had been at the heart of the process. To suddenly begin making vehement denunciations of the Nazis' murder of the Jews might trigger a so-that's-the-real-reason reaction in the minds of millions of anti-Roosevelt Americans.

II

FDR was also aware that not far beneath the surface of American life lay a psychological minefield where anti-Semitism as well as prejudice against blacks and other ethnic groups flourished. His attempts to skirt the Bill of Rights and pressure his attorney general into silencing the Jew-baiting loudmouths of the lunatic fringe in court were evidence that this problem loomed large in his mind. The mainstream media added to his uneasiness. In March of 1942, the *Saturday Evening Post*, the nation's largest weekly magazine, had run an article, "The Case Against the Jew," that caused a huge uproar. Written by a thirty-three-year-old ex-newspaper reporter named Milton Mayer, it excoriated Jews for abandoning their ancient faith to assimilate into America's materialistic gentile culture. Mayer predicted an explosion of anti-Semitism at the end of the war. "A bitter and bewildered nation" would blame the war on the Jews—and Mayer gloomily declared the Jews would deserve it because they had "changed their noses" but forgot they could not "change their Moses."[5]

The *Saturday Evening Post*'s editor had resigned and Wendell Willkie had been drafted to write a rebuttal, "The Case for Minorities," in which he meandered through a history of American prejudice, from hanging Quakers in Puritan Boston to burning Catholic Churches in the 1840s to the Ku Klux Klan of the 1920s. At one point Willkie claimed that Hitler's persecution of the Jews gave Germany "the momentary strength of regimentation" that enabled them to conquer Europe. He never dealt with Mayer's claim that anti-Semitism was a huge American problem that "had reached an all time high in this country before Pearl Harbor" and was going to get worse the moment the war ended.[6]

One keeper of a daily diary of the war noted that in the Midwest, the global struggle was called "The Jew's War" as often as it was called a war to save the British empire. The director of the

Selective Service, General Lewis Hershey, had to issue a specific denial to a widespread rumor that Jews were evading the draft. In late 1942, when Roosevelt proposed an extension of his war powers to give him the freedom to suspend the immigration laws and admit refugees, Congress rejected the idea. "The ugly truth," *Newsweek* magazine reported, "is that anti-Semitism was a definite factor in the bitter opposition to the President's request."[7]

<h1 style="text-align:center">III</h1>

Even more problematic was the propaganda emanating from the Nazis, who repeatedly told the German people and the rest of the world that the Jews were behind the Bolsheviks in Russia and the capitalists in America. To turn the war into a crusade to save the Jews would have seemingly confirmed this Nazi big lie. At the Overseas branch of the OWI, the New Dealers who had begun the war with apostrophes to "the strategy of truth" had already drawn this hard-eyed conclusion. When Paul Tillich, a German refugee theologian, proposed a broadcast to the German people, warning them that if they allowed the Nazis to continue their ghastly pogrom, they might meet the same fate, he was turned down. The only standard by which the OWI now judged a story was whether it would help or hinder the war effort. Tillich's proposal fell into the latter category.[8]

The OWI, reflecting the all-Germans-are-guilty mindset that emanated from the policy of unconditional surrender, may have missed a great opportunity to both help the Jews and disrupt the German war machine. The latest historical evidence suggests the extermination of the Jews was not a long-range plan concocted by Hitler and his henchman the moment they took power. The Nazi Party was not elected on an anti-Semitic platform. There were several other parties far more obsessed with this issue. The Nazi's chief appeal was their social program, which appealed to middle- and lower-middle-class voters who distrusted big business and big labor.[9]

Even after the Nazis, goaded by Hitler's virulent hatred of Jews, made anti-Semitism one of their leading policies, their original program called for the expulsion of the Jews from Germany and other parts of Europe. At one point, when a negotiated peace with England and a quick victory over Soviet Russia seemed possible, there was talk of resettling them in Madagascar, with the collaboration of the cowed Vichy-French government. When England declined to negotiate peace, a plan to transport Jews to conquered areas of Russia as part of a megalomaniacal "ethnic redistribution" of Europe became the program of choice. Only when the Red Army's resistance revealed this to be another bureaucratic chimera did the shift to methodical extermination begin in early 1942.[10]

Why the Nazis kept the mass murder of the Jews a secret is visible in the regime's reaction to the exposure of an extermination program that preceded the holocaust—and may justly be considered its precursor—Hitler's decision to gas the inhabitants of Germany's psychiatric hospitals. On August 3, 1941, the Roman Catholic bishop of Munster, Clemens August Graf von Galen, denounced the "cleansing" of the nation's mental hospitals as "pure murder." The city had recently been hit hard by British bombers, which the Nazis had shrilly denounced as "cowardly aerial terror." Bishop von Galen disagreed. He said the bombing was God's punishment because Germans were allowing innocent people to be killed without a word of protest.[11]

Almost instantly, the Nazis abandoned the psychiatric extermination program. Propaganda chief Joseph Goebbels nervously told his diary a public debate on the "euthanasia problem" would not be a good idea at the moment, with the blitzkrieg in Russia starting to stall and the air raids causing alarming "setbacks in mood" among the civilian population. This reaction of the Nazi regime to a single speech by a local bishop revealed how nervous Hitler and his henchmen were about their grip on the predominantly Catholic cities of western Germany.

One wonders what might have been accomplished by a massive propaganda campaign from the OWI, including denunciations of the slaughter of the Jews by prominent Catholic and Protestant clergymen from around the world—and finally, perhaps scathing statements by Roosevelt and Churchill. To launch such a campaign required a belief in the existence of decent Germans, a point of view that had been firmly excluded from the White House, and to a considerable extent from 10 Downing Street.[12]

IV

In the minds of Roosevelt and Churchill and the diplomats at the Foreign Office and the State Department, the news of the unfolding holocaust was fatally entangled with the refugee problem. The British were running Palestine under a mandate from the League of Nations. Next door were oil-rich, restless Iraq and Saudi Arabia, who both took extremely dim views of Jewish calls for a homeland in Palestine. An attempt to transform the war into a crusade to save the Jews would almost certainly have led to pressure to open Palestine to refugees. The British feared that would trigger a massive Arab shift to the German side of the war.

Roosevelt had sent an army officer, Lieutenant Colonel Harold Hoskins, on a three-month information-gathering tour of the Middle East in the winter of 1942/43, to provide him with enough background to judge the situation without any help from the British Foreign Office. Hoskins returned with a gloomy assessment. American prestige was sinking throughout the region because of the perception that American Jews had too much influence in the American government. Hoskins warned that the Arabs might start waging "outright warfare" against the Allies, unless they were reassured that no commitments to the Jews would be made during the war.[13]

When Zionist spokesman David Ben-Gurion visited the United States, FDR curtly forbade Supreme Court Justice Felix Frankfurter to meet with him. "The less said by everybody of all creeds, the better," he said. Henry Wallace and Harold Ickes, both pro-Zionists, discussed their unhappiness with Roosevelt's supercautious approach. He was letting oil triumph over morality, they mournfully agreed. Sam Rosenman became so exercised over FDR's hesitation on the Jewish question that he testily predicted the Democrats might lose the Jewish vote in 1944.[14]

Another complication was the Stern Gang, a group of Jewish guerillas in Palestine who specialized in assassinating British policemen and public officials. In February 1942 the British had killed the founder, Abraham Stern, in a shootout. But his followers continued to set off bombs and stage ambushes with deadly skill, hoping to drive the British out of the country. Their activities did not endear the Jews to the British Foreign Office or the British public. In America, where at least half the Jews opposed Zionism and non-Jews had only a dim idea of its history, the Stern Gang's impact was almost as negative.

Early in March 1943, the increasingly desperate American Jewish Congress called on the American and British governments to do something to save the 5 million Jews left in Europe. The AJC claimed 2 million Jews had already been massacred in Poland in the previous twelve months. It was not enough to indict the murderers, the AJC declared. If the surviving Jews were allowed to perish, it would be "an eternal badge of shame on the soul of mankind."[15]

Again, the story did not make the front pages of most newspapers. *Time* ran it on page 29 of their March 8, 1943, issue. Many supposedly well informed observers simply did not believe it. Once more, World War I's shadow was distorting perceptions and opinions. So many of the German atrocity stories floated by the British propaganda machine in that war turned out to be fakes, sophisticated thinkers vowed never to be deceived again by tales of blood and gore. Moreover, the dimension of the crime was too monstrous for many people to comprehend. One of the major civilized nations of the world, famed for its contributions to culture and science, simply could not perpetrate such a barbarity.

Whereas New Dealers Ickes and Wallace and the covert New Dealer in Republican costume, Wendell Willkie, followed Roosevelt's policy of playing down the annihilation of Europe's Jews (although Willkie became an outspoken Zionist), Harry Truman felt no such compunction. Once more displaying his independence of the White House, in April 1943 the senator from Missouri spoke at a huge rally staged by the American Jewish Committee in Chicago. He asked how any nation that was fighting under the standard of the Four Freedoms could ignore what the Nazis were doing in Europe. "Merely talking about the Four Freedoms is not enough," he said. He went even further, declaring that "today—not tomorrow" the United States must use its power to find a haven for "all those who can be grasped from the hands of the Nazi butchers."[16]

V

The senator's indignation was obviously genuine. But he was not in charge of the executive branch of the American government. There, for most of 1943, very little was done to stop the slaughter. What little was cosmetic. Palestine became the focus of whatever hope existed for a refuge, presuming Hitler would allow Jews to emigrate. The State Department arranged for a meeting between British foreign secretary Anthony Eden and leading American Jews when Eden visited Washington in March of 1943. The meeting went nowhere. Eden rejected the idea of the Allies calling on Hitler to let Jews emigrate. He dismissed the possibility of Jews going to Turkey. He refused even to consider shipping food to Jews in Europe because the Germans would undoubtedly seize it.

The foreign secretary was even more intransigent when he conferred with Secretary of State Hull, Harry Hopkins, and other top Roosevelt aides. He claimed the British were willing to accept 30,000 Jews in Palestine but there were no ships available to take them there. Eden feared if the allies expressed a willingness to accept the Jews as refugees the Germans would use the policy shift to negotiate the war to a dead stop. Above all, he warned the Americans against making grandiose promises on which neither they nor the British could deliver.

With great fanfare, British and American diplomats met in Bermuda to discuss the refugee problem. Assistant Secretary of State Breckinridge Long led the American delegation. Old and ill, Long had acquired his job mostly by making large donations to the Democratic Party and agreeing with Cordell Hull about everything. He was neither a bright nor a sensitive man. The chief British representative had been handpicked by Anthony Eden and his correspondence with the foreign secretary made it clear that the main goal of the conference was to guarantee neither group try to pull a fast one by placing the blame for the nightmarish situation on the other side.

Eden's man was soon reporting with relief that the Americans were mainly looking for support from the British so they could tell "unpalatable facts" to their people. They were not going to embarrass the British about Palestine. The goal of the conference was evolving toward defining the problem in terms of "practical possibilities." That meant trying to save "thousands instead of hundreds of thousands." The British also hoped to persuade the Americans to agree on what should not be done, such as trading German POWs for the Jews.

Breckinridge Long's diary confirms one of the chief concerns of the Roosevelt administration. Long fretted over the aggressive way "one Jewish faction" led by Rabbi Stephen Wise was pushing for action. "One danger is . . . their activities may lend color to the charges of Hitler that we are fighting this war on account of and at the instigation of and direction of our Jewish citizens. . . . It might easily be a detriment to our war effort."[17]

While the diplomats exchanged generalities in the sunshine, the Warsaw ghetto exploded in a desperate revolt against the by now obvious fate the Germans had in store for Poland's Jews. Malnutrition, disease, and deportations to the death camps had reduced the ghetto's numbers from a half-million to about 60,000, whom the Germans decided to eliminate in one final sweep. Members of the Jewish Combat Organization attacked the Nazis with guns and Molotov cocktails. Only a handful of Jews survived the savage house-to-house fighting that lasted four weeks. The revolt triggered similar uprisings in Kraków and other Polish cities.[18]

Perhaps embarrassed by this excruciating reminder of the horror the diplomats were trying to evade, the proceedings and even the final agreement of the Bermuda conference remained secret. Its only achievement was the creation of another wartime committee, an intergovernmental affair that was supposed to meet periodically to assess the problem. Beyond that gesture was a proposal to build camps for a few thousand refugees somewhere in North Africa. A British participant was not exaggerating when he later called the conference "a facade for inaction."[19]

The fault, it soon became clear, was at the top of the American government, not at the middle or bottom of the State Department, where anti-Semitism at worst or indifference at best supposedly lurked. Early in May, Assistant Secretary of State Adolf A. Berle Jr., perhaps the most tough-minded member of Roosevelt's original brain trust, gave a speech in Boston. He accused the Germans of "national murder" but he told his audience there was nothing the United States or its allies could do about it for the time being. Berle's numerous enemies promptly labeled him an anti-Semite and soon spread an even more ingenious smear: he had secretly converted to Catholicism.[20]

VI

Throughout the rest of 1943, American Jews continued to stage rallies in public arenas such as Madison Square Garden. They marched to the White House and Capitol Hill. But their impact on American popular opinion was slight. As late as December 1944—two years after the first news story on the Holocaust appeared in America—a poll revealed that a majority of Americans still refused to believe in the existence of a Nazi campaign to exterminate the Jews.

Secretary of the Treasury Henry Morgenthau Jr. became more and more upset over Franklin Roosevelt's silence and the State Department's stalling tactics. As a Jew, he at first had hesitated to involve himself in the controversy because he feared an anti-Semitic backlash. Also, he was not a Zionist, and most of the demonstrators and ralliers in the Jewish community were of this persuasion. But the failure of the Bermuda Conference changed Morgenthau's mind. He ordered his staff to investigate the situation and the Treasury Department soon became involved in an attempt to provide funds for the emigration of 70,000 Jews from Romania. They collided with maddening delays in the State Department and in the British Foreign Office about licenses to transfer funds and arguments that no neutral country in the Near East or Europe would accept that many refugees.

The Treasury men also discovered that the State Department had concealed another cable from Gerhart Riegner to Rabbi Wise, estimating that the Germans were killing 6,000 Polish Jews a day. State's desk men had ordered the ambassador in Berne to stop transmitting messages intended for private individuals and Riegner had thus been effectively silenced. In a tense scene, Morgenthau asked Assistant Secretary of State Breckinridge Long if he was anti-Semitic. Long vehemently denied the charge, which his diary amply substantiated.[21]

As months passed and hope of saving Romania's Jews dwindled, Morgenthau grew weary of the struggle. Secretary of State Cordell Hull repeatedly claimed he was supporting the Treasury's efforts. But when the treasury secretary confronted him with evidence of the bureaucrats' foot-dragging, Hull could only express shock and bewilderment. His indifference to the administration of his department left him out of touch with what was happening all around him. "Roosevelt wouldn't move on Hull, he never has; and Hull wouldn't move on Long," Morgenthau morosely concluded.[22]

Morgenthau's aides were even more exasperated. One of them, Randolph Paul, prepared a memorandum summarizing the saga of delay and obfuscation. It had an explosive title: *Report to the Secretary on the Acquiescence of this Government in the Murder of the Jews*. Did Morgenthau have the courage to show it to FDR at their weekly White House luncheon? For the moment, the answer was no.

VII

Meanwhile, Roosevelt's antipathy toward the one group that could have rescued the Jews, the German resistance to Hitler, was hardening. In May 1943 Churchill came to Washington for a conference code-named Trident. Probably reacting to Admiral Canaris's attempts to reach him through OSS chief William Donovan, Roosevelt told the prime minister he wanted to issue a declaration that he would refuse to negotiate with the Nazi regime, the German army high command or any other group or individual in Germany. Churchill, once more demonstrating his dislike for taking such an intransigent public stand, managed to talk him out of it.[23]

But the prime minister himself was not innocent of calling for total war and total victory in terms that made unconditional surrender seem like a threat of annihilation. In a speech to the House of Commons in September 1943, Churchill distinguished between the treatment he planned to mete out to the Italian and the German people. He saw little or no obstacles to the Italians regaining "their rightful place among the free democracies of the modern world."

Not so the Germans. "Twice within our lifetimes, three times counting that of our fathers, they have plunged the world into their wars of expansion and aggression. They combine in the most deadly manner the qualities of the warrior and the slave. They do not value freedom themselves and the spectacle of it among others is hateful to them." He went on to denounce Prussia as "the core of the pestilence." Nazi tyranny and Prussian militarism had to be "rooted out" before Germany could return to the family of nations.[24]

This was pure Vansittartism. Lord Robert was saying virtually identical race-baiting words in the House of Lords. "The German Reich, which twice in our lifetime has nearly destroyed the world, was mainly the creation of Prussian militarism united with German nationalism. . . . Germans must now learn to speak humbly, lowly, with downcast eyes, in half tones."[25]

In his message to Congress on September 17, 1943, Roosevelt was an echo of this British venom. "This is one thing I want to make perfectly clear: when Hitler and the Nazis go out, the Prussian military clique must go with them. The war-breeding gang of militarists must be rooted out of Germany . . . if we are to have any real assurance of peace."[26]

Roosevelt's—and Churchill's—and Vansittart's—attribution of evil to the German general staff and Prussian militarism was a compound of the shallowest kind of newspaper journalism and race-baiting propaganda from World War I. The German general staff actually protested against the civilian government's plunge into World War I. On the eve of World War II, General Ludwig Beck, the German army's chief of staff, resigned in protest against Hitler's seizure of Prague in violation of the Munich agreement. Hitler himself decried the cautious defensive mentality of the general staff. It repeatedly tried to discourage his adventurism, from the seizure of Austria to the invasion of Russia. The Führer said he had always thought of the general staff as a "butcher's dog," a creature that had to be restrained from attacking everyone in sight. Instead, he found "it is I who have always had to goad on this butcher's dog."

As for Churchill's claim that Prussia was the source of Germany's aggressions, plunging Europe into three wars, in the first of these, the Franco-Prussian War of 1870, it was France who declared war, confident of an easy victory in the tradition of Napoleon I. The American ambassador in Paris at the time issued a statement, unequivocally branding France the aggressor. Who started the First World War is a murky business that historians are still debating. The only certainty is that no one on either side had any idea it would consume a generation.

Between the wars, Prussia and its capital, Berlin, were the stronghold of the German Social Democratic Party. The Nazis never won a majority there in any election. Most members of the Nazi Party were from Bavaria. Munich was its spiritual home, not Berlin. Their vulgar uniforms, their gaudy banners, their macho posturing were polar opposites of the austere style of the Prussian aristocracy.[27]

The policy of unconditional surrender was aimed at a target that did not exist. No one put this more forthrightly than a group of German anti-Nazi refugee scholars (many of them Jews) who were working for the OSS in the Office of Research and Analysis.

They produced studies aimed at correcting Allied denunciations of "Prussian militarism" and "the Teutonic urge for domination." These knowledgeable men dismissed such terms as anachronisms left over from World War I. In modern Germany power was not in the hands Prussian aristocrats; they had been discredited by defeat in the previous war. The executives of I. G. Farben, Krupp, and the other big corporations were the power brokers of the Third Reich.

The scholars especially deplored the way unconditional surrender played into the hands of Nazi propagandists by enabling them to tell the German people they had no choice between resistance and the annihilation of the nation. They also saluted the courage of the anti-Hitler plotters, calling their existence "a tribute to human endurance and courage, and the revelation of a great hope." They urged the Allied governments to make contact with the resisters to "give some substance to the hope." Their advice was totally ignored.[28]

In a final irony, unconditional surrender made no impression whatsoever on the man for whom Roosevelt claimed to have designed it: Josef Stalin. The Soviet dictator considered it a blunder and said so, making much the same point that Generals Eisenhower, Wedemeyer, and Eaker made: it would only make the Germans resist to the bitter end. In July 1943 Stalin demonstrated his idea of how to approach the Germans. A National Committee of Free Germans—high-ranking prisoners taken at Stalingrad—began broadcasting from Moscow, assuring the Germans that the Soviet Union had no desire to destroy them as a people. They only wanted to help them get rid of Hitler.

The Russian leader was saying the very thing that Admiral Canaris and his friends wanted so desperately to hear from President Roosevelt. Inside the resistance movement, younger people began considering a switch to Moscow, but the older leaders, Canaris, Oster, Beck, Goerdeler, and Von Hassell, remained adamantly opposed to such a reversal. Much as they detested Nazism, they loathed Communism even more.[29]

VIII

On the other side of the world, race hatred was being preached with a ferocity that equaled anything Joseph Goebbels was producing in his Berlin propaganda mill. Here, the preachers were Americans. The surprise attack on Pearl Harbor sent Americans into paroxysms of racial and even genocidal rage against the Japanese. *Time* summed up the standard American reaction: "Why the little yellow bastards!" Yellow became an epithet as well as a descriptive adjective in innumerable references to the Japanese.

One American weapons manufacturer boasted his new submachine gun was especially good at "blasting red holes in little yellow men." *Reader's Digest* featured an article on Japanese psychology that began: "Let us look into one of these yellow heads and see what it contains." Newsreels regularly referred to the Japanese as "yellowbellies" and "yellow bastards." One shortened the epithet "little yellowbellies" to "LYBs." Songwriters followed the national trend with such ditties as "We're Gonna Find a Fellow Who Is Yellow and Beat Him Red White and Blue."[30]

Admiral William "Bull" Halsey, the most outspoken of the Pacific's military commanders, was fond of saying that after the war, Japanese would be spoken only in hell. "The only good Jap is a Jap who's been dead six months," Halsey said, topping the savagery of the frontier attitude toward Indians. Even after the war, in his memoirs, Halsey referred to the Japanese as "animals."

The concept of the decent German, trapped in the evil Nazi undertow, remained alive in most American minds throughout the war. There was little or nothing to be found in film or print or speech that encouraged the idea of a decent Japanese, also trapped by his nation's headlong plunge into militarism. Everyone from journalists to President Roosevelt routinely used the dehumanizing slang term "Jap," and regularly compared Japanese soldiers and civilians to monkeys, baboons, and gorillas. Admiral Halsey was especially fond of the monkey metaphor, invariably attaching "yellow" to it. At one point Halsey said he could hardly wait to put to sea "to get some more monkey meat."

Even the *New Yorker* magazine saw nothing wrong with imitating the admiral, publishing a cartoon of Americans firing at Japanese snipers in a jungle. Several monkeys were visible beside the snipers in the trees and one of the Americans says: "Careful now. Only those in uniform."[31]

Rats was another favorite metaphor to describe the Japanese. A huge patriotic parade in New York in 1942 featured a float with an American eagle leading bombers in an assault on a group of scurrying rats. It was one of the most popular exhibits in the parade. Small wonder that American marines went into action in the Pacific with "Rodent Exterminator" stenciled to their helmets. Or that Americans and Australians found it easy to kill the few Japanese who offered to surrender on Guadalcanal, New Guinea, and other islands.[32]

New Dealers and others around the president made no attempt to alter this dehumanizing war against the Japanese. In September 1942, Admiral William Leahy, Roosevelt's White House chief of staff, told Vice President Henry Wallace that Japan was "our Carthage" and "we should go ahead and destroy her utterly." Wallace noted this sentiment without objection in his diary. Elliott Roosevelt, the president's son, told Wallace some months later that he thought Americans should kill "about half the Japanese civilian population." New Dealer Paul McNutt, chairman of the War Manpower Commission, went him one better, recommending "the extermination of the Japanese in toto."[33]

IX

In Europe, during the last half of 1943, the war seemed to be stumbling into a stalemate. On the Italian peninsula, the Americans and British slugged it out with the Germans entrenched in the mountainous Gustav Line. On the eastern front, huge armies clashed in massive tank and infantry battles about which the West learned little. In many ways the ground war began to look like a replay of World War I. But a new and very different war was being fought in the skies. It was a conflict that eluded traditional morality and succumbed more and more to hatred, in this case disguised as military policy.

The generals who commanded the fleets of bombers that began pounding German cities in 1943 had drunk deep of the doctrines of the Italian airman General Giulio Douhet, who had written his seminal 1921 book, *Command of the Air*, in the shadow of the World War I's four years of slaughterous trench warfare. Douhet predicted victory in the next war would be won by massive aerial bombardment of the enemy's civilian population. Although the results would be "tragic"—and seemingly immoral—according to Douhet such tactics were actually merciful because civilians, lacking the military discipline and endurance of trained soldiers, would panic and force their rulers to conclude an immediate peace. Thanks to the airplane, wars would be barbaric but brief.

General Billy Mitchell, the 1920s advocate of air power for the American army and navy, subscribed wholeheartedly to Douhet's ideas. In some ways he was even more ruthless than his mentor. He enthusiastically endorsed wiping out entire cities with poison gas. He saw nothing wrong with killing masses of civilians because they were helping to manufacture the enemy's guns and ammunition, making them as much a part of the war as the men in the trenches. He too argued that such terror tactics would shorten wars and thereby make air warfare "a benefit to civilization."[34]

274 THE NEW DEALERS' WAR

Interlarded with these apocalyptic visions was the influence of
the various American antiwar groups who flourished in the
1930s. The men at the head of the army air forces had to temper
their Douhetian ruthlessness to get appropriations out of congressmen who listened to these pioneer peaceniks. Congress also
demanded an early version of more bang for the buck. They were
not about to finance the fleets of planes that would be needed to
demolish large cities. So the army air forces switched to the concept of a relatively few planes equipped with precision bombsights that could target factories and power stations and cripple
an enemy economy. As a pious dividend, these new tactics were
also sold as a moral way to wage air warfare, minimizing civilian
casualties.

The German air attacks on London and other British cities inspired in many AAF officers a revival of Douhetian thinking.
General Henry H. "Hap" Arnold, the AAF commander, visited
London in April 1941 and came away impressed by the damage
500 German planes, few of them heavy bombers of the sort the
British and the Americans were developing, had inflicted on the
city. However, Arnold thought the Germans had failed to learn
the fundamental lesson of the use of airpower, "[the] employment of airplanes in numbers large enough to secure complete
destruction."[35]

When the Americans began bombing Germany in the spring of
1943, Arnold sent the commanders of the Eighth Air Force a
memorandum that recommended "selective bombing" of economic and military targets, with great stress on accuracy. The
general saw himself as being both practical and idealistic here—a
neat straddle of the great American dichotomy. Accurate bombing would save the lives of the bomber crews, who would not
have to return to the same target again. It would also avoid
killing civilians, whom Arnold called "victim populations." The
general thought bombing them would only lead to a cycle of ha-

tred between nations that would breed future wars. Arnold ended his epistle with an apostrophe to the bomber as potentially "the most humane of all weapons."[36]

This unstable mixture of barbarism and humanitarianism soon collided with ugly realities in the skies above Germany. Accurate selective bombing of economic and military targets could be conducted only in daylight. When the Americans arrived at English air bases in the spring of 1942, the British told them that they had tried daylight bombing and after horrendous losses in planes and men had switched to night bombing. They had also abandoned any pretense of aiming at a particular target. Their goal was pure Douhetism, to break the morale of Germany's civilian population by smashing their cities to rubble and killing huge numbers of people. General Douhet had an especially strong appeal to His Majesty's generals, who dreaded a repetition of World War I's toll of almost 1 million dead infantrymen.

The Americans informed the British that they disapproved, though not for moral reasons. They felt that the German bombing of London entitled the British to a payback in kind. The Americans thought morale bombing would not work. Among themselves, they also exchanged uneasy memorandums admitting that American voters and congressmen would take a dim view of slaughtering defenseless women and children. "We want the American people to understand and have faith in our way of making war," Arnold told one of his top commanders.[37]

The two air forces worked out a compromise, which was formally ratified by Churchill and Roosevelt at Casablanca. The Americans would precision-bomb by day, the British would area-bomb by night. It would be like a one-two punch, leaving the Germans groggy. With no control over British tactics or intentions, the Americans soon found themselves involved in some very messy operations. In July and August of 1943, Air Marshal Sir Arthur Harris, head of the RAF's Bomber Command, decided to destroy the city of Hamburg. Operation Gomorrah sent 728 planes loaded with incendiary bombs to attack the sprawling port on July 27/28. The result was a firestorm that created temperatures high enough to melt metal and bricks and consumed all the oxygen in the center of the city, asphyxiating and incinerating 45,000 people. The bodies of small children looked like fried eels on the livid pavement. In air-raid shelters people became bones suspended in congealed fat. More than a million Germans fled into the countryside. Half of the houses in the city were destroyed.[38]

During this epic of destruction, the Americans bombed the burning city in daylight, aiming at shipyards and factories. But the smoke was so thick, they ruefully admitted they missed most of their targets. Their bombs fell on the hapless civilians. It would be hard to deny they participated in the slaughter but most of the onus for the raid fell—deservedly—on the British. Not that any serious blaming occurred. As one RAF airman put it, "To whom could you express doubts? . . . What would have been the result? Court martial!" FDR thought Hamburg was "an impressive demonstration" of air power's potential and hoped it would soon be applied to Japan, an idea in which General Arnold eagerly concurred.[39]

Harder questions were asked when the Americans bombed two industrial cities deep in Germany, Regensburg and Schweinfurt. Regensburg, on the Danube in Bavaria, produced Germany's crack fighter plane, the ME-109, in huge factories just outside the town. Schweinfurt was the home of equally vital ball bearing factories. German antiaircraft guns and swarms of fighter planes exacted an horrendous toll on the attackers. Over Regensburg, 84 out of 146 bombers went down; over Schweinfurt, 36 succumbed and another 27 were so badly shot up they were junked when they staggered back to England. Worse, they made so few hits on Schweinfurt's ball bearing factories they had to return for a second try.

These were unacceptable losses. The B-17 bomber, the so-called Flying Fortress, was clearly unable to defend itself against German fighters. Frantic conferences between American air commanders led to new tactics. Instead of aiming at industrial targets, they would simply dump their bombs on the city's center and get home as fast as possible. General Curtis LeMay, who led the Regensburg raid, saw no difference between bombing civilian houses and the factories in which the civilians worked. Soon the Americans were bombing exclusively in this Douhetian style. Some people were even frank enough to call it area-bombing.

For a while, no one objected. Then Vera Brittain, a World War I British nurse who had written a best-selling book about her experiences, published an article in a pacifist journal, denouncing area-bombing by the RAF and the Americans. Twenty-eight British clergymen and antiwar activists joined her in deploring "this carnival of death." The British ignored them but the *New York Times* picked up the story and it became a political uproar in America, where everyone thought their airmen were still carefully selecting targets with maximum care to avoid killing women and children. The *New Republic* deplored "bombing defenseless people merely to instill terror in them" but piously declared such tactics were "not the practice of the RAF and the AAF."⁴⁰

FDR ordered his press secretary, Steve Early, to issue a reply to the British pacifists. Early said the president was "disturbed and horrified" by the killing. But he saw no other way to stop it but by forcing the Germans and Japanese to change their militaristic philosophy. This idea of changing a nation's philosophy was intimately linked to FDR's unconditional surrender policy. In his mind he seemed to envision unconditional surrender as making Germany and Japan tabulae rasae, swept bare of all their bad ideas, awaiting American infusion of good ideas. Area-bombing—which provided a somewhat gruesome metaphor of razing the enemy's landscape literally, if not philosophically—may have found a link in FDR's subconscious on this basis, although he did not need any metaphors to fuel his hatred of Germany.

Further evidence of American uneasiness was a hurried visit to Europe by Under Secretary of War for Air Robert A. Lovett, who warned AAF commanders that not a few Americans, including members of Congress, were becoming upset about area-bombing. Lovett was not personally troubled. In fact, he wrote to a British friend that he had enjoyed looking at the pictures of a recent RAF "obliteration" raid on Essen with "sadistic barbarism." Like many other Americans in and out of the AAF, Lovett found the quarrel over area-bombing a test of how macho a man was. The British regularly put the argument on this basis.[41]

The American public remained largely unaware of this contretemps. In *Bombardier*, a 1943 RKO film made with the assistance of the army air forces, audiences saw Americans demonstrating their amazing bombsight to skeptical congressmen. From 20,000 feet they planted a bomb in a barrel. When one beginning bombardier got a letter from his mother, urging him to quit the air force lest he become guilty of killing women and children, his commanding officer blithely assured him he would do no such thing. American wizardry would enable him to obliterate enemy factories producing evil weapons, without harming a single woman or child. The reassured bombardier flew into the wild blue yonder with a happy smile on his face.[42]

X

As the year 1943 lengthened, polls revealed that unconditional surrender had become a very popular slogan with the American people. It was identified in many minds with the promise of a peaceful postwar world. No one noticed that it was tinged with hate. In a world where hatred was being preached and practiced by hateful foes, this defect was scarcely discernible. Not a word about the German resistance to Hitler had reached the American public. The president was determined to maintain this wall of silence about the Front of Decent People.

In England, however, unconditional surrender was being viewed with growing skepticism by a number of prominent people, including Winston Churchill. In August of 1943, the prime minister told Foreign Secretary Anthony Eden he opposed "continually uttering the slogan 'Unconditional Surrender' . . . . We certainly do not want, if we can help it, to get them [the Germans] all fused together in a solid desperate block for whom there is no hope." He told Eden he was now opposed to rejecting all peace feelers out of hand. They should encourage anything that promises a "disintegration of the Nazi machine . . . and consequently the saving of hundreds of thousands of British and American lives."[43]

In December 1943, a British intelligence subcommittee reported to the war cabinet that the "formula of unconditional surrender . . . is having a big effect in making the Germans afraid of the consequences of defeat to themselves individually and collectively." The report went on to say Goebbels's use of the slogan was having some success "amongst the uneducated masses" and was also affecting industrialists, bankers, and senior civil servants who had no sympathy with the Nazi regime.[44]

The British military analyst, Captain Basil Liddell Hart, studying the war with expert eyes, wrote a memorandum in which he concluded that every German general knew the war was lost. They were fighting on the defensive against overwhelming odds. Strategically, their situation was hopeless. Liddell Hart thought there was a real possibility of a coup d'état that would remove Hitler. (He knew nothing about the existence of the German resistance movement.) But he pointed out that unconditional surrender was an insuperable barrier to such a move. People who feel themselves "the target of an unlimited attack," Liddell Hart concluded, would be inclined to "rally to the regime, tyranny though it is, which at least organizes their defence."[45]

In Rome, Pope Pius XII sent a message to Roosevelt through the American ambassador to the Vatican, Myron Taylor. The pontiff told the president that the "temple of peace" could endure only if it were based on Christian charity and forgiveness, unalloyed by "vindictive passions or any elements of hatred." Using the oblique diplomatic style with which he had feebly opposed Nazism, the pope added that the demand for unconditional surrender was "incompatible with Christian doctrine."[46]

This was another cry of anguish from tormented Europe that Franklin D. Roosevelt made sure never reached American voters.

12

RED STAR RISING

In the spring of 1943, a political earthquake struck the U.S. State Department. It emanated from a conversation Harry Hopkins had with wealthy Joseph Davies, ambassador to the Soviet Union from 1936 to 1938. Still living in the White House with his new wife, Hopkins retained his role as Roosevelt's most trusted assistant and presidential spokesman within the government and the Washington establishment. Hopkins told Davies the president was extremely worried about Josef Stalin's reaction to the news that there would be no second front in France in 1943, only diversionary attacks on Sicily and Italy. The president feared Stalin might sign a separate peace with Hitler once he had expelled German troops from Soviet soil, leaving the British and Americans to face the full might of the Wehrmacht's 200-plus divisions when the Western allies invaded Europe.

Davies rushed to the Russian embassy to see Maxim Litvinov, the Soviet ambassador, who was delighted to stoke the president's fears. A consummate actor, Litvinov said he was "almost despondent" about the Russian alliance with Great Britain and America and claimed everyone in the Kremlin felt the same way. "The faith of [my] government has been all but destroyed over the second front," he said.[1]

Davies assured Litvinov he would give this message to Harry Hopkins immediately, with the presumption that it would reach Roosevelt within the hour. Meanwhile, the emboldened Litvinov paid a visit to Under Secretary of State Sumner Welles. The Russian handed him a list of State Department employees whom he found obstacles to better understanding between the United States and Moscow. Would the under secretary please arrange for them to be transferred elsewhere?

The astounded Welles was faced with the most difficult decision of his life. For the last ten years, he had walked a precarious path between placating his putative superior, Secretary of State Cordell Hull, and serving his patron, President Roosevelt. Hull had never forgiven Welles (or Roosevelt) for the 1941 snub that humiliated him before the Washington establishment—the president's decision to take Welles rather than the secretary with him to the Atlantic Charter conference with Churchill off Newfoundland. The secretary of state seldom spoke to the under secretary. The door between their adjoining offices was permanently locked.

Hull also blamed Welles for the New Dealers' criticism of the Department that erupted when the United States made its "deal with the devil" and accepted Admiral Darlan and his circle of Vichy French bureaucrats in North Africa. The under secretary was a social friend of columnist Drew Pearson—proof of his perfidy, in Hull's opinion.

II

Paradoxically, Hull let Welles more or less run the State Department. The secretary was a hopeless administrator and had only the dimmest interest in personnel. Welles, who had been in the department since 1915, except for a hiatus of several years in the 1920s, knew the people and the organization intimately. To some extent the department ran itself. The old hands such as James Dunn were in charge of the cable traffic that poured in from all parts of the world, and prepared answers that often set or at least reinforced policy.

Son of a New Jersey builder, Dunn had joined the State Department during World War I, married an heiress, and became a specialist in Western European affairs. A Catholic like Robert Murphy, he was fiercely anticommunist and had earned the enmity of Washington's liberals by supporting General Francisco Franco in the Spanish Civil War. Dunn complacently ignored their name-calling. He had devoted his diplomatic skills to charming Cordell Hull. His wife became one of Mrs. Hull's best friends. The Hulls were frequent dinner guests at Dunn's splendid mansion, next door to the British embassy.[2]

Dunn and the other veteran foreign service officers had very little enthusiasm for New Dealers and One Worlders and their utopian ideas about universal brotherhood. Instead, the diplomats presumed human nature was not going to change. Nations would continue to pursue their individual interests and politicians would be driven by the same hunger for fame and power that had motivated them since history began. In particular, throughout the 1930s they disagreed with Roosevelt and the New Dealers in their attempts to align America with Soviet Russia against the fascist dictatorships in Italy and Germany. They were appalled by the ignorance New Dealers such as Harold Ickes displayed when he declared that Communism was the "antithesis of Nazism" because it was founded on "belief in the control of the government, including the economic system, by the people themselves."[3]

On the whole, Welles agreed with his fellow professionals. He supported them in their turf wars with New Dealers on the Board of Economic Warfare and elsewhere. He sat at the top of the State Department's bureaucratic pyramid and approved or disapproved all the important cables and memoranda prepared by the specialists at the various "desks" that handled specific areas of the world. In 1937, he had even risked Roosevelt's disapproval when the president essayed a much publicized reorganization of the department to move it closer to a New Deal point of view. Welles rearranged and promoted and transferred but there was little if any serious change in the department's power structure. Above all, Welles had protected most of the men whom Litvinov was now trying to obliterate: the Russian specialists.[4]

III

This small but elite cadre had been put together back in the 1920s when it became apparent that the Soviet Union was going to be around for a while. They had gone to Europe and studied the Russian language and the Soviet system from the vantage point of the Baltic states, Berlin, and Paris. They emerged from this experience profoundly disillusioned with the Communist experiment in remaking human nature. Russia was a brutal totalitarian state, especially dangerous because Communist ideology had a huge appeal to Western intellectuals.

In 1937, Welles had gone along with abolishing the Division of Eastern European Affairs, where these experts worked. He had merged it with the European Division, and he had exiled the founder of the EE, Robert Kelley, and the division's most brilliant thinker, George Kennan, to posts outside Russia's orbit. But the core of the group remained intact within the larger European Division.

Loy Henderson, Elbridge Durbrow, and Charles Bohlen were not far behind Kennan in brainpower, and they had absorbed the essence of Kennan's harsh judgment of Russia. As Kennan put it in his *Memoirs*, "Never—neither then (1937) nor at any later date—did I consider the Soviet Union a fit ally or associate, actual or potential, for this country."[5] Almost as important to the EE operation was Ray Murphy, who maintained voluminous files on Communist activity in the United States and around the world, on which the Russian experts could draw for documentation. Only the FBI, with whom Murphy often exchanged information, could equal the depth and breadth of his dossiers.

Kennan, Henderson, Durbrow, and Bohlen had all served in the American embassy in Moscow during the 1930s and came away even more convinced that Soviet Russia was a morally degraded country. Someone described Kennan's dispatches as diapasons of gloom that counterpointed the chirps of praise for Stalin emitted by Joseph C. Davies. Henderson, watching Stalin murder hundreds of thousands in the "Great Purge" of the late 1930s, became even more convinced that he was face-to-face with evil and acted accordingly. He had declined to succumb to the heavy-handed charm of Maxim Litvinov, who had been Soviet foreign minister at the time, and was proud of his ability to relate to Westerners.

For a man in the diplomatic service, Loy Henderson had little use for tact. In 1940, Soviet Russia attacked tiny Finland, outraging many Americans. Eleanor Roosevelt told Cordell Hull that she had heard Finland was the aggressor, and urged him to create a committee of experts to look into the question. Hull asked Henderson how to handle this request. "Tell Mrs. Roosevelt that I've been watching the situation from the beginning and I don't need to make a study. Russia is the aggressor," Henderson said. Two years later, Mrs. Roosevelt tried to get one of her liberal friends appointed to the Moscow embassy. Henderson curtly vetoed the suggestion.[6]

IV

After Germany invaded Russia and the Soviet Union became an ally, Sumner Welles had tried to play a mediator's role between the prevailing skepticism of the Russian experts and the wishes and hopes of the White House. In late 1942, the Metropolitan (bishop) of Kiev proposed that the Russian Orthodox Church and England's Anglican Church exchange official visits. The British ambassador asked Welles if the U.S. would object. Welles asked for an opinion from the Russian experts. Charles Bohlen scorned the idea, calling the metropolitan nothing more than an agent of the Soviet government, who was "permitted to exist" and tell lies for propaganda purposes. Welles, who knew FDR wanted to promote the myth that religious freedom existed in Russia, argued that approval should be granted because it might lead to liberalizing the Soviets' attitude toward religion. The under secretary tacitly admitted the metropolitan was a fake but tried to convince himself (and Bohlen) that fakery might produce the real thing. Such tortured logic only revealed Welles's underlying predicament.[7]

The British decided to admit the metropolitan without U.S. approval so the disagreement between Welles and Bohlen became moot. On other matters, Welles often sided with the Russian experts. Litvinov tried to bypass the specialists by persuading Lawrence Duggan, the head of the South American division, to urge Welles to let Spanish communists into Mexico as a counterweight to the "fascists" in that country. The under secretary showed Duggan's memo to Loy Henderson, who denounced the idea in his usual scathing style.[8]

Whenever possible, Litvinov ignored Henderson and the other Russian experts and dealt with the White House through Harry Hopkins and former ambassador Davies, whose 1941 book, *Mission to Moscow*, praised everything Russian, including Stalin. Henderson had registered a sharp protest against letting Litvinov go out of channels. Now here was the Russian ambassador, asking—even telling—the State Department that Henderson should be purged. Henderson was not entirely surprised. The department's Soviet watcher, Ray Murphy, had warned him in early 1942 that the Communists were launching a campaign to "force from the government service any public official who will not go along with what they conceive to be the best interests of the Soviet Union."[9]

Secretary Hull was outraged from the moment he heard about the Russian ambassador's campaign to get Henderson. "Litvinov doesn't decide these matters. It can't be tolerated," he roared. If Welles had agreed, the matter would have been dropped. But something strange and sad was happening to Sumner Welles. He was under covert attack for a side of his personality that had nothing to do with his skills as a diplomat. He was bisexual and word of some of his homosexual indiscretions had begun swirling through Washington. Whether the Russians were using the stories to put pressure on him is uncertain. Welles had enemies in the American government ready and willing to play such a dirty game. Either way, he felt compelled to go along with Litvinov, perhaps thinking if he pleased FDR and Eleanor Roosevelt he would survive a confrontation with Hull—and become secretary of state.[10]

V

America's relationship to Soviet Russia was a large problem that had roiled New Dealers and their political opponents inside and outside the Democratic Party since 1933. Communism and its offshoots, anarchism and socialism, had been divisive issues in the United States for decades before the New Deal came to power in Washington. Anarchist bombs had killed Chicago policemen in the Haymarket Square riot in 1886 and an anarchist had assassinated President William McKinley in 1901. When the Bolsheviks, a Communist minority who preached violent overthrow of the existing order, seized power in Russia during World War I and proclaimed the dawn of a worldwide revolution that would destroy capitalism, not a few Americans reacted with fear and loathing. The Great Red Scare of 1919, led by Mitchell Palmer, Woodrow Wilson's attorney general, threw thousands of Communists, socialists, and anarchists in jail on the flimsiest charges and deported hundreds of others. In retaliation, radicals had detonated a bomb outside J. P. Morgan and Company in Wall Street in 1920, killing 33 and wounding more than 400 passersby.

Liberals nonetheless criticized President Wilson's refusal to recognize the Bolshevik regime, because it had never held a free election to prove its legitimacy. Throughout the 1920s, the intelligentsia's fascination with the experiment in Communist rule grew more and more intense. Writers and thinkers trekked to the Soviet Union and sent back glowing reports. Upton Sinclair, whose iconoclastic critiques of American society sold widely in Russia, was typical of those who closed their eyes to the Communist Party's dictatorship and insisted the Soviet Union was "democratic in the broad sense."[11]

When FDR took office in 1933, he had already decided to recognize the Soviet Union. But he moved cautiously toward this goal. The administration argued that trade with Russia would be large and profitable and would help revive the American economy. Unfortunately, there was a serious obstacle to these profits: a Stalin-instigated terror famine in the Ukraine that had killed an estimated 10 million people in 1932/33. These farmers, known as kulaks, were murdered because they belonged to the middle class and had resisted Stalin's order to destroy private farms and collectivize agriculture. It was the first of many mass slaughters inspired by Communism's doctrine of class hatred. Stalin sent in troops who seized the kulaks' crops and arrested them. In an eerie foreshadowing of the Holocaust, many were put on trains and shipped to death camps in Siberia. Often their children were left behind to starve in the streets. Because the kulaks had large amounts of land under cultivation, their removal had a catastrophic impact on the food supplies of those left behind. Soon people were dying at the rate of 25,000 a day.[12]

The American government apparently made no attempt to discover the truth about the famine. Instead, Roosevelt and the New Dealers embraced the conclusions of reporter Walter Duranty of the *New York Times*, who grandly assured his readers that the famine was "mostly bunk." To the astonishment and outrage of his numerous critics on the *Times,* Duranty had won a Pulitzer Prize in 1932 "for dispassionate interpretive reporting of the news from Russia." Others thought Duranty's reporting made the *Times* the "uptown *Daily Worker*" (the Communist Party's newspaper). But the Pulitzer made Duranty virtually untouchable.[13]

The English-born journalist had carved a newsworthy niche for himself by foreseeing the durability of the Soviet experiment and predicting the rise of Stalin. The *Times* remained largely conservative and anticommunist but many of its readers accepted Duranty's thesis that Communism was the right government for the "Asiatic" Slavs. He was famous for his bland dismissal of reports of Soviet brutality: "You can't make an omelet without breaking eggs." A glimpse of his popularity—and the passion of the intelligentsia to believe in Stalin's Russia—was the moment in late 1933 when Duranty was introduced during a 1,500-seat banquet at the Waldorf-Astoria celebrating Roosevelt's recognition of the Soviet Union. Duranty's name, the *New Yorker* magazine reported, evoked "the only really prolonged pandemonium" of the evening. The entire audience leaped to their feet and cheered.[14]

Other reporters were telling quite a lot of the truth about the Stalin-created famine. Duranty's fellow Timesman in Moscow, Frederick T. Burchall, estimated the deaths at 4 million and stressed this was a very conservative figure. Two English journalists, Malcolm Muggeridge and Gareth Jones, wrote more accurate estimates of the toll. Their reward for telling the truth about this stupendous barbarity was savage attacks by Communists and liberals in the West accusing them of being enemies of the great Soviet experiment.[15]

<h1 style="text-align:center">VI</h1>

The New Dealers' prophecies of lucrative commerce between Russia and America soon fizzled. Even more disappointing was Stalin's failure to pay Russia's World War I debt to America and his cavalier indifference to his foreign minister's promise that the Soviet Union would order American communists to stop agitating for revolution in the United States. Not a little of the fault for these lapses lay with FDR, who had negotiated the treaty personally and in typical style paid scant attention to the details. He also revealed a worrisome tendency to paper over differences when the Russians resisted American demands.[16]

The failure of this first rapprochement did not spell the end of the Roosevelt administration's interest in Moscow. As the Great Depression continued to grip the globe and dictatorships of the right emerged in Germany, Italy, and other countries to counter the Communist challenge, liberals found new reasons to support the Soviet Union. Stalin announced a policy of "socialism in one country" and supposedly abandoned the call for world revolution. Communists forged alliances with noncommunists in what came to be called "popular front" governments, opposed to Fascism and Nazism. Liberals in America and Europe supported this turnaround virtually in a body.

No one summed it up better than the poet and literary critic Malcolm Cowley: "All through the 1930s the Soviet Union was a second fatherland for millions of people in other countries, including our own. It was the land where men and women were sacrificing themselves to create a new civilization, not for Russia alone but for the world. It was not so much a nation . . . as it was an ideal, a faith and an international hope of salvation."[17]

The passions aroused by the Spanish Civil War, in which Stalin supported the Republicans while Hitler and Mussolini supported General Franco and his Nationalists, only intensified this mindset. From 1936 to 1939, the Soviet Union seemed the only power willing to confront fascism in Spain or elsewhere. The democracies hid behind a timid mask of neutrality and gaseous rhetoric such as FDR's 1937 call to quarantine aggressors.

Stalin's purge trials of the late 1930s shook the faith of many true believers in Soviet Russia. But astonishing numbers of other liberals were able to talk themselves into believing that the procession of top Communists who confessed to spying and other forms of betrayal were telling the truth. In *Mission to Moscow*, Joseph C. Davies, who attended some of the trials during his two years in the Soviet capital, blandly called the auto-da-fé "this purging process" as if murdering people judicially was an acceptable technique for reforming society. So totally did Davies swallow Stalin's claim that traitors were sabotaging his five year plan to make Russia an industrial power, the ambassador wrote a letter to Secretary of State Cordell Hull predicting a breakdown of the Soviet economy.

Davies's motto was see no evil, hear no evil, think no evil about Russia. In his lone reference to the terror famine, Davies wrote that "hundreds of thousands were alleged to have died." George Kennan and Loy Henderson were so distressed by Davies's attitude, they considered resigning from the foreign service.[18]

VII

On August 14, 1939, came a stunning turnaround that left true believers in the Soviet Union in a daze. Hitler and Stalin signed a nonaggression pact, freeing Germany of the nightmare that had tormented her during World War I: a two-front war. Two weeks later, Hitler and Stalin jointly invaded Poland and divided it between them. As a dividend, Stalin swallowed the Baltic states and invaded Finland. A year later, Hitler's war machine, with oil and other raw materials supplied by Russia, crushed France and isolated England.

The cynicism of Stalin's about-face was ignored by hard-core communists in other countries. No less than 20,000 New Yorkers rallied in Madison Square Garden to cheer Poland's dismemberment. In the ensuing months, Communists, who had been among the loudest screamers for America to join a united democratic front against the Nazis and Fascists, became passionate supporters of America First and nonintervention. Not a few of the strikes that tied up war plants when Roosevelt started to rearm in 1941 were Communist-led. Many liberals and moderates declared they could see no difference between the two dictatorships and called on Roosevelt to denounce both of them. Liberal columnist Max Lerner ruefully admitted, "You can scarcely think nowadays because of the noise made by those who are eating their words." A poll revealed 99 percent of the American people were hoping tiny Finland could defeat the Russian giant. Newspapers and their columnists rushed to denounce Hitler and Stalin as "brother dictators, swindlers of the same breed." [19]

In yet another dizzying turnaround, Hitler invaded Russia and FDR joined Winston Churchill in extending aid and encouragement to the embattled Soviets. The president sent Harry Hopkins to Russia for face-to-face talks with Stalin, and he returned declaring his admiration for the Soviet leader. As it became apparent that Russia would survive the Nazi onslaught, the liberal love affair with the dictatorship of the proletariat underwent an amazing resurrection. The New Dealers and their allies in the media began to find in the Red Army's increasingly successful resistance proof of the hidden virtues of the Communist system and Stalin. Max Lerner, the word-eater of 1939, led the way, proclaiming that he was sure the fires of war would somehow purify Stalinism and make Russia a "responsible partner in a common peace." It was a harbinger of rationalizations to come.[20]

VIII

In late 1941, the *New Republic* published a special issue, "Russia Today," in which various liberal icons, such as Roger Baldwin, founder of the Civil Liberties Union, told readers that Russia was a democratic society because it had achieved "economic democracy." Others claimed the German assault proved Stalin had been telling the truth about the Nazi-sympathizing tendencies of the Bolsheviks he had purged. Others, such as the malleable Max Lerner, decided that Hitler's hands on Stalin's gullet proved the two totalitarian systems were not identical after all.

Stalin played expertly on this will to believe. His gave speeches in which he rallied his people with calls to defend "Holy Russia." He rehabilitated various clergymen, such as the pliable Metropolitan of Kiev, and even received several Orthodox church leaders in the Kremlin. More important, he announced he was dissolving the Comintern, the arm of the Soviet apparatus that linked Russia with communist parties around the world. Conservative Senator Tom Connally of Texas, chairman of the Senate Foreign Relations Committee, hailed this step as proof that the Soviet Union would henceforth respect the independence of foreign nations.[21]

By the spring of 1943, when Maxim Litvinov presented his ultimatum to Under Secretary of State Sumner Welles, pro-Russian articles, books, and films were deluging America. *Mission to Moscow*, a huge best-seller in 1941, had blazed the trail, with FDR's enthusiastic endorsement. He wrote on the flyleaf of his copy, "This book will last." In 1943, it appeared as a film, reportedly at FDR's express request to Jack Warner, head of Warner Brothers studio. In the book, Davies had tempered his pro-Soviet effusions with an occasional doubt. The film eliminated all such hesitations. It portrayed Stalin as a beaming pipe-smoking "easy boss" of Russia, a kind of old-fashioned Tammany leader writ large. The Soviet Union was a land of happy collective farmers and cheerful factory workers. The appalled Russian experts in the State Department called it "Submission to Moscow." [22]

The Davies film was not an isolated phenomenon. No less a capitalist organ than *Life* magazine devoted its entire March 29, 1943, issue to unqualified praise of Soviet Russia. Stalin was portrayed as a diplomatic and political genius and the ubiquitous Joseph C. Davies assured one and all that in the glorious future there was not the slightest chance that the Soviet Union would "promote dissension in the internal affairs of other nations." Collective farms and state-owned factories received effusive tributes.[23]

Other magazines were equally rapturous. The big weekly *Colliers* devoted article after article to making Russians and Americans as similar as peas from the same pod. In the *Saturday Evening Post*, almost everything on Russia (and China) was written by Edgar Snow, author of the procommunist *Red Star Over China*. Even *Reader's Digest*, a frequent prewar critic of the Soviet Union, printed scarcely a negative word. Their correspondent in Moscow during the war years was Maurice Hindus, a wholehearted apologist who wrote fervent apostrophes to the Russian peasant.

Book publishers were of the same Moscow-admiring state of mind. Scarcely a single negative book about the Soviet Union was published throughout 1943. Bennett Cerf, the president of Random House, suggested that the publishing industry declare a moratorium on books critical of Russia until the war ended. It should hardly be surprising to discover that polls reported 93 percent of the American people believed Russia would be the friendly partner of the U.S.A. in creating a peaceful postwar world.[24]

IX

Maxim Litvinov's March ultimatum to Sumner Welles coincided with this cresting public enthusiasm for Russia and with a new spate of media attacks on the State Department for its reluctance to commit the United States to an all-out effort to save Europe's Jews. The White House was happy to let the diplomats and desk men in State take the heat for a policy that FDR secretly supported.

The *Nation* saw the conservatives at State plotting to construct a "Washington-Madrid-Rome" axis to resist the coming military triumph of Communist Russia. The editors made much of the fact that Archbishop Francis Spellman of New York had recently conferred with General Franco and then flown to Rome to see the pope. The *Nation* saw this trip as a harbinger of the Vatican's determination to rally the forces of reaction. "A new Holy Alliance is in gestation," the magazine declared, referring to the conservative coalition that dominated Europe after the Napoleonic wars. Simultaneously, the New Dealers' chief spokesman, Vice President Henry Wallace, was noting similar ideas in his diary.[25]

This pro-Soviet atmosphere almost certainly contributed to Sumner Welles's decision to side with Litvinov and abandon the State Department's Russian specialists. Welles was backed by administration spokesmen in Congress. They said Loy Henderson was the evil genius behind the American ambassador to Moscow, Admiral William Standley, who chose this moment to criticize the Russians for their lack of appreciation of the billions in lend-lease aid they had received from America. An infuriated FDR disowned the admiral's remarks and sent Joseph Davies to Moscow with a sealed personal letter to Stalin, asking for a face-to-face meeting. When Davies returned in June of 1943 he brought word that the Russians were insisting on action on Litvinov's demands.

Welles served as the reluctant go-between in Henderson's decapitation. Also on the hit list was Ray Atherton, acting head of the European desk, the Russian experts' theoretical boss. (In fact, they operated more or less independently.) The message was clear. If Atherton's successor took too much advice from the surviving Russian experts, Elbridge Durbrow and Charles Bohlen, he would meet the same fate.

Secretary of State Hull was furious, but as usual he did nothing when confronted with yet another Roosevelt insult to his prerogatives. Instead, he made his displeasure clear by promoting Henderson two full grades to the rank of chief of mission. Unfortunately, the only opening for a diplomat at this level was in Baghdad, the capital of backwater Iraq. That was where Henderson went, after a brief talk with FDR at the White House, in which, Henderson recalled, "he was very nice to me."[26]

X

Cordell Hull now regarded Welles as worse than disloyal to him personally. He had become a traitor to the foreign service and even to his country. Hull was ready to entertain any and all attacks on his under secretary. Unfortunately for Welles, there was a man waiting in the wings of this imbroglio who had a lurid story to tell.

William C. Bullitt was the scion of a distinguished Philadelphia family that went back to the American Revolution. He had accompanied Woodrow Wilson to Versailles and became a self-made expert on European politics. Roosevelt had chosen him to be the first American ambassador to Soviet Russia in 1933, an assignment Bullitt had accepted with the same high optimism the president displayed. Bullitt's exposure to Josef Stalin's blood-soaked regime had turned him into a passionate anticommunist.

Transferred to Paris, Bullitt filled the Atlantic cables with advice, little of which Roosevelt accepted. Bullitt urged French-German reconciliation for a united front against Soviet Russia. After France fell to Hitler's panzers, Bullitt demanded a cabinet post. FDR ignored him. Bullitt was singing a song Roosevelt did not want to hear.[27]

Lacking a job commensurate with his high opinion of his talent, Bullitt had taken to brooding about why he had been pushed out of the White House circle. More and more, he saw Welles as the sycophant who had replaced him as Roosevelt's chief advisor on foreign affairs. He picked up rumors of Welles's homosexual episodes, which he began whispering to Hull.

One Welles indiscretion was documented beyond the realm of gossip. On a 1940 trip to the funeral of a prominent southern senator, the under secretary had gotten extremely drunk and propositioned several black porters on the train. The porters had complained to the railroad, and the president of the railroad had given Bullitt the incriminating statements. Bullitt gave them to Roosevelt and told Hull about them. The secretary began demanding Welles's resignation but Roosevelt said he needed Welles and temporized. He ordered the Secret Service to assign a man to Welles when he traveled to make sure he did not repeat his 1940 performance.[28]

XI

Seething beneath the surface of the protoscandal was an unpleasant use of homosexuality by New York liberals in 1942. Democratic Senator David I. Walsh of Massachusetts had been caught in a police raid on a gay brothel in Brooklyn. The *New York Post*, encouraged by the prominent liberal lawyer, Morris Ernst, had been the only paper that printed the story. Walsh had been a leading isolationist before Pearl Harbor. The liberals piously claimed they were motivated by patriotism. They feared German spies might get evidence of Senator Walsh's sexual orientation and blackmail him. The Senate's anti-Roosevelt coalition called it a vendetta and accused Ernst of being a secret agent for the White House.

FDR told Henry Wallace that "everyone knew" about Walsh. But he countenanced an FBI investigation that whitewashed the senator, who of course denied all. Walsh's anti-Roosevelt allies in the Senate, such as Burton K. Wheeler, still seethed about the incident. It was not hard to imagine what they would do with the Welles story if it surfaced.[29]

Welles's attempt to propitiate the White House by abandoning the Russian experts gave Hull and Bullitt the opening they needed to renew their attack on the under secretary. Welles's betrayal of Henderson and Atherton destroyed his support among State's professionals, particularly the members of the elite European division. The plotters enlisted the aid of several Republican senators, who threatened to call for an investigation, possibly by the Truman Committee.

The *New York Times* weighed in with a front-page story accusing FDR of maladministration in the State Department. For years, the *Times* reporter intimated, the president had permitted the department to be paralyzed by the feud between Hull and Welles. Almost identical stories appeared in the *Chicago Tribune* and the *Washington Times-Herald*. Arthur Krock, the *Times's* chief Washington correspondent, went for the kill in a series of columns that deplored FDR's tendency to favor Welles and humiliate Hull. A jubilant Hull decided it was time to lay his trump card on FDR's desk. He told the president to choose between him and Welles.

XII

By now it was the summer of 1943. The sealed letter Roosevelt had sent via Joseph Davies had persuaded Stalin to agree to a face-to-face meeting in December, but the Russian leader insisted on a preliminary conference of foreign ministers in Moscow first. Now Hull had the president in an impossible bind. If he fired Hull and made Welles secretary of state, Hull and Bullitt would play their ultimate trump, Welles's homosexuality, possibly when he was in the midst of crucial diplomacy in Moscow. FDR decided Welles had become a political liability and agreed to his departure.

In an attempt to turn the tables, FDR called Welles to the Oval Office and asked him to go to the foreign ministers' conference in Moscow as his special envoy. But Welles was a bitter burnt-out man. He rejected the president's proposal and retreated from Washington, leaving Roosevelt without the professional foreign policy advisor he badly needed.

The winners in this tangled personal and ideological struggle were the Communists. The liberal media assailed Hull and State's professionals, accusing them of ousting Welles because he was pro-Russian. Drew Pearson said this explicitly in one of his columns, infuriating the secretary of state so much that Hull convened a press conference to deny it, and persuaded FDR to call Pearson "a chronic liar." Hull, a politician first and a diplomat second, decided to go to Moscow for the foreign ministers' conference and prove he could be as friendly to Stalin as Sumner

Welles. It did not matter that Welles had never been any such thing. Political perceptions were steadily replacing reality in the New Dealers' war.[30]

XIII

In the midst of the Welles-Henderson-Litvinov hugger-mugger, the Berlin radio reported the discovery of a huge grave in the Katyn Forest, near Smolensk in eastern Poland. In it, trumpeted Hitler's propaganda chief, Joseph Goebbels, were the bodies of perhaps 10,000 Polish army officers who had surrendered to the Russians in 1940 and had been murdered at Stalin's order.

Berlin's outrage was hard to swallow for anyone who knew that the Germans were killing 6,000 Jews a day. But the story nevertheless sent an uneasy chill through the New Dealers and their media allies. Could it be true? It was a reminder that they were dealing with a man, Stalin, whom many people believed was a mass murderer, no matter how many nice things Joseph Davies and Walter Duranty said about him.

In London, the Polish government in exile called for the International Red Cross to investigate the story. Moscow angrily denied its guilt and broke off diplomatic relations with the Poles. In the White House, Harry Hopkins took the lead in dismissing the Poles as troublemakers who were endangering the alliance with Russia. He said their government in exile was controlled by "large landlords" who feared the Russians would confiscate their estates.

The president was even more vehement. He considered the story Nazi propaganda and was furious with the Poles for demanding an investigation. The OWI, abandoning any and all shreds of a strategy of truth, rushed to purvey this White House line. In a widely circulated statement, Elmer Davis called the massacre story a classic example of the Big Lie propaganda technique preached by Hitler in *Mein Kampf*. When Polish-American radio stations in Detroit and Buffalo began broadcasting facts that suggested the Big Lie was emanating from the Oval Office, the OWI and the Federal Communications Commission brusquely silenced them. [31]

The Katyn story refused to go away. In London, Colonel Henry I. Szymanski, a West Point graduate who was liaison officer to the Polish army in exile, compiled a report based on the evidence smuggled out of Poland. It included a statement by Lavrenti Beria, head of Stalin's secret police, admitting the crime; a report of a Polish officer who had escaped from the Russian prison camps just before the slaughter; and numerous requests for information on the missing men addressed to Stalin by the leaders of the Polish army in exile. Szymanski remarked that he was having the information delivered by hand to the head of army intelligence in Washington because he knew it contained "too much dynamite to be forwarded through regular channels." The U.S. Army thoroughly agreed with that estimate. Szymanski's report was sent to a warehouse outside Washington and stayed there for the rest of the war.[32]

In Istanbul, the U.S. naval attaché, Lt. Commander George H. Earle, FDR's special emissary to the Balkans, who had tried to get him to listen to spokesmen from the German resistance to Hitler, undertook his own investigation of Katyn, using his many contacts in the Balkans. He gathered photographs and testimony, and became more and more convinced that the Russians were guilty. However, he decided to say nothing until he had a face-to-face talk with Roosevelt to show him the evidence.[33]

XIV

In London, Winston Churchill ordered an investigation of Katyn by Sir Owen O'Malley, ambassador to the Polish government in exile. In June of 1943, O'Malley submitted a massive report to the king and the war cabinet, prepared with the help of the Poles. The British career diplomat concluded there was not a shadow of a doubt that the Soviets were guilty. They had "broken apart the heads of [the] . . . Polish officers with the insouciance of a monkey cracking walnuts." The report included vivid descriptions of how the Russians marched the Poles into the forest, shot them in the back of the head, and shoved them into the huge gravesite. "Up and down on the bodies the executioners tramped . . . treading in the blood like butchers in a stockyard." O'Malley left it up to his superiors to decide what to do with his conclusion. But he warned that the crime could cause enduring "moral repercussions."[34]

Sir Alexander Cadogan, the permanent British under secretary of state, called O'Malley's report "very disturbing." He wondered how the British and Americans could possibly ask the Poles to live in peace with the Russians "for generations to come." But he concluded that for the moment, "there is nothing to be done." The report "cannot affect the course of action or policy." He even wondered about the wisdom of circulating the report, exposing more people to the "spiritual conflict" that reading it "excites."[35]

Cadogan and Foreign Secretary Anthony Eden decided to circulate the O'Malley report. One reason may have been O'Malley's eloquent commentary on the moral problem it posed—and the temporary solution he offered. He admitted the Allies were "constrained by the urgent need for cordial relations with the Soviet government." But he regretted being "obliged to distort the normal and healthy operations of our moral and intellectual judgments." It pained him to see "the good name of England" being used to cover up such an appalling crime. For the time being he thought the only solution lay "inside our own hearts and minds, where we are masters." In this realm, the reader of his report could make "a reaffirmation of our allegiance to truth and justice and compassion."[36]

A month after O'Malley's report was circulated to the war cabinet, Churchill sent it to FDR with a personal letter, urging him to read it carefully. There was no response. Ten days later, on August 23, 1943, Churchill wrote to Harry Hopkins, asking if the president had read the report, and requesting its return. Again, there was no response. Only after Churchill wrote another letter did a member of the White House staff confirm that the president had been given the report.

By the time FDR received the O'Malley account, Lt. Colonel Szymanski's report had been in Washington for three months. The president undoubtedly had read it—or a condensation of it—and approved its interment in a government warehouse. If he read the O'Malley report, there is no record of him saying a word to Churchill about it, nor did he discuss it with anyone in the White House, much less circulate it among his cabinet or other high-ranking members of his administration.

Instead, FDR chose a backstairs method of dealing with the problem. He ordered John F. Carter, a member of a special intelligence team that monitored Radio Berlin and analyzed Nazi propaganda, to make an investigation of Katyn for the president's eyes only. FDR told Carter before he began this task that he thought the Russians were probably guilty. But officially and publicly, he intended to tell those around him that he "didn't want to believe it" and if eventually he did believe it, he would "pretend not to." Carter's report concluded the Polish government "was fully justified in demanding that an impartial investigation [of Katyn] be held."[37]

The strategy of truth, the New Dealers' dream of reducing the global conflict to a moral issue, had gone glimmering. Some would say it had already vanished in the 1,000°C flames of Hamburg, in the race hatred that permeated the Pacific war and the White House's covert acquiescence in the slaughter of the Jews. But the refusal to admit the truth about the Soviet regime, at least within the upper level of the American government, has a starker, more unnerving dimension.

In both Britain and America, the truth about Katyn was successfully suppressed. From the British embassy in Washington, Isaiah Berlin reported with evident relief that even among those who believed the Russians were guilty, the story was received "more in sorrow than in anger." In the White House, Roosevelt prepared to meet Stalin in the Iranian capital of Teheran. FDR was clinging to a prediction he had made to Churchill the previous year: "I know you will not mind my being brutally frank when I tell you that I think I can personally handle Stalin better than either your Foreign Office or my State Department."[38]

13

SHAKING HANDS
WITH MURDER

Roosevelt took only one member of the State Department to Teheran: Charles "Chip" Bohlen, who succeeded Loy Henderson as chief of the Russian desk in the European section. But Bohlen did not go to the conference as a presidential advisor. He was there only to serve as FDR's interpreter and notekeeper in his discussions with Stalin. Bohlen made no objection. If anything, he was relieved.

Bohlen was living proof of the effectiveness of the Litvinov purge of Henderson and the European section chief, Ray Atherton. The suave handsome Harvard graduate was walking a tightrope between loyalty to Henderson and a readiness to hew the White House line on Soviet Russia. As he put it in his memoirs: "Like Henderson, I, too, thought we were dealing with the Soviets on an emotional rather than a realistic basis." But he "did not feel as strongly as Henderson" about it. He agreed with Roosevelt that the "grim military situation" made it necessary to appease—or at least please—Stalin. Throughout the last years of the war, Bohlen admitted he "rarely tried to convince anyone" that admiration for Russia's military prowess was "blinding Americans to the dangers of the Bolshevik leaders."[1]

On the way to Teheran, Roosevelt stopped in Cairo to confer with Winston Churchill and China's leader, Chiang Kai-shek. While the top men talked, Bohlen found himself having long conversations with Harry Hopkins. The president's right-hand man questioned Bohlen intensely about his attitude toward the Soviet Union. Was he part of State's "anti-Soviet clique"? Bohlen's tactful responses satisfied Hopkins that he could be trusted to promote—or at least not oppose—the president's point of view.

A shrewd, astute man, Chip Bohlen was not selling out, as fiercely anti-Soviet William Bullitt accused him of doing. He was simply going with the pro-Russian flow, which was no longer emanating only from the White House. As a trained foreign service officer, he was supposed to resist fluctuations of popular opinion but there are limits to such maxims. Bohlen did not change his opinions. He simply decided to keep his head down for the time being because he saw that it could be separated from his shoulders, Henderson style, if he were too frank.

II

Bohlen's immediate boss, Secretary of State Cordell Hull, had come back from the October 1943 foreign ministers' conference in Moscow breathing apostrophes to the Soviet Union and basking in an unprecedented shower of praise from the liberal press for his supposedly masterful performance there. Hull had submitted a statement calling for postwar international cooperation between China, the United States, Great Britain, and Soviet Russia, a document written, ironically, by his departed enemy, Sumner Welles. The foreign ministers had accepted this Four Power Declaration with little argument, raising everyone's hopes for a peaceful future.

On the last night of the conference, a jovial Joseph Stalin had given a dinner in the Kremlin for the diplomats and their staffs. The Soviet dictator had sat Hull at his right hand and after the usual toasts had leaned over and informed the dazzled secretary of state that as soon as the European war ended, the Soviet Union would join the United States in a decisive assault on Japan.[2]

Hull accepted this offer as a further tribute to his ability to charm the Russians. On top of the Four Power Declaration, it made him look like the foreign policy leader he had hoped to become until he discovered Roosevelt intended him to be a mere figurehead. It was a delicious triumph for the seventy-two-year-old Tennessean after the pounding he had taken from the liberal press over Sumner Welles's dismissal.

Was this sudden Russian bonhomie, six months after Ambassador Litvinov told Sumner Welles his government was in despair over their relations with Washington, an amazing piece of luck? Or had Roosevelt the juggler told the Soviets through various back channels that Hull could be converted from foe to friend? Since the Atlantic Charter conference, while Roosevelt and Churchill talked constantly about the "United Nations" as a peacetime as well as a wartime entity, Hull had remained stonily silent. He had been equally mute about Soviet-American friendship, reflecting instead the skepticism he heard from his Russian experts at the State Department.

Roosevelt did his share to inflate Hull's new sense of importance. The president praised the secretary's Moscow performance at a press conference, singling out for special commendation his statements on behalf of the policy of unconditional surrender. When Hull deplaned at Washington's airport, a beaming FDR and a cheering congressional delegation greeted him.[3]

Roosevelt also arranged with Democratic legislative leaders to make Hull the first secretary of state to address a joint session of Congress. Storms of applause greeted his declaration that the Moscow Conference and the global war had transformed international relations. "There will no longer be need for spheres of influence, for alliances, for balances of power or any of the other special arrangements through which, in the unhappy past, the nations strove to safeguard their security and promote their interests," he declared. Hull characterized the Communists as being "like your country cousins come to town a little slow but well worthwhile." He saw no barriers whatsoever to future Soviet-American cooperation.[4]

III

Roosevelt's real opinion of Hull and the rest of the State Department was revealed the day before he left for Teheran. He spent the morning secretly conferring with Sumner Welles in the White House. Later in the day, with Bohlen, Harry Hopkins, and several other members of the White House staff, he began the 6,000-mile trip to the Iranian capital. The president had done everything in his power to persuade Stalin to agree to some other site—Alaska, North Africa, Iceland—but the Russian dictator had been immovable. Stalin wanted a psychological victory over his allies before they sat down at the conference table, and he got it.

The Soviet dictator followed this victory with another preliminary triumph. The day Roosevelt arrived in Teheran, Stalin claimed his secret police had learned there was a Nazi plan to assassinate the three leaders, and he urged Roosevelt to leave the relatively small American embassy and join him in the Russian compound. Roosevelt accepted and Stalin moved out of the embassy's main building into smaller quarters. No one bothered to

On the way back from the Teheran summit, FDR conferred with General Dwight D. Eisenhower. The president would soon appoint Ike commander of Overlord, the invasion of France. Eisenhower repeatedly made it clear that he disagreed with the policy of unconditional surrender.

Roosevelt speech writer and confidant Sam Rosenman of New York invented the term "New Deal" in 1932. Here he chats with Dr. Howard Bruenn, the navy physician who discovered in early 1944 that FDR was suffering from potentially lethal heart disease and high blood pressure.

Commander of the U.S. Army air forces General Henry A. "Hap" Arnold (right) became an advocate of "morale bombing" aimed at killing and "dehousing" German civilians. Other AAF generals vehemently disagreed with this policy, calling it "baby-killing."

In the spring of 1944, FDR sent Vice President Henry Wallace to Siberia and China. After conferring with General Chiang Kai-shek, leader of the Chinese nationalists, Wallace concluded he was a "short term investment," because he refused to form a coalition government with the Chinese Communists. (Corbis)

Missourian Robert Hannegan became chairman of the Democratic Party in 1944. Convinced that Roosevelt was dying, he decided to jettison Henry Wallace and replace him with Harry S. Truman. Hannegan persuaded party bosses such as Ed Flynn and Ed Kelly of Chicago to agree. (Acme)

Delegates demonstrate in favor of FDR at the 1944 convention in Chicago. New Dealers put enormous pressure on Roosevelt to run again. Without him the Republicans would have won in a landslide. Polls predicted that if the war had ended before the election, even with FDR on the Democratic ticket the GOP candidate would have been a runaway winner. (Acme)

Ben Cohen (left) was the only New Dealer with the courage to tell the mortally ill Roosevelt that he should not run for a fourth term. With his partner, Tommy Corcoran (right), Cohen wrote much of the New Deal's 1930s reform legislation. Cohen warned FDR he had been in office too long and the coalition that had elected him had fallen apart.

Labor leader Sidney Hillman acquired great influence in the Democratic Party thanks to his ability to raise money and turn out union voters. At the 1944 convention, FDR told the party bosses that they would have to "clear it with Sidney" before deciding on a vice presidential candidate. (Photograph by T. McAvoy)

"Assistant President" Jimmy Byrnes (right), head of the Office of War Mobilization, welcomes FDR back from Teheran (along with Secretary of State Cordell Hull). Roosevelt told Byrnes he had his backing for vice president in 1944. But the president abandoned his friend of thirty-two years when Sidney Hillman objected to Byrnes's anti-labor voting record in Congress.

Speaking from San Diego, FDR accepted the Democratic Party's nomination for a fourth term in 1944. Navy photographers, indifferent to camera angles, made him look like a dying old man. The Chicago Tribune *blew the picture up to twice the usual size and splashed it on their front page.*

Admiral Wilhelm Canaris was head of the Abwehr, the German secret service. He was also one of the leaders of the German resistance to Hitler. They hoped to persuade Germany's military leaders to overthrow the dictator and negotiate peace. Canaris was dismayed by Roosevelt's announcement of the policy of unconditional surrender. "The other side have now disarmed us of the last weapon with which we could have ended [the war]," he said.

General Henning von Tresckow was a central figure in the German army's opposition to Hitler. Three times he came close to assassinating the German dictator. He believed Hitler was "the arch enemy, not only of Germany but of the whole world." When the final attempt to kill Hitler failed, Tresckow committed suicide rather than surrender to the Gestapo.

Former mayor of Leipzig Carl Goerdeler was another leader of the German resistance to Hitler. Here he stands trial in a Nazi "People's Court" after the failed attempt to assassinate the dictator. Goerdeler and over seven hundred others were executed in a Sippenhaft—*a Nazi blood purge. (Corbis)*

President Roosevelt and the 1944 Democratic vice presidential nominee, Senator Harry S. Truman of Missouri, confer in the White House garden after the Democratic convention. A worried Truman later told one of his Senate staff, "Physically, he's just going to pieces."

check with the Iranian government, who later angrily denied any such plot existed.

If Loy Henderson or George Kennan had been with Roosevelt, they would have warned the president that henceforth, everything the Americans said to each other would be bugged and all their servants would be members of the NKVD, the Soviet secret police. Chip Bohlen said nothing—his opinion was not solicited—and volunteering it would have led Harry Hopkins to change his mind and decide he was part of the State Department's anti-Soviet clique, after all.[5]

IV

Churchill was not invited to enjoy this greater Russian security—Stalin's rather pointed way of saying he would not miss the prime minister if Nazi secret agents started shooting. (The prime minister had no serious worries on this score; the British embassy was guarded by a regiment of Sikhs.) For twenty years Churchill had repeatedly opposed and denounced Bolshevism. When Hitler invaded Russia, the prime minister had declared he was ready to supply the Soviets with all the aid Britain could spare. But no apostrophes to the Soviet system came with this offer, and Churchill's previous meetings with Stalin had been marked by angry exchanges and even insults. The Russian dictator remembered that Churchill had once said an alliance with Stalin would be like "shaking hands with murder."[6]

Originally FDR had proposed that he and Stalin meet without Churchill and only vehement protests by the British prime minister had changed FDR's mind. Churchill had argued that such a unilateral move would humiliate him before the British people, something he thought his fellow leader of a democracy ought to understand.

The attempt to sideline Churchill was a manifestation of Roosevelt's underlying hostility not merely to the prime minister but to Britain and its colonial empire. From his hero, Woodrow Wilson, Roosevelt had inherited the opinion that British imperialism was a malign force. From his Democratic predecessor had also come the conviction that the New World was morally superior to the Old World. In FDR's political cosmology, Russia was exempted from this negative judgment. Like the United States, she was not part of Europe. Ever since his recognition of the Soviet Union in 1933, Roosevelt had envisioned a Russian-American entente as the answer to the fratricidal tendencies of Europe's great powers.[7]

Within fifteen minutes of FDR's arrival in the Russian compound, he was embarked on solidifying this unspoken alliance with the Soviet Union. Roosevelt's eager acceptance of Stalin's invitation encouraged the Soviet dictator to pay the president an unscheduled visit. The stocky Russian leader was dressed simply, in a khaki tunic, with a single decoration, the Order of Lenin, on his chest. He was accompanied only by a translator and an escorting U.S. Army officer who quickly vanished.

After an exchange of greetings, Stalin asked if Roosevelt had a list of the topics they were going to cover at the conference. Roosevelt dismissed the idea, saying he disliked "rigidly" adhering to an agenda. He thought a "general discussion" would be better.

After a passing mention of a second front and the problem of maintaining it, the talk turned to France. Stalin made some uncomplimentary remarks about General de Gaulle, the leader of the Free French. Roosevelt agreed with him completely. In fact, he declared that no one over the age of forty should be allowed in the postwar French government because they had all collaborated with Hitler.

Roosevelt's opinion of the French was almost as low—and as hostile—as his opinion of the Germans. In 1942 he had told

Henry Wallace that "neither France nor Germany were going to have any army at all when this war was over."[8] Roosevelt agreed when Stalin said France's Indochina colonies were an imperialist disgrace and should not be returned to her after the war. FDR said the same policy should be applied to India, which was more and more restless under British rule. He contemptuously added that "Mr. Churchill" had no solution to offer. Roosevelt said the best answer would be "reform from the bottom, somewhat on the Soviet line."

This remark must have made Stalin wonder if he were dreaming. The president of the United States, the headquarters of world capitalism, found no fault with reform, Soviet style? The Russian dictator obviously thought this endorsement of Leninism was too good to be true. He said India was a "complicated" problem. "Reform from the bottom would mean revolution." Roosevelt dismissed this observation with a toss of his head, as if to say, What's a Bolshevik upheaval or two among friends?[9]

V

This opening exchange set the pattern Roosevelt followed at the Teheran conference. Again and again, Roosevelt agreed with Stalin and tried to use his fabled warmth to make the Russian leader unbend. But Stalin declined to cooperate most of the time. With an absolute minimum of charm he told Roosevelt at their first plenary session that his policy of unconditional surrender was a very bad idea.

The Russian leader said he thought its vagueness and implied threat only served to unite the German people. He favored an explicit statement of terms and an appeal to the German people to discard Hitler—a strategy Russia was already pursuing with the National Committee of Free Germans recruited from officers captured at Stalingrad. Churchill emphatically endorsed this idea, revealing his underlying hostility to unconditional surrender. Neither man changed Roosevelt's mind.[10]

Before the first plenary session began, Churchill asked to see Roosevelt privately. FDR bluntly, even rudely, declined. When the session convened that afternoon, with the three leaders and their top aides and interpreters at a central table in a large ornate hall next to Roosevelt's quarters, FDR sided with Stalin against Churchill's argument for operations in the eastern Mediterranean and the Balkans, using troops from Italy and North Africa. Churchill wanted a Western presence in these areas to encourage non-Communist politicians. Roosevelt made it clear that he had no interest in this aspect of the war.[11]

By the end of the afternoon, Churchill was in a rage. He knew that his country was being shunted aside by the two stronger powers. That injured his pride. But he was also appalled at FDR's indifference to the prospect of Communism moving with the Soviet armies into Eastern Europe and the Mediterranean basin.

For two more days, the leaders wrangled over the date of Overlord, the invasion of northern France and a simultaneous invasion of the south of France. Stalin demanded a commitment to both operations. The American Joint Chiefs of Staff were emphatically in favor of Overlord. But they had no opinion on the landing in southern France, on which Stalin grew insistent. Roosevelt backed him and it became an adjunct of Overlord.

Later, General Mark Clark, the American commander in Italy, would protest this decision, claiming he could invade the Balkans with the troops that were being siphoned off to southern France. But FDR was indifferent to Stalin's desire to confine the British and Americans to Western Europe. In fact, the president told Averell Harriman, the American ambassador to Moscow, that he "didn't care whether the countries bordering Russia became communized or not."[12]

VI

That night at dinner, Stalin held forth on the postwar treatment of France and Germany. He reiterated his contempt for the French ruling class and dismissed Churchill's assertion that a restored and prosperous France was essential to the civilized world. Roosevelt said nothing. Nor did he object when Stalin launched a hate-filled diatribe against the German people, declaring Germany was an outlaw nation and should be rendered "impotent" forever.

When the conversation turned to Lithuania, Latvia, and Estonia, Stalin growled that the Baltic states were not a subject for discussion. They had voted "by an extension of the will of the people" to join the Soviet Union in 1940. This was a Russian version of democracy. Anyone who did not vote in these supposedly free elections was shot or shipped to Siberia. Again, the Americans and British waited for Roosevelt to say something.

To their horror, FDR slumped in his wheelchair, writhing with awful stomach cramps. As Charles Bohlen later recalled it, "he turned green and great drops of sweat began to bead off his face; he put a shaky hand to his forehead." An agitated Harry Hopkins ordered the president wheeled to his bedroom, where his personal physician, Admiral Ross McIntire, examined him. By that time he had revived and McIntire dismissed the episode as indigestion. It was not the first nor would it be the last of McIntire's misdiagnoses.

The next day, Stalin had another private meeting with Roosevelt. He descanted on the menace of Germany and said "strong points" either inside or just outside Germany should be occupied by the victors. Roosevelt again displayed an amazing indifference to the idea of Soviet troops in Central Europe. Instead, he proposed the idea of the great powers acting as "four policeman" to prevent future wars, wherever they might break out. They would be the linchpin of the world organization that he outlined in very rough terms to an obviously skeptical Stalin.

The next plenary session produced more wrangling about Overlord in which Stalin beat down Churchill's continuing hesitations and objections. The British prime minister dreaded a replay of the World War I's horrendous casualties and apparently hoped Allied air power alone might batter the Third Reich into surrender. Churchill's doubts contributed to Roosevelt's tilt toward Stalin. The president let the Soviet leader do all the talking but FDR obviously agreed with him.

That night, Stalin hosted a dinner at which he began accusing Churchill of having a secret affection for Germany and wanting a "soft peace." Abruptly, Stalin revealed his real intentions for Germany. These had little to do with the generous sentiments displayed by his Free Germans Committee. He favored dismembering the country into four or five ineffective parts—and shooting between 50,000 and 100,000 officers of the German army.

Although the Russian dictator made this latter recommendation in a sardonic tone, Churchill exploded and cried that the British people had always been opposed and always would be opposed to mass vengeance. Stalin, his tone still sardonic—or sadistic—insisted at least 50,000 German officers should be shot.

"I would rather be taken out into the garden here and now and be shot myself than sully my own and my country's honor by such infamy," Churchill roared.

The prime minister was obviously aware that he was dealing with the man who had massacred 10,000 Polish officers in the Katyn Forest. Roosevelt's reaction alarmed Churchill even more. The president suggested a compromise: shooting 49,000. Recalling how seriously the British took the moral significance of Katyn—and how earnestly Churchill tried to make Roosevelt face the truth about the crime—it is easy to imagine the prime minister's dismay at the president's offhand approval of another mass slaughter.[13]

Churchill sprang to his feet and bolted into the garden rather than continue the argument. Later, Stalin and Molotov joined him there with broad smiles and claimed that Stalin had only been joking. Calmer and more resigned to shaking hands with murder for the time being, Churchill summoned a smile and the incident was passed off as the Russian idea of humor.[14]

VII

At the final plenary session, as Churchill walked toward the conference room beside Roosevelt in his wheelchair, FDR said: "Winston, I hope you won't be sore at me for what I am going to do."

When the session began, Roosevelt started making fun of the prime minister as a typical Brit, who drank too much brandy and was "John Bullish" about his pompous little island and its pretensions to imperial glory. Churchill turned red, while Stalin's smile grew broader. Finally, the Soviet dictator "broke out into a deep hearty guffaw" (according to FDR's version of the story). A delighted Roosevelt asked Stalin if he minded being called "Uncle Joe." Stalin was supposedly so pleased, he came around the table and shook Roosevelt's hand. Other versions of the story claim Stalin was not even slightly amused.[15]

The reason for this sophomoric humor, Roosevelt later explained, was his feeling that he had not been able to "get at" Stalin. The phrase is an interesting insight into how FDR related to people. When he "got at" someone, he apparently thought he had power over them. In America, this was often the case. But was it true of Stalin, with whom FDR was conversing through a screen of interpreters? In America, Roosevelt wielded enormous power, whether or not he "got at" anyone. He did not wield much, if any, power over Stalin.

Charles Bohlen watched this presidential performance with growing dismay. Bohlen thought Roosevelt was making a "basic error," trying to ingratiate himself with Stalin at Churchill's expense. It stemmed from Roosevelt's lack of understanding of the Bolsheviks—and it was "transparent" in the bargain.[16]

At this final plenary session, Roosevelt continued his policy of agreeing with Stalin and denigrating Churchill. He consented to Stalin's demand for most of eastern Poland, asking only that his approval be kept quiet until after the 1944 elections, lest it cost him votes among the Polish-Americans.[17] He also tacitly agreed to Stalin's demand for a "friendly Poland," knowing it meant Moscow would refuse to deal with the Polish government in exile, which was still demanding an investigation of the Katyn massacre. Roosevelt seemed utterly indifferent to Poland's contribution to the war effort. The Poles had the fourth largest number of men under arms on the Allied side of the war. Moreover, they produced no Nazi puppet government nor any collaborators. Yet Roosevelt's sympathy for Poland was as nonexistent as his support.[18]

VIII

This indifference to Poland's fate was doubly regrettable, because Stalin felt a special enmity for the Polish people. In 1920, a war-desolated Europe looked ripe for conquest by Communism. Germany was an especially inviting target; the kaiser had abdicated, the establishment was tottering. Lenin sent the Red Army into Poland with orders to march to the aid of the German Communists. Stalin was the overall boss of the operation.

To everyone's amazement, the Poles refused to let their country become a highway to a Communist Europe. They organized a ferocious resistance. In a tremendous battle outside Warsaw, they sent the Red Army reeling back to Russia. It took Stalin years to recover from the impact of this defeat on his reputation as a leader of men.

As a result, the Soviet leader nursed a profound hatred for Poland. In the part of the nation occupied by Russia in 1939, when Russia and Germany were allies, state terrorism reached levels unusual even for the Stalin era. In two years, at least 1 million people—10 percent of the population—experienced the harsh hand of the NKVD, the Russian secret service. Most were deported to the Siberian gulag. About 100,000 died on the trains or in the camps; some 30,000 were shot. Roosevelt never displayed the slightest awareness of these awful realities.[19]

Over Churchill's objections, FDR agreed to breaking Germany up into five smaller states. The prime minister protested the creation of a "Europe of little states, all disjointed, with no larger units at all"—except Russia. But he might as well have talked gibberish. Stalin and FDR ignored him. Teheran marked the beginning of a bitter decline in Churchill's friendship with Roosevelt.[20]

IX

Charles Bohlen emerged from Teheran deeply alarmed by Roosevelt's acquiescence to Stalin's ideas about everything, from eliminating the independence of the Baltic states and vassalizing Poland to dismembering Germany. The Soviet Union obviously hoped to dominate Europe and Roosevelt seemed to be totally unbothered by this fact. Bohlen, on the other hand, saw a strong postwar Germany and a revived France as the only way to bar Bolshevism from Western Europe. But he kept these opinions to himself for the time being.[21]

FDR and Harry Hopkins went home from Teheran exultant. They were convinced that Stalin was now "get-attable" and a postwar world of peace and cooperation was assured. Eleven days after Teheran, on December 12, 1943, Stalin met with Edvard Benes, the president of the Czechoslovak government in exile. Benes was amazed to find the usually dour Russian dictator in a jubilant mood. Stalin told the Czech president a new era was dawning. Teheran had convinced him that the Slavs, under Soviet leadership, would soon dominate the politics of Europe and Asia.[22]

A few months later, Stalin had a conversation with Milovan Djilas, the Yugoslav partisan leader, in Moscow. The Soviet dictator volunteered his impression of Churchill and Roosevelt. "Churchill is the kind who, if you don't watch him, will slip a kopeck out of your pocket! And Roosevelt? Roosevelt is not like that. He dips his hand in only for bigger coins." The Soviet leader added that Teheran had also helped him draw another more fateful conclusion. "Whoever occupies a territory imposes on it his own social system. Everyone imposes his own system as far as his army can reach."[23]

So much for Stalin being get-attable.

X

Stalin did not have to worry about "getting at" Roosevelt. Before the Soviet dictator went to Teheran, he had been thoroughly briefed on what the president thought about him, the second front, Poland, and most of the other topics discussed at the summit meeting. Ever since Roosevelt opened diplomatic relations with Moscow, the NKVD had been recruiting agents in the American government. Thanks to the 1995 release of secret U.S. decrypts of NKVD cables to Moscow, code-named Venona, and the more recent release of other information from Russia's archives, we now know that Stalin orchestrated a massive espionage operation against his capitalist allies throughout World War II.

One of the most important spies was Lauchlin Currie, the president's Canadian-born senior administrative assistant. Currie reported what FDR was thinking and saying to a Soviet network led by an American Communist Party member named Nathan Gregory Silvermaster. Currie's close friend Assistant Secretary of the Treasury Harry Dexter White was another Soviet spy with frequent access to Secretary of the Treasury Henry Morgenthau Jr., a man who lunched with the president once a week and was the recipient of much of his thinking on a wide range of subjects. At the State Department, Alger Hiss headed the Office of Special Political Affairs, an umbrella title that enabled him to lay his hands on secret documents from other departments and bureaus, including the project to build an atomic bomb.

Almost as important was Lawrence Duggan, a protégé of Sumner Welles, who was chief of the State Department's South American division from 1935 to 1944. Duggan gave his Soviet contacts inside information on the invasion of Italy and secret discussions of British-American problems in the oil-rich Middle East. He had accompanied Vice President Wallace on his trip to South America and they had become close friends, enabling Duggan to inform the Russians about a wide range of topics that Wallace discussed in cabinet meetings and elsewhere.[24]

There was scarcely a branch of the American government, including the War, Navy, and Justice Departments, that did not have Soviet moles in high places, feeding Moscow information. Wild Bill Donovan's Office of Strategic Services, the forerunner of the CIA, had so many informers in its ranks, it was almost an arm of the NKVD. Donovan's personal assistant, Duncan Chaplin Lee, was a spy.

In London, Moscow's penetration of His Majesty's Secret Intelligence Service and Churchill's war cabinet was even more complete. A group of Cambridge University graduates, now known to espionage historians as "the Cambridge Five," had reached the highest levels of trust and power. If international diplomacy can be compared to high stakes poker—a not unrealistic equation—

when Churchill and Roosevelt sat down with Stalin at Teheran, they were facing a man who knew every card in their hands and how they were going to play them.

XI

In 1939, a disillusioned ex-Communist named Whittaker Chambers went to Assistant Secretary of State Adolf Berle, who was Roosevelt's advisor on internal security matters. Chambers named Lauchlin Currie, Harry Dexter White, Alger Hiss, and a baker's dozen other administration officials as Soviet spies.

Berle sent Roosevelt a report of the conversation, with all the names. The president dismissed it as absurd. There are conflicting versions of what happened next. One has Berle notifying the FBI, who ignored him because they were more interested in hunting Nazi spies. Another has him putting his memorandum in a filing cabinet and more or less forgetting about it. One thing seems certain. He did not inform the State Department's security people, although several of the men named were high-level State officials.

It is hard not to think conspiratorially about such foot-dragging. But Berle was a staunch anti-Communist. A more likely explanation is FDR's evident determination to see no evil and hear no evil about Soviet Russia. To have raised a hue and cry would have put Berle at odds with a man to whom he was deeply devoted.[25]

Other New Dealers took their cues from FDR's presidential example. When Harry Hopkins learned from an FBI report that the Bureau had caught a member of the Russian embassy staff—an NKVD man in disguise—giving money to Steve Nelson, a West Coast Communist whom the FBI had under surveillance, Hopkins quickly informed the Russian ambassador of this faux pas. He warned him that such behavior could cause political problems for the administration on Capitol Hill. It might even make some people wonder if the American Communist Party was an arm of the Soviet government, instead of the independent 100 percent American organization it claimed to be.

In 1943, OSS chief William Donovan flew to Moscow to propose a formal relationship with Soviet intelligence. To prove his sincerity, Wild Bill offered them information on OSS operations in Bulgaria, which undoubtedly consigned to postwar firing squads or the Siberian gulag all those involved. Only a ferocious objection from J. Edgar Hoover stopped Donovan from persuading Roosevelt to allow the NKVD to have an official presence in Washington, D.C. When an OSS agent obtained a copy of an NKVD codebook from a Finnish contact, FDR ordered Donovan to return it to the Soviet embassy. Donovan did so and got a letter of thanks from the no doubt secretly chortling Russian ambassador.[26]

XII

When Roosevelt abolished Henry Wallace's Board of Economic Warfare and shifted its powers to the Foreign Economic Administration, the president appointed Lauchlin Currie the deputy director of that important organization, making him the agency's chief administrator and a man of substance in Washington. The position gave Currie links to the State Department and the War Department and enabled him to place other Soviet agents on his staff.[27]

Currie knew how to throw his White House weight around on Moscow's behalf. He intervened with Under Secretary of War Robert Patterson to obtain a security clearance for Nathan Gregory Silvermaster when the Russian-born economist was challenged by Army counterintelligence for his Communist Party connections. When the FBI questioned Currie about Silvermaster's Communist links, Currie promptly reported the interview in detail, enabling the NKVD to ponder the questions and decide that the bureau did not suspect Silvermaster of spying.[28]

Through Currie and other members of his network, Silvermaster gave his Russian handler a wealth of information, ranging from British hopes of postwar influence in the Balkans and copies of American diplomatic cables about negotiations with the USSR to American plans to drastically reduce their army at the end of the war. One of the most interesting reports described the tense relations between FDR and Secretary of State Hull—a piece of information that may have had something to do with Stalin's decision to charm Hull at the Moscow foreign ministers' conference.[29]

By count from the Venona decrypts, there were 329 Soviet agents inside the U.S. government during World War II. The number of rolls of microfilm shipped to Moscow from the NKVD's New York headquarters leaped from 59 in 1942 to 211 in 1943, the same year during which the American press and publishing industry were gushing praise of the Soviet Union. In the single year 1942, the documents leaked by one member of England's Cambridge Five filled forty-five volumes in the NKVD archives. The Russian agent in charge of Whittaker Chambers's spy ring boasted to Moscow: "We have agents at the very center of government, influencing policy." The OSS and the British SIS did not have a single agent in Moscow.[30]

XIII

Roosevelt returned from Teheran "bone tired," and "exhausted," according to one of his aides. There were no triumphal greetings from Secretary of State Hull or anyone else. Instead, the atmosphere in Washington was "tepid", and rancid with gossip. There was a rumor that someone, perhaps a Russian, had poisoned the president during the dinner at which he had suffered his attack of stomach cramps. Columnist Drew Pearson reported more or less accurately that the president and Prime Minister Churchill had quarreled acrimoniously at the conference.

A State Department official told a British embassy staffer that Roosevelt had given Stalin everything he asked for and made Secretary of State Hull look like a master diplomat in comparison. The Greek ambassador was telling people that Roosevelt had sold out Poland and the Baltic states. Others were exercised by a rumor, equally accurate, that the Allies had abandoned plans to send troops across the Adriatic to Yugoslavia, meaning that country was likely to drift into the Communist orbit under a partisan leader named Tito.[31]

Secrecy had been clamped on Teheran's proceedings. No one knew whether any or all of these rumors were true. But that did not slow their circulation. What is evident from their negative tone and the overall unenthusiasm that greeted the returning president was lack of confidence in Roosevelt as a diplomat, suspicion of Roosevelt-the-Trickster, and a backlash against the twelve-month orgy of Soviet Union worship in the media.

More and more journalists had begun to criticize the praise bestowed on the Soviets by New Dealers and their media allies. The blatant propaganda of the movie, *Mission to Moscow*, was the focus of much of this acrid rebuttal. An undercurrent of suspicion was threatening FDR's vision of a postwar world in which democrats and communists would lie down together like lambs.[32]

Publisher Joe Patterson of the *New York Daily News*, his sister Cissy at the helm of the *Washington Times-Herald*, and their cousin Robert McCormick at the *Chicago Tribune* continued to warn their almost 4 million readers that Communism was as bad as or worse than Nazism, and the New Dealers, with their fondness for "Commufascist" government decrees, were not much better. The Hearst papers, with 8 million readers, repeatedly sent a similar message.

Catholic leaders remained inveterately hostile to the Soviet regime. When Stalin rehabilitated the Metropolitan of Kiev to create the illusion of religious freedom in Russia, Monsignor Fulton Sheen scoffed: "What were his first words? Thanks to God? No, he asked for a second front." The mostly Irish-American leaders of the 4-million-man American Federation of Labor deplored communism at home and abroad. In 1943, they stonily refused to join British and Russian workers in an Anglo-Soviet Trade Union Council. That same year, in a Labor Day speech, AFL's president William Green declared he saw no difference between the Nazis and the Communists.[33]

XIV

Perhaps the most important factor in the president's lukewarm reception on his return from Teheran was the calendar. As 1943 ebbed into 1944, the country began thinking about the presidential election in November. Not a few Republicans were exuding confidence that Roosevelt was all but a lame duck, if not a dead one. The Democratic Party remained in a state of torpor. When National Chairman Frank Walker sent letters to 3,048 Democratic county chairman, asking them to tell him about political problems in their locales, he received only 108 replies—an alarming indication of apathy and even despair.[34]

Few emanated deeper gloom than Indiana Democratic National Committeeman, Frank McHale, who said: "If an election were held . . . at the present time . . . the chances are five to one against the Democratic Party." The off-year election returns had continued to show a strong Republican trend. The GOP elected governors in New Jersey and Kentucky. Pennsylvania, Connecticut, and California went heavily Republican in local elections. The GOP now controlled 26 states with an electoral vote of 342.[35]

In California, Democratic liberals and moderates were still at each other's throats. Similar fratricide was wrecking the party in Illinois. Liberals called on Roosevelt to sponsor a left-wing platform, even if it cost him the election. Thomas E. Dewey's political stature grew larger in New York when the voters elected the lieutenant governor of his choice in a special election. (The incumbent had died.) Jim Farley wondered if a Democratic victory was possible, even if the president ran.[36]

Polls revealed a dismaying anti-Roosevelt trend among the voters. Asked how they would vote if FDR's opponent were the probable Republican nominee, Governor Thomas E. Dewey of New York, some 51 percent said they would back FDR if the war was still on. But if the war was over on election day 1944, Dewey was a runaway winner, 51 to 30 percent, with the rest undecided. No wonder one Republican opined: "The GOP could win with a Chinaman."[37]

To these voices of gloom and doom, Roosevelt produced a stunning answer at a press conference soon after he returned from Teheran. A reporter asked him if he would use the term "New Deal" to describe the government's current domestic policies. Roosevelt coolly replied that he considered the New Deal an obsolete term. It described policies that were needed in 1932 but not in 1943. A better slogan would be Win the War. In a follow-up press conference, he improved on this reply by personifying the two ideas. Dr. New Deal's medicine was what the United States needed to get it up and running in 1932. But in 1943, the aging physician had been replaced by brisk, determined Dr. Win-the-War.

Projecting this image as a national leader above the political fray, Roosevelt gave a Christmas eve report on Teheran that was aglow with optimism. In a fireside chat from Hyde Park, he told the American people that he and Marshal Stalin had talked with "complete frankness" and had reached agreement on every point

"concerned with the launching of a gigantic attack on Germany."
He did not think that "any insoluble differences" would arise between the English, the Americans, and the Russians. He "got
along fine" with Marshal Stalin, who impressed him as a man
who "combines a tremendous relentless determination with a
stalwart good humor." He was "truly representative of the heart
and soul of Russia." With Rooseveltian gusto, FDR predicted
"we are going to get along very well with him and the Russian
people—very well indeed."[38]

In another apparent demonstration of his political agility, two
weeks after FDR declared that Dr. New Deal had been retired for
the duration, he presented a state of the union address in which
he called for an "economic bill of rights" to sustain the American
people after the war. He wanted the Congress and the executive
department to begin drawing up plans to guarantee everyone a
rewarding job and an acceptable standard of living, decent housing, adequate medical care and educational opportunity, plus security in old age. A lot of people began to wonder if Dr. New
Deal was only taking a wartime furlough.

XV

FDR did not deliver this state of the union message. It was released to Congress and the press in written form. The White
House explained that the president was afflicted with a wracking
bronchial cough that made speaking difficult if not impossible.
There are grounds for suspecting FDR paid only perfunctory attention to the message. The call for an economic bill of rights was
an old Democratic Party chestnut that went back to Woodrow
Wilson.[39] A more immediate source of these postwar ideas was
the National Resources Planning Board, the agency that had enraged Congress unto extermination in early 1943 with its call for
a Washington-centered postwar economy.

Politically, it made no sense to announce that the New Deal was over and put it back in business two or three weeks later. This was not the shrewd political tactician at work. It had the rank smell of ideological ghostwriters—not very original ones. What makes this scenario seem likely was the dolorous state of the president's health. Within a week of his return from Iran he developed a case of what he called "Teheran flu." He ran a high fever and his racking cough made sleeping difficult. Worse, the illness resisted his doctor's treatment.

For those few who were paying attention to FDR's physical condition, this bout of flu was not blamable on Teheran. He had suffered several similar attacks of grippe and fevers as high as 104 degrees in the fall of 1943, continuing a history of respiratory problems, especially when he was under stress.[40]

When Harold Smith, the director of the budget, saw FDR in his White House bedroom early in January 1944, he was still complaining about the way his flu bug refused to go away. More alarming to Smith was the cursory way Roosevelt read the budget message, one of the most important statements on a president's agenda. "I have never seen him so listless. He is not his acute usual self," Smith wrote in the notes he kept on his meetings with FDR. "At one stage, when he was about two-thirds through the message . . . I saw his head nod. I could not see his eyes but it seemed as though they were completely shut. Yet he said something to the effect that 'this paragraph is good.'" Never, Smith concluded, had he seen the president so "groggy."[41]

A week's vacation in Hyde Park, often a restorative, failed to work its usual magic. Headaches tormented FDR almost every evening. Back in the White House, he regularly told his devoted secretary, William Hassett, that he felt "rotten" or "like hell." Long weekends at Hyde Park failed to alter his malaise. He complained constantly of being tired and unable to concentrate. Reporter Allen Drury, a longtime Roosevelt watcher, saw the president in a newsreel and was dismayed by how he had become "an aging man." At a White House dinner, Aubrey Williams, former head of the terminated National Youth Administration, was "shocked" by FDR's ashen gray skin color, his trembling hands, the dark circles beneath his eyes.[42]

As February 1944 ebbed into March with little or no improvement in the president's condition, nobody seemed to know what to do about the health of arguably the most powerful human being on the planet. His doctor, Admiral Ross McIntire, was a medical ignoramus. FDR got more and possibly better advice from his cousin, Daisy Suckley, who often visited him at Hyde Park and suggested nostrums such as mineral salts and lemon juice in hot water before breakfast. His wife, Eleanor, was too busy pursuing her own political agenda to notice, much less worry about, his health.

FDR's daughter Anna, who had moved into the White House when her husband, Major John Boettiger, was appointed an aide to the Joint Chiefs of Staff, decided her father needed serious medical attention. She demanded a physical examination by a team of specialists at Bethesda Naval Hospital. A reluctant Dr. McIntire consented and the examination took place on March 28, 1944.[43]

XVI

Thirty-nine-year-old cardiologist Howard Bruenn, a graduate of Johns Hopkins Medical School, conducted the examination. He had joined the navy in 1942 with the rank of lieutenant commander. The examination included X rays and a careful physical scrutiny of the patient. When Bruenn helped the president out of his wheelchair and stretched him on the examining table, he noticed that his breathing immediately became labored. When he percussed FDR's chest, he found his heart was seriously enlarged.

The X rays confirmed this diagnosis and also revealed the imminence of congestive heart failure.

There was a bluish tinge on the president's lips and fingernails, caused by fluid in his lungs. The specialist heard a "blowing sound" when he listened to FDR's heart with his stethoscope, indicating that dangerous pressure was being exerted on the aortic valve. Worse, the president's blood pressure was 186/108, indicating severe hypertension. He was also suffering from bronchitis, the only illness Admiral McIntire, who saw him every day, had diagnosed. The appalled Bruenn concluded that the president could die at any moment. His condition was "God-awful."[44]

Bruenn reported these findings to Admiral McIntire but not to the president, who seemed totally uninterested in what the young cardiologist had found. The same day, at a White House press conference, FDR breezily told reporters that the examination had found nothing but bronchitis. He told Daisy Suckley that the doctors had found nothing "drastically wrong." Strictly speaking, these statements cannot be called lies. But on April 4, Admiral McIntire went before reporters and told a whopper. He said the examination showed nothing wrong but a respiratory infection. The only thing the president needed to do was get rid of his chest problem and find time for more sunshine and exercise. Seemingly quoting Dr. Bruenn, McIntire declared that "we decided that for a man of 62-plus we had very little to argue about."[45]

In fact, McIntire and a backup squad of navy doctors had been having screaming arguments with Dr. Bruenn at Bethesda for the previous six days. Dr. Bruenn wanted to start giving FDR digitalis for his congestive heart condition and confine him to bed. "You can't do that," McIntire roared. "This is the President of the United States." McIntire assembled a board of navy doctors, all captains, to go over Bruenn's findings. They insisted no treatment was necessary and tried pulling rank on the lieutenant commander. But Bruenn gamely stood his ground and threatened to resign from the case if the senior ranks' judgment prevailed. Two of the board members went to the White House and examined the president. They returned considerably sobered and agreed that Franklin D. Roosevelt was a very sick man.[46]

There were no drugs for high blood pressure in 1944. But digitalis worked wonders for the president's heart. The drug reduced the enlargement, especially in the left ventricle, the fluid in FDR's lungs disappeared, and so did his cough. For the first time in months, the president began getting a good night's sleep. Bruenn used this marked improvement to exercise some doctorly authority. He persuaded Roosevelt to take a vacation at Hobcaw Barony, Bernard Baruch's South Carolina estate, where he did little or nothing but fish and otherwise relax for the month of April.

Back in Washington, Bruenn and McIntire worked out a White House regimen that was designed to give FDR as much rest as possible without alarming president watchers in the press and on Capitol Hill. FDR breakfasted in his bedroom and arrived in the Oval Office about eleven for two hours of appointments. After lunch he lay down for an hour, then spent another two hours in the Oval Office doing paperwork, followed by a rubdown and another hour of bed rest. Night work was banned and the office work was supposed to involve little or no irritation.

The mere idea that the president of the United States, a man running a global war, dealing with a hostile Congress and a suspicious press corps, could avoid irritation was so fanciful, it belies the desperation Dr. Bruenn felt about FDR's precarious condition. Irritation, Bruenn feared, could lead all too easily to a fatal heart attack or stroke. That was the way men and women with serious hypertension died. Dr. Bruenn apparently did not ask himself if there was a moral or political problem in restricting the commander in chief of the free world to a twenty-hour week.

He defined his job as keeping his patient alive as long as possible. What the patient and others thought about the situation was their business.

XVII

For the next three months, Roosevelt took his digitalis and obeyed his doctor's orders. Never once did he ask Bruenn for an opinion of his condition. When Bruenn checked his blood pressure, FDR never inquired about the numbers. He did not even seem to be aware that Bruenn's specialty was cardiology. But this was a typical Roosevelt deception. At Hobcaw Barony, when his cousin Daisy Suckley visited him, FDR referred to Bruenn as "one of the best heart men," a designation that obviously came from Admiral McIntire.

In another private conversation, FDR told Daisy his systole and diastole, the terms for the upper and lower blood pressure readings, were not working properly. On the sly, the president was having his physical therapist, George Fox, take his blood pressure. So he knew, more or less, how sick he was. He confided to Daisy that his doctors were afraid to tell him the truth. Even here, the Rooseveltian desire to feel superior in a relationship prevailed.[47]

In a few weeks, the digitalis, a very toxic drug, began to have a negative effect. While it improved FDR's heart function, it began to destroy his appetite. He frequently complained of overeating, of having to force down his food. His unappealing low-fat diet may have had something to do with this reaction. In spite of his cardiac improvement, he remained a man who tired easily and developed some physical problems distressing to those around him.

His secretary, Grace Tully, noticed that Roosevelt would doze off while reading the mail or even while dictating replies to her. Doze is probably the wrong word to describe this tendency, which is a symptom of secondary metabolic encephalopathy, the result of an insufficient blood supply to the brain. We now know that FDR had uncounted numbers of these cerebral episodes. One of the White House secret service agents later recalled that six times in the last year of the president's life, he found FDR lying on the floor beside his wheelchair in his bedroom. He had toppled out of the chair during one of these attacks.[48]

While watching a movie at night with his daughter, Anna, the president's mouth often fell open and remained that way, giving him the look of a senile old man. Reporters noticed FDR's voice had grown so weak, those in the back rows at press conferences had trouble hearing him. He was also easily irritated, especially when the newsmen asked him about his health, a question that arose no less than five times in the spring of 1944.

The question almost asked itself in many minds. The president's diminished appetite had produced a growing weight loss that gave him a gaunt, even a ravaged look. If the reporters had bothered to consult a medical textbook, they would have discovered that this physical trait was not unusual among persons with serious heart problems. It was called "cardiac cachexia."[49]

XVIII

Compounding the physical symptoms were signs that the commander in chief was also suffering from clinical depression. He was by no means the first chief executive to contract this malady. Herbert Hoover had similar symptoms in the closing months of his disastrous presidency. Henry Stimson, his secretary of state, said cabinet meetings with Hoover became like taking a bath in black ink. Roosevelt's depression had both physical and political roots. Ever since polio struck him down, he had been forced to

fight against the cruel incapacity it had inflicted on his once mus-
cular athletic body.

FDR managed this feat through a combination of will power
and ingenuity. In spite of his wasted legs, he learned to drive
his own car with special controls on the steering wheel, to walk
with the aid of braces and a sustaining arm from a son or Secret Service agent. Now, his helplessness became acute. His
hands trembled so much he could no longer shave himself. His
arms lost much of their strength. He could no longer lift himself from bed to his wheelchair, or from the wheelchair to his
desk chair. His valet, Arthur Prettyman, had to do everything
for him, down to bathing him in the tub and carrying him to
the toilet.

Coupled with this loss of personal control was his growing loss
of political control. FDR was no longer in charge on Capitol Hill.
Congress was dominated by men who disliked him or at best
gave him only grudging respect. Was there also an intuition that
he was losing control of the political side of the war? His stubborn refusal to face the truth of the Katyn Massacre and numerous other ugly facts about Stalin's Russia was typical of the man.
FDR had always had a unique capacity to ignore unpleasant
truths. But that ability may have dwindled when other truths—
age and physical decay and imminent death—began to loom.

The signs of the president's clinical depression were numerous.
His recurrent headaches, his inability to concentrate, his broken
sleep, his bouts of exhaustion, in spite of the improvement in his
heart condition. His doctors inadvertently added to his woes by
denying him favorite pleasures. Swimming in the White House
pool was banned because it seemed to lead to colds and respiratory infection. Cigarettes were reduced from forty a day to five or
six. Most of his food became bland and tasteless in the name of
health.[50]

XIX

Around this depressed dying man, the global war churned on. In London, newly appointed General Dwight Eisenhower was overseeing plans for the assault on northern France. In the Pacific, U.S. Marines and Navy ships were advancing across the center of that vast ocean, capturing islands that would soon enable American planes to bomb Japan. In the South Pacific, soldiers and sailors under Douglas MacArthur were grimly fighting their way toward the Philippines.

On the home front the race for the presidency was gathering similar momentum. The New Dealers in the White House inner circle had to ask themselves a difficult question. Should this dying man run for a fourth term? Without FDR, the polls showed the Democratic Party faced horrendous defeat. Would the war within the war end in the rout and humiliation of the New Dealers? Ignoring the evidence before their eyes, liberals in and out of the White House vowed not to let the unthinkable become reality. They deluged Roosevelt with calls and letters and public statements, urging him to serve another term.

Only one New Dealer had the courage to tell Roosevelt the truth. He was Ben Cohen, the brilliant lawyer who had done great service for the New Deal in a half-dozen roles, notably in drafting much of the 1930s reform legislation, such as the Securities and Exchange Act. Cohen was currently serving as general counsel to Jimmy Byrnes in the Office of War Mobilization, in the East Wing of the White House. Cohen saw Roosevelt frequently and knew how sick he was. On March 8, 1944, Cohen sent the president an eight-page memorandum, analyzing the "difficulties which would confront the administration during a fourth term."

Cohen had no doubt that Roosevelt could be reelected. But he bluntly declared he had been in office too long. The coalition that elected him had fallen apart. "The conservative friends of the

President are ever fearful of a revival of radicalism, while his liberal and labor supporters are ever suspicious of being let-down. Jealousies and enmities within the Administration even in the higher echelons are faintly concealed." Worse, there was no ground to expect "an improved political situation during a fourth term." Cohen feared a fourth term might become "an anti-climax" that would leave "Rooseveltian ideas" as discredited as those of Woodrow Wilson.

Cohen wondered if there were not a "practical alternative" to a fourth term, a compromise that would make Rooseveltian ideas enduring. Even if this meant a Republican victory, Cohen was sure the Democrats would make a "quick comeback" after the American people watched the GOP grapple with the problems of peacemaking and postwar adjustment. He suggested Roosevelt negotiate with the Republicans to create "a common foreign policy platform," including an agreement to nominate FDR as the first president of the United Nations.

Another possibility was a constitutional amendment to delay federal elections for a year, giving the war a chance to end—with the guarantee that FDR would not be a candidate. Cohen reported this alternative had been "favorably considered by some prominent Republicans," intimating he or some of his friends had floated the idea. But he admitted that the time for cutting such a deal was short and the difficulties "very great." Cohen closed by urging the president not to abandon searching for "a practical alternative" to a fourth term.

The president responded on March 13 with a two-sentence letter. He called Cohen's memorandum "a tremendously interesting analysis—and I think a very just one." Cohen had left out only one thing: "the matter of my own feelings!" He was, FDR said, "feeling plaintive."[51]

The fatalism that had engulfed Roosevelt when he committed himself to a third term, telling Jim Farley that he did not care if he lived only a month after his election, was more than ever in command of his soul. The war, with its brutal demands on his time and its indifference to domestic political concerns, also played a part in his loss of enthusiasm for the New Deal. FDR's followers would soon discover that their faltering leader meant what he said when he declared Dr. Win-the-War was the country's new physician—and Dr. New Deal had been relegated to history's attic.

14

GODDAMNING ROOSEVELT AND OTHER PASTIMES

On Capitol Hill and in the state capitals of the no longer solid South, Roosevelt's name was being uttered with epithets as the year 1944 began. Congress's attitude toward the New Dealers and the president was dramatized by two major brawls in which the southern Democratic–Republican coalition scored bruising victories.

The first round was a ferocious clash over the soldier vote. By this time the Democrats had been advised by their pollsters that turnout was the crucial factor in their hopes for 1944. Soldiers and sailors, most of them young and presumably admirers of their commander in chief, were a vital component of this thesis. The White House made the first move with a proposal for a federal ballot that would be delivered to every serviceman before the election, enabling them to vote for presidential candidates but no one else.

The Republicans, convinced that everyone overseas was being brainwashed into Roosevelt worship by the OWI, violently opposed this idea. They argued for ballots from individual states, and their southern Democratic allies emphatically agreed. The southerners instinctively resisted all attempts by the federal government to encroach on states' rights. A federal ballot would enable blacks to vote without paying a poll tax—the by now traditional way of keeping African-Americans out of the elective process.

Seldom did a piece of legislation reveal more starkly the schizoid personality of the Democratic Party. Senator John McClellan of Arkansas and Senator Kenneth McKellar of Tennessee proposed an alternative "state control" bill that would enable servicemen to cast absentee ballots if they wrote and asked for them. The debate in the Senate was vitriolic. Senator Harry Byrd of Virginia predicted if the Roosevelt federal ballot passed, the South would abandon the Democratic Party. Fellow Democrat Joseph Guffey of Pennsylvania said this only proved that treason was still alive in the souls of southerners.[1]

The White House—if not the ailing president—got into the fray, urging Congress not to approve the "meaningless" state ballot bill. Alas, Roosevelt's stock was so low, this tactic only angered both houses of Congress. Senator Robert Taft castigated the president for intervening in "legislative matters." He added that the president's condescending language was "a direct insult to the members of this body."

The Senate ignored Senator Guffey and the president and voted for the state control bill. New Dealers in the House managed to tack on some amendments, permitting states to use a federal ballot if they preferred one. A serviceman could also get one of these ballots if his state refused to send him the home variety. Liberals denounced the bill as a "shameful farce." The president chose to let the measure become law without his signature, signifying his displeasure, and possibly persuading soldiers to cast a protest vote for him. Cartoonist Bill Mauldin dramatized the outcome from the pro-FDR side when he sketched his favorite soldier characters, Joe and Willie, reading about the bill in their jeep, their faces stamped with disgust and disbelief. "That's okay Joe," Willie said. "At least we can make bets."[2]

II

In his rambling state of the union message, the president had included a demand for a revised tax law, one that would limit corporate profits and otherwise give voters the feeling that the government was treating all Americans evenhandedly. Muddling this good idea was a proposal by the chairman of the New York Federal Reserve Bank, Beardsley Ruml. The Treasury Department had proposed that Americans should begin coughing up their 1943 taxes on a pay-as-you-go basis. To lessen the pain, Congress, over the president's objections, forgave taxpayers 75 percent of their 1942 IRS obligations. Ruml argued that the Treasury would not miss the money until Judgment Day. But the New Dealers around Henry Morgenthau Jr. in the Treasury were outraged to think of rich Americans getting such a fat almost-free pass.

The Treasury men claimed this congressional largesse meant the government needed another $12 billion right away to prevent the national debt from looming to Mount Everest proportions, triggering runaway inflation. Roosevelt persuaded Morgenthau to shave this figure to $10.5 billion and let Congress take the heat on how to raise the money. The House of Representatives, where tax bills get written, consigned Morgenthau's message to the circular file and produced a law that raised only $2.1 billion. As is their wont, the congressmen added a few tax breaks for friendly constituents, mostly owners of mines and timberland. The Senate pondered, pontificated, and added several more of these acts of legislative benevolence.[3]

When the bill reached the White House, the sick president was bombarded with contradictory advice. A discouraged Morgenthau advised FDR to let it become law without his signature. Others, such as Sam Rosenman, Roosevelt's speechwriter, denounced it as a "vicious piece of legislation" and declared that Roosevelt would be all but derelict if he did not veto it. Homefront czar Jimmy Byrnes, usually far more conservative than Rosenman, agreed. Speaker of the House Sam Rayburn of Texas and Senate Majority Leader Alben Barkley of Kentucky strongly urged the president to sign the bill.[4]

Roosevelt debated with himself and others for two weeks and decided on a veto. The accompanying message, on which Rosenman later claimed he did not work, nonetheless echoed his sentiments so vividly that Press Secretary Steve Early was compelled to issue a formal denial that Rosenman wrote it. Significantly, Rosenman admitted that the president approved the message "pretty much in the form in which it had come to him"—supposedly from Jimmy Byrnes's Office of War Mobilization—an indication that a sick FDR was already becoming the passive voice of the White House inner circle.[5]

Targeting the special interest legislation rather than the puny size of the levy (which troubled no one in the country but the Treasury bureaucrats) the veto message condemned the bill as "tax relief . . . not for the needy but for the greedy." Some people had advised FDR to accept the bill, the message continued, "on the ground that having asked the Congress for a loaf of bread to take care of this war for the sake of this and succeeding generations, I should be content with a small crust. I might have done so if I had not noted that the small piece of crust contained so many extraneous and inedible materials."[6]

Senate reporter Allen Drury, normally a Roosevelt admirer, called it "a smart-aleck" veto message. Congress exploded with near maniacal fury. Denunciations of Roosevelt rained down on the White House. The House Ways and Means Committee called the Treasury's $10.5 billion dollar goal "oppressive," not a bad adjective to flaunt in an election year. Particularly enraged was Senate majority leader Barkley. His struggles on Roosevelt's behalf in the hostile Congress had produced little but humiliation and defeat. He felt the veto message's language made any hope of future cooperation with the White House impossible. Back in Kentucky, the senator's campaign for reelection was faltering. His opponents were painting him as Roosevelt's errand boy.

In an impassioned speech on February 23, 1944, Barkley announced his resignation as majority leader. He called the president's veto message "a calculated and deliberate assault upon the legislative integrity of every member of Congress." If the Congress had "any self respect left," Barkley thundered, it would override the veto immediately. The House promptly overrode and the Senate followed suit, with three-fourths of the Democrats voting against the president. It was the first time in the history of the country that Congress had overridden a veto of a tax bill.[7]

The sick president got the news at Hyde Park, to which he had been retreating almost every weekend in a vain search for better health. FDR seemed bewildered by the ferocity of Congress's reaction, evidence that he had not given much thought to the veto message that Jimmy Byrnes's staff (or Sam Rosenman) had written for him. "Alben must be suffering from shell shock," he told his secretary, William Hassett. FDR speculated to an ex-senator and mutual friend that Mrs. Barkley's serious illness probably explained the majority leader's outburst.

The White House staff prepared a soothing reply to Barkley, in which Roosevelt denied any intention to attack the integrity of

Congress. Still trying to blame the senator, FDR claimed he had read part of the message to Barkley before he sent it to Capitol Hill and the majority leader had not tried to alter the "basic decision," nor had he expressed how strongly he disliked the message. This pas de deux conveniently forgot that both Barkley and House Speaker Rayburn had strongly urged the president not to veto the bill.

Barkley's reply to the president was acerbic. Washington insiders agreed that the senator was now almost certain to win reelection. An appalled Allen Drury wrote in the journal he was keeping of his days reporting on the Senate: "When Roosevelt finally leaves the White House, the Presidency will have been reduced nearer impotency than it has been for many years." The *Chicago Tribune* gloatingly declared the New Deal was dead and, politically speaking, so was Roosevelt.

The ill and depressed president seemed to agree with these judgments. He told one correspondent: "There are a very small number of people who would rather nail my hide onto the barn door than win the war." This was undoubtedly true, except for the arithmetic. The number was dismayingly large. A gloomy FDR told Budget Director Harold Smith that "for all practical purposes we have a Republican Congress now."[8]

III

This sense of national malaise was soon compounded by the Roosevelt administration's maladroit handling of a labor dispute with the giant mail order company, Montgomery Ward. Here the New Dealers came a cropper when they tried to protect one of their chief constituencies, the labor unions. Early in the war, Roosevelt had extracted a no-strike pledge from the reluctant unions. To console them, he had created an executive entity called the War Labor Board, which would supposedly resolve most disputes in their favor. As an additional sweetener, the WLB promulgated a "maintenance of membership" rule that required employers not only to accept the concept of the closed shop, but to threaten any employee with dismissal if he or she refused to join the union. For a final touch of Washington power-playing, the companies were also ordered to collect the unions' dues. Not surprisingly, with this kind of Big Brotherish backing, union membership soared from 10 million to 15 million during the war.

Montgomery Ward was headed by an unreconstructed conservative named Sewell Avery, who disliked Franklin D. Roosevelt and unions, especially those affiliated with the Communist-tinged CIO. When the United Mail Order, Warehouse and Retail Employees Union won a WLB supervised election, supplanting the company union, Avery refused to bargain with them unless they dropped the maintenance of membership clause from the contract. Avery argued that the regulation only applied to war plants. Montgomery Ward was a civilian operation. The union naturally refused and called on the WLB for help. As far as the WLB was concerned, there was nothing to arbitrate. The maintenance of membership rule was virtually the only reason for their bureaucratic existence.

After an exchange of threats and defiances, Commerce Secretary Jesse Jones was ordered to seize the company. He dispatched several of his top people, including a lawyer who was an old Avery friend. They found the Montgomery Ward CEO intransigent. When they enlisted the aid of a federal marshal, Avery scoffed at this pathetic show of government force and refused to leave his desk. The White House, growing more and more exercised, summoned a platoon of soldiers from a nearby army base and asked Attorney General Francis Biddle to fly to Chicago in an army plane to take charge of the situation.

On the morning of April 27, 1944, Avery showed up at his office to find it crowded with Biddle, several Justice and Commerce

Department aides, and a number of soldiers. Biddle tried to be polite at first. But Avery refused to obey his order to turn over the company's books, or to call a meeting of his staff to urge them to cooperate with the government. "To hell with the government," Avery snarled.

Biddle was "deeply shocked." He later claimed he saw Avery's defiance endangering the entire war effort. Exactly how, the attorney general never adequately explained. More likely, he saw an economic royalist in the flesh, threatening one of the New Deal's key power bases. Biddle was also more than a little frazzled: the White House had had trouble finding an army plane and he had landed in Chicago at 4 A.M. Turning to the top Commerce Department man, Biddle snarled: "Take him out!"

The Commerce man ordered the soldiers to remove Avery. Apologizing elaborately, a young officer ordered two of his men to link hands and create a seat to carry Avery out of the building. As he departed, Avery glared at Biddle and roared: "You—you New Dealer!"

Downstairs, a photographer snapped a picture of the slight silver-haired Avery as he was carried onto the street by the steel-helmeted soldiers. Hands folded across his stomach, Avery looked almost relaxed, but still defiant. The picture made the front page of virtually every newspaper in the country, and a typhoon of abuse descended on the White House.

The *Denver Post* declared "a more infamous outrage had never before been perpetrated under the cloak of government. Hitler's thugs . . . never did a more efficient job." The *Fort Wayne News Sentinel* called it "government not by law but by bayonet." The *Washington Post* and the *New York Times* also disapproved, if not quite as vehemently. So did columnist Walter Lippmann and many other pundits. The *Chicago Tribune* ran a cartoon portraying Attorney General Biddle as an axe-wielding executioner beneath a sign that read: "No business is immune from our power."[9]

Avery received over 3,000 letters, 95 percent of them supporting him. FDR got several hundred telegrams and letters, split
about fifty-fifty between approval and disapproval. More alarming was a Gallup poll that showed 60 percent of the country favored Avery's side of the argument. This inspired the *Chicago
Tribune* to run another cartoon, showing two voters carrying
Franklin D. Roosevelt out of the White House. An agitated FDR
devoted an entire press conference to defending the government's
actions.[10]

IV

FDR's allies fought this conservative tide with some negative
skullduggery of their own. The Friends For Democracy, a group
that had played a leading role in fighting America First before
Pearl Harbor, hired a writer named Avedis Derounian, who infiltrated various right-wing groups, pretending to be sympathetic, and then surfaced under the pseudonym John Roy
Carlson to accuse them of being a vast fascist and/or right-wing
conspiracy. Carlson's book, *Undercover*, roared to the top of
the best-seller list, backed by fervent praise from numerous liberal reviewers.[11]

Assistant Attorney General O. John Rogge read *Undercover*
carefully and decided it had the sort of material he needed to proceed with the long-delayed sedition trial of the lunatic-fringe
right-wingers the Justice Department had indicted back in 1942.
Adding George Sylvester Viereck and several leaders of the German-American Bund to the list of hatemongers, Rogge procured
new indictments and the trial began on April 17, 1944. FDR remained enthusiastic about the business. He saw political capital
in implicitly linking those who criticized the administration to
genuine German agents such as Viereck and the assorted extremists already in the dock. Some historians have christened this

episode the "brown smear" (in contrast to a "red smear") campaign.[12]

The trial rapidly turned into one of the most bizarre circuses in the history of American jurisprudence. The defendants hired a total of forty lawyers, many of whom were as unstable as their clients. Each day saw a bedlam of shouted objections, cries of rage, and antic behavior such as everyone pounding their fists on the defense tables in unison and denouncing "Vishinsky" Rogge, implying this was a replay of Stalin's 1930s purge trials. One of the women defendants wore her long blue nightgown to court each day, under her dress. The mild-mannered judge struggled in vain to maintain order. Losing his reputed Ivy League cool, Prosecutor Rogge waved Nazi flags at the jury and read strident passages from *Mein Kampf*.

Rogge was reduced to these tactics because his legal arguments were weak. Following Carlson's book, he maintained that the defendants were guilty of sedition because passages in their writings and speeches were very close to Nazi statements on Roosevelt, the Jews, and similar topics. Civil libertarians grew more and more aghast at the spectacle. Only ultra liberals cheered on the maniacal proceedings. Eventually, the exhausted judge died of a heart attack and a mistrial was declared.

Rogge wanted to bring new indictments but Attorney General Biddle, who had gotten into the mess only to please the president, demurred. "Everyone was sick of the farce," he said.[13]

V

Against this backdrop of home-front disarray Wendell Willkie, that covert New Dealer in a rumpled Republican suit and tie, got more attention than the ailing president in the first months of 1944. Buoyed by the spectacular sales of his book, *One World*, the hoarse-voiced Hoosier declared himself his party's front-runner and roamed the country giving speeches to often surly Republican audiences, reiterating the need for the GOP to convert from isolationism to internationalism.

Willkie's claim that the Grand Old Party had its head in the sand in regard to the rest of the world infuriated not a few Republicans with some knowledge of the GOP's history. Until Woodrow Wilson reached the White House, it had been the Democratic Party, not the Republicans, who veered toward the stance known as isolationism. Particularly annoyed was Senator Robert Taft of Ohio, whose father, President William Howard Taft, had been among the strongest supporters of a league of nations to maintain world peace, before Wilson made it his brainchild.[14]

What the Republicans disliked was the utopian idealism of Woodrow Wilson, with its vision of a world that would dissolve into instant brotherhood at the mere mention of the word democracy. This unrealism had produced terrific disillusion after World War I when Americans saw the supposedly redeemed globe veer toward mass hatred and tyranny.

Willkie was a 1940s version of this utopian strain in the great American dichotomy between idealism and realism. He told columnist Samuel Grafton that every American should "feel in his belly" the need for "the closest possible relations with Britain and Russia." The Indianian claimed this was the "touchstone," the only political position that mattered in 1944. "You cannot be wrong on this issue and right on any other," he declared. Willkie was saying things that Roosevelt believed but said far more cautiously if at all. The Republican was also ignoring polls that showed voters were more interested in domestic issues than international relationships.

In September of 1943, the GOP had organized a mini-convention of forty-eight "elected Republicans" (governors and congressmen and senators) at Mackinac Island in the straits between the upper and lower Michigan peninsulas to formulate a postwar foreign policy. Willkie was not invited, an omission that drew a rebuke from the *New York Times*. But the rules also excluded ex-president Herbert Hoover and the party's 1936 candidate, Governor Alfred Landon. Michigan's Senator Arthur Vandenberg told J. P. Morgan banker Thomas Lamont that he was "hunting for the middle ground" between extremists on the left who "would cheerfully give America away" and extremists on the right who wanted to turn the country into an isolated fortress. In his diary, Vandenberg added a comment that revealed his thoughts about Willkie: "I have no sympathy whatever with our Republican pollyannas who want to compete with Henry Wallace."[15]

After much wrangling, the Mackinac meeting produced a statement in favor of a cautious internationalism. The delegates called for Republicans to commit the party to "responsible participation in a postwar cooperative organization among sovereign nations." Willkie said it was a "move in the right direction" but wished his fellow Republicans had been more specific.

Willkie supplied specifics in plenty when he announced his candidacy in a special issue of *Look* magazine, whose owner, Gardner Cowles, was a devoted admirer. The candidate called on the Republicans to again become "the great American liberal party" that had put Lincoln in the White House, fought the Civil War to free the slaves, and backed Theodore Roosevelt's criticism of "malefactors of great wealth" (half-truths at best). He urged a renewed commitment to civil rights and a foreign policy that scoured the word "isolation" from the GOP's vocabulary.[16]

VI

There was an American everyman quality about Willkie that appealed to many voters. But his condescending lectures did not please Republican professional politicians, especially in the Midwest, Willkie's native territory. His speaking tour was marred by incidents that revealed visceral hostility among the party's leaders. In Missouri, one of his biggest 1940 backers, Edgar Monsanto Queeny, introduced the candidate at a luncheon for 150 Republican business and political leaders as "America's leading ingrate." Queeny said he had raised $200,000 for Willkie's run against Roosevelt and never got a word of thanks.

A furious Willkie leaped to his feet and shouted: "I don't know whether you're going to support me or not and I don't give a damn. You're a bunch of political liabilities anyway!"[17]

John D. M. Hamilton, whom Willkie had fired as GOP chairman in 1940, ignoring the large role he had played in getting him the nomination, was behind these insults. With money from Queeny, an heir to the Monsanto chemical fortune, Hamilton toured the country as vigorously as Willkie, preaching a devastating message: Willkie was a political incompetent, out for nobody but himself—and secretly in bed with Franklin D. Roosevelt. The latter charge hit home with particular force to a growing number of Republicans.[18]

Other blows came from supporters of Governor Thomas E. Dewey. The president of New York's National Republican Club, Thomas J. Curran, warned that voters would see no point in switching from "a Democrat who knows he is bigger than his party to a Republican who thinks he is bigger than his party." Congressman Louis Miller of Missouri, who had been Willkie's convention floor manager in 1940, wondered aloud whether the Hoosier was a true liberal or a left-wing "neoliberal" who was actually advocating a postwar totalitarian state like Soviet Russia. Congresswoman Clare Boothe Luce took a similar line, urging Willkie to wake up to the Soviet Union's undoubted determination to rule the world. She also told him to lose forty pounds and quit drinking.[19]

Competing candidates surfaced. Governor Harold Stassen of Minnesota, who had resigned to enter the navy, let it be known from the South Pacific that he was available. Senator Vandenberg and a contingent of Midwesterners, led by Colonel Robert McCormick of the *Chicago Tribune*, turned to General Douglas MacArthur as the man to save them from another four years of Franklin D. Roosevelt. John Hamilton and other GOP operators urged popular Republicans such as Governor Earl Warren of California to run as favorite sons in their state primaries to deny Willkie delegates.[20]

Willkie continued to lecture Republicans on their shortcomings. One California speech was virtually a paean of praise to FDR and the New Deal. "If you had been half as smart as President Roosevelt, the Republicans would have advocated the legislation that brought the New Deal to power," he bellowed. Although such over-the-top statements gave him a bounce in the polls, mail to Republican national headquarters starting running 9-1 against him.[21]

Democrats watched Willkie's performance with a mixture of admiration and amazement. Columnist I. F. Stone remarked in the *Nation* that if Roosevelt continued to move to the right—as evidenced by his retirement of Dr. New Deal—and Willkie continued to move left, they would soon reverse the platforms they had run on in 1940. Harold Ickes confided to his diary that Willkie's "free swinging liberalism" was what the Democratic Party needed as much as the GOP. Ickes hoped Willkie would "force the President" to give liberal leadership to the Democrats. Robert Sherwood privately speculated that if Willkie won the nomination, Roosevelt might not run for reelection.[22]

In February 1944, at a big rally in New York, Willkie made more headlines when he called for a $16 billion tax increase to forestall a crippling postwar national debt. At a press conference a bemused FDR, who was trying in vain to get Congress to increase taxes by little more than half that amount, said he "did not have the nerve" to agree with Willkie. The *New York Times* declared Willkie was "head and shoulders" above any other Republican candidate. Professional politicians in both parties thought a candidate who urged a huge tax rise in an election year was idiotic at best and suicidal at worst.

VII

Ironically, the *New York Times*'s endorsement coincided with a Willkie downward slide in the polls. Although he won a majority of the delegates in New Hampshire in mid-March, a nationwide Gallup poll reported he was running 36 points behind Governor Thomas E. Dewey, who had thus far carefully avoided announcing he was a candidate. Even more ominous, the poll revealed Willkie's following was mainly in New England and the mid-Atlantic states.[23]

It was now apparent to Willkie and his backers that he had to prove he had support in other sections of the country, especially the Midwest. One of the earliest primaries was in Wisconsin. Willkie's entourage told him he had to carry this state if he expected any more financial support from them. Without giving it serious thought, Willkie agreed.

Wisconsin was a formidable challenge for a man who preached one world as the wave of the future. Numerous German-Americans still resented Roosevelt's prewar anti-German foreign policy. Even the state's liberal leader, Senator Robert LaFollete, the sole surviving elected member of the Progressive Party, had opposed Roosevelt's interventionist tactics. The *Chicago Tribune*, which editorially loathed Willkie's tendency to be a Roosevelt clone, circulated widely in southern Wisconsin.

For thirteen days, Willkie crisscrossed Wisconsin, often plowing through snowdrifts, at one point resorting to a horse-drawn sleigh. His advance planning staff was nonexistent. He was constantly behind schedule, frequently keeping audiences waiting an hour or more. But he drew big crowds as he damned Republican reactionaries and criticized the mess FDR's New Dealers had created in wartime Washington. Willkie's opposition did not even make an appearance. Governor Dewey tried to withdraw from the race. General MacArthur and Governor Harold Stassen remained on active duty in the South Pacific. All three had busy surrogates, but Willkie's ebullient personality and energy seemed to give him a big advantage.

The results of this Wisconsin blitz, which reduced Willkie's voice to a rasp and its owner to exhaustion, were stunning. In the April 4 primary, Dewey won seventeen delegates, Stassen four, MacArthur three—and Willkie none. His delegates ran last in every district. Not one received more than 49,535 votes—a third of Dewey's top man. Willkie unquestionably got a chance to tell Wisconsin's voters what he thought about politics, domestic and international. Most of them unquestionably did not like it.[24]

Willkie's first reaction was rage. Consuming scotch by the gulp, he refused to quit the race and threatened to bolt the party and endorse Roosevelt. In the morning the candidate awoke a sadder but wiser man. In Omaha, Nebraska, where he was supposedly campaigning for that state's delegates, he gave a speech on foreign policy that many considered brilliant. He damned Roosevelt's secret diplomacy and his dealings with fascists in North Africa and Italy. Above all he excoriated the president for failing to state "in plain terms what we stand for and what we are fighting for." Then came an unscheduled announcement: he was withdrawing from the race. The coupling of the incisive speech and the withdrawal emphasized the odd, immature emotionalism in Willkie's nature. He seemed to be saying to his fellow Republicans: see how hard I can hit Roosevelt? See what you're losing?[25]

It was not a graceful departure. In a prepared statement, Willkie castigated both the Republican Party and the citizens of Wisconsin as moral midgets who had failed to respond to the great crusade for international peace to which he had summoned them. Collectively, their failure gave him a "sense of sickening." He even dredged up the fact that the Dewey delegate who had won the most votes had once been a member of America First. Obviously, Willkie had learned nothing from Roosevelt's 1942 attempt to make isolationism a badge of shame.[26]

The *New York Times* tut-tutted editorially that Willkie's collapse left a void in the Republican Party. Liberals lined up to issue consoling eulogies. Walter Lippmann predicted Willkie would exert a more positive influence on American life by eschewing political power. William Shirer praised him for clarifying "the fundamental issues facing this country." The *Chicago Tribune* more accurately remarked that from now on Willkie could safely be regarded as a minor nuisance.[27]

Sidney Hillman, the political spokesman for the labor movement's left wing, saw Willkie's defeat as a triumph for "the camp of reaction." A few political realists viewed the Hoosier's crushing repudiation as part of the mounting tide against the New Dealers, another victory in the political war within the military war. Unquestionably, it was not good news for the man who was determined to march into the future flaunting the banner of a New Deal for the world: Vice President Henry Wallace.[28]

VIII

In January 1944, Wallace was the principal speaker at the Democrats' annual Jackson Day dinner, a fete at which the faithful regularly reaffirmed their allegiance to the party's ideals. The president's illness had eliminated him as a participant, which was just as well. The vice president came very close to openly challenging FDR's leadership. Speaking only a few weeks after Roosevelt had retired aging Dr. New Deal, Wallace declared the New Deal was anything but dead. If that were the case, the Democratic Party would also be dead, "and well dead."

On the contrary, Wallace said he looked forward to the day when Roosevelt would have a chance to give the New Deal "a firmer foundation than it ever had before." Looking down the head table, Wallace saw irritated disagreement on many faces. They were not happy with his opposition to FDR's apparent strategy for 1944, to downplay liberalism and conciliate big business and the southern wing of the party. But Wallace declined to throw "a few extra shovelsful of dirt" on the grave of the New Deal. He was thinking ahead to the 1944 convention and "what type of thought" would control the Democratic Party. He was convinced, from talking to his fellow liberals and reading their letters to him, that unless someone made "a real fight," the party would wind up in the hands of "reactionaries."[29]

Since his public defenestration by Roosevelt in July 1943, Wallace had continued to speak out on behalf of the century of the common man. He also gave long interviews to reporters and columnists deemed sympathetic to his views. In these chats, he regularly praised President Roosevelt, repeatedly predicting that he would and should run for a fourth term. "It is unthinkable that Mr. Roosevelt not be at the peace table," he told reporters in Chicago.[30]

A larger question was how hard Wallace should campaign for his renomination as Roosevelt's vice president. Here Wallace wavered between admitting he wanted the job and saying it was up to the president. To one reporter, he declared he was mainly interested in getting his ideas over. The reporter, a savvy AP hand named Jack Bell, bluntly remarked: "I suppose you know some of the men around the White House are against your being nominated again."

Wallace claimed total ignorance of this conspiracy. But he admitted he had heard from "general conversation" that some of the Oval Office inner circle had been "active" against him in "the Jesse Jones affair." In fact, Wallace was well aware that several members of the inner circle were his secret enemies. Presidential man for all seasons and assignments Harry Hopkins, and home-front czar Jimmy Byrnes were the leaders of this cabal. On January 3, Eugene Casey, a White House executive assistant, gave Wallace "specific details as to how Hopkins had tried to cut my throat at various times." Wallace confided to his diary that he had "no doubt" Casey was telling him the truth.[31]

Wallace also noted Casey's claim that Roosevelt was drifting into associating too much with men of wealth, a failing Casey implicitly attributed to Hopkins's influence. Roosevelt had appointed U.S. Steel millionaire Edward Stettinius under secretary of state to replace Sumner Welles, and multimillionaire Averell Harriman ambassador to Russia. Too often FDR spent his White House Sunday nights with these men or their friends, rather than entertaining senators and congressmen.

Wallace said he had known Harry Hopkins was "wholeheartedly against me" for years but he was also "wholeheartedly for winning the war," so Wallace had never tried to counterattack him. The overwrought Casey told Wallace he was too Christian for his own good. Harry Hopkins was "a selfish no good" and he was going to "get him."[32]

This vendetta turned out to be superfluous. Hopkins's rare form of stomach cancer flared up and he was soon far sicker than the president. Lord Root of the Matter retreated to the Mayo clinic for treatments and surgery that left him barely clinging to life for the first seven months of 1944. Adding to his physical burden was the news that his eighteen-year-old son, Stephen, had been killed in the U.S. Marines' assault on Kwajalein Atoll in the mid-Pacific.[33]

In February 1944 Wallace made a two-week swing through the west, giving several major addresses. Once more he aggressively defended the New Deal, declaring it was under attack by American fascists—people who believed "that Wall Street comes first and the country second and who are willing to go to any length . . . to keep Wall Street safely sitting on top of the country." Wallace darkly declared that these plotters on the right were trying to elect delegates to state and national political conventions. In Chicago, pressed by reporters to name some of these *fascisti*, Wallace could only come up with Colonel McCormick of the *Chicago Tribune*.

More alarming to many was Wallace's postwar vision. He wanted to see a "general welfare economy" and a "profound revolution" that could be "gradual and bloodless" if the men of wealth went along with it. He also called for a federal "job authority" to advise the president on how to create full employment when peace came. Although these ideas won FDR's covert praise, Wallace still resisted his friends' attempts to persuade him to start campaigning actively for renomination as vice president.[34]

IX

Henry Wallace had no illusions about the absolute control Franklin Roosevelt liked to exercise about such important matters. "I felt in 1944 as I felt in 1940 that a man who went out to get delegates would inevitably get his throat cut," the vice president said. "Roosevelt wouldn't tolerate that kind of thing." Wallace had a built-in distaste for that sort of "practical politics" anyway. He was probably reassured by a March 1944 Gallup poll that showed him with a commanding lead over potential vice presidential contenders. He had 46 percent of the Democrats sampled; Secretary of State Hull was a distant second with 21 percent, and Jim Farley was even farther behind with 15 percent.

Moreover, Wallace seemed to be popular with southern rank-and-file Democrats, although their leaders viewed him with dislike and distrust.

Wallace was also reassured by the enthusiasm for him among labor leaders, in particular Sidney Hillman, the aggressive president of the Amalgamated Clothing Workers of America, who had frequent access to the Oval Office. Responding to the Smith-Connally Act's ban on union contributions, Hillman had invented something he called the Political Action Committee, which was raising huge sums of money for the 1944 election. CIO-PAC was behind Wallace one hundred percent, Hillman assured him.

Being human, Wallace was also flattered by the admiration Eleanor Roosevelt bestowed on him. At a White House lunch, Mrs. Roosevelt startled Wallace by telling him she thought he could run for president and win if FDR decided not to seek a fourth term. She confided that both she and the president regarded him as the heir best qualified to succeed FDR, thanks to his outspoken liberalism. But she admitted that southern resistance to his candidacy would be fierce. She also feared the president himself faced defeat if he tried for a fourth term.[35]

A few weeks later, at a White House dinner, Mrs. Roosevelt and Wallace had a long earnest talk about the future of the Democratic Party. They agreed that it had to retain its liberal essence. She told him with evident regret that FDR was putting liberalism on hold until the primary season ended. He feared the possibility of a third party emerging in the South. Wallace in turn told her some people were urging him to convene a sort of liberal Mackinac Island convention to issue a fighting statement that would fill the political vacuum the president's swing to the right was creating. They agreed that such a move would be unwise for the time being. The subtext: it would only irritate—and possibly infuriate—FDR.[36]

Hanging over a Wallace candidacy were the "Dear Guru" letters to his old friend and spiritual companion, Nicholas Roerich. The president had seen these murky epistles during the 1940 campaign. He was unlikely to forget them or underestimate the possibility that they could surface again in 1944, when damage control might be more difficult. This specter suddenly acquired substance when Charles Michelson, the ousted former publicity director of the Democratic Party, published something he called his autobiography. It was much closer to a compilation of his press releases, with some wry commentary. Among his remarks was a discussion of the guru letters, the last thing Wallace wanted or needed. Reviewers zeroed in on Michelson's enigmatic references to the letters and soon Washington was buzzing with prurient curiosity about them.[37]

Not a few capital insiders began wondering why Michelson had chosen this moment to publish his half-baked book. In January, the president had installed a new chairman of the Democratic Party, Robert Hannegan of St. Louis. He had been something of an emergency appointment. Postmaster General Frank Walker, Ed Flynn's successor, hated the job and starting talking about resigning the day after he accepted the post. Word reached the vice president that Hannegan was telling everyone in sight that it was "thumbs down" for Wallace on the 1944 ticket.[38]

This animosity must have struck Wallace as a bit odd. One of Hannegan's best friends was another potential candidate, Senator Harry S. Truman of Missouri. Hannegan had saved Truman's neck in 1940 by delivering several St. Louis wards in the senator's run for a second term. But Truman repeatedly told Wallace that he was "eager to support [him]" for another term as vice president. When the Missouri politicians had introduced Hannegan to the Democratic Party establishment at a reception in the Mayflower Hotel, Truman had made a point of inviting Wallace.[39]

Whether this invitation was sincere or the gesture of a shrewd politician is unclear. Six months earlier, Senator Joseph Guffey of Pennsylvania, an outspoken liberal, had invited Truman to lunch and asked him for a candid off-the-record opinion of Henry Wallace as vice president. Truman grinned and said Wallace was "the best secretary of agriculture the country ever had." Guffey had asked Truman if he was interested in the job—and got an emphatic no thank you.[40]

By this time, Wallace was incapable of being totally surprised by the atmosphere of Byzantine intrigue that Roosevelt's political style encouraged in Washington, D.C. Another friend had told him that Ed Flynn, still the extremely potent boss of the Bronx Democratic machine and a close friend of the president, was working hard to dump Wallace from the ticket. When someone reproached Flynn for this sort of back-stabbing, reminding him that Wallace was his friend, Flynn had shrugged and said he was acting under orders "from the top."[41]

More than once, Wallace noted with wry bemusement in his diary Roosevelt's habit of lying to him or others. On March 10, 1944, Roosevelt held forth to a cabinet meeting about his recent conference with two American Zionists, Rabbis Abba Hillel Silver and Stephen S. Wise. Roosevelt said he had thrown them on the defensive before they could even begin arguing about letting more Jews into Palestine. "Do you want to be responsible by your action for the loss of hundreds of thousands of lives? Do you want to start a Holy Gehad?" he supposedly said. The president gleefully recounted the grisly picture he painted of a Middle East in bloody turmoil as enraged Arabs ran amok.

The vice president had talked to Rabbi Silver the night before the cabinet meeting and the clergyman had told him how delighted he and his colleague Rabbi Wise were by Roosevelt's positive attitude toward Zionism. The president had assured them he was on their side and it was only a question of political timing that was forcing him to hold his tongue. With an almost audible sigh, Wallace told his diary: "The President certainly is a waterman. He looks one direction and rows the other with the utmost skill."[42]

In spite of this foreknowledge, Wallace seems to have suspected nothing when Roosevelt took charge of a trip to Russia that the vice president proposed making in March of 1944. Wallace said he wanted to meet ordinary Russians and get a feel for the country. Roosevelt vetoed that idea because too many people would be "shooting at you during the campaign for being too far to the left." Roosevelt suggested a compromise: a trip to China by way of Siberia, where he could meet plenty of Russians and then try to solve the ugly problems that were developing in Chungking. Because of the long Siberian winter, Wallace would have to delay the trip until early June and return a few days before the Democratic convention on July 17.[43]

The president was getting Wallace out of the country at the precise time that the struggle over who would be nominated for vice president would come to a climax. Wallace later claimed to have no suspicions that he was being sandbagged. But he seems to have had some doubts about the way Roosevelt had scheduled the trip and made a halfhearted try to escape. On March 13, 1944, he told FDR that he had discussed the journey with Secretary of State Hull and Army Chief of Staff George C. Marshall, who had warned him China was an unholy mess. Since Wallace had no background on China, he began to wonder if there was any point in going so far unless he could do "some real good."

"Oh you must go," FDR said. "I think you ought to see a lot of Siberia." Wallace noted glumly in his diary that the president was "much stronger for the trip than I had ever thought." Trapped by Roosevelt's charming indirection, Wallace began boning up on Siberia and China with the help of Washington experts. When political insiders heard about the trip, most shook their heads and declared the vice president had received the kiss of death, FDR style.[44]

<h1 style="text-align:center">X</h1>

While Wendell Willkie self-destructed and Henry Wallace prepared to vanish over the horizon, Senator Harry S. Truman of Missouri remained hard at work scrutinizing the war effort for corruption and inefficiency. He also continued to expose, without quite saying it, how Franklin D. Roosevelt had handed over the vast enterprise to big business. Truman still thought small and medium-sized companies should share in the bonanza of cash flowing out of Washington. Before the war began, they had accounted for roughly 70 percent of the goods and products made in America. In a year of war production, their share slipped to 30 percent and the giants had cornered the rest.

Truman had strongly supported the creation of a Smaller War Plants Corporation (SWPC) early in the war and the establishment of $150 million fund to help small and medium-sized manufacturers convert their plants to war work. He had backed his friend Lou E. Holland, a successful small businessman from Kansas City, as the first chairman of the SWPC. Holland had spent a year in Washington, D.C., negotiating with the generals and admirals—and gotten next to nowhere. The military preferred to deal only with the big companies, and let them subcontract what one small-business advocate called "crumbs from the table" to the little companies. Secretary of War Henry Stimson and his top aides emphatically backed the brass. Republicans all, they had a natural affinity for big business—and they shared the military's insistence on a massive superiority in the weapons of war to guarantee victory.

Holland quit in disgust and went home to Kansas City. Brigadier General Robert Wood Johnson replaced him. Truman was not happy. "I believe uniforms should be reserved for the purposes for which they were adopted: namely to distinguish the combatants on the field of battle," he said. Truman saw "so-called officers" such as Johnson as big businessmen in disguise. This was certainly true of Johnson—in civilian life he was chairman of the board of Johnson and Johnson, the nation's largest drug company.[45]

The general turned out to be a sincere advocate of small business. But he confirmed Truman's fears by having the patronizing air of both an army procurement officer and a big businessman. He campaigned to get more subcontracting business from the major firms, a policy that wounded the pride of many small businessmen, who felt they had the expertise and competence to deal directly with the government. At the end of 1943, Johnson too quit, declaring the problem insoluble.

Although Truman was frustrated by the triumph of the corporate giants, he did not go public with an apocalyptic criticism of Henry Stimson and his lieutenants as enemies of the New Deal in the manner of Henry Wallace's attack on Jesse Jones. Nor did he lament, like Harold Ickes, that FDR was "abandoning advanced New Deal ground with a vengeance," with the tax breaks and cost-plus incentives the government showered on big business. Truman recognized there was some merit in the military's desire for mass production of tanks, guns, and planes. The generals' and admirals' attitude might be narrow-minded politically, but it was getting results on the battlefronts.

Truman got more results with his criticisms of the military for their insensitivity to the civilian needs of the wartime economy. His opposition played a large role in forcing the generals to reduce their manpower goals from 215 divisions to 90. Truman also opposed on the Senate floor the National Service bill that Secretary of War Stimson sponsored, giving the military the power to draft workers into war plants far from their homes. Like his earlier op-

position to a similar proposal by Paul McNutt, the war manpower czar, the Missouri senator's opinion persuaded his fellow
solons to let the idea drift into legislative oblivion.[46]

Truman also played a major role in the Senate dispute over
sponsoring a bipartisan resolution supporting the creation of an
international organization to foster peace in the postwar world.
Three members of his committee joined with Democrat Lister Hill
of Alabama to introduce Senate Resolution 114, which became
known as B^2H^2 after the last names of its sponsors. Although
FDR privately approved this move, he gave them very little public
support. With Henry Wallace talking about a New Deal for the
world, Roosevelt worried about arousing the antagonism of the
Republican–southern Democratic coalition. The debate over B^2H^2
led to a resolution by Senator Tom Connally, head of the Senate
Foreign Relations Committee, calling for "the establishment and
maintenance of international authority with power to prevent aggression and preserve the peace of the world." A huge majority of
the Senate voted for this step beyond isolationism.

The quiet man from Independence continued to grow in stature
in the eyes of many Washington insiders. When fifty press gallery
reporters were asked to name the ten Americans who had contributed the most to the war effort, Senator Truman was the only
member of Congress on the list. In the spring of 1944, Truman
made several speeches urging FDR's renomination for a fourth
term, insisting that he deserved reelection. His role as a critic of
the way the war was being fought on the home front gave added
weight to his words. The *New York Times* noted that praise from
Truman was a "stamp of approval . . . from a source that commands considerable respect."[47]

Senator Truman injected himself into another home front battle
as 1944 unfolded. He began recommending that the government
set up a bureau or commission to study how to convert the war

economy to peacetime production without sending Wall Street into a tailspin, panicking the big corporations into unwarranted cutbacks and layoffs, and driving labor unions berserk. Abrupt moves could also create economic chaos on the home fronts of allies such as Great Britain, who had become dependent on lend-lease. This subject was not popular with the generals and admirals and their allies grouped around Secretary of War Stimson. They feared, with some justice, that people would assume the war was as good as won, and perform accordingly in the workplace. Again, General Brehon Sommervell summed up the military's view of the civilians: "They have never been bombed, they have little appreciation of the horrors of war and only a small percentage . . . have enough hate."[48]

If Congress had not eliminated the National Resources Planning Board and—an even bigger what-if—the NRBP had not been stubbornly committed to turning postwar America into a New Dealish centralized economy, this agency might have done the job. But the NRPB was in the government warehouse graveyard where terminated bureaucracies go. Instead, Senator Truman nudged Donald Nelson, whom he had backed to head the War Production Board, into the fray. Having discovered the hard way that the WPB had little real power to control the military procurement barons, Nelson had mutated into a sort of imitation New Dealer, a people's advocate. Conversion looked at first like a battle he could win.

The argument swiftly turned ugly. Demonstrating how totally they had taken over most of the levers of government, the War Department ordered the OWI, the agency the New Dealers had once so proudly manned in the name of a strategy of truth, to unleash a ferocious attack on Nelson's proposal. Crucial members of the White House inner circle, in particular Jimmy Byrnes, did not agree with the WPB chairman's initiative. This meant that the enfeebled president, still limited to a bare twenty hours a week of serious work, never came to Nelson's aid. Senator Truman, seeing the way things were tilting, remained silent too.

Nelson was soon in Henry Wallace's footsteps, en route to China on a vague economic mission that became an assignment to oblivion. Around this time Budget Director Harold Smith told speechwriter Sam Rosenman: "I would like to have a solid commitment from you that you will let me know the first time you hear the words 'Smith' and 'China' in the same breath."[49]

Senator Truman's early political education in the Pendergast machine had given him a healthy respect for the realities of power. Even while losing the peacetime conversion battle, the man from Independence demonstrated the kind of savvy a politician needed to survive in wartime Washington. One might justly conclude he was running for something. Not a few people decided it was vice president. But Senator Truman spent the spring of 1944 strenuously denying that he wanted Wallace's job.

"I have no intention of running for vice president," he told a Missouri friend who urged him to seek the nomination. He pointed out to another friend that after nine years in the Senate he was on three of the most powerful committees in the upper chamber, Appropriations, Military Affairs, and Interstate Commerce. These slots plus his Special Committee to Investigate the War Program gave him all the power he wanted or needed. He told a third friend that he thought the vice presidency was a poor trade for his present status. "The vice president merely presides over the Senate and sits around waiting for a funeral."[50]

Senator Truman obviously had no idea that Franklin D. Roosevelt was a dying man.

15

DEMOCRACY'S
TOTAL WAR

Back in 1941, Harry Hopkins declared that the forces of democracy had to exceed the Nazis in "fury and ruthlessness." In the skies above Europe in 1944, these concepts were put into practice by the British and American bomber fleets with increasing candor. "Breaking civilian morale," the phrase that the British air generals had whispered behind their hands to the shocked Americans in 1942, was swiftly becoming official policy. Soon shortened to "morale-bombing," it was a step beyond area-bombing, which could be rationalized by arguing that there were war plants and railroad yards within the districts being smashed. Morale-bombing was aimed at German civilians, without apology or subterfuge.

The Americans had already moved in this direction, using a rationalization called "radar bombing." This idea utilized radar supposedly to find targets when the weather over Germany was too cloudy to see the ground. Its real purpose was visible in the terminology used in memorandums discussing it. One remarked it would do a good job of "dehousing" civilians in wintertime. The goal, said the radar proponents, would be "one Hamburg a month."[1]

General Henry H. Arnold, commander of the army air forces, gave the green light to a series of massive radar raids on Berlin in March of 1944. One AAF general was soon exulting that if they kept it up, "there won't be a damn house left." This was not exactly the language of pinpoint bombing. Yet the British were unsatisfied. They regularly ran stories in their newspapers about the Americans being too timid to bomb the center of cities where the antiaircraft fire was heaviest. Their macho reputations challenged, the AAF generals proceeded to plaster the center of Berlin in another series of massive raids during April and May 1944.

Yet the American commanders remained uneasy about the home-front image of the AAF. When a staff committee began considering morale-bombing as the next step, presuming that all strategic targets had been eliminated, an explosion of protest took place within the American command structure. It was led, with the irony that war seems fond of improvising, by an American staff officer of English birth, Colonel Richard D. Hughes. He was head of the Enemy Objectives Unit, in charge of selecting targets for the Eighth Air Force. The son of a doctor, Hughes struggled to keep "vestiges of decency" in the bombing campaign. He attacked the "terror raids" for both moral and practical reasons.

Hughes argued that morale was a will-o'-the-wisp. German civilians were already terrorized by Hamburg and Essen. They were living under a total dictatorship that was ready and willing to shoot anyone who tried to oppose the war or shirk his or her responsibilities. Hughes reminded his fellow airmen that Congress and the American people were seriously concerned about killing civilians needlessly and he warned the air force against losing public support.

The proponents of morale-bombing admitted the tactics were "repugnant" and even "deplorable." But the Germans deserved to have their women and children killed because they had been "brought up on doctrines of unprecedented cruelty, brutality and disregard of basic human decencies." The influence of the German hatred fanned by Vansittart and the policy of unconditional surrender is all too visible in this rhetoric. If morale-bombing shortened the war by even a day, argued its inflamed backers, it would be worth it, because it would save Allied lives.[2]

Other officers supported Hughes as the quarrel proceeded through channels to the higher echelons of the air forces. There, after more debate, the commander of the U.S. Strategic Air Forces in Europe, General Carl Spaatz, decided not to pursue morale-bombing. General Eisenhower gave his emphatic approval to the decision. But General Spaatz ordered that morale-bombing should be included in future Strategic Air Forces planning, and radar or "blind" bombing was still authorized when the weather made visual bombing impossible. This policy gave tacit permission to go on flattening German houses rather than factories, and suggested to not a few of the participants in the argument that they had not heard the last of morale-bombing.[3]

By this time, German civilians had no illusions about Allied bombing policies. Airmen who were shot down were often menaced by mobs of angry nomcombatants, who wanted to lynch the *terrorflieger*—"the terror flyer"—on the spot. One American pilot who went through the experience ruefully admitted: "The civilians had been bombed and shot, their houses had been burned and they were . . . angry." Another downed pilot and two of his crew were dragged to the center of a German town, where a crowd began chanting: "Kill them! Hang the scoundrels!" The mob's leader was a woman whose child had been killed by a bomb the day before. An elderly member of the German reserve army appeared with a rifle and rescued the flyers. German soldiers and public officials repeatedly saved airmen in similar situations and escorted them to prison camps, where they were treated as prisoners of war in accordance with the Geneva Convention.[4]

II

The cross-channel invasion now became the focus on both sides of the battle lines. With the Russians advancing relentlessly from the east, the leaders of the German resistance to Hitler realized they were running out of time. Early in 1944, Canaris's Nazi enemies succeeded in ousting the elusive admiral from control of the Abwehr. However, they were unable to make their suspicions of his treason into a factual case against him, and Hitler appointed Canaris head of a small agency in charge of the civilian war effort. He was able to leave behind in the Abwehr a number of subordinates who were still committed to Hitler's destruction.

A younger man now assumed the active leadership of the plot to get rid of Hitler. Thirty-seven-year-old Colonel Claus von Stauffenberg had no connection to the Protestant East German Junkers and Prussians on whom Churchill, Roosevelt, and Vansittart focused their antipathy. He was a Catholic and a descendant of the nobility of the principality of Württemberg, in south Germany, an area that even Vansittart admitted in an unguarded moment had democratic tendencies. Nazism's vicious deeds had filled Stauffenberg with loathing for Hitler, and the Anglo-American bombing offensive convinced him that it was time to act. "A thousand years of civilization are being destroyed," he said.

Stauffenberg had no doubts or hesitations about the necessity of killing Hitler—and he was in a position to do it—as well as to seize control of Germany. Badly wounded by an allied air attack in Tunisia in which he had lost an arm, an eye, and all but two fingers on his remaining hand, the colonel had become chief of staff of the Replacement Army, a forty-one division force that consisted of training units, convalescents, and reserves numbering over 500,000 men. They were well-armed and organized to keep order should Germany's millions of slave laborers attempt an uprising. Stauffenberg proposed to kill Hitler and use the Replacement Army to wrest power from the Nazis.[5]

With growing desperation, the Front of Decent People continued their efforts to win some sort of recognition from London and Washington. In several visits to Stockholm, diplomat Adam von Trott zu Solz was reduced to begging for even a small gesture, a hint of an eventual willingness to modify the unconditional surrender formula—to no avail. Hans Gisevius, under suspicion as the Nazis probed the Abwehr, finally had to take refuge with Allen Dulles in Berne. Complicating the resisters' problem was another irony. Certain Nazis, notably SS leader Heinrich Himmler, had become convinced the war was lost and were also sending emissaries to probe an opening to the West. The German-haters in the British Foreign Office accused Trott of being an agent of the Hitler regime.[6]

Around this time the Berlin conspirators won an important new ally. Hitler had appointed Field Marshal Erwin Rommel to command the western front. The former leader of the Afrika Korps was by far the most popular general in the German army. In February 1944, Dr. Karl Stroelin, an old friend from World War I days, visited him in his headquarters. The mayor of Stuttgart, Stroelin was an ally of Carl Goerdeler's, and he boldly asked Rommel to accept the leadership of the movement after Hitler was killed. Only a man of Rommel's stature could prevent a civil war, Stroelin argued. After a moment of deep inner struggle, Rommel said: "I believe it is my duty to come to the rescue of Germany."[7]

Unknown to the Front of Decent People, they were acquiring allies on the other side. As British and American planners contemplated the harsh realities of attacking Rommel's 1.5 million man army in France, doubts about the policy of unconditional surrender escalated in the Pentagon and State Department. Similar concerns grew in Parliament and among powerful branches of the British government, notably the army and the intelligence community, which did not share the Vansittartism of the Foreign Office. In America, Wild Bill Donovan's OSS was violently opposed to the policy and so was the Office of War Information, where New Dealers no longer reigned. The new leaders of the OWI regarded unconditional surrender as a propaganda disaster of the first order.[8]

It soon became evident that few top people in either government supported the policy except Roosevelt and his White House circle. (Vansittart, ranting in the House of Lords, had influence but no power.) On March 25, 1944, General George Marshall and his fellow chiefs of staff submitted a memorandum to Roosevelt, urging "that a reassessment of the formula of unconditional surrender should be made ... at a very early date." The chiefs proposed a proclamation that would assure the Germans that the Allies had no desire to "extinguish the German people or Germany as a nation." Unconditional surrender would be described, not as a policy of vengeance but as a "necessary basis for a fresh start" to a peaceful democratic society.[9]

On April 1, 1944, Roosevelt replied with an outburst that revealed as never before his hatred of Germany. "A somewhat long and painful experience in and out of Germany leads me to believe that German Philosophy cannot be changed by decree, law or military order. The change must be evolutionary and may take two generations." Any other alternative risked "a third world

372 THE NEW DEALERS' WAR

war." The president bluntly told the joint chiefs he was going to "stick to what I have already said," that the Allies were determined to inflict a "total defeat" on Germany. Although he insisted he did not intend to destroy the German people, he had no intention of saying the same thing about the German nation. In his opinion, the very word Reich had to be scoured from the German soul.[10]

General Marshall was dismayed by this response. He told Field Marshal Sir John Dill, the British liaison officer in Washington. that they were "up against an obstinate Dutchman." In London, Marshall's protégé and Overlord's commander, General Dwight Eisenhower, was even more disappointed. At the urging of his chief of staff, General Walter Bedell Smith, Ike decided to try to change the president's mind on his own. On April 14, 1944, Ike met with Under Secretary of State Edward Stettinius and asked him to request Cordell Hull to intercede with Roosevelt to give the Germans a "white alley," a path down which they could surrender with honor.[11]

Eisenhower was drawing on his experience in Italy, reasoning that if the Allies had gone along with installing Italian Field Marshal Pietro Badoglio as premier, what was wrong with the same approach for Germany? In his cable to Hull, Stettinius, obviously quoting Eisenhower, said they should try to encourage the emergence of a German Badoglio. The cable also added the suggestion that after the beachhead was established in France, Eisenhower should call on the German commander in the West to surrender.[12]

Stettinius emboldened Ike by revealing that he and other high-ranking Democrats were hoping the obviously ill Roosevelt would not seek a fourth term. They wanted him to give a rousing farewell speech at the 1944 Democratic convention—and nominate General Marshall as a "win-the-war" candidate. Stettinius intimated that he planned to propose this idea to the president. The portrait of Roosevelt as a dying, all-but-incapacitated man added urgency to Eisenhower's proposal, which both men saw as a way to end the war quickly.[13]

From the White House in response to the Stettinius-Eisenhower message came only silence. General Eisenhower was encouraged and ordered the preparation of a proclamation that became, under the influence of his psychological warfare experts, a warm personal chat with the German soldier, urging him to trust the Allies. A copy of the speech was rushed to the White House, and again the response was silence. Was it a sign of approval or further evidence that Roosevelt was out of the loop?

On May 31, 1944, General Ike's chat with the German soldier was attacked from an entirely unexpected quarter. Winston Churchill wrote a violent letter to the Supreme Commander, accusing him of "begging before we have won the battle." Never, he claimed, had he ever read anything "less suitable" for soldiers.[14]

Unknown to Eisenhower, Roosevelt had sent a "most secret" message to Churchill about Eisenhower's proposal. Instead FDR offered to make a unilateral declaration to the Germans. It did little but repeat some of the things he had said at Casablanca: the Allies did not seek the "total destruction of the German people." Brendan Bracken, the British minister of information, dismissed it as "sloppy and silly." Churchill told Roosevelt he and his cabinet were alarmed by its "tone of friendship." The British attitude toward Germany vacillated between Vansittartist hatred and the possibility of an honorable accommodation. At this point, Vansittartism was in the ascendancy. Ike's appeal for an early surrender got scrubbed. Stettinius, chastened by the oblique Rooseveltian rebuke, dropped all thoughts of urging FDR not to run for a fourth term.[15]

In France, Admiral Canaris emerged from the shadows to make one last effort to cut a deal. In the months before D day, he leaked vital intelligence to the British and Americans, including the German army's order of battle, an invaluable insight into the

Wehrmacht's intentions. Through intermediaries, he made a final plea to Stewart Menzies, head of England's secret intelligence service, offering, among other things, the support of General Rommel for a bloodless conquest of the western front if the Anglo-Americans would give the slightest sign of a disposition for an armistice. In a convent outside Paris, one of Menzies's most trusted aides delivered the British reply: there was no alternative to unconditional surrender. Canaris gasped with pain as he read the letter. "Finis Germaniae," he sighed.[16]

III

Elsewhere, the U.S. Army's air forces was putting to the test another principle of the New Dealers' war: America's Russian allies were people with whom Americans could get along "very well indeed," as FDR put it in his report to the nation on the Teheran conference. One of the topics discussed at Teheran was the possibility of using bases in the Soviet Union to "shuttle-bomb" targets in eastern Germany. This arrangement would save an immense amount of fuel, not to mention the lives of airmen as well as wear and tear on planes, if Americans did not have to make the long dangerous flight back to bases in England.

At Teheran, Stalin said he agreed "in principle" to the idea but in Moscow in the ensuing months the Russians stonewalled and evaded American requests for six air fields. Simultaneously, they demanded a copy of the famed Norden bombsight, an early version of the automatic pilot and other top secret technology that the Americans were not even sharing with the British. General Arnold agreed to these gifts, stunning the army air forces officers doing the negotiating in Moscow. They did not realize that the White House had ordered the AAF to give the project top priority.

Behind the military arguments was FDR's hope that if large numbers of Americans and Russians worked together, it would give a people-to-people impetus for other forms of cooperation during and after the war. The donation of the top secret technology extracted seeming agreement from the Russians and a pleased General Spaatz authorized five freighters to be loaded with 21,717 tons of fuel, bombs, vehicles, signals, and other devices to equip the bases.[17]

Three airfields were given to the Americans, all in the Ukraine in the vicinity of Kiev, with Poltava, named for a nearby agricultural town, as the headquarters. None were suitable for heavy bombers and all had been badly damaged by the retreating Germans. The Americans had to expend much time and money lengthening runways and repairing bomb holes. The goal was to get things up and flying before the invasion of France, scheduled for early June. Someone with a sense of humor on the air force staff named the troubled experiment Operation Frantic.

The Russians continued to haggle over everything. The Americans wanted 2,100 ground personnel. The Russians limited them to 1,200. When the first sixteen officers and six enlisted men flew to Teheran, the Russians refused to let them into the Soviet Union until the Americans agreed to let Stalin station a Russian air force unit in Italy. Things did not improve in the ensuing weeks. At first the Russians insisted that only their people could man the radio equipment to communicate with the planes when they were airborne, an idea that drove the Americans to the brink of insanity, imagining harried pilots, possibly under German attack, trying to understand Russian-English or waiting for an interpreter to tell them what was just said.

The Russians were equally intransigent about who would protect the air bases. They insisted this was their responsibility. But no Russian fighter planes or antiaircraft guns appeared as the time approached for the arrival of the first American bombers. More American protests produced a few fighters and some trucks with fifty-caliber machine guns mounted on them—hardly the last word in antiaircraft defense.

When the first American reconnaissance planes tried to land at the bases, the Russians opened fire on them, then claimed they had not given permission for them to arrive and cancelled all future reconnaissance flights, making intelligent planning for assaults on specific targets next to impossible. One exasperated American officer asked: "Is Russia on our side in this war?"

Next, the Russians objected to every target the Americans selected, most of them in the vicinity of Riga, Latvia. Instead they insisted the Americans should bomb railroads and war plants in Hungary, easily within range of the Fifteenth Air Force in Italy, with no need to shuttle on to Poltava. Again, the cursing Americans swallowed their objections and agreed. Finally, on June 2, 1944, with all the air crews sworn to secrecy, the first Operation Frantic mission took off from Italian bases. With D day imminent, Allied planners had decided they needed all the Britain-based Eighth Air Force's planes to support the invasion.

The Fifteenth Air Force planes hit railyards in Hungary with devastating effect. Flying on toward the Ukraine, they were supposed to pick up a Russian direction-finding beacon. It never appeared on their instruments and they flew all over the map before making a visual landing with their gas gauges on empty. In spite of this Soviet snafu, sixty-five bombers and fifty fighters made the trip with the loss of only a single plane.

The American airmen and the local Russians got along well and Stalin had Frantic One's commander, General Ira Eaker, flown to Moscow to be his guest at a dinner. The Russians, who had no heavy bombers or a strategic air force, were impressed by the big B-17s. Their planes flew in support of their ground army.

But General Eaker grew more and more concerned about the lack of air defenses around Poltava and the other two fields. He was also frustrated by a continuing Soviet refusal to approve reconnaissance flights. The Russians were clearly hostile to the idea of Americans building up a file of pictures on targets in or near the Soviet Union. When reconnaissance planes strayed out of specified corridors, they were attacked by Russian fighter planes and landed full of bullet holes. Meanwhile, Stalin stonewalled on assigning more bases to the Americans, and refused to discuss the possibility of arranging for bases in Siberia from which American planes could attack Japan, when and if Russia entered the war.

When the D day landings were made with relatively light casualties, the Eighth Air Force undertook Frantic 2, the first shuttle bomb raid from England. Everything went well; the Russian direction-finding equipment worked perfectly and losses were light. Some of the fliers noticed they had been trailed to Poltava by a German plane but no one worried about it. According to recent estimates, the Russian air force had 23,000 planes and what was left of Hitler's Luftwaffe was fighting the British and Americans over France.

On June 22, 1944, there were some seventy-three B-17s on the ground at Poltava. Around midnight, as the Americans slept in their tents—there were still no barracks at the ruined field—Russian antiaircraft guns began firing and an air-raid siren wailed. The airmen dashed to the shelter of crude slit trenches. Seconds later, flares drifted down, turning the airfield into a good approximation of daylight. Minutes later, bombs exploded among the flying fortresses parked wing-to-wing off the runways. The Luftwaffe was attacking.

After turning the big planes into a mass of flaming wreckage, the Germans roared in at treetop level with antipersonnel bombs. Then came incendiaries that set 200,000 gallons of high-octane fuel ablaze, followed by ingenious land mines that burrowed into the soggy spring earth. For an hour and a half eighty German planes plastered the field without encountering a single Russian night fighter. American P-51 fighter pilots, who had accompanied the bombers to Russia and were at the two nearby fields, rushed to their planes as soon as they saw the flames and heard the explosions, but the Russians refused to let them take off.[18]

When the crews of the ruined bombers finally returned to England aboard transport planes, they were greeted with an order from General Carl Spaatz's headquarters, forbidding them to say anything to reporters that would be "offensive to the Russian government." This censorship did not stop a lot more American airmen from wondering if they and the Soviet Union were on the same side in the war.[19]

IV

In the same spring of 1944, Roosevelt's old friend, Commander George Earle, returned from Istanbul to Washington, bringing with him his report on the Katyn Massacre. In the Oval Office, he showed the president gruesome pictures of the site and reams of testimony from Poles, confirming the Russians' guilt. FDR dismissed it all with a wave of his hand. "George," he said, "this is entirely German propaganda and a German plot. I am absolutely convinced the Russians did not do this."[20]

George Earle left the White House an unhappy man. He had the distinct impression that he was no longer Franklin D. Roosevelt's friend.

V

In the Pacific, the war with Japan mounted in intensity. Americans were staggered by the ferocity and tenacity of the Japanese resistance. The first island chain attacked were the Gilberts, with the atoll of Tarawa the main target. Surrounded by an air and sea armada that rained more than 3,000 tons of bombs and shells on their sandspit, the 5,000 Japanese refused to surrender, and inflicted horrendous casualties on the assaulting marines as they waded ashore. After a day and a half of sanguinary combat, the remaining Japanese radioed Tokyo: "Our weapons have been destroyed and everyone is attempting a final charge." Screaming the emperor's name, they flung themselves into the muzzles of the marines' machine guns.

This heroic behavior provoked a new level of race hatred. The Americans begin writing in popular magazines that the Japanese soldier was "a moronic individual." A marine wrote that the Japanese were "plain crazy, sick in the head." The *American Legion Magazine* ran an article entitled: "These Nips Are Nuts." This belief in Japan's national insanity was combined with a growing perception that race was at the root of the struggle. A Hearst paper portrayed the war in Europe as a "family fight" whereas in the grapple with Japan the future of Western civilization was at stake. Another Hearst paper saw it as a "war of the Oriental races against the Occidental races for the domination of the world."[21]

Some Western writers with a knowledge of Asia were appalled at this rampant racism. Pearl Buck risked her status as a best-selling author to condemn it in speeches and in her 1943 novel, *The Promise*, about the British and Chinese fighting the Japanese in Burma. She depicted the British as infected with all but incurable racist attitudes, which led them to see Asians as subhuman, even when they were allies. Buck warned that the white men were blundering into a ruinous future war between the East and the West.[22]

On January 28, 1944, the U.S. government released the story of the Bataan Death March, the ordeal that the victorious Japanese had inflicted on the Americans who surrendered in the Philippines in March of 1942. The Roosevelt administration had kept the information secret for over six months, and released it as a calculated step to intensify American determination to defeat Japan. The Death March convinced most Americans of "the true nature of the enemy . . . an enemy that seems to be a beast which sometimes stands erect." Stories of Japanese cruelty to prisoners became a staple diet of the daily papers and newsreels for the rest of the war.[23]

VI

Revealing the Bataan Death March was part of the Roosevelt administration's continued manipulation of the American people's emotions about the war. In September, 1943, the censors in the army and navy information services and their by now subservient collaborators in the Office of War Information had decided their sanitized version of the war was working almost too well. Labor unrest, race riots, brawls between Washington power brokers such as Henry Wallace and Jesse Jones gave the impression that it was business as usual on the home front. The Italian surrender was another factor in the bureaucrats' changing mindset. They feared it would give Americans the feeling the war was all but over. Another worry was Hollywood's approach to the war. Their films, all of whose scripts were carefully reviewed by the Office of War Information before production, showed few American casualties. Washington became concerned that Americans might conclude that only Germans and Japanese were willing to die for their country.[24]

The censors decided to break the taboo on American dead with the cooperation of *Life* magazine. On a September 1943 cover, *Life* carried a picture of three American dead soldiers on the beach in Buna, New Guinea, with a wrecked landing craft behind them. *Life* backed up the photograph with an editorial, declaring it was time for Americans to confront "war's terror." American dead were in danger of dying in vain "if live men refused to look at them." This was disingenuous to say the least; by this time tens of thousands of Americans had already received telegrams informing them that their husbands or sons had been killed in action.

Newspaper comment revealed how uncomfortable the media was with the Roosevelt administration's policy of feeding the war to the public in carefully calculated doses. Approving the *Life* picture, the *Washington Post* declared it was time the government treated the American people as adults. The paper added that government manipulation of the people's emotions was "intolerable." Then, nervously revealing ongoing uneasiness about public support for the war, the *Post* reversed its field and tut-tutted that "an overdose of such photographs would be unhealthy."

A month later, the OWI took a survey in five war plants in the New York area and reported that 75 percent of those polled approved of pictures of American dead. In fact, the OWI concluded that the public had been barraged with so much preachy propaganda, they were somewhat immune to it. Only "hate pictures" made people mad enough to "dig deep" and buy war bonds. Topping this bizarre conclusion was a telegram to the OWI from New Orleans: *Please rush airmail gruesome photos of dead American soldiers for plant promotion Third War Loan.*[25]

VII

In Moscow, George Kennan was back in the Soviet Union after an absence of ten years, thanks to Charles Bohlen. Proving he had by no means abandoned his convictions about the Communist dictatorship, Bohlen had persuaded the new ambassador, Averell Harriman, to accept Kennan as counselor of the embassy, even though Kennan made it clear that he did not agree with FDR's policy toward Stalin's Russia.[26]

Kennan found himself brooding on the isolation that the Soviet system inflicted on all foreign diplomats. They were forbidden to travel and their access to average Russians was severely restricted. One day Kennan got into a conversation with a Soviet acquaintance, a dedicated Communist. Why, Kennan asked, do you teach everyone to assume that every foreigner is a spy? The Russian replied it was necessary because that was the only way they could instill the proper "self-control" in their citizens and make them measure up to the standards of a great power.

The two men argued this point for several minutes and the Russian suddenly blurted: "We cannot permit you to associate closely with them. You will tell them all sorts of things . . . about your higher standard of living, about what you consider to be your happier life. You will confuse them. You will weaken their loyalty to their own system."

Kennan gave up and warned the man that the consequences of this policy would spread a sense of resentment and grievance against Russia throughout the rest of the world.

The Russian laughed. "We're not afraid of that!" he said. After a pause he added. "We are being very successful these days [on the battlefield]. The more successful we are, the less we care about foreign opinion."[27]

VIII

As D-day loomed, Vice President Henry Wallace found himself absorbed by his preparations for a visit to Siberia and China. By now Wallace must have known he was leaving the country at the worst possible time. A successful Allied landing would be likely to restore American confidence in the Roosevelt administration. It would be the ideal time for a vice president to stay as close as possible to the president, to have his picture taken beside FDR, to be seen coming and going at the White House.

Instead, the president had consigned him to the tutelage of Laughlin Currie, second in command of the Foreign Economic Administration, the agency that had absorbed the Board of Economic Warfare. The Canadian-born economist had gone to China at the president's behest in 1942. For further advice, Currie selected John Carter Vincent, a State Department expert on China, and Owen Lattimore, deputy director of the overseas branch of the OWI and an old China hand. Also in the picture was Harry Dexter White, the assistant secretary of the treasury, who was an expert on international monetary matters. Finally, Alger Hiss, a specialist in international organization at the State Department, sent Wallace a long memorandum on who to trust and who not to trust in the American embassy in Chungking.[28]

All these people had something in common: they were deeply sympathetic to Communism. In fact, we now know from the Venona transcripts that Currie, Hiss, and White were Soviet agents. Vincent and Lattimore were strongly inclined to view the political situation in China with fellow-travelers' eyes. They both thought Communism offered China the best hope of escaping Western—in essence British—domination.

Under Currie's direction, Vincent prepared a set of position papers for the vice president. One consisted of a savage attack on Winston Churchill and the entire British war leadership. It accused them of playing a "save the empire" game in the Far East and around the world. Another paper declared that China's leader, Chiang Kai-shek, had "no appreciation of what genuine democracy means." The Chinese Communists, on the other hand, held local elections regularly. Vincent maintained that their regime had no resemblance to "orthodox Communists." They encouraged "individual economic freedom." All in all, it was a mistake even to call them Communists. A better term would be agrarian democrats.[29]

The Chinese ambassador to the United States, Wei Tso-ming, tried to give the vice president another point of view. He told him the Chinese Communists were ruthless murderers who regularly shot everyone who did not go along with their class-hatred ideology in areas of China they controlled. He spoke disparagingly of Theodore White, a journalist who had written an admiring article about the Communists in *Life* magazine. Wallace confided to his diary that he strongly suspected White was "accurate."[30]

IX

Finally, there was the advice Wallace got from the president. FDR started by telling Wallace how to solve the problem of China's runaway inflation. He wanted Wallace to urge Generalissimo Chiang Kai-shek to call in one person from each of China's provinces, and make them agree to issue a new currency based on $200 worth of the new money to $1 of the old money. Then he should fix prices and enforce them. Wallace managed to conceal his amazement at this example of Roosevelt's total incomprehension of basic economics. When the president had said similar things to Henry Morgenthau Jr., the Treasury secretary had informed his diary that he had never heard FDR so "ill informed" on any subject.

"Don't you think I had better talk to Harry White . . . about this inflation problem?" Wallace asked. The president agreed he should talk to Harry. He was obviously unaware that White had been worsening the Chinese inflation problem for the better part of a year. In 1943 the Chinese had asked for $200 million in gold to back up their depreciating paper currency. It was to be charged against a $500 million loan Congress had authorized in 1942. Roosevelt approved the gold transfer but Assistant Secretary of the Treasury White, with the cooperation of two other Communists in the Treasury department, convinced Secretary Morgenthau to delay shipping the gold until China had adopted a long list of financial reforms. Meanwhile inflation rocketed to 1,000 percent a year, destabilizing the country.[31]

FDR now launched into the way the generalissimo should handle the Chinese Communists. He should follow the motto of William Jennings Bryan, "Nothing should be final between friends." Roosevelt went on to quote Al Smith on how to conciliate warring factions. "Let me get them all into the same room with good chairs to sit on where they can put their feet on the table, where they can have cold beer to drink and cigars to smoke. Then I will knock their heads together and we will settle everything."

FDR said he would be happy to serve as arbiter between the Nationalist and Communist Chinese. He would follow the example of Charles Francis Adams, the minister to England during the Civil War. Adams dealt evenhandedly with Englishmen who favored the South and those who favored the North, because he saw they were all "friends of the entire United States." The president said he was a friend of "all China."

More somberly, FDR told Wallace he had persuaded Stalin to agree to stay out of China's mineral-rich northern province of Manchuria. He wanted Wallace to tell this to Chiang Kai-shek. But if the generalissimo could not compose his differences with the Communists, the president was not sure he could "hold the Russians in line."[32]

Exactly how or why FDR thought the Chinese—heirs to a 4,000 year old civilization thronged with wise men and philosophers who had commented on war, peace, and politics while Europeans were still living in caves—should be impressed by the wisdom of Bryan and Smith, two defunct Democratic politicians who had failed to win races for the presidency, must have puzzled Wallace. But he had no difficulty swallowing the rest of the president's advice about telling Chiang to cut a deal with the Communists or else.

It would be crude though not completely erroneous to claim Wallace had been brainwashed by his State Department advisors. His mystic vision of the century of the common man predisposed him to accept their belief that Communism was just a stage on the road to universal democracy. He was like France's popular front politician, Leon Blum, who was asked why he believed in the eventual triumph of socialism. "Because I hope for it," he said.

X

With a stopover in Alaska, Wallace flew to Siberia, arriving on May 23, 1944. Over the next twenty-five days, he visited eighteen cities and made numerous side trips to the countryside, where he used his fluency in Russian to talk to average people. He gave speeches in Russian to several audiences, predicting a world in which the USSR and the U.S.A. would become partners in peace and joint promoters of the century of the common man. Moscow reprinted the speeches in *Pravda* and lavished praise on the vice president.

Wallace was delighted by his warm reception, especially by average Russians. He was even more impressed by the "respect" the common folk paid his escorts. With a naïveté that almost passes comprehension, he explained they were "old soldiers . . . members of the NKVD." Wallace seemed to think the Russian secret police were benevolent despots, beloved by the people.[33]

The major in command of the NKVD detachment charmed the Americans by revealing a sense of humor. He had escorted Wendell Willkie on his tour of Russia. Asked to compare the Hoosier statesman's trip to Wallace's, the major said that would require two stories with different titles: for Willkie it would be "Vodka, Vodka, Vodka." For Wallace it would be called "Kipicheonia, Kipicheonia," loosely translated as boiled water, Wallace's staple drink.[34]

Everywhere Wallace went, he was told that the people of Siberia were all volunteers, eager to be pioneering in the Asian wilderness, like the frontiersmen in the American west of the previous century. At Kolyma, a gold- and coal-mining center, he met "big husky young men" who told him they wrote to Stalin begging to be sent to the front but their Great Leader had decreed they were doing more important work in Siberia. Wallace had no idea he was in the heart of the Soviet gulag. The watchtowers that normally frowned over the Kolyma barracks had been torn down and the half-starved prisoners hidden in remote villages. The big bruisers were probably the guards, masquerading as workers.

At another stop Wallace was introduced to a group of cheerful well-fed women working as swineherds. They were all office workers, assigned to the pigs for the day. The real swineherds were off in the woods, starving. The gullible vice president told one audience that Americans had long associated Siberia with "frightful suffering and sorrow, convict chains and exile." He was ecstatic to discover Communism had transformed the meaning of the word into enterprise and progress.

In fact, during World War II, conditions in the Siberian gulag were, if possible, worse than ever. Stalin deported some 1.3 million ethnic groups from European Russia to join 1.2 million "specially displaced" victims already there, lethally overcrowding the work camps. They soon had a mortality rate of 25 percent. At one point, Lavrenti Beria, the head of the NKVD, reported that 30 percent of one deported group were unable to work because they had no shoes. Bare feet would be a problem in Siberia, where winter temperatures frequently sank to 40 below zero.

Obviously, the vice president's trip was known well in advance, thanks to Soviet spies Currie, Hiss, and White, and the Russians had ample time to prepare for it. By way of a little icing on this piece of intelligence-war cake, Owen Lattimore, traveling with

Wallace, wrote an article, "New Road to Asia" for the *National Geographic* when they returned to America. The essay described Siberia in glowing terms. All the Russians Lattimore and Wallace met had "a sensitive interest in art and music and a deep sense of civic responsibility." There was no mention of the millions of political prisoners slaving in the gulag.[35]

XI

In China, Wallace sat down for several long talks with Generalissimo Chiang Kai-shek. After seven years of war against a Japanese army of 2 million men, Chiang's regime was on the ropes. Inflation was at the runaway level. Local corruption was rampant. Army and civilian morale was low. The Japanese still had Chiang cut off from almost all outside aid, and at Teheran Roosevelt had acquiesced in a British request to delay an offensive in Burma, which would have opened a supply line into south China.

If anyone around Wallace had a sense of history, they might have reminded him that China's desperate situation closely paralleled another undeveloped country that had fought a seemingly endless war against a far stronger invader, the United States of America in 1781. Thanks to the British blockade, the infant U.S.A.'s economy had sunk to barely 20 percent of its prewar level and its inflated currency had become a bad joke. Defeatism and disloyalty were rampant in all directions. The leader of the Revolution, George Washington, filled his diary with predictions of imminent collapse.[36]

Instead, Wallace and his advisors saw China's situation as an indictment of Chiang. Wallace insisted on Roosevelt's solution: an alliance with the Chinese Communists. Again, some historical knowledge might have helped the vice president see how fatuous this idea was. Chiang had fought a civil war with the Communists in the 1920s and had no illusions about their murderous tendencies. In 1928, when they created "Soviets" in the part of China they controlled, a reign of "democratic terror" ensued. Whole villages were invited to trials of landowners and other "counterrevolutionaries" who were invariably condemned to death. While crowds shouted "Kill! Kill!" Red Guards hacked the victims to pieces. Later, a Communist speaker would address a revolutionary meeting with a row of severed heads on stakes in front of the platform.

When Chiang refused to consider the proposal to form a government with these blood-drenched enemies, Wallace could only report the Generalissimo's "prejudice" against the Communists, as if it were a personal aberration. Under pressure from the vice president, Chiang reluctantly agreed to let the Americans consult the Communists about setting up air bases in their part of China—another example of what might be called FDR's Poltava approach to international diplomacy.[37]

Wallace would tell Roosevelt that China's only hope was "agrarian reform," ignoring how difficult it would be to pursue such an agenda in the middle of a war. He was aware that Roosevelt himself had given up all pretenses to reform in the United States in order to win the war. "Dr. New Deal" was in the discard dumpster. But neither the vice president nor his entourage were ready to cut any similar slack for the embattled Chinese leader. Wallace saw no alternative to supporting Chiang for the present but he called him "a short term investment."[38]

As he boarded his plane to return to the United States, the vice president did not realize that Franklin D. Roosevelt had already made the same harsh judgment on Henry Agard Wallace.

16

OPERATION STOP HENRY

While Henry Wallace traversed Siberia and China, orating on the century of the common man, Democratic politicians in Washington, D.C., were discussing the vice president in a very different context. They were a loose-knit group, united by a single conviction: Franklin D. Roosevelt was a dying man, and virtually anything short of assassination must be considered to prevent Wallace from becoming the next president.

Leading this informal coalition was Robert Hannegan, the new chairman of the Democratic Party. Even more important in some opinions was California oilman Edwin W. Pauley, the treasurer of the party and the man who had given Roosevelt blunt advice about getting back to practical politics after the 1942 midterm debacle. Not far behind him were Boss Ed Flynn of the Bronx and Mayor Ed Kelly of Chicago, a duo with the power to win—or lose—two crucial states, New York and Illinois. Backing them was another party leader, Postmaster General Frank

Walker. Inside the White House was an ally, Appointments Secretary General Edwin "Pa" Watson. More than anyone else, he knew the truth about the president's condition—and he controlled access to the Oval Office.[1]

None of these men were New Dealers. But Wallace was also under fire from two of that dwindling band, both close to Roosevelt. In May Harold Ickes had warned FDR that Wallace could cost the ticket 3 million votes, enough to swing the election. Ickes found ominous an upheaval at the Texas Democratic state convention, at which a majority of the delegates refused to endorse Roosevelt for a fourth term. Many thought Jesse Jones was behind this defiance, but among most delegates hatred of Wallace seemed genuine.

A few weeks later Henry Morgenthau Jr. got into a discussion with the president about Wallace. FDR remarked that Eleanor Roosevelt was hounding him day and night to "insist" on Wallace as his vice president. Morgenthau abruptly replied: "If something should happen to you, I certainly wouldn't want Wallace to be president." The secretary had recently noted in his diary that at the Kentucky state Democratic convention, delegates had ripped Wallace's picture off the wall while onlookers cheered.[2]

Ed Pauley had toured the country for the previous year, telling Democratic leaders Roosevelt was a sick man and Wallace would be an impossible president. He found a confederate in Pa Watson, who was born in Alabama and graduated from West Point in 1908. Appointed FDR's military aide in 1933, he became a White House fixture, largely because of his talent as a raconteur. Watson collaborated in arranging for a steady stream of visitors who told the president Wallace was a political cancer that had to be excised. Hannegan, who traveled 12,000 miles around the United States in the first six months of 1944 talking to troubled Democrats, also sent numerous messages reporting strong anti-Wallace sentiment—and many favorable opinions of his fellow Missourian, Senator Harry S. Truman.[3]

In a late June meeting with Hannegan and speechwriter Sam Rosenman, Roosevelt took the lead in stating his unenthusiasm for Wallace. He said he was "just not going to go through" the 1940 experience of dictating his choice to the Democratic convention again. He feared it would "kill our chances for election in the fall." Hannegan grimly concurred and Rosenman added his assent—a crucial vote. He had been an early Wallace backer in 1940. With Harry Hopkins ill for the previous six months, no one was closer to Roosevelt than "Sammy the Rose."[4]

FDR began sorting through alternative candidates. He personally leaned toward Supreme Court Justice William O. Douglas, an outspoken liberal who was being pushed by Harold Ickes and Attorney General Francis Biddle. (Ickes, never one to scant his own gifts, also let it be known that he would accept an invitation to board the ticket.) Others such as Ed Pauley urged Jimmy Byrnes, the "assistant president," as a good possibility. FDR dismissed Speaker of the House Sam Rayburn because he could not control the violently anti-Roosevelt delegation from his own state, Texas. The president seemed cool to Harry Truman, claiming he "did not know much about him."

II

FDR suddenly launched a political romance with Jimmy Byrnes. Roosevelt took the balding beak-nosed South Carolinian with him for a weekend at Shangri La, the retreat in the Maryland mountains (which became Camp David under President Eisenhower). In bucolic privacy, FDR told Byrnes he was the man best qualified to succeed him as president and therefore was his choice for vice president. Roosevelt urged him to start campaigning for the job. Byrnes informed his staff of this startling news and added wryly that they should believe it only when and if it happened.

Byrnes would have been even more cautious if he had known that FDR was also exploring the possibility of running with Wendell Willkie. In early July Harold Ickes, claiming to be speaking for the president, met Willkie in New York and asked him if he would accept the nomination as vice president on the Democratic ticket. Willkie did not say yes or no at first. But his closest advisor, Gardner Cowles, urged him to turn down the offer. By this time, a lot of people knew FDR had a bad habit of dangling nominations in front of too many people for arcane, often self-interested, reasons.[5]

At the same time, Roosevelt sent out feelers to the man who controlled the bulk of Wallace's support in the Democratic Party, labor leader Sidney Hillman, head of the CIO's Political Action Committee, CIO-PAC. By now, the CIO's unions had put $650,000 into this operation (reminder: multiply by 10 to estimate this value in today's dollars), which was denounced by conservatives as a violation of the Smith-Connally Act ban on union contributions to political campaigns. (Corporation money had been banned since 1907.) But Attorney General Francis Biddle had ruled there was nothing wrong with using the money to "educate" voters on the issues and to organize "get out the vote" drives to persuade people to register and cast their ballots on election day. Fortunately for the Democrats, the term "soft money" had not yet been invented.

Hillman was soon throwing CIO-PAC's weight around at the grass roots and in the White House. Down in Texas, the PAC gave shipyard and oilfield workers money to pay their poll taxes if they promised to vote against Martin Dies, head of the House Un-American Activities Committee. Dies abandoned his run for reelection. Similar tactics beat two other members of his committee in primaries. This was vendetta politics, without much national significance. The PAC had numerous Communists among its managerial staff and they had urged Hillman to settle some scores for them.

Jimmy Byrnes was another matter. Hillman told Roosevelt that CIO-PAC violently opposed him because of his antiblack, antilabor voting record during his long years as a congressman and senator from South Carolina. However, when Harold Ickes asked the labor boss if he was totally committed to Henry Wallace, Hillman said he would back anyone the president suggested, as long as the new face had an "acceptable" record as a supporter of labor.[6]

The stage was now set for dumping Wallace. The vice president's journey to Siberia and China was coming to an end. Roosevelt summoned Sam Rosenman to the Oval Office and asked him if he remembered when FDR was governor of New York he regularly asked Sam to take bad news to the bosses of New York City's Tammany Hall. Rosenman was now going to take similar news to Henry Wallace. "Tell him that I'd like to have him as my running mate but I simply cannot risk creating a permanent split in the party," the president said. "I am sure he will understand and be glad to step down."[7]

FDR would soon discover how wrong he was. The man who said the New Deal was not dead had no intention of letting Franklin D. Roosevelt kill it, or him. The president was inadvertently setting the stage for the climactic battle of the war within the war.

III

Arriving at Fairbanks, Alaska, on July 5, 1944, Wallace called Senator Joseph Guffey of Pennsylvania to find out what was happening politically. Wallace had been gone forty-six days. He was totally out of touch. Guffey, once one of his strongest backers for renomination, said: "Things are not going well. Some of the people around the White House are saying, 'We need a new face.'"[8]

Wallace also talked to his assistant, Harold Young, who had been rounding up delegates while the vice president was away. Young had good news and bad news. A poll showed Wallace was now the favorite candidate of 65 percent of the Democrats, with the remaining 35 percent supporting a half-dozen other names. But the pressure coming from the White House and the party bosses made for doleful delegate counting at the upcoming convention, scheduled for July 19 in Chicago.

Wallace had barely hung up when he got a call from Sam Rosenman, who said he and Secretary of the Interior Harold Ickes wanted to have lunch with him on Monday, July 10, in Washington, D.C. Wallace replied that he was going to make a major radio address to the nation from Seattle on July 9, reporting on his trip to Siberia and China. Rosenman was undeterred. He urged him to take a night plane to Washington. Secretary Ickes had a train to catch for the West Coast. Ickes had a mortal fear of flying. Wallace noted in his diary he was being asked to fly all night so Ickes could avoid flying at all.

On July 9, Wallace sent Rosenman a wire, saying he wanted to see the president before he saw Rosenman and Ickes. Nevertheless, the Iowan made his speech and rushed to catch the night plane. As he flew through the darkened skies, the angry vice president must have realized he was already being treated as a political has-been. But he refused to believe it. Sleepless in the droning plane, he clung to his faith in Franklin D. Roosevelt.

Wallace's speech on China and Soviet Siberia said only nice things about both places, and, at Harold Young's suggestion, carefully stated that Communism did not jibe with the American philosophy of government. Young was desperately trying to turn

Wallace into a candidate. Arriving in Washington, D.C., on the morning of July 10, the vice president called the White House for an appointment. It was 10 A.M. Pa Watson blandly told him the president was bathing. A little later, General Watson called back to say Wallace had an appointment at 4:30 but FDR wanted him to see Rosenman and Ickes first.[9]

Wallace invited his two fellow New Dealers to have lunch at his apartment at the Wardman Park Hotel. It was a tense meeting. Ickes, who had frequently quarreled with Wallace when he was secretary of agriculture over interdepartmental turf wars, listened while Rosenman soothingly assured the vice president that Roosevelt wanted him as a running mate but did not think he could win at the convention, or would help the party win in the fall.

Ickes intruded at this point, saying Wallace had "grown in his esteem." Carried away by his own insincerity, the Old Curmudgeon added that Wallace was "a true liberal" and he (Ickes) and the vice president were "the only two real liberals left in the government."

Rosenman indignantly asked: "What about me?" Ickes said he was talking about liberals in the "western sense of the word." Apparently Honest Harold did not regard New York City Democrats as liberals, no matter what they claimed to believe. It required the bracing air and open spaces of the west to breed a true liberal.

Wallace presented them with a face that might have been carved in stone: "I am seeing the president at four thirty. I have a report to make on my mission to China. I don't want to talk politics."[10]

Ickes and Rosenman retreated, the latter fuming to himself that he could have handled Wallace if Ickes had not been there to get his back up. Rosenman was, of course, desperately trying to reduce the pressure on the sick president. But Wallace remained oblivious to FDR's condition and arrived for his 4:30

meeting eager to do battle with his enemies, if not with Roosevelt.

FDR greeted the vice president with his usual warmth. Wallace gave the president some stamps from Outer Mongolia for his collection and for two hours they discussed China. Not until 6:30, when, according to Dr. Bruenn, Roosevelt was supposed to have long since finished his working day, did they get around to American politics. FDR's first words were cautionary: when Wallace left, he was to tell reporters no politics were discussed. They only talked about China.

"I am now talking to the ceiling about political matters," FDR declared. He told Wallace he preferred to have him on the ticket. Tomorrow, Robert Hannegan was going to give him a letter, declaring that the party wanted him (FDR) for a fourth term. He would accept and announce his candidacy. His fourth term was going to be "progressive." He was going to get rid of conservatives like "Jesus H" Jesse Jones and his friend Will Clayton and others who "were thinking only about their own money." But a lot of people had told him that Wallace could not be nominated unless the president repeated his 1940 performance and insisted on him. Even then many delegate counters were not sure. Wallace interjected that he would not let the president repeat 1940. He would have objected in 1940 if he had known about it.

Wallace asked him if he would be willing to say: "If I were a delegate to the convention I would vote for Henry Wallace."

"Yes I would," FDR said.

But the president went back to quoting the naysayers, who kept telling him Wallace would sink the ticket. Wallace declared himself ready to step aside for anyone who would strengthen the ticket.

FDR said he "could not bear the thought" of Wallace being rejected by the convention. "Think of the catcalls and jeers and the definiteness of the rejection. You have your family to think of."

Wallace found himself thinking: I am much more concerned about the Democratic Party and you than I am about myself and my family. The vice president said he was at a disadvantage, having been out of the country for so long. He was going to talk things over with Joe Guffey that evening, hoping to get "current."

Roosevelt seemed to like that idea. He told Wallace to return for lunch the following day (Tuesday), and again on Thursday. Back in his apartment, Wallace got in touch with Harold Young, who had been doing a state-by-state tabulation of his strength, based on polls and data from Hillman's CIO-PAC. Young now predicted Wallace would win on the first ballot at the convention. On Tuesday morning, Joe Guffey arrived and at first tried to talk Wallace out of staying in the contest. When the vice president resisted, Guffey produced a draft of a statement that Guffey claimed would guarantee Wallace's nomination on the first ballot, if FDR agreed to make it.

On Tuesday, Wallace was told to arrive for his White House lunch via "the back way" (the south entrance). Wallace brought along the Guffey statement and a copy of the Harold Young state-by-state tabulation. He did not know that Guffey had already reported to the president that Wallace was being "quite stubborn" about stepping down. Roosevelt read the Young memorandum, "page by page," Wallace noted in his diary. Roosevelt carefully dated the report and said he wanted to keep it.[11]

FDR went back to telling Wallace other reasons why he would be a liability on the ticket. Roosevelt mentioned the numerous people who thought Wallace was "a Communist or worse." FDR waxed indignant, claiming he did not know a man who was more "American . . . no one more of the American soil." Next he mentioned the gibe that Wallace wanted to give a daily quart of milk to every Hottentot. "You know, Mr. President, I never said that!"

Wallace exclaimed. "That was said by the President of the National Association of Manufacturers."

Roosevelt professed amazement. He talked about the numerous times he had defended Wallace against these slanders. At the close of the lunch, the president said he would keep the Guffey statement, although he had worked out "another wording." Wallace left the White House feeling pleased with the progress he thought he was making.

Back in the Oval Office, FDR handed the Young memorandum with its optimistic polling numbers and Guffey's statement to his secretary, Grace Tully, and ordered her to "sink it in our files and NO ONE IS TO SEE IT." The only exception to this command was his son-in-law, Anna Roosevelt's husband, Major John Boettiger, who was living in the White House, functioning as an informal presidential aide, when he was not working for the Joint Chiefs of Staff.[12]

IV

That night, after dinner, Roosevelt met in his second floor oval study with a majority of the anti-Wallace phalanx—Robert Hannegan, Ed Flynn, Ed Kelly, Frank Walker, and George Allen, a Democratic fundraiser and VIP-about-Washington who had joined the parade. With them was John Boettiger, functioning as a secretary. The weather was hot muggy Washington at its July worst. Gulping drinks, the pols did most of the talking at first. They discussed and dismissed various candidates, such as Senator Alben Barkley (too old) and Jimmy Byrnes (because of CIO-PAC's opposition). Hannegan pushed vigorously for Senator Truman, pointing out that he appealed to all factions in the party. The others emphatically agreed with him. FDR asked his age. He thought Truman was rather old (he was sixty) and remarked that they needed youth on the ticket. The Republicans had just nominated forty-two-year-old Thomas E. Dewey as their candidate for president.

FDR astounded everyone by suggesting John Winant, the ambassador to England. He had no following anywhere, as far as anyone could discern. Next the president suggested Justice William O. Douglas, saying he would appeal to labor because he had worked as a logger, and he "looked like a boy scout." His hair had a tousled western look that people seemed to like. The president was obviously thinking of two other tousled liberals, Wallace and Willkie. No one showed an iota of enthusiasm.

As the meeting dragged on in the stifling heat, FDR grew more and more listless. The month-long vacation he had taken at Bernard Baruch's South Carolina estate in April had given the president a patina of health. When he returned in May, he seemed bronzed and rested to many visitors, almost his old cheerful zesty self. (Henry Wallace was one of these optimists.) But FDR was still a very sick man and any extra effort beyond his twenty-hour-a-week work schedule revealed it. The tremor in his hands returned and weariness induced an uncharacteristic passivity. Later, Frank Walker said he had never seen Roosevelt assume a spectator's role at a meeting as important as this one.

Finally, the weary president put his hand on Hannegan's knee and said: "Bob, I think you and everyone else here want Truman." Ed Pauley decided this was a good time to call the meeting to a close. He stood up and the group said good night. As they departed, FDR said: "I know this makes you boys happy and you are the ones I am counting on to win this election. But I still think Douglas would have the greater public appeal."[13]

This was not exactly a rousing endorsement. Downstairs, Walker urged Hannegan to go back and get something in writing. Roosevelt scrawled on a piece of paper: "Bob, I think Truman is the right man. FDR." This was better than nothing, but not a lot better. It read like something that could easily be dismissed as a passing thought, if time and circumstance required it.

V

On July 12, Robert Hannegan called on Henry Wallace at the Wardman Park. Hannegan said he had come at the president's behest to tell Wallace to withdraw. Wallace replied that the president wanted him to stay in the race—that FDR wanted him as vice president—in effect calling the party chairman a liar. In a rage, Hannegan all but gave away the game plan. Scornfully, he told Wallace that Roosevelt was going to say Wallace was his first choice and name "someone else" as his second choice. This would "automatically" result in the second choice getting all the dissident votes, which were unquestionably a majority. Wallace replied: "Bob, we might as well understand each other. I am not withdrawing as long as the president prefers me."[14]

On the way out, Hannegan encountered a reporter from the *St. Louis Post-Dispatch*, who asked him if he supported Wallace for vice president. Hannegan replied heatedly that he would sooner support %#—@&!! (many expletives deleted). He added that he was not going to Chicago until "this vice-presidential thing" was settled. The newsman made notes on the conversation and passed them to a Wallace aide.

Senator Claude Pepper of Florida visited Wallace to tell him that he would back him "on the early ballots, at least." This was ominous proof of the long reach of the rumor of FDR's decision to dump the vice president. Other liberals were equally luke-warm, thanks in large part to Harry Hopkins, who was back from the Mayo Clinic. In recent conversations, Pepper said Hopkins had "Yes butted" Wallace every time his name was mentioned.

Other insiders were downright hostile. Frowning fiercely, manpower czar Paul McNutt had told Pepper, "it won't be Wallace this time. I do not give a damn what Roosevelt says." McNutt's 1940 vice presidential ambitions had been crushed by FDR's insistence on Wallace. His comment was an interesting hint that some people still feared FDR was again backing Wallace.[15]

On the evening of July 12, Sidney Hillman arrived at the Wardman Park for a conference with the vice president. Hillman reported Harold Ickes had told him Wallace did not have a chance and CIO-PAC better have a second choice. Hillman was admittedly concerned but Wallace thought FDR was "standing fairly firm." The vice president recorded in his diary Hillman's boast that the PAC had a payroll of $65,000 a month, several times larger than the Democratic National Committee staff's take-home pay. They discussed the dirty game *Time* was playing. They were coming out with a picture of Hillman on the cover—"a very Semitic likeness," Wallace noted. They agreed it was part of a Republican plan to make it look like Jewish-led labor was running the Democratic Party.[16]

VI

The next day, Wallace returned for his second lunch of the week with the president, again entering the White House the back way. Wallace began the conversation by asking if he could nominate the president at the upcoming convention. Roosevelt shook his head. He had already agreed to let Alben Barkley do it. Warm words from the Kentuckian would remove the sting of his Senate denunciation over the vetoed tax bill. Roosevelt said he was going to send a letter to Senator Samuel D. Jackson of Indiana, the chairman of the convention, saying if he were a delegate he would vote for Wallace. He planned to add he "did not wish in any way to dictate to the convention." He wanted to "get the wording just right" so it would be "just" to Wallace but would avoid any hint of bossism.[17]

Wallace was delighted with this proposal. He listened complacently while Roosevelt told him about the interminable meeting with Ed Flynn, Frank Hague, Ed Kelly, and the other "professionals," as Wallace described them. Again, the vice president offered to withdraw if Roosevelt agreed with their insistence that his name would harm the ticket. Roosevelt shook his head. He "would not think of accepting" the offer, "mighty sweet" though Wallace was to make it. But FDR fretted that he did not know if the bosses were right or wrong. He could only find out by talking to farmers in the towns around Hyde Park. But he did not have time to make such a foray. Roosevelt was scheduled to leave in a few days for the West Coast and a sea voyage to Hawaii to review the progress of the war in the Pacific—part of his above-politics-commander-in-chief performance.

The two men discussed other vice presidential candidates in a dismissive way, going down the usual list—Byrnes, Barkley, Douglas. FDR noted the professionals preferred Truman. Wallace abruptly tried to use the information he had gotten from the hotheaded Hannegan about the second choice strategy. He told FDR the nasty epithets Hannegan had used when the reporter had irked him and asked the president if he was going to give Hannegan a second name in his letter to Convention Chairman Samuel Jackson. FDR looked him in the eyes and said no. That would be "too much like dictation."

As Wallace got up to leave, a smiling Roosevelt shook hands and drew the vice president close to his chair. "While I cannot put it just that way in public," he said, "I hope it will be the same old team." Then he added words that could not have thrilled Wallace. "Even though they do beat you out at Chicago, we will have a job for you in world economic affairs."[18]

VII

On July 14, Postmaster General Frank Walker and Democratic Party Chairman Robert Hannegan invited Jimmy Byrnes to lunch at the Mayflower Hotel and told the South Carolinian the decision to support Truman. Back at the White House, Byrnes called Roosevelt at Hyde Park and asked him if he had agreed with the bosses, that Truman was the nominee. "That is not what I told them," Roosevelt said. "That is what they told me. I did not express myself. . . . I had nothing to do with it." He unhesitatingly urged Byrnes to stay in the race. Some labor people had objected to him but he, FDR, still believed he was "the best qualified man in the whole outfit." He added that he "hardly knew Truman."[19]

Byrnes, no slouch at political infighting, now called Senator Truman, who remained oblivious to this maze of intrigue. The assistant president asked the senator if he would nominate him for vice president at the convention. Truman cheerfully agreed. He still did not want to become vice president. Byrnes thought, not without reason, that he had taken some of the steam out of the senator's prospects.[20]

What was Roosevelt trying to do? Some have attributed this web of lies and evasions and agreements that were not agreements to his dislike of telling anyone bad news face-to-face. Others, such as Henry Wallace, later saw it as the product of a man whose brain was no longer getting an adequate supply of blood. But an equally good argument can be made that amid the twists and turns Roosevelt was trying to procure a victory for Wallace while seeming to agree with the Democratic professionals. Although he considered the Iowan an inept politician, FDR was tempted by his fervid liberalism to back him covertly.

One thing stands out. The president had very little enthusiasm for Harry S. Truman. FDR's agreement that the Missourian had adequate liberal credentials was grudging, at best. Roosevelt admitted the senator was a loyal Democrat but added no praise to that concession. There was no sign of fondness and not a trace of admiration in the president's comments. He undoubtedly knew Truman remained a close friend of former vice president John Nance Garner, a man who now made no secret of his loathing for Roosevelt and New Dealers, and of Senator Burton K. Wheeler, by now FDR's most inveterate congressional enemy. The Truman Committee's reports had supplied Republicans and southern conservatives with too much ammunition for their claim that the White House was botching the war effort.

Agreeing to Truman's candidacy and at the same time encouraging Byrnes to run was a good way to kill off both men by splitting their conservative and moderate support. Into the vacuum would surge the passionately enthusiastic CIO-PAC financed backers of Henry Wallace. If the bosses, who had already dismissed Byrnes, concentrated too much on stopping Wallace, another kind of vacuum could develop, making a dark horse such as Douglas the compromise victor.

FDR was a very sick man but he was still the master manipulator, the juggler who seldom let his right hand know where his left hand was wandering. He was doing his utmost, at this point, to prevent Harry S. Truman from becoming his vice president.

VIII

All the players in this drama now headed for Chicago and the final act. Quite a lot was at stake and many people knew it. If Wallace won, there was a very good chance that the southern Democrats would walk out of the convention and form a third party, handing the election to the Republicans. Far more important to people were the rumors about Roosevelt's health. They shuddered at the prospect of Henry Wallace as commander in chief. The vantage point of another half-century only makes the shudders more intense. Wallace was clearly incapable of discerning the malevolent spirit of violence and hatred at the heart of totalitarian Communism. He was in the hands of men who were eager to manipulate him for the benefit of the Soviet Union. He later said that if he became president, he had intended to make Harry Dexter White secretary of the treasury and appoint Lawrence Duggan to a powerful post in the State Department. Thanks to the Venona decrypts, we now know both these men were Soviet agents.[21]

In Europe, the war was exploding into furious violence. The Germans had revealed a secret "vengeance" weapon, rockets that could bombard London from Antwerp and other areas still under their control along the channel coast. The American and British armies were struggling to break out of their Normandy beachhead. The Russian Army was storming into Poland. The banner headlines in the *New York Herald Tribune* on July 19 read:

BRITISH CROSS ORNE, BREAK LINES BELOW CAEN
AMERICANS SEIZE ST. LO; REDS DRIVE ON LWOW[22]

Wallace reached Chicago on the morning of July 19. By then, on Hannegan's orders, Senator Samuel Jackson of Indiana, the convention chairman, had released FDR's letter about the vice president. He claimed to have written it because "I expect to be away from Washington for the next few days." The letter said much of what Roosevelt had promised Wallace it would say.

I have been associated with Henry Wallace during
his past four years as Vice President, for eight years

*earlier while he was secretary of agriculture, and well
before that. I like him and I respect him, and he is
my personal friend. For these reasons, I personally
would vote for his renomination if I were a delegate
to the convention.*

*At the same time I do not wish to appear in any way
to be dictating to the convention. Obviously, the
convention must decide. And it should—and it will—
give great consideration to the pros and cons of its
choice.*[23]

IX

Released on July 17, the letter was quickly labeled "the kiss of death" by many newsmen. But Wallace did not seem to think so. He held a press conference for 150 reporters and told them he was "in this fight to the finish." He knew the president was writing the letter and he, Wallace, warmly approved of it. He did not want "anything in the nature of dictation to the convention."[24]

On July 15, the train carrying FDR to the West Coast had stopped on a siding in the Chicago railyards at the request of Robert Hannegan and Ed Pauley. They had gone over the Wallace letter with the president and persuaded him to weaken it considerably. One suspects that the previous version (lost or destroyed) was much closer to the Joseph Guffey original, which was designed to win Wallace the nomination on the first ballot.

Hannegan thought that the toned-down Wallace letter was anything but a dismissal. He decided that he needed something more substantial than the one-line scrawl endorsing Truman that FDR had given him in the White House on July 11. The party chairman persuaded the president to write the following:

Dear Bob:

You have written me about Harry Truman and Bill Douglas. I should, of course, be glad to run with either of them and believe that either one of them would bring real strength to the ticket.

Always sincerely,
Franklin D. Roosevelt

Hannegan was less than thrilled by FDR's insistence on adding Douglas's name to the letter. It was one more example of the president's unenthusiasm for Truman. But it was still a large improvement over the one-line scrawl—and Douglas could be construed to be FDR's way of not seeming to dictate to the convention. One could even argue it shed some of the associate justice's ultra-liberal glow on the senator from Missouri. Moreover, there was not even a tiny boomlet for Douglas among the delegates.

Hannegan had also been hard at work eliminating Jimmy Byrnes. At dinner with the assistant president on Sunday, July 16, Byrnes told Hannegan and several other party leaders that he was the president's choice. Hannegan said that was fine with him, but they would have to "clear it with Sidney." FDR had left explicit orders to give Sidney Hillman and the CIO-PAC veto power over the choice of a candidate, the party chairman claimed.

This, not the letter about Wallace, was the real kiss of death at the Chicago convention. On Monday, July 17, Hannegan went to see Hillman and told him Byrnes had Roosevelt's backing and the party leaders were ready to support him. Then came the deal: "We will withdraw Byrnes if you will withdraw Wallace." Hillman agreed, leaving the field to Truman. But Hillman's putative boss, CIO head Philip Murray, remained stubbornly committed to Wallace.[25]

Another name remained in curious circulation on the eve of the convention: Wendell Willkie. Several New Yorkers, including Senator Robert F. Wagner and Edward Loughlin, the head of Tammany Hall, were toying with a push to draft the barefoot Wall Street lawyer as the vice presidential candidate. Columnist Drew Pearson was also among the plotters of this unlikely coup. It collapsed when Loughlin talked to fellow Irish-American Leo Crowley, who was the convention's floor manager. Crowley told the Tammany boss to forget it. The word from the White House and the party hierarchy was Truman. Later, Pearson claimed that Crowley admitted talking to the president about Willkie and Roosevelt said he would be "favorably disposed" if there was a "spontaneous movement" toward the liberal Republican. It was clear that Crowley did not intend to let that happen.[26]

X

On July 19, Governor Robert S. Kerr of Oklahoma opened the convention with a stem-winding keynote speech that the sweltering delegates thought would never end. His verbosity terminated the vice presidential boomlet a small band of Kerr admirers were nurturing on the fringes. Other rumors swept the convention as favorite sons were nominated. A few true believers still thought Wendell Willkie had Roosevelt's secret backing. Southerners thought the answer to Wallace was a Dixie liberal, such as Senator John H. Bankhead of Alabama or Senator Alben Barkley of Kentucky. Wallace made a brief appearance on the convention floor and drew a roar of approval from the crowd, deepening the anxiety of his foes.[27]

The next afternoon, Thursday, July 20, Alben Barkley nominated Roosevelt for a fourth term and the delegates shouted themselves hoarse with approval. Now came Wallace's moment. He had persuaded convention chairman Samuel Jackson to let him second Barkley's speech. As the demonstration for Roosevelt churned around the convention hall, Wallace and his assistant, Harold Young, hurried to a small office under the platform, where he planned to wait until he was introduced and go over the text of his speech one more time.

As Young and Wallace entered the office, they found Ed Pauley talking on the telephone to FDR. The demonstration drowned out most of the conversation, but the name "Truman" reached their ears. Pauley hung up and glanced uneasily at Wallace and Young, who said nothing. Finally, Pauley said: "Well at least you've heard it play-by-play."

Wallace tapped the text he was carrying in his hand. "This is my campaign speech," he said. "This is the one that will do it."[28]

On the rostrum, Wallace came on like a New Deal firestorm. He said the Democratic Party could win "only if and when it is the liberal party." He called Roosevelt "the greatest liberal in the history of the United States."[29]

Then came words of uncompromising defiance: "The future belongs to those who go down the line unswervingly for the liberal principles of both political democracy and economic democracy regardless of race, color or religion. In a political, educational, and economic sense there must be no inferior races. The poll tax must go. Equal educational opportunities must come. The future must bring equal wages for equal work regardless of sex or race."[30]

Harold Young and others had begged Wallace to avoid such a confrontational approach. They told him that if he did not mention the poll tax, the nomination could still be won. Their advice was amply confirmed by operatives Roosevelt had sent into the South. Aubrey Williams of the abolished National Youth Organization had returned telling FDR the southerners would not tolerate an attack on racial discrimination in the platform. Jimmy Byrnes, intimately in touch with South Carolina and other states, had warned Roosevelt that any mention of the poll tax, black voting rights, or school segregation would doom the Democrats. Roosevelt had made sure the party's platform contained not a word about these issues. It merely affirmed that "racial and religious minorities have the right to live, develop and vote equally with all citizens and share the rights that are guaranteed by our Constitution."[31]

Wallace's closing words continued his determination to make hope triumph over experience. "Roosevelt is a greater liberal today than he has ever been. His soul is pure. The high quality of Roosevelt liberalism will become more apparent as the war emergency passes. The only question ever in Roosevelt's mind is how to serve the cause of liberalism."[32]

Roars of approval greeted these declarations of the Democratic Party's supposed principles, which were, in fact, only shared by an aggressive minority. The galleries were crowded with Wallace backers, thanks to the ample coffers of the CIO-PAC and identically colored convention tickets that made it difficult to restrict access to the hall. For an hour, the vice president looked unbeatable.

XI

That same afternoon, Senator Harry S. Truman was summoned to a meeting of the anti-Wallace men in Robert Hannegan's suite at the Blackstone Hotel. They told him he was their candidate and the president backed him. Truman stubbornly insisted he did not want the job and did not believe Roosevelt would accept him. Hannegan put through a call to San Diego and soon Truman heard the president's voice.

"Bob," FDR asked, "have you got that fellow lined up yet?"

"No," Hannegan said. "He is the contrariest goddamn mule from Missouri I ever dealt with."

"Well, you tell him if he wants to break up the Democratic Party in the middle of the war, that's his responsibility."

Clunk. The line went dead. Truman, who had been sitting beside Hannegan on a twin bed, leaped up and paced the room. "Well if that's the situation, I'll have to say yes. But why the hell didn't he tell me in the first place?"[33]

The question was more than a little apt. It reflected Truman's perception that Roosevelt had no real enthusiasm for him. If one compares this third-party conversation to the oozing solicitude with which FDR talked to Henry Wallace in the White House, it is obvious, again, that Roosevelt did not want Truman as his vice president any more than the senator wanted the job.

XII

Selected he was, Truman realized, and got down to business with his fellow Democrats. They decided that the best man to nominate him was Bennett Clark, the senior senator from Missouri, who had carved a career as an outspoken anti-Roosevelt Democrat and pre–Pearl Harbor isolationist. The choice of Clark signaled that Truman was not running as a New Dealer. Senator Clark was a symbol of an earlier conservative disappointment. His father, Champ Clark, had been Speaker of the House of Representatives and the odds-on favorite to win the Democratic nomination in 1912. But he had seen it snatched away by Roosevelt's liberal forerunner, Woodrow Wilson.

Party Chairman Hannegan decided now was the time for reporters to see the letter from Roosevelt, endorsing Truman and/or Douglas. For many, the two names considerably lessened the letter's impact. Knowing FDR's wily ways, they wondered if he was backing either man.

In the evening session, Roosevelt was formally nominated with only token opposition from Senator Harry Byrd of Virginia. FDR accepted the nomination, speaking by radio from the San Diego naval base. More than one delegate had the eerie feeling that he sounded like a voice from the grave. Few noticed at the time that the speech could have been considered an obituary for the New Deal. The president announced he would severely limit his campaigning because of his responsibilities as commander in chief. The New Deal was mentioned only as a memory, not a program for the future.

After cheers for Roosevelt, the convention hall swirled with barely suppressed excitement. By agreement with the newspaper and radio reporters, the nominations for vice president would come the following night, so the newsmen could give them full attention the next day. But few delegates were aware of this arrangement.[34]

In spite of all the promises and counterpromises and backroom deals, Sidney Hillman and his CIO-PAC still felt free to make an effort to elect their favorite candidate. Hillman was pushed hard in this direction by Philip Murray, the head of the CIO, who had remained aloof from the deal-making. Thousands of PAC enthusiasts in the galleries began chanting: "We want Wallace! We want Wallace!" The huge convention hall electric organ began playing over and over again "Iowa, That's Where the Tall Corn Grows." An infuriated Ed Pauley ordered a Democratic Party official to chop the wires if some other songs were not added to the repertoire instantly. Delegates and PACers began prancing in the aisles. It looked for a few minutes like the convention would be stampeded.

Senator Claude Pepper of Florida began fighting his way to the platform, frantically signaling Chairman Jackson that he wanted to speak. He was sure Wallace would be nominated overwhelmingly if he could place his name before the convention. Jackson, a party regular, just as persistently ignored him, while Bob Hannegan ordered the convention doors thrown open to permit a milling crowd in the corridors to join the frenzy. Soon the number of people in the convention hall was close to 40,000—and

Mayor Ed Kelly called for an adjournment because the fire laws were being violated.

Chairman Jackson asked for a voice vote on adjournment. "Aye!" screamed a sizeable number of delegates. "No no no," shouted the Wallace backers. Jackson said the ayes had it and gaveled the convention into recess, aborting the Wallace stampede.

"This convention is in the hands of the enemy!" screamed Wallace's assistant, Harold Young. A frantic Harold Ickes, forgetting his role in trying to ditch Wallace, rushed out and sent FDR a five-page telegram of protest. The New Deal was going down to calamitous defeat and the president did not seem to care. The hard-eyed realists were in charge of America's destiny.[35]

XIII

The rest of the night was devoted to furious politicking by both sides. Hannegan, Pauley, and company toured the hotel rooms where the state delegations were headquartered, reporting their conversation with Roosevelt and his choice of Truman. Not everyone was convinced by it. They knew something about FDR's habit of promising without delivering. But Hannegan's ability to produce the signed letter he had obtained on the railroad siding on July 15 swung more than a few waverers to Truman's side.

The next day, newspapers carried a photo of FDR making his acceptance speech. He looked ghastly. His mouth was open and the camera angle made his face look especially elongated and the muscles out of control, as if he were a stroke victim. The *Chicago Tribune* blew the picture up to twice the usual size and splashed it on their front page. Memories of a shriveling dying Woodrow Wilson flashed through many minds, reminding them that they might be choosing a president, not a vice president.[36]

Truman had spent half the night hunting for Senator Bennett Clark. He found him holed up in another hotel, almost too drunk to talk. The ferocious politicking had evoked painful memories of his father's defeat in 1912, and the realization that Clark had failed to realize his own presidential ambitions. Worse, the senator was facing almost certain defeat in an upcoming Democratic primary contest in Missouri. Sobered up by the desperate professionals in the next twelve hours, Clark had neither the time nor the inclination to make much of a speech for Truman. He proposed him as a man who "would not only not cause weakness in the ticket headed by President Roosevelt, but will be an element of possible strength in every part of the United States." The delegates' response was tepid. The galleries were silent.[37]

Wallace's nominator, an Iowa judge named Richard Mitchell, said more meaningful things. While the vice president supported the free enterprise system, he did not think it gave the powerful "the freedom . . . to dominate or crowd out their weaker brothers." Henry Wallace not only had faith in the common man, he "also believes in his rights." Seconding the judge were speakers who underlined the liberals' desperation with over-the-top rhetoric. Ellis Arnall, governor of Georgia, declared the Democratic Party "would not go to Munich" and betray Henry Wallace. Senator Claude Pepper shouted that "Henry Wallace bears upon his body the scars of many daggers. Those daggers were meant for Franklin Roosevelt."

But CIO-PACers were no longer cheering in the galleries, which were mostly empty. Mayor Kelly's sergeants at arms at the convention hall's entrances turned away some 1,500 would-be Wallace supporters because they lacked official tickets. Chastened by the previous night's close call, the professionals were making sure there would not be another Wallace stampede. The frustrated CIO leaders surrounded the convention hall with college and high school students carrying placards for Wallace. But they had little or no impact on the proceedings inside.[38]

After the speeches on behalf of Truman and Wallace, numerous favorite sons were proposed by admirers from their home states. The professionals' strategy called for the state delegations to hold their votes for these candidates, while the Wallace men tried for a first ballot victory. Careful head counting had convinced the professionals that Wallace would fall short.

On the make or break first ballot, Wallace came close, rolling up 429 votes. (He needed 589 to win.) Truman had 319 and the other votes were scattered among the favorite sons. By this time it was six o'clock. The convention had been in session for six hours. To some it might have made sense to adjourn for dinner. But Robert Hannegan, the mastermind of the Truman movement, shook his head and called for a second ballot. It was a terrific gamble. If Truman did not win, Wallace might well inspire some wavering moderates to switch, or there might be a bolt to one of the favorite sons.[39]

Once more the states were polled, with Wallace again in the lead at first. But the favorite son strategy began to work. Ed Pauley ordered Governor Robert Kerr to switch Oklahoma to Truman. Maryland and several other states also switched, but the race stayed close until the tally reached 477 for Truman to 473 for Wallace. For a moment, deadlock loomed. Then favorite sons with substantial numbers of votes—Senators Bankhead of Alabama, Lucas of Illinois, and Barkley of Kentucky—threw their votes to Truman. Pandemonium erupted as other states rushed to board the Truman bandwagon. By the time it was over, the senator from Missouri had 1,051 votes and Wallace had dwindled to a stubbornly loyal 105 from Iowa, Minnesota, North Dakota, Oregon, and Wisconsin. Harry S. Truman had become the most unwilling vice president in American history. The New Dealers had lost the biggest battle of the war within the war.[40]

XIV

Henry Wallace spent a fair amount of time trying to explain to himself why Roosevelt had failed to support him. In his diary, he noted all sorts of stories about backstairs knifings by Leo Crowley, Bob Hannegan, and Ed Flynn, among others. In one version, Flynn was marked as the evil genius behind Wallace's downfall. He had supposedly convinced Hannegan that big money could be raised for the campaign "if the President would ditch me." Ed Pauley played a large role here as well. He had "enormous political influence," Wallace later observed, "because of his ability to raise funds."[41]

Harder to bear was the message from an insider on the Democratic National Committee that "the attitude" toward Wallace did not originate with Hannegan but "with the President himself." Hannegan had gotten FDR to break his promise not to introduce a second name. Wallace, drawing on his flashes of realism about Roosevelt, glumly noted that FDR's explanation "doubtless would be that all he meant to say . . . was that he would not introduce a second name in his letter to Jackson." With an almost audible sigh, Wallace concluded the president had agreed to dump him "in spite of his very real affection for me. He tried to wiggle out but could not. The money boys meant business." A few years later, in response to a question about his defeat, Wallace said: "You could say I was taken in by him."[42]

On Friday evening, July 21, Wallace received a telegram from Roosevelt. "You made a grand fight and I am very proud of you. Tell Ilo not to plan to leave Washington next January." Ilo was Mrs. Wallace. FDR was renewing his promise to find Wallace a job in the new administration. One wonders if Wallace recalled the president's habit of being very nice to someone after he had finished hitting him. The vice president might have been even less consoled if he had seen the cynical telegram Roosevelt sent to

Hannegan, congratulating him on his management of a Democratic convention that "deserved to be called democratic."[43]

Time, obviously enjoying itself, played up Roosevelt's treachery and saw the outcome of the convention as a crushing defeat for liberalism. The *New Republic* glumly agreed. So did a disgusted Drew Pearson. The *New York Times* coolly summed up "the New Missouri Compromise" by saying the bosses had beaten the CIO. On his way out of Chicago, a disgusted Jimmy Byrnes leaked to the *Times*'s Turner Catledge FDR's injunction to "clear it with Sidney." When it appeared in the *Times* under Arthur Krock's byline, Republicans seized on it to portray the Democrats as in thrall to the CIO-PAC, although the results of the convention proved the precise opposite. Probably the most perceptive comment came some weeks later in the *Progressive* magazine, which saw the convention as a contest between "Wallace, the reformer who had failed at politics and Roosevelt the politician who had failed at reform."[44]

A story whizzed around Washington, D.C., about Missourian Paul Porter, a veteran New Dealer—he was associate director of the Office of Price Stabilization—who had helped to dump Wallace. "You better get over to the White House and straighten yourself out with Anna Boettiger," a friend told Porter. "She told me the other day that you are a son of a bitch because of the way you treated Wallace in Chicago."

"You go tell Anna," Porter supposedly said, "so's your old man."[45]

Instead of seeking out Truman to congratulate him face-to-face, Wallace sent the senator a telegram, in which he reiterated the message of his convention speech: The future of the Democratic Party rested with liberalism. Senator Truman undoubtedly got the sarcastic undertone. On August 5 he visited Wallace in Washington, D.C., assured him he had not conspired against him in Chicago, and hoped they were still friends. In his diary, Wallace recalled Truman's statement earlier in the year that he supported him for another term as vice president. The senator's protestations only convinced Wallace "beyond doubt that he is a small opportunistic man, a man of good instincts, but, therefore probably all the more dangerous." Although Henry Wallace struggled to conceal it from himself, he was a bitterly disappointed man.[46]

17

Death and
Transfiguration
in Berlin

W hile the New Dealers were meeting political Armageddon in
Chicago, the policy of unconditional surrender was producing
another kind of ultimate confrontation in Germany. On July 20,
1944, Colonel Claus von Stauffenberg flew to the Wolfschanze
(Wolf's Lair), Adolf Hitler's headquarters in eastern Germany,
near Rastenburg, to confer with the Führer about the readiness of
Germany's Home Army. In his briefcase the colonel carried two
extremely powerful bombs supplied by the Abwehr. Giving up on
making a deal with Roosevelt or Churchill, the Front of Decent
People had decided to remove Hitler unilaterally.

"The assassination must be attempted, at any cost," said General Henning von Tresckow, sponsor of three previous failed plots
to kill the Führer. "Even should that fail, the attempt to seize

power in the capital must be undertaken. We must prove to the world and to future generations that the men of the German resistance movement dared to take the decisive step and to hazard their lives upon it. Compared with this object, nothing else matters."[1]

At Rastenburg, where Hitler was guarded by a regiment of fanatical SS troops, Stauffenberg joined a staff conference composed of a half-dozen generals and colonels. It was a very hot day and someone suggested moving the meeting from the stifling underground bunker to a wooden hut just outside it. Hitler agreed and Stauffenberg could hardly demur.

On the way to the hut, the colonel slipped into a men's room and tried to set the timing devices on the two bombs, a difficult task for a man with only two fingers. He managed to set one of them before, in his judgment, suspicion might be aroused, and he hurried into the conference hut. Other topics preceded the Home Army briefing, and after several minutes, Stauffenberg excused himself to answer a prearranged telephone call from his aide. A few minutes later the bomb exploded with terrific force, killing two staffers and injuring others severely.

Outside, Stauffenberg and an aide waited until they saw a man being carried from the hut, covered in Hitler's cloak. Certain the Führer was dead, they raced to the airport in a waiting car to take a plane to Berlin. By 1 P.M. they were airborne. When news of the blast reached the Bendlerblock, the huge German army headquarters on the Bendlerstrasse in the German capital, staff officers of the Home Army, fellow plotters, put a code word, "Valkyrie," on the army's teleprinter circuit. This was an alert that was supposed to bring all units of the Home Army rushing to their assigned posts, guns in their hands. Former chief of staff General Ludwig Beck planned to broadcast a statement to these reserve soldiers, announcing he was their new commander. Stauffenberg had a speech ready to transmit to the nation, announcing

Hitler's death and the formation of a republic with Carl Goerdeler and Beck among the chief figures—and their determination to bring the war to a swift end.[2]

But Hitler, the seat blown out of his trousers, his coat ripped up the back, both eardrums ruptured, had survived the blast. Many members of the Home Army, particularly the young commander of a battalion of elite Prussian Guards who was ordered by Beck to arrest Joseph Goebbels, wanted proof that Hitler was dead. At Goebbels's headquarters, the propaganda chief put through a call to Rastenburg, and proved Hitler was still alive. The Führer had been saved by the thin walls of the hut, which dissipated most of the explosion's force. Also, a staff colonel, leaning over a map to explain a troop movement, had moved Stauffenberg's briefcase a few crucial feet away from the Nazi leader.

In France, Field Marshal Erwin Rommel had been wounded in an air attack and Field Marshal Guenther von Kluge had replaced him. Kluge, who had already participated in one attempt on Hitler's life, had been approached by Beck and promised to join the July 20 plot. But when Kluge found out Hitler had survived, his resolution dissolved. General Karl Heinrich von Stuelpnagel, the commander in Paris, another conspirator, rushed to Kluge's headquarters and tried to persuade him to stick with the revolt anyway. Stuelpnagel had already arrested all the Nazis in Paris. He begged Kluge to seize the moment. "The fate of the nation is in your hands!" he cried.

"It would be so," Kluge said, "if only that swine were dead." He could not break his oath of loyalty to the Führer.[3]

In Berlin, the Prussian Guards battalion commander and other younger officers turned violently against the conspirators. Before the night was over, Beck was dead by his own hand and Stauffenberg and three others had been executed against the wall of the Bendlerblock. "Long live Germany!" Stauffenberg cried as the bullets struck him.

On the eastern front, General Henning von Tresckow told Major Fabian von Schlabrendorff: "Now they will all fall upon us and cover us with abuse. But I am convinced more than ever that we have done the right thing. . . . A man's moral worth is established only at the point where he is prepared to give his life for his convictions." Whereupon Tresckow blew off his head with a grenade.[4]

Hitler ordered a *Sippenhaft*, a blood purge of the conspirators and their families. Generals Rommel and von Kluge committed suicide. Virtually everyone connected to the resistance—about 7,000 by one estimate—was arrested by the Gestapo within a few days. Even diplomat Ulrich Von Hassell's grandchildren, aged two and three, were seized and confined in a Nazi orphanage under false names, to be raised as brainwashed disciples of the Reich. The chief conspirators were brutally tortured by the Gestapo but in most cases they refused to testify against each other.[5]

In Washington and London, the reaction to this heroic attempt to redeem Germany's honor was total silence. Most of the American government's leaders were in Chicago, absorbed in the vice presidential contest. Roosevelt was en route to Hawaii on his Pacific inspection tour. Churchill was aboard the cruiser HMS *Arromanches*, off Normandy. Both knew about the failed attempt almost immediately. Roosevelt said nothing and Churchill confined himself to a gloating remark about "a very great disturbance in the German machine."[6]

II

Thus did the Western leaders vitiate a great propaganda opportunity, and an even greater moral opportunity. Through Allen Dulles's reports from Berne and other sources, the British and Americans had an intimate knowledge of the men involved in the coup. They could have painted them as moral heroes and urged other Germans to follow their example. But the hate-tinged aura of the unconditional surrender policy refused to acknowledge the possibility of German moral heroes. The only nation that praised the conspirators was the Soviet Union. A member of Stalin's Free Germans Committee broadcast: "Generals, officers, soldiers! Cease fire at once and turn your arms against Hitler. Do not fail these courageous men!"[7]

Western press comment was totally unsympathetic—hardly surprising, because no one outside the topmost government circles had a clue about the existence of the Front of Decent People. The *New York Herald Tribune* editorialized that Americans ought to rejoice that Hitler had survived and was wiping out the "militarists" who had tried to get rid of him. The Führer was "doing a large part of the Allies' work for them." The flagship of liberal Republicanism maintained that Americans "hold no brief for aristocrats as such, especially those given to the goose step." They were "the chief exponents of [the] master race" and the "personification of German arrogance."

The *Nation* indulged in similar anachronistic German-hating fantasies. They saw the coup as a plot by the "Junker chiefs" who realized the war was lost and were trying to save themselves and their "caste." They were trying to escape the jaws of unconditional surrender but they were only "fooling themselves." The Allies would not consent to any terms that allowed German militarism to recover.

The English were even more savage. One journalist gloated that the bomb's failure had enabled Hitler to remove "an appreciable . . . selection of those who would undoubtedly have posed as 'good' Germans after the war, while preparing for a third World War." He hoped the purge would continue: "The killing of Germans by Germans" would save the Allies from doing the messy job after unconditional surrender.[8]

III

In Hawaii, on July 29, 1944, President Roosevelt gave a press conference at which someone asked him whether unconditional surrender also applied to Japan. After answering in the affirmative, Roosevelt heaped scorn on those who had criticized the policy. He claimed they did not understand his historical comparison. He then proceeded to give a totally erroneous description of Robert E. Lee's conversation with Ulysses Grant at Appomattox, in which the president maintained that Grant kept insisting on unconditional surrender while Lee pleaded with him for food for his starving soldiers. When Lee finally accepted unconditional surrender, Grant supposedly gave him food and permitted his officers to keep their horses for spring plowing.[9]

This history lesson, which no one in the press or anywhere else corrected, demonstrated the dangers of a gentleman's C, FDR's usual grade, at Harvard. General Lee, as he set out to see General Grant at Appomattox Court House, said to one of his officers: "I can tell you one thing for your comfort. Grant will not demand an unconditional surrender; he will give us as good terms as this army has a right to demand." Grant proceeded to do exactly that. He did not even mention unconditional surrender at Appomattox. He simply accepted Lee's surrender and paroled his men, allowing them to return to their homes with a promise that they would not take up arms against the United States again. At Lee's request, he allowed them to keep their horses, and ordered federal rations sent through the lines to feed the half-starved former rebels.[10]

The president was apparently unaware that Grant had acquired his unconditional surrender nickname when he besieged Fort Donelson on the Cumberland River in 1862. When the defending Confederate general attempted to negotiate a deal that would permit his men to withdraw, Grant crisply informed him that his terms were unconditional surrender, which were not unusual for a military commander besieging a fort or city. Roosevelt seemed to think Lee had surrendered the entire Confederacy at Appomattox; he only surrendered the Army of Northern Virginia. The only man who had the right to insist on the unconditional surrender of the Confederate States of America was President Abraham Lincoln—and he never uttered the term. Roosevelt remained oblivious to how unusual, even unique, it was to demand the unconditional surrender of an entire country.

Roosevelt's argument that unconditional surrender was necessary to teach Germany the lesson it had not learned from World War I was dubious at best. But it was completely inappropriate to apply the policy to Japan. The Americans and the Japanese had been allies during World War I and for many previous years the United States regarded Japan with an almost fraternal affection. It was the United States in the person of Commodore Matthew Perry who had persuaded the Japanese to leap from feudalism to the modern world in the mid-nineteenth century. One of FDR's heroes, Theodore Roosevelt, deeply admired the Japanese; during his presidency, T.R. called war between the two nations "unthinkable."[11]

Add to the debit account the way FDR covertly goaded Japan into attacking the United States and the application of this faulty formula for ending a war becomes even more inappropriate. But the race hatred the war had unleashed (on both sides, it should be added) made it easy for Roosevelt to insist on unconditional surrender as Japan's only option.

IV

In his Hawaiian history lesson, Roosevelt seemed to imply that if the Germans surrendered unconditionally, they could expect decent treatment. But he soon revealed that he had a very different policy in mind. In August, Secretary of the Treasury Henry Morgenthau Jr. visited England, accompanied by Assistant Secretary Harry Dexter White. Morgenthau was horrified by the damage Hitler's V rockets were doing to London. Like Henry Wallace, he sought wisdom from the common people and asked a hotel employee what they should do with the Germans after the war. "We want to stamp them out, but the high finance doesn't!" the man said.

This advice apparently carried great weight with Morgenthau and White. They were soon telling British political leaders that Germany should be dismembered into small states and all her heavy industry destroyed. Most of the British, especially the members of Winston Churchill's Conservative Party, politely disagreed, insisting a strong Germany was vital to Europe.

The secretary of the Treasury and his right-hand man said the same thing to American ambassador John Winant and his staff, who were organizing the European Advisory Commission to determine how to handle a prostrate postwar Europe. Harry Dexter White did most of the talking, declaring that Germany should be reduced to a "fifth rate power." Several members of Winant's staff vigorously demurred, pointing out that smashing the German economy would expose all of Europe to Moscow's control. None of these earnest men, including Morgenthau, had any idea that White was a Soviet agent and this was precisely the objective he had in mind. Even without this knowledge, Winant immediately cabled Roosevelt requesting instructions that would enable him to countermand the Morgenthau-White program. He did not get an answer.[12]

With British foreign secretary Anthony Eden's help, Morgenthau read the still secret minutes of the Teheran conference, where Roosevelt and Churchill agreed Germany should be dismembered. This discovery only reinforced Morgenthau's determination to push for a punitive approach. Back in Washington, he revealed his program to Secretary of State Cordell Hull, who could barely contain his astonishment at discovering that the secretary of the Treasury was up to his eyes in foreign policy. Hull said he had yet to read a line of the Teheran minutes. No one had even bothered to summarize them for him. The secretary of state favored punishing Germany's Nazi leaders but was noncommittal about the rest of Morgenthau's ideas.

V

At the White House on August 19, 1944, Henry Morgenthau told Roosevelt the British were much too benevolent in their postwar plans for Germany and so were the State Department and the European Advisory Commission. The secretary was, incidentally, "shocked" by FDR's appearance. "He is a very sick man and seems to have wasted away," he told his diary. But that observation did not deter him from urging the president to stop this soft approach to Germany.

Roosevelt's animus against the Germans erupted into fury. "Give me thirty minutes with Churchill and I can correct this," he told Morgenthau. "We have got to be tough with Germany and I mean the German people, not just the Nazis. You either have to castrate [them] or you have got to treat them . . . so they can't just go on reproducing people who want to continue the way they have in the past."[13]

Morgenthau left the White House convinced that he had a mandate to create a better plan to deal with postwar Germany. He put Harry Dexter White in charge of a special committee "to draft the Treasury's analysis of the German problem." The result was the Morgenthau Report. It proposed to divide Germany into four parts. It also recommended destroying all the industry in the

Ruhr and Saar basins and turning Central Europe and the German people into agriculturists. At one point Communist agent White, who was described by his Soviet handler as "a very nervous cowardly person," feared they were going to extremes. He warned Morgenthau this idea was politically risky; it would reduce perhaps 20 million people to starvation. "I don't care what happens to the population," Morgenthau said.[14]

In another visit to the Oval Office, Morgenthau added fuel to the presidential ire by showing FDR a copy of a "Handbook of Military Government" that the U.S. War Department had prepared under the supervision of Robert Murphy, Eisenhower's top political advisor. Unaware (like everyone else) of the decisions made at Teheran, Murphy assumed Germany would remain a single unified nation and advised military personnel to work with the existing government to restore order as quickly as possible. Roosevelt denounced this approach in a fiery letter to Secretary of War Henry Stimson because it "gives me the impression that Germany is to be restored just as much as the Netherlands and Belgium, and the people of Germany brought back as quickly as possible to their pre-war estate." Roosevelt emphatically disagreed. "It is of the utmost importance that every person in Germany should realize that this time Germany is a defeated nation."

His hatred of Germany rising as he dictated, Roosevelt ranted on: "Too many people here and in England hold to the view that the German people as a whole are not responsible for what has taken place—that only a few Nazi leaders are responsible. That unfortunately is not based on fact. The German people must have it driven home to them that the whole nation has been engaged in a lawless conspiracy against the decencies of modern civilization." The July 20 attempt by the Front of Decent People to rescue Germany from Hitler had made no impression on the president.[15]

VI

Over the 1944 Labor Day weekend, FDR and Eleanor Roosevelt drove over from Hyde Park to Henry Morgenthau's nearby Fishkill mansion and spent an hour and a quarter discussing a preliminary draft of the Morgenthau Report. Revealing their joint ignorance of basic economics, the Roosevelts agreed that destroying German industry would promote prosperity in England and Belgium, Germany's chief industrial competitors. Morgenthau suggested transporting most of the Germans between the ages of twenty and forty out of Germany to toil on "some big TVA project" in Central Africa for the rest of their lives. They were supposedly too tainted by Nazism to reeducate. What to do with their children, he admitted, would be "a big problem." Roosevelt was in "complete sympathy" with what the secretary was saying and so was Mrs. Roosevelt, Morgenthau delightedly noted in his diary.[16]

Emboldened by Mrs. Roosevelt's backing, Morgenthau launched an attack on Robert Murphy, asking FDR why he ever appointed him Eisenhower's political advisor. The secretary brought up Murphy's negotiation of the deal with Admiral Darlan in North Africa and Mrs. Roosevelt chimed in, vigorously denouncing it. FDR just as angrily defended it, growing "quite excited," Morgenthau noted. Mrs. Roosevelt added that she thought it was especially deplorable to have a Catholic involved in dealing with defeated Germany, because of "the attitude of the Pope." Presumably she meant the pope was pro-Nazi.

FDR, irked to find himself accused of being an accomplice in the Darlan mess through his choice of Murphy, defended the pope for upholding the right to private property and being "against Communism," an odd stance for a man who had exiled State Department professionals for displaying doubts about the Soviet Union. It was the sort of agitation that Dr. Bruenn wanted the president to avoid. FDR's incoherence suggested he was no longer thinking very clearly.[17]

VII

Roosevelt remained so enthusiastic about the Morgenthau Report, he invited the secretary of the Treasury to accompany him to a conference with Churchill in Quebec on September 14, 1944.[18] When Morgenthau outlined his program to the British prime minister at a state dinner, Churchill was aghast. He said the working people of Great Britain would never agree to it. They still felt considerable solidarity with the German working class. Moreover, he agreed with the great eighteenth-century Anglo-Irish politician Edmund Burke that you cannot indict an entire nation. At his most vehement, Churchill said it would be like chaining England to a dead body.[19]

The next day, while Roosevelt watched with icy amusement, Churchill had to negotiate with Morgenthau about how much lend-lease aid the bankrupt British government could expect from America after the Germans surrendered. Morgenthau dangled $3 billion in front of the prime minister and Roosevelt made it very clear that the money would not be forthcoming until Churchill agreed to "cooperate" on their plan for postwar Germany. Swallowing his previous protestations, the mortified Churchill initialed the Morgenthau plan. When he revealed his decision to Foreign Secretary Anthony Eden, even he, long considered Lord Vansittart's voice in the cabinet on matters German, recoiled and the two leaders had a violent public quarrel.

Back in Washington, Secretary of War Henry Stimson and Secretary of State Cordell Hull launched an all-out assault on the Morgenthau plan. Stimson said he had "yet to meet a man who was not horrified at the 'Carthaginian'-attitude of the Treasury. It is Semitism gone wild for vengeance and will lay the seeds of another war in the next generation." The secretary of war pointed out the plan violated the Atlantic Charter, which promised equal opportunity for the pursuit of happiness to both victors and vanquished. He claimed it would create 40 million unemployed Germans, 19 million in the Ruhr alone.

Hull was outraged by Morgenthau's "inconceivable intrusion" into foreign policy. The secretary of state told the president the plan would inspire last-ditch resistance and cost thousands of American lives. Hull was so upset, he was unable to sleep and ate next to nothing. His wife finally checked him into Bethesda Naval Hospital. She later told *New York Times* columnist Arthur Krock that "the Morgenthau business" was the final blow that made Hull decide to resign.[20]

By that time Krock had been invited for a drink with an official he described as "just below the presidential echelon." The official had asked Krock if he knew where Henry Morgenthau was. Krock didn't. The official had urged Krock to find out. The reporter soon learned that Morgenthau was in Quebec, "pressing his mad scheme." Soon the story was in the *New York Times*, and that, Krock gleefully recalled, "really stirred up the animals."[21]

Within days, Drew Pearson, the *Wall Street Journal,* and a swarm of other columnists and newspapers were writing about the Morgenthau Report and their reactions were less than rapturous. Congressmen and senators by the dozen began firing from the lip. A firestorm of reproof and disapproval engulfed the White House.

In Germany, Goebbels seized on Morgenthau's and Roosevelt's brainchild as final proof that the United States was determined to destroy Germany. "The Jew Morgenthau" wanted to make Germany into a giant potato patch, Goebbels declared. This White House propaganda disaster coincided with the collapse of optimistic Allied hopes that the German army would crumble after the British and Americans broke out of Normandy and captured Paris. Instead, the Wehrmacht smashed a British attempt to slash into the Reich from the north at Arnhem and began fighting the Americans to a standstill along the German border. The Republican candidate for president, Thomas E. Dewey, joined the chorus of disapproval, accusing Roosevelt of inspiring the Germans to resist to the last man.

Roosevelt responded by demonstrating why he deserved nicknames such as "the juggler." He summoned Secretary of War Stimson to the White House and said he agreed with him completely. FDR claimed he never had the slightest intention of implementing the Morgenthau Report. When Stimson read him portions of the document, calling for the virtual abolition of Germany, FDR claimed to be aghast and could only wonder why he or Churchill ever initialed it. The secretary of the Treasury and his friends had, the president solemnly declared, "pulled a boner."[22]

Roosevelt told Cordell Hull he was now opposed to making any postwar plans for "a country we do not yet occupy." FDR seemed to be saying it would be better to make things up on the spur of the moment to create a policy for dealing with a nation of 70 million people. This reversal could not undo the damage of handing Goebbels an immense propaganda victory. Coupling unconditional surrender with the Morgenthau plan gave the Nazis a rallying cry that was certain to inspire fanatical German resistance.[23]

VIII

While this charade was being performed in Washington, the leaders of the Front of Decent People were being tortured by the Gestapo and tried before Nazi judges in a so-called People's Court, packed with party members who jeered and hooted at them. Field marshals, generals, colonels, and former officials of the foreign office and the Abwehr were forced to wear clothes that were either ridiculously large or small, to make them look as much like buffoons as possible.

Yet these brave men managed to defend themselves with calm dignity, testifying that they had tried to overthrow Hitler because Nazism filled them with moral and spiritual revulsion. In the case of Helmuth James von Moltke, who had been in jail for six months before the attempt to remove the Führer, the judge told him he was condemned because he was friendly with certain people who took part in the plot and because "you think differently"—that is, as a Christian—he was opposed to Nazism. In a letter to his wife, Moltke wrote: "If we are to die, I am in favor of dying on this issue."[24]

On August 8, 1944, another conspirator, a cousin of von Stauffenberg, Count Peter Yorck von Wartenburg, wrote to his mother shortly before he was hanged:

> At the end of a life greatly blessed with love and friendship, I have only gratitude toward God and humility before His will. . . . I can assure you no ambitious seeking after power motivated my actions. [They] were motivated only by my patriotic feelings, the concern for Germany as it has developed over two millennia. . . . Therefore I stand unashamed before my ancestors, my father and my brothers. Perhaps a time will come when people will arrive at a different evaluation of our conduct, when we will be considered not bums but warners and patriots. I pray that the wonderful way in which we have been called will serve to honor God.[25]

Not a word of sympathy or regret was uttered for these men by Churchill, Roosevelt, or any of their spokespeople. Instead, the Anglo-Americans showered Germany with mocking leaflets, sneering that the conspiracy was a sure sign of Hitler's imminent collapse. At one of the trials, a Nazi judge read from one of these pamphlets: "Those who cooperated, those who engineered it—all of them are not worth anything. At best they had a perverted love of Germany."

IX

Meanwhile, the Soviet Union, the nation with whom America was going to get along very well indeed, was perpetrating one of the great barbarities of the war. By August 1, 1944, the Red Army was poised to cross the Vistula and attack Warsaw. Its tanks were in the Warsaw suburb of Praga, just east of the river, which divided the city. The thud of Russian artillery was more than audible. Inside Warsaw, a force of about 40,000 men, armed with weapons air-dropped by the British, had gathered under the leadership of General Tadeusz Bor-Komorovski. They were loyal to the Polish government in exile in London, an entity the Soviets no longer recognized, because they had called for an investigation of the Katyn Massacre.

Elsewhere in Poland, this Home Army had cooperated with the Russians, playing an important role in the capture of Lublin. As the Red Army approached Warsaw, Russian planes had dropped leaflets in the city and the vicinity, urging armed resistance to help their assault. On July 29, the Poles picked up a radio message from Moscow, declaring: "The time of liberation is at hand! Poles, to arms!" Further encouragement came from reports that the exiled government's premier, Stanislaw Mikolajczyk, was in Moscow and had been warmly welcomed by Stalin. General Bor-Komorovski decided this was the time to rise in revolt and seized two-thirds of Warsaw from the startled Germans.

The Russian army suddenly developed a strange paralysis. It sat on the east bank of the Vistula for two months and allowed the noncommunist Poles to be slaughtered by the infuriated Germans in horrific street fighting. The Soviets later claimed their rapid advance had outrun their supply lines, but this story was disproved by the way they crossed the Vistula south of Warsaw while the Home Army was being exterminated.[26]

The Polish government in exile begged the British and the Americans for help. The Americans decided their air base in Poltava could prove useful at last. On August 14, 1944, they requested permission from the Russians to drop supplies to the embattled Poles. The Soviet Foreign Office stonily refused. Ambassador Averell Harriman took the request all the way up to Foreign Minister Vyacheslav Molotov and got nowhere. The Royal Air Force attempted to fill the gap without asking the Russians for permission but the Luftwaffe swarmed into the skies over Warsaw and shot down a heavy percentage of their planes. Not a single Russian fighter plane appeared to oppose the Germans.

Pleas to Moscow from the government in exile in London drew only a response from Tass, the Soviet news service, claiming that the uprising had been started without consulting the Russian Army High Command. The statement complained of "a libel" against the Soviet army in Western newspapers and blamed "Polish émigré circles in London" for the disaster. An angry telegram from Ambassador Harriman to Roosevelt produced a strong reply from the president, authorizing him to protest in his name. But another talk with Molotov drew only the insolent remark that the uprising was a "purely adventuristic light-minded affair," and Moscow had no intention of assisting it. By way of final insult, the Soviet foreign minister informed Harriman that Stalin wanted Poltava and the other shuttle air bases returned to Russia as soon as possible.[27]

Only in mid-September, when most of the Polish Home Army had been killed, did Stalin permit a flight of B-17s from England to air-drop supplies to the Poles. Flying at 14,000 feet, the Americans suffered few losses. But most of the guns and food and ammunition drifted down into German hands. By that time, the area of Warsaw controlled by the Home Army was too small for successful airdrops from such an altitude.[28]

On October 1, the remnant of the Home Army surrendered. Most of Warsaw was in ruins. Over 250,000 civilians had died along with the freedom fighters. Stalin was now ready to resume the Red Army's advance, certain that there would be no armed Polish resistance to his rule—and no one to accuse him of the Katyn massacre and the other crimes the NKVD had committed in Poland.

Back in August, a distraught Averell Harriman had wired the State Department that "when the American public understands fully the facts, there will be serious repercussions in the public opinion of the United States towards the Soviet Union." But Franklin D. Roosevelt, the one man who could have made sure the Americans fully understood the facts, never said a word about Stalin's betrayal of Warsaw. Instead, he did everything in his power to conceal it.

X

The German army's unexpectedly fierce resistance after the fall of Paris in late August 1944 reignited Allied airmen's ambition to end the war from the skies. The British air ministry proposed a plan of unabashed terror raids, which would include strafing German civilians in the streets and bombing attacks on small and medium-sized cities where there were no military objectives.

Top American officers objected with a variety of arguments, some pragmatic—they doubted terror would lower German industrial production. In fact, it might embitter the civilians and make them work even harder. A new moral leader emerged on the American side, General Laurence Kuter, the assistant chief of air staff for plans. (He was the officer who had assailed Frank Waldrop, the *Washington Times-Herald*'s foreign editor, for publishing Rainbow Five.) Kuter pointed out that German civilians, no matter how terrorized, had no political power. They were living under a dictatorship. Even more to the point, Kuter thought terror-bombing was "contrary to our national ideals." Americans did not "wage war against civilians."[29]

General Henry Arnold, Kuter's boss, was less inclined to let ideals get in the way of a Douhetian victory. But he disliked playing second fiddle to the British. He ordered American planners to come up with variations on the air ministry's scheme—with the same objective, terrorizing German civilians into mass surrender. One proposal called for announcing in advance that certain cities and towns were about to be destroyed, and then obliterating them one by one, inducing despair in enemy hearts. General Kuter objected to these ideas too. He suspected that the Royal Air Force was trying to lure the Americans into doing "the majority of the dirty work," to share the guilt for their eagerness to kill German civilians.

Undeterred, the air ministry proposed Thunderclap, a gigantic raid on the center of Berlin by huge numbers of British and American bombers, aimed at killing everyone still living there. The moralists on the American side reacted with horror and disgust. One said it would be "a blot on the history of the Air Forces and the U.S." It was not war, it was "baby killing." Some top commanders concurred. General Carl Spaatz told General Arnold the British were trying to get the Americans "tarred with morale bombing." Spaatz feared the "aftermath"—public reaction at home—would be "terrific."[30]

XI

General Arnold persisted in calling for a workable American morale-bombing plan. The first proposal was the War Weary Bomber project. Worn-out B-17s and other aircraft would be converted into robot planes loaded with as much as 20,000 pounds of high explosives and launched at German cities and towns. The British cabinet, already concerned about German rocket attacks on London, was horrified. The Germans might retaliate with their own robot bombers, which would be far more deadly than the relatively small warheads on V-1 and V-2 rockets. Some AAF generals also recoiled from such blatant morale-bombing. But General Arnold liked the idea and kept pushing it.[31]

One of the early experiments with the war-weary bombers ended in a tragedy that could be said to have altered the course of American history. Joseph P. Kennedy Jr. had volunteered to fly one of these explosive-crammed planes against an enemy objective on the Belgian coast. The plan called for Kennedy to bail out once the plane was aimed at its target. Instead, as the bomber flew over the English Channel, it exploded with a blinding flash. No trace of Kennedy's body was found. Gone was his father's dream of making this gifted oldest son governor of Massachusetts and eventually president of the United States.

XII

Instead of the war-weary bombers, several air force staffers proposed a program called Shatter, which would attack the German railroad stations and marshaling yards. These were surrounded by civilian homes, which would be blasted with the same bombs. Again the moralists objected, this time led by Colonel John Hughes, the officer who had aroused the original resistance to terror raids. "Do we want a Germany virtually de-housed, lacking all public utility services, whose population is little better than a drifting horde of nomads ripe for any political philosophy of despair?" Hughes asked.[32]

Hughes did not realize it, but he was describing an army air force variation on the Morgenthau plan. Into this debate dropped

Roosevelt's Morgenthau-inspired letter to Secretary of War Stimson about the handbook for the military government of Germany, in which FDR declared "the German people as a whole" must be punished for the Nazis' "lawless conspiracy against the decencies of modern civilization." A copy was soon on General Arnold's desk, giving him the green light he wanted for American terror-bombing.

By September 9, the AAF had drafted a letter for the president's signature, establishing a group to study the effects of American strategic bombing on Germany and Japan. The letter requested information on how bombing hampered the enemy war effort by saddling them with the problem of evacuating thousands of civilians from wrecked cities. In particular, it recommended a study of "the psychological and morale effect on an interior community, which had hitherto been free from attack, of a large influx of evacuees." The implication, that the commander in chief of the U.S. armed forces approved of terror-bombing, was clear. Roosevelt signed the letter, which was addressed to Secretary of War Stimson. A copy also soon reached General Arnold's desk.[33]

Planners began putting together Clarion, a variation on Shatter, which called for all-out American bombing and strafing of German civilian targets. One disgusted air force general said it would show the Germans "we are the barbarians they say we are." Another dissenter wrote on his copy of the proposal: "It is the same old baby killing plan." But the debate over baby-killing was over. The baby-killers had won.[34]

18

THE DYING CHAMPION

In the United States, the 1944 presidential election was churning toward a climax. The contest started out badly for the Democrats. On FDR's return from his Pacific trip, the president all but revealed he was a mortally ill man. At Bremerton, Washington, at the end of August, Roosevelt gave a speech reporting on his journey, which had included a stopover in the Aleutian Islands, now cleared of Japanese troops. FDR had written the speech without the aid of Sam Rosenman or Robert Sherwood; instead he had dictated most of it to a navy stenographer. It was a flabby, rambling affair.

Standing on the forecastle of a destroyer to accentuate his commander in chief role, FDR wore his braces for the first time in months. Because of his weight loss, they did not fit very well. The sloping deck and a high wind added to his instability. The crowd, mostly workers coming off a shift at the navy shipyard, stood on the shore and was obviously bored. In the middle of the speech, Roosevelt experienced agonizing chest pains that radiated to both shoulders. It did nothing for his concentration or his delivery. Listening on the radio in Washington, D.C., an appalled Sam Rosenman had a "sinking sensation" and thought, *Something must have happened to the president.*[1]

When FDR finished the speech, he tottered to Dr. Howard Bruenn and gasped: "I had a severe pain!" Rushing him to the nearest cabin, Bruenn took some blood and gave him an electrocardiogram. There was no sign of a heart attack but the pain was unquestionably angina pectoris, caused by a constricting of the heart muscle, often under stress. Bruenn took grim satisfaction in noting it was the first time FDR had ever admitted having chest pain. "This was proof positive he had coronary disease," Bruenn said later.[2]

The awful performance in Bremerton was quickly coupled with the ghastly picture taken in San Diego as FDR gave his acceptance speech to the Chicago convention. Governor Thomas E. Dewey's poll ratings leaped. Both images fit neatly into the Republican candidate's strategy. He and his advisors had decided to avoid at all costs Wendell Willkie's me-too 1940 strategy. Dewey offered himself as a youthful vigorous alternative to the "tired old men" in the Roosevelt administration, implying without quite saying it that the most tired old man of all was the president. The New York governor also deplored the New Dealers as "quarrelsome," reminding voters of the headline-making brawls between Henry Wallace and Jesse Jones, Henry Morgenthau and Henry Stimson. He cited the disastrous failure of the stroke-crippled Woodrow Wilson to deal with the problems of peace and implied Roosevelt would repeat the experience.[3]

II

Dewey's strategy looked shrewd and effective. The war was obviously on its way to being won, weakening the Democrats' "Don't change horses in midstream" argument. Roosevelt's pollster, Hadley Cantril, nervously reported that the "overwhelming majority" of the voters thought the next president's most important problem would be how to maintain the full employment of the wartime boom. Dewey, his conservative vice presidential nominee Senator John Bricker of Ohio, and their Republican businessmen backers seemed to be better equipped to handle the challenge. Dewey struck a telling blow in his speech accepting the Republican nomination. Noting the New Dealers' failure to achieve full employment in the 1930s, he asked: "Do we have to have a war in order to get jobs?"[4]

Accentuating the Democrats' woes was a boner by General Lewis Hershey, the head of Selective Service, who remarked that the government might decide to keep soldiers and sailors in uniform after the war to prevent them from swamping the job market. The delighted Republicans flung ads on billboards: "If You Want To Bring The Boys Home Sooner Vote For Dewey And Bricker." Dewey also reminded the voters that the New Dealers had spent billions trying to solve the Depression and failed. He called the Rooseveltians "the most wasteful, extravagant administration in the history of the nation." Dewey's campaign spent over $2 million in radio broadcasts to get out this message.[5]

In deep background, a crisis occurred that could have drastically altered the campaign. An army officer leaked to Dewey that the United States had broken the Japanese codes before Pearl Harbor and knew Tokyo was going to war. Someone told General George Marshall that Dewey was thinking of making a major speech, blaming Pearl Harbor on Roosevelt. The general rushed a letter to Dewey, sternly urging him to remain silent. He outlined the naval victories the U.S. had won thanks to knowing the Japanese codes. A fuming Dewey said FDR ought to be impeached rather than reelected. But he decided not to use the information.[6]

As the campaign picked up momentum, Republican attacks on Roosevelt's health became more overt. Clare Boothe Luce spoke of the president's "tired and shaking hands." Republican oilman Joseph Pew flatly declared voters should realize they were deciding whether to make Harry Truman, not Roosevelt, the president. Joe Patterson's *New York Daily News* called for "our elderly president" to have a physical examination and tell the people the results.[7]

III

Democrats responded to these potentially lethal attacks by telling very big lies. Party Chairman Robert Hannegan later told close friends that he wanted only one thing on his tombstone: "*He stopped Henry Wallace from becoming president of the United States.*" For public consumption Hannegan denounced the Republican "whispering campaign" about Roosevelt's fitness. "The president is very vigorous, the picture of health," Hannegan insisted. Oscar Cox, vice chairman of the Democratic National Committee, who sometimes assisted in drafting FDR's speeches, sent Harry Hopkins a proposed oration: "The False Fiction of the President's Health." Most deceitful of all was Admiral Ross McIntire, who told the *New York Times:* "The President's health is perfectly OK."[8]

The Democrats fought back by trying to focus voters' attention on Dewey's youth and supposed inexperience, conveniently ignoring that he had been a more than creditable governor of New York, the nation's most populous state. Vice presidential candidate Harry S. Truman warned that there was "no substitute for experience." Jimmy Byrnes, reconciled by Roosevelt's strenuous apologies for his treatment at the convention, went even further, saying Dewey's election would "jeopardize the peace."

Not a few Democrats took up a theme launched by Oklahoma's governor, Robert Kerr, at the Chicago convention: Admirals Chester Nimitz was fifty-nine, William (Bull) Halsey was sixty-two, Generals Douglas MacArthur and George Marshall were both sixty-four, and Admiral Ernest King was sixty-six. If these "tired old men" were winning the war, why couldn't the sixty-two-year-old Roosevelt do likewise? In logic, this is known as begging the question. In politics it was a good comeback.[9]

IV

These lies and half-truths were helpful, but Roosevelt knew that the voters wanted more than statements from third parties. Husbanding his strength, FDR hid behind his commander in chief's role and did no campaigning for most of September. But he and Sam Rosenman and Robert Sherwood were working on a speech that was designed to answer the overconfident Dewey with an unexpected ingredient: ridicule. Their target date was a Teamsters Union dinner in Washington, D.C., on September 23.

Determined to give the illusion of vitality, Roosevelt used his ill-fitting braces to stand at the podium. He began by remarking he had spoken to the union members in 1940. "You know, I am actually four years older, which is a fact that seems to annoy some people," he said. "In fact there are millions of Americans who are more than eleven years older than when we started in to clear up the mess that was dumped in our laps in 1933."

He proceeded to pin the Depression on the Republicans, mocking their attempt to turn the failure to solve it on the Democrats. He accused the GOP of importing "propaganda techniques invented by the dictators abroad," rhetoric more usually associated with Henry Wallace. He talked about the "twelve ill-fated years when the Republicans were in power," and recalled an old saying, "Never speak of rope in the house of a man who has been hanged." He thought the Republicans ought to remember that when they brought up the word "Depression."

Can the Old Guard pass itself off as the New Deal?
I think not.
We have all seen many marvelous stunts in the circus but no performing elephant could turn a hand-spring without falling flat on his back.

Roars of laughter greeted these gibes.

Growing serious, FDR dismissed the Republicans' use of the Hershey statement—described as a remark by a high government official—"as a callous brazen falsehood . . . to stimulate fear among American mothers, wives and sweethearts." He praised the workers of America for their war production and sneered at Republican assertions that they were better qualified to negotiate a lasting peace.

Then he swung back to ridicule. Some Republicans had claimed that when Roosevelt stopped in the Aleutians on his way back from Hawaii, he had left behind his pet Scottie, Fala, and the navy had sent a destroyer racing back to get him, at vast cost in fuel and wear and tear on the ship.

These Republican leaders have not been content with attacks on me, on my wife, or on my sons. . . . They now include my little dog, Fala. Well, of course, I don't resent attacks, and my family doesn't resent attacks, but Fala *does* resent them. You know, Fala is Scotch, and being a Scottie, as soon as he learned that the Republican fiction writers in Congress and out had concocted a story that I had left him behind on the Aleutian Islands and had sent a destroyer back to find him—at a cost to the taxpayers of two or three or eight or twenty million dollars—his Scotch soul was furious. He has not been the same dog since. I am accustomed to hearing malicious falsehoods about myself—such as the old worm-eaten chestnut that I have represented myself as indispensable. But I think I have a right to resent . . . libelous statements about my dog.

More howls of laughter greeted this riff. FDR closed with a promise of a durable peace and a full-employment economy and a final gibe at the GOP about the Depression. "The fruits of victory this time," he said, "will not be apples sold on street corners." [10]

The Republicans were staggered. They had expected to campaign against the enfeebled man they saw in San Diego and Bremerton. Instead of answering FDR's ridicule with better ridicule, Dewey chose to be offended. He said Roosevelt had given a speech full of "mud-slinging and wisecracks." It plumbed "the depths of demagoguery." Americans dislike pomposity and Dewey displayed it in capital letters with these words. A gleeful Paul Porter told Sam Rosenman the election had become a contest between "Roosevelt's dog and Dewey's goat." [11]

V

Yet polls showed the contest remained very close, and nervous Democrats began telling Roosevelt he could not win without making some kind of campaign tour. Isador Lubin, former head of the Bureau of Labor Statistics, who had moved to the White House to provide FDR with an independent source of data on the war effort—and help Sam Rosenman with the factual side of FDR's speeches—warned that Roosevelt had to appear at least once "before a huge public gathering" to dispel the health issue.

FDR accepted the advice with not a little weariness. "There has been this constant rumor that I'll not live if I am elected," he said at a cabinet meeting. "You all know that is not so but apparently 'Papa has to tell them'."[12]

Evidence of how seriously the Democrats took the health issue has emerged from FBI files. Assistant Secretary of State Breckinridge Long heard that a doctor in the office of the army surgeon general's office was telling people Roosevelt had a serious heart problem. Long rushed a letter to Press Secretary Steve Early at the White House who got on the telephone to J. Edgar Hoover. Soon FBI agents were swarming into the surgeon general's office, as well as Bethesda Naval Hospital and the Mayo Clinic in Minnesota, where doctors were also gossiping about Dr. Bruenn's constant presence in Roosevelt's entourage. The doctors hastily admitted they did not know all the facts about the president's condition and the gossip ceased.[13]

On October 21, FDR was scheduled to go to New York for an evening speech before the Foreign Policy Association. The Democratic National Committee urged him to tour the city in a motorcade to give people a chance to see him. The president asked Ed Flynn's advice; Flynn, deeply concerned about FDR's health, urged him to tell the committee to go to hell. But FDR chose to make the tour. He arrived in a cold, wind-lashed downpour, the tail end of a northeast storm, and decided the weather gave him the opportunity to prove "Papa" was hale and hearty. For almost five hours, he rode in an open car through fifty-one miles of New York's streets while at least a million people cheered. To survive he wore flannel underwear and wrapped most of his body in a fur robe beneath his heavy Navy cape; under his legs was a special heater. At a prearranged stop, the president was lifted from the car, given a drink of brandy and a rubdown, and thrust into a dry suit. The public saw a magnificent performance. Ed Flynn was so afraid the ordeal would be fatal, he retreated to his country house, lest he be blamed for FDR's demise.[14]

VI

For a man in FDR's condition, the tour of rain-lashed New York was the equivalent of bungee jumping. Elated to discover he was still alive, the president displayed more than a little hubris in his speech to the Foreign Policy Association. Recalling the flawed diplomacy after World War I, he told the audience this war had given everyone a second opportunity to achieve a peaceful world. He held up the United States' "Good Neighbor" policy toward South America as a model for the rest of the globe. Another example of being a good neighbor, he maintained, was his recognition of the Soviet Union in 1933.

At this point, while FDR was working on the speech, he had told Sam Rosenman and his helpers that here he wanted to insert a story told to him by Mrs. Roosevelt. She had visited a classroom in a rural schoolhouse in which a map of the world contained a large white space where the Soviet Union existed. The teacher told Mrs. Roosevelt that the school board had decided not to teach the children anything about Russia.

The speechwriters, already jittery about Dewey-Bricker attacks on Communists in Sidney Hillman's CIO-PAC, urged FDR to omit this passage, arguing it was "irrelevant." Realists, they were also remembering the Katyn Massacre, the Poltava double cross, and the Warsaw betrayal. They wanted FDR to skate over the reference to Russia as fast as possible and get to the main purpose of the speech, a condemnation of the Republicans' isolationist past.

Each time they gave the president a draft without the schoolhouse story, FDR insisted on putting it back into the speech. Finally, when it was omitted in a final draft, Roosevelt agreed to leave it out—and added: "I'll just ad-lib it."

In his memoirs, Sam Rosenman recalled that everyone assumed the president was joking. To their astonishment, he ad-libbed the entire story in the actual speech, revealing the centrality of his 1933 recognition of Russia in his thinking about the Soviets. Not only was he proud of this step, FDR was determined to maintain its wisdom by asserting the Communist empire's virtues and suppressing whenever possible reports of Russian actions that revealed the truth about Josef Stalin's brutal dictatorship.[15]

With similar stubbornness, the president refused to abandon Republican isolationism as an issue, in spite of the disaster that policy had inflicted on the Democrats in 1942. Now FDR used it to impugn the Republicans' ability to forge a lasting postwar peace. The argument may have carried some weight with voters who worried about Governor Dewey's all but total inexperience in foreign affairs.

VII

As the campaign began, FDR invited the vice presidential nominee, Senator Harry Truman, to the White House for lunch. The meeting went well. Roosevelt poured on the charm and Truman thanked him "for putting the finger on me" for vice president—an interesting choice of words, if one stops to analyze it. Fingering people, in the slang of the 1920s and 1930s, meant execution, gangland style.

For several minutes the two men talked seriously about the current political situation. Roosevelt gave Truman an assessment of the nation's mood that he shared with very few other politicians. He thought the war-weary American people had absorbed about all the reforms they were able to handle. FDR implied that this realization lay behind his decision to discard Henry Wallace.

Truman later said the conversation was about "making the country run for the Democrats." It covered "sealing wax and many things." The latter quote is from one of Truman's favorite passages in Lewis Carroll's *Through the Looking Glass*. FDR was telling Truman he had been chosen to be the conserver of the New Deal's legacy. But Truman, resisting the notion that he might soon become that least enviable of political beings, an accidental president, dismissed the words as harmless nonsense.[16]

The candidates went outside and had lunch under a magnolia tree supposedly planted by Andrew Jackson, with Anna Roosevelt Boettiger as the hostess. Photographers and movie cameramen swarmed around them until the food was served. Roosevelt asked Truman how he planned to campaign. Truman said he was thinking of using an airplane. FDR vetoed the idea. "One of us has to stay alive," he said—a graphic glimpse of his awareness that the demands of the campaign might kill him.

Leaving the White House, Truman told reporters: "He's still the leader he's always been. Don't let anybody kid you about it. He's keen as a brier." Back in his Senate office, Truman confided to an assistant that he had no idea the president was in such "a feeble condition. . . . It doesn't seem to be any mental lapse of any kind but physically, he's just going to pieces."[17]

VIII

Truman campaigned vigorously. So did Henry Wallace. The source of the rejected vice president's vigor was a conversation with Roosevelt as the campaign was beginning. Wallace had told the *New York Times* that he would not campaign unless Roosevelt convinced him in a "completely frank" talk that he was going to pursue a liberal course in his fourth term. FDR invited him to lunch and gave Wallace a full blast of the old charm. Roosevelt quickly "skated over the thin ice" of the convention (as Wallace put it in his diary) and told the vice president his only political problem was being four or six years ahead of his time.[18]

Subtly rebuking Wallace (or trying to teach him basic politics) FDR told the Iowan he could have won if he had made a deal with some of the opposition. That was what Roosevelt had done with John Nance Garner in 1932. Wallace replied that he did not like to make deals, no doubt further confirming Roosevelt's judgment that he did not have "it," the makeup of a politician. Wallace said he had backed Roosevelt only because his name was a "symbol of liberalism." The vice president was choosing his words very carefully. He did not say Roosevelt was a liberal. As one biographer has noted, Wallace was dumping coals of fire on the president's head.[19]

Nevertheless, FDR promised to give Wallace any cabinet post he wanted after the election. The only exception was the State Department, because Cordell Hull was an "old dear" and he could not bear to break his heart by dismissing him. Roosevelt did not bother to tell Wallace that Hull had already informed FDR he was planning to resign. Roosevelt knew Hull would never tolerate Henry Wallace as his successor.

If they won the election, Roosevelt said he and Wallace would draw up a list of who they wanted to get rid of. At the head of FDR's list would be Secretary of Commerce Jesse Jones. Wallace promptly asked for Jesse's cabinet job with Jones's two powerful loan funds, the Reconstruction Finance Corporation and the Foreign Economic Administration, "thrown in." He remarked that would be poetic justice for his humiliation in the Board of Economic Warfare brawl. Roosevelt beamed and agreed wholeheartedly.[20]

Changing his mind about how many speeches he would give, Wallace traveled widely and spoke often to groups that admired him, labor unions and minorities. Almost alone among the speakers in either party, he called for a commitment to civil rights and justice for African Americans. Again and again he urged a "rebirth of liberalism"—an interesting choice of words. He was admitting that liberalism had all but expired since 1940. At the same time he exhibited his readiness to demonize his fellow

Americans. He told his audiences that every vote for Dewey and Bricker would be applauded in Berlin.[21]

Wallace and Truman appeared together only once, in New York's Madison Square Garden on October 31, a week before the election. It was not the happiest occasion for either man. Wallace did not arrive on time and several Wallaceites urged Truman to go out on the platform alone. Truman's people flatly declined to let him do any such thing. They knew they were in Wallace territory and feared their man would be booed—and when Wallace appeared the applause would be so tremendous, the story would make headlines.

When Wallace finally arrived, with a weak excuse about forgetting his glasses, he looked extremely annoyed to find Truman waiting for him. "They walked out . . . arm in arm and smiling at each other," said a Truman man, "but I think they were about ready to cut each other's throats."[22]

When Truman was introduced, the applause was tepid; Wallace received an ovation and cries of "Wallace in '48." Truman praised FDR and Wallace with equal fervor, calling the Iowan "the greatest secretary of agriculture this country ever had." One wonders if the senator remembered the ironic way he had used these words to Joe Guffey, or if Guffey had passed on the wisecrack to Wallace.

The lame duck vice president declined to say anything complimentary about Truman, beyond noting he was not "a reactionary Democrat." Wallace spent most of his time extolling the Roosevelt administration, which he urged his fellow liberals to support.[23]

IX

In the Oval Office, FDR was hard at work enlisting another outspoken liberal under his banner. Wendell Willkie loathed the Republican candidate, Governor Thomas E. Dewey, and declined to endorse him. At the Republican convention in Chicago, Willkie had called a press conference and denounced the GOP plank affirming support for international cooperation but opposing U.S. membership in a world state. FDR began harvesting some of the seeds he had planted by dangling the vice presidential nomination in front of Willkie in July.

Roosevelt had followed up this move by dispatching Sam Rosenman to confer with Willkie in New York to see if he was interested in a "long range" plan to reorient politics in the United States by grouping all the liberals, labor unions, and minorities in a single party and letting the southern conservatives and the Republicans and the party bosses go their errant ways. A tremendously excited Willkie said he was very interested. "Tell the president," he said, "I'm ready to devote almost full time to this."[24]

In his conversations with Henry Wallace, FDR deprecated Willkie. Roosevelt told the vice president he did not think the Republican was "really a liberal." This suggests that FDR was wooing the Hoosier politician with something less than wholehearted sincerity. During the summer, Roosevelt wrote two letters to Willkie, urging an off-the-record meeting. Both were leaked to the press and a furious Willkie, suspecting he was being used, barred further contacts with the White House. But he remained intrigued and after the party conventions his disgust and disdain for Dewey continued to grow, although the Republicans did everything in their power to persuade him to endorse the New York governor.[25]

On August 11, 1944, Harry Hopkins got a surreptitious phone call from visiting Lord Beaverbrook, the British press baron, with some interesting news. Willkie had told him—and authorized him to tell Hopkins—that he was not going to endorse Dewey. Instead, he planned to come out for Roosevelt in October. The fish was hooked and FDR continued to play him with superb skill. Roosevelt told his son Elliott, a notorious leaker to the press, that he was thinking of backing Willkie for secretary general of the as yet unborn United Nations. Later, FDR contacted Willkie and suggested a talk in Hyde Park over Labor Day.[26]

Willkie remained wary of an early embrace but he performed ably as a pro-Roosevelt operative inside the Republican Party. He leaked information about the isolationist background of Dewey's campaign manager to the liberal newspaper, *PM*. He told Drew Pearson about the way Herbert Hoover was supposedly becoming a major Dewey campaign advisor, linking the New York governor with the Democrats' favorite target. When Dewey rebuked Congressman Hamilton Fish for making anti-Semitic remarks in his campaign for reelection, Willkie managed to find fault with the governor's statement because he failed to condemn Fish's isolationist past.[27]

Whether the strain of playing the double-crosser got to Willkie, or his heavy drinking and indifference to exercise and a sensible diet eroded his health, the Hoosier suffered a serious heart attack in late August. He ignored it at first but finally sought help at New York's Lenox Hill Hospital, where he had thirteen more attacks as the doctors struggled to save his life. On October 7, another seizure killed him.

Some of Willkie's followers made good on his promise to Hopkins. After Roosevelt's speech to the Foreign Policy Association, in which he called for a United Nations with the authority and military power to keep the peace, they published an "Open Letter to Fellow Republicans," urging support of Roosevelt. They assailed Dewey's foreign policy as vague and timid and said there were still too many isolationists in the Republican Party. FDR's fishing expedition had not been entirely in vain.[28]

X

In Washington, D.C., Roosevelt was coping with a large worry. The Russian betrayal of Warsaw's freedom fighters had put the nation's 6 million Polish-American voters in a foul mood. In March of 1944, they had formed a Polish-American Congress to make their voices heard. They of course knew nothing about FDR's betrayal of Poland at Teheran—not even Secretary of State Hull knew about it—and the president's remark that he wanted to keep his agreement with Stalin a secret because, "as a practical man," he did not want to lose the Polish vote.

With no fear of contradiction, the president assured a gathering of Polish-American congressmen that he had not made any secret agreements about Poland at Teheran. The Republicans tried to play on Polish suspicions but they too were ignorant of what went on at Teheran. "We cannot prove they have been sold down the river (if they have)," Michigan's Senator Arthur Vandenberg ruefully admitted in late October.[29]

On Pulaski Day (October 11) commemorating the Polish patriot Casimir Pulaski who fought as a cavalryman in the American Revolution, FDR met with leaders of the Polish-American congress and assured them that he wanted to see Poland "reconstituted as a great nation." Later in the month he said the same thing to the president of the congress. Newspaper stories about Warsaw's betrayal were sufficiently blurred to obfuscate Stalin's responsibility and there was still an illusion that wrongs could be righted at a peace conference. The Polish-American politicians urged their followers to go down the line for Roosevelt.

Henry Wallace, voice of the New Dealers in the administration, did not say a word of protest about the massacre of Warsaw's liberation army. On October 6, he met Charles Bohlen, Roosevelt's translator at Teheran and the current head of the Russian Section in the State Department, thanks to Harry Hopkins's blessing. Bohlen began talking about the Warsaw betrayal. Obviously deeply disturbed, the diplomat dropped his customary caution about expressing his opinions and said the Russian action (or inaction) was "very hard to explain."

Instead of sympathy, in his diary Wallace expressed doubts that the Russians had broadcast a call for the Warsaw Poles to revolt. He told himself the question was "still open in his mind." But there was "no question" in his mind that Bohlen was "definitely anti-Russian in his attitude." If Wallace had been renominated as vice president, that observation would have been the death knell of Charles Bohlen's career in the foreign service.[30]

XI

The Poles were not the only people who were unhappy with the way Roosevelt and the New Dealers were throwing themselves and the nation into Soviet Russia's embrace. A poll showed a steep decline in FDR's support among Catholics of all ethnic varieties, amounting to a defection of 10 percent or 730,000 votes. Among the most disillusioned was Joseph P. Kennedy. After cajoling him into the radio address that played a crucial role in the 1940 election victory, Roosevelt had let Kennedy sit out the war without offering him any job worthy of his prestige or talents.[31]

Kennedy knew he had been seduced, and grew bitter. He deplored the policy of unconditional surrender—he considered writing an article for Reader's Digest, denouncing it—and was appalled by the Morgenthau Plan for Germany. His negative attitude was exponentially compounded by his son Joe's death flying a war-weary bomber. In the middle of the campaign, Kennedy had dinner with the vice presidential candidate, Harry Truman, in Boston. The meeting turned into a Kennedy diatribe against the president. "Harry," Kennedy cried, "what are you doing campaigning for that crippled son of a bitch who killed my son Joe?"

The implication was all too clear. Kennedy knew Truman's personal opinion of Roosevelt was not much higher than his own. But Truman was not about to be drawn into saying things about the president that could easily get into the newspapers. He knew Kennedy was very close to Arthur Krock of the *New York Times*, among other FDR critics in the press. "If you say another word about Roosevelt, I'm going to throw you out that window," Truman snapped.[32]

XII

The Republicans handled the Communist issue gingerly at first. They let Dewey's vice presidential candidate, Ohioan John Bricker, hammer away at the Democrats' connection with the CIO and the Communist Party, knowing he would not attract major press attention. When an apparently vigorous Roosevelt made outdoor speeches in Philadelphia and Chicago, further defusing the health issue, Governor Dewey decided Soviet subversion might jump-start his faltering candidacy.[33]

On November 1, Dewey charged that Roosevelt had handed control of the Democratic Party to Sidney Hillman and Communist Party boss Earl Browder "to perpetuate himself in office for sixteen years." Hillman and his Communist allies in CIO-PAC had been well publicized in *Time* and elsewhere. For a while the combative Hillman fired back. But his heavy Lithuanian accent and unmistakably Jewish features made the White House nervous. One aide rushed a letter to Roosevelt begging him to find a way to keep Hillman quiet. Party Chairman Robert Hannegan told a friend he hoped a heart attack would remove the high-strung labor leader from the scene.[34]

Dewey's charge of Communist influence gave FDR a chance to answer the Republicans on this issue. In a sarcasm-laced speech in Boston on November 4, he accused the Republican candidate of taking the low road. "Never before in my lifetime has a campaign been filled with such misrepresentation, distortion and falsehood," he said. Any candidate for high office who claimed the American government was infiltrated by Communists was re-vealing "a shocking lack of trust in America."[35]

As we have seen, Roosevelt had no less than 329 Communist spies in his administration, including several at the higher levels of the White House, the State Department, and the Treasury De-partment. But no one in either party, including the president, was even faintly aware of this sobering fact—perhaps the most sober-ing of the New Dealers' war. Politically, FDR's words were a dev-astating answer to a candidate whose strategy had gone awry.

By this time, Roosevelt had also demolished the argument that the Republicans would do a better job maintaining peacetime prosperity. In several speeches he assured Americans that the ad-ministration was hard at work, planning an economy that would guarantee 60 million jobs. In fact, nothing of the sort was being done anywhere in the government. In his diary, Henry Wallace noted that Lauchlin Currie complained to him about the lack of postwar planning, in spite of the way the war was obviously churning toward a conclusion.[36]

XIII

To the relief of his doctors, the president's speaking schedule in the final weeks of the campaign had no immediate impact on his precarious health. On October 29, Dr. Bruenn noted "during the past month he has engaged in more than the usual amount of ac-tivity [and] a complete disregard of the rest regime." But the pres-ident's pulse and blood pressure readings were relatively good. He almost seemed to be thriving on the extra effort he was making.[37]

As election day approached, *Newsweek*'s poll of political ex-perts concluded that the race was too close to call. *Time* pre-dicted a narrow Roosevelt victory. Roosevelt himself was pessimistic. He too thought it would be very close. In an informal bet with Sam Rosenman and others of his inner circle about how many electoral votes he would receive, the president insisted on tearing up the figure he wrote on his slip of paper, lest it somehow get leaked. Apparently he did not believe his private pollster, Hadley Cantril, who told him he was going to win 53 percent of the vote and do very well in the electoral college.[38]

Cantril proved to be a reliable prophet. On election day the Champ rolled to his fourth presidential victory, winning 53.8 percent of a huge turnout—48 million votes—almost 10 million more than the Gallup Poll had predicted. CIO-PAC had spent its money wisely. Roosevelt and Truman ran extremely well in the cities, carrying every urban center over 500,000 except Cincinnati.

In the electoral college it was a Democratic landslide, 36 states and 432 votes to a pathetic 99 for the hapless Dewey-Bricker team. In the popular vote, however, Roosevelt's 3.5 million margin made it the closest presidential election since Woodrow Wilson's victory in 1916. The Republicans gained a seat in the Senate and the Democrats gained thirty seats in the House, bolstering their nominal control. But the southern conservative-Republican coalition remained in charge of Congress.[39]

Harry Truman's congratulatory telegram zeroed in on the issue on which he wholeheartedly agreed with Franklin Roosevelt: "I AM VERY HAPPY OVER THE OVERWHELMING ENDORSEMENT YOU HAVE RECEIVED. ISOLATIONISM IS DEAD. HOPE TO SEE YOU SOON."

In Hyde Park, Roosevelt and his family and friends celebrated their victory over Thomas E. Dewey, a man they had come to detest. As he was wheeled away to bed, FDR called over his shoulder: "I still say he's a son of a bitch."

Merrimam Smith, a veteran White House reporter, was shocked by Roosevelt's exhausted appearance. "He looked older than I had ever seen him," Smith said. "His conversation was irrelevant, much of the time."[40]

In Kansas City, Missouri, Harry Truman escaped a victory party at the Muehlebach Hotel in the wee hours of the morning and threw himself down on a bed. He told an old friend from southwest Missouri what was on his mind: "The last time that he saw Mr. Roosevelt the pallor of death was on his face and he knew that he would be president before the term was out."[41]

XIV

FDR returned to Washington the day after the election. He was greeted at Union Station by cabinet members and aides—and by Harry S. Truman and Henry Wallace—a symptom of trouble to come. Wallace was determined to assert himself as the leader of the liberal wing of the Democratic Party. The president offered them both a seat in the back of his touring car, and insisted on leaving the top down, even though it was raining hard. He was still playing the vigorous candidate.

The president's health was much on Wallace's mind. A week after the election, Wallace attended a cabinet meeting and informed his diary that the conclave had proceeded in "the usual futile way" with FDR talking off the top of his head about a dozen different topics, none of them relevant. He thought from "the character and quality of his remarks" that FDR's intellect "will now begin to fade pretty rapidly."[42]

One of Roosevelt's first moves vis-à-vis Congress was an attempt to block a bill to continue the work of the departed Martin Dies's House Un-American Activities Committee. This was a payoff to the CIO-PAC, who had done so much to elect him. The results of FDR's initiative demonstrated how little the election had altered the fundamental balance of power in Washington. The congressmen not only defied the president, they increased the committee's budget, added apostrophes to HUAC's achievements in exposing Communist influence in the government and made it a permanent committee of the House.[43]

XV

This liberal defeat was only a minor ripple compared to the tidal wave of protest that arose when Cordell Hull, seriously ill with tuberculosis, resigned and checked into a hospital. Roosevelt attempted one last time to reorganize the State Department to his and Harry Hopkins's satisfaction. Joseph C. Davies of *Mission To Moscow* fame was still sending Roosevelt memos, warning him that the Russians found too many department professionals guilty of "prejudice and hostility."

This time Davies was aiming at Russian experts Charles Bohlen and Elbridge Durbrow. Davies's wealthy wife, Marjorie Meriwether Post, also played the please-Stalin game, telling Henry Wallace that Bohlen and his friends "looked down on the Russians, suspect them, [and] make . . . difficulty."[44]

In the fall of 1943, when FDR appointed Edward Stettinius under secretary of state to replace Sumner Welles, Roosevelt ordered him to "raise hell" in the department. Nothing happened. Stettinius, a genial glad-hander with no background in foreign policy, was co-opted by the professionals—all skilled diplomats, after all—and intimidated by Hull, who told him: "Watch out for extremists and do not bring in any leftists."[45]

Totally outmaneuvered, Stettinius had launched a reorganization plan under the tutelage of the old pros. To no one's surprise except FDR's, the professionals ended up with far more power than they had enjoyed under Sumner Welles. Favorite liberal target James Dunn became director of the Office of European Affairs as well as acting chief of Special Political Affairs, an umbrella title that gave him a say in everything, including planning for the UN.

In the past, the heads of the various area and country "desks" had reported to the under secretary. Now they reported to Dunn. The emboldened Dunn also rehabilitated Ray Murphy, the keeper of anticommunist files, whom Welles had twice banished, in obedience to Roosevelt's and Hopkins's demands.[46]

This was only a warm-up to the reorganization that took place after the 1944 election. Theoretically, the president was on a roll, with the political momentum to have his way, if not in Congress, then certainly in the executive branch. But there was a wide gap between theory and reality, filled largely by Cordell Hull. Roosevelt was still spooked by a dread of repeating Woodrow Wilson's post–World War I failure to win the backing of the conservative opposition in the Senate for the League of Nations. The president regarded Hull as his bridge to the Senate's southern conservatives—and Hull knew it.

By this time FDR realized Stettinius was putty in the hands of the department's professionals. But he made him secretary of state with the understanding that Harry Hopkins would work with him to bring in a layer of New Dealers at the top of the department who would do battle with the "reactionaries." FDR planned to make Joseph C. Davies under secretary; as assistant secretaries he readied Ben Cohen, hard-nosed general counsel to Jimmy Byrnes's War Mobilization Board, and Archibald MacLeish, late of the vanished Office of Facts and Figures and more recently assistant director of the OWI.

To Roosevelt's dismay, the plan swiftly unraveled. In an ironic echo of FDR's declining health, Davies reported that his doctor would not let him take the job. Hull probably would have vetoed him away. New Dealer Cohen refused his appointment because it was "abundantly clear to me that I am not really wanted in the State Department."[47] The outgoing secretary proceeded to make his own choices through the complaisant Stettinius. Forty-year foreign-service veteran Joseph Grew, whose last assignment had been ambassador to Japan (where he had opposed Roosevelt's provocative pre–Pearl Harbor policy) became under secretary.

Instead of Ben Cohen, James Dunn became assistant secretary of state with virtually global responsibilities. Only South America, assigned to Republican Nelson Rockefeller, another new assistant secretary, was excluded from Dunn's bailiwick. Semi–New Dealer Dean Acheson was downgraded to assistant secretary for congressional affairs and Jesse Jones's right-hand man, Will Clayton, was given his far more potent job of assistant secretary for economic affairs. Two other assistant secretaries, Roosevelt loyalists Breckinridge Long and Adolf Berle, were fired.

The liberal press erupted with rage. I. F. Stone, Walter Lippmann, and others tut-tutted and sputtered. Stone declared that all Roosevelt needed to do was add Republican foreign-policy guru John Foster Dulles to the group and "Wall Street would have no cause to regret the failure to elect Dewey." Liberal senators announced they would launch a filibuster to block the appointments.

Eleanor Roosevelt was "alarmed and outraged" and exploded into anti-Catholic vituperation at Dunn's appointment. She accused her husband of "poor administration" to put such a man in power, knowing that he had backed Franco. She claimed Dunn was now arguing "in favor of using German industrialists to rehabilitate Germany. . . . The fine Catholic hand is visible in Europe and in our State Department." She agreed with I. F. Stone that the "set-up" would not be much different from what it might have been under Dewey.[48]

XVI

This imbroglio put a huge strain on the already exhausted president. Eleven days after the election, Dr. Bruenn took his blood pressure and found it had risen to an alarming 210/112. FDR continued to lose weight, even when the doctor took him off digitalis. Worse, he had abandoned the "regime of rest" and was working all day and into the night. The State Department brawl involved long talks with Secretary of State Stettinius and others, including the infuriated Ben Cohen, who resigned from the government when he was blocked by Hull and only changed his mind after a lengthy discussion with FDR.[49]

An enraged Adolf Berle did everything but roar curses in Roosevelt's face. "A secretary of state should be able to read and write and talk," he snarled. "He may not be able to do all these but Stettinius can't do any of them."

"I know that, Adolf," Roosevelt said. "But I was pressed to take two men who would have upset postwar agreements in the Senate—Wallace and Byrnes. So I just stuck Stettinius in there to stop it. I realize that I'll have to do the work now, but I have no choice."[50]

Here, truly, was the saddest moment of the New Dealers' war. Their fall was so complete, the man who was their leader, the president who reveled in exercising power, was humbly confessing his impotence. A contrite Berle accepted a face-saving appointment as ambassador to Brazil.

XVII

Late in 1944, Associated Press reporter Louis Lochner, the man who had tried to put FDR in touch with the German resistance in 1942, reached Paris as a war correspondent. He began interviewing numerous German civilians left behind in the city by the retreating Wehrmacht. They were still trying to operate an anti-Nazi movement, sending agents with money and information into the Reich. When Lochner filed a story on them, the U.S. Army's censors killed it. The reporter was infuriated and demanded an explanation. He was told a special regulation was in force "from the President of the United States in his capacity as commander in chief, forbidding all mention of any German resistance."[51]

In his memoir of his World War II experiences, William Casey, who served as London director of covert operations for the OSS (he later headed the CIA under President Ronald Reagan) recalled how unconditional surrender cost thousands of lives in the September 1944 battle for Aachen. The German general in command wanted to declare Aachen an open city and spare its Romanesque cathedral and other treasures from the age of Charlemagne. But the Americans ignored his offer and Aachen was captured after eight days of bloody street-fighting that left the city a ruin full of German and American corpses.

Appalled, the OSS canvassed the prison camps and found five captured German generals who offered to serve as intermediaries to persuade other generals to capitulate in similar situations. The idea was rushed to Washington with the full backing of General Omar Bradley, the American ground commander in Europe. "Weeks passed before an answer came," Casey wrote. "No. The project had been considered and rejected." Why? The American government "did not propose to use German militarists to defeat German militarism."[52]

On the battlefield, meanwhile, the combination of unconditional surrender and the Morgenthau Plan guaranteed a ferocious German resistance. In November the Wehrmacht inflicted a strategic defeat on the immense American army that was trying to reach the Rhine. On November 22, 1944, a worried Dwight Eisenhower cabled the Joint Chiefs of Staff urging "that we should redouble our efforts to find a solution to the problem of reducing the German will to resist."[53]

The Joint Chiefs turned to Roosevelt, who stubbornly refused to say a word. But he asked Churchill to broadcast a redefinition of unconditional surrender, inviting the Germans to join in "this great effort for decency and peace among human beings." Churchill replied that the war cabinet disapproved of the idea, because it would "confess our errors." With more than a touch of savage sarcasm, Churchill added: "The General Grant attitude 'to fight it out on this line if it takes all summer' appears one to which I see no alternative. In the meantime I shall remain set in unconditional surrender, which is where you put me."[54]

The OWI was reduced to cooking up a clumsy translation of unconditional surrender into German, *bedingunglose waffeniederlegung*, which suggested the goal was surrender of the armed forces and not the German people. It did not have much effect. On December 21, the Wehrmacht stunned the British and Americans by assembling 250,000 men and 1,000 tanks and smashing out of the forest of the Ardennes in a daring lunge to recapture the port of Antwerp and strand the Allied army on the battlefield without food or gasoline. The desperate fighting and dying in the mud and snow at Bastogne and other more obscure crossroads in the ensuing Battle of the Bulge cost 80,000 American casualties.

Overall, the Americans lost 418,791 dead and wounded in the fighting after the breakout from Normandy and the capture of Paris. The British and Canadians lost another 107,000.[55] These figures do not include air force losses, or casualties in other theaters, such as Italy. If we include Russian and German losses, including German civilian casualties from Allied bombing, the total number of post–D day dead and wounded approaches 2 million. If we add to this toll the number of Jews who were killed in the last year of the war, the figure can easily be doubled. If we add all the dead and wounded since 1943, when unconditional surrender was promulgated, destroying the German resistance's hope of overthrowing Hitler, that figure too could be doubled—to 8 million. Unquestionably, this ultimatum was written in blood.[56]

XVIII

The enfeebled man who had created this nightmare within the larger nightmare of the war was slipping toward death, in spite of the best efforts of his doctors. After encountering the intransigence of the conservative coalition in Congress about the House Un-American Activities Committee and the stubbornness of Cordell Hull in the attempted overhaul of the State Department, FDR retreated to Warm Springs, a shaken, utterly weary man. He sent out a call for help to his cousin Daisy Suckley, who had become one of his favorite companions, and she soon joined him there.

Daisy, another diary keeper, was dismayed by FDR's appearance. "He looks ten years older than last year. Of course I wouldn't confess that to anyone, least of all to him, but he knows it himself." Even in Warm Springs, the president could not escape his faltering heart and deteriorating blood vessels. Dr. Bruenn had to watch him constantly. One day, Roosevelt stayed in the swimming pool twenty minutes instead of his allotted ten. When Bruenn took his blood pressure, it was an alarming 260/150, a level at which a stroke could occur at any moment. FDR complained constantly of feeling "logy"; he was clearly depressed by his physical condition and the immense political challenges he was facing in Washington and Moscow.

Daisy Suckley and Dr. Bruenn became so concerned about FDR's fragility, they began to dread every visitor. The president could not resist playing the cordial host, telling stories and becoming more excited and tense than they wanted him to be. On December 15, Democratic Party chairman Robert Hannegan came for lunch and stayed three hours, discussing patronage and policies. By the time he left, Roosevelt was gray and enfeebled. A distraught Daisy told her diary somehow they would have to limit every visitor to "shorter sessions." In her anguished affection, she seemed to forget she was writing about the president of the United States, the commander in chief of a global war machine of 10 million men, the chief executive of a quarrelsome war-weary nation of 138 million, first among equals in a deteriorating grand alliance.[57]

Ignoring his anxious doctors, President Roosevelt toured New York in a cold, drenching rain during his 1944 campaign for reelection. He was trying to refute rumors about his failing health. Five months later he was dead. (UPI)

Secretary of the Treasury Henry Morgenthau Jr. (seated, center) was a Roosevelt intimate. With the help of Assistant Secretary Harry Dexter White (standing, left) he concocted the Morgenthau Plan, which called for dismembering Germany and destroying its heavy industry. Morgenthau was unaware that White was a Communist agent. (Corbis)

FDR's fourth inaugural address on January 20, 1944, was the shortest on record, lasting barely five minutes. One witness said he "seemed to tremble all over" while he spoke. Back in his private quarters, the president discussed his will with his son James (in Marine Corps uniform at right) as well as the ceremony he wanted at his burial. (Acme)

At the Yalta summit in February 1945, President Roosevelt offered little or no resistance to Stalin's clear intention to dominate Poland and the other nations of Eastern Europe. FDR told his son Elliott that he thought the Soviet Union would be a "constructive force" once it got most of Europe under its control.

Secretary of State Edward Stettinius (far left) poses with one of his top assistants, Alger Hiss (second from left). The gifted Harvard graduate was one of 329 Soviet agents operating inside the Roosevelt administration during World War II. The Russian in charge of one Washington spy ring boasted, "We have agents at the very center of government, influencing policy."

An obviously ill Franklin D. Roosevelt reports to Congress and the nation on the Yalta summit meeting. Several times FDR lost his place in the text and ad-libbed comments that "bordered on the ridiculous," speech writer Sam Rosenman later said.

Tokyo, the capital of Japan, was virtually razed by American incendiary bomb attacks. An air raid on March 9, 1945, created a firestorm that killed at least 87,000 people and left over a million homeless. (Carousel)

In April 1945 General Dwight D. Eisenhower viewed bodies of concentration camp prisoners murdered by their Nazi guards. As he left the camp, Ike turned to an American enlisted man and asked, "Do you still have trouble hating them?" (Carousel)

This is the last photograph of Franklin D. Roosevelt. It was taken on April 11, 1945, the day before he died of a cerebral hemorrhage in Warm Springs, Georgia. For the final year of his life, doctors restricted the president to a twenty-hour work week in a desperate attempt to keep him alive. (American Heritage Library/Carousel)

On April 12, 1945, with Mrs. Truman and his daughter Margaret watching, along with members of Roosevelt's cabinet and White House staff, Vice President Harry S. Truman took the oath as president in the Cabinet Room of the White House. Bess Truman remarked, "This will be a terrible load on Harry. Roosevelt has told him nothing."

*When the Japanese refused to accept unconditional surrender,
President Truman and his advisors ordered the use of the atomic
bomb on Hiroshima. Here the mushroom cloud rises in the aftermath
of the explosion, which killed 220,000 people, a death rate of 54
percent. (Corbis)*

XIX

Back in Washington, the president had to run another gauntlet over his State Department appointments. In his first press conference, reporters asked him how appointing five conservatives and one liberal jibed with the New Dealish tone of his election campaign. FDR dodged expertly, claiming he was running things the way he had always run them, "a little left of center." Reporters also pressed him about the rumor that there would soon be another meeting between him and Churchill and Stalin. Defensively, he said the time and place was "a question of geography."

Behind the scenes, Stalin was putting on a repetition of his Teheran performance, insisting that Churchill and Roosevelt had to come to him. He proposed the Black Sea resort of Yalta—even more inaccessible than Teheran for Roosevelt and Churchill—and on Russian soil in the bargain. The thought of such a long exhausting journey horrified Roosevelt's doctors and must have troubled him too. By now he had few illusions about his illness.

In Europe, omens of larger political troubles to come flared in Italy and Greece. Prime Minister Churchill had already warned Roosevelt that Italy seemed to be drifting toward what he called "rampant Bolshevism." When the Italian government made anti-monarchist liberal Count Carlo Sforza the foreign minister, the British tried to block the appointment, calling Sforza an intriguer who might destabilize the fragile coalition government. Roosevelt let Secretary of State Stettinius fire off a telegram, reprimanding Churchill for interfering in Italian domestic politics. The British prime minister was infuriated and bombarded Roosevelt with telegrams demanding a retraction.[58]

In Greece, as the German army fled, armed Communists tried to seize power. Churchill ordered British troops in Athens and elsewhere to meet force with force. He begged Roosevelt for support but all he got was a telegram that FDR could do or say nothing because American public opinion would disapprove of interfering in the Greeks' right to self-determination. Privately, Roosevelt remarked to Harold Ickes that he thought the best solution was "to give every Greek a rifle and then let them fight it out."[59]

Hadley Cantril, FDR's private pollster, reported a worrisome trend in American public opinion. Americans saw, and disliked, the way both Great Britain and Soviet Russia were playing power politics in an all too familiar way. The Soviet army's betrayal of Warsaw had a particularly negative impact. The number of Americans who "trusted" the Soviet Union sank to 44 percent in October 1944.[60]

XX

In the meantime, there was an inauguration to plan, a state of the union address to write for Congress. Others handled the details, of course. But there were constant conferences with the president about everything. To the dismay of his doctors, Roosevelt ignored their plea for a return to the twenty-hour-week "regime of rest." Dr. McIntire glumly noted that not even his daughter Anna could stop FDR "from working through the entire day and well into the night." As a result, even McIntire, the perpetual optimist, admitted his condition had "worsened."[61]

By now, almost every visitor took one look at FDR and realized he was a very sick man. On January 4, 1945, Harold Smith, the director of the budget, wrote in his notes of a meeting that Roosevelt was "still in possession of his very great faculties" but "seemed tired in using them." Newly promoted aide Jonathan Daniels noted with alarm the odd signature on his White House commission. It was tilted off the line at a weird angle, suggesting Roosevelt no longer had the strength to grip a pen firmly.[62]

Perhaps the most grisly testimony came from Frances Perkins, the secretary of labor. On January 19, a final cabinet meeting of the outgoing administration was scheduled for the afternoon. Perkins had decided to retire and sent the president a note that morning, informing him of her decision. FDR did not mention her departure at the cabinet meeting. Alarmed and a little annoyed, Perkins waited while several other cabinet members talked business. She finally got to see FDR at about 4 P.M. She was stunned at his condition. His lips were blue, his skin a darkish gray. He could not even hold his head erect. He had to support it with one of his hands.

When Perkins reminded the president of her resignation, he became almost maudlin. "No, Frances. You can't go now," he said. "You mustn't put this on me now. I just can't be bothered now. I can't think of anyone else and I can't get used to anyone else. Not now!" Ms. Perkins withdrew her resignation.[63]

XXI

Inaugural day was cold and snowy. Using the war as an excuse, FDR canceled the usual parade and ride down Pennsylvania Avenue. He took his fourth presidential oath of office on the south portico of the White House while a small crowd stood on the lawn, up to their ankles in slush and mud. A secret service man and FDR's son James, in his marine dress blues, lifted Roosevelt from his wheelchair and stood him before the lectern in his ill-fitting braces.

All too conscious of his dwindling strength, FDR gave the shortest inaugural speech in American history, less than five minutes. The president said the future called for patience and faith. He warned that "things in life will not always run smoothly." He urged the American people to remember the great lesson the war had taught, that they had to become "citizens of the world, members of the human community." He quoted Ralph Waldo Emerson: The only way to have a friend is to be one."[64]

Dr. Bruenn, watching from a comparative distance, thought the president got through the address "quite easily." Those standing closer did not agree. Vice President Harry Truman saw flashes of pain on FDR's face and Secretary of State Edward Stettinius noted in his diary that "he seemed to tremble all over. It was not just his hands that shook but his whole body as well." Twenty-year-old Margaret Truman thought FDR looked "so worn and spent," she felt depressed.

Afterward, waiting for the reception to begin, FDR confided to James Roosevelt that he could not handle the ordeal of greeting 1,805 guests. James wheeled him back to the private quarters, where the president discussed his will and the ceremony he wanted for his burial—a stark indication of how he was feeling. The Trumans and Mrs. Roosevelt undertook the hand-shaking chores. During the reception, Woodrow Wilson's widow told Frances Perkins that the president looked "exactly as my husband did when he went into his decline."[65]

When the celebrating ended, it occurred to Sam Rosenman and his wife that they had not seen Henry Wallace at the reception. As friends and liberal allies, they decided to console the fallen standard-bearer. Perhaps Rosenman was also trying to assuage his guilt for telling Roosevelt that Wallace had to be dumped.

The Rosenmans found Wallace alone in his suite at the Wardman Park Hotel. "No person had been there even to say hello to him now that he wasn't vice president," Sam Rosenman later said. This strange antipolitical politician probably preferred it that way. While others partied, he was listening to Russian records, trying to improve his speaking skills in that difficult language. Although it did not occur to Rosenman, it was a sign that Henry Wallace thought he was still in the political game.[66]

19

LOST LAST STANDS

Not even someone as intimate as Sam Rosenman knew what Franklin Roosevelt was doing while his guests celebrated his fourth inaugural. The president was writing a letter to Jesse Jones, asking him to resign as secretary of commerce so Henry Wallace could get the job. He began by telling "Dear Jesse" that the letter was "very difficult" to write. He thanked him for his "splendid services" to the public and then launched into a veritable eulogy of the former vice president.

> Henry Wallace deserves almost any service which he believes he can satisfactorily perform. I told him this at the end of the campaign, in which he displayed the utmost devotion to our cause, traveling almost incessantly and working for the success of the ticket in a great many parts of the country. Though not on the ticket himself, he gave of his utmost toward the victory which ensued.

He told me he thought he could do the greatest amount
of good in the Department of Commerce, for which he
is fully suited. And I feel, therefore, that the Vice-Presi-
dent should have this post in the new Administration.
It is for this reason only that I am asking you to relinquish this present post to Henry, and I want to tell you
that it is in no way a lack of appreciation for all that
you have done, and that I hope you will continue to be
part of the government.[1]

This sloppy letter was a sad example of FDR's dwindling faculties. The timing could not have been worse. Presidents are not
supposed to do business on inauguration day. The presumption
that Jesse Jones would go quietly into the night and let his chief
political enemy triumph over him was almost ludicrously wrong.
The added presumption that the Senate, which had the constitutional power to advise and consent on cabinet appointments,
would tolerate the replacement of Jones, a man they liked, with
Wallace, a man they detested, was an even greater misjudgment
of political realities.

Worst of all was the presumption that this was a private letter
that would never become public. This illusion was all too evident
in the closing paragraph. The president suggested that Jones pay
Ed Stettinius a visit at the State Department to talk over an ambassadorship.

II

The dimensions of Roosevelt's misjudgment became visible the
next day. Jesse Jones demanded an interview with the president
and got it. What was left of FDR's charm had no effect on the enraged Jones. The Texan spurned the ambassadorship and told

FDR appointing Henry Wallace secretary of commerce was the craziest thing he had ever done.

Later that day, Jones held a press conference and released FDR's letter, along with a devastating reply. He zeroed in, not on the Commerce Department, which was a sort of Washington attic full of random agencies that had little impact on business, but on the Reconstruction Finance Corporation and the Foreign Economic Administration, which had, thanks to the billions in their coffers, a huge potential influence on the political future of America and the world.

> I have had satisfaction in my Government service because I have had the confidence of Congress, as well as your own. I have had that confidence because I have been faithful to the responsibilities that have been entrusted to me. For you to turn over all these assets and responsibilities to a man inexperienced in business and finance will, I believe, be hard for the business and financial world to understand.[2]

Newspaper reaction more than confirmed this prophecy. The *New York Sun* called the appointment "a heavy blow to business confidence in this country." The editors called Wallace "the most radical, impractical and idealistic dreamer" in Roosevelt's entourage. To put him in charge of "billions of dollars" was certain to make everyone on the private enterprise side in America wonder "if the wolf has not been appointed as . . . shepherd."

The *Knickerbocker News* of Albany resorted to satiric verse:

EXPLANATION TO JESSE JONES
Of financial experience
You've surely had a lot

So kindly scram and give the job
To some who has not.[3]

The *Detroit Free Press* declared "it would be difficult to imagine any man in all the United States who is as thoroughly disliked by American businessmen—big and little—as Henry Wallace." Even pro-Roosevelt newspapers found it hard to defend the appointment. It made a mockery of FDR's frequent calls to put politics aside for the duration of the war.[4]

III

A major congressional battle erupted between the conservatives and the New Dealers. The man in the middle was not President Roosevelt but Vice President Harry S. Truman. On January 22, FDR departed on his journey to Yalta to meet Josef Stalin and Winston Churchill. When FDR called Truman a day or two before the inauguration and told him he was going to make Henry Wallace secretary of commerce, the new vice president had said: "Jesus Christ!" But Truman went to work on the problem, drawing on the not inconsiderable influence he had acquired in his ten-year Senate career.[5]

After hours of cajoling southern conservatives, Truman concluded they would never permit Wallace to take charge of the Reconstruction Finance Corporation and the Foreign Economic Administration, which controlled between $30 and $40 billion in funds. Truman decided the nomination could only be saved if the Commerce job was separated from the loan agencies. With the help of Senator Tom Connally of Texas, the vice president persuaded Senator Walter George of Georgia, a survivor of Roosevelt's 1938 purge, to introduce a bill, severing the loan agencies from the Commerce Department and creating a new office, Federal Loan Administrator, to handle the money side. Truman then rounded up a majority of senators who agreed to confirm Wallace as secretary of commerce if the president promised to sign the George bill.[6]

Henry Wallace would have none of it. He insisted he wanted both jobs. Anticipating the Truman solution, the Iowan had visited the White House in late December and obtained a pledge of support from FDR. On January 17, Wallace had written to him, claiming that "certain financial people both in this country and south of the Rio Grande . . . are especially interested in your signing executive orders, one of which would take the RFC out of Commerce. If we give in to the financial gang at this time, the people will say that you and I have lost another battle to the reactionaries."

When Senator Tom Connally and Senator Josiah Bailey, the head of the Senate Commerce Committee, visited Roosevelt that same day with the proposal to separate the two jobs, FDR had opposed them. But the president's departure from the battlefield was a not so subtle statement of how much (or little) importance he attached to it. Even if he had been there to fight, the president had been outgeneraled by Jones's defiance and his release of FDR's careless letter.[7]

IV

Senator Bailey scheduled Commerce Committee hearings and to no one's surprise called Jesse Jones as his first witness. Jones and his friends made sure the hearing chamber's benches were packed with his supporters. When he appeared on January 24, they cheered him as if he were a heavyweight boxer entering the ring. Jones joked that he wished he had a piece of the gate receipts.

The ousted secretary of commerce read a prepared statement in which he defended his record and insisted the RFC had become a force for good in America under the leadership of men "experienced in business . . . men who haven't any ideas about remaking the world" or an inclination to "jeopardize the country's future with untried ideas and idealistic schemes." Senator Walter George read a list of the staggering number of federal loan operations in Jones's bailiwick. It took him twenty minutes. Whereupon Chairman Bailey asked: "Have you ever used your powers as Loan Administrator and RFC chairman for the purpose of determining the economic or the social character of the country?"[8]

"I certainly have not!" Jones declared. The spectator benches burst into cheers and applause.

Other questions revealed the awesome powers of the RFC, with the implication that it had to be kept in the right (pun only half intended) hands.

"What are the limits? How far can you go"? Senator Bailey asked.

"We can lend anything that we think we should," Jones replied. "Any amount, any length of time, or [at] any rate of interest . . . to anybody that we feel is entitled to the loan."

Wallace's only supporter on the Commerce Committee was Senator Claude Pepper of Florida. He asked Jones if he expected to become federal loan administrator if the George bill passed. Jones said that would be up to the president. Shifting his point of attack, Pepper asked why, if he had held both the Commerce and the loan jobs, another man could not do the same thing, "assuming his competence."

"If you are trying to ask me if Henry Wallace is qualified for both jobs, I will say: No," Jones said.

Again the benches erupted with cheers and applause.[9]

V

The next day, January 25, Henry Wallace was the witness. This time the spectator benches were packed with his supporters. They cheered lustily when he appeared. He too began with a prepared statement, which rambled at first, but soon got to a rather sharp point. "You know and I know that it is not a question of my lack of experience. Rather it is a case of not liking the experience I have."

The applause was thunderous. Wallace attacked the claim that he had no business experience, pointing out that the Agriculture Department had loaned $6 billion while he was secretary, comprising 11,500,000 separate commodity credit loans and 1,208,000 rural rehabilitation loans, most of them repaid. Wallace said the real motive for stripping the Commerce Department of its "vast financial power . . . is whether the Reconstruction Finance Corporation and its giant subsidiaries are to be used to help only big business or whether these powers are also to be used to help little businesses and to help carry out the President's commitment of 60,000,000 jobs." The quarrel was not "a petty question of personalities. It is the question of the path which America will follow in its future."[10]

Wallace assailed Jones and his backers as "persons of limited vision and stunted imagination." They lacked faith in America, the kind of faith that Roosevelt had when he predicted in 1941 that America would build 50,000 planes in one year. Wallace remained uncompromising during a long question and answer session, insisting at one point that the president had a right to appoint him to the Commerce job because the Democrats had won the election.

Again and again, as Wallace declaimed and argued, applause from his backers filled the hearing chamber. If a stranger had arrived from some isolated island country unaware that World War II was raging around the globe and attended these two days of hearings, he might have concluded that the United States of America was on the brink of civil war or revolution.

VI

The puzzled visitor might have drawn the same conclusion if he read the newspaper comments on the clash. Liberal I. F. Stone praised Wallace for his refusal "to placate the committee, to trim his sails, to gloss over his fundamental beliefs. He laid out his post-war full employment program with courage, zest and a passionate sincerity. He has Jefferson's wide-ranging mind and Lincoln's homely human goodness and the committee was impressed despite itself. . . . Wallace is a hard man to hate face to face and the hearing must have disappointed the Jones supporters."[11]

Hearst columnist Westbrook Pegler saw it differently. He found Wallace a "not too bright and, by himself, an amiable and harmless bleeding heart." But he was also a dangerous man because of his far-left followers, and their joint naïveté about the nature of Communism, their New Dealish hunger for power, and their ability to dupe sentimental journalists. These "yearning essayists" were "forever seeking another Lincoln." They pounced on "any untidy man with a bang over his eyes . . . and a clumsy fumbling public manner." Add to these characteristics "some generalities stolen from Jesus Christ such as the brotherhood of all mankind and the great virtue of the poor and the people can be fooled."[12]

The Times of London followed the Jones-Wallace struggle with fascination. In a long article on January 30, 1945, it wondered whether the collision would come to rank in American history with the Hayne-Webster debate as "pregnant with significance for the future." (Senator Robert Hayne of South Carolina and Daniel Webster of Massachusetts had tangled in 1830 over a state's right to secede from the Union, with Webster the victor.) "The issue which antagonizes Mr. Wallace and Mr. Jones is the issue which divided Jefferson and Hamilton, Washington's Secretary of State and Secretary of the Treasury—the rights of the 'common man' as against the privileges of the money power . . .

the central political conflict that has agitated the Republic since its birth."[13]

VII

Wallace may have impressed I. F. Stone and the readers of the *Nation* and the *New Republic*—but he did not impress the people who counted—the ninety-six members of the U.S. Senate. Wallace's spokesman, Senator Claude Pepper, tried in vain to raise the flag of party solidarity. He reminded the Senate that Franklin D. Roosevelt, the president who had just won reelection for a fourth term, wanted this man to be both secretary of commerce and the federal loan administrator. On January 29, 1945, liberals gave Wallace a testimonial dinner in New York, at which he probably did his cause no good by warning Congress against an "economic Munich or Dunkirque." This rhetoric no doubt reminded many people of his fondness for implying that those who opposed him were crypto-Nazis. Simultaneously waffling, Wallace said he might still take the Commerce job if Roosevelt appointed a liberal as the new federal loan administrator.

Behind the scenes, Eleanor Roosevelt, Sam Rosenman, and Henry Morgenthau Jr. were sending frantic cables to Roosevelt, who was aboard USS *Quincy* heading for Yalta. The president did not respond. On January 30, he celebrated his sixty-third birthday with no less than five cakes on the table in his quarters. There seems to have been no mention of Henry Wallace during the festivities.[14]

On February 1, 1945, the Senate's conservative coalition came within a whisker of rejecting Wallace for both jobs. The Commerce Committee had voted 15-5 in favor of this solution and on February 1, Senator Josiah Bailey made a motion to consider Wallace's nomination ahead of the George bill, severing the two jobs. The Senate tied 42-42 and Senator Robert Taft, a Wallace foe, moved for reconsideration, certain he could pick up a wavering moderate or conservative and rid Washington of Wallace once and for all. But Vice President Harry S. Truman, divining what Taft had in mind, instead recognized Democratic Majority Leader Alben Barkley, who brought up the George bill, with the promise that the president would sign it.[15]

Trying to avoid unconditional surrender, Senator Pepper and his dwindling band of Wallace supporters ran up the legislative equivalent of the white flag, saying they would be grateful to their fellow solons if they let Wallace have the Commerce job. The Senate responded by passing the George bill, 72-12. The House of Representatives completed the humiliation of the New Deal's battered standard-bearer by outdoing the Senate, 400-2. The congressmen apparently agreed with Republican Leonard Hall of New York, who declared that Wallace planned to change the New Deal to the New Communism. This staggering wipeout was accomplished by a Senate with a nineteen-vote Democratic majority and a House with a twenty-vote edge, three months after the Democratic Party had triumphed at the polls. A vote on approving Wallace as neutered secretary of commerce was put off until March 1.[16]

Thus did FDR's attempt to pay off Henry Wallace for his support in the 1944 election become the New Dealers' Little Big Horn. Their confidence inflated by their recent victory at the polls, they had ventured into enemy territory and met Custer's fate.

VIII

While this domestic massacre was taking place, FDR continued wending his way to Yalta. The USS *Quincy* carried him to the Mediterranean island of Malta, where he met Churchill. There they boarded planes for a seven-hour flight to Saki, on Russia's Crimean peninsula. It was a dangerous trip. The Germans still controlled Crete and a fighter escort was added to make sure the Luftwaffe did not try to shoot down the unarmed planes in which FDR and his entourage were flying. Because of the president's deteriorating heart and blood vessels, his doctors forbade the planes to go above 6,000 feet, lest the decreased pressure in the cabin prove fatal.

From Saki the mortally ill president endured an eighty-mile, five-hour car ride over unbelievably rough roads to reach the outskirts of Yalta, where accommodations in a fifty-room bedbug-ridden former czarist palace were awaiting him. Along the entire route, at least two divisions of Russian soldiers lined the road. Ignoring icy rain and occasional snow, they came to attention as the president's car passed. Was it Stalin's way of reminding his visitors of the might of the Red Army?

The inner thoughts of William Hassett, FDR's devoted secretary, were not reassuring as he watched Roosevelt depart for Yalta. He understood better than almost anyone what Roosevelt was thinking. "Having achieved every political ambition a human being could aspire to, there remains only his place in history." That place was at stake in Yalta's outcome, and Hassett was by no means optimistic. "Stalin remains an enigma, Churchill has brains, guts, courage . . . everything but vision. And FDR, outside of his military and naval advisors, is leaning on some pretty weak reeds."[17]

Hassett was undoubtedly thinking of Secretary of State Edward Stettinius, who was generally recognized as less than brilliant. Hassett may also have had in mind Harry Hopkins, whose stomach cancer and acute colitis had reduced him to a state of debility approaching Roosevelt's. FDR also brought Jimmy Byrnes and Ed Flynn, two people with no background in foreign policy.

Flynn was supposedly planning to travel from Yalta to other parts of Russia, gathering data on religious freedom under Stalin. Roosevelt was still trying to sell this idea to the American public.

Byrnes was invited as a consolatory gesture, because FDR had double-crossed him at the Democratic convention and compounded the insult by not making him secretary of state.

Stettinius wanted to bring Assistant Secretary of State James Dunn along as his chief advisor. But Roosevelt shook his head and snapped: "He'll sabotage everything." Dunn was unacceptable because he did not trust the Russians. Stettinius then suggested Alger Hiss, who was heavily involved in planning for the United Nations. Roosevelt agreed, thus putting one of Russia's secret agents at the heart of the conference.[18]

IX

Charles Bohlen, still Roosevelt's choice as interpreter and White House liaison with the State Department, met Roosevelt at Malta, after detouring to London and Paris with Harry Hopkins. Like so many others, Bohlen was shocked by FDR's appearance. "His condition had deteriorated markedly in the less than two weeks since I had seen him. He was not only frail and desperately tired, he looked ill . . . despite a week's leisurely voyage at sea."[19]

Thanks to Stettinius's readiness to consult the State Department's professionals, Bohlen was pleased to see Roosevelt had numerous "black books" on the subjects to be discussed at Yalta. Bohlen took great satisfaction in examining them. He thought they covered "every problem likely to come before the conference." Only later did he learn that the enfeebled president had barely looked at a single page during his week-long sea voyage.[20]

On his first night in Yalta, Bohlen received a letter from the deepest thinker among the State Department's Russian experts, George Kennan. From his office in the Moscow embassy, Kennan told Bohlen that he was "aware of the realities of this war, and of the fact that we were too weak to win it without Russian cooperation." As a realist, he recognized that the Soviet Union would undoubtedly "find its reward at the expense of other peoples in eastern and central Europe." Nevertheless, Kennan reiterated his stance that the Soviet Union was not a "fit ally" for America. Two days after Hitler attacked Russia, Kennan had told Loy Henderson the United States should do its utmost to distance herself politically from the Soviet Union. He still saw no need to "associate ourselves with this [Communist] political program, so hostile to the interests of the Atlantic community as a whole, so dangerous to everything which we need to see preserved in Europe."

Kennan thought the United States should frankly abandon Eastern and Southeastern Europe to a Soviet sphere of influence and concentrate on forming a Western European Federation. He was so leery of the United States getting involved in defending "a swollen and unhealthy" Russian sphere of power, he was even inclined to junk the United Nations and "stop wandering about with our heads in the clouds of Wilsonian idealism and universalistic conceptions of world collaboration."

Bohlen, harassed with preparations for the conference, wrote a hasty reply. He strongly disagreed with Kennan—showing the influence of his exposure to Roosevelt's and Hopkins's desire to achieve some kind of understanding with Russia. He no longer saw it as an "emotional rather than a realistic" approach. He told Kennan there was no alternative to the president's policy. He went so far as to call Kennan "naive to a degree" because he was thinking too abstractly. "Foreign policy of that kind cannot be made in a democracy," Bohlen wrote. Democratic leaders had to create "a climate of public opinion." Forgetting that Kennan had already conceded the point, he added impatiently: "The simple fact is if we wanted to defeat Germany, we could never have even tried to keep the Soviet armies out of Eastern Europe and Germany itself."[21]

Bohlen's letter shows how the pressure of events can change the minds of even the most intelligent men. By this time Bohlen clearly sympathized with Roosevelt's desperate wish to fashion a lasting peace out of the New Dealers' war. The sheer physical effort of the journey to Yalta and the all but visible proof that the president was a dying man made this reaction understandable. What Bohlen could not face was Kennan's pessimism about the climate of public opinion Roosevelt had created. By selling the American people a vision of Russia as a democratic nation not much different from America, the president had painted himself into an agonizing political corner. If the Russians acted as Kennan predicted they would, FDR would look like a fool, and there was a veritable horde of conservative enemies in the United States eager to help the American people draw that conclusion.

X

One of the leitmotifs of Yalta was struck the next day, when Roosevelt, repeating his Teheran performance, met Stalin without Churchill. On the car ride from Saki, FDR had noticed the war-ravaged landscape, dotted with burnt-out tanks and charred automobiles. "I'm more blood thirsty than a year ago," he said to the Soviet leader. "I hope you make another toast proposing the execution of 50,000 German officers."

FDR also resumed his habit of denigrating the British, hoping it would further ingratiate him with Stalin. Roosevelt told the Soviet leader the British were trying to reestablish France as a great power, because they wanted a French army to oppose an invasion from the east. The British, he sneered to Stalin, were "a very peculiar people."[22]

These attempts to charm a mass murderer show Roosevelt, the master American politician, sadly out of his depth. Stalin, already well informed by his spies of what to expect, listened with barely concealed satisfaction to Roosevelt's naive admission that the American people probably would not tolerate a large American army in Europe for more than two years. This jibed neatly with the Soviet leader's expectation that Communist parties in France and Italy and Germany would soon convert Central and Western Europe into pro-Soviet territory.

At Yalta's second plenary session, Roosevelt seemed to fulfill everyone's worst fears. He launched a rambling discussion of Germany that revealed once more how little he knew about the country. He talked of visiting it as a boy in 1886, when some parts of the Reich were still semiautonomous, and declared that the centralization of the government in Berlin was the reason Germany had become a dictatorship.

To an appalled Charles Bohlen, the president's discourse "didn't even hang together." Stalin said he presumed this meant FDR still favored German dismemberment. FDR replied that he leaned toward "five or seven" small states. Churchill said he supported the idea "in principle," which was a polite way of saying he had grave doubts about it.

Stalin let the discussion drift away for the time being. He had gotten on the record what he wanted: Allied agreement to partition Germany. A year later he would tell the German people Soviet Russia had never favored partition, it was a British-American idea, as the minutes of the Yalta conference proved.[23]

XI

Again and again, Stalin raised FDR's hopes by being remarkably agreeable. He endorsed the policy of unconditional surrender, which he had criticized at Teheran. He yielded to the British request to give France a share in the administration of conquered Germany. He declared Russia's readiness to join the United Nations and seemingly accepted the idea of discussing international problems by a majority vote in the security council. Only on deciding a plan of action did the Russians request a UN veto, which sounded reasonable.

When the discussions turned to Poland, Stalin was not so agreeable. By this time he had installed a pro-Communist government, the Lublin Committee, in the ruins of Warsaw. They were running the country and the Soviet secret police were rounding up thousands of members of the Polish Home Army, claiming they were fascist saboteurs. Roosevelt pleaded for free elections and a representative government. But he did not argue for these fundamentals on the basis of democratic principles. He talked about his anxiety to bring something back to America that would satisfy the 6 million suspicious Polish-American voters. For him, Poland's hard fate was part of the war within the war at home. At one point FDR declared that on Poland's future might depend the American people's willingness to participate in international affairs.[24]

Unmoved, Stalin insisted that for Russia, Poland was a matter of life and death. He claimed to fear another German invasion; that was why he wanted a Poland friendly to Russia. Over the next few days, the Russians negotiated the British and Americans down to something very close to zero. Instead of their ambassadors and embassy staffs in Warsaw making sure future elections were free, they would simply keep their governments "informed about the situation in Poland." Instead of the Lublin Committee being only a third of the provisional government, they would be an overwhelming majority, with "other" unnamed democratic leaders added to the Communist sandwich—if any could be found willing to risk their lives by returning to Poland or, if they were still at large after the NKVD's sweeps, by coming out of hiding.

Admiral William Leahy, Roosevelt's chief of staff, read this agreement before it was signed, and gasped: "This is so elastic the Russians can stretch it all the way from Yalta to Washington without even technically breaking it." Roosevelt wearily admitted this was the case. But it was good enough to keep the 6 million Polish-American voters quiet for a while.[25]

Stalin also got his way on Poland's boundaries, carving off a huge chunk of eastern Poland, including the valuable Drohobycz oil fields, and adding it to Russia. Eleven million Poles became Russians in this transfer, without anyone asking if they wanted to change their citizenship. Roosevelt resisted this piracy at first, suggesting a plebiscite. The transfer made a mockery of Woodrow Wilson's supposedly sacred principle of self-determination, but FDR added that he was "merely suggesting this for consideration rather than insisting on it." Even Edward Stettinius was dismayed by such flabby negotiating, which practically invited Stalin to dismiss it, which he did.

By way of compensation, Stalin proposed giving Poland a swath of East Prussia, which would turn 8 or 10 million Germans into refugees from land they had inhabited for six hundred years. Roosevelt (and a reluctant Churchill) acquiesced to this arrangement, another byproduct of unconditional surrender's implicit savagery.

As for the rest of Eastern Europe, Stalin clearly intended to follow the principle he had enunciated to Tito's lieutenant, Milovan Djilas: Everyone imposes his own system as far as his army can reach. More than once the Soviet leader hinted that he was merely imitating the sphere-of-influence politics the Allies were playing, by putting General de Gaulle in charge of France, and Greek nationalists, backed by British guns, in charge of Greece. Since spheres of influence were supposedly one of the evils that the century of the common man was going to eliminate, Roosevelt papered over this difference by proposing that everyone sign a "Declaration on Liberated Europe."

The professionals, returned to power in the reorganized State Department, had paid careful attention to the wording of this document. So did Harry Hopkins, who did his utmost to water down the original draft, prepared under the guidance of James Dunn. That document had an unmistakable call for free elections, supervised by a European Commission to which each of the Great Powers would appoint a representative. Hopkins persuaded Roosevelt to veto the European Commission, to the great disappointment of Secretary of State Stettinius. Free elections were called for at the "earliest possible" time, but who would decide this crucial point was muddied by a paragraph saying the three governments would "consult" on this and other matters to discharge their "joint responsibilities." Still, one British diplomat thought the end result, though a whittled down version of the idealistic original, was not "irremediably" damaged.[26]

Stalin agreed to sign the declaration, after scanning it to find several sentences that pleased him. One was a passage calling for the destruction of the "last vestiges of Nazism and Fascism" in the liberated countries. He also liked the sentence that defined these countries as nations where self-government had been destroyed by "the aggressor nations." This eliminated the Baltic states, Lithuania, Latvia, and Estonia, which he had acquired before his war with Germany began.

Almost as important as Poland to Stalin was an agreement on the repatriation of prisoners. The Soviets wanted the Allies to hand over the thousands of Russians who were fighting in the ranks of the German army. Many were prisoners of war who had volunteered to fight against Communism. Others were émigrés who had fled the Russian Revolution and fought beside the Germans to prevent Bolshevism from engulfing them again. The Allies made no attempt to distinguish between these two groups. While it was traditional for a defeated army to hand over turncoats, the émigrés had become citizens of other countries. Many would commit suicide rather than accept a return to Soviet Russia.

The president's military advisors convinced Roosevelt to sign the agreement because they feared thousands of American and British prisoners of war captured by the Germans and held in camps in eastern Germany would fall into the Russians' hands and they might refuse to return them if their demand for total repatriation was not met. The arrangement violated basic principles of human rights, not to mention self-determination. Once more, Roosevelt chose the brutally realistic side of the great dichotomy.[27]

XII

Before Roosevelt left for Yalta, he had been briefed on the atomic bomb. General Leslie Groves, the man in charge, had reported the first bomb would be available in August 1945. But there was wide disagreement among the scientists and resident experts on how powerful it would be, or whether it would work in the first place.

The uncertainty about the bomb led to another private FDR meeting with Stalin on the last day of the Yalta summit to discuss Russia's entry into the war against Japan. The U.S. Army, shaken by the high casualties Americans experienced in the Pacific fighting Japanese infantrymen, feared that Japan might ship a hefty portion of its 2 million man army in China to the home islands to meet a prospective American invasion. They urged the president to obtain Stalin's guarantee to join the war in the Far East. As with the repatriation of prisoners, and the deals with Darlan and Badoglio, the soldiers continued to pursue the goal so bluntly stated by Admiral Leahy in 1942—a disregard of any and all political calculations—to reduce the length of the casualty list.

Russia had signed a nonaggression pact with Japan in the spring of 1941 but this piece of paper did not prevent Stalin from playing power politics with cold-blooded intensity. In previous discussions with Ambassador Averell Harriman, the Russian leader had demanded that the Americans equip an entire Russian army of 1,500,000 men with 3,000 tanks, 75,000 trucks and jeeps, and 5,000 planes. Much of this hardware was being shipped to Siberia.[28]

Now Stalin asked for Russian control of the railroads in Manchuria, a not so subtle way of giving him virtual dominance of this vast northern province of China. FDR agreed, forgetting— or ignoring—that at Teheran he had taken pains to procure Stalin's promise to stay out of Manchuria. Next was a demand for a warm water port in the Pacific—China's Darien—and control of nearby Port Arthur under a long-term lease. Also, the status quo in Outer Mongolia was to be confirmed—Soviet agents had turned this remote Chinese province into a Russian puppet.

In return Stalin promised to unleash the Red Army on Japan three months after the war in Europe ended. He also promised to conclude a treaty of friendship and alliance between Russia and China and to put pressure on the Chinese Communists to enter a coalition government with Chiang Kai-shek.

Roosevelt uneasily remarked that he had no authority to give Stalin access to vital parts of China. But he agreed to the terms, promising to persuade Chiang Kai-shek at some unspecified future date. He would not tell Chiang for the time being because the Chinese were supposedly not good at keeping secrets. But FDR was enthused by Stalin's promise to press the Communists to join Chiang in governing China and the offer of the treaty of friendship with the Nationalists.[29]

Why did the president think Stalin took a treaty with China any more seriously than the one he was about to violate with Japan? FDR apparently thought he had "gotten at" Stalin, and his personal influence on the Russian dictator would restrain him from breaking his word here and elsewhere in the world, notably Poland.

XIII

The apparent rapport with Stalin on the Japanese war and his readiness to sign the Declaration on Liberated Europe enabled the Americans to convince themselves that Yalta was a success. Some members of the delegation felt almost euphoric as they headed home. Harry Hopkins believed they had achieved "the dawn of the new day we had all been praying for." Charles Bohlen, aware of George Kennan's pessimism, clung to wary hope. "The general mood was one of satisfaction," he recalled. Admiral Leahy was among the few pessimists. He saw future "international disagreements" if Russia became the most powerful nation in Europe. But he said nothing, publicly.[30]

At home, the Yalta agreements were hailed from all points of the ideological compass. Liberals, desperate to believe their faith in Communist Russia was being vindicated, praised them extravagantly. Even ex-president Herbert Hoover, in a speech to 1,000 Republican leaders, commended them as a "grand hope" for a durable peace. The audience responded with prolonged applause.[31]

There were some negative voices. One of the most powerful was Whittaker Chambers, the Communist defector who had warned the Roosevelt administration back in 1939 that Harry Dexter White, Alger Hiss, Lauchlin Currie, and many other New Dealers were Soviet spies. Chambers had become foreign editor of *Time*, where almost single-handedly he fought the correspondents who sent back optimistic reports about the Russian and Chinese communists.

Chambers's commentary on Yalta was a *Time* essay, "The Ghosts on the Roof," in which he imagined the last Romanov czar, Nicholas II, and his family, executed by the Communists in 1918, gathering on the roof of their rundown summer palace in Yalta to observe the politicians conferring inside. Their spectral

Russian hearts were gleeful, and full of admiration for Stalin. This stocky Georgian peasant was extending the Russian empire farther than any czar had ever dared to dream. He was on the brink of seizing Europe and China. Iran, Turkey, the oil fields of the Middle East would be next. No one could resist the "international social revolution," the marvelous device Stalin had perfected for "blowing up other countries from within."

The staffs of *Time* and *Life* sent a delegation to Henry Luce, trying to block the article. They called Chambers "a well poisoner." Readers bombarded *Time* with angry letters, accusing Luce of sabotaging Roosevelt's struggle for peace. *Time*'s correspondent in Moscow, John Hersey, reported that no Russian would talk to him. *Time* apologized in all directions.[32]

XIV

On February 13, the day after Yalta ended, the American and British air forces combined to produce the ultimate terror raid of the European war. One would almost think Roosevelt's comment to Stalin that he felt more bloodthirsty than a year ago had been passed on to them. Such an unlikely leak was not necessary. Armed with the presidential authority to "dehouse" Germans in the name of the Strategic Bombing Survey, General Arnold had already ordered his subordinates to cooperate with the British in morale- (a.k.a. terror-) bombing.

The USAAF had signed aboard the British proposal, Thunderclap, a joint assault on cities in Eastern Germany. Adding to everyone's enthusiasm was the belief that a demonstration of British-American air power would "add immeasurably" to FDR's strength in negotiating with the Russians at the postwar peace table.[33]

On February 3, while the Yalta conference was convening, the Americans hit Berlin in the first act of Thunderclap. Over 900

American bombers took part, killing an estimated 25,000 civilians. Almost all the bombing was done by radar, the by now standard code word for blind. In the next few days, Munich and Leipzig received the Thunderclap treatment, a combination of high explosives and incendiary bombs.

From February 13 to 15, it was Dresden's turn. This old city, rich in architecture and history, was often called "the German Florence." Bombed by two waves of British planes followed by a massive American assault, which dropped 475 tons of general bombs and 292 tons of incendiaries, Dresden was engulfed in a Hamburg-like firestorm that incinerated tens of thousands of people. No one will ever know the exact number of deaths because the city was jammed with at least 500,000 refugees who had fled eastern Germany to escape the oncoming Red Army. After much debate, an original figure of 300,000 was reduced to 60,000 dead and another 30,000 injured. More than 7,000 public buildings and 30,000 houses were destroyed. A German war correspondent who visited the ruins wrote: "A great city has been wiped from the map of Europe."[34]

When the story of Dresden's immolation appeared in Swiss and other neutral country newspapers, U.S. Army Air Force officers grew more than a little alarmed for their reputations. Various generals hastily put on the record their hitherto unmentioned opposition to the Thunderclap raids. The British reacted with considerable nastiness. One of their top RAF officers gave an interview to an AP reporter, frankly admitting both the Americans and British were aiming at killing and dehousing civilians and creating chaos in Germany. The newsman reported that "Allied air bosses" had decided to adopt "deliberate terror bombing . . . to hasten Hitler's doom."[35]

What do we say? asked a frantic information officer at USAAF headquarters. The American air chiefs huddled and decided there was only one solution: lie. They claimed the censor had erred in clearing the AP reporter's story and solemnly declared there had been no change in American bombing policy: attacks were still directed "against military objectives." General Marshall got into the act, asserting that at Yalta the Russians had asked for Dresden to be bombed. The record shows that the Russians requested raids on Berlin and Leipzig but never mentioned Dresden.

Secretary of War Henry Stimson backed up the army air forces in a Washington press conference, roundly denouncing terror-bombing. But Stimson, nobody's fool, was uneasy with the ongoing controversy over Dresden. In England, Churchill was under fierce attack in Parliament for resorting to barbarism. Stimson asked for photo-reconnaissance pictures of Dresden to prove that "our objectives were, as usual, military in character."

The request was nervously forwarded to General Arnold, who was recuperating from a heart attack in Florida. He wrote in the margin: "We must not get soft." Whether Stimson ever saw any pictures is doubtful. Dresden had no war industries worth mentioning, except a small factory that made lenses for gunsights. The secretary of war dropped the subject.[36]

XV

As Roosevelt sailed home from Yalta aboard the USS *Quincy*, cables from U.S. ambassadors in Bulgaria and Rumania began arriving at the State Department, describing how the Russians were honoring the Declaration on Liberated Europe. In Rumania, one of Josef Stalin's most ruthless followers, Andrei Vishinsky, the prosecutor at the Moscow purge trials of the late 1930s, unilaterally demanded the dismissal of the present government and the appointment of what the U.S. ambassador called "a puppet government." With the country full of Russian soldiers, Vishinsky soon got his way. Needless to say, there had been no consultation with anyone about this transition to Russian-style democracy.

In Bulgaria, local Communists, again backed by Russian troops, rounded up thousands of supposedly fascist heretics and condemned them to death before "people's courts." The American ambassador reported the Communists intended to liquidate all democratic opposition. He told of prominent Bulgarians who had read the Declaration on Liberated Europe asking him if Washington meant these bold words on behalf of freedom—or were they abandoning them to the Russians?[37]

Not a word of these reports reached the American press or people. On the contrary, the White House was hard at work maintaining the patina of triumph created by the joint communiqué the three leaders had issued at the end of the Yalta conference. Great care was devoted to the photos released to the press. White House aide Jonathan Daniels was in charge of this chore, which was not easy. Army signal photographers had taken the pictures and many of them revealed all too visibly that Roosevelt was close to death. "Some of them were appalling," Daniels later admitted.[38]

At Roosevelt's request, Sam Rosenman had boarded the *Quincy* at Algiers to work on a speech to Congress reporting on Yalta. Later, Rosenman said he was "disheartened" by the president's appearance. "He was listless and apparently uninterested in conversation—he was all burnt out." For a week, on the voyage home, the frustrated Rosenman could not get the president to work on the speech. FDR spent the day either in his cabin or staring out at the ocean. Not until February 26, when the *Quincy* was approaching the American coast, did he go over the draft Rosenman had prepared from minutes of the Yalta conference and notes supplied by Charles Bohlen.

As they worked, FDR told Rosenman he was sure Yalta had laid the foundation of a peaceful world. He felt he "understood Stalin and that Stalin understood him." He believed the Soviet leader had a "sincere desire" for peace so he could make "industrial and social changes" in Russia that would lead to true democracy. FDR's only worry was the possibility that others "back in the Kremlin" might oppose Stalin.[39]

The worshipful Rosenman did not utter a word of disagreement to this monologue. A very different scenario unfolded when Roosevelt discussed Yalta with ex–brain truster Adolf Berle soon after he returned to the White House. Roosevelt found himself confronted by someone who was no longer a true believer in FDR—and never a believer in the Russians. Berle apparently reviewed Yalta with a scathing eye. Roosevelt threw up his hands and cried: "Adolf, I didn't say the result was good. I said it was the best I could do!"[40]

XVI

On March 1, when the president appeared before a joint session of Congress, there was no trace of caution or pessimism. Instead, FDR all but announced world salvation was at hand. Yalta, he said, would spell the end of the old way nations related to each other. There would be no more unilateral action, exclusive alliances, balances of power, spheres of influence, "and all the other expedients that have been tried for centuries—and have always failed." Instead, the United Nations would admit all the nations on the globe and its machinery would create "permanent peace." If Congress and the American people did not accept this arrangement, they would have to "bear the responsibility for another world conflict."[41]

Along with a vision of a permanently peaceful future came a renewed declaration of FDR's hatred for Germany. He reiterated that at Yalta everyone had endorsed the policy of unconditional surrender. He also spelled out what the policy meant for Germany: temporary occupation by the four "great powers," the end of Nazism and the Nazi Party, the end of militarism, speedy and severe punishment for war criminals, complete disarmament, the destruction of the industries that built weapons, the permanent abolition of the German general staff and reparations in cash and goods. There was, he declared, "not room on earth for both German militarism and Christian decency." But he carefully avoided mentioning his desire to dismember Germany into "five or seven" states. American resistance to the Morgenthau Plan was still a painful political memory.[42]

The president's appearance—his gaunt face, hollowed dark-circled eyes—shocked his audience. FDR delivered the speech sitting in his wheelchair, the first time he had ever made a public appearance that acknowledged his disability. He seemed to have no strength in his right arm, and had to turn the pages of the speech with his left hand, an awkward motion. Often he slurred his words and stumbled over phrases and sentences. Several times he lost his place in the text and ad-libbed comments that to a dismayed Sam Rosenman were "wholly irrelevant." Some "bordered on the ridiculous."[43]

Nevertheless, the speech was considered a success. There was no significant opposition in Congress to sending an American delegation to a conference on the United Nations, scheduled to meet in San Francisco on April 25.

XVII

Back in the White House, cables from European embassies continued to remind the president of the gap between his wishful thinking and reality. With Harry Hopkins in the Mayo Clinic fighting off imminent death, Charles Bohlen came to the Oval Office almost daily to help the president respond to these disturbing messages. Communist rule was being clamped on Poland without even an attempt to stage-manage anything resembling a free election. The same thing was happening in Hungary, Bulgaria, Rumania, Albania, and Yugoslavia.

Even worse was the way the Russians were abusing American and British prisoners of war as the Soviet army advanced through eastern Germany. Ambassador Averell Harriman reported that they were not allowing any American officers to visit them. The men had been thrown into refugee camps with civilians. Food was minimal and sanitary facilities nonexistent. This was the Russians' way of putting pressure on the American and British military to repatriate any and all Russians who fell into their hands.

A glum Charley Bohlen was forced to admit to himself that George Kennan's pessimistic letter to him at Yalta had been "soundly based." The Soviets were showing that the Declaration on Liberated Europe "meant nothing." Their hostility to Americans, demonstrated repeatedly in the Poltava experiment, persisted. Stalin was doing "exactly as Kennan had predicted." Nevertheless, Bohlen told himself it was better in the long run that America had "stood up" for the human rights of people on the Soviet borders. That may have been true, although one wonders whether publishing brave words on liberation and human rights and doing nothing to support them should be called "standing up."

Was it better in the long run for the president of the United States to tell the American people they could and should trust Stalin and his regime? One of the bitterest legacies of the New Dealers' war was the political animosity this misjudgment bred between different groups of Americans.[44]

XVIII

In Roosevelt's congealing brain, much of this mounting evidence of Stalin's contempt for democracy probably came and went in fits and starts of painful luminosity, like cosmic flare-ups on a dying star. A good part of the time he was not in touch with reality. When General Lucius Clay visited the Oval Office in mid-March 1945 to discuss his assignment as Eisenhower's deputy in occupied Germany, the president rambled on for a half-hour about his boyhood visits to Germany and switched to urging Clay to consider building a huge TVA-type dam in Central Europe. The appalled Clay never had a chance say a word. Emerging, he said to Jimmy Byrnes, who had escorted him: "We've been talking to a dying man."

"He's been like this for a long time," Byrnes replied, revealing how much White House insiders had known about the president's health well before the run for a fourth term.[45]

Gerald Murphy, Eisenhower's chief civilian advisor and the man who had negotiated the deal with Admiral Darlan so hated by New Dealers, was summoned to Washington to confer with the president and General Clay. Since there was still no written statement of German occupation policy, Murphy was especially anxious to see Roosevelt. But he cooled his heels around Washington for days with no word from the White House.

Suddenly an urgent phone call invited him to dinner with FDR on a few hours' notice. Murphy appeared at the White House at the appointed time and was stunned by FDR's ghastly appearance. As he stared, dumbfounded, the president said: "Well it's almost over!" For a weird moment Murphy thought FDR was talking about his life.

After dinner with Anna and John Boettiger and Canadian prime minister Mackenzie King, Roosevelt invited Murphy into his study for what the diplomat hoped would be a serious discussion. But Murphy soon realized this was not going to take place. Roosevelt talked aimlessly for over an hour, again reminiscing about his boyhood trips to Germany, remembering German men's fondness for uniforms. Somehow the Germans had to be "kept out of uniform." Murphy tried several times to draw the president out on urgent matters—how the occupying powers could share Germany's natural resources; how FDR saw the future of Europe. It was hopeless. The president was "in no condition to offer balanced judgments upon the great questions of war and peace."[46]

A would-be visitor was Lieutenant Commander George Earle, who was still tormented by the information he had gathered on the Katyn Massacre. He was also bitter because Roosevelt had refused to transfer him to Germany, where he hoped to organize anti-Communist opposition. Instead, Roosevelt had ordered him placed on the retired list, in effect ousting him from the navy. On March 21, Earle, giving up on reaching Roosevelt directly, wrote an angry letter to Anna Roosevelt Boettiger, whom he knew well, announcing his intention to write an article, revealing the truth about Katyn and the Soviets' murderous repression in the Balkans.

He was being "forced out of the picture," Earle wrote. "Because I told your father the truth about conditions in Russia and countries occupied by Russia." But before he departed, he was determined to tell the American people that "Russia today is a far greater menace than Germany ever was." Twenty-five years after the Revolution, Russia was "exactly the same Red Terror it was then." Americans needed to know of the "15 million people in concentration camps, of [the] treatment of the Jews and of labor." He had learned the truth from interrogating hundreds of refugees from Soviet terror. He could name numerous courageous Bulgarian "democrats" who had fought the Nazis and were now being sentenced to long prison terms. But no matter now "hurt" he was "because your father resents the fact that I told him the truth," he would remain silent if Roosevelt insisted. "I shall never do anything to hurt or embarrass him as long as we both live."[47]

Earle said he would wait a week. If he heard nothing, he would begin talking to the press. On March 24, Roosevelt wrote to

"Dear George," saying: "I have noted with concern your plan to publish your unfavorable opinion of one of our allies at the very time when such a publication from a former emissary of mine might do irreparable harm to our war effort. . . . I not only do not wish it, but I specifically forbid you to publish any information or opinion about an ally that you may have acquired while in . . . the service of the United States Navy."[48]

Roosevelt added that since Earle evinced an interest in "continued active service," he would "direct the Navy Department to continue your employment wherever they can make use of your services." But FDR was withdrawing "any previous understanding that you are serving as an emissary of mine." A few weeks later, Earle was transferred to Samoa, where he stayed until the war ended. When Earle returned to the United States, his embarrassed superiors in the navy apologized to him, explaining they had sent him to the South Seas at the express order of the president.[49]

XIX

In Europe, continued German resistance prompted First Army censors to pass a story by American war correspondent John Thompson. He reported a study of 130 German prisoners—officers, noncommissioned officers, and privates—seeking to answer the question: Why do they still fight?

More than one hundred of these men considered the war lost beyond all hope. Only ten clung to faith in a miracle. Most of those questioned asserted that the German army was still fighting because "terror bombings" and statements by Lord Robert Vansittart, Secretary of the Treasury Morgenthau, and other spokesmen only served to deepen in the average German the feeling that "he will be hopelessly caught in the same trap that threatens Nazi criminals." For the soldier at the front, the battle has become "a fight of despair," with no future but "deportation to Siberia, mass sterilization and eternal slave labor. And so he continues firing his gun until he is hit." The U.S. Army was still waging an underground war against the folly of unconditional surrender.[50]

Postwar testimony by German generals revealed a similar state of mind in the high command. British military writer B. H. Liddell Hart interviewed over a dozen generals for a book. "Throughout the last nine months of the war, they spent much of their time discussing ways and means of getting in touch with the Allies to arrange a surrender," Liddell Hart concluded. "All . . . dwelt on the effect of the Allies 'unconditional surrender' policy in prolonging the war."[51]

XX

Among the other men who wanted to see Roosevelt during the month of March 1945 was Vice President Harry S. Truman. He reached the Oval Office exactly twice, and each time the president rambled and said nothing about any important political issue. Truman saw the same dying man that others saw, but he desperately tried to convince himself that the exhausting journey to Yalta and back was the reason for FDR's desuetude. At home, Truman talked over his dilemma with his astute wife, who had been his closest advisor throughout his political career.

Since the president's two-faced treatment of her husband in his 1940 race for reelection to the Senate, Bess Truman was not a Roosevelt admirer. She thought there might well be some malice in FDR's distant manner. She could not help comparing it to the way the president had handed out responsible jobs to his former vice president, Henry Wallace, and regularly had lunch with him in the White House.

Exactly what Vice President Truman thought about the situation is hard to assess. His daughter Margaret, looking back, is convinced that her father simply tried to put the worst version of the future out of his mind for the time being. He knew the president was "a very weary man." But Truman complained off the record to at least one reporter that he felt cut off from the entire Roosevelt administration.[52]

This sense of distance between the two men worked both ways. After the president's Yalta speech, some friendly reporters asked Truman what he thought of it. "One of the greatest ever given," the vice president said—and joined the reporters in sarcastic laughter. Henry Wallace, determined to keep FDR on a pedestal as the New Deal's hero, would never have said such a thing, although he might have confided it to his diary.[53]

Truman was also deeply concerned about Roosevelt's deteriorating relationship with Congress. The brawl over making Wallace secretary of commerce was only the most notorious example of the seething hostility with which the southern conservative-Republican majority regarded FDR. Not long after the Senate eviscerated Wallace, the solons rejected veteran New Dealer and Eleanor Roosevelt favorite Aubrey Williams for rural electrification administrator, a minor post at best. Congress had already gutted the agency's budget.

Another attempt to pass a compulsory manpower bill, giving the government power to force workers to fill jobs in war plants and otherwise "work or fight" was buried in a 46–29 Senate vote. On April 10, the Senate deadlocked 39–39 on an amendment to the Lend-Lease Act, terminating it as soon as the war ended. The vice president rescued the president from humiliation with a curt: "The Chair votes No."[54]

XXI

While the New Dealers dwindled into impotence in Washington, the United States was demonstrating the awesome power of the war machine that the dollar-a-year big businessmen and their army and navy partners had created with the encouragement of Dr. Win-the-War. As the year 1945 began the immense Third Fleet under the command of Admiral "Bull" Halsey dominated the waters of the Pacific. By the time Douglas MacArthur led his troops ashore on Luzon on January 7, 1945, to begin the recapture of the Philippines, Halsey had annihilated what was left of the Japanese fleet in the battle of Leyte Gulf.

The war was rapidly becoming a hopeless mismatch for the Japanese. One historian has calculated that every American soldier and sailor in the Pacific was backed by four tons of equipment, ammunition, and supplies. His Japanese opposite number was relying on two pounds. There was scarcely a single Japanese code, naval or diplomatic, that the U.S. cryptographers had not broken, enabling the Americans to know Tokyo's strategy in advance, obviously an incalculable advantage in war.[55]

Yet the Japanese remained lethal foes on the battlefield. Their readiness to die rather than surrender was typified by the appearance of the kamikazes, suicide pilots who dove their bomb-laden planes into American ships, creating fearful havoc. Japanese foot soldiers inflicted heavy casualties on marines and army infantry in death-before-dishonor stands on islands such as Iwo Jima, adding to the steep rise in American dead and wounded in the first months of 1945.

This intransigence inspired American airmen to launch a war of terror from the skies, aimed at proving General Douhet was right, even if his doctrine had failed to bring Germany to her knees. The weapon of choice was a new plane, the B-29. Roosevelt had backed General Henry H. Arnold's desire to develop this machine, which had cost $3 billion to develop—more than the price of the atomic bomb. Three stories high, with a wing span of 141 feet, the plane's immense range and load capacity had only one purpose: to cross the Pacific's vast distances and bomb Japan.

American experience with incendiary bombs in Europe had convinced the army air forces generals that Japan's cities, mostly wood and paper houses, were uniquely vulnerable to this device. On March 9, 1945, 172 B-29s took off from American air bases on Guam and nearby islands and headed for Tokyo. Their commander, General Curtis LeMay, told the airmen their mission was terrible but simple: "to shorten the war." LeMay had stripped the big planes of most of their defending machine guns to add to their bomb loads. They had orders to attack at extremely low altitudes, something the Americans never tried against Germany's tough air defenses. Comparatively speaking, Japan's air defense system was nonexistent.

XXII

Tokyo, a city of 5 million, had only 8,100 professional fire fighters. The Japanese expected civilians in the various parts of the city to put out most fires with bags of sand, brooms, and hand pumps. The city also had very few air-raid shelters. The Japanese leaders wanted the civilians to remain in their neighborhoods and do their duty as defenders of the empire. All of them—middle-aged and old men, women and teenage girls—had taken an "air defense oath" that bound them to "refrain from selfish conduct," i.e., running away.

Bombing at altitudes as low as 4,900 feet, the B-29s dropped 1,165 tons of incendiary bombs on an area in which the population density was 135,000 per square mile. Soon a stupendous conflagration—a literal sea of fire—was raging. Rising currents of superheated air almost flung some of the bombers out of control. General Thomas Powers, whose plane flew back and forth over the conflagration throughout the raid, tried to tell himself there was "no room for emotions in war." But he realized he was seeing something so awful, he would remember it for the rest of his life.

On the ground the firestorm devoured everything in its path. The neighborhood fire-fighting associations fled in terror. Most of them did not get very far. Men and women literally caught fire and burned like sticks of wood. Women carrying infants on their backs suddenly realized their babies were on fire. People who retreated to small shelters under houses were roasted alive. Those who took refuge in brick schools and theaters suffered a similar fate.

Others who leaped into canals or lakes were boiled to death in the superheated water. In the few deeper shelters, people died en masse of carbon monoxide poisoning when the firestorm consumed the oxygen in the air. The conflagration soon destroyed most of the Tokyo Fire Department's engines and hose, and organized resistance to the flames collapsed.

After the last B-29s departed at 3:45 A.M., Tokyo burned for another thirteen hours. Streets became carpeted with charred bodies. Rivers grew choked with corpses. Thousands fled into icy Tokyo Bay and died of hypothermia. The fire was kept alive by a diabolical wind that rose in intensity throughout the day.

The United States Strategic Bombing Survey later estimated that 87,793 Japanese died, 40,918 were injured, and 1,008,005 were dehoused. The specificity of the figures stirs instant skepticism. No one, including the Japanese, knows how many people died. In the days following the raid the authorities collected 69,164 charred mostly unidentifiable corpses. Only 64 were claimed by families and buried privately. The rest were interred in mass graves. General Powers later called the raid "the greatest single disaster incurred by any enemy in military history. . . . There were more casualties than in any other military action in the history of the world."

The B-29s lost only two planes to antiaircraft fire. When they returned to Guam and the other airfields in the Mariannas, General Curtis LeMay showed them a wire from General Arnold. "Congratulations. This mission shows your crews have got the guts for anything."

Not a word was spoken in England or America against this escalation of terror-bombing. The Office of War Information had taken care of this problem in advance. Early in 1944, OWI chief Elmer Davis had told the War Information Board, which played an advisory role in the government's manipulation of the news, that there was another reason for revealing Japanese atrocities such as the Bataan Death March, beyond intensifying support for the war. The goal was to "nullify any voices that might be raised here if we should undertake bombing of Japanese cities."[56]

XXIII

On March 29, the president fled the White House to the isolation of Warm Springs. He would let others deal with contentious telegrams from Stalin and Churchill. He would sign them but the words were written by Charles Bohlen. He would let a discouraged Senator Alben Barkley and a frustrated Vice President Harry Truman grapple with the hostile Congress. As FDR departed, a grieving William Hassett told Dr. Bruenn: "He is slipping away from us."

In Europe, the war was boiling to a climax. Combining luck and dash, the Americans finally crossed the Rhine on March 7, 1945, by seizing the Ludendorff Bridge near the town of Remagen. Thereafter, the German army's collapse accelerated as utter hopelessness overwhelmed the ranks. Armored columns trapped 400,000 Germans in the Ruhr pocket while tank-led task forces raced east and south. The Ninth Army, under blunt-talking General William Simpson, began a dash to the Elbe, the last natural barrier between the Americans and Berlin.

In Germany, the remaining survivors of the resistance to Hitler, including Admiral Wilhelm Canaris and his Abwehr second in command, General Hans Oster, were moved to the Flossenburg concentration camp in Bavaria. Heinrich Mueller, the head of the Gestapo, was determined to make sure the rampaging Americans would not rescue them. On April 9, with American tanks less than fifty miles away, they were taken from their cells, stripped naked, and hanged.

Shortly before he died, Canaris tapped out a farewell message to a Danish secret agent in the next cell. "I die for my country and with a clear conscience." An SS witness to his execution sneered: "The little Admiral took a very long time—he was jerked up and down once or twice." But a doctor who watched the grisly event said: "Admiral Canaris died a staunch and manly death."[57]

XXIV

On April 11 an American armored task force of the Third Army captured the village of Ohrdruf. Outside it was a complex of buildings surrounded by a barbed wire fence. Inside Americans gaped in disbelief at the ragged skeletons that stumbled toward them. In the buildings bodies of those who had starved to death were stacked like cordwood. The outside world had discovered the first German concentration camp. On the same day other units of the Third Army reached Buchenwald, and tankers of the Ninth Army discovered Nordhausen. The next day an appalled Eisenhower visited Ohrdruf and ordered every American unit within traveling distance to be taken to see the horror. As he left the camp he turned to a sentry and said: "Still having trouble hating them?"[58]

This startling question sums up in five words the New Dealers' failure to turn the war against Germany into a hate-filled cru-

sade. No one knew better than Eisenhower this central but seldom mentioned problem in the minds and hearts of his men, as
he demonstrated in his repeated attempts to repeal the policy of
unconditional surrender. Germany had not attacked the United
States and most Americans never found a good reason to fight
her soldiers to the death.

XXV

On April 11, in Warm Springs, Roosevelt received a visit from
Henry Morgenthau Jr. He was on his way to Florida to see his
ailing wife. Like so many others in recent months, the secretary
of the treasury was "terrifically shocked" when he saw FDR—
further evidence of the president's accelerating deterioration from
a man who saw him regularly in the White House. At dinner
Roosevelt seemed in a daze, barely listening to the conversation.
During cocktails, he could not seem to remember many things
and he was "constantly confusing names." His hands shook so
badly he "started to knock the glasses over" and Morgenthau
had to hold each glass while FDR poured cocktails.

After dinner, Morgenthau started talking about the postwar
treatment of Germany, which still obsessed him. He again denounced Robert Murphy as an appeaser and Nazi collabora-
tionist and urged the president to "break the State Department
crowd" once and for all. Instead of Murphy as Eisenhower's political advisor, the secretary urged Roosevelt to appoint Claude
Bowers, author of a book on Thomas Jefferson and Alexander
Hamilton, which made the man from Monticello the hero and
the New York financial genius the villain of the early Republic.
Bowers was currently in the State Department's approximation of
outer darkness, serving as ambassador to Chile.

FDR said appointing Bowers was a wonderful idea. In 1925 he
had given the diplomat's book a glowing review in the *New York*

Times.[59] A delighted Morgenthau persuaded FDR to write down Bowers's name, so he wouldn't forget it. The secretary launched into an impassioned plea for his punitive solution to Germany's future. "Mr. President, I am going to fight hard [for] this," Morgenthau said. He was so overwrought, he repeated this statement two or three times.

"Henry," Roosevelt said. "I am with you a hundred percent."[60]

There is little doubt that the news of Ohrdruf, Nordhausen, and Buchenwald would have given Morgenthau and Roosevelt the ammunition they needed to demolish Secretary of War Henry Stimson and other foes of the Morgenthau Plan. Germany would have been dismembered, its industries destroyed, its people reduced to the desperate poverty in which another creed that preaches radical hatred, communism, would have flourished. The future of Europe, and the world, hung in the balance for twenty-four hours, while proof of Nazism's ruthlessness began circulating on the radio and in the newspapers. But history, that seemingly blind force, decreed that the New Dealers would lose this final round in their spasmodic struggle to control the ideology of the war.

XXVI

On April 12, FDR awoke complaining of a headache. In the pouch of correspondence from the White House was a cable from Winston Churchill, asking Roosevelt what he should tell the House of Commons about the Soviet seizure of Poland. FDR replied that he would "minimize the general Soviet problem as much as possible because these problems, in one form or another, seem to arise every day and most of them straighten out. . . . We must be firm, however, and our course thus far is correct." Ignoring what had already happened in Hungary, Rumania, and Bulgaria, Roosevelt was still clinging to his illusion that Stalin could be charmed into liberal democracy.[61]

Later in the morning, the president sat for a portrait while he went through a batch of letters William Hassett had prepared for his signature. The painter was surprised to notice that FDR's gray pallor had disappeared. His skin had the ruddy glow of seeming health. Not long after Hassett left with the signed letters, FDR's right hand jerked to his head several times in an almost convulsive manner. "I have a terrific headache," he said. He slumped forward in the armchair and the portrait painter frantically called for help.

The president's valet and another servant carried Roosevelt into his bedroom and summoned Dr. Howard Bruenn. The heart specialist found FDR unconscious, his pupils dilated, his neck rigid—symptoms of a massive brain hemorrhage. The ruddy skin color had been another sign of oncoming arterial collapse. Three hours later, the big lie about FDR's health that the Democrats had told the American people in the 1944 election was exposed to a dismayed nation. Eighty-two days after he began his fourth term, President Franklin D. Roosevelt died.[62]

A New President
and an Old Policy

At 4:35 P.M. the news of the president's death was flashed to the White House, triggering a frantic search for Vice President Harry S. Truman. He was in the Capitol, having a postadjournment drink with Speaker of the House Sam Rayburn. A telephone call from Press Secretary Steve Early brought him to the White House. When Truman arrived, a somber Eleanor Roosevelt greeted him with the momentous words, "Harry, the president is dead."

A staggered Truman asked if there was anything he could do for her.

"Is there anything we can do for you?" Mrs. Roosevelt asked. "You are the one in trouble now."[1]

Not long after Bess Truman heard the news, she said to one of her husband's close friends: "This is going to put a terrific load on Harry. Roosevelt has told him nothing."[2]

At the time, these words were interpreted as evidence of Mrs. Truman's fear of her husband's ability to handle the presidency. In fact, they were a criticism of the distant, subtly contemptuous way Franklin D. Roosevelt had dealt with Harry Truman since he won the nomination as vice president.

After the new president took the oath of office, he held his first cabinet meeting. Truman told the shaken official family that he intended to pursue FDR's domestic and international goals. At the same time, he intended to be "president in my own right." Later in the evening he made this very clear with a telephone call to Mexico City, where his old friend John Snyder was attending a banking conference. The president told Snyder he wanted him to become federal loan administrator, the post Congress had recently created to prevent Henry Wallace from lending billions to the liberals of his choice.

Was Truman aware that he was sending a signal to the New Dealers that their reign was over? If so, he did not let it worry him. He wanted a man he could trust in this potentially explosive job. Snyder was more than qualified. As head of the Defense Plant Corporation in Jesse Jones's financial empire, the ex-banker had spent $11 billion to build the factories that created the American war machine. A few days later, Truman telephoned Jesse Jones to tell him Snyder was taking charge. This was not mere courtesy. Truman wanted Jones's numerous Capitol Hill friends on his side in future dealings with Congress. He knew they—and Jesse—would be pleased that a Jones man was getting this much-disputed job.[3]

At the same time, Truman was careful not to affront the party's liberal wing. When FDR's body arrived in Washington, he invited Henry Wallace to ride with him to Union Station to meet the funeral train. He also invited Jimmy Byrnes, the former assistant president, with whom Truman had already conferred about Yalta and many other matters. In the limousine, Byrnes and Wallace, like a sotto voce Greek chorus, began discussing FDR's political mistakes. They agreed that his worst blunder was his attempt to purge the Democrats who had not supported his Supreme Court–packing plan. That act of hubris unraveled the fragile consensus holding the New Dealers and the rest of the Democratic Party together.[4]

Back in the White House, the new president received a message from Winston Churchill, asking his opinion of the War Weary Bomber project, the USAAF plan to launch pilotless planes loaded with explosives against German cities. General Arnold had persuaded Roosevelt to write to the prime minister, urging him to support the idea. Churchill had done so with great reluctance. Now, shaken by the uproar over the incineration of Dresden, the prime minister wondered if such a terror weapon was necessary. President Truman replied that he wanted no part of it. He asked Churchill to make sure the project was postponed indefinitely.[5]

II

FDR's death swept away the rancor and hostility that was engulfing his fourth term. An inspired bureaucrat put his name at the head of the casualty lists the following day. The millions of Americans who regarded him as a father—even a savior—figure for his leadership in the dark days of the Great Depression mourned him in private and in public. After the burial service at Hyde Park, President Truman returned to Washington and addressed a joint session of Congress. He reiterated his intention to pursue Roosevelt's goals in the war and the postwar peace. He was interrupted by applause no less than forty times.

When the new president stated his support for unconditional surrender, the legislators leaped to their feet and gave him a standing ovation. As the war had dragged on and casualty lists grew, bitterness had seeped into the American soul. Unconditional surrender had now become enormously popular with Congress and the American people. Polls gave it an approval rating of 90 percent.

Toward the Japanese, the bitterness had become even more tinged with hatred. As Truman spoke, American marines and army infantrymen were encountering fierce resistance in the struggle for Okinawa, the sixty-mile-long island south of Japan. Japanese soldiers fought to the death while kamikaze planes ravaged the 1,000 ship American fleet offshore.[6]

Japan was only one of a staggering array of problems facing the new president. Averell Harriman flew from Moscow to tell him about the deteriorating relationship with Soviet Russia. The State Department sent Truman a stream of reports from East European ambassadors about what the Russians were doing in Hungary, Rumania, Bulgaria, and, above all, Poland. For State's professionals, the change in leadership was electrifying. Assistant Secretary of State James Dunn recalled showing Roosevelt a proposed telegram about Poland, the last time he saw him alive: "He was seeing the paper but not reading it . . . picking out something to show he was alert. He was in no shape to do anything."[7]

Now there was a man in the Oval Office with the energy and concentration to absorb information. Truman worked a twelve-hour-day, pausing only for lunch and a nap. Under Secretary Joseph Grew expressed his delight after one early meeting. "I had fourteen problems to take up with him and got through them in less than fifteen minutes with a clear directive on each of them," he said.[8]

One of Truman's early conclusions from reading the flow of reports from Eastern Europe was: "Stalin is not keeping his bargain." When Soviet foreign minister Vyacheslav Molotov arrived in Washington, D.C., on his way to the April 25 San Francisco conference on the United Nations, he called on the president. Charles Bohlen was on hand as interpreter. In his usual peremptory manner, Molotov wanted to know if Truman was going to honor the agreement Roosevelt had made with Stalin about Russian entry into the war against Japan, giving Moscow control of Manchuria's railroads and access to north China ports. Truman assured him he would keep FDR's promises, and then added that the United States was "getting tired" of waiting for the Soviet Union to implement the principles of the Declaration on Liberated Europe in Poland and the other countries occupied by the Red Army.

Molotov interrupted him to bluster that many Poles were profascists who were sabotaging the Red Army's supply lines. "I'm not interested in propaganda," Truman said, and ordered the foreign minister to tell Stalin that he was concerned about the situation in Eastern Europe. Friendship required both countries to live up to their obligations. It could not be maintained on the basis of "a one way street."

Molotov turned "a little ashy," Bohlen later recalled, and huffed: "I have never been talked to like that in my life."

"Carry out your agreements and you won't get talked to like that," Truman said.

When Molotov tried to get the conversation back to the Far East, Truman said: "That will be all, Mr. Molotov."

Charles Bohlen never forgot how much he enjoyed translating Truman's sentences. "They were probably the first sharp words uttered during the war by an American president to a high Soviet official," he said. Freed of the constraints Hopkins and other New Dealers had woven around him, Bohlen was amazed and delighted to find a president who was ready to hear the truth about the Soviet Union—and do something about it. Loy Henderson, recently returned from exile in Iraq, said "morale began to soar" in the State Department when others heard the news.[9]

III

At the same time, Truman's political antennae told him he could not say in public what he had told Molotov in private. The optimism about Soviet Russia that Roosevelt had created in many Americans was too potent to disturb, especially while the war was still raging. The Russians, well aware of this protective cover, ignored the new president's warning and became even more outrageous.

The Soviets invited sixteen leaders of the Polish underground to Moscow to discuss the formation of an interim government in Warsaw. The moment the Poles emerged from hiding, they disappeared. At the United Nations conference in San Francisco, Secretary of State Stettinius asked Vyacheslav Molotov about the missing men. Without even a hint of an apology, Molotov said: "They have all been arrested by the Red Army." Whereupon he turned away to greet another diplomat. "Stettinius was left standing there with a fixed smile on his face," recalled Charles Bohlen, who witnessed this calculated insult.[10]

An appalled Averell Harriman decided it was time to get newsmen in touch with reality about the Soviets. He invited a number of prominent journalists and radio broadcasters to a series of off-the-record talks about what was happening in Poland and elsewhere. Harriman bluntly told them that "our objectives and the Kremlin's objectives were irreconcilable. They wanted to communize the world, and we wanted a free world." It was time to recognize this fact before trying to work out some sort of compromise that would enable us to "live in peace on this small planet."

Two columnists, Walter Lippmann and broadcaster Raymond Gram Swing, were so shocked they stormed out of the meeting. Several newsmen, including Swing, violated the off-the-record agreement and attacked Harriman as something close to a traitor. Swing echoed the Harry Hopkins–Henry Wallace line that any diplomat hostile to Moscow should be kicked out of the State Department. A few years later, Wallace told an interviewer this talk by Harriman "decisively changed" American relations with Soviet Russia.[11]

IV

While the statesmen dickered at San Francisco, the war in Europe hurtled to an end at a speed that exceeded everyone's expectations. After a final attempt by Heinrich Himmler, Hitler's SS chief, to arrange a surrender with the West, which Truman and Churchill quickly rejected, the German army collapsed, Adolf Hitler committed suicide in his Berlin bunker, and unconditional surrender became a fait accompli on all fronts. On May 7 it was ratified by the signature of Colonel General Alfred Jodl, Hitler's chief of staff, on a formal surrender document.[12]

Perhaps the most significant eyewitness account of VE day came not from reporters describing joyous celebrations in Paris, London, and New York, but from George Kennan in Moscow. When the news reached the Soviet capital on May 9, Kennan, the ranking officer in the American embassy, ordered the American flag displayed. The sight of Old Glory soon attracted a crowd that rapidly swelled to gigantic proportions, filling the huge square in front of the building. American diplomatic personnel came out on the balconies of the embassy and waved in response. The crowd's excitement grew when Kennan hung a Soviet flag beside the Stars and Stripes.

Accompanied by a marine sergeant, Kennan went downstairs and mounted the pedestal of a column in front of the building to say a few words. "Congratulations on the day of victory. All honor to our Soviet allies," he shouted in Russian. The crowd roared its appreciation and hoisted a young Russian soldier aloft and passed him over their heads until he was at the foot of the pedestal. He climbed up and kissed the marine sergeant and dragged him into the crowd. The sergeant did not return until the next day, no doubt somewhat the worse for wear after a night of partying, Russian style.

All day and into the evening the crowd remained in front of the building, cheering the Americans. It was totally spontaneous, and the Soviet regime did not like it at all. Again and again police tried to get the crowd to move along. They were ignored. Officials set up a bandstand on the other side of the square to lure the cheerers away. The music was also ignored. For two decades, Kennan mused, the Soviets had heaped slanders and abuse on America as a "bourgeois power." This outburst of warmth, friendliness, enthusiasm from the hearts of the Russian people disturbed the Communists enormously—and saddened Kennan.

That night, Kennan told a journalist friend he felt deeply sympathetic to the Russian people, who had suffered so much. They were hoping for better times but he did not think they were going to see them under the Soviet regime. The friend, a former *New York Times* correspondent named Ralph Parker, had a Russian wife. Later he defected to the Communist side and published a book about V-E Day in Moscow. In his account, there was no crowd in front of the American Embassy, there were no flags, no Americans on balconies, no speech by Kennan. Instead, Kennan was pictured lurking behind drawn curtains, glaring out at the crowd, muttering: "They think the war has ended. But it is really only beginning."[13]

V

The abrupt end of the war in Europe intensified the already prickly relationship between President Truman and the New Dealers. Truman adopted a Roosevelt tactic, and seemingly agreed with everything they said at first. Henry Wallace, no friend of the new president, sourly informed his diary: "It almost seemed as though he was eager to decide in advance of thinking." Wallace recorded Anna Boettiger's fear that Truman was failing to follow her father's example in keeping relations with Russia "on a constructive and stable basis." After talking with Cordell Hull, Wallace gleefully concluded: "It is obvious that [he] feels Truman is pretty ignorant of foreign affairs."

Mrs. Roosevelt continued to give the new secretary of commerce the illusion that he was liberalism's only hope. She told him that New York's liberals, who had been gravely disturbed by FDR's dismissal of Dr. New Deal, were waiting for him to give them "the word," presumably to launch an attack on Truman.[14]

The new president seemingly tolerated downright rudeness from Harold Ickes. When the secretary of the interior did not get a prompt reply to a letter about a timetable for granting independence to the Philippines, he followed it up with a peremptory note demanding an answer. Truman invited the self-styled Old Curmudgeon to the Oval Office and told him he was "perfectly free to come over here at any time and call me any kind of an S.O.B. you want to."[15]

Henry Morgenthau did his utmost to poison Truman's mind against the professionals in the State Department. In one of his early visits, the secretary of the treasury launched into his by now all-but-patented attack on Robert Murphy as a Catholic and Nazi appeaser and urged his replacement with Claude Bowers. Truman said he thought that was a "wonderful" idea. But Bowers stayed in Chile. Morgenthau told him General Lucius Clay was a fascist and Truman assured him he knew all about General Clay. But the general remained the man in charge of defeated Germany when the Third Reich surrendered.[16]

The secretary of the treasury gradually realized the Morgenthau Plan for Germany was dead on arrival in Harry Truman's Oval Office. The new president gave Morgenthau a fair hearing.

In spite of the immense pressures on him from all quarters, Truman read several chapters of the book Morgenthau was proposing to publish to promote the plan, and told him he did not want it to see the light of day. By that time, Truman knew he would soon have to deal with Stalin face-to-face at another summit conference, and he did not want to go there with one of his cabinet officers publicly backing an approach to Germany the president did not endorse.[17]

Morgenthau seemed to have an almost compulsive need to give advice to the new president. On the funeral train returning from Hyde Park, he had told Robert Hannegan to tell Truman not to appoint Jimmy Byrnes secretary of state. Morgenthau hated Byrnes almost as much as he hated Robert Murphy, supposedly because Byrnes could not "play on anyone's team." This antagonism went back to Byrnes's dislike of Morgenthau's habit of interfering in many matters outside the purview of the Treasury Department, relying on the weight of his long friendship with FDR to get his way.

On June 1, Morgenthau issued the same anti-Byrnes warning to Truman directly and proposed liberal Senator Harley Kilgore of West Virginia as secretary of state. This intrusiveness, which implied that he did not think Truman knew what he was doing, may have led the new president to a rude conclusion he later stated to aide Jonathan Daniels: "Morgenthau did not know shit from apple butter."[18]

When Morgenthau expressed a desire to go to France to open a Paris exhibit on war bonds, Truman said no. He was obviously determined to bar Morgenthau from further dabbling in foreign policy. A few days later, Truman announced Jimmy Byrnes was his new secretary of state and the secretary of the treasury knew his days in the cabinet were numbered. The final blow was the discovery that Truman was not taking him to the upcoming summit conference in Potsdam, Germany.

The secretary tried a power play. On July 5, he went to the White House and told Truman if he was not invited to Potsdam, he would resign. Truman told him to go ahead, he had been thinking of getting a new secretary of the treasury anyway. Moreover, he was bringing Secretary of War Henry Stimson, the chief foe of the Morgenthau Plan, to Potsdam.[19]

VI

At the same time, Truman demonstrated he was no reactionary. He kept Sam Rosenman, a quintessential New Dealer, in his White House circle, characterizing him as "a loyal Roosevelt man and an equally loyal Truman man." He strove to maintain a good relationship with Eleanor Roosevelt, keeping her in the political loop with a stream of informative letters and eventually convincing her that he deserved her support.[20]

Soon after Truman took office, David Lilienthal, the chairman of the Tennessee Valley Authority, faced a Senate fight for another term. Jimmy Byrnes had told Roosevelt back in November to begin looking for a replacement. Lilienthal had a powerful enemy in the Senate, Tennessee's senior senator, crusty Kenneth McKellar. When the TVA chairman visited the new president, he was amazed to discover Truman not only had every intention of reappointing him, but he had no worries about Senator McKellar.

There was no moaning about what a "rap" the president was facing for his support. McKellar ranted and raved against Lilienthal but in the final count the senator was able to muster only two votes. Truman demonstrated how many friends he had in the U.S. Senate—and how deftly he could handle them in a tough fight.[21]

Truman also staunchly opposed an attempt by the conservative coalition in the House of Representatives to abolish the Fair Employment Practices Committee by canceling its annual appropriation. After creating it in 1941 to quiet black resentment of their second-class-citizen status, FDR had paid little or no attention to the committee during the war. Responding to a plea from Walter White, head of the NAACP, the new president wrote a forthright letter to the chairman of the House Rules Committee, telling him that abandoning the FEPC was "unthinkable." Instead, Truman wanted to change the committee's status from a temporary wartime measure to a permanent government agency. This tough stand soon persuaded the House to work out a compromise with the Senate, keeping the FEPC in business.[22]

Truman did not oppose most liberal goals, but he was wary of liberals as a pressure group. With their numerous supporters in the media, and the knowledge that they had opposed him vehemently in Chicago, he regarded them as a potential threat to his presidency. He considered himself a liberal, although he preferred "forward-looking Democrat." He intensely disliked "professional liberals," people who put their ideology at the forefront of their relationships and were ready to attack anyone who did not measure up to their lofty ideals.[23]

VII

In the sixth week of his presidency, Harry S. Truman sent another signal that the New Deal was out of fashion in his White House. On May 24, 1945, the president wrote a letter to ex-president Herbert Hoover. "If you should be in Washington, I would be most happy to talk over the European food situation with you. Also, it would be a pleasure for me to become acquainted with you." It was a letter Franklin D. Roosevelt would never have written.

Truman knew exactly what he was doing. As his daughter Margaret later recalled, "he was resolved to right a wrong that history—and the publicity mavens of the Democratic Party—had done to Mr. Hoover. He also thought the country needed Hoover's talents as a thinker and manager of great humanitarian enterprises."[24]

Years later, a grateful Hoover would write to Truman: "Yours has been a friendship that reached deeper into my life than you know. . . . When you came to the White House, within a month you opened the door to me to the only profession I know, public service, and you undid some disgraceful actions that had taken place in prior years."

Ex-presidents are a small, extremely select group. They think about the country in ways that differ from ordinary citizens. Truman sought Hoover's advice, not only on how to feed war-devastated Europe, but on how to deal with a reeling Japan. The cornerstone of Hoover's advice on Japan was: abandon unconditional surrender. The Japanese knew they were beaten and were ready to admit it. An invasion was unnecessary and would cost between 500,000 and 1,000,000 American lives.[25]

VIII

Harry Hopkins, in Truman's opinion, was an "advanced" liberal but he was not a professional one. The two men had enjoyed a cordial relationship when Hopkins headed the WPA. These were among several reasons why Truman chose him as a special envoy to Stalin, to see if the damage inflicted on the alliance by the Communists' destruction of freedom in Poland and other East European countries could be repaired. Although his health was extremely precarious, Hopkins undertook the exhausting journey to Moscow to see if he could salvage the policy of trust and forbearance that he and Franklin D. Roosevelt had launched. He took Charles Bohlen with him as interpreter; Averell Harriman returned to the Soviet capital at the same time and joined in the talks with Stalin.

For ten days Stalin and Molotov met with the three Americans for sessions that lasted as long as four hours. Stalin's manner was conciliatory most of the time. He listened politely as Hopkins warned him that the Soviets' actions and policies were alienating Americans' positive attitude toward Russia, which Roosevelt had worked so hard to create. Stalin followed the negotiating style he had initiated at Yalta. "Outwardly agreeable, he would not yield an inch," was the way Charles Bohlen described it.

Bohlen's skill in Russian picked up some slips in Stalin's performance that revealed his Bolshevik point of view. Hopkins asked if he was ready to honor the Yalta agreement on entering the war against Japan. "The Soviet Union always honors its word," Stalin replied, and then muttered in an undertone, "except in cases of extreme necessity." The Soviet interpreter omitted this phrase— until Bohlen told him to include it.

In the midst of this deadlock, word arrived from the San Francisco conference on the United Nations that the Russians were insisting the veto given to the Great Powers at Yalta extended not only to substantive decisions but also to the subjects that could be discussed in the security council. The conference was teetering toward collapse unless Stalin altered this position, which had been asserted by Molotov. Responding to Hopkins's appeal, the Russian leader reaffirmed the original agreement and the UN was rescued from premature dissolution.

Except for resolving this clash, which never should have occurred, Hopkins's visit to Moscow changed nothing, although the newspaper stories suggested it had repaired the alliance. "All the evidence indicated there was no possibility of a just solution," Bohlen concluded. Stalin was only willing to grant four or five out of twenty positions in Poland's provisional government to noncommunists. There would be no "democratic freedoms" permitted for fascists, a term the Communists used to describe anyone who disagreed with them. As for the sixteen arrested Polish underground leaders, Stalin insisted they were all criminals, and they soon received harsh prison sentences. Only six survived the gulag, and they were rearrested as soon as they returned to Poland.[26]

In the midst of these fruitless talks, Harry Hopkins asked George Kennan to visit him to discuss Stalin's terms on Poland. It was an encounter freighted with symbolic power. The dying Hopkins, the ultimate New Dealer, was seeking advice from the leader of the State Department's cadre of trained Russian experts, whom he and FDR had contemptuously ignored, slandered, and even purged at the behest of the Soviets.

Hopkins asked Kennan if he thought there was any hope of improving Stalin's terms on Poland. Kennan said no.

Did Kennan think the United States should accept the terms and come to an agreement? Kennan again said no. He thought "we should accept no share of the responsibility for what the Russians proposed to do in Poland."

"Then you think it's just sin," Hopkins said. "And we should be agin it."

"That's just about right," Kennan said.

"I respect your opinion," Hopkins said sadly. "But I am not at liberty to accept it."[27]

On the long flight back to Washington, D.C., Hopkins talked for hours with Charles Bohlen. For the first time he confessed to serious doubts about the possibility of "genuine collaboration" with the Soviet Union. The heart of the disagreement, Hopkins realized, was the "absence of freedom" under Communism. Listening to this admission, Bohlen must have wondered why something so obvious could have escaped such an intelligent man for so long. Perhaps it can only be explained by the mesmerizing power of FDR's will to believe his ability to "get at" Stalin could overcome this crucial flaw.

Hopkins clung to his New Dealers' belief that "German militarism" represented a greater danger to the postwar freedom than the Soviet Union. No longer fearful of falling out of favor with the Roosevelt White House, Bohlen bluntly disagreed. Germany, he told Hopkins, "was crushed flat." He simply did not believe she would ever "tread the same path" she had followed from 1933 to 1939.[28]

Back in Washington, Hopkins reported to President Truman on his mission, stressing Stalin's agreeable manner, and their failure to agree on anything except the United Nations veto argument, which had not been part of his assignment. A discouraged Lord Root of the Matter returned to the Mayo Clinic, a dying man.

IX

Before President Truman left for the summit meeting at Potsdam, he held lengthy talks with his top advisors on the atomic bomb and the possibility of peace negotiations with Japan. Since the March 10 incendiary bombing of Tokyo, the army air forces' B-29s had continued to ravage the capital and other Japanese cities with the same fiery formula. Nagoya, Osaka, Kobe, and Yokohama burned. The Japanese government had moved millions of people out of the cities into the countryside, reducing the number of casualties. But the impact on Japan's infrastructure was devastating. They were rapidly approaching the goal enunciated by an AAF staff officer: to lay waste Japan's major cities "not leaving one stone lying on another."[29]

Ironically, around the same time reports were arriving from Germany on the effect of British and American terror-bombing of the Third Reich's cities. The Strategic Bombing Survey ordered by Roosevelt as a pretext for this tactic was finding that morale-bombing did not work. There was little evidence that it lowered defense production and, as the AAF critics feared, some data suggested the tactic may even have made enraged workers toil harder and longer to defeat such a barbaric enemy. The top AAF generals dismissed the findings and continued to firebomb Japan.

The AAF also ordered light bombers and fighter planes to attack Japanese civilians at treetop heights. Passenger trains became favorite targets. The AAF rationale was Tokyo's decision to enlist all men from fifteen to sixty and women from seventeen to forty in a last-ditch defense force. That supposedly made every civilian a legitimate target.[30]

America's overwhelming air superiority convinced many Japanese the war was lost. Since April, Tokyo's Foreign Office had been sending out peace feelers. Thanks to the ability to break Japan's secret codes, the United States knew all about these probes. Ironically, Tokyo's biggest effort was aimed at Moscow. Relying on the nonaggression treaty they had signed in 1941, the Japanese thought Stalin would be willing to act as an intermediary with the United States. They knew nothing of the secret Yalta agreement Stalin had made with Roosevelt to enter the war.

From reading the intercepts, the Americans soon perceived that the chief obstacle to an immediate peace was the policy of unconditional surrender. Tokyo reiterated to their Moscow ambassador that they would never accept this demand, which they considered an ultimate humiliation, and a threat to Emperor Hirohito, whose sacred presence everyone regarded as a necessity for the nation's survival.

X

Distaste, if not outright disapproval for terror-bombing was beginning to emerge at the top of the Truman administration. On June 1, Secretary of War Stimson called General Arnold to his Pentagon office and asked him to explain the way the AAF was bombing Japan. Stimson growled that he had been promised by

Under Secretary for Air Robert Lovett that only precision-bombing would be used. How did Arnold explain these fire raids? The AAF commander was momentarily speechless. They had been burning Japan's cities for three and a half months without any objections from Stimson or anyone else.

The general offered the AAF rationale that in Japan a lot of industrial work was done at home and that was why it was necessary to use incendiary bombs. Stimson was not satisfied with this specious argument and made that clear to Harry Truman in a conversation the next day. But he did not feel he had the political power to intervene. Neither did the new president.[31]

For several previous weeks, an Interim Committee had been debating the use of the atomic bomb. Whether to make a demonstration on some uninhabited part of Japan or drop it at sea, whether to give prior warning of its use, were among the options discussed. No one knew exactly how powerful the bomb would be but most members of the committee, which included politicians, soldiers, and scientists, were beginning to think its impact would be awesome. Unfortunately, no one could think of a convincing demonstration. During the debates, Stimson revealed his deep conflicts about terror-bombing. He talked about "the appalling lack of conscience and compassion the war had brought about . . . the complacency, the indifference, the silence with which we greeted the mass bombings . . . of Hamburg, of Dresden, of Tokyo."[32]

The soon-to-be secretary of state, Jimmy Byrnes, played a decisive role in these discussions. His opinion had added weight because of his previous intimacy with FDR. On June 1, he told the committee it was time to stop debating. The bomb should be dropped on a "war plant surrounded by workers' homes and it should be used without warning." The committee agreed with this by now standard rationalization for killing civilians and

Byrnes informed Truman of their decision. The president accepted it "with reluctance."[33]

XI

Joseph Grew, the former ambassador to Tokyo, and currently acting secretary of state while Edward Stettinius was in San Francisco dealing with the birth of the United Nations, approached President Truman with an alternative plan. He reminded the president that the Japanese were trying to find a way to surrender. American readings of the messages traveling between Moscow and Tokyo made that clear.

Grew's long years in Japan had convinced him that if the president agreed to let the emperor remain on the throne, a peaceful capitulation was more than possible. But the policy of unconditional surrender barred the way to this solution. Was there some way in which it could be altered?

Like Bohlen in the case of Germany, Grew discounted the likelihood that Japanese militarists would ever return to power and launch a new war of conquest. Japan's defeat was already so total, the generals had been completely discredited with the Japanese people. Truman replied that he was interested "because his own thoughts had been following the same line."

The next day, Grew convened a meeting with Stimson, General George Marshall, Secretary of the Navy James Forrestal and a number of other high-ranking officials to discuss his proposal. Marshall and the military secretaries favored it. The liberals in the group, OWI head Elmer Davis and assistant secretaries of state Archibald MacLeish and Dean Acheson, disagreed with Grew. They argued that unconditional surrender was a sacred principle that could not be altered. The American people would rise up in wrath at the mere idea.[34]

The following day, May 30, 1945, Grew told President Truman of the strong opposition to his proposal. That same day, Truman learned from Harry Hopkins that Stalin had told him the Soviet Union would be ready to attack Japan on August 8. The Russian leader also reported in very cryptic fashion that the Japanese envoy in Moscow was putting out peace feelers. With supreme cynicism, Stalin added that he had ignored the envoy because he now firmly backed the policy of unconditional surrender. Stalin also added that he expected to share in the government of occupied Japan.[35]

XII

On June 18, Truman convened a meeting of his top military advisors to discuss the bomb. General Marshall reported the army, navy, and marines were planning to invade Kyushu, the southernmost Japanese island, on November 1. It was a make-or-break date. Weather conditions would not permit another try for six months. If the 350,000 Japanese troops on the island fought to the last man, as they had on Okinawa, American casualties would be between 70,000 and 280,000, with the lower figure more probable.

Secretary of War Stimson and one of his top assistants, John McCloy, now weighed in for the civilian side. Stimson said there was still a chance to persuade the Japanese to surrender by altering the unconditional surrender formula. To everyone's amazement, Admiral William Leahy, FDR's military chief of staff, now serving Truman in the same capacity, backed Stimson. Leahy declared unconditional surrender should not be applied to Japan, no matter what FDR said in Hawaii in 1944. Truman said he agreed with him but he did not see how he or anyone else could change American public opinion within the painfully small window of time in which they were working.[36]

The *Washington Post* entered this fray with a series of editorials questioning the unconditional surrender formula. They argued that the Japanese needed to be told that they could keep the emperor. The paper urged the Truman administration to "spell out" what they expected the Japanese to do after they surrendered. This was a sign that a few intelligent journalists had begun to see something wrong with unconditional surrender. But the *Post*'s shift was unlikely to alter public opinion. Then as now, few Americans read newspaper editorials and even fewer took them seriously.[37]

XIII

Meanwhile, the specter of a Soviet occupation of a part of Japan impelled Under Secretary of State Joseph Grew to renew his proposal to bypass unconditional surrender. On July 2, he was joined by Henry Stimson, who presented Truman with a variation on Grew's idea. Stimson argued that the "liberals" in Japan had been forced to surrender power to the militarists "at the point of a gun" and now, if they were permitted to retain the emperor, they would pursue a peaceful path for the future.

Dismissing the rampant Japanese hatred that was still being spewed in American newspapers and radio broadcasts, Stimson argued that Japan was "susceptible to reason." She was "not a nation composed wholly of mad fanatics of an entirely different mentality from ours." He pointed to Japan's amazing hundred-year leap from medieval feudalism to a modern nation. It was "one of the most astounding feats of national progress in history." Stimson ended his plea by suggesting that "a carefully timed warning" be given to Japan about the atomic bomb—and a reassurance that they could retain the emperor as a constitutional monarch.[38]

Before he left for Potsdam, Truman gave Jimmy Byrnes a copy of Stimson's proposal. Byrnes immediately rushed it to the still-hospitalized Cordell Hull, who was operating as a sort of shadow secretary of state from his sickbed. Remembering the deceptions practiced on him by the Japanese envoys before Pearl Harbor, the Tennessean forgot he had originally denounced unconditional surrender. With a vindictiveness worthy of FDR, he dismissed Stimson's idea as "appeasement of Japan." Two weeks later, after Truman and Byrnes had sailed for Potsdam aboard the cruiser USS *Augusta*, Hull sent them a cable adding even more negative thoughts. He said the Japanese might reject such a surrender offer. This would lead to "terrible political repercussions" in the United States.[39]

Spawned by FDR's attempt to repair his sinking domestic political power in 1942, unconditional surrender was now wielded as a political threat to a harassed new president facing one of the most momentous, and most complex, decisions in world history. Harry Truman's humane instincts urged him to somehow rid himself of this ideological albatross. But around him were too many men who were determined not to let him do it.

XIV

At Potsdam President Truman met Josef Stalin and Winston Churchill for the first time. Stalin put on his agreeable act and Churchill made speeches that Truman found too long and ultimately irritating. Stalin said he appreciated Truman's pledge to be frank. But several times the Russian dictator was disconcerted by just how frank the new president could be. When Poland's government and borders were on the table, Truman brought up a subject that FDR had tried to conceal as deeply as he had buried the German resistance to Hitler: the Katyn Massacre.

Truman asked Stalin what had happened to all those Polish officers? The Russian dictator did not try to blame the Germans—

Moscow's previous tactic. He simply said they "went away." Truman dropped the subject. But Stalin now knew he was dealing with a man who understood the real reason why Moscow could not tolerate an independent Poland.

Although Truman had few illusions about Stalin, the president dealt straightforwardly with the Soviet leader at Potsdam. It did not take him long to conclude Stalin was "smart as hell." The Russian brought to the conference a list of proposals aimed at expanding Soviet power in several directions. He wanted Truman and Churchill to join him in ousting General Franco in Spain and he saw no reason why Russia could not take over several of Italy's African colonies. He also wanted a naval base at the straits of the Dardenelles and a large slice of Armenia that he claimed Turkey had stolen from Russia at the end of World War I. Stalin did not get affirmative answers to any of these proposals.

The Russian dictator inadvertently revealed his thinking about the future of Europe in an early conversation with American ambassador Averell Harriman. When Harriman congratulated him for the Red Army's advance to Berlin, Stalin shrugged and said, "Czar Alexander got to Paris." He was referring to the Russian army that participated in the occupation of the French capital after Napoleon's final defeat in 1815.[40]

The Kremlin's boss tried to take a large step in that direction by proposing his own version of the Morgenthau Plan for Germany. Stalin wanted to make the Ruhr, Germany's industrial heartland, an international entity, with Russia one of the four controlling powers. The Ruhr was in the British zone, and Churchill flatly rejected the idea. Truman concurred. Charles Bohlen later opined that Moscow would have "undoubtedly used the privilege to paralyze the German economy and push West Germany toward Communism."[41]

XV

The main drama at Potsdam took place behind the scenes and it had only an oblique connection to the Big Three's discussions on how to deal with a prostrate Europe. The Americans—and the British, who were soon consulted—waited impatiently for news from New Mexico about the final tests of the atomic bomb. It arrived in a coded telegram on July 16: "*Operated on this morning. Diagnosis not yet complete but results seem satisfactory and already exceed expectations . . . Dr. Groves pleased.*"

The bomb worked. Subsequent telegrams revealed its terrifying power, the equivalent of 20,000 tons of TNT. Truman decided he should tell Stalin about it as a gesture of solidarity in the final assault on Japan. After one of Potsdam's plenary sessions, he strolled around the table and said in a casual tone that the United States had developed a new weapon of "great explosive power." Stalin evinced only minimal interest. He said he was glad to hear it and hoped the United States would "make good use of it" against Japan.

Charles Bohlen, who was standing nearby, studied Stalin closely as this message was delivered. The Soviet dictator seemed so off-hand, Bohlen wondered if he had understood it. Only in later years did Bohlen realize that Stalin, thanks to his spies, knew as much about the new weapon as Truman. When Stalin returned to his private quarters, he ordered a telegram sent to the head of Russia's atomic program, telling him to "speed things up."[42]

Truman now knew the power of the weapon that the S-1 project had created. He also learned that General Dwight Eisenhower had joined the list of those who did not think the bomb should be used on Japan. The general grew "more and more depressed" as he thought about it. He told the Truman staff members who consulted him that "the Japanese were ready to surrender and it was not necessary to hit them with that awful thing." He also "hated to see our country be the first to use such a weapon."[43]

Truman and his advisors made a final attempt to get around the unconditional surrender impasse. They decided to issue a declaration, calling on the Japanese to lay down their weapons. As the text was being drafted, Henry Stimson tried once more to persuade Truman to tell the Japanese they could keep the emperor. The president assured him it was still under consideration.

Contending with this plea was a memorandum from the Joint Chiefs of Staff that criticized the language Stimson proposed. They argued against saying the Allies would tolerate "a constitutional monarchy under the present dynasty." Instead they recommended much vaguer terminology, along the lines of the Atlantic Charter, guaranteeing the Japanese the eventual freedom to choose "their own form of government." This was woefully short of Stimson's goal and everyone seems to have known it.[44]

On July 26, Truman issued the Potsdam Declaration. Its language is a study in semantic agony. The president and his advisors were trying to evade unconditional surrender and yet somehow live with it. The opening sentence was a ferocious trumpet blast. "*Following are our terms. We shall not deviate from them. There are no alternatives. We shall brook no delay.*"

From there, the declaration insisted "there must be eliminated for all time the authority and influence of those who have deceived and misled the people of Japan into embarking on world conquest." But it also assured Tokyo that the Japanese military forces overseas would be permitted to return to the homeland "with the opportunity to lead peaceful and productive lives." It insisted there was no intention to enslave the Japanese people or destroy them as a nation. Japan would be permitted to maintain "industries" and the occupying forces would be withdrawn as soon as "respect for fundamental human rights" was established, and a government created by the "freely expressed will" of the Japanese people.

Finally, the declaration called for "the unconditional surrender of all Japanese armed forces." The alternative was "prompt and utter destruction."[45]

The mention of unconditional surrender in the final paragraph was window dressing. The previous paragraphs of the document offered the Japanese all sorts of conditions. Only the armed forces would be required to surrender unconditionally. But the Japanese, reading the document in Tokyo the next day, were totally unaware of the Americans' tormented state of mind, and focused on the use of the two words they could not accept.

Tokyo's leaders also had no inkling of the existence of the atomic bomb. Moreover, the government ministers read the words under the baleful influence of the Imperial Army's generals, who were still confident they could inflict unacceptable casualties on the Americans in their expected invasion of Kyushu.

The Japanese took a full day to reply. They were still hoping for some sort of response from their diplomatic efforts in Moscow. Finally, the prime minister, Baron Kantaro Suzuki, held a press conference. He said the government saw "no important value" in the Potsdam Declaration and could only resolve to continue fighting for "a successful conclusion of the war." Those fateful words gave the decision to drop the bomb irresistible force. Truman issued the order, specifying only that he wanted the explosion to occur after he left Potsdam.

The president's anguished state of mind was all too visible in his diary jottings. After detailing what he had heard about the power of the test bomb in New Mexico—it had blasted a hole 6 feet deep and 1,200 feet wide and knocked men down 10,000 yards away—he wrote: "I have told the Sec. of War, Mr. Stimson, to use it so that military objectives and soldiers and sailors are the target and not women and children." The distraught president was trying to conceal from himself what he already knew: a weapon of such stupendous power was going to kill everything and everyone in its vicinity.[46]

In an official government film, *Action At Anguar*, issued in the spring of 1945 to support the seventh war-bond drive, footage showed Japanese soldiers being burned alive by flamethrowers while the narrator said: "By this time we had shot, blasted or cooked six hundred of the little apes." In his diary, President Truman showed he too could be infected by this kind of thinking, as FDR was by the German hatred spewed by American propagandists in World War I. Truman described the Japanese as "savages, ruthless, merciless and fanatic." But the president still concluded that Americans, as the leader of the free world, could not drop "this terrible bomb" on Japanese civilians.[47]

XVI

On August 6, 1945, a B-29 nicknamed *Enola Gay* after the pilot's mother roared down the runaway on Tinian in the Mariana Islands and lumbered aloft with a 9,700 pound atomic bomb in its belly. Weather planes had preceded the bomber to the target, the port of Hiroshima, on the Ota River in Honshu, Japan's main island. A war plant surrounded by worker's homes was the aiming point, precisely as the Interim Committee had recommended. At 8:15 A.M., a twenty-four-year-old bombardier with sixty-three combat missions in Europe pressed the bomb-release mechanism. The bomb dropped toward the city. Less than a minute later, a stupendous flash engulfed the plane, followed by a terrific shock wave. "Fellows," the pilot said, "you have just dropped the first atomic bomb in history."[48]

On the ground were about 290,000 civilians and some 43,000 soldiers. Hiroshima was not the "purely military target" that

President Truman had wanted. That did not exist in Japan. But Hiroshima was a city of some military importance. It was the headquarters of the Japanese Second Army, which was in charge of defending Kyushu. To the soldiers and civilians in the vicinity of the aiming point, it was a distinction without a difference. All vanished in the explosion that the bomb unleashed.

At the center of the blast, temperatures above 5,400 degrees Fahrenheit melted tile 1,300 yards away. Human bodies were reduced to thousands of charred bundles that stuck to streets and walls. Birds caught fire in midair. In a circumference of six miles, almost everyone who was out of doors died instantly. Doctors had to develop a new terminology to describe the "thermal burns" of those who survived. One witness remembered seeing "very young girls, not only with their clothes torn off but with their skin peeled off as well." Thousands of survivors were burned alive in the wreckage of their homes. "Citizens who lost no family members in the holocaust were as rare as stars at sunrise," wrote the author of a Japanese study of Hiroshima.

After much argument, statisticians concluded 140,000 people died in Hiroshima, either immediately or of burns that killed them before the end of 1945. Over the next five years, radiation poisoning claimed another 60,000 victims, giving Hiroshima a death rate of 54 percent. In Tokyo's worst raid, the March 9/10 firestorm, the death rate was about 10 percent. Vastly increasing both civilian and military casualties was the surprise element of the Hiroshima attack. Almost no one was in air-raid shelters. A lone B-29 was not regarded as a threat.[49]

XVII

President Truman heard the news aboard the USS *Augusta*, on the way back from Potsdam. He told the excited sailors it was "the greatest thing in history."

At Los Alamos, General Leslie Groves and physicist J. Robert Oppenheimer, the scientific director of the atomic project, congratulated each other. At U.S. training camps and army bases around the world, celebrations took place. Especially elated were the men who were preparing for the invasion of Kyushu. In Chicago physicist Leo Szilard, who had tried to prevent the bomb's use, called it "one of the greatest blunders in history."[50]

The White House released a stern warning, calling on the Japanese to surrender unconditionally without delay. But the Japanese dithered and debated, trying to grasp the nature of the weapon that had leveled Hiroshima. In Moscow, the Japanese ambassador tried once more to persuade Foreign Minister Molotov to mediate peace. Instead, Molotov told him that the Soviet Union was declaring war on Japan the next day, August 9. The Soviet Far East army, magnificently equipped thanks to American generosity, rumbled into Manchuria at midnight.

The Americans, astonished that the Japanese were holding out, decided to shower the nation with 6 million leaflets warning them that more Hiroshimas were to come. The idea that the Japanese man or woman in the street could do something about forcing an early surrender was as illusory as the air force generals' presumption that bombed German civilians would somehow arise from their smashed incinerated houses and overthrow Nazism.

XVIII

On August 10, another B-29, *Bock's Car*, rumbled down the Tinian runway with a second atomic bomb in its belly. This time the target was Kokoura Arsenal on the north coast of Kyushu. But haze and clouds obscured this military target and the pilot, low on fuel, decided to bomb his designated second choice, the port city of Nagasaki. Cloud cover complicated the bomb run here too. The selected aiming point was invisible and the bombardier had to resort to that familiar device of Europe's terror-bombers, radar.

At the last moment, the clouds parted long enough for the bombardier to see the city, but the bomb fell several miles from the original aiming point. It destroyed the Mitsubishi factory, maker of the shallow water torpedoes that had stunned Americans at Pearl Harbor. It also demolished Urakami Catholic Cathedral, center of the Christian faith in Japan, and killed thousands of Japanese Catholics who lived in the vicinity.

In Nagasaki, 70,000 people died either immediately in the fireball or by the end of the year from thermal burns and other injuries. Eventually, radiation poisoning raised the death toll to 140,000, making the casualty rate roughly equal to Hiroshima. Similar scenes of horror were also reenacted: charred bodies, children with skin seared from their flesh, dazed survivors wondering what had hit them.[51]

XIX

Not long after the Nagasaki bomb exploded, Harry Truman wrote to his old Senate friend, Richard Russell of Georgia, revealing how deeply disturbed he was by the moral problem that unconditional surrender had inflicted on him. Russell had urged Truman to "carry the war to them [the Japanese] until they beg us to accept unconditional surrender."

Truman did not share this Rooseveltian vindictiveness. "I know that Japan is a terribly cruel and uncivilized nation in warfare," he told Senator Russell. "But I can't bring myself to believe that because they are beasts, we should ourselves act in the same manner. . . . My object is to save as many American lives as possible but I also have a humane feeling for the women and children of Japan."[52]

In Tokyo, the government's leaders argued for an entire day about whether to accept the Potsdam Declaration or attach to it other conditions, among them, a refusal to permit a military occupation. Meanwhile, the Red Army was rampaging through Manchuria and General Groves reported from Los Alamos that he would have another atomic bomb ready for delivery on August 17. Emperor Hirohito finally took charge of the situation and ordered Prime Minister Suzuki to issue a statement that Japan would accept the Potsdam Declaration, with the one condition: "the prerogatives of his Majesty as a Sovereign Ruler" would remain intact.

This was not unconditional surrender. But Henry Stimson, James Forrestal, and Admiral Leahy urged President Truman to accept it. Secretary of State Jimmy Byrnes grimly demurred. He remained married to unconditional surrender and warned that any deviation from it might lead to "the crucifixion of the president" by American voters.

Once more, the Casablanca edict looked as if it might lead to an impasse and thousands more charred bodies. But Harry Truman overruled the secretary of state. He ordered Byrnes to issue a statement announcing that the United States would accept the Japanese offer, but to word the response in a way that reiterated the Potsdam Declaration's insistence that the emperor and the government of Japan would be under the authority of the commander of the Allied occupation army. Byrnes, who drafted the statement, added a requirement that Hirohito sign the surrender document.

That same day, Truman ordered a halt to atomic bombing and General Groves decided not to ship the third bomb to Tinian. The president told a cabinet meeting that "the thought of wiping out another 100,000 people [is] too horrible." He recoiled from the idea of "killing all those kids." He also reported he had received 170 telegrams from Americans, urging him to insist on unconditional surrender and the harshest possible peace terms.[53]

The Chinese accepted President Truman's statement without demur. The British thought it might be improved by removing the requirement that Hirohito himself sign the surrender document. Truman agreed. Even before the statement reached Moscow, the Russians told Ambassador Harriman that they thought the Japanese offer should be rejected out of hand, claiming that the request to keep the emperor violated unconditional surrender.

When Truman's statement arrived at midnight, Harriman was meeting with Molotov. The Soviet foreign minister said he would give Harriman a reply the following day. Harriman informed him that he wanted an answer that night. "He gave me the definite impression that he was willing to have the war continue," Harriman reported.[54]

An hour or so later, Molotov summoned Harriman to the Kremlin again and accepted the statement. He coolly added that his government expected to participate in "candidacies" for representatives on the Allied High Command to which the emperor was to be "subordinated." Harriman told him the American government would never accept this idea. After a "most heated discussion," Harriman agreed to send the proposal to Washington. Before it could be wired, Molotov called to tell Harriman that Stalin had backed down and only wished to be "consulted" on the occupation government.

Harriman was acting in accordance with instructions he had received at Potsdam from the president. "I was determined that the Japanese occupation should not follow in the footsteps of our German experience," Truman later wrote. The decision was a significant step toward George Kennan's proposed policy of distancing the United States from any and all forms of political collaboration with Russia, whenever possible.[55]

On August 11, the Truman statement was transmitted to Tokyo by way of Berne, Switzerland, where the Japanese maintained an embassy. That day, the president ordered a halt to conventional bombing of Japan. Instead, the B-29s showered Tokyo and other cities with more leaflets urging the citizens to tell their government they wanted peace.

If and when bombing was resumed, General Carl Spaatz ordered the Strategic Air Force to abandon the use of incendiaries. Henceforth, the targets would be strictly military and economic. Spaatz had been troubled about terror-bombing both in Germany and Japan.

XX

In China, as President Truman later put it, "complications were . . . beginning to arise." The American embassy reported that the Chinese Communists' commanding general had announced he would accept the surrender of Japanese units in his area. The general also declared his intention to occupy towns and cities and set up governments in them, a gesture of open defiance to the authority of Chiang Kai-shek. The American ambassador predicted a "fratricidal civil war" would be certain if the Communists were permitted to pursue this policy and arm themselves with captured Japanese weapons. Unfortunately, there was little or nothing the American government could do. In that summer of 1945, Truman later ruefully recalled, "the American people wanted nothing more . . . than to end the fighting and bring the boys home."[56]

August 12 and 13 passed with no word from the Japanese. Some American officials began to consider shipping the third atomic bomb to Tinian. On August 14, the Japanese government, having overcome resistance from die-hard militarists, sent a message via Berne, accepting the terms of the Potsdam Declaration. The emperor declared himself ready to issue commands to "all the military, naval and air authorities" of Japan to cease operations and surrender their arms. On August 15, Emperor Hirohito broadcast to his nation, urging his subjects to "pave the way for a grand peace for all the generations to come by enduring the unendurable and suffering the insufferable."

There was no reference to unconditional surrender. President Truman nevertheless said the statement was "a full acceptance of the Potsdam Declaration, which specifies the unconditional surrender of Japan." He added that in the Japanese reply "there was no qualification." That was true enough, but everyone knew that the condition of permitting the emperor to remain in power had been yielded, in an elaborate back-and-forth dance of phrasing and invisible negotiation. The most ruinous policy of the New Dealers' war had finally been discarded in the name of sanity and peace.[57]

21

ASHES OF VICTORY

For the New Dealers, the war's outcome created a world starkly distant from their early hopes and illusions. At home their political power was shattered beyond recall. Their leader, Franklin D. Roosevelt, was dead and his widow had anointed an antipolitician, Henry Wallace, as their standard-bearer. The war against fascism had been won by the awesome production machine created by free enterprise, under the direction of the largely Republican corporate executives whom Roosevelt and the New Dealers had once smeared as economic royalists lusting for a coup d'état. Side by side with the stupendous outpouring of weaponry, these businessmen had created a prosperous civilian economy that made New Deal–style reform politics superfluous.

Although President Harry Truman declared his commitment to New Deal goals such as full employment and public housing, his proposals went nowhere in Congress. In the 1946 elections the Republicans won control of both houses of the national legislature by comfortable margins. Pundits of the period blamed the Democratic Party's defeat on Truman's lack of charisma and the chaotic, unplanned transition to a peacetime economy. From a distance of a half-century, the Republican victory was also a repudiation of the New Deal and the New Dealers by the American people. Unlike 1942, the soldiers, sailors, and marines were almost all home from the war. Neither they nor the rest of the voters had much interest in supporting a program that constituted a Roosevelt legacy. Particularly striking was the falloff in the normal Democratic vote—about 8 million Democrats stayed home.[1]

The Republican slogan in 1946 began as "Have You Had Enough of the Alphabet?"—galvanizing voters tired of the New Deal's "alphabet soup" of government agencies. Shortened to "Had Enough?" it made no bones about calling on Americans to bury the New Deal. The congressional Republicans were soon trumpeting the repeal of 77,000 government regulations left over from the Democrats' days of power.[2]

This remarkable revival of confidence suggests that the roots of the modern conservative movement can be found in the New Dealers' war. The conservatives' political victories on the home front coincided with America's military victories on the battlefronts to restore convictions shaken by the trauma of the Great Depression. Over the next five decades, Republicans, the party of free enterprise, controlled the White House for twenty-eight years.

Even before the voters spoke in 1946, there had been a veritable exodus of middle-level New Dealers from Washington, D.C. One newsmagazine reported they were departing "by the dozen." According to the magazine's national affairs reporter, the explanation was twofold. No longer did the New Dealers have their "personal devotion" to FDR to inspire them. More important, they no longer felt their ideas on how to run the nation got a sympathetic hearing at the White House. Most of their proposals wound up spiked by John W. Snyder, who had become Truman's secretary of the treasury, and "the pet hatred" of the departing New Dealers.[3]

Harold Ickes made a more spectacular departure after an attempt to stage a rear-guard skirmish with one of the winners of the war within the war. When Truman appointed Ed Pauley secretary of the navy, Ickes saw a chance to even the score against the man who had played a leading part in the New Deal rout at the 1944 Chicago convention. Without warning the president, Ickes attacked Pauley as a man who represented California oil interests, eager to poach on the nation's petroleum reserves. When Truman reiterated his support for Pauley, Ickes sent in his resignation, a ploy that had worked numerous times with FDR. The Old Curmudgeon was more than a little astonished to get a phone call from the White House, telling him his resignation had been accepted and he had two days to clean out his desk.[4]

II

The feisty man from Independence managed to revive the Democratic coalition to become president in his own right in 1948. Truman managed this feat by retaining the loyalty of Democratic core groups—labor, big city ethnics and African-Americans—while professional liberals and southern conservatives defected to the left and right. When southerners walked out of the 1948 convention because Truman accepted a strong civil rights plank in the party's platform, someone asked their leader, Strom Thurmond, why he was bolting. Roosevelt had put similar planks in previous platforms. "But Truman really means it," Thurmond replied.[5]

Missing from Truman's administration was the New Deal's fondness for a command economy. John Snyder later said that the Truman economic agenda was the precise opposite, "to get as much of the government out of Washington as possible."⁶ Truman's Fair Deal was, by its very nomenclature, a moderation of the New Deal. It harked back to Teddy Roosevelt's Square Deal. There was no intimation of toppling the establishment or altering basic American values. As for a New Deal for the world, that slogan was deep-sixed by everyone, even Henry Wallace. So was the Century of the Common Man. In that contest, Henry Luce's American Century of triumphant capitalism was a hands-down winner.

A few months after Harry Truman took office, Congressman Joseph Baldwin of New York, a liberal Republican, visited him in the Oval Office. He told the new president of a conversation he had with Roosevelt in early 1945. Baldwin had asked FDR why he had dumped Henry Wallace. Roosevelt replied that he thought Wallace was too liberal for the temper of the country. The American people were tired of political experiments. FDR wanted someone slightly to the right of center to succeed him, if he could not complete his term, so they could digest the changes wrought by the New Deal.

Truman nodded and drew Baldwin to the French windows overlooking the White House rose garden. He pointed to the wooden bench where he and Roosevelt had sat at the start of the 1944 campaign. Truman told Baldwin that Roosevelt had said the same thing that day, and he was using it as one of the domestic guidelines of his presidency.⁷

Some may ask if this glimpse of FDR's intentions does not conflict with his covert attempt to make Henry Wallace his running mate again in 1944. The answer may lie in the great American dichotomy. During the war years, Wallace had come to personify the idealist side of this perpetual clash, while FDR embraced the brutal realism of Dr. Win-The-War. Roosevelt felt compelled to make one last gesture toward the idealism he had abandoned.

Another perhaps more probable explanation is Henry Wallace's observation that FDR always wanted to be in the dominant position in a face-to-face encounter. By pretending he had intended to dump Wallace, Roosevelt was able to play the wise man's role with both Truman and Baldwin. When the juggler tried to reverse course and give Wallace control of Jesse Jones's Department of Commerce–RFC empire, FDR discovered the hard way that his trickster days were over.

III

Routed on the home front, the New Dealers fought a rear-guard struggle on foreign policy. After a Truman cabinet meeting on August 10, 1945, Henry Wallace gloomily informed his diary: "It is obvious to me that the cornerstone of the peace of the future consists in strengthening our ties of friendship with Russia." This was "the word" that Wallace began passing to fellow liberals. Two weeks after V-J day, he told Congressman Adolph Sabath of Chicago: "I would place friendship with Russia as number one in our foreign policy."[8]

Recent research in the archives of the Russian secret service has revealed how far Wallace was prepared to go in pursuit of this goal. On October 24, 1945, the ex–vice president—now Truman's secretary of commerce—invited Russian diplomat Anatoly Gorsky to breakfast. Gorsky was the chief Soviet intelligence agent in Washington.

The Iowan spoke contemptuously of Truman as a "petty politico" who had gotten to the presidency by accident. Wallace told the amazed Soviet spy that there were two groups fighting for the "soul" of the new president, pro-Soviet liberals led by him and anti-Soviet conservatives led by Jimmy Byrnes. The ex–vice president admitted his group was smaller and weaker and needed assistance. "You could help this smaller group considerably," he said. When Gorsky conveyed the conversation to Moscow, Foreign Minister Molotov attached a note to the report: "It must be sent to Comrade Stalin!"[9]

Wallace would stubbornly pursue Franklin D. Roosevelt's naive view of Soviet Russia unto his own political destruction. Ironically—the word has become overused but it is inescapable—the man who administered the coup de grâce to the Iowan's quixotic crusade was George Kennan, the leader of the State Department's cadre of Russian experts that the New Dealers had repeatedly tried to obliterate.

As 1946 began, the Truman administration had grown more and more dubious about the chances of reaching an accommodation with the Soviets. In February the professionals in the State Department told Kennan that the Russians were being difficult about participating in organizations such as the World Bank and the International Monetary Fund. Compounding the irony was the source of the cry of woe, the U.S. Treasury Department, where, under the guidance of Soviet spy Harry Dexter White, rosy estimates of Soviet cooperation had often originated. Kennan responded with a document that was to make him famous, the Long Telegram.

In this 8,000-word message, sent in five parts, Kennan described the Soviet regime as incurably hostile and grimly committed to expansion, either by force or by proxy politicians, front organizations, and "stooges of all sorts" in other countries. The message would have been dismissed if it had been sent a year earlier, when FDR and Harry Hopkins were alive to intimidate dissent in the State Department. It arrived in the Truman White House just as the last dregs of optimism about Russia had vanished. Averell Harriman had dozens of copies made and circulated them throughout the government.[10]

President Truman read the Long Telegram, and two weeks later journeyed to Fulton, Missouri, and sat on the platform while

Winston Churchill made an historic speech. "A shadow has fallen upon the scenes so lately lighted by the Allied victory," the former prime minister (British voters had ousted him in the summer of 1945) declared. "From Stettin in the Baltic to Trieste in the Adriatic, an iron curtain has descended across the continent. . . . The Communist parties, which were very small in all these Eastern states of Europe, have been raised to pre-eminence and power far beyond their numbers and are seeking everywhere to obtain totalitarian control."[11]

The *Nation* called Truman "inept" and Walter Lippmann declared Churchill's speech and Truman's obvious approval of it— the president applauded several times during its delivery—were an "almost catastrophic blunder." Although Truman bobbed and weaved through these volleys of criticism in a style FDR would have approved, he was reassured by the polls of what the American people were thinking about the Soviet Union. In August 1945, Gallup reported 54 percent were optimistic about Russia's cooperation in the postwar world. By February 1946, this figure had declined to 35 percent. By March 7, after the Soviet Union threatened to seize northern Iran and only withdrew after Truman warned them off in the grimmest terms, the optimists had dwindled to a minuscule 7 percent.[12]

On September 18, 1946, Secretary of Commerce Wallace and President Truman had a confrontation in the Oval Office over Wallace's pro-Soviet speeches on foreign policy, in which he savagely criticized Secretary of State Jimmy Byrnes, and, by implication, the president. Truman ordered an absolute ban on further speeches. Echoing his stubbornness—and his unrealism—with Jesse Jones, Wallace shot back: "Can you get the State Department to stay out of foreign economic affairs if I stay out of foreign political affairs?" Truman promised to discuss this with State and the conversation continued, ranging over many aspects of America's relationship with Russia and other countries.[13]

The two men parted with a show of amiability. The next day, Truman wrote a summary of their talk on his desk diary, disguising Wallace as X. The president began with a grim conclusion: his visitor was not as "sound" intellectually as Truman had thought. "X is a pacifist one hundred percent. He wants us to disband our armed forces, give Russia our atomic secrets and trust a bunch of adventurers in the Kremlin Politbureau. I do not understand a 'dreamer' like that." Truman soon asked for Wallace's resignation.[14]

IV

In 1948 Henry Wallace ran for president as the candidate of the Progressive Party. His chief plank was a call for reconciliation with Russia. In the campaign, all Wallace's flaws and past failings returned to haunt him. The Hearst newspapers got their hands on the Roerich letters and had them authenticated by a handwriting expert. Unable to call them forgeries, Wallace simply refused to discuss them, dismaying even his supporters in the press. He defended the Soviet seizure of Czechoslovakia in early 1948 and sent an open letter to Stalin with a six-point program for peace that the Soviet dictator accepted, all but smacking his lips over such an easy propaganda victory.

As a presidential candidate, Wallace proved beyond question Harry Truman's contention that he was the best secretary of agriculture the country ever had. Even his original sponsor, Eleanor Roosevelt, deserted him and declared for Truman. On election day, Wallace got 1,157,140 votes—2.37 percent of the national total—and failed to prevent Truman's victory, the real purpose of his bizarre campaign. Wallace's political career was over.[15]

In saying farewell to Henry Wallace, justice requires a recognition of his importance as an American philosopher-prophet. Like the original inventors of the role in ancient Greece and Israel, he was not honored in his time. But some of his ideas have retained their vitality, especially his call to give blacks and women a more equal share of American liberty.

Wallace's unyielding stances may have been poor politics but he personified for a little while the idealism that America can only forswear at her peril. In his generation he was Theodore Roosevelt's "man in the arena" who spent himself unstintingly in worthy causes, and though he failed, he went down "daring greatly." Unlike those aloof prophets of New England, Ralph Waldo Emerson and Henry Thoreau, who eschewed the gritty realities of the struggle for power, Wallace fought hard and, except for his tendency to rhetorical excess, honorably for his beliefs.[16]

When Wallace was wrong, as on the nature of the Soviet Union, he was very very wrong. But some of his wildest flights of idealism, such as a New Deal for the world, have proved surprisingly durable. More attainable versions of this vision reappeared in Harry S Truman's Point Four plan for international development and in John F. Kennedy's Peace Corps. Even Whittaker Chambers, surveying the postwar world from a very different point of view, warned that "there will be no peace for the islands of relative plenty until the continents of proliferating poverty have been lifted to something like the general material level of the islanders."[17]

V

Driven from electoral power, liberals in academia and the media clung to faith in a future that would reconcile American liberty and Soviet totalitarianism. The triumphs of the Red Army gave Communism a second wind and a facade of respectability that persuaded many people to ignore the absence of freedom that the ultimate New Dealer, Harry Hopkins, "Lord Root of the Matter," finally discerned was the fatal flaw in this admiration for Soviet-style economic democracy. This postwar refusal to face reality inflicted wounds on American liberalism that still fester.

The heirs of the New Dealers were not the only ones at fault. The excesses of the anticommunists, especially Senator Joseph McCarthy, the demagogue who seized the leadership of their movement, also exacerbated the situation. Not to be omitted in the blame game is the U.S. Army, who decided to keep the Venona transcripts secret from everyone, including President Harry S. Truman and his successors. As Senator Daniel Patrick Moynihan put it in his farewell newsletter: "A generation of American politics and government was tormented by reciprocal charges of 'red baiting' and 'comsymp' charges because they did not know that Whittaker Chambers . . . was telling the truth."[18]

Fortunately for the future of genuine democracy, the Truman administration ignored these powerless heirs of the New Dealers' war and created the Marshall Plan to rescue prostrate Europe from economic despair and the North Atlantic Treaty Organization to forestall any attempt to use the Red Army to advance Bolshevism beyond the borders of East Germany. Unfortunately, there was little Truman could do to prevent the peoples of Eastern Europe from living for forty-four years in the gray netherworld of Stalinist dictatorships, with ubiquitous secret police, a muzzled press, and stagnant economies.

Even more unfortunately, the Truman administration, preoccupied with rescuing Western Europe, based its Asian policy on the naive "agrarian reformers" view of the State Department's China experts toward Chinese Communism. Chiang Kai-shek was repeatedly urged to form a coalition government with the Communists while they grew in strength and confidence. In 1949, they won control of the most populous nation on earth. Much too late, Secretary of State Dean Acheson admitted that the U.S. had sought "the reconciliation of irreconcilable factions."[19]

VI

Meanwhile, the mixture of memory and history that constituted America's vision of World War II underwent a remarkable transformation. Forgotten were the reluctance to take up arms, the double-talk Franklin D. Roosevelt used to conceal his intention to make war on Germany—revealed so graphically in the leak of Rainbow Five—and the provocative policies that lured Japan into the attack on Pearl Harbor. Also lost to memory was the ferocious antagonism between Roosevelt and Congress. Perhaps most forgotten were the consequences of the policy of unconditional surrender and the hateful tactics it legitimized, terror-bombing of civilians and the use of the atomic bomb.

Instead, the deepening realization of the horror of Hitler's campaign of extermination against the Jews, which only a few Americans understood during the war, justified in many people's minds unconditional surrender, the ruthless air war, and even the atomic bomb. The global conflict slowly became the Good War, something that few of its participants would have called it at the time.[20]

VII

Perhaps the supreme irony in the web of ironies that surround the New Dealers' war is how un-Rooseveltian was America's rigid adherence to unconditional surrender as a policy. In one of his more brilliant essays, the British philosopher Isaiah Berlin, whose wartime observations in Washington, D.C., are an invaluable window on the politics of the American capital, called Roosevelt a "perfect chameleon." It was not a criticism. That was, Berlin maintained, exactly what a politician should be. Almost certainly, FDR could have abandoned unconditional surrender and persuaded a majority of Americans to approve the decision.

The seldom considered factor of Roosevelt's health should mitigate a harsh judgment, insofar as FDR's personal responsibility is concerned. After the war, one of Churchill's aides blamed the president's illness for the "costly enfeeblement" of Anglo-American unity in the closing years of the war. It also had much to do with his rigid commitment to unconditional surrender, in spite of the urgent pleas of so many of his top military and political advisors. A man with a deteriorating brain was unlikely to be flexible or even reasonable, especially when he was temperamentally inclined never to admit a mistake.

VIII

Winston Churchill, the only member of the three Allied leaders to leave behind him a personal account of the conflict, candidly admitted his share of the responsibility for the failure to recognize the German resistance to Hitler. When one of the survivors, Fabian von Schlabrendorff, visited him after the war, Churchill apologized to him and blamed his staff and the British Foreign Office for not telling him the truth about the movement.

The former prime minister was evading several German-hating speeches he made during the war that contributed to this British attitude. But in 1947 he abandoned Vansittartism. Rising in Parliament, he described Canaris, Moltke, Trott, and their fellow conspirators as men who "belonged to the noblest and greatest [of resistance movements] that have ever arisen in the history of all peoples."[21]

IX

At the end of Robert Sherwood's generally admiring book about the partnership of Roosevelt and Harry Hopkins, FDR's speechwriter brooded on "the risks that we [Americans] run of disastrous fallibility at the very top of our constitutional structure." There was, he said, "far too great a gap between the president and congress," particularly in wartime, when the "solitary powers" of the presidency were exercised under the title of commander in chief. Sherwood speculated that George Washington's character may be the origin of the problem. The presidency was tailored for his awesome talents, among which was an almost superhuman objectivity, and an equally superhuman integrity.[22]

Blaming Roosevelt's presidential behavior on George Washington is, of course, a rather large non sequitur. Far better if we cast a cold eye on the legacy of White House deceit—and suspicion of deceit—that FDR left behind him. Equally dubious was his use of the implied powers of the presidency to wage an undeclared war in 1941. Perhaps it was not an accident that the president who considered himself Roosevelt's heir, Lyndon Johnson, fought another undeclared war in Vietnam. There is a dark penumbra to what one admiring historian has called the shadow of FDR.[23]

X

Twenty-five years after World War II ended, a combination of luck and circumstance gave this writer a chance to spend several days talking to Harry S. Truman in Independence, Missouri. One evening, I asked him what he really thought of Franklin D. Roosevelt.

The eighty-six-year-old ex-president hesitated for a moment, then spoke in a calm, steady voice. "Inside he was the coldest man I ever met. He didn't care about you or me or anyone else in the world on a personal level, as far as I could see. But he was a great president. He brought this country into the twentieth century."[24]

Mr. Truman was praising the man who had rescued America from the despair of the Great Depression. He was remembering the creation of social security, the passage of laws that encouraged the formation of labor unions, the renewal of America's commitment to a more equal liberty. But Harry S. Truman had not a word of praise for the man who led America in World War II. Perhaps that presidential silence is the most revealing comment on the New Dealers' war.

NOTES

CHAPTER 1: THE BIG LEAK

1. *Chicago Tribune* and *Washington Times-Herald*, December 4, 1941; Albert C. Wedemeyer, *Wedemeyer Reports*, New York, 1958, 15.

2. Kenneth S. Davis, *FDR: Into the Storm, 1937–40*, New York, 1993, 621. On October 23, 1940, Roosevelt said: "To Republicans and Democrats, to every man, woman and child in the nation, I say this: Your President and your Secretary of State are following the road to peace" (617).

3. *Chicago Tribune* (editorial page), December 6, 1941.

4. *Congressional Record*, 77th Congress, 1st session, 1941, 87, pt. 14: A5448–A5451.

5. *Chicago Tribune*, December 6, 1941.

6. Wayne S. Cole, *Roosevelt and the Isolationists*, Lincoln, Neb., 1983, 468; Burton K. Wheeler, *Yankee from the West*, Garden City, N.Y., 1962, 27.

7. William L. O'Neill, *A Better World: The Great Schism, Stalinism and the Intellectuals*, New York, 1982, 37.

8. Davis, *FDR: Into The Storm*, 618.

9. Cole, *Roosevelt and the Isolationists*, 480. Ted Morgan, *FDR: A Biography*, New York, 1985, 600ff.

10. Personal Communication (hereafter PC), Albert Wedemeyer; also see Wedemeyer, *Wedemeyer Reports*, 15ff.

11. PC, Wedemeyer.

12. O'Neill, *A Better World*, 15.

13. PC, Wedemeyer; Fleet Admiral William D. Leahy, *I Was There*, New York, 1950, 339.

14. PC, Wedemeyer; also see Wedemeyer, *Wedemeyer Reports*, 24.

15. *Chicago Tribune*, December 6, 1941, for the Stimson quotation; also see Wedemeyer, *Wedemeyer Reports*, 21.

16. PC, Frank Waldrop. The author interviewed Mr. Waldrop at length in 1986.

564NOTES

17. Federal Bureau of Investigation report of the leak of Rainbow Five, approximately 1,200 pages in four volumes, memorandum on unnumbered page.

18. PC, Wedemeyer.

19. *New York Times*, December 6 and 7, 1941.

20. Harold L. Ickes, *The Secret Diary of Harold L. Ickes,* vol. 3, *The Lowering Clouds,* New York, 1955, 659–660.

21. Robert E. Sherwood, *Roosevelt and Hopkins*, rev. ed., New York, 1950, 418.

22. *Chicago Tribune*, December 5, 1941; *New York Times*, December 6, 1941.

23. *Chicago Tribune*, December 5, 1941, 10.

24. Kemp Tolley, "The Strange Mission of the Lanikai," *American Heritage,* October 1973, 57ff.

25. Kemp Tolley, *Cruise of the Lanikai: Incitement to War*, Annapolis, Md., 1973, 14–15, 277.

26. Tolley, *Cruise of the Lanikai,* 21ff; Edward S. Miller, *War Plan Orange: The U.S. Strategy to Defeat Japan, 1897–1945*, Annapolis, Md., 1991, 134.

27. *Congressional Record,* 1941, A5449 (Details of Rainbow Five).

28. Martin Weil, *A Pretty Good Club: The Founding Fathers of the U.S. Foreign Service*, New York, 1978, 105.

29. Richard M. Ketchum, *The Borrowed Years, 1938–41: America on the Way to War*, New York, 1989, 589; Ickes, *The Secret Diary*, vol. 3, 630.

30. Edward S. Miller, *War Plan Orange*, Annapolis, Md., 1991, 269–270.

31. Waldo Heinrichs, *Threshold of War: Franklin D. Roosevelt and American Entry into World War II*, New York, 1988, 135, 177–179.

32. *Time*, September 22, 1941.

33. Heinrichs, *Threshold of War,* 213.

34. Ibid., 211.

35. Jonathan G. Utley, *Going to War with Japan*, Knoxville Ky., 1985, 173.

36. Heinrichs, *Threshold of War,* 203; William L. Langer and S. Everett Gleason, *The Undeclared War,* New York, 1953, 893, 898.

37. Utley, *Going to War with Japan,* 175. In Langer and Gleason, *The Undeclared War,* the phrase, "fire the first shot" is discussed at length. It is from Henry Stimson's diary. These two historians, determined to minimize American responsibility for being on the brink of war, argue that the Army Secretary's choice of words was "infelicitous and hurried" and was supposedly contradicted by his and the Army's desire to postpone a conflict.

38. Heinrichs, *Threshold of War,* 217–218.

39. Ibid., 217.

40. Tolley, "Strange Mission of the Lanikai," 95. Also see Tolley, *Cruise of the Lanikai*, 42ff. The two other small craft that were dispatched on similar missions were also recalled when the Japanese struck Pearl Harbor. In Gordon W. Prange, *Pearl Harbor: The Verdict of History* (New York, 1986, 46ff.), the two actual authors of the book, Donald M. Goldstein and Katherine V. Dillon (Prange was dead when the book was written), pooh-pooh Tolley's claims and those of authors such as Harry Elmer Barnes and George Morgenstern, who found the mission suspicious.

But it is difficult if not impossible to argue away Admiral Hart's eyewitness testimony. In W. G. Winslow, *The Fleet the Gods Forgot*, Annapolis, Md., 1982, the author, a U.S. Navy captain, concentrates on the *Isabel*, one of the other small ships sent into the Japanese sea lanes. Winslow makes it clear that Admiral Hart considered it a suicide mission. The author quotes Hart as saying he received Roosevelt's order to dispatch the ships "with consternation." Winslow notes Hart already had the area that these ships were supposed to penetrate "under surveillance by air." He acerbically records that the *Isabel*'s captain and crew were told they were searching for survivors of a downed PBY flying boat—a lie that breached the code of honor by which army and navy officers live. When they returned to Manila on December 7, 1941, Admiral Hart greeted the captain with: "Well, I never thought I'd see you again" (250–255).

CHAPTER 2: THE BIG LEAKER

1. Johanna Menzel Meskill, *Hitler and Japan: The Hollow Alliance*, New York, 1955, 40.

2. Warren Kimball, *The Juggler: Franklin D. Roosevelt as Wartime Statesman*, Princeton, N.J., 1991, 7.

3. Burton K. Wheeler, *Yankee from the West*, 32–33; PC, 1956 interview with Edward Wheeler, Senator Wheeler's son.

4. *Washington Post*, January 6, 1963.

5. PC, Frank Waldrop.

6. Letter from Murray Green, Arnold's official biographer, to J. E. Hoover, September 19, 1967 (copy in author's possession, from the files of Gen. Wedemeyer).

7. FBI investigation of the leak of Rainbow Five, letter in opening pages of vol. 4.

8. William Stevenson, *A Man Called Intrepid*, New York, 1976, 298–299.

9. Utley, *Going to War with Japan*, Knoxville, Ky., 1985, 174.

10. Langer and Gleason, *The Undeclared War*, 703. Also see Gerhard L. Weinberg, *A World in Arms*, New York, 1994, 250.

11. After the war, Ribbentrop claimed to have taken this position. In his surviving statements immediately after Pearl Harbor, he evinced no hesitation, publicly, about joining the war on Japan's side. Since he was the architect of the Tripartite Pact, this was hardly surprising. He would not have been the first foreign minister to say one thing in public and the opposite to his master. Michael Bloch, *Ribbentrop: A Biography*, New York, 1992, 344–345.

12. The Pearl Harbor attack was a late addition to Japan's war plans, imposed over many objections by strong-willed Admiral Irosoku Yamamoto. The original plan called for an attack on the British and Dutch in the Far East and a war of attrition if the Americans attempted to sortie from Pearl Harbor to join the fighting. The Japanese saw it ending in an all-or-nothing fleet-to-fleet battle that the weakened Americans would lose. Ronald Spector, *Eagle Against the Sun: The American War with Japan*, New York, 1983, 44–45.

13. Langer and Gleason, *The Undeclared War*, 749.

14. Gerhard L. Weinberg, *Germany, Hitler, and World War II*, New York, 1995, 203.

15. *New York Times,* December 9, 1941. Also see Franklin D. Roosevelt, *The War Message, Being the addresses of the President to the Nation and Congress Concerning the Involvement of the United States in a War with the Empire of Japan and the Axis Powers,* St. Louis, Mo., 1942, 15–31.

16. Meskill, *Hitler and Japan: The Hollow Alliance,* 1–47, is the best summary of how far from the truth Roosevelt strayed in his speech. The book describes the astonishing cross-purposes at which the German-Japanese alliance worked. Meskill also sees the leak of Rainbow Five as a contributor to the German declaration of war.

17. Captain Tracy B. Kittredge, "A Military Danger, The Revelation of Secret Strategic Plans," U.S. Naval Institute Proceedings, July 1955, 737–739. Captain Kittredge based this study on translations of the German Naval Staff Diary, Part A, December 1941. For further light on Hitler's decision see *Inside the Third Reich: Memoirs of Albert Speer,* translated by Richard and Clara Winston, New York, 1970, 356: "Press reports were crucially important in forming his [Hitler's] opinions; they also had a great deal to do with his mood. Where specific foreign news items were concerned, he instantly formulated the official German position, usually highly aggressive."

18. Kittredge, "A Military Danger," 740; Weinberg, *Germany, Hitler, and World War II*, 203.

19. Wedemeyer, *Wedemeyer Reports*, 186.

20. David Kahn, *Hitler's Spies*, New York, 1978, 617; Kittredge, "A Military Danger," 740–741.

21. Walter Warlimont, *Inside Hitler's Headquarters*, New York, 1964, 208.

22. Kittredge, "A Military Danger," 742–743.

23. Frances Perkins, *The Roosevelt I Knew*, New York, 1946, 379–380.

24. Ketchum, *The Borrowed Years*, 782–785.

25. Tolley, *Cruise of the Lanikai*, 302.

26. Ibid., 302.

27. James O. Richardson, *On the Treadmill to Pearl Harbor*, Washington, 1973, 435.

28. Tolley, *Cruise of the Lanikai*, 165–166.

29. Edward S. Miller, "Kimmel's Hidden Agenda," *Military History Quarterly*, Autumn, 1991, 36 ff. Miller explores the plan and overall Navy strategy for the war against Japan at more length in his book *War Plan Orange*. On page 282, he notes that CNO Stark bombarded Kimmel with cautionary cables, warning him against excessive risks. It was an indirect admission that Admiral Richardson was right when he said the fleet did not have the men or the ships for a sustainable sea offensive against the Japanese.

30. George Morgenstern, *The Secret War*, New York, 1947, 17.

31. Ibid., 54.

32. John W. Dower, *War Without Mercy: Race and Power in the Pacific War*, New York, 1986, 102–103.

33. Ickes, *The Secret Diary,* vol. 3, 387; Bruce Catton, *The War Lords of Washington*, New York, 1948, 9. Knox's remarks reflected his confidence in Kimmel's battle plan. "We've had our plans worked out for twenty years. Once it starts, our submarines will go in to blockade them, and sooner or later our battle fleet will be able to force an action."

34. Gordon W. Prange, *At Dawn We Slept: The Untold Story of Pearl Harbor*, New York, 1981, 332–333; Dower, *War Without Mercy*, 105.

35. Spector, *Eagle Against the Sun*, 133–135.

36. Ibid., 119. These words were aimed at Douglas MacArthur but they can be applied to everyone in the chain of command who mismanaged the Philippines defense.

37. Ward Bronson, Unpublished diary in the author's possession, 41.

38. Richardson, *On the Treadmill to Pearl Harbor*, 461.

39. Tolley, *Cruise of the Lanikai*, 272, 279. Thanks to his skills as a sailor and a tremendous amount of luck, Tolley was one of the few survivors of the Asiatic Fleet. After the Japanese invasion, he was ordered to take six members of Hart's staff south aboard the *Lanikai*. They made it to Australia after four months of dodging Japanese planes and ships. In Prange, *Pearl Harbor: The Verdict of History*, Goldstein and Dillon attempt to discount Hart's testimony by arguing that when he testified before Congress during postwar Pearl Harbor hearings, he declined to comment on the *Lanikai*. But it is obvious from his statement to Morison that Hart felt the Navy as well as FDR had dishonored themselves with the *Lanikai*, and as a loyal Navy man he had no desire to publicize this conclusion.

40. Richardson, *On the Treadmill to Pearl Harbor*, 460.

41. Lloyd C. Gardner, *A Covenant with Power*, New York, 1984, 50. In *The German Wars, 1914–45* by D. J. Goodspeed (New York, 1977), the author's focus on Germany gives him an interesting perspective on the war with Japan. He points out (413) that if Roosevelt had agreed to the Japanese proposal for a partial withdrawal from Indochina and a relaxation of the oil embargo for three months, there might never have been a Pacific war. In the next three months, the Russian armies defeated the Germans before Moscow and the tide of war changed drastically. The Germans no longer looked like winners and Japan would have seen no further advantages in the Tripartite Pact. They would have been far more amenable to a face-saving agreement with America. But this, Goodspeed admits, is hindsight. As Harry Truman has noted, any six-year-old's hindsight is worth a president's foresight.

42. Roy Hoopes, *Americans Remember the Home Front*, New York, 1977, 74.

CHAPTER 3: FROM TRIUMPH TO TRAUMA

1. Nathan Miller, *FDR: An Intimate History*, New York, 1983, 252.

2. Morgan, *FDR: A Biography*, 405.

3. Katie Loucheim, ed., *The Making of the New Deal: The Insiders Speak,* with Historical Notes by Jonathan Dembo, Cambridge, Mass., 1983, 176.

4. Arthur Krock, *Memoirs: Sixty Years on the Firing Line*, New York, 1968, 216–217. Krock, who published the statement in the *New York Times*, offers convincing evidence that Hopkins said it.

5. Reminiscences of Adolf A. Berle, Columbia University Oral History Collection, 187.

6. Fulton Oursler, *Behold This Dreamer!,* edited with commentary by Fulton Oursler Jr., New York, 1964, 173–175.

7. Oursler, *Behold This Dreamer!*, 373–393; Reminiscences of Henry A. Wallace, Columbia University Oral History Collection, vol. 8, 1427.

8. Loucheim, *The Making of the New Deal*, 15.

9. Ibid., xvi.

10. Morgan, *FDR: A Biography*, 422.

11. Ibid., 431–432.

12. Otis L. Graham, Jr., ed., *The New Deal: The Critical Issues*, Boston, 1971, 123.

13. Winston Churchill, *Great Contemporaries*, London, 1932, 241.

14. Stephen Skowronek, *The Politics Presidents Make: Leadership from John Adams to George Bush*, Cambridge, Mass., 1993, 303. This was a sharp reversal of Roosevelt's policy in the early years of his presidency. He began by attempting to portray himself as a father figure, above politics. In March 1934, he declined to take part in a Jefferson Day Dinner, unless it was "nonpartisan" and included Republicans. Graham, *The New Deal,* 123.

15. FDR's plurality of 11 million has since been exceeded by Richard Nixon's 18 million in 1972 and Ronald Reagan's 17 million in 1984.

16. Kenneth S. Davis, *FDR: The New Deal Years , 1933–1937*, New York, 1986, 649.

17. Ibid., 70–71.

18. Ibid., 77–78.

19. Harold L. Ickes, *The Secret Diary of Harold L. Ickes,* vol. 2, *The Inside Struggle*, New York, 1954, 170.

20. Morgan, *FDR: A Biography*, 496.

21. Fulton Oursler Papers, Georgetown University.

22. John A. Garraty, "The New Deal, National Socialism and the Great Depression," *American Historical Review* 78 (October 1973), 920.

23. Herbert Hoover, *Memoirs,* vol. 3, *The Great Depression*, New York, 1952, 474–475; Garraty, "The New Deal," 944. Mr. Garraty states: "The Nazis were far more successful in curing the economic ills of the 1930s."

24. James A. Farley, *Jim Farley's Story: The Roosevelt Years*, New York, 1948, 101.

25. Miller, *FDR: An Intimate History*, 405.

26. Farley, *Jim Farley's Story*, 106.

27. Ferdinand Lundberg, *America's 60 Families*, New York, 1937, 484–486.

28. Alan Brinkley, *The End of Reform: New Deal Liberalism in Peace and War*, New York, 1995, 57–58.

29. *New York Times,* January 10, 1940, editorial page.

30. Davis, *FDR: Into the Storm,* 129–133, 336.

31. Samuel I. Rosenman, *Working with Roosevelt,* New York, 1952, 71, 167.

32. Davis, *FDR: Into the Storm*, 415.

33. Ibid., 584–585.

34. Ibid., 589–591.

35. Dennis Tilden Lynch, *Criminals and Politicians*, New York, 1932, 64; Jack Lait and Lee Mortimer, *Chicago Confidential*, New York, 1950, 177, 184; Lyle W. Dorsett, *Franklin D. Roosevelt and the City Bosses*, Port Washington, N.Y., 1977, 92–93.

36. Robert H. Ferrell, *Truman and Pendergast*, Columbia, Mo., 1999, 55. In the 1950s the author discussed Hague's mail tampering with Mr. Farley. He shook his head ruefully and said: "We had a hell of a time getting Hague out of that one."

37. Davis, *FDR: Into the Storm,* 596–597.

38. Ibid., 601.

39. Graham White and John Maze, *Henry A. Wallace: His Search for a New World Order*, Chapel Hill, N.C., 1995, 137.

40. Ferrell, *Truman and Pendergast*, 48–53. The Kansas City boss contributed to his own downfall with bizarre behavior. He began betting huge sums on horses and demanded gigantic bribes to cover his losses. Some people attributed his unbosslike antics to a mental breakdown, brought on by alcoholism and/or syphilis.

41. Margaret Truman, *Harry S. Truman*, New York, 1972, 122–125.

42. Robert H. Ferrell, ed., *Dear Bess: The Letters from Harry to Bess Truman, 1910–1959*, New York, 1983, 446.

43. Morgan, *FDR: A Biography,* 531.

44. Michael Beschloss, *Kennedy and Roosevelt: The Uneasy Alliance*, New York, 1980, 213.

45. Davis, *FDR: Into the Storm*, 613.

46. White and Maze, *Henry A. Wallace*, 65–66.

47. Morgan, *FDR: A Biography,* 533–534.

48. Davis, *FDR: Into the Storm*, 623–624.

49. Beschloss, *Kennedy and Roosevelt*, 215.

50. Ibid., 218–221.

51. Davis, *FDR: Into the Storm,* 625; Morgan, *FDR: A Biography*, 540.

52. John Pritchard, "Ring Around Roosevelt," *Coronet*, June 1941.

53. Graham, *The New Deal*, 88.

54. William K. Klingaman, *1941: Our Lives in a World on the Edge*, New York, 1988, 59.

55. Torbjorn Sirevag, *The Eclipse of the New Deal and the Fall of Vice President Wallace*, New York, 1985, 266.

56. Morgan, *FDR: A Biography*, 579.

57. Ibid., 581; Ketchum, *The Borrowed Years*, 578–579.

58. *The Presidential Press Conferences of Franklin D. Roosevelt*, New York, 1972, vol. 17, 86–87.

59. Morgan, *FDR: A Biography*, 579.

60. Sirevag, *The Eclipse of the New Deal*, 273.

61. Dwight William Tuttle, *Harry L. Hopkins and Anglo-American-Soviet Relations, 1941–1945*, New York, 1983, 41–42.

62. Ibid., 42.

63. Morgan, *FDR: A Biography*, 590.

64. Sirevag, *The Eclipse of the New Deal*, 273–275.

65. Langer and Gleason, *The Undeclared War*, 796–797. Pius XII's predecessor, Pius XI, had issued an encyclical, *Divini Redemptoris*, forbidding all forms of collaboration with Communism. The pope's concession came with a warning that if Communism remained an "active force" after the war, in a few years it would dominate Europe and attack England and the United States.

66. Ketchum, *The Borrowed Years*, 58.

67. Tolley, *Cruise of the Lanikai*, 274. The author quotes from minutes of a 1941 British cabinet meeting, part of a mass of secret documents declassified in 1971.

68. Theodore A. Wilson, *The First Summit: Roosevelt and Churchill at Placentia Bay 1941*, Boston, 1969, 265–267.

69. Langer and Gleason, *The Undeclared War, 1940–41*, 757.

70. Sherwood, *Roosevelt and Hopkins*, 382.

71. Morgan, *FDR: A Biography*, 599–603.

72. Sherwood, *Roosevelt and Hopkins*, 383.

73. Sirevag, *The Eclipse of the New Deal*, 275–279.

CHAPTER 4: THE GREAT DICHOTOMY

1. John Morton Blum, ed., *The Price of Vision: The Diary of Henry A. Wallace, 1942–1946*, Boston, 1973, 21.

2. Sirevag, *The Eclipse of the New Deal*, 68.

3. Reminiscences of Henry A. Wallace, Columbia University Oral History Collection, vol. 7, 1152.

4. Catton, *The War Lords of Washington*, 3–12.

5. Sirevag, *The Eclipse of the New Deal*, 55.

6. Blum, *Price of Vision*, 17–19.

7. Ibid.

8. Catton, *The War Lords of Washington*, 69.

9. *Time*, January 19, 1942, 11.

10. Catton, *The War Lords of Washington*, 72.

11. Steven Fraser, *Labor Will Rule: Sidney Hillman and the Rise of American Labor*, New York, 1991, 469, 485–486.

12. Truman, *Harry S. Truman*, 145.

13. Richard Norton Smith, *An Uncommon Man: The Triumph of Herbert Hoover*, New York, 1984, 309.

14. Reminiscences of James A. Farley, Columbia University Oral History Collection, 375–376.

15. Ralph G. Martin, *Cissy: The Extraordinary Life of Eleanor Medill Patterson,* New York, 1979, 415.

16. Ibid., 419.

17. Richard R. Lingeman, *Don't You Know There's A War On?,* New York, 1980, 36–39.

18. Dan Van Der Vat, *The Atlantic Campaign: World War II's Great Struggle at Sea,* New York, 1988, 267.

19. Michael Gannon, *Operation Drumbeat,* New York, 1990, 176.

20. Ibid., 267ff.

21. Dower, *War Without Mercy,* 81.

22. Paul Milkman, *PM: A New Deal in Journalism,* New Brunswick, N.J., 1997, 162–163.

23. Morgan, *FDR: A Biography,* 628; Otis L. Graham Jr. and Meghan Robinson Wander, eds., *Franklin Roosevelt: His Life and Times,* New York, 1985, 209.

24. Morgan, *FDR: A Biography,* 629.

25. Francis Biddle, *In Brief Authority,* New York, 1962, 237–238.

26. Richard Gid Powers, *Not Without Honor: The History of American Anticommunism,* New York, 1995, 158, 183.

27. Biddle, *In Brief Authority,* 238–239.

28. Ibid., 246–247. For FDR's use of tax investigations to silence critics, see Morgan, *FDR: A Biography* (555–556), where the prosecution of Moses Annenberg, the Philadelphia newspaper publisher, is detailed.

CHAPTER 5: WHOSE WAR IS IT ANYWAY?

1. George H. Roeder Jr., *The Censored War: American Visual Experience During World War II,* New Haven, 1993, 87; Jerome S. Bruner, *Mandate from the People,* New York, 1944, 136.

2. *Time,* January 26, 1942, 8.

3. Fulton Oursler papers, Georgetown University, Sinclair letter to Sherwood, February 11, 1942.

4. Oursler papers, Sinclair letter of March 9, 1942; Allan M. Winkler, *The Politics of Propaganda: The Office of War Information, 1942–1945,* New Haven, 1978, 77.

5. Winkler, *The Politics of Propaganda,* 28.

6. Oursler papers, Sinclair letter of March 25.

7. Oursler, *Behold This Dreamer!,* 453.

8. White and Maze, *Henry A. Wallace,* 158–159.

9. Norman D. Markowitz, *The Rise and Fall of the People's Century,* New York, 1973, 48; Sirevag, *The Eclipse of the New Deal,* 246. Also see full text of this crucial speech in Blum, *The Price of Vision,* 635–640.

10. Reminiscences of Henry A. Wallace, Columbia University Oral History Collection, vol. 8, 1533.

11. H. G. Nichols, ed., *Washington Dispatches, 1941–45,* with an introduction by Isaiah Berlin, Chicago, 1981, 38.

12. Ibid., 46–47.

13. Markowitz, *The Rise and Fall of the People's Century,* 52.

14. Richard Polenberg, *War and Society: The United States, 1941–1945,* New York, 1972, 220. John Morton Blum, *V Was For Victory: Politics and American Culture During World War II,* New York, 1976, 122. Keith Eiler, *Mobilizing America: Robert Patterson and the War Effort, 1942–45,* Ithaca, N.Y., 1997, 324–325. Eiler notes that Patterson kept a rein on profits by renegotiating final payments when the figures seemed out of line. By the end of the war, $7.5 billion had been refunded to the government by defense contractors.

15. Brinkley, *The End of Reform,* 119.

16. Blum, *V Was For Victory,* 133–135. Also see Polenberg, *War and Society,* 77–78. No less than twenty-five antitrust suits were "deferred" and eventually abandoned. A disgusted Arnold quit the business and became a federal judge.

17. Ibid., 135.

18. Winkler, *The Politics of Propaganda,* 12.

19. Ibid., 24.

20. Blum, *V Was For Victory,* 24.

21. Roeder, *The Censored War,* 8–10.

22. "On the Progress of the War," Fireside chat, February 23, 1942, The Fireside Chats of Franklin D. Roosevelt, URL http://www.mhric.org/fdr/chat20.html. For losses see: Spector, *Eagle Against the Sun,* 5–6, 108; Jack Sweetman, *American Naval History,* Annapolis, Md., 1984, 160–161.

23. Roeder, *The Censored War,* 13.

24. Scott Donaldson, *Archibald MacLeish: An American Way of Life,* New York, 1992, 356–357. Few writers came to MacLeish's defense. He had alienated large sections of the literary community in 1940–41 by denouncing their unenthusiasm for intervention. He castigated by name writers such as Ernest Hemingway and John Dos Passos as "Irresponsibles" because their view of life was so negative, they had bred cynicism about all wars and governments in their readers. When his targets fired back, MacLeish revealed no small talent for name-calling. His critics, he told one of his dwindling band of literary friends, were all "isolationists, pro-fascists, communist-fascists, and the whole literary gang who always run with the cur dogs" (Donaldson, 337).

25. Ibid., 354–355.

26. *Time,* February 23, 1942.

27. Winkler, *The Politics of Propaganda,* 24.

28. Ibid., 27.

29. Ibid., 28–29.

30. Ibid., 34.

31. Reminiscences of Henry A. Wallace, Columbia University Oral History Collection, vol. 8, 1550.

32. Roeder, *The Censored War,* 9–10.

33. Peter Hoffmann, *The History of the German Resistance 1933–1945,* translated from the German by Richard Barry, Cambridge, Mass., 1988, 214–215; Anne

Armstrong, *Unconditional Surrender: The Impact of the Casablanca Policy on World War II,* New Brunswick, N.J., 1961, 210–211.

34. Louis P. Lochner, *What About Germany?*, New York, 1942, 216–237.

CHAPTER 6: SOME NEGLECTED CHICKENS COME HOME TO ROOST

1. Reminiscences of Henry A. Wallace, Columbia University Oral History Collection, vol. 8, 1467.

2. Roeder, *The Censored War,* 8.

3. Blum, *V Was For Victory,* 233.

4. Robert Edwin Ficken, "The Democratic Party and Domestic Politics During World War II" (Ph.D. dissertation, University of Washington, 1973), 15–16; Roland Young, *Congressional Politics in the Second World War,* New York, 1956, 169.

5. Ficken, "The Democratic Party," 18–19; Young, *Congressional Politics,* 170.

6. Charles Michelson, *The Ghost Talks,* New York, 1944, 213ff.

7. Ibid., 216–219.

8. Catton, *The War Lords of Washington,* 151–167; Young, *Congressional Politics,* 100.

9. Ficken, "The Democratic Party," 19, 21, 22; Young, *Congressional Politics,* 14–15.

10. Ficken, "The Democratic Party," 30, 34.

11. Ibid., 66.

12. Ibid., 40–41.

13. Ibid., 41–43.

14. Farley, *Jim Farley's Story,* 350.

15. Ibid., 353–354.

16. *New York Herald Tribune,* June 5, 1942.

17. Ficken, "The Democratic Party," 48–49.

18. *New York Herald Tribune,* June 22, 1942.

19. *New York Daily News,* August 21, 1942; Ficken, "The Democratic Party," 50.

20. Ficken, "The Democratic Party," 50–51.

21. *New York Herald Tribune,* August 31, 1942.

22. Ibid., August 23, 1942.

23. Warren Moscow, *Roosevelt and Willkie,* Englewood, N.J., 1968, 206.

24. Steve Neal, *Dark Horse: A Biography of Wendell Willkie,* New York, 1984, 201ff; Donald Bruce Johnson, *The Republican Party and Wendell Willkie,* Urbana, Ill., 1960, 198.

25. Neal, *Dark Horse,* 217.

26. Ibid., 219–220.

27. Ficken, "The Democratic Party," 61.

28. Unpublished autobiography of Mary T. Norton, New Jersey Room, Jersey City Public Library, 200.

29. Ficken, "The Democratic Party," 69, 70, 74.

30. Milton H. Leff, "The Politics of Sacrifice In World War II," *Journal of American History*, March, 1991, 1298–1300.

31. Ibid., 1301.

32. *New York Times*, October 2, 1942.

33. *New York Herald Tribune*, October 2, 1942.

34. *New York Herald Tribune* and *New York Times*, October 2, 1942.

35. *American Magazine*, November, 1942.

36. Ficken, "The Democratic Party," 77–79; Blum, *The Price of Vision*, 131.

37. *Time*, November 16, 1942, 20; Ficken, "The Democratic Party," 73.

38. Blum, *V Was For Victory*, 221; *Time*, November 16, 1942, 19.

39. Ficken, "The Democratic Party," 80–81.

40. Blum, *V Was For Victory*, 232.

41. Marie B. Hecht, *John Quincy Adams*, New York, 1972, 330–331. Adams, Secretary of State in Monroe's administration, was replying to an insulting article in the *Edinburgh Review*, "What Has America Done for Mankind?" in which the British took Americans to task for not supporting liberals in Spain, France, and Italy. Other parts of Adams's speech have an eerie relevance to modern times. An America that relied on force, he said, "might become dictatress of the world. She would be no longer the ruler of her own spirit." For a more complete excerpt, see John Bartlett, *Familiar Quotations*, 15th ed., Boston, 1980, 418.

42. Sirevag, *The Eclipse of the New Deal*, 287; Ficken, "The Democratic Party," 92.

43. Henry H. Adams, *Harry Hopkins*, New York, 1977, 302.

44. Ibid., 303.

45. Nichols, *Washington Dispatches*, 113. Also see Lewis Atherton, *Main Street on the Middle Border*, Bloomington, Ind., 1984, 282. Atherton too notes the contrast between World War I's enthusiasm and World War II's "grimmer" mood of "loyal determination."

46. Benjamin L. Alpers, "This Is the Army: Imagining a Democratic Military in World War II," *Journal of American History* 85(1) (June 1998), 159.

CHAPTER 7: IN SEARCH OF UNCONDITIONAL PURITY

1. Winston S. Churchill, *Their Finest Hour*, New York, 1949, 232.

2. Harry H. Semmes, *Portrait of Patton*, New York, 1955, 121–128. Colonel Semmes received his third Distinguished Service Cross in this action. He had won his first two in World War I, serving under Patton in the U.S. Tank Corps.

3. Ronald Steel, *Walter Lippmann and the American Century*, Boston, 1980, 401–402; John Morton Blum, ed., *From the Morgenthau Diaries: Years of War, 1941–1945*, Boston, 1967, 148.

4. Blum, *From the Morgenthau Diaries: Years of War*, 148–149.

5. Ibid., 151.

6. Leahy, *I Was There*, 135, 137.

7. Nichols, *Washington Dispatches*, 119, 127.

8. *Time,* November 30, 1942; Rosenman, *Working with Roosevelt,* 363–364; Winkler, *The Politics of Propaganda,* 86–87.

9. Morgan, *FDR: A Biography,* 649.

10. Blum, *The Price of Vision,* 132.

11. Ibid., 138.

12. *Time,* February 1, 1943, 12.

13. Morgan, *FDR: A Biography,* 654.

14. Morgan, *FDR: A Biography,* 657; Armstrong, *Unconditional Surrender,* ix.

15. Robert Dallek, *Franklin D. Roosevelt and American Foreign Policy, 1932–1945,* New York, 1979, 374–375.

16. Frances L. Lowenheim et al., eds., *Roosevelt and Churchill, Their Secret Wartime Correspondence,* New York, 1975, 309.

17. Anthony Cave Brown, *Bodyguard of Lies,* New York, 1975, 248.

18. Sir John Slessor, *The Central Blue,* New York, 1957, 434.

19. Lord Maurice Hankey, *Politics, Trials and Errors,* Chicago, 1950, 29. Hankey overlooked the German demand for Belgium's unconditional surrender in 1940. But this was a mere fillip of arrogance in a clash that the Germans (and the Belgians) knew was a foregone conclusion.

20. E. R. Dupuy, *Men of West Point,* New York, 1951, 324.

21. Wedemeyer, *Wedemeyer Reports,* 186. Wedemeyer opposed Roosevelt's (and Churchill's) tendency to demonize Germany as a "power of darkness" (90).

22. Reminiscences of General Ira Eaker, Columbia University Oral History Collection, 131.

23. Brown, *Bodyguard of Lies,* 249.

24. Armstrong, *Unconditional Surrender,* 160.

25. Ian Colvin, *Vansittart in Office,* London, 1965, 149–155, 205–206.

26. Klemens Von Klemperer, *German Resistance Against Hitler: The Search for Allies Abroad, 1938–1945,* New York, 1992, 343–344; Brown, *Bodyguard of Lies,* 239.

27. Brown, *Bodyguard of Lies,* 234.

28. Hans Hohne, *Canaris: Hitler's Master Spy,* translated by Maxwell Brownjohn, New York, 1979, 480–481.

29. The Rt. Hon Lord Vansittart, *Bones of Contention,* New York, 1945, 41; Norman Rose, *Vansittart: Study of a Diplomat,* London, 1978, 242; John Colville, *The Fringes of Power: Downing Street Diaries,* London, 1985, 162.

30. Armstrong, *Unconditional Surrender,* 119.

31. Ulrich von Hassell, *The Von Hassell Diaries, 1938–1944,* New York, 1947, 281.

32. Sherwood, *Roosevelt and Hopkins,* 696. Map Room Files, FDR Library, box 165, folder 3, three-page typewritten manuscript entitled "Notes for FDR." Above, in FDR's handwriting, is: "Notes for my press conf.—dictated by me January 22."

33. Morgan, *FDR: A Biography,* 657; Raymond G. O'Connor, *Diplomacy for Victory: FDR and Unconditional Surrender,* New York, 1971, 36–37.

34. Armstrong, *Unconditional Surrender,* 17. In 1935, the *Philadelphia Record* had called Davis "a menace at large" because he called on FDR to take a belligerent

stance toward Germany's decision to rearm (Davis file, Franklin D. Roosevelt Library).

35. Martin E. Marty, *Pilgrims in their Own Land: 500 Years of Religion in America*, Boston, 1984, 363, 370.

36. *Holmes Pollock Letters*, vol. 1, 250, cited in Morton White, *Social Thought in America*, Boston, Mass., 1957.

37. Donald Smythe, *Pershing, General of the Armies*, Bloomington, Ind., 1986, 220–222.

38. Noel F. Busch, *T.R.: The Story of Theodore Roosevelt and his Influence on our Times*, New York, 1963, 328–329. Also see John Milton Cooper, *The Warrior and the Priest*, Cambridge, Mass., 1983, 306ff.

39. Sherwood, *Roosevelt and Hopkins*, 603. Another rationale for unconditional surrender offered by postwar defenders was its value as a safeguard against a repetition of Germany's "stab in the back" (*Dolchstoss*) explanation for their defeat in World War I. Hitler and others maintained that the German army had not been defeated on the battlefield and blamed the loss of the war on the collapse of civilian morale and a Communist revolt led by Jews. FDR did not mention *Dolchstoss* as an argument for unconditional surrender, nor did the Davis Committee. Their simplistic stance was summed up by one of its members, Assistant Secretary of State Breckinridge Long: "We are fighting this war because we did not have an unconditional surrender at the end of the last one." (Raymond G. O'Connor, *Diplomacy for Victory: FDR and Unconditional Surrender*, New York, 1971, 37.) Apparently, they had concluded that any attempt to negotiate with the Germans would be a mistake because negotiations had failed to secure a lasting peace in 1918–19.

40. Dallek, *Franklin D. Roosevelt and American Foreign Policy*, 375.

41. Brown, *Bodyguard of Lies*, 249.

42. Armstrong, *Unconditional Surrender*, 187–188.

43. Ibid., 218. Also see *Washington Post*, February 19, 1943.

44. Joachim Fest, *Plotting Hitler's Death: The Story of the German Resistance*, translated by Bruce Little, New York, 1996, 189–196, 224–225.

45. Nichols, *Washington Dispatches*, 134.

CHAPTER 8: WAR WAR LEADS TO JAW JAW

1. Morgan, *FDR: A Biography*, 658; James McGregor Burns, *Roosevelt: The Soldier of Freedom*, New York, 1970, 324.

2. Weil, *A Pretty Good Club*, 121.

3. Harold Macmillan, *The Blast of War*, New York, 1968, 201.

4. Weil, *A Pretty Good Club*, 126.

5. Winkler, *The Politics of Propaganda*, 100–101.

6. Weil, *A Pretty Good Club*, 125.

7. *Time*, March 15, 1943, 11.

8. Biddle, *In Brief Authority*, 186–187.

9. Ficken, "The Democratic Party," 94.

10. Ibid., 96.

11. Ibid., 97.

12. Nichols, *Washington Dispatches,* 124; Young, *Congressional Politics,* 23.

13. Francis Neilson, *The Tragedy of Europe*, Appleton, Wisc., 1940–1946, vol. 3, 393–394.

14. Nichols, ed., *Washington Dispatches,* 129.

15. Young, *Congressional Politics*, 25.

16. Blum, *The Price of Vision,* 165.

17. Polenberg, *War and Society,* 194–195.

18. Blum, *V Was For Victory,* 240.

19. Ibid., 236–237.

20. Sirevag, *The Eclipse of the New Deal,* 217–223.

21. Leff, "The Politics of Sacrifice in World War II," 1299.

22. Winkler, *The Politics of Propaganda,* 66–72.

23. "Pennsylvania Governors Past and Present," URL http://www.state.pa.us/PA_Exec/Historical_Museum/DAM/governors/earle.html

24. Hans Hohne, *Canaris: Hitler's Master Spy,* translated by Maxwell Brownjohn, New York, 1979, 483–484.

25. Hoffmann, *The History of the German Resistance,* 226–227; Hohne, *Canaris,* 484.

26. Allen Dulles, *Germany's Underground,* New York, 1947, 128ff. Also see Peter Grose, *Gentleman Spy: The Life of Allen Dulles,* New York, 1994, 176ff.

27. Grose, *Allen Dulles,* 180.

28. Hoffmann, *The History of the German Resistance,* 228–229.

29. Hans Hohne, *Canaris,* 486ff.

30. Armstrong, *Unconditional Surrender,* 83; Michael S. Sherry, *The Rise of American Air Power*, New Haven, Conn., 1987, 152.

31. Eric Morris, *Circles of Hell: The War in Italy 1943–1945*, New York, 1993, 11–12, 97–98. Earlier, in a cable to Washington Eisenhower recommended offering the Italians a "peace with honor." After much jockeying, Roosevelt persuaded Churchill to sign a joint telegram, telling Eisenhower, "We cannot get away from unconditional surrender." Eisenhower's subsequent statement tried to evade this directive by omitting any mention of the phrase.

32. On July 26, Roosevelt had told Churchill he was willing to accept a deal "as close to unconditional surrender as possible." FDR's change of mind revealed how much the phrase had become an article of political faith to him and his inner circle. Morris, *Circles of Hell*, 97.

33. Ibid., 175ff.

34. Armstrong, *Unconditional Surrender*, 83–84. Paul Kecskemeti, *Strategic Surrender: The Politics of Victory and Defeat,* Stanford, Calif., 1958, 116. Badoglio refused to commit Italy to what the allies called "co-belligerency," a call to Italians to join the war against the Germans. He let King Victor Emmanuel declare war on Germany on October 11—a virtually meaningless gesture. Morris, *Circles of Hell,* 200–201.

35. Morris, *Circles of Hell*, 135–138. The impact of Italian disenchantment with unconditional surrender was especially visible in Tirana, Albania, headquarters of

Italian Army Group East. A handful of German paratroopers seized the commanding general and his staff, immobilizing a quarter of a million men.

36. John Ellis, *World War II: A Statistical Survey: The Essential Facts and Figures for all the Combatants,* New York, 1993, Table 53, 255; Morris, *Circles of
Hell,* notes that the Allies originally sought only to capture Naples and the complex
of airfields around Foggia, and committed only nine divisions to the invasion. But
the Italian campaign soon acquired a momentum of its own, requiring ever larger
numbers of troops, to prevent the Germans from inflicting a serious wound on Allied prestige.

37. Winkler, *The Politics of Propaganda,* 88.

38. Ibid., 94–95.

39. Ibid., 95–97.

40. Ibid., 99–100.

41. Ibid., 108–111.

CHAPTER 9: FALL OF A PROPHET

1. White and Maze, *Henry A. Wallace,* 166.

2. Reminiscences of Isador Lubin, Columbia University Oral History Collection, 123.

3. Sirevag, *The Eclipse of the New Deal,* 527; Edward L. Schapsmeier and
Frederick H. Schapsmeier, *Prophet in Politics: Henry A Wallace and the War Years,
1940–1965,* Ames, Iowa, 1970, 55.

4. Sirevag, *The Eclipse of the New Deal,* 540–542; White and Maze, *Henry A.
Wallace,* 165.

5. Sirevag, *The Eclipse of the New Deal,* 540–541.

6. Ibid., 118.

7. Ibid., 120.

8. White and Maze, *Henry A. Wallace,* 166–168.

9. Schapsmeier and Schapsmeier, *Prophet in Politics,* 58–61.

10. White and Maze, *Henry Wallace,* 172–173.

11. Schapsmeier and Schapsmeier, *Prophet in Politics,* 46–49.

12. Ibid., 51–52.

13. Sirevag, *The Eclipse of the New Deal,* 542.

14. Russell Lord, *The Wallaces of Iowa,* Boston, 1947, 506–507.

15. Blum, *The Price of Vision,* 219–220.

16. Ibid.

17. Ibid.

18. Ibid., 222.

19. Ibid., 224–225.

20. White and Maze, *Henry A. Wallace,* 176.

21. Blum, *The Price of Vision,* 226 (footnote); Sirevag, *The Eclipse of the New
Deal,* 543.

22. *Washington Times-Herald,* July 15, 1943.

23. Jones did have a habit of acquiring "chits" from FDR authorizing or supporting potentially controversial decisions. See Sirevag, *The Eclipse of the New Deal*, 532–533.

24. White and Maze, *Henry A. Wallace*, 178; Schapsmeier and Schapsmeier, *Prophet in Politics*, 71.

25. Blum, *The Price of Vision*, 228; Schapsmeier and Schapsmeier, *Prophet in Politics*, 71.

26. Blum, *The Price of Vision*, 228.

27. Nichols, *Washington Dispatches*, 221.

CHAPTER 10: WHAT DO YOU GET, BLACK BOY

1. Polenberg, *War and Society*, 127.

2. Blum, *V Was For Victory*, 200–202.

3. Robert Shogan and Tom Craig, *The Detroit Race Riot*, New York, 1964, 32.

4. *Time*, June 21, 1943; Polenberg, *War and Society*, 127–128.

5. *Time*, June 21, 1943.

6. Polenberg, *War and Society*, 128.

7. Blum, *V Was For Victory*, 184–185.

8. Ibid., 206.

9. Blum, *The Price of Vision*, 243; Blum, *V Was For Victory*, 204–205.

10. Shogun and Craig, *The Detroit Race Riot*, 114.

11. Polenberg, *War and Society*, 159–160.

12. Morgan, *FDR: A Biography*, 663–664; James F. Byrnes, *All in One Lifetime*, New York, 1958, 179–183.

13. Polenberg, *War and Society*, 166–167; Ficken, "The Democratic Party and Domestic Politics During World War II," 104–105.

14. Ibid., 104.

15. Nichols, *Washington Dispatches*, 210.

16. Ibid.

17. Sirevag, *The Eclipse of the New Deal*, 247.

18. Ibid., 247–248.

19. Ibid., 249.

20. Ibid.; Schapsmeier and Schapsmeier, *Prophet in Politics*, 75.

21. White and Maze, *Henry A. Wallace*, 180.

22. White and Maze, *Henry A. Wallace*, 182; Schapsmeier and Schapsmeier, *Prophet in Politics*, 77; Blum, *The Price of Vision*, 227.

23. Blum, *The Price of Vision*, 228.

24. Ibid., 236.

25. Ibid., 237.

26. Memoirs by Harry S. Truman, *Year of Decisions*, New York, 1955, 179.

27. Truman, *Harry S. Truman*, 155.

28. Donald L. Riddle, *The Truman Committee: A Study in Congressional Responsibility*, New Brunswick, N.J., 1964, 123; Truman, *Harry S. Truman*, 154.

29. Truman, *Harry S. Truman*, 146–147.

30. Ibid., 155–156.

31. *Time*, March 8, 1943, 13.

32. Riddle, *The Truman Committee*, 159–160.

33. Truman, *Harry S. Truman*, 162.

34. Neal, *Dark Horse*, 230–258; Morgan, *FDR: A Biography*, 647.

35. Johnson, *The Republican Party and Wendell Willkie*, 219.

36. Neal, *Dark Horse*, 261.

37. Blum, *The Price of Vision*, 128.

38. Neal, *Dark Horse*, 264–265.

39. Ibid., 230; Johnson, *Republican Party and Wendell Willkie*, 235.

40. Johnson, *The Republican Party and Wendell Willkie*, 237; Neal, *Dark Horse*, 280.

41. Blum, *The Price of Vision*, 127–128; Morgan, *FDR: A Biography*, 647.

42. *Time*, March 8, 1943, 12.

CHAPTER 11: LET MY CRY COME UNTO THEE

1. Richard Breitman, *Official Secrets: What the Nazis Planned, What the British and Americans Knew*, New York, 1999, 139.

2. Ibid., 92ff.

3. Ibid., 142.

4. William Vanden Heuvel, "America and the Holocaust," *American Heritage*, July-August 1999. Eighty-three percent of German Jews under twenty-five escaped Germany before the war began. Also see Joseph Tenenbaum, *Race and Reich*, New York, 1956, 255.

5. *Saturday Evening Post*, March 28, 1942.

6. *Saturday Evening Post*, June 27, 1942.

7. Neilson, *The Tragedy of Europe*, vol. 3, 400; Blum, *V Was For Victory*, 174.

8. Breitman, *Official Secrets*, 135–136.

9. William Brustein, *The Logic of Evil: The Social Origins of the Nazi Party, 1925–1933*, New Haven, Conn., 1996, 25–29.

10. Götz Aly, *Final Solution: Nazi Population Policy and the Murder of the European Jews*, translated from the German by Belinda Cooper and Allison Brown, New York, 1999, 59–148. Aly probes the files of the midlevel bureaucrats who worked for Himmler, Heydrich, and other Nazis leaders to reveal how their policy of "ethnic redistribution" to create a greater German heartland gradually transmuted into extermination of the Jews.

11. Ibid., 203.

12. Ibid., 204–205. Aly points out that no book has yet been written on what the Germans thought during World War II about the "solution of the Jewish question."

13. Sirevag, *The Eclipse of the New Deal*, 354.

14. Ibid.

15. *Time*, March 8, 1943, 29.

16. Richard Lawrence Miller, *Truman: The Rise To Power*, New York, 1986, 390–391. Also see David McCullough, *Truman*, New York, 1992, 286.

17. Henry L. Feingold, *The Politics of Rescue: The Roosevelt Administration and the Holocaust*, New Brunswick, N.J., 1970, 197.

18. Weinberg, *Germany, Hitler and World War II*, 225–228.

19. Breitman, *Official Secrets*, 181–186; Blum, *V Was For Victory*, 178.

20. Breitman, *Official Secrets*, 186; Jordan A. Schwarz, *Liberal: Adolf Berle and the Vision of an American Era*, New York, 1987, 198–205.

21. Blum, *From the Morgenthau Diaries: Years of War*, 218.

22. Ibid., 220.

23. Sherwood, *Roosevelt and Hopkins*, 791.

24. Winston Churchill, *The Hinge of Fate*, Boston, 1950, 685–657.

25. Vansittart, *Bones of Contention*, 62, 76.

26. War Messages of Franklin D. Roosevelt, U.S. Government Printing Office, 85.

27. Armstrong, *Unconditional Surrender*, 32–33.

28. Barry M. Katz, *Foreign Intelligence, Research and Analysis in the Office of Strategic Services, 1942–1945*, Cambridge, Mass., 1989, 39–40.

29. Armstrong, *Unconditional Surrender*, 56–57.

30. Dower, *War Without Mercy*, New York, 1986, 162.

31. Ibid., 85.

32. Ibid., 92.

33. Ibid., 54–55.

34. Ronald Schaffer, *Wings of Judgment: American Bombing in World War II*, New York, 1985, 24–26.

35. Thomas M. Coffey, *"Hap": The Story of the U.S. Air Force and the Man Who Built It, General Henry A. "Hap" Arnold*, New York, 1982, 228.

36. Schaffer, *Wings of Judgment*, 61.

37. Ibid., 37.

38. Eric Markusen and David Kopf, *The Holocaust and Strategic Bombing: Genocide and Total War in the 20th Century*, New York, 1995, 158–160. Also see Martin Caidin, *The Night Hamburg Died*, London, 1966.

39. Sherry, *The Rise of American Air Power*, 1987, 156.

40. Schaffer, *Wings of Judgment*, 59; Sherry, *The Rise of American Air Power*, 139–141.

41. Schaffer, *Wings of Judgment*, 69–70.

42. Roeder, *The Censored War*, 84.

43. Richard Lamb, *The Ghosts of Peace, 1935–1945*, London, 1987, 224.

44. Ibid., 225–226.

45. Armstrong, *Unconditional Surrender*, 156.

46. Ibid., 262.

Chapter 12: Red Star Rising

1. Weil, *A Pretty Good Club*, 134.

2. Ibid., 49–50; Hugh De Santis, *The Diplomacy of Silence: The American Foreign Service, the Soviet Union, and the Cold War, 1933–1947*, Chicago, 1980, 23.

3. Weil, *A Pretty Good Club*, 101.

4. Ibid., 130–133. Also see Charles Bohlen, *Witness To History*, New York, 1973, 39–41.

5. George F. Kennan, *Memoirs,* vol. 1, Boston 1967, 57.

6. Weil, *A Pretty Good Club*, 135–136.

7. Ibid., 132.

8. Ibid., 133.

9. Ibid., 139

10. Ibid., 134–135. For the rumor campaign about Welles's bisexuality, see Otis L. Graham Jr. and Meghan Robinson Wander, eds., *Franklin D. Roosevelt: His Life and Times,* Boston, 1985, 453.

11. O'Neill, *A Better World,* 22–23. Also see Eugene Lyons, "Apologists Do Their Stuff," in *The Red Decade,* New York, 1941, 114–127.

12. S. J. Taylor, *Stalin's Apologist,* New York, 1990, 220. Thomas R. Maddux, *Years of Estrangement: American Relations with the Soviet Union, 1933–1941,* Tallahassee, Fla. 1980, 11–26.

13. Taylor, *Stalin's Apologist,* 182. Laying it on with a trowel, the Pulitzer Committee added that Duranty's dispatches glittered with "scholarship, profundity, impartiality and sound judgment and exceptional clarity."

14. Robert Conquest, "Liberals and Totalitarianism," *The New Criterion,* February 1999, 7.

15. Taylor, *Stalin's Apologist,* 206–208.

16. Maddux, *Years of Estrangement,* 25.

17. O'Neill, *A Better World,* 20.

18. Joseph C. Davies, *Mission to Moscow,* New York, 1941, 167, 178; Weil, *A Pretty Good Club,* 92.

19. Oursler, *Behold This Dreamer!,* 363; O'Neill, *A Better World,* 22, 43; Maddux, *Years of Estrangement,* 103.

20. O'Neill, *A Better World,* 46.

21. Christopher Andrew and Oleg Gordievsky, *KGB: The Inside Story of its Foreign Operations from Lenin to Gorbachev,* New York, 1990, 331.

22. Weil, *A Pretty Good Club,* 92.

23. O'Neill, *A Better World,* 60.

24. Ibid., 61.

25. Weil, *A Pretty Good Club,* 127–128.

26. Ibid., 138. Also see Loy W. Henderson, *A Question of Trust: The Origins of U.S.-Soviet Diplomatic Relations,* edited, with an introduction, by George W. Baer, Stanford, Calif., 1986, 513–514.

27. Weil, *A Pretty Good Club,* 140.

28. Benjamin Welles, *Sumner Welles: FDR's Global Strategist,* New York, 1997, 343ff. For secret service protection, PC with Frank Waldrop, former managing editor of the *Washington Times-Herald.*

29. Reminiscences of Henry A. Wallace, Columbia University Oral History Collection, vol. 8, 1536, 1586, 1611.

30. Welles, *Sumner Welles,* 350.

31. Amos Perlmutter, *FDR and Stalin: A Not So Grand Alliance*, Columbia, Mo., 1993, 121; Paul, *Katyn,* 314.

32. Ibid., 307.

33. Ibid., 314.

34. Ibid., 302, 304.

35. Ibid., 302–303.

36. Ibid., 305–306.

37. Robert Szymczaki, "The Unquiet Dead: The Katyn Forest Massacre as an Issue in American Politics" (Ph.D. dissertation, Carnegie-Mellon University, 1980), 119–120.

38. Lloyd C. Gardner, *A Covenant with Power*, New York, 1984, 57.

Chapter 13: Shaking Hands With Murder

1. Bohlen, *Witness to History,* 121, 125–126.

2. Irwin F. Gellman, *Secret Affairs: Franklin Roosevelt, Cordell Hull and Sumner Welles*, Baltimore, 1995, 337; Keith Eubank, *Summit at Teheran, The Untold Story*, New York, 1985, 120.

3. Ibid., 337.

4. Ibid., 338.

5. Bohlen, *Witness to History*, 135. Bohlen was "skeptical about the plot."

6. Neilson, *The Tragedy of Europe*, vol. 3, 417.

7. John Lamberton Harper, *American Visions of Europe*, New York, 1996, 75.

8. Reminiscences of Henry A. Wallace, Columbia University Oral History Collection, vol. 8, 1571.

9. Eubank, *Summit at Teheran,* 247.

10. Sherwood, *Roosevelt and Hopkins,* 782.

11. Harper, *American Visions of Europe,* 89.

12. Ibid.

13. Bohlen, *Witness to History,* 147.

14. Eubank, *Summit at Teheran,* 315–316.

15. Ibid., 351; Harper, *American Visions of Europe,* 117–118.

16. Bohlen, *Witness to History,* 146.

17. Harper, *American Visions of Europe,* 89. Averell Harriman noted that Roosevelt "consistently show[ed] very little interest in Eastern European matters except as they affect sentiment in America."

18. John Keegan, *The Battle for History: Re-Fighting World War II,* New York, 1996, 111. Charles Bohlen was "dismayed" by Roosevelt's readiness to abandon Poland if Stalin helped him deceive the Polish-American voters in the United States (*Witness to History*, 151).

19. Stephane Courtois et al., *The Black Book of Communism: Crimes, Terror, Repression*, Cambridge, Mass., 1999, 367–372.

20. FDR expressed his indifference to Russian domination of Europe to a number of people. In September 1943, he told Francis, Cardinal Spellman he expected Russia to control Germany, Austria, Croatia, as well as the states on her borders. He hoped "European influence would bring the Russians to become less barbarian." Earlier, he

told his son Elliott that an aggrandized Russia, with most of Europe under its control, might be a constructive force. Harper, *American Visions of Europe*, 88.

21. Bohlen, *Witness To History*, 153.

22. Edward Taborsky, *President Edvard S. Benes: Between East and West, 1938–1948*, Stanford, Calif., 1981, 19–20. Stalin assured the gullible Benes that Moscow would permit the other Slav nations to choose their own system of government.

23. Milovan Djilas, *Wartime*, New York, 1977, 388–389, 437. Stalin also added a comment on his "Panslavic" policy. "If the Slavs keep united and maintain solidarity, no one in the future will be able to move a finger." Other historians have stressed Stalin's personality as resistant to Rooseveltian charm, or any other external influence. "Stalin's suspicious nature was inherent, not contingent. . . . A man who ordered the execution of millions of loyal Bolsheviks during the purges, who had his leading generals shot just before the outbreak of the war, and arranged the murder of Leon Trotsky in Mexico, was a man pathologically determined to see conspiracies everywhere." John Patrick Diggins, *The Proud Decades: America in War and in Peace, 1941–1960*, New York, 1988, 68.

24. John Earl Haynes and Harvey Klehr, *Venona: Decoding Soviet Espionage in America*, New Haven, Conn., 1999, 140–150, 201–204.

25. Christopher Andrew and Vasili Mitrokhin, *The Sword and the Shield: The Mitrokhin Archive and the Secret History of the KGB*, New York, 1999, 107. In 1941, Berle consulted Dean Acheson, assistant secretary of state, and Associate Justice of the Supreme Court Felix Frankfurter about Chambers's revelations. They assured him that the accusations were "groundless." Allen Weinstein, *The Haunted Wood*, New York, 1999, 48. When the FBI interviewed Chambers in 1941, he was distressed to learn they had never seen Berle's memorandum and, fearing a plot to ruin him, told them little or nothing. Sam Tanenhaus, *Whittaker Chambers*, New York, 1997, 162–163, 170.

26. Andrew and Mitrokhin, *The Sword and the Shield*, 107–108; Weinstein, *The Haunted Wood*, 241ff. Donovan disobeyed Roosevelt's orders and made a copy of the codebook before returning it.

27. Haynes and Klehr, *Venona*, 146.

28. Ibid., 134.

29. Ibid., 136.

30. Andrew and Mitrokhin, *The Sword and the Shield*, 111; Allen Weinstein, "Nadya: A Spy Story," *Encounter*, June 1977, 75.

31. Nichols, *Washington Dispatches*, 287–288.

32. O'Neill, *A Better World*, 78.

33. George Sirgiovanni, *An Undercurrent of Suspicion: Anti-Communism in America During World War II*, New Brunswick, N.J., 1990, 106–109, 122–3, 152.

34. Ficken, "The Democratic Party," 182–183.

35. Johnson, *The Republican Party and Wendell Willkie*, 253.

36. Ibid.; Ficken, "The Democratic Party," 185; Stanley Walker, *Thomas E. Dewey: An American of this Century*, New York, 1944, 144–145.

37. Ficken, "The Democratic Party," 184; Nichols, *Washington Dispatches*, 291.

38. Eubank, *Summit at Teheran*, 426–427.

39. John M. Blum, *Joe Tumulty and the Wilson Era*, New York 1953, 150, 250, 263.

40. Robert Ferrell, *The Dying President*, Columbia, Mo., 1998, 28–29.

41. Ibid., 30.

42. Ficken, "The Democratic Party," 201.

43. Ferrell, *The Dying President*, 34–35.

44. Robert E. Gilbert, *The Mortal Presidency*, New York, 1992, 55; Ferrell, *The Dying President*, 37.

45. Ibid., 38–39.

46. Ibid., 39–41.

47. Ibid., 72.

48. Gilbert, *The Mortal Presidency*, 62; For the comments of the Secret Service agent who found Roosevelt beside his wheelchair, see *The American Experience—FDR*, Episode 3, "The Juggler," PBS, 1994.

49. Gilbert, *The Mortal Presidency*, 57.

50. Hugh Gregory Gallagher, *FDR's Splendid Deception*, New York, 1985, 86–91.

51. Roosevelt Library, President's Secretary's File (PSF: Cohen), March 8, 13. Roosevelt's reply is attached to this memorandum.

Chapter 14: Goddamning Roosevelt and Other Pastimes

1. Blum, *V Was For Victory*, 251.

2. Ibid., 251; Ficken, "The Democratic Party," 111.

3. Blum, *From the Morgenthau Diaries: Years of War*, 74–75.

4. Ficken, "The Democratic Party," 113.

5. Rosenman, *Working with Roosevelt*, 429.

6. Ficken, "The Democratic Party," 113.

7. Roland Young, *Congressional Politics in the Second World War*, New York, 1956, 140–143; Morgan, *FDR: A Biography*, 708–709; Blum, *V Was For Victory*, 243–244.

8. Ficken, "The Democratic Party," 117–118.

9. Biddle, *In Brief Authority*, 317–318.

10. Nancy Allen Hobor, "The United States Vs Montgomery Ward" (Ph.D. dissertation, University of Chicago, 1973), 202–203.

11. Powers, *Not Without Honor*, 184–185.

12. Biddle, *In Brief Authority*, 242; Powers, *Not Without Honor*, 187. Biddle wrote: "Nothing like the trial had ever happened in an American court of law."

13. Biddle, *In Brief Authority*, 243.

14. In 1915 Taft became head of the League to Enforce Peace, which launched a publicity campaign for a league of nations. Its 22 vice presidents were a who's who

of distinguished Republicans. Henry F. Pringle, *The Life and Times of William Howard Taft*, New York, 1939.

15. Neal, *Dark Horse,* 284.

16. Johnson, *The Republican Party and Wendell Willkie,* 246–247.

17. Ibid., 290–291.

18. Ibid., 112.

19. Neal, *Dark Horse,* 286; Johnson, *The Republican Party and Wendell Willkie,* 249–250.

20. Neal, *Dark Horse,* 286–287.

21. Ibid., 288; Johnson, *The Republican Party and Wendell Willkie,* 252.

22. Neal, *Dark Horse,* 288.

23. Ibid., 294–295.

24. Nash, *Dark Horse,* 305; Johnson, *The Republican Party and Wendell Willkie,* 280.

25. Blum, *The Price of Vision* 322.

26. Johnson, *The Republican Party and Wendell Willkie,* 280.

27. Neal, *Dark Horse,* 306; Johnson, *The Republican Party and Wendell Willkie,* 282.

28. Johnson, *The Republican Party and Wendell Willkie,* 281.

29. White and Maze, *Henry A. Wallace,* 187–188.

30. Schapsmeier and Schapsmeier, *Prophet in Politics,* 78.

31. White and Maze, *Henry A. Wallace,* 187; Blum, *The Price of Vision,* 289.

32. Blum, *The Price of Vision,* 289.

33. Morgan, *FDR: A Biography,* 707–708.

34. White and Maze, *Henry A. Wallace,* 188.

35. Blum, *The Price of Vision,* 263.

36. Ibid., 269–270.

37. White and Maze, *Henry A. Wallace,* 194.

38. Blum, *The Price of Vision,* 317.

39. Ibid., 295.

40. McCullough, *Truman,* 292.

41. White and Maze, *Henry A. Wallace,* 191.

42. Blum, *The Price of Vision,* 313.

43. Ibid., 308, 310.

44. Ibid., 315.

45. Truman, *Harry S. Truman,* 153; Brinkley, *The End of Reform,* 193. A friend to FDR, Johnson was serving as a colonel in the army ordnance department when he was appointed head of SWPC. In a vain attempt to give him more clout he was promoted to brigadier general. Franklin D. Roosevelt Library, Official Files, file 4735F, Box 4.

46. Ibid., 155–156.

47. Ibid., 163.

48. Polenberg, *War and Society,* 229–230.

49. Ficken, "The Democratic Party," 217.

50. Truman, *Harry S. Truman,* 166–167.

Chapter 15: Democracy's Total War

1. Schaffer, *Wings of Judgment*, 67.

2. Ibid., 77.

3. Ibid., 79. Michael S. Sherry also notes in his chapter, "The Dynamics of Escalation" the influence of what he and other historians of the air war call "operational necessity." The heavy bombers had to be used to destroy cities because they were good for little else. (*The Rise of American Air Power*, 175.)

4. John C. McManus, *Deadly Sky: The American Combat Airman in World War II*, Novato, Calif., 2000, 202–203.

5. Thomas Parrish, ed., *The Simon and Schuster Encyclopedia of World War II*, New York, 1973, 223 (for size of replacement army).

6. Hoffmann, *The History of the German Resistance*, 31, 235ff.

7. Brown, *Bodyguard of Lies*, 430.

8. Winkler, *The Politics of Propaganda*, 133–134.

9. Brown, *Bodyguard of Lies*, 587–588.

10. Ibid., 588–589.

11. Ibid., 589.

12. Ibid., 589–590.

13. David Eisenhower, *Eisenhower at War*, New York, 1986, 204.

14. Brown, *Bodyguard of Lies*, 591.

15. Lamb, *The Ghosts of Peace*, 234–235.

16. Brown, *Bodyguard of Lies*, 592, 598–599.

17. Glenn B. Infield, *The Poltava Affair*, New York, 1973, 28–31.

18. Ibid., 160–162.

19. Ibid., 167.

20. Allen Paul, *Katyn: The Untold Story of Stalin's Polish Massacre*, New York, 1991, 314.

21. Dower, *War Without Mercy*, 144, 161.

22. Ibid., 160.

23. Ibid., 51–52.

24. Roeder, *The Censored War*, 21.

25. Ibid., 14.

26. Kennan, *Memoirs*, 180.

27. Ibid., 195–197.

28. Blum, *The Price of Vision*, 331.

29. Schapsmeier and Schapsmeier, *Prophet In Politics*, 85–86.

30. Blum, *The Price of Vision*, 326–327.

31. Haynes and Klehr, *Venona*, 142–143.

32. Blum, *The Price Of Vision*, 333.

33. White and Maze, *Henry A. Wallace*, 195.

34. O'Neill, *A Better World*, 150–151.

35. White and Maze, *Henry A. Wallace*, 194–195; O'Neill, *A Better World*, 151; Courtois et al., *The Black Book of Communism*, 111–115; Owen Lattimore, "The New Road to Asia," *National Geographic*, December 1944.

36. Richard Buel, *In Irons,* New Haven, Conn., 1998, 36ff. This book is an excellent account of the impact of the war on the American economy.

37. Courtois et al., *The Black Book of Communism,* 470–471; Schapsmeier and Schapsmeier, *Prophet in Politics,* 85.

38. Schapsmeier and Schapsmeier, *Prophet in Politics,* 95–96.

CHAPTER 16: OPERATION STOP HENRY

1. Schapsmeier and Schapsmeier, *Prophet In Politics,* 102.

2. Morgan, *FDR: A Biography,* 725–726; Ficken, "The Democratic Party," 207.

3. Ibid., 214.

4. Rosenman, *Working with Roosevelt,* 439.

5. Neal, *Dark Horse,* 313–314.

6. Ficken, "The Democratic Party," 212.

7. Rosenman, *Working with Roosevelt,* 441.

8. Blum, *The Price of Vision,* 360.

9. Lord, *The Wallaces of Iowa,* 525; Blum, *The Price of Vision,* 361.

10. Blum, *The Price of Vision,* 361.

11. Ibid., 362–363. In his diary, Wallace refers to the tabulation as "the Marsh Memorandum." It had been prepared by Young's assistant, Charles Marsh. Also see Markowitz, *The Rise and Fall of the People's Century,* 104.

12. Ficken, "The Democratic Party," 219.

13. Schapsmeier and Schapsmeier, *Prophet in Politics,* 104.

14. Blum, *The Price of Vision,* 364.

15. Ibid., 365.

16. Ibid.

17. Ibid., 365–366.

18. Ibid., 366–367.

19. Morgan, *FDR: A Biography,* 728.

20. Byrnes, *All in One Lifetime,* 225–226.

21. Andrew and Mitrokhin, *The Sword and the Shield,* 109.

22. Lord, *The Wallaces of Iowa,* 530–531.

23. Ibid., 531–532.

24. Ibid., 531.

25. Byrnes, *All in One Lifetime,* 227; White and Maze, *Henry A. Wallace,* 205.

26. Neal, *Dark Horse,* 315.

27. White and Maze, *Henry A. Wallace,* 203; Lord, *The Wallaces of Iowa,* 532.

28. Schapsmeier and Schapsmeier, *Prophet in Politics,* 105.

29. Lord, *The Wallaces of Iowa,* 532.

30. Ibid., 533.

31. Ficken, "The Democratic Party," 221–222.

32. Schapsmeier and Schapsmeier, *Prophet in Politics,* 106.

33. Truman, *Harry S. Truman,* 177.

34. Lord, *The Wallaces of Iowa,* 535.

35. Ibid. Also see Truman, *Harry S. Truman,* 177, and Schapsmeier and Schapsmeier, *Prophet in Politics,* 107.

36. Ferrell, *The Dying President,* 79; Lord, *The Wallaces of Iowa,* 535.

37. Truman, *Harry S. Truman,* 177–179.

38. Blum, *The Price of Vision,* 370; Markowitz, *The Rise and Fall of the People's Century,* 112.

39. Truman, *Harry S. Truman,* 181.

40. Ibid., 181–182.

41. Blum, *The Price of Vision,* 369; Reminiscences of Henry A. Wallace, Columbia University Oral History Collection, vol. 8, 1442.

42. Blum, *The Price of Vision,* 369–370; Reminiscences of Henry A. Wallace, Columbia University Oral History Collection, vol. 8, 1427.

43. Markowitz, *The Rise and Fall of the People's Century,* 114.

44. Ibid., 117; Krock, *Memoirs: Sixty Years on the Firing Line,* 218. Krock published the "Clear it with Sidney" line because Byrnes was a close friend of *Times* editor Turner Catledge. If he had written it, Byrnes would have been quickly identified as the source. Everyone involved denied it until Byrnes admitted the story in his memoir, *All In One Lifetime.*

45. Blum, *V Was For Victory,* 292. Early in 1945, FDR made Porter chairman of the Federal Communications Commission.

46. Blum, *The Price of Vision,* 370.

CHAPTER 17: DEATH AND TRANSFIGURATION IN BERLIN

1. Weinberg, *Germany, Hitler and World War II,* 249.

2. Peter Hoffmann, *Stauffenberg: A Family History,* Cambridge and New York, 1995, 266–267.

3. Brown, *Bodyguard of Lies,* 768ff; Fest, *Plotting Hitler's Death,* 280–282.

4. Klemperer, *German Resistance Against Hitler,* 385.

5. Ibid., 426 (note); Von Hassell, *The Von Hassell Diaries,* 566–567.

6. Brown, *Bodyguard of Lies,* 768.

7. Armstrong, *Unconditional Surrender,* 209.

8. Theodore S. Hamerow, *On the Road to the Wolf's Lair: German Resistance to Hitler,* Cambridge, Mass., 1997, 357–358.

9. Rosenman, *Working with Roosevelt,* 371–372.

10. Douglas Southall Freeman, *R. E. Lee,* vol. 4, New York, 1936, 123.

11. Edward Wagenknecht, *The Seven Worlds of Theodore Roosevelt,* New York, 1958, 238. Roosevelt added that a war with Japan could only begin "as the result of such folly and wickedness as to stamp all who were responsible for it, no matter in which country they dwelt, with eternal infamy."

12. Blum, *From the Morgenthau Diaries: Years of War,* 338.

13. Frank Friedel, *Franklin D. Roosevelt: Rendezvous with Destiny,* Boston, 1990, 350–351; Blum, *From the Morgenthau Diaries: Years of War,* 342. It is inter-

esting to note FDR's fondness for castration as a solution—evidence of his psychological link with German-haters of World War I.

14. Blum, *From the Morgenthau Diaries: Years of War,* 342ff.; Weinstein, *The Haunted Wood,* 158.

15. Blum, *From the Morgenthau Diaries, Years of War,* 349.

16. Ibid., 353–354.

17. Ibid., 353–354.

18. FDR told Secretary of State Hull he wanted Morgenthau along to discuss England's financial problems. Franklin D. Roosevelt Library, Morgenthau Diaries, Box 516, vol. 6, July-December, 1944.

19. Morgan, *FDR: A Biography,* 734.

20. Krock, *Memoirs: Sixty Years on the Firing Line,* 209.

21. Ibid., 208.

22. Morgan, *FDR: A Biography,* 735–736.

23. Sherwood, *Roosevelt and Hopkins,* 818–819.

24. Hoffmann, *The History of the German Resistance,* 524ff.; Helmuth James von Moltke, *Letters to Freya, 1939–1945,* edited and translated from the German by Beate Rhum von Oppen, New York, 1990, 404.

25. Weinberg, *Germany, Hitler and World War II,* 253.

26. Weinberg, *A World in Arms,* 709–712.

27. Kennan, *Memoirs,* 210.

28. Infield, *The Poltava Affair,* 202–203.

29. Schaffer, *Wings of Judgment,* 80–81.

30. Ibid., 83–84; Michael S. Sherry notes that by this time, three-fourths of all American missions relied on radar or blind-bombing techniques, with terror their "inevitable consequence" (*The Rise of American Air Power,* 261).

31. Schaffer, *Wings of Judgment,* 85–86.

32. Ibid., 88.

33. Ibid., 88–89.

34. Ibid., 91–92; Sherry, *The Rise of American Air Power,* 262.

CHAPTER 18: THE DYING CHAMPION

1. Rosenman, *Working with Roosevelt,* 461–462.

2. Ferrell, *The Dying President,* 83.

3. Richard Norton Smith, *Thomas E. Dewey and His Times,* New York, 1982, 403–404.

4. Rupert Hughes, *The Story of Thomas E. Dewey, Attorney for the People,* New York, 1944, 399.

5. Ficken, "The Democratic Party," 249.

6. Smith, *Thomas E. Dewey and His Times,* 426–427.

7. Ficken, "The Democratic Party," 251–252.

8. Ibid., 253–255.

9. Ibid., 255–256.

10. Rosenman, *Working with Roosevelt*, 475–478.

11. Smith, *Thomas E. Dewey and His Times*, 422; Rosenman, *Working with Roosevelt*, 479.

12. Ficken, "The Democratic Party," 260.

13. Ferrell, *The Dying President*, 86–88.

14. Ibid., 91–92; Gilbert, *The Mortal Presidency*, 58. A. Merriman Smith, *Thank You, Mr. President: A White House Notebook*, New York, 1946, 156.

15. Rosenman, *Working with Roosevelt*, 483–485.

16. Sirevag, *The Eclipse of the New Deal*, 457–459.

17. Ferrell, *The Dying President*, 89.

18. White and Maze, *Henry A. Wallace*, 208; Blum, *The Price of Vision*, 381–382.

19. White and Maze, *Henry A. Wallace*, 209.

20. Blum, *The Price of Vision*, 382.

21. Schapsmeier and Schapsmeier, *Prophet in Politics*, 115; Lord, *The Wallaces of Iowa*, 544.

22. Truman, *Harry S. Truman*, 1972, 189.

23. Ficken, "The Democratic Party," 280; Markowitz, *The Rise and Fall of the People's Century*, 127.

24. Rosenman, *Working with Roosevelt*, 463–467; Neal, *Dark Horse*, 317.

25. Blum, *The Price of Vision*, 384; Neal, *Dark Horse*, 318.

26. Ficken, "The Democratic Party," 269–270.

27. Neal, *Dark Horse*, 320.

28. Ibid., 323.

29. Ficken, "The Democratic Party," 273.

30. Blum, *The Price of Vision*, 387–388.

31. After the 1940 election, Kennedy had visited Roosevelt at Hyde Park and reportedly got into an argument about intervening in the war. Roosevelt had become so angry, he ordered Kennedy off the estate. The two men never spoke again. Seymour M. Hersh, *The Dark Side of Camelot*, New York, 1997, 80–81.

32. Beschloss, *Kennedy and Roosevelt*, 259.

33. Smith, *Thomas E. Dewey and His Times*, 433.

34. Fraser, *Labor Will Rule*, 529–530.

35. Ficken, "The Democratic Party," 283–284.

36. Blum, *The Price of Vision*, 394.

37. Ferrell, *The Dying President*, 93.

38. Rosenman, *Working with Roosevelt*, 506; Ficken, "The Democratic Party," 283.

39. Ibid., 284–285.

40. Gilbert, *The Mortal Presidency*, 59.

41. Truman, *Harry S. Truman*, 190.

42. White and Maze, *Henry A. Wallace*, 211.

43. Nichols, *Washington Dispatches*, 496–497.

44. Weil, *A Pretty Good Club*, 179.

45. Ibid., 145–146.

46. Ibid., 147–148.

47. Cohen letter of January 16, 1945, Franklin D. Roosevelt Library, President's Secretary File (PSF).

48. Weil, *A Pretty Good Club*, 184–185.

49. Gilbert, *The Mortal Presidency*, 59; Ferrell, *The Dying President,* 93; Weil, *A Pretty Good Club*, 181.

50. Weil, *A Pretty Good Club*, 183.

51. Armstrong, *Unconditional Surrender,* 211.

52. William Casey, *The Secret War Against Hitler*, Washington, D.C., 1988, 179–180. Also see R. Harris Smith, *OSS*, Berkeley, Calif., 1978, 226–227. Smith confirms Casey's account.

53. Brown, *Bodyguard of Lies*, 797.

54. Eisenhower, *Eisenhower At War*, 529–530.

55. Brown, *Bodyguard of Lies,* 796; Armstrong, *Unconditional Surrender*, 158. Armstrong's figures differ slightly.

56. Armstrong, *Unconditional Surrender*, 158.

57. Ferrell, *The Dying President*, 96–97.

58. Dallek, *Franklin D. Roosevelt and American Foreign Policy,* 504.

59. Ibid., 505.

60. Ibid., 506.

61. Gilbert, *The Mortal Presidency*, 59.

62. Ferrell, *The Dying President,* 98.

63. Gilbert, *The Mortal Presidency*, 59.

64. Rosenman, *Working with Roosevelt*, 517. Roosevelt took three drafts of the inaugural speech and produced a final version that was shorter than any of them.

65. Gilbert, *The Mortal Presidency*, 60; Ferrell, *The Dying President*, 103; Truman, *Harry S. Truman*, 195.

66. White and Maze, *Henry A. Wallace*, 212.

CHAPTER 19: LOST LAST STANDS

1. Lord, *The Wallaces of Iowa*, 544–545.

2. Bascom N. Timmons, *Jesse H. Jones, The Man and the Statesman*, New York, 1956, 358–359.

3. Ibid., 360.

4. Ficken, "The Democratic Party," 292–293; Markowitz, *The Rise and Fall of the People's Century,* 132.

5. White and Maze, *Henry A. Wallace*, 213.

6. Truman, *Harry S. Truman*, 197.

7. Markowitz, *The Rise and Fall of the People's Century*, 132.

8. Lord, *The Wallaces of Iowa*, 547–548; Markowitz, *The Rise and Fall of the People's Century*, 131.

9. Lord, *The Wallaces of Iowa*, 548–549.

10. Ibid., 549–550.

11. Ibid., 554.

12. Ibid., 555.

13. Ibid., 546–547.

14. Leahy, *I Was There*, 293–294.

15. Truman, *Harry S. Truman*, 198; Markowitz, *The Rise and Fall of the People's Century*, 133–134.

16. Schapsmeier and Schapsmeier, *Prophet In Politics*, 123–124.

17. Perlmutter, *FDR and Stalin: A Not So Grand Alliance*, 180.

18. Weil, *A Pretty Good Club*, 186.

19. Bohlen, *Witness to History*, 171.

20. Ibid.

21. Bohlen, *Witness to History*, 175–176; De Santis, *The Diplomacy of Silence*, 131.

22. Dallek, *Franklin D. Roosevelt and American Foreign Policy*, 509; Bohlen, *Witness to History*, 173.

23. Bohlen, *Witness to History*, 183.

24. Dallek, *Franklin D. Roosevelt and American Foreign Policy*, 516.

25. Burns, *Roosevelt: The Soldier of Freedom*, 572.

26. Weil, *A Pretty Good Club*, 197–198; Edward R. Stettinius, *Roosevelt and the Russians: The Yalta Conference*, edited by Walter Johnson, New York, 1949, 36–37.

27. Bohlen, *Witness to History*, 199.

28. John Costello, *The Pacific War*, New York, 1981, 80. When Stalin signed his nonaggression pact with Tokyo, he told the Japanese foreign minister: "Now that Japan and Russia have fixed up their problem, Japan can straighten out the Far East and Germany can handle Europe. Later, together all of us will deal with America." It is an interesting glimpse of Stalin's worldview before Hitler invaded the Soviet Union.

29. Bohlen, *Witness to History*, 196–198.

30. Ibid., 200; Dallek, *Franklin D. Roosevelt and American Foreign Policy*, 520; Leahy, *I Was There*, 323.

31. Sirevag, *The Eclipse of the New Deal*, 655 (note).

32. Tanenhaus, *Whittaker Chambers*, 190–191.

33. Schaffer, *Wings of Judgment*, 96.

34. Knightley, Philip, *The First Casualty*, New York 1975, 315.

35. Schaffer, *Wings of Judgment*, 98–99; Sherry, *The Rise of American Air Power*, 261. The British, led by Air Marshal Sir Arthur Harris, never tried to apologize for Dresden. Harris sneered that protestors were motivated by a sentimental attachment to "German bands and Dresden shepherdesses." He insisted the city was "a mass of munitions works"—a lie. John Ellis, *Brute Force: Allied Strategy and Tactics in the Second World War*, New York, 1990, 187–188.

36. Schaffer, *Wings of Judgment*, 102–103. Dresden apparently never came to Roosevelt's attention—hardly surprising; by this time he was barely functioning. Sherry, *The Rise of American Air Power*, 262.

37. De Santis, *The Diplomacy of Silence*, 133–135.

38. Ferrell, *The Dying President*, 108.

39. Rosenman, *Working with Roosevelt*, 526.

40. Beatrice Bishop Berle and Travis Beal Jacobs Berle, eds., *Navigating the Rapids, 1918–1971: From the Papers of Adolf Berle*, New York, 1973, 477.

41. Dallek, *Franklin D. Roosevelt and American Foreign Policy*, 520.

42. Rosenman, *Working with Roosevelt*, 529.

43. Ibid., 527.

44. Bohlen, *Witness to History*, 207–208.

45. Morgan, *FDR: A Biography*, 758.

46. Robert Murphy, *Diplomat Among Warriors: The Unique World of a Foreign Service Expert*, New York, 1964, 247–248.

47. Anna Roosevelt Halsted Papers, Franklin D. Roosevelt Library.

48. Ibid. A copy of this letter is attached to Earle's letter in the Anna Roosevelt Halsted Papers, Franklin D. Roosevelt Library.

49. Crister S. Garrett and Stephen A. Garrett, "Death and Politics: The Katyn Massacre and American Foreign Policy," *Eastern European Quarterly* 20(4), 1986: 439–440.

50. Neilson, *The Tragedy of Europe*, vol. 3, 270.

51. B. H. Liddell Hart, *The German Generals Talk*, New York, 1948, 292–293.

52. Allen Drury, *A Senate Journal*, New York, 1963, 410.

53. Truman, *Harry S. Truman*, 203.

54. Ibid., 204–205.

55. David M. Kennedy, *Freedom From Fear*, New York, 1999, 668.

56. Schaffer, *Wings of Judgment*, 128–135; Roeder, *The Censored War*, 15. Also see Spector, *Eagle Against the Sun*, 504–505; Costello, *The Pacific War*, 530–533.

57. Hohne, *Canaris*, 595–596.

58. Charles MacDonald, *The Mighty Endeavor*, New York, Oxford University Press, 1965, 479; Eisenhower, *Eisenhower at War*, 763.

59. FDR called Bowers's book "thrilling." Harper, *American Visions of Europe*, 44.

60. Blum, *From the Morgenthau Diaries, Years of War*, 417–419.

61. Chester Wilmot, *The Struggle For Europe*, New York, 1952, 695.

62. Ferrell, *The Dying President*, 118–119; Neilson, *The Tragedy of Europe*, vol. 5, 308.

CHAPTER 20: A NEW PRESIDENT AND AN OLD POLICY

1. Truman, *Harry S. Truman*, 208–209.

2. Margaret Truman, *Bess W. Truman*, New York, 1986, 253.

3. Ibid., 253; Truman, *Harry S. Truman*, 220.

4. Ibid., 221–222.

5. Ibid., 222–223.

6. Harry S. Truman, *Memoirs*, New York, 1955, 42; Richard B. Frank, *Downfall: The End of the Imperial Japanese Empire*, New York, 1995, 215.

7. Weil, *A Pretty Good Club*, 189.

8. Ibid., 220.

9. Bohlen, *Witness to History,* 213. Truman, *Harry S. Truman,* 237.

10. Bohlen, *Witness to History,* 214–215.

11. W. Averell Harriman, *America and Russia in a Changing World,* New York, 1971, 42; Reminiscences of Henry A. Wallace, Columbia University Oral History Collection, vol. 7, 1407.

12. Some historians have argued that the failure to fight to the last man proved unconditional surrender did not prolong the struggle with Germany. This conclusion omits the ferocious resistance the Wehrmacht offered the British and Americans for ten months after D day. In his book *Strategic Surrender: The Politics of Victory and Defeat,* Paul Kecskemeti focuses on the final days and draws this inference. Yet two pages later he admits "the war may have been needlessly lengthened by the unconditional surrender policy." He tries to distinguish between the slogan and "rules" of non-negotiation that made it difficult for the allies to handle "surrender situations." To this writer, the argument seems to beg the question (226–228).

13. Kennan, *Memoirs,* 241–242.

14. Blum, *The Price of Vision,*437, 448, 457, 458.

15. Ibid., 458.

16. Weil, *A Pretty Good Club,* 222–223; Blum, *From the Morgenthau Diaries: Years of War,* 464.

17. Blum, *From the Morgenthau Diaries: Years of War,* 459–460. After Morgenthau left the government, he published the book *Germany Is Our Problem,* New York, 1945.

18. Weil, *A Pretty Good Club,* 224.

19. Blum, *From the Morgenthau Diaries: Years of War,* 464.

20. Robert H. Ferrell, ed., *Off the Record: The Private Papers of Harry S. Truman,* New York, 1980, 46.

21. Truman, *Harry S. Truman,* 248–249.

22. Mary B. Hinchey, "The Frustration of the New Deal Revival" (Ph.D. dissertation, University of Missouri, 1965), 112–113. Robert J. Donovan, *Conflict and Crisis: The Presidency of Harry S. Truman, 1945–1948,* New York, 1977, 32–33.

23. Ferrell, *Off the Record,* 35. Truman considered professional liberals "the lowest form of politician." At another point he told his diary: "No professional liberal is intellectually honest." Truman, *Harry S. Truman,* 8.

24. Margaret Truman, *First Ladies,* New York, 1995, 276.

25. Frank, *Downfall,* 133, citing *Harry Truman and Herbert Hoover,* a documentary history by Timothy Walch and Dwight M. Miller.

26. Bohlen, *Witness to History,* 219.

27. Kennan, *Memoirs,* 212–213.

28. Bohlen, *Witness to History,* 222.

29. Schaffer, *Wings of Judgment,* 140.

30. Ibid., 140. Sherry, *The Rise of American Air Power,* 308–311.

31. Godfrey Hodgson, *The Colonel: The Life and Wars of Henry Stimson,* New York, 1990, 324.

32. Richard Rhodes, *The Making of the Atomic Bomb,* New York, 1986, 647.

33. Ibid., 647, 651.

34. Frank, *Downfall*, 218–219.

35. Ibid., 217.

36. Ibid., 143.

37. Hoopes, *Americans Remember the Home Front*, 77.

38. Rhodes, *The Making of the Atomic Bomb*, 684.

39. Ibid., 684–685.

40. Ferrell, *Off the Record*, 53; Truman, *Harry S. Truman*, 270.

41. Bohlen, *Witness to History*, 234.

42. Ibid., 237.

43. Rhodes, *The Making of the Atomic Bomb*, 688.

44. Frank, *Downfall*, 219–220.

45. Rhodes, *The Making of the Atomic Bomb*, 692.

46. Ferrell, *Off the Record*, 55.

47. Roeder, *The Censored War*, 87; Ferrell, *Off the Record*, 55–56.

48. Rhodes, *The Making of the Atomic Bomb*, 708–711.

49. Ibid., 733–734; Frank, *Downfall*, 284–286.

50. Rhodes, *The Making of the Atomic Bomb*, 735.

51. Ibid., 740–741.

52. Schaffer, *Wings of Judgment*, 174.

53. Blum, *The Price of Vision*, 474.

54. Truman, *Memoirs*, vol. 1, 430.

55. Ibid., 432.

56. Ibid., 434–435.

57. Ibid., 436.

CHAPTER 21: ASHES OF VICTORY

1. Hinchey, "The Frustration of the New Deal Revival," 233.

2. Diggins, *The Proud Decades*, 102.

3. "New Deal: This Way Out," *Newsweek,* July 8, 1946, 25.

4. Truman, *Harry S. Truman*, 291. President Truman later remarked that "Honest Harold . . . was never for anyone but Harold [and] would have cut FDR's throat—or mine for his 'high minded' ideas of a headline—and did." Ferrell, *Off the Record*, 174.

5. Truman, *Harry S. Truman*, 8.

6. PC, interview with John Snyder, May, 1980.

7. Sirevag, *The Eclipse of the New Deal*, 468–469.

8. Blum, *The Price of Vision*, 475; Markowitz, *The Rise and Fall of the People's Century*, 173.

9. Weinstein, *The Haunted Wood*, 284.

10. Harper, *American Visions of Europe*, 190–194.

11. Winston Churchill, *The Second World War*, New York, 1959, 582.

12. Alonzo Hamby, *Man of the People: A Life of Harry S Truman*, New York, 1995, 346.

13. Blum, *The Price of Vision*, 617–626.

14. William Hillman, ed., *Mr. President: The First Publication from the Personal Diaries, Private Letters, Papers and Revealing Interviews of Harry S. Truman*, New York, 1952, 128.

15. White and Maze, *Henry A. Wallace*, 270–283.

16. The full quotation is: "It is not the critic who counts, not the man who points out where the strong man stumbled, or where a doer of deeds could have done them better. The credit belongs to the man in the arena whose face is marred by dust and sweat and blood, who strives valiantly, who errs, and who comes up short again and again, who knows great enthusiasms, the great devotions and spends himself in a worthy cause. The man who at best knows the triumph of high achievement and who, at worst, if he fails, fails while daring greatly, so that his place will never be with those cold timid souls who never know victory or defeat." *Citizenship in a Republic*, Speech delivered at the Sorbonne, Paris, April 23, 1910.

17. Tanenhaus, *Whittaker Chambers*, 506.

18. Daniel Patrick Moynihan, "Letter to New York," August 2000.

19. J. Robert Moskin, *Mr. Truman's War: The Final Victories of World War II and the Birth of the Postwar World*, New York, 1996, 246–248. The author wryly describes "the great American illusion" of a democratic China.

20. Similar things have happened to American memories of other major wars. The American Revolution was won by a small "band of brothers," the officers and men of Washington's Continental Army, who stayed in the ranks to the bitter end of the eight-year struggle, while the rest of the country did as little as possible to aid the Glorious Cause. In the years after independence was secured in 1783, this dolorous truth was transformed. Every militiaman who had served thirty or sixty days in the ranks of his local regiment in an emergency told his children and grandchildren of his magnificent contributions to the triumph of American liberty. Bunker Hill, a battle fought before the Continental Army was formed, became enshrined by poets and Fourth of July orators as the epitome of American heroism and proof that the militia had really won the war while the regulars were mostly expensive spectators. See Charles Royster, *A Revolutionary People At War: The Continental Army and the American Character*, Chapel Hill, N.C., 1979, 331 ff. No one does a better job of mocking the "public virtue" that supposedly won the war, according to the Fourth of July orators.

The Civil War—at least in the North—underwent a similar transformation in memory. The terrorist, John Brown, who dreamt of starting a race war by distributing the guns of the Harper's Ferry arsenal to the enslaved blacks, and the Yankee abolitionists who financed him, became elevated to the status of heroes. No one remembered that among the many condemners of Brown was the would-be Republican presidential candidate, Abraham Lincoln. Equally forgotten was the attitude of the men of General William Tecumseh Sherman's army, the unbeatable host who marched through Georgia from Atlanta to the sea. These Midwesterners often said they would much rather shoot an abolitionist than a rebel. In memory the war became a crusade to end slavery and the terrific acrimony over its purpose—and the widespread loathing for Lincoln—were forgotten. See Michael Kammen, *The Mystic Chords of Memory*, New York 1991, 101ff.

21. Brown, *Bodyguard of Lies*, 820.

22. Sherwood, *Roosevelt and Hopkins,* 931.

23. Dallek, *Franklin D. Roosevelt and American Foreign Policy*, 289. The author quotes Senator William Fulbright's 1971 remark: "FDR's deviousness in a good cause made it easier for LBJ to practice the same kind of deviousness in a bad cause."

24. PC, interview with Harry S. Truman, April 1970.

INDEX